ENCYCLOPEDIA OF
AFRICAN-AMERICAN EDUCATION

ENCYCLOPEDIA OF AFRICAN-AMERICAN EDUCATION

EDITED BY
Faustine C. Jones-Wilson, Charles A. Asbury,
Margo Okazawa-Rey, D. Kamili Anderson,
Sylvia M. Jacobs, and Michael Fultz

GREENWOOD PRESS
WESTPORT, CONNECTICUT • LONDON

Library of Congress Cataloging-in-Publication Data

Encyclopedia of African-American education / edited by Faustine C.
   Jones-Wilson . . . [et al.].
      p.   cm.
   Includes bibliographical references and index.
   ISBN 0–313–28931–X (alk. paper)
      1. African-Americans—Education—Encyclopedias.   I. Jones-Wilson,
   Faustine C. (Faustine Childress).
   LC2717.E53   1996
   371.97'96'073—dc20   95–42918

British Library Cataloguing in Publication Data is available.

Library of Congress Catalog Card Number: 95–42918
ISBN: 0–313–28931–X

First published in 1996

Greenwood Press, 88 Post Road West, Westport, CT 06881
An imprint of Greenwood Publishing Group, Inc.

Printed in the United States of America

The paper used in this book complies with the
Permanent Paper Standard issued by the National
Information Standards Organization (Z39.48–1984).

10 9 8 7 6 5 4 3 2 1

CONTENTS

PREFACE

The *Encyclopedia of African-American Education* is an essential, comprehensive reference tool for researchers, teachers, scholars, students, and laypersons who need information under a single cover on significant issues, policies, historical events, laws, theories, organizations, institutions, and people incident to the education of African-Americans in the United States. This segment of the American population is unique in that its educational history includes as law and public policy the systematic, long-term denial of the acquisition of knowledge. Initially, African-Americans were legally forbidden to be schooled in the American South, where most of them had lived as slaves from the 1600s. The attitude was cultivated by policymakers and slaveholders that blacks were incapable of mastering academic subjects. This period, which ended about 1865 with the conclusion of the Civil War and the establishment of the Freedmen's Bureau, was followed by sixty-nine years of laws, policies, and practices providing for rudimentary and vocationally oriented education under the dual-school, separate-but-equal policies established by *Plessy v. Ferguson* in 1896. These policies did not end until the 1954 and 1955 Supreme Court decisions in *Brown v. Board of Education of Topeka, Kansas* were reinforced by the passage of civil rights and equal educational opportunity legislation in the mid-1960s. African-Americans and some whites of this era worked assiduously to effect the repeal of discriminatory laws and to revise public policies and attitudes in order to secure educational equality for African-Americans. Attitudes about appropriate schooling and the education provided (or lacking) for blacks have been and remain unresolved moral, political, legal, economic, and psychological dilemmas for our nation.

In this reference tool, the coeditors sought to provide a rich, extensive resource characterized by breadth and depth on each topic. Important local and regional information has been presented, along with that which is national in scope. A difficult editorial problem occurred when the number of pages of manuscript copy we originally submitted to the publishers exceeded the prescribed contract limitation, resulting in our having to eliminate or shorten many entries.

A decision was made to retain as many topical entries as possible and to reduce the biographical entries because they are available in other sources. Forthcoming from Greenwood Press is the *Biographical Dictionary of African-American Educators*, to which the reader is referred.

This effort began in September 1992; entries were received from authors through December 1994. Their participation in this research and publication effort is deeply appreciated. During this period, the coeditors have benefitted immensely from the highly competent and dedicated services of Mr. Wayson Jones, editorial assistant, who coordinated most of the day-to-day activities associated with this complicated project, beginning in the spring of 1994. Graduate students Ms. Tracey T. Jones, Mr. John Taborn, and Ms. Susan Montello also lent valuable support. The continuous cooperation of Dr. Sylvia T. Johnson, Mrs. Geraldine C. Bradner, and Mr. Mahmoud Gudarzi of the *Journal of Negro Education* at Howard University has been invaluable.

Lastly, tribute must be paid to those who came before us, those who presently labor in the vineyards, and those who will follow in our footsteps. As such, this work is dedicated to the legions of African-Americans who have sought, in their respective times and with the resources available to them, to improve and facilitate educational opportunity, both qualitatively and quantitatively, for our people. We stand on their shoulders.

—Faustine C. Jones-Wilson

A

A BETTER CHANCE, INC. A Better Chance is the oldest and only nation-wide academic talent search agency for minority youth. Headquartered in Boston, Massachusetts, this nonprofit organization was founded in 1963 by representatives of twenty-three independent schools who convened at Phillips Academy (Andover, Mass.) "to consider ways and means of helping Negro high school students who, because of the lack of resources or cultural advantages, would be hampered in their ambitions to enter college." Initially based at Dartmouth College, A Better Chance sought to identify entering secondary-school students of color with excellent academic potential, develop their academic skills through intensive study, and prepare them for college entrance. Since its founding, A Better Chance's mission has rested on a single goal: to increase substantially the number of well-educated minority youth capable of assuming positions of responsibility and leadership in American society.

Through its largest program, the College Preparatory Schools Program, A Better Chance identifies, recruits, selects, and places talented and motivated minority students in academically rigorous private and public high schools. Under the leadership of its current president, Judith Berry Griffin, the organization has expanded its focus to include programs that provide minority high school students with academic enrichment, preparation for college entrance, and career options. In addition, A Better Chance offers access to enrichment programs in such fields as academic and leadership skills, introduction to business careers, outdoor living, and study and residence abroad. In 1993, the organization's membership consisted of 177 schools and an annual average of 70 affiliated colleges and universities. Approximately 2,000 students are enrolled in colleges and member schools during a given year.

A Better Chance has developed a network of some three thousand volunteers who recruit at four hundred "feeder schools" to identify promising student applicants. The application process is rigorous, including essay responses, academic transcripts, teacher recommendations, and personal interviews. Over 12,000 applications are distributed annually; more than 2,300 students usually apply to the program. Applicants are also required to take the Secondary School Admissions Test (SSAT); however, the agency does not rely heavily on standardized evaluative measures. Rather, test results are considered against a more comprehensive backdrop of demonstrated ability. After eligibility has been determined, students are matched with schools that most closely fit their individual characteristics and interests. Member schools provide more than $12 million in financial aid for admitted students.

Each year, approximately 160 A Better Chance high school students are enrolled in the unique Public Schools Program, attending outstanding public high schools in twenty-three suburban communities. Under the aegis of a local A Better Chance board of directors, these students live in a dormitory setting that enables them to attend local public institutions during the school year.

Better than 99 percent of A Better Chance graduates immediately go on to college, and more than 90 percent receive degrees. As of 1993, the organization had a total of 7,800 alumni, who are pursuing a wide variety of professions.

SELECTED BIBLIOGRAPHY

Judith B. Griffin, "Developing More Minority Mathematicians and Scientists: A New Approach," *Journal of Negro Education* (Yearbook Issue, 1990); Judith B. Griffin and Sylvia T. Johnson, "Making a Difference for a New Generation: The ABC Story," in Diana T. Slaughter and Deborah J. Johnson, eds., *Visible Now: Blacks in Private Schools* (1988); Sylvia T. Johnson and S. Prom-Jackson, "Career Choice in Science and Mathematics–Related Areas among Talented Minority Youth," in A. O. Harrison, ed., *The Eleventh Conference on Empirical Research in Black Psychology* (Rockville, MD: National Institute of Mental Health, 1988): 32–51; Charlisle Lyles, *Do I Dare Disturb the Universe? From the Projects to Prep School* (1994); Sylvester Monroe, "Brothers," *Newsweek* (23 March 1987): 54–63.

JUDITH BERRY GRIFFIN

ACADEMIC ACHIEVEMENT AND AFRICAN-AMERICANS. Many theories have been proposed to explain the problem of academic underachievement among African-American students. Historically, the most popular explanations have focused on home background, motivation, and socioeconomic status, too often ignoring the role of the school. Although issues related to students' backgrounds can and do contribute to low achievement for some children, a growing body of recent literature clearly indicates that factors such as teacher expectations, assessment and instruction, and the structure and organization of schools must also be considered in order to improve the academic achievement of African-American students.

It is important to recognize that the images that teachers hold about children and their potential can have a major influence on the self-efficacy as well as the achievement of any youngster. Research indicates that race and socioeconomic status influence teacher expectations and the ways in which the students' actions are interpreted. It has often been noted that characteristics specific to African-American students can help shape expectations. For example, one body of evidence indicates that kindergarten teachers lowered their expectations of the academic abilities of African-American students who used dialect or spoke "Black English" and raised their expectations of African-American students who spoke "Standard English." Moreover, teachers exhibit fairly consistent patterns of behavior toward students for whom they have low expectations ("lows"). For example, such teachers call on lows less often to respond to questions, wait less time for lows to answer questions, and often give lows the answer or call on someone else rather than repeating the question or asking a new question. These teachers also generally praise lows less frequently than those students for whom they have high expectations ("highs"), demand less from them, and give them less information and feedback to their questions. Lows are also usually seated farther away from the teacher and generally receive less friendly interaction, such as smiling and eye contact from the teacher within the classroom setting. Ability grouping and tracking resulting from these negative teacher expectations and behaviors have been found to adversely affect African-American student achievement. Substantial evidence exists that while white students are often placed into higher academic groups, African-Americans, particularly African-American males, are tracked into lower academic groupings such as vocational, remedial reading, and general math, often because of negative teacher expectations. Indeed, students of color are less likely to be enrolled in programs for the gifted and talented and are disproportionately placed in special education programs.

Another factor that affects the educational achievement of African-Americans is the tension and conflict between students' cultural knowledge and school knowledge. Cultural knowledge is the set of assumptions, perspectives, and insights that students may derive from experiences in their homes and communities that can be used to interpret the knowledge and experiences they encounter in the school and in other institutions within the larger society. The cultural knowledge of African-American students is often devalued in school and often conflicts with mainstream group interaction and with the communication styles and perspectives that constitute school knowledge. The challenge facing teachers is that of making effective instructional use of the personal and cultural knowledge of students while also helping them to reach beyond their own cultural boundaries. Teachers can use such information to motivate students and as a foundation for more effective teaching. By allowing students the opportunity to investigate how cultural biases influence the way knowledge is perceived, teachers are able to facilitate students' potential to create knowledge and to enhance their academic achievement. This type of climate allows the inclusion of the voices and perspectives of not only teachers and textbooks but also students in the curriculum.

Assessment is another factor in the achievement of African-American students. In 1983, the National Commission of Excellence in Education produced a report that stated that "our nation is at risk." Educational institutions reacted by focusing more on tightening standards for educational outcomes rather than by ensuring that every child has a reasonable chance of attaining them. Consequently, standardized test scores continually reflect racial disparities, while data on suspensions, expulsions, and dropout rates indicate that too many African-American students are being distanced from mainstream America.

In response to ongoing criticisms of standardized tests, many researchers have endorsed a move toward more authentic and constructive forms of assessment. One of the major distinctions between alternative and traditional forms of assessment is that alternative forms are aimed at providing students with systematic opportunities to gain insight about their own learning, while traditional forms are aimed at grouping and sorting students according to standards. A key argument for teachers' use of alternative assessments is that they provide a more accurate basis for making pedagogical decisions about the instruction of African-American students. Thus, in the politics of assessment, the most basic challenge is to assist teachers in raising their expectations about children's potential.

SELECTED BIBLIOGRAPHY

J. A. Banks, "The Canon Debate, Knowledge Construction, and Multicultural Education," *Educational Researcher* 22, no. 5 (1993): 4–14; L. Darling-Hammond, "Performance-based Assessment and Educational Equity," *Harvard Educational Review* 64 (1994): 5–30; L. Delpit, "The Silenced Dialogue: Power and Pedagogy in Educating Other People's Children," *Harvard Education Review* 58 (1988): 280–98; P. DeMeis and R. Turner, "Effect of Student Race, Physical Attractiveness and Dialect on Teacher Evaluation," *Contemporary Educational Psychology* 3 (1978): 77–86; J. Dusek and G. Joseph, "The Basis of Teacher Expectancies: A Meta Analysis," *Journal of Educational Psychology* 75, no. 3 (1983): 327–46; T. Good and J. Brophy, *Looking in Classrooms* (1991); J. E. Hale-Benson, *Black Children: Their Roots, Culture and Learning Styles*, rev. ed. (1982); D. L. Jones and D. G. Winborne, "Consideration for Cultural Diversity in Education Reform: Elements of Positive Change," *New Directions for Educational Reform* 1, no. 1 (1992): 5–12; M. Lockheed and D. G. Morgan, *Research Report: A Causal Model of Teachers' Expectations in Elementary Classrooms* (1979); D. Neill and N. Medina, "Standardized Testing: Harmful to Educational Health," *Phi Delta Kappan* (May 1989): 688–97; J. Oakes, *Keeping Track of How Schools Structure Inequality* (1985); R. Rist, "Student Social Class and Teacher Expectations: The Self-Fulfilling Prophecy in Ghetto Education," *Harvard Educational Review* 40, no. 3 (1970): 411–51; P. Winograd and D. L. Jones, "The Use of Portfolios in Performance Assessment," *New Directions in Education Reform* 1, no. 2 (1992): 37–50.

                                                              DENEESE L. JONES

ACCESS TO AND PARITY IN HIGHER EDUCATION. As the demographic face of the United States is undergoing fundamental change, the consequences of this change pose a serious challenge to American higher education with respect to both access and parity in enrollment and degree completion for minority students, especially African-Americans. In 1988, findings from the National Center for Education Statistics (NCES) revealed that African-Americans earned fewer degrees in 1985 than in 1977 at all degree levels except the first professional degree. The report further documented the fact that black males accounted for two thirds of the drop in the number of African-Americans receiving degrees between 1977 and 1985. It concluded that the ability of America's colleges and universities to attract and retain minority students is important to the nation's success in achieving its goal of equal opportunity. It also stated that change in the number of degrees earned by minorities in relation to their population provided one measure of higher education's progress in this direction.

A 1991 analysis of trends in racial/ethnic enrollment in higher education indicated that approximately 1,335,000 African-American students were enrolled in American institutions of higher education. However, of that number, just 758,000 (57 percent) were enrolled in four-year institutions, while 578,000 (43 percent) were enrolled in two-year institutions. An overview of studies comparing baccalaureate degree completion for students who start at the two-year and the four-year levels has found that (a) roughly 15 to 25 percent of two-year college students transfer to four-year institutions, while just 10 to 15 percent ever receive a B.A. degree; (b) African-American students are less likely than white or Asian-American students to transfer to a B.A.-granting institution; and (c) white community college students are more likely to earn a B.A. than are African-American and Hispanic students.

In 1991, African-Americans enrolled in four-year institutions of higher education in the United States represented 8.7 percent of total four-year enrollment. Yet they received just 5.8 percent of a total of 1,046,930 bachelor's degrees conferred. White student enrollment represented 78 percent of total four-year enrollment, and white students received 84.3 percent of the total number of B.A. degrees conferred. The B.A. completion rate of African-American students at American colleges and universities would be a good deal lower than it is were it not for the productivity of historically black colleges and universities (HBCUs) in awarding B.A. degrees to African-American students. While HBCUs constituted only 3 percent of the nation's 3,559 institutions of higher education in 1990, the eighty-six HBCUs that award bachelor's degrees enrolled 28 percent of all African-American students enrolled at four-year colleges and universities (257,804) and awarded 27 percent (19,734) of all B.A. degrees earned by African-Americans nationwide.

In addition to enrolling in college at lower rates than white students, African-American students tend to leave college without a bachelor's degree at higher rates. For example, among those who entered post-secondary institutions by 1982, 71 percent of African-American high school graduates, 66 percent of Hispanics, and 65 percent of Native Americans left by 1986 without a bachelor's degree. Research by the College Board indicated that most reasons given by African-American students for leaving college are financial. Need notwithstanding, however, between 1978 and 1989, the proportion of African-American students receiving Pell Grants declined from 55 percent to slightly over 41 percent because of the federal government's failure to index Pell Grant eligibility levels to inflation. The percentage of white students receiving grants during the same period remained constant at 20 percent. Astin and Cross found that 63 percent of African-American students surveyed reported parental incomes of less than $12,000, as opposed to 10 percent of their white counterparts in the same survey.

Findings of the American Council on Education indicate that during the late 1970s and the early 1980s, as the number of white high school graduates began to decline and as the number of African-American and Hispanic graduates continued to increase both absolutely and proportionately, the gap in relative enrolled-in-college participation rates of 18-to-24-year-olds increased in favor of whites. The ACE report further found that, despite declines in the number of white high school graduates in this age group, whites maintained an enrolled-in-college participation rate that increased from 33.9 percent in 1978 to 35.8 percent in 1985, while the African-American rate dropped from a high of 33.4 percent in 1976 to a low of 26.1 percent in 1985.

In America, the earning power of a college education as compared to a high school education is considerable. Census Bureau figures on 1990 median annual income indicated that whites with four or more years of college earned an average salary of $30,431, while whites with four years of high school earned only $15,570. In 1990, African-Americans with four or more years of college earned on average $27,256 annually, while those with four years of high school earned $12,665—a difference of $14,591. Census Bureau statistics also indicate that individuals with bachelor's degrees earn $6,000 per year more than those with associate degrees only and $7,464 more per year than those with vocational certificates only.

African-American students' access to the B.A. degree has been restricted far more than white students'. In the states of Mississippi, Alabama, and Louisiana, the African-American percentage of total elementary and secondary headcount enrollment in 1986 was 55.5 percent, 37.0 percent, and 41.3 percent respectively. However, the African-American percentage of higher education headcount enrollment in 1986 for the same three states was 28.5 percent, 20.8 percent, and 22.9 percent respectively. Aside from the increased income it ensures, the B.A. degree serves as a passport to postgraduate work at every level.

Current patterns of racial disparity in higher education access and parity are reinforced by the fact that most of the decline in minority enrollment between 1976 and 1986 was due to a decline in African-American enrollment at the baccalaureate level. In four-year institutions of higher education, African-American enrollment grew by just 1.8 percent between 1976 and 1986 (from 604,000 to 615,000), while Hispanic enrollment grew by 120 percent (from 119,000 to 262,000). Clearly, the pattern of restricted access to higher education indicates that the obstacles to access and completion faced by African-American youth are more intractable than those faced by other minority groups.

SELECTED BIBLIOGRAPHY

H. S. Astin and P. H. Cross, *The Impact of Financial Aid on Student Persistence in College* (1975); Deborah Blum, "Foreign Students Said to Get Aid Preference over U.S. Minorities," *Chronicle of Higher Education* 38, no. 27 (March 1992); Bureau of the Census, *Black Population of the United States, 1991* (1992); Deborah J. Carter and Reginald Wilson, *Minorities in Higher Education: Tenth Annual Status Report, 1991* (1991); C. Leatherman, "After 10-Year Decline, Number of Black Ph.D.'s Begins to Increase," *Chronicle of Higher Education* 37, no. 36 (May 1991); Douglas Lederman, "Black Athletes Graduate at a Higher Rate Than Other Blacks, NCAA Reports," *Chronicle of Higher Education* 38, no. 44 (July 1992); C. A. Ottinger, "College Going, Persistence, and Completion Patterns in Higher Education: What Do We Know?" *American Council on Education Research Briefs* 2, no. 3 (1991); Fred L. Pincus and Elayne Archer, *Bridges to Opportunity: Are Community Colleges Meeting the Transfer Needs of Minority Students?* (1989); Oscar Porter, *Undergraduate Completion and Persistence at Four-Year Colleges and Universities: Completers, Persisters, Drop-Outs and Stop-Outs* (1992); Christopher Shea, "Fewer Test Takers Get Top Scores on the Verbal SAT," *Chronicle of Higher Education* 39, no. 19 (January 1993); U.S. Department of Education, National Center for Education Statistics, *1989 Digest of Educational Statistics* (1990).

BARBARA FLEMING

ACCREDITATION IN HIGHER EDUCATION. In 1871, the University of Michigan developed an arrangement by which high schools in that state were accredited after inspection by a college faculty committee. Graduates of those schools were to be admitted without examination. In 1873, the state of Indiana asked the state board of education to evaluate and accredit schools. The accreditation movement first extended beyond the state level with the formation in 1885 of the New England Association of Colleges and Preparatory Schools. Other regional associations were soon established: the Association of Colleges and Preparatory Schools of the Middle States and Maryland in 1892, the North Central Association of Colleges and Secondary Schools in 1894, and the Southern Association of Colleges and Secondary Schools* (the "Southern Association") in 1895. The Southern Association published its first list of member colleges in 1920; as African-American schools were not accepted as members, this list did not contain African-American schools or colleges.

In an attempt to fill this void, the Association of Colleges for Negro Youth (ACNY) was organized in 1913. At its first meeting, the ACNY adopted a standard of entrance into college requiring fifteen units of high school work. At the second meeting in 1914, the representatives of the organization's member colleges composed a list of secondary schools whose graduates, based on experience, might be admitted to their institutions. Another topic of discussion was the content of the basic college curriculum. ACNY members also agreed that any schools with the "time and facilities" might offer the M.A. degree, but not the Ph.D. At its 1920 annual meeting, the ACNY urged member institutions to eliminate duplication of secondary school studies and deplored what it viewed as an overemphasis on athletics. As a result, four southern colleges were denied membership in the ACNY. In 1923, a set of formal standards for colleges was adopted. Membership in the ACNY was thus limited to those colleges that required fifteen high school units for admission and 120 semester hours for graduation; had at least six departments with six full-time professors, all of whom held the bachelor's degree and three-fourths of whom had one year of graduate work; enrolled at least fifty students; and had at least 4,000 volumes in the library. With regard to medical school candidates, the American Medical Association agreed to admit African-American students to medical school who had graduated from schools approved in a 1928 federal Office of Education survey.

In 1930, the Southern Association began inspecting African-American colleges. Although they were not admitted as members, the schools were evaluated and rated by a Committee on Negro Schools. As a result of the first inspection, one college was rated *A* and six were rated *B*. Three years later, six colleges were rated *A* and twenty-two were rated *B*.

In 1934, the ACNY was reorganized to parallel the Southern Association and was renamed the Association of Colleges and Secondary Schools for Negro Youth in the Southern Region (commonly referred to as the Association of Colleges and Secondary Schools for Negroes, or the ACSSN). About thirty-five four-year colleges and seven junior colleges held membership in this association. Its mission was conceived as working within the framework of segregation to improve educational opportunities for African-American youths at both the high school and the college levels, so that the same standards set for white schools could be met.

Recognizing that its own ratings had little credibility and that it had no voice in ratings by the Southern Association, the ACSSN formed a liaison committee in 1948 to work toward full membership in the Southern Association. This intention was made clear when A. D. Beittel spoke at the annual meeting of the Southern Association on the topic "Knocking at Your Door." A grant in 1955 from the General Education Board enabled the Southern Association to inspect all colleges in the ACSSN. In 1957, fifteen African-American colleges and three junior colleges were admitted to full membership in the Southern Association; in 1958, fourteen more colleges were admitted. With colleges and high schools being admitted to full membership in the Southern Association and with racial barriers to admission to predominantly white institutions falling, the ACSSN held its last meeting in 1964.

The struggle for accreditation by African-American schools exhibits a conflict between two views. The paternalistic view, largely adopted by white institutions, held that nothing much could be expected of African-American institutions and therefore lower standards should be set. From its inception, the Association of Colleges and Secondary Schools for Negroes held that, although its schools required understanding and help, there should be no double standard. Whatever standards were accepted as appropriate for white schools should be met without exception by African-American schools. The latter view prevailed.

SELECTED BIBLIOGRAPHY

Leland Stanford Cozart, *A History of the Association of Colleges and Secondary Schools, 1934–1965* (1966); *Minutes* of the Association of Colleges for Negro Youth (various years); *Proceedings* of the Annual Meetings of the Association of Colleges and Secondary Schools for Negroes (various years); papers of the Association of Colleges and Secondary Schools for Negroes, Atlanta University Library.

EARLE H. WEST

ADAMS v. RICHARDSON, 480 F.2d 1159 (D.C. Cir. 1973). This case established that the U.S. Department of Health, Education, and Welfare (HEW) had an affirmative obligation to enforce its duties under the Civil Rights Act of 1964,* with respect to educational programs that receive federal funds. Title VI of the Civil Rights Act prohibits discrimination on the basis of race, color, or national origin in any program receiving federal financial assistance. Nonetheless, HEW refused to take action against several entities receiving federal funds despite its findings that (a) ten states (Arkansas, Florida, Georgia, Louisiana, North Carolina, Maryland, Mississippi, Oklahoma, Pennsylvania, and Virginia) were operating segregated systems of higher education; (b) seventy-four public school districts had reneged on approved desegregation plans; (c) forty-two public school districts were in presumptive violation of the Supreme Court's desegregation order in *Swann v. Charlotte-Mecklenburg Board of Education*, 402 U.S. 1 (1971); and (d) eighty-five school districts were in apparent violation of *Swann*. The plaintiffs also sought to have HEW monitor all school districts then under court desegregation orders and report its progress in each of these four areas.

HEW contended that its discretion in enforcing Title VI precluded judicial review of its actions. The District of Columbia federal Circuit Court of Appeals disagreed that HEW had absolute authority to act independently of judicial review and noted that such review was appropriate to ensure that HEW complied with the specific enforcement procedures (ending the provision of federal funds, or any other means authorized by law) provided in Title VI. Further, the Court of Appeals held that judicial review was especially appropriate in this situation, where HEW had abdicated wholly its responsibility to ensure that segregated educational facilities did not receive federal funds.

The Court of Appeals ordered HEW to act immediately to ensure compliance in all of the areas described above except with respect to the systems of higher education. Because HEW had less experience in dealing with higher education than with primary and secondary school systems, it also directed HEW to confer with those states and within 180 days develop a plan to rectify desegregation in those facilities. Thus, private citizens secured court assistance to compel a federal agency to enforce provisions of the Civil Rights Act of 1964.

On the strength of the decision in *Adams*, federal district courts subsequently oversaw HEW's enforcement activities under Title VI. In 1975, in *Adams v. Weinberger*, the D.C. District Court ordered HEW to initiate enforcement activities against jurisdictions that had not desegregated their school systems as of 1975. Later, in *Adams v. Califano* (1977), the D.C. District Court ordered HEW to revoke its acceptance of desegregation plans submitted by six states because the plans did not meet the requirements of Title VI.

SELECTED BIBLIOGRAPHY
Adams v. Califano, 430 F. Supp. 118 (D.D.C. 1977); *Adams v. Richardson*, 480 F.2d 1159 (D.C. Cir. 1973); *Adams v. Weinberger*, 391 F. Supp. 1269 (D.D.C. 1975).
                                                                        STEVE ROYSTER

ADULT EDUCATION OF AFRICAN-AMERICANS. An analysis of the significant historical events related to the evolution of adult education can be made over the course of six overlapping historical periods. They are the antebellum and civil war period (1619–1863); the emancipation and Reconstruction era (1863–1877); the post-Reconstruction era (1878–1915); the world wars and postwar developments era (1914–1959); the civil rights era (1960–1980); and the modern era (1981–present).

Essentially, two broad streams reflect the operational practice of adult education: formal adult education and nonformal adult education. Formal refers to organized, purposeful learning activities that are designed specifically for adult learners. The learning activities contain goals and objectives and are offered under the sponsorship of an educational institution. Nonformal refers to all of the aforementioned elements except the sponsorship by an educational institution.

During the antebellum and Civil War period, a small percentage of slaves were trained to become skilled and semiskilled technical workers; but, prior to the 1850s, there were very few schools in the North and none in the South that provided formal adult education. Early in 1863, the Union Army began to recruit freed African-Americans for military duty. As African-American regiments were organized, the Army set up schools to teach these soldiers how to read and write. The Union Army's role in adult education was significant because of the estimated 180,000 African-American soldiers who served in the military during the Civil War, and its occupation of the South brought further educational and employment benefits to African-American adults.

During the early period of Reconstruction, hundreds of schools were set up to provide adult education for a limited number of freed African-American men and women. These schools were established by the federal government Bureau of Refugees, Freedmen, and Abandoned Lands,* more commonly known as the Freedmen's Bureau, the American Missionary Society,* the African Methodist Episcopal Church, and other antislavery groups. The 1860s also witnessed the founding of a large number of African-American colleges. Although they were called "colleges," their programs essentially offered elementary and secondary education designed to provide basic academic and vocational skills for adult students. Adult education, the most urgently needed type of education during this era, continued to be a major component of many schooling activities during Reconstruction and until about the 1930s.

The Great Depression of the 1930s was devastating to African-American education in general, and to adult education in particular, as African-American unemployment reached crisis levels. African-American churches, fraternal orders, branches of the YMCA and YWCA, the NAACP,* and the National Urban League* came forward with support for elementary education and set up classes for adult education. However, efforts from the private sector were insufficient. In 1933, President Franklin D. Roosevelt established a number of emergency agencies to provide federal assistance to the states to address poverty, homelessness, unemployment, and education. The main agency handling adult education was the Federal Emergency Relief Administration. In 1935, that role was taken over by the Works Progress Administration. Other important adult education programs were instituted by the Department of Agriculture; vocational training programs were handled by the National Youth Administration. African-Americans participated in all of the adult education programs initiated during the New Deal era, even though these programs were segregated in the South and parts of the Northeast.

During World War II adult training programs were organized to prepare the unskilled to become defense and military workers. The aftermath of World War II and the Korean War brought a broad increase in vocational programs because of technological changes in U.S. industry. The G.I. Bill of Rights had perhaps the greatest impact on adult education and higher education for African-American veterans. This act provided federal funds to cover a four-year period for the education of veterans. It is estimated that about two million African-American veterans served during these two wars and were thus eligible to receive a college education.

The 1960s saw a large increase in federal legislation and funding for a diversity of adult education initiatives. Two conditions accounted for most of the federal programs—increased poverty and rising unemployment. The Manpower Development and Training Act (MDTA) of 1962 was a skills-training program for unemployed heads of households, through which thousands were trained and found employment. The Economic Opportunity Act (EOA) of 1964 was the major legislation that supported the Johnson Administration's "War on Poverty," by providing for a number of employment related programs. Seven major manpower programs under EOA served a substantial number of African-Americans, including the Neighborhood Youth Corps, Operation Mainstream, Public Service Careers, the Concentrated Employment Program, Job Corps, the Work Incentive Program, and the Public Employment Program. The Adult Education Act of 1966 supported adult basic education (ABE) in public schools across the country, providing instruction in basic reading, writing, and computation. It also provided secondary education and high school equivalency completion. ABE programs have not been successful in recruiting and retaining sufficient percentages of African-American inner-city residents, although the target populations for these districts are extremely large. It is estimated that African-American adults represent less than 10 percent of ABE enrollment nationally, whereas the African-American target population exceeds 30 percent.

The current period is characterized by a retrenchment of federal, state, and local governments and consequently by minimal funding to support adult education. Fee-based adult education programs appear to be expanding, particularly in the area of employment-related, short-term training. The rapid growth of these human resource development programs has come primarily from the business sector and university-based continuing education programs. However, there is a consensus among adult educators that the percentage of participation by African-Americans has been disproportionately low.

SELECTED BIBLIOGRAPHY

Diane B. Brisco and Jovita M. Ross, "Racial and Ethnic Minorities and Adult Education," in Sharon B. Merriam and Phyllis M. Cunningham, eds., *Handbook of Adult and Continuing Education* (1989); Virginia L. Denton, *Booker T. Washington and the Adult Education Movement* (1993); Edwin Hamilton, *Adult Education for Community Development* (1992); Jonathan Kozol, *Illiterate America* (1985); National Center for Education Statistics, *National Adult Literacy Survey* (1993); Harvey G. Neufeldt and Leo McGee, eds., *Education of the African-American Adult* (1990).

EDWIN HAMILTON

AFRICAN-AMERICAN STUDIES DEPARTMENTS. Whether identified as African-American Studies, Afro-American Studies, Africana Studies, or Black Studies, academic departments exclusively devoted to research and teaching some multi-or interdisciplinary aspects of the African-American experience have been a significant aspect of higher education in America for the last quarter century. These departments have had an importance and impact in education far in excess of their small number. They will be referred to here by the generic term "African-American Studies," since most of their curricula focuses on black people in the United States.

The history of departments of African-American Studies is a relatively recent aspect of a much older intellectual tradition of self-help among African-Americans. A few educated African-Americans attempted to counter the racist propaganda of the post-Reconstruction era through short-lived history appreciation groups such as the Bethel Literary and Historical Society, established in Washington, D.C., in 1881, the American Negro Historical Society (Philadelphia, 1897) and the Negro Society for Historical Research (New York, 1911). At the initiative of clergyman Alexander Crummell, in 1897 the American Negro Academy* became the first truly national association of African-American intellectual leaders. Consisting of a learned membership of almost a hundred ministers, professors, lawyers, and successful businessmen, scattered across the country, the American Negro Academy published a number of seminal papers on different aspects of African-American life and culture during the quarter century of its existence.

Organized by Carter G. Woodson* in 1915, the Association for the Study of Negro Life and History* came to be black America's most influential institutional vehicle for promoting scholarly inquiry on topics related to African-American history and literature. The Woodson organization linked its members through the *Journal of Negro History* (1916) and the *Negro History Bulletin*

(1937). From its beginnings, the association has kept alive a sense of the legitimacy of the black experience as a topic of formal study in scores of local chapters around the nation. The association has also retained its operational independence from higher education institutions despite its dependence on academic leadership. During the first decades of the association's existence, no predominantly white American educational institution welcomed the inclusion of black social and historical issues into its curriculum. The reluctance to offer formal instruction about blacks was evident even among the faculties at predominantly black institutions. Although he had some supporters, Woodson survived only one year in the history department at Howard University. In 1933, in his *The Mis-Education of the Negro*, Woodson pleaded with African-American educators to make and sustain a declaration of intellectual independence in the study and interpretation of the black experience throughout the world. In 1935, W. E. B. Du Bois* produced *Black Reconstruction*, a thoughtful, sensitive reinterpretation of the role of African-Americans during the tumultuous aftermath of the Civil War. Like Woodson and many other pioneer African-American scholars Du Bois produced most of his work independent of formal institutional support and outside the academy proper.

Mainstream institutional support for African-American Studies emerged only in the late 1960s, concomitant with the protests of the Civil Rights Movement, the rise of a Black Power consciousness, and the admission of a critical mass of African-American students to hitherto nearly all-white college and university campuses in the wake of the assassination of Dr. Martin Luther King Jr.

African-American Studies departments were created in an environment of confrontation and the rejection of traditional curricula content and prevailing theories of basic social reality. Initially, many African-American students indicated the topics or subject in which they wished to be instructed. Virtually all African-American Studies departments began by offering history courses. Some institutions classify history as a social science; others see it as part of the humanities, which complicates classification of African-American Studies departments. However, over 60 percent of African-American Studies curricula are made up primarily of social science courses, with the Department of African-American Studies at Ohio State University being perhaps most representative of this model. Temple University's doctoral curriculum is roughly divided between courses cited in its catalog as "social/behavioral" and "cultural/aesthetic." More recently, African-American Studies units have come to be seen as incubators of the philosophical and ideological ideas associated with the concept of Afrocentrism.

According to a major 1983 survey covering 1,333 colleges and universities, 193 responded that they had some sort of administrative structure housing an African-American Studies department, program, or institute. This survey also showed that black students initiated the formation of two thirds of these units; faculties and administrative officers initiated most of the remaining third. This study identified the following African-American Studies administrative configurations: fifty-six full-fledged departments, nine academic department/cultural center combinations, fifty-four nondegree academic units, five research institutes, five nondegree academic and cultural centers, one cultural center only, and forty-eight other units definable as related to African-American Studies. In 1990, at least ten master's degree–level programs were likewise housed in predominantly white institutions. Of the predominantly African-American institutions, only Howard University had an autonomous undergraduate African-American Studies department; and Atlanta University had the only graduate (M.A.) department. Other predominantly African-American institutions such as Morgan State University or North Carolina A & T (Greensboro) had African-American Studies concentrations within traditional departments.

African-American Studies instructional units have undergone several evolutionary phases. The first involved the issues of staffing and structural relations: What should be the technical qualifications of African-American Studies faculty? What should be the salience of ethnicity in staffing these units? Should there be an intellectual resocialization of persons trained in traditional fields and disciplines? What should be the relationship between the African-American Studies entity and other instructional units on campus? What should be the role of students in faculty recruitment and curriculum development? Should faculty members hold joint or department-only appointments? Each of these questions was answered differently by different institutions, but the record is clearest on the matter of single versus joint appointments. According to a 1985 Ford Foundation study, joint appointments were the rule in African-American Studies departments. Reasons for this involved (a) the scarcity of black faculty in general, (b) a hesitation to sever administrative connections with traditional disciplines, (c) the prospect of less difficulty with tenure aspirations, (d) perceived more positive attitudes by funding agencies, and (e) a desire to keep confrontation issues to a minimum.

Whatever might be the eventual outcome of any particular debate about its structure or evolution, the existence of African-American Studies institutional vehicles has raised profound questions about the education of Americans in general and African-Americans in particular. As this debate continues, the African-American Studies department may become even more important in the educational systems of this nation.

SELECTED BIBLIOGRAPHY

Russell L. Adams, "African-American Studies and the State of the Art," in Mario Azevedo, ed., *African Studies: A Survey of Africans and the African Diaspora* (1993); "An Assessment of Black Studies in American Higher Education," *Journal of Negro Education* 53, no. 3 (Summer 1984), entire issue; Philip T. K. Daniel and Admasu Zeke, "Northern Illinois University Black Studies Four Year College and University Survey," *Journal of Negro Education* (May 1983); Robert Harris et al., *Three Essays: Black Studies in the United States* (1990), passim; Nathan I. Huggins, *Afro-American Studies: A Report to the Ford Foundation* (1985), passim; David Mill, "The West Alternative," *Washington Post Magazine* (8 August, 1993): 14–19, 24–25; Henry Louis Gates, Jr.,

"Academe Must Give Black-Studies Programs Their Due," *Chronicle of Higher Education* (20 September, 1989): A56; James Traub, "The Hearts and Minds of City College," *New Yorker* (June 1993): 42–53.

RUSSELL L. ADAMS

AFRICAN METHODIST EPISCOPAL ZION CHURCH AND AFRICAN-AMERICAN EDUCATION. The African Methodist Episcopal Zion (A.M.E.Z.) Church had its beginning in New York State in the eighteenth century. John Wesley, the father of Methodism, had established several Methodist churches in the New York area. From the early records kept by missionaries, it was determined that a large portion of the membership of these churches consisted of African-Americans. Wesley noted that many of New York's legal prohibitions against African-Americans—for example, not permitting them to have public meetings—created some perplexing situations. As a result, a group of free African-Americans led by James Varick, Abraham Thompson, June Scott, William Miller, and others withdrew from the John Street Methodist Episcopal Church. They organized a new church in 1796, named Zion, which was constructed in 1800. The founders chose the name Zion because it was frequently used in the Bible to designate the Church of God. However, the church was incorporated in 1801 as the African Methodist Episcopal Church in New York. (It was not until 1848 that the church's general conference voted to make "Zion" an official part of the denominational name; henceforth, it became known as the African Methodist Episcopal Zion Church.) In 1820 the group, again led by James Varick, voted themselves out of the Methodist Episcopal Church and published their first *Book of Discipline*. Varick was elected the first bishop of the A.M.E.Z. Church in 1822.

The idea of establishing a college for African-American youth was the result of a conference of A.M.E.Z. ministers who wished to promote a type of education that would make the race self-sufficient. The Church eventually established six colleges: Livingstone College* (1879), Lomax–Hannon Junior College (1893), Clinton Junior College (1894), Hood Theological Seminary (1903), A.M.E. Zion Community College (1981), and Hood–Speaks Theological Seminary (1992).

SELECTED BIBLIOGRAPHY

David H. Bradley, Sr., *A History of the A.M.E. Zion Church*, vol. 2, *1872–1968* (1970); William J. Walls, *The African Methodist Episcopal Zion Church, Reality of the Black Church* (1974).

HAROLD O. ROBINSON

AFROCENTRISM AND AFROCENTRIC (AFRICAN-CENTERED) EDUCATION. Afrocentrism is the interpretation of reality from perspectives that are centered by and within the processes that maintain and perpetuate the life and culture of people of African descent. Afrocentric or African-centered education is the means by which the attributes of African culture are developed and advanced, along with the knowledge and skills needed to maintain and perpetuate it. Both concepts are corollaries of the "African worldview," a term first coined by Senegalese anthropologist Cheikh Anta Diop (1923–86), whose 1978 work, *The Cultural Unity of Black Africa*, is generally regarded as the cornerstone of the Afrocentric idea, which has since been amplified and popularized by African-American Studies theoreticians in Africa, the Caribbean, and the Americas.

Essentially, Diop's thesis is that European and African cultural orientations represent antithetical worldviews. Instead of a universal hierarchy of cultures in which Western European culture represents the epitome, Diop suggested that African and European cultures developed within two axiomatic and divergent "cradles" of civilization. The environmental harshness of the northern cradle (Europe) gave rise to individualism, possessiveness, and forms of social organization reflective of the scarcity of natural resources within the European environment. Conversely, the warmth and fertility of the southern cradle (Africa) and the absence of moral and material misery produced a sense of collectivism and benevolence among precolonial Africans. The following attributes of the African worldview have been identified in the literature: (a) an emphasis on the family as a source of personal identity and reference; (b) a far-reaching and abiding spirituality; (c) respect for elders and ancestral figures; (d) a preference for communal and societal arrangements; (e) a live-and-let-live philosophy of coexistence and cooperation among individuals, communities, and cultures; and (f) an optimistic and holistic disposition toward life.

While, as Diop contends, the Afrocentric worldview has existed from antiquity, Afrocentrism is a contemporary concept. Afrocentrism shares with earlier constructions such as negritude, Black nationalism, and early pan-Africanism an emphasis on the need for people of African descent to resist the Western cultural hegemony. What sets Afrocentrism apart, however, is its focus on recovery and restoration of the African worldview as a means of locating and centering present conceptions of reality and analyses of phenomena. Among contemporary scholars, Molefi K. Asante* is perhaps the most widely known and prolific proponent of Afrocentrism and Afrology, a term he has coined to refer to "the science or study of all modalities related to people of African descent from an Afrocentric perspective." Other African-American Studies scholars such as Karenga, Azibo, Carruthers, and Ani have focused on the ideological function of culture in European and African societies and the personal transformation facilitated by the concept of the "de-Europeanization" of culture.

Afrocentric education is part of the same process of cultural restoration and promulgation that is inherent to Afrocentrism. Schools are among the institutions through which the process of cultural assault upon Africans has been facilitated. African students are taught to think in non-African ways, using Western orientations to knowledge as the foundation for learning. Carter G. Woodson* provides a treatise on this process in his classic 1933 text, *The Mis-Education of the Negro*. As a countervailing force, African-centered education contributes to the development of African-American people's sense of history, pride, and collective belonging through a reinforcement of their culture. Some of the major assumptions underlying Afrocentric education are that (a) it acknowledges African spirituality as an essential aspect of our uniqueness as a people and makes it an instrument of liberation; (b) it facilitates participating in the affairs of nations and defining (or redefining) reality from the perspectives of African people's needs and interests; (c) it prepares people of African descent for self-reliance and governance in every regard; (d) it emphasizes the fundamental relationship between the strength of African-American families and the strength of their communities and nations; (e) it ensures that the historical role and function of the customs, traditions, rituals, and ceremonies that have protected and preserved our culture are maintained and perpetuated; (f) it facilitates African people's spiritual expression; (g) it ensures harmony in social relations between people of African descent and others; (h) it prepares African-American youth to meet their responsibilities as adults; and (i) it sustains the continuity of African life over successive generations.

Because Afrocentric education is a process dependent upon human perception and interpretation, it follows that it can be systematically facilitated only by people who themselves are consciously engaged in Afrocentric personal transformation. Correspondingly, a curriculum cannot be Afrocentric independent of an educator's capacity to perceive and interpret it in an Afrocentric manner. Afrocentric education is thus both complex and straightforward. It facilitates preparation for African life, self-determination, a link between spirituality and liberation, a bond connecting family and nation, and an acknowledgment of cultural artifacts and their meanings. Moreover, Afrocentric education facilitates recognition of the continuity of African cultural history, commitment, personal transformation, and recognition of the future of African people.

SELECTED BIBLIOGRAPHY

K. A. Akoto, *Nationbuilding: Theory and Practice in Afrikan-Centered Education* (1992); M. Ani, *Yurugu: An African-Centered Critique of European Cultural Thought and Behavior* (1994); S. Anwisye, "Education Is More Than the Three 'Rs,' " *Harvard Journal of African-American Public Policy* 2 (1993): 97–101; M. K. Asante, *The Afrocentric Idea* (1987); M. K. Asante, *Kemet, Afrocentricity and Knowledge* (1990); D. A. Azibo, "Articulating the Distinction between Black Studies and the Studies of Blacks: The Fundamental Role of Culture and the African-Centered Worldview," *Afrocentric Scholar* 1, no. 1 (1992): 64–97.

MWALIMU J. SHUJAA AND KOFI LOMOTEY

AGRICULTURAL EDUCATION AND AFRICAN-AMERICANS. Agriculture and mechanical arts were among the first areas in which federal and state governments set aside funds and facilities for the instruction of African-Americans. The purpose of the Morrill Act of 1862 was to establish institutions of higher learning for the express purpose of educating the children of farmers and laborers. Sponsored by Representative Justin Morrill of Vermont, the act

provided for the creation of land-grant colleges,* which would include agricultural, mechanical, and technical arts curricula. Unfortunately for the freedmen,
the 1862 Morrill Act made no reference to color. As a result, the southern states
opened several land-grant institutions that were closed to African-Americans.
The second Morrill Act of 1890* changed this by demanding that the Southern
states equitably provide the monies and land for institutions that would admit
the freedmen. Even though an equal distribution of the monies between the two
land-grant systems never came to fruition, this second Morrill Act did eventually
give rise to several historically black agricultural and mechanical colleges.

By the late 1920s, many of the land-grant institutions had dropped such names
as ''Normal School'' or ''Mechanical College for Colored Youth'' and had
begun to refer to themselves as colleges and universities. As the literacy rate of
their students rose, the land-grant colleges began to implement more collegiate-
level instruction. By the late 1930s, the land-grant colleges were starting to
receive accreditation by the Southern Association of Colleges and Secondary
Schools*; by the early 1940s, they had become full-fledged institutions of higher
education, having added courses in many disciplines besides agriculture and
offering four-year courses leading to B.A. and B.S. degrees. In some institutions,
postgraduate degrees were offered as well.

Although the first extension work was actually begun in 1906 by Thomas
Monroe Campbell, cooperative agricultural extension did not reach substantial
numbers of African-American farmers until the passage of the Smith–Lever Act
in 1914. This legislation made possible the ''Movable School,'' a staple of
extension work. This teaching facility on wheels went to remote areas of the
counties to give various home demonstrations on methods and procedures for
canning, hog killing, home sanitation, sewing, planting, and crop rotation—
anything to help African-American farmers improve their quality of life. The
Movable School was also the pride of Dr. George Washington Carver, one of
the pioneers in cooperative extension work. Working in his laboratories at Tuskegee Institute*, Dr. Carver developed many different strains of hybrid seeds
and a host of chemicals, paints, and dyes. Because long-distance communication
was virtually nonexistent and because many African-American farmers were
unable to read the trade journals published by Dr. Carver, an alternative means
of bringing new technologies to these farmers became necessary; hence, the
movable school came into being.

Another type of extension work consisted of teams of two or three agents,
usually based at land-grant colleges. These extension teams typically included
a teacher from the college, a county agent who was directly under the aegis of
the state and/or federal agriculture board, and a nurse or, in some cases, a female
agent who gave home demonstrations to the farmer's wife. Together, these extension teams kept African-American farmers up-to-date on the news and technology in agricultural advances. The extension teams also serendipitously

provided another important service. They became the first recruiters for the historically black colleges.

Out of the extension workers' interest in the farmers' lives grew a need to provide services that included programs for children. Thus, organizations like the New Farmers of America (NFA) and the New Homemakers of America (NHA) were established. Young boys and girls of NFA and NHA got hands-on training in farming, homemaking, and technical arts. NFA also provided a social outlet for young African-American males. There were fairs, competitions, opportunities for public speaking, and lessons in parliamentary procedures. NFA was often the only organization in which African-American male youth could hold office. NHA offered similar experiences for African-American females, although not to the extent that NFA did for males. Many of NFA's intramural activities were held on land-grant college campuses. Because all land-grant colleges had cooperative extension departments and worked closely with extension agents, admissions officials began to recruit the young members of NFA, often while they were still in junior high school.

By the early 1970s, NFA was defunct. It had merged with the Future Farmers of American (FFA), its white-dominated counterpart. After integration, African-American youths left NFA to join FFA, where they were not welcomed by the young white members. African-American youth were prevented from holding office or participating in any meaningful way in FFA. By the time African-American youths realized what they had sacrificed by joining the white organization, NFA no longer existed.

Today, African-Americans no longer own or farm the amount of land they once did. In the early 1900s, African-American farmers owned over fifteen million acres of land. By the early 1990s, that acreage had dwindled to fewer than two million. During that same period the total number of African-American farmers declined from one million to approximately twenty-three thousand. Some of this land was simply lost, but much of it was sold by the farmers, often to provide college tuition for their children. Though African-Americans may never again become holders of major tracts of land, they may be able to capitalize on technological advances to maximize their resources. Agriculture always will be important to all societies. African-Americans cannot be content to be relegated to a role as mere consumers of goods and services. In order to achieve economic independence, African-Americans must assume a major role in the nation's production of food and fiber.

SELECTED BIBLIOGRAPHY

B. D. Mayberry, *The Role of Tuskegee University in the Origin, Growth and Development of the Negro Cooperative Extension System 1881–1990* (1989); B. D. Mayberry, *A Century of Agriculture in the 1890 Land-Grant Institutions and Tuskegee University 1890–1990* (1991); "The Tuskegee Institute Movable School 1906–23," *Agricultural History* 45 (July 1971): 101–6; Ledell W. Neyland, *Historically Black Land-Grant Institutions and the Development of Agriculture and Home Economics 1890–1990* (1990); Barbara

Cotton, *The 1890 Land-Grant Colleges: A Centennial Review* (1992); Wayne D. Rasmussen, *Taking the University to the People: Seventy-Five Years of Cooperative Extension* (1989).

ERICA JOCELYN CHEW

ALABAMA A&M UNIVERSITY. Situated in Huntsville, Alabama, Alabama A&M University is a coeducational land-grant institution of higher learning. Founded in 1875, the university has a strong commitment to academic excellence. Alabama A&M University also fosters well-rounded character growth among its diverse student population through numerous extracurricular activities for students' involvement. The academic programs at AAMU are fully accredited by several associations, and the academic offerings include five undergraduate areas of concentration, in its schools of agriculture and home economics, arts and sciences, business, education, and engineering and technology. Together, these schools offer more than seventy majors. A school of graduate studies, offering master's and doctoral degrees, forms a sixth school. With the approval of Ph.D. programs in applied physics, plant and soil sciences, and food science, the university offers courses and degrees at the doctorate level. A strong research and training program is supported by local, federal, and private funds.
SELECTED BIBLIOGRAPHY
National Association for Equal Opportunity in Higher Education, *Profiles of the Nation's Historically and Predominantly Black Colleges and Universities* (1993).

SAMUEL L. MYERS

ALABAMA STATE UNIVERSITY. Alabama State University began in Marion, Alabama, in 1866, as the Lincoln Normal School, a private institution. It had as its aim ''the Higher Education of the Colored Race.'' In 1874, it became the first state-supported historically black institution and was for many years the only school of its kind in the southern states. The university in recent years has expanded its role from that of a teacher-training institution to that of a multipurpose university whose degree-granting programs and offerings are changing and growing to respond to the needs of a dynamic society. Today, ASU houses seven major units: the University College, the College of Arts and Sciences, the College of Business Administration, the College of Education, the School of Music, the School of Graduate Studies and Continuing Education, and the Division of Aerospace Studies. Academic offerings range from a two-year associate's degree to the bachelor's and master's degrees and through the educational specialist degree programs. The institution's physical plant is approximately 138 acres.
SELECTED BIBLIOGRAPHY
National Association for Equal Opportunity in Higher Education, *Profiles of the Nation's Historically and Predominantly Black Colleges and Universities* (1993).

SAMUEL L. MYERS

ALCORN STATE UNIVERSITY. Established in 1871, Alcorn State University is one of Mississippi's two land-grant universities. It has an enrollment of approximately 2,900 students and more than five hundred faculty and staff members. Approximately 50 percent of the 151 members of the faculty hold earned doctoral degrees. The university offers instruction in seven divisions: General College for Excellence, Agriculture and Applied Science, Arts and Sciences, Business and Economics, Education and Psychology, Nursing, and Graduate Studies. More than fifty undergraduate majors are offered, and the university's graduate division offers the master's degree in elementary education, secondary education, and agriculture and the educational specialist in elementary education. Alcorn State University is accredited by the Southern Association of Colleges and Schools,* the National Association of Schools of Music, the National Council for the Accreditation of Teacher Education (NCATE), the National League for Nursing, and the National Association for Industrial Technology. Alcorn has an extensive research program, a program of cooperative extension, and an agricultural and forestry experiment station.

SELECTED BIBLIOGRAPHY

National Association for Equal Opportunity in Higher Education, *Profiles of the Nation's Historically and Predominantly Black Colleges and Universities* (1993).

SAMUEL L. MYERS

ALEXANDER v. HOLMES COUNTY BOARD OF EDUCATION, 396 U.S. 19 (1969). In *Alexander*, the United States Supreme Court ordered that its school desegregation decree in *Brown v. Board of Education** be implemented immediately in elementary and secondary public school systems. In the 1954 *Brown* decision, the Supreme Court had urged that schools be desegregated with ''all deliberate speed.'' In 1969, some fifteen years later, the Supreme Court decreed that school systems could no longer operate segregated schools. Instead, ''the obligation of every school district is to terminate dual school systems at once and to operate now and hereafter only unitary [desegregated] schools.'' This order required school districts to convert immediately to unitary systems. The districts were permitted to submit objections to or propose amendments to desegregation orders, but only after they had converted to unitary systems. Thus, desegregation in the schools was no longer to be delayed by legal challenges to desegregation orders.

SELECTED BIBLIOGRAPHY

Alexander v. Holmes County Board of Education, 396 U.S. 19 (1969).

STEVE ROYSTER

ALLEN, WALTER RECHARDE (3 February 1949, Kansas City, Missouri). A sociologist by training, Walter R. Allen has developed a comprehensive understanding about students of color at institutions of higher education through many research undertakings. He holds a B.A. from Beloit College (Wisconsin, 1971), an M.A. and a Ph.D. in sociology from the University of Chicago (1973 and 1975, respectively). In addition, he has taught at the University of North

Carolina–Chapel Hill and the University of Michigan and currently is a professor of sociology at the University of California, Los Angeles.

Most notably, Allen's involvement with the National Study of Black College Students (NSBCS) at the University of Michigan has served African-American education by using empirical methods to present a thorough picture of the experiences of African-American college students at both traditionally white and historically black institutions. The findings and implications of Allen's research are exigent to the amelioration of the situation of African-Americans in society. *College in Black and White*, a book that reports some findings from the NSBCS, is replete with major studies based on data that are the first of their kind. Allen and the two other editors (Edgar G. Epps, University of Chicago, and Nesha Z. Haniff, University of Michigan) have included in this work analyses that challenge the prevailing misunderstandings and assumptions about African-American college students.

Allen has been the recipient of the distinguished leadership award from the United Negro College Fund (1985), the Rockefeller Foundation fellowship (1982–83), a Fulbright scholarship to the University of Zimbabwe (1984, 1986–87), and the American Educational Research Association distinguished scholar award (1987).

SELECTED BIBLIOGRAPHY
Walter Recharde Allen and Reynolds Farley, *The Color Line and the Quality of Life* (1987); Walter Recharde Allen, "Black Student, White Campus: Structural, Interpersonal, and Psychological Correlates of Success," *Journal of Negro Education* 54, no. 2 (1985): 134–47; Walter Recharde Allen, "The Color of Success: African-American College Student Outcomes at Predominantly White and Historically Black Public Colleges and Universities," *Harvard Education Review* 62, no. 1 (1992): 26–44.

TIMOTHY K. EATMAN

ALLEN UNIVERSITY. Allen University in Columbia, South Carolina, is the oldest historically black college in that state. It was founded in 1870 under the auspices of the African Methodist Episcopal Church. Allen recognizes the unique characteristics of its students by emphasizing personalized instruction in four major academic divisions—education, humanities, natural sciences and behavioral sciences. Academic programs for future emphasis include the health sciences, nutrition, gerontology, computer science, energy technology, urban studies, public administration, and adult and continuing education. Students are encouraged to maximize their academic program with practical work experiences. Five buildings on the twenty-acre campus have been officially awarded the "Historic District Status" by the U.S. Department of the Interior.

SAMUEL L. MYERS

ALSTON v. BOARD OF EDUCATION OF THE CITY OF NORFOLK, 112 F.2d 992 (4th Circuit, 1940), cert. denied 311 U.S. 693 (1940). The NAACP* and African-American teachers in the public schools of the South began a campaign in the late 1930s to achieve a single salary schedule that raised African-American teachers' pay to parity with white teachers'. Victories in state court in Maryland encouraged efforts elsewhere. But when Aline E. Black, a teacher at Booker T. Washington High School in Norfolk, Virginia, sued for salary equalization, she lost her case in June 1939 in local court. The school board took the position that it had absolute discretion in hiring matters, including establishing salary levels. Before she could appeal to Virginia's supreme court, the school board declined to renew her contract. However, upon losing her job, she lost her standing to sue. The board made it clear that she could not teach as long as she pursued her litigation.

Later that year, Black's colleague Melvin O. Alston, a teacher and principal at Norfolk's Booker T. Washington High School, initiated action against the school board. Alston, who had been teaching in the system since 1935, was making an annual salary of only $921, while a white male high school principal could make no less than $1,200 even in his first year. Alston's lawyers were the same as Black's—the NAACP's Thurgood Marshall,* Leon A. Ransom, and William H. Hastie, as well as Virginia attorney J. Thomas Hewin, Jr.—together with newcomer Oliver W. Hill. When the Norfolk School Board did as it had with Black and rejected Alston's petition for salary equalization, he took the case to the U.S. District Court. Though Judge Luther B. Way dismissed the suit in February 1940, he expected the case to be appealed and gave the city a verbal lashing for refusing to rehire Aline Black in the earlier case.

Alston's case went to the Fourth Circuit Court of Appeals, which accepted Thurgood Marshall's major arguments and, in June 1940, handed Alston and the NAACP a major victory. Did the teachers have a constitutional right that was being violated? They did. Was there a remedy? There was. For the Fourteenth Amendment to come into play, Alston's plight had first to involve state action. As the court noted, the Virginia state constitution mandated the establishment and maintenance of a system of free public schools throughout the state. The Norfolk city schools were "under the direct control and supervision" of the school board and the school superintendent. "Solely upon" the basis of "race or color," the court declared, defendants had long pursued a policy "of paying Negro teachers and principals in the public schools in Norfolk less salary" than their white counterparts "possessing the same professional qualifications, certifications and experience, exercising the same duties and performing the same services as Negro teachers and principals." Alston and all other African-American teachers in Norfolk were "being denied the equal protection of the laws." The court went on to reject the school board's "position that no one but a teacher holding a contract with the Board has any such interest in the rate of pay as would give him standing to sue concerning it," and that, having signed a contract, he had waived any right to challenge its provisions. Teachers' waivers of the right to contest their salaries could not extend beyond their one-year contracts. Thus the court reversed the lower court ruling and sent the case back for trial in district court. There, Alston and the NAACP could be confident of securing a declaratory judgment against the school board's previous policy and a permanent injunction against further racial discrimination in teachers' salaries.

It was a victory of enormous magnitude, if it could be made to stick. The city appealed the case, but on 28 October 1940 the Supreme Court denied certiorari—declined to review it—and Alston's victory stood. Yet agreement seemed difficult to achieve. The Norfolk teachers accepted a school board offer that would raise their salaries in increments over a three-year period to parity with white teachers. Attorneys for the school board and the African-American teachers differed, however, over what the agreement should say. The city objected to inclusion of such terms of enforcement as "declaratory judgment" and "permanent injunction," while Hill insisted on them. Even as African-American teachers received pay checks that included the increment that had been agreed upon, the case was scheduled for hearing in the federal district court after all. Some teachers, wishing to avoid further court action, favored accepting the school board's version, but the NAACP legal staff threatened to walk away from the case if the teachers did so. The week before the case was scheduled for trial on its merits, final agreement was reached in February 1941. The city capitulated. The consent decree was entered.

African-American teachers and the NAACP had secured a powerful precedent. Following the victory in the Alston case, they followed the strategy in that case as they initiated efforts to equalize salaries in various southern states. To be sure, outside Norfolk there was nothing automatic, certainly nothing swift, about compliance with the spirit of the Alston decision. Even in Virginia, further cases were filed in District Court regarding salary schedules in Newport News and Richmond (an out-of-court settlement in Richmond, reached in 1942, called for equalization in five annual increments). Nevertheless, great progress was made in the next few years in achieving racial equality in teachers' salaries. Moreover, Oliver Hill and the NAACP brought successful subsequent litigation in federal court in Virginia that addressed such questions as equalizing curricular offerings and physical facilities in public high schools. In 1950, the NAACP changed its strategy regarding public schools to attack segregation rather than inequality within segregation.

SELECTED BIBLIOGRAPHY

George M. Fredrickson, *The Black Image in the White Mind: The Debate of Afro-American Character and Destiny, 1817–1914* (1971); Mark V. Tushnet, *The NAACP's Legal Strategy against Segregated Education, 1925–1950* (1987); *Norfolk Journal and Guide* (10 June 1939): 8, (7 February 1940): 1, (5 February 1941): 1–2.

PETER WALLENSTEIN

AMERICAN MISSIONARY ASSOCIATION. The American Missionary Association (AMA) began its existence on 3 September 1846, in Buffalo, New York, as a result of the merger of the Union Missionary Society, the Committee for West Indian Missions, and the Western Evangelical Missionary Society. The coalition's initial interests focused upon founding Christian missions around the world, but it soon shifted attention to the nonviolent overthrow of slavery in the United States. In 1847, as one of the organization's first active steps toward this goal, the AMA initiated relief services for slaves who had successfully escaped into Canada. The commitment to African-American education, which became the AMA's hallmark, began in 1859 with the founding of Berea College* in Kentucky. Outspoken abolitionist Cassius M. Clay donated the land to John G. Fee, who opened the institution to African-Americans and whites alike. Shortly after opening, however, the school closed as a result of pressures from local whites frightened by John Brown's raid on Harper's Ferry in neighboring Virginia. Berea College reopened in 1865 with three African-American students in attendance, marking the first time in higher education that blacks and whites attended classes together in the South.

The AMA continued its commitment to African-American education during and after the Civil War. The first AMA school for freedmen opened at Fortress Monroe, Virginia, under the direction of Mary S. Peake* on 17 September, 1861. AMA volunteers provided relief services and education for the growing number of former slaves throughout the war. During Reconstruction, a network of over five hundred colleges and normal schools developed in the South. AMA educators from the North often faced open hostility to their presence in southern states. Several schools were burned, and many teachers became victims of attacks by racist organizations such as the Ku Klux Klan. Southern whites perceived African-American education as a threat to their political dominance, and others claimed that AMA schools provided blacks with training not available to whites of the same regions. As a result of the AMA's commitment to education, however, the work continued. Seven thousand of the fifteen thousand African-American teachers in the South in 1870 had attended AMA schools. In an attempt to gain white support, the AMA also opened schools for the predominantly poor white children living in the mountains of Virginia.

Today, most of the five hundred schools founded by the AMA have been absorbed by state and local education systems. Of the ten surviving colleges founded by the AMA, six remain in close association with the organization: Dillard University* (New Orleans, La.), Fisk University* (Nashville, Tenn.), Tougaloo College* (Tougaloo, Miss.), Huston-Tillotson College (Austin, Tex.), LeMoyne Owen College* (Memphis, Tenn.), and Talladega College* (Talladega, Ala.). The national headquarters are currently located in New York, N.Y.

SELECTED BIBLIOGRAPHY

American Missionary Archives, Fisk University, Nashville, Tennessee; *The American Missionary* 1–89 (1846–1934); Augustus-Field Beard, *A Crusade of Brotherhood* (1972 reprint of 1909 edition); F. Q. Blanchard, "A Quarter Century in the American Missionary Association," *Journal of Negro Education* 6 (April 1937): 152–56; Edmund L. Drago, *Initiative, Paternalism and Race Relations: Charleston's Avery Normal Institute* (1990); Clifton H. Johnson, "The American Missionary Association, 1846–1861: A Study of Christian Abolitionism," Ph.D. diss., University of North Carolina, 1958; Lewis C. Lockwood, "Mary S. Peake, the Colored Teacher at Fortress Monroe" (1874), reprinted in William L. Katz, ed., *Two Black Teachers during the Civil War* (1969); Joe M. Richardson, *Christian Reconstruction: The American Missionary Association and Southern Blacks, 1861–1890* (1986).

JAMES W. STENNETT

AMERICAN NEGRO ACADEMY. The American Negro Academy, founded in 1897 in Washington, D.C., was the first major African-American learned society in the United States. Its purpose was the promotion of intellectual activity and leadership among African-Americans. The organization was established by African-American Episcopal clergyman Alexander Crummell, its first president, with the help of such noted African-American scholars and intellectuals as W. E. B. Du Bois,* William Crogman, and Francis J. Grimké.

The ANA was launched during an era marked by the infamous *Plessy v. Ferguson* (1896)* segregation ruling and by the burgeoning Jim Crow, Social Gospel, and Social Darwinism* movements, which respectively proclaimed the social, moral, and intellectual inferiority of nonwhites. To counter this climate of racial hostility and refute the arguments advanced by "cultured despisers" of people of African descent in both the North and the South, the organization held annual meetings at which its members engaged in discussion and critical reflection on issues incident to African-Americans. They presented scholarly papers on topics related to black culture, history, religion, civil and social rights, and institutions. Twenty-two of these presentations were published by the ANA as occasional papers between 1897 and 1924. ANA members also organized historical exhibits and established an archival collection of books by and about people of African descent.

For thirty-one years, until its dissolution in 1928, the ANA struggled to survive in a climate of tumultuous social change and race relations. Throughout its history, its membership remained relatively small for several reasons. Educated African-Americans constituted less than 3 percent of the African-American community prior to 1900. Moreover, because the ANA was comprised of a select group of individuals who sought to function as intellectuals, it never received the support of Tuskeegee Institute* president Booker T. Washington,* the influential leader whose ideas about vocational education and African-American acquiescence dominated the African-American community during over half the organization's lifetime. Despite these obstacles, the ANA became a significant clearinghouse and strategy center for African America. Prominent members who joined the ANA after the turn of the century include John Hope, president of Morehouse College* and later Atlanta University (now Clark Atlanta University*); Alain L. Locke,* Howard University* professor, critic, and key figure in the Harlem Renaissance; historian Carter G. Woodson*; and poet, writer, and civil rights leader James Weldon Johnson.

SELECTED BIBLIOGRAPHY
Alfred A. Moss, Jr., *American Negro Academy* (1981); Rayford W. Logan and Michael R. Winston, eds., "Grimké, Francis J.," *Dictionary of American Negro Biography* (1982): 273–74.

D. KAMILI ANDERSON

AMERICAN TEACHER CORPS. Established in 1965, this U.S. Office of Education federal discretionary grant program was part of President Lyndon B. Johnson's Great Society efforts. Its purpose was to strengthen the educational opportunities available to children in areas having concentrations of low-income families; to encourage colleges and universities to broaden their program of teacher preparation; and to encourage institutions of higher education and local educational agencies to improve programs of training and retraining for teachers, teacher aides, and other educational personnel. Teacher Corps provided opportunities for thousands of African-American educators to achieve prominence and have influence in the nation's educational system. It brought over thirteen thousand African-American, Hispanic, Asian-American, Native American, and European American liberal arts college graduates into the teaching profession during its first ten years of operation. Nearly 70 percent of those who participated in the program remained in teaching or education, as teachers, principals, superintendents, professors, and senior university educators.

Teacher Corps was the cornerstone of pioneering efforts to develop and support educational innovation and change in public schools and in teacher preparation programs in colleges and universities. It implemented team teaching, flexible grouping of students, individualized and personalized instruction of students, bilingual and multicultural education, competency-based teacher education, alternative schools, collaborative planning and site-based decision-making, community and school-based teacher education, and community councils that directed the efforts of each project.

As a federal program, the Teacher Corps was unique in its mission and longevity and in its ability to respond to the changing needs of the urban educational environments and the youth they serve. Approximately fifty million children and their parents were served by interns and other Teacher Corps participants over the seventeen-year life span of the program.

H. JEROME FREIBERG

ARKANSAS BAPTIST COLLEGE. Arkansas Baptist College, a four-year historically black church-related institution, offers a liberal arts–oriented academic program leading to terminal degrees in the natural and physical sciences, social sciences, education, and business administration. The college, organized in 1884, provides, in addition to its academic program, service programs that benefit the state and local community. The programs include a Kiddie Kollege for preschoolers and noncredit courses through an extended career arrangement with the Arkansas Baptist Convention. Arkansas Baptist College participates in the Greater Little Rock Center for Higher Education, a consortium of historically black colleges in the Little Rock area. The college's student body is composed of students from the local community, rural Arkansas, and major urban centers throughout the country.

SELECTED BIBLIOGRAPHY

National Association for Equal Opportunity in Higher Education, *Profiles of the Nation's Historically and Predominantly Black Colleges and Universities* (1993).

SAMUEL L. MYERS

ARMED FORCES, AFRICAN-AMERICAN EDUCATION IN THE. Historically, African-Americans have benefitted from the instruction and services provided by the U.S. armed forces. Although the reason for this instruction was often the self-interest of a government needing men to go to war, it remains that African-Americans' involvement in the armed forces provided them, often for the first time, an opportunity to acquire a basic education.

In 1862, a year after the start of the Civil War, African-Americans were accepted into the nation's military services. General Benjamin F. Butler initiated African-Americans' recruitment into the U.S. Army, but black soldiers were remunerated with lower wages than were whites and were further placed in segregated units. Nearly two hundred thousand African-Americans served in combat units during the Civil War, and about 20 percent of them gave their lives for the survival of the Union. During the war, and during the early years of Reconstruction, the chaplains of the African-American regiments often served a dual role as literacy instructors. The most influential of these clergymen was Chaplain George Gatewood Mullins, who started his tour of duty with the Twenty-Fifth Infantry at Fort Davis, Texas, in 1875. Observing among his students a correlation between the acquisition of literacy and an increase in their sense of self-respect, pride, and dedication to military duties, Chaplain Mullins became a strong supporter of education in the armed forces. His advocacy was supported in 1878 by an order from the War Department asking all military units to provide education for enlisted men. Chaplain Allen Allensworth, an ex-slave who had served in the Union Navy during the war, was another preeminent clergyman who promoted education among African-American soldiers and devised a comprehensive curriculum for them.

The Servicemen's Readjustment Act of 1944 (popularly known as the G.I. Bill of Rights), sponsored by President Franklin D. Roosevelt, offered monetary, employment, and educational assistance to veterans. These benefits included up to four years of education and vocational training, in the total amount of two thousand dollars, with additional living allowances. Amendments in 1945 raised both tuition and living allowances. Preceding the desegregation of the armed forces in 1948, the G.I. Bill was instrumental in promoting education among African-Americans and consequently improving their socioeconomic condition. Postwar enrollment of African-American veterans at black colleges rose from 43,003 in 1940 to 76,000 by 1950. To enforce educational opportunities for

African-American soldiers, the Defense Department ruled in 1964 that academic institutions practicing racial discrimination would not receive federal financial assistance. Among veterans of the Korean and Vietnam wars, who were also entitled to educational benefits for a period of ten years following their discharge, participation rates in academic programs were higher for African-Americans than for other veterans.

SELECTED BIBLIOGRAPHY

Ira Berlin, ed., *Freedom: The Black Military Experience* (1982); Dudley Taylor Cornish, "The Union Army as a School for Negroes" *Journal of Negro History* 37 (October 1952): 368–82; John W. Blassingame, "The Union Army as an Educational Institution for Negroes, 1862–1865," *Journal of Negro Education* 34 (Spring 1965): 152–59; Veterans Administration, *Report of Educational Testing Service on Educational Assistance Programs for Veterans* (1973); Keith W. Olson, *The GI Bill, the Veterans, and the Colleges* (1974).

CONSTANCE A. BURNS

ARMSTRONG, SAMUEL CHAPMAN (30 January 1839, Maui, Hawaii–11 May 1893, Hampton, Virginia). The founder in 1868 of Hampton Normal and Agricultural Institute (now Hampton University*) the first black vocational training school in the South, Samuel Chapman Armstrong devoted his life to promoting the "Hampton-Tuskegee Idea," the model of black industrial and missionary education that formed so large a part of the southern education movement.

Raised in Hawaii by missionary parents, Armstrong, who was white, observed firsthand the principles of agricultural and industrial training. He later applauded the "reinforcement of mechanics to train and harden the soft Hawaiian hand, to establish industrious habits, and thus to supply a stamina which the native character lacked." This kind of education was not just practical; it was considered "wise missionary work," endowing native Hawaiians with both the work skills they would need to survive in a market society and the moral and spiritual values that make work itself not only a necessity but also an act of Christian redemption.

After his father's sudden death in 1860, Armstrong left the islands to complete his education at Williams College in Massachusetts, graduating there with honors in 1862. Seeing in the plight of African-American slaves a cause worthy of the moral idealism taught to him as child, Armstrong joined the Union army with a captain's commission, moving quickly up the ranks from lieutenant colonel to colonel of the Eighth and Ninth Regiments of the United States Colored Troops.

Armstrong left the war a Brevet Brigadier General, but instead of returning to Hawaii or New England he remained in the South, taking a job as the Freedmen's Bureau officer in charge of ten counties of eastern Virginia, with headquarters at Hampton. Already persuaded of the benefits of manual training through his Hawaiian upbringing and convinced through his war experience of the "excellent qualities and capacities" of the freedmen, Armstrong approached the American Missionary Association* about supporting a manual training school for blacks—"an industrial system, not only for the sake of self-support and intelligent labor, but for the sake of character."

The Hampton Normal and Agricultural Institute opened its doors in 1868 and was chartered by the State of Virginia in 1870. The school was from the first devoted to the method of learning by doing, with the belief that the salvation of the African-American race would have to "be won out of the ground. Skillful agriculturalists and mechanics are needed," Armstrong wrote in the Annual Report for 1872, "rather than poets and orators." Armstrong's most famous student at Hampton, Booker T. Washington,* would go on to enshrine these sentiments at his own manual training school in Tuskegee, Alabama. Washington's message to African-Americans in 1895 was to "cast down your bucket where you are" and to develop first and foremost their economic prospects, realizing that "there is as much dignity in tilling a field as in writing a poem."

The "New Education" spread from Hawaii to the post–Civil War South and to the United States as a whole in the twentieth century. It spread even further, to as many corners of the world as there were American missionary outposts. Armstrong's life and work and its widespread influence during and after Reconstruction came to exemplify the major social, religious, and educational ideals that by the twentieth century had come to dominate American policy, foreign as well as domestic.

SELECTED BIBLIOGRAPHY

James D. Anderson, *The Education of Blacks in the South, 1860–1935* (1980); Samuel Chapman Armstrong, *Education for Life* (1914); Ronald Butchart, *Northern Schools, Southern Blacks, and Reconstruction: Freedmen's Education, 1962–1875* (1980); Robert F. Engs, *Freedom's First Generation: Black Hampton, Virginia, 1861–1890* (1979); Fritz J. Malval, ed., *A Guide to the Archives of Hampton Institute: Bibliographies and Indexes in Afro-American and African Studies*, vol. 5 (1985).

JOHN M. HEFFRON

ARNEZ, NANCY L. (6 July 1928, Baltimore, Maryland). An educator, administrator, college dean, and author, Nancy L. Arnez is the daughter of Milton Emerson Levi and Ida Barbour Rusk. She received an A.B. in English in 1949 from Morgan State College and an M.A. in English (1954) and an Ed.D. in educational administration (1958) from Columbia University, Teachers College. She did postdoctoral study at Harvard University (1962) and Loyola College (1965).

Arnez taught English in Baltimore, Maryland, public schools from 1949 to 1958. In 1958 she served as an English department head. In 1962, Arnez went to Morgan State University* to become the director of student teaching. In 1966 she became assistant director of the Center for Inner City Studies (CICS) at Northeastern Illinois University, Chicago, one of the first multidisciplinary, multicultural centers in the nation. As director of CICS from 1969 to 1974, Arnez was responsible for obtaining approximately two million dollars in federal, state, and local funds for the university.

One of the most outstanding programs developed for lower-income African-American children was the Cultural Linguistic Follow-Through Approach, co-founded by Arnez in 1969. In 1974, she became associate dean of the School of Education at Howard University* and acting dean in 1975. In 1976, she became a full-time professor of educational administration, served as chairperson of the department from 1980 to 1986, and subsequently became coordinator of the Educational Administration Program.

Arnez is the recipient of numerous honors and awards. These include an appointment as an Honorary Citizen of Compton, California, 1972, for bringing her Cultural Linguistic Follow-Through Program there; the Howard University distinguished faculty research award, 1983; and first placement in the Regional Phi Delta Kappa Biennial Research Competition for Outstanding Research, 1985. Arnez has been a member of numerous professional organizations, including the African Heritage Studies Association, *Phi Delta Kappan*, and the American Association of School Administrators, and a board member of the *Journal of Negro Education*.* From 1981 to 1984, she served as editor of the National Alliance of Black School Educators'* *Newsbrief*.

A prolific writer, Dr. Arnez has at least 168 significant educational and creative publications to her credit. These include ten book chapters, nineteen books and manuals, forty articles, twenty curriculum pieces written for the Association for the Study of Afro-American Life and History,* twenty-nine poems, and fifty book reviews. At least seven of her books, manuals, and articles deal directly with administrative issues affecting African-Americans, including her best-known book, *The Besieged School Superintendent* (1981). Her other publications deal with various aspects of the effective teaching of African-American inner-city children.

SELECTED BIBLIOGRAPHY

Nancy L. Arnez, *Cultural Linguistic Approach to Education* (1972); Nancy L. Arnez, *Partners in Urban Education: Teaching the Inner City Child* (1973); Nancy L. Arnez, "Implementation of Desegregation as a Discriminatory Process," *Journal of Negro Education* 47 (Winter 1978); I. Cloyd and W. Matney, Jr., eds., *Who's Who Among Black Americans 1990/1991* (1990); *Who's Who in America* (1992–93).

MYSCHELLE W. SPEARS

ARTHUR v. NYQUIST, 712 F.2d 816 (2d Cir. 1983). *Arthur v. Nyquist* is a leading case on the remedial authority of federal trial courts to impair the seniority rights of teachers in order to eliminate the vestiges of racial segregation in public education. Decided in the context of the more than decade-long battle to dismantle de facto segregation in the Buffalo, New York, public school system, the influential Second Circuit Court of Appeals affirmed the most significant aspects of a race-conscious plan for the hiring and laying off of teachers as a means of achieving desegregation despite contractually or statutorily established seniority systems. In *Arthur v. Nyquist* the Second Circuit joined the First Circuit as the only federal courts to have upheld faculty layoffs as a tool to establish equitable staffing patterns in the face of de facto segregation. Although the continued viability of *Arthur* is questionable after the Supreme Court's ruling in *Wygant v. Jackson Board of Education*,* it does represent the proposition that trial courts may use their equitable powers in fashioning remedies in the continuing struggle to eradicate the vestiges of de facto segregation.

In March 1979, subsequent to the initial round of litigation, the district court issued a two-part desegregation order. First, the percentage of minorities in all job classifications was to equal the 21 percent minority population in the community at large. Second, the targeted rate was to be achieved by a "one-to-one" hiring plan, under which the Board was required to hire one minority teacher for each majority teacher hired. Problems with implementation surfaced in August 1979 when tenured teachers who had been laid off by the district a year earlier due to fiscal difficulties sought to return to work. The crux of the problem was fourfold. First, state law and the operative collective bargaining agreement established preferred eligibility lists based on seniority. Second, the lists were composed largely of white applicants. Third, there was a paucity of minority applicants. Finally, the order denied many long-term substitute teachers, most of whom were white, the opportunity to be offered appointments on the basis of seniority.

After the trial court modified its plan as a result of challenges by the Buffalo Teachers Federation, the union sought further review from the Second Circuit. The union argued that the trial court's order exceeded its equitable powers. At the outset, the Second Circuit rejected the union's claim that the trial court's order was invalid simply because it infringed upon the statutory and contractual rights of teachers who had not contributed to the pattern of segregation practiced by the Board. It noted succinctly that a state law could not impede a remedy designed to redress a constitutional violation such as segregation. The Second Circuit held that, given the finding of intentional discrimination in Buffalo's staffing practices, which contributed to the continuation of a racially segregated school system, the trial court had the authority to impose an equitable remedy. This meant that it could override seniority schemes that helped perpetuate segregation. At the same time, the Second Circuit cautioned that, in fashioning its remedy, a trial court had to be careful not only to avoid excessive use of its power but also to balance individual and collective interests.

The Second Circuit affirmed the three most salient aspects of the plan. First, it found the "one-to-one" formula to be acceptable because it was imposed only after Buffalo failed to take steps to increase significantly the number of minority teachers it employed. Second, it held that the district could be ordered to utilize long-term substitutes rather than hire new tenure-track teachers in areas where there were insufficient minority applicants. It opined that to do otherwise would permit the then-current shortage of minority teachers to be reflected in the system's tenured faculty for years to come. Finally, the court upheld the directive calling for any future layoffs on a percentage basis, as this would guarantee the maintenance of the existing ratio of minority to majority staff. It reasoned that if prospective layoffs were based on seniority alone, the progress made in increasing the number of minority teachers would be eroded because, as educators with the least seniority, they would be at the greatest risk of being laid off.

The Second Circuit reversed that part of the trial court's order that dealt in a needlessly harsh manner with the rights of laid-off teachers. It ruled that it was acceptable to place teachers on preferred eligibility lists in the order in which they were laid off rather than recall them pursuant to a "one-to-one" plan. The court adopted this approach because it protected the statutory and contractual rights of the teachers; it also hoped that this would eventually establish percentage rehiring equal to the rate of layoffs ordered below, even though white teachers with greater seniority would be more likely to be rehired prior to their minority colleagues. The Supreme Court denied certiorari to a further appeal filed by the union in *Buffalo Teachers Federation v. Arthur.*

SELECTED BIBLIOGRAPHY

Arthur v. Nyquist, 712 F.2d 816 (2d Cir. 1983).

CHARLES J. RUSSO AND J. JOHN HARRIS III

ASANTE, MOLEFI KETE (14 August 1942, Valdosta, Georgia). Molefi K. Asante is professor and chair, Department of African-American Studies at Temple University. Considered to be one of the most distinguished contemporary scholars, Professor Asante has published more than two hundred articles and is the author or editor of thirty-three books, including seminal works on the Afrocentric theory, *Afrocentricity, The Afrocentric Idea*, and *Kemet, Afrocentricity and Knowledge.*

Asante received his Ph.D. in 1968 from UCLA at the age of twenty-six and was appointed a full professor at the State University of New York at age thirty. He is the creator of the world's first doctoral program in African-American Studies at Temple University and is the founder of the National Afrocentric Institute. An activist scholar, Asante is a member of the numerous pan-African organizations, including the Institute of the Black Peoples–Ouagadougou, the African Continental University, and the National Council for Black Studies.* Since 1969 he has edited the *Journal of Black Studies* and served as associate editor of eighteen journals. Dr. Asante has guided the dissertations of more than fifty students.

SELECTED BIBLIOGRAPHY

Christa Brelin and William C. Matney, Jr. eds., *Who's Who among Black Americans, 1992/1993* (1992).

MYSCHELLE W. SPEARS

ASSOCIATION FOR THE STUDY OF AFRO-AMERICAN LIFE AND HISTORY. Carter Godwin Woodson* founded the Association for the Study of Negro Life and History (later renamed the Association for the Study of Afro-American Life and History, or ASALH) in 1915. He brought national attention to African-American history and enabled the world to learn of the significant past contributions and rich heritage of African-Americans. Woodson described the role of the association as an organization "which publishes an historical magazine, researches the achievements of Negroes, directs a home study program along with writing and publishing books and monographs." He gave priority to the collection and preservation of documents concerning African-American history. Woodson's book, *The Education of the Negro Prior to 1861,* published in 1915, stimulated an even stronger interest in the work of the association.

Among the most prolific writers of African-American history in the twentieth century, Woodson's scholarly works paved the way for African-American Studies programs and the recent interest in Afrocentric education. Woodson believed that racial prejudice resulted from the miseducation of both races. In order to combat this, on 1 January 1916, he founded the *Journal of Negro History,* the association's official scholarly organ, which is widely subscribed to by educators and historians. In 1926, Woodson initiated the annual observance of "Negro History Week" (now known as "National Black History Month"). In 1937, he initiated the *Negro History Bulletin,** which addressed the need for African-American historical materials to be included in elementary and secondary schools.

In 1936, Mary McLeod Bethune, noted educator, was selected as the first woman president of ASALH. A tremendous leadership void was created when Dr. Woodson passed away at the age of 75 on 3 April 1950, in Washington, D.C. The association was then guided by a committee that included such prominent African-American historians as Rayford W. Logan,* Lorenzo Greene, John Hope Franklin,* and Louis R. Mehlinger. Two years later, noted historian and scholar Charles Wesley became president. In 1993, Dr. Janette Hoston Harris was elected national president, becoming the second woman in forty-two years to hold this position.

The Association for the Study of Afro-American Life and History exists today as a testament to the research and writing of Afro-American life and history worldwide. Fulfilling Dr. Woodson's mission to educate youth and the community, the Carter G. Woodson Leadership Institute of the ASALH was launched in 1993. This educational center was established to teach junior high school students the basics of citizenship, African-American history, and leadership development.

SELECTED BIBLIOGRAPHY

"Carter G. Woodson: Mirror and Molder of His Time, 1875–1950," *Journal of Negro History* 58 (January 1973): 4–5, 7; Rayford W. Logan, "An Evaluation of the First Twenty Volumes of the Journal of Negro History," *Journal of Negro History* 20 (October 1935): 397; Patrice Gaines, "Finding the Story in History's Footnote," *Washington Post District Weekly,* D.C.1, 17 March 1994.

JANETTE HOSTON HARRIS

ASSOCIATION OF DEANS OF WOMEN AND ADVISORS TO GIRLS IN NEGRO SCHOOLS. Determined to confront the deplorable living conditions of women students, the inequity in women's salaries, and the exclusion of women from boards of trustees, administrations, and faculties at African-American colleges, Lucy Diggs Slowe,* the first permanent dean of women at Howard University* and founder of the National Association of College Women (NACW), convened a conference at Howard University in March 1929 to address these and other issues. This conference, sponsored by the Committee on Standards of the NACW, gave birth to the Association of Deans of Women and Advisors to Girls in Negro Schools.

Among those attending the Washington, D.C., meeting were Elsie Brown, Carol Cotton, Otelia Cromwell, Marian Cuthbert, Sadie Daniels, Hilda A. Davis,* Johanna Houston, Juanita Howard, Ruth Howard, Bertha McNeil, Anna Payne, Ruth Rush, Georgina Simpson, Alethia Washington, Tossie Whiting, and Gertrude Woodard, as well as Dean Slowe. At the close of this historic conference, five problems in African-American institutions were identified: (a) the lack of African-American women on boards of trustees and college administrations; (b) the need for academically qualified and equitably salaried deans of women and advisors to girls; (c) the lack of adequate and properly equipped housing for female college students; (d) the absence of wholesome extracurricular and well-planned recreational activities for female college students; and (e) the need for separate housing and developmentally appropriate regulations and activities for girls attending high school on college campuses.

For the next five years, these women met annually under the sponsorship of the NACW. At the sixth conference, held at Howard University in 1935, twenty-eight women from eleven states and the District of Columbia voted to establish an independent organization. The founding officers were Lucy Diggs Slowe of Howard University, president; Dorothy Hopson of Hampton Institute,* first vice president; Georgia Myrtle Teale of Wilberforce University,* second vice president; Eva Burrell Holmes of Howard University, second vice president; and Tossie P. Whiting of Virginia State University,* treasurer.

In 1938, the organization adopted its first constitution and took as its name the Association of Deans of Women and Advisors to Girls in Negro Schools. Its purposes were (a) to bolster a spirit of unity and cooperation among deans and advisors of Negro women and girls; (b) to create a recognized professional status for deans, advisors, counselors, and others engaged in the physical, social, and moral uplift of girls and young women in education, civic, and economic life; and (c) to study the best methods of counseling girls and young women. Hilda A. Davis of Talladega College* was elected president of the reconstituted organization.

In 1946 the Association of Deans of Women and Advisors to Girls in Negro Schools held the first joint conference with the National Association of Personnel Deans and Advisors of Men in Negro Institutions. Eight years later, at a joint meeting hosted by Howard University in 1954, the groups voted to merge. The new body formed was the National Association of Personnel Workers

(NAPW). Among its founding officers were many women deans: Sadie M. Yancey of Howard University, president; Arlynne Jones of Grambling State University,* recording secretary; Jean Spinner of North Carolina Agricultural and Technical College,* assistant recording secretary; and Vallete H. Bell Linnette of Virginia State College,* first regional vice president.

In its twenty-five-year history, the Association of Deans of Women and Advisors to Girls in Negro Schools played a critical role in the academy as a professional network for women deans and educators. It provided a setting where role models could be observed and institutional politics candidly discussed. Its conferences represented one of the few training opportunities for African-American women, who were routinely denied full participation at meetings of white associations in which similar activities took place. The Association of Deans of Women and Advisors to Girls in Negro Schools became a national voice for African-American women's educational concerns, as its members were among the most highly placed and articulate women in the academy and the nation.

SELECTED BIBLIOGRAPHY

Mary M. Carter, *The Educational Activities of the National Association of College Women, 1923–1960*, master's thesis, Howard University, Washington, D.C., 1962; Hilda A. Davis and Patricia Bell-Scott, Association of Deans of Women and Advisors to Girls in Negro Schools, *Black Women in America: An Historical Encyclopedia* (1993); Lucy Diggs Slowe, "Some Impressions from Two Conferences of Deans of Women," *Journal of the National Association of College Women* (1935); Lucy Diggs Slowe, "Summary of the Conference of Deans and Advisors to Women in Negro Schools," *Journal of the National Association of College Women* (April 1928); Lucy Diggs Slowe, "Summary of the Seventh Deans' Conference," *Journal of the National Association of College Women* (1936); Elaine Tacil, "The Deans of Women Hold Their Second Conference," *Journal of the National Association of College Women* (1930–31).

HILDA ANDREA DAVIS AND PATRICIA BELL-SCOTT

ATTRITION. Attrition is defined as a gradual reduction in numbers of membership as a result of constant stress. Attrition among college students, which results from several factors, is an issue that has been widely addressed by researchers and scholars.

The study of attrition among African-American college students, in particular, has been addressed by many studies, which have provided empirical evidence that the attrition process among African-American students results from several complex factors. Some of these factors included academic problems related both to inadequate preparation and to the quality of teaching and academic support in colleges, insufficient financial support, interpersonal complications, difficulties with faculty or family life, health problems, and a hostile institutional environment.

As opportunities increased for African-Americans to attend institutions of higher education during the late 1960s and throughout the 1970s, the high school completion rate among African-American students also improved significantly.

As a result, the pool of potential college students among African-American students also increased. This expanded pool resulted in a substantial improvement in the overall participation of African-American students in predominantly white colleges and universities. This growth in enrollment continued throughout the 1970s and 1980s despite social and institutional obstacles. However, although African-American students were increasingly able to enter college, many were not progressing through to graduation, but were dropping out. The problem of attrition among African-American students in the nation's institutions of higher education remains an ongoing challenge.

Researchers have pointed to the social environment of predominantly white campuses as a factor in the attrition of African-American students. They note that these students often experience feelings of loneliness and isolation, withdrawal, and cultural alienation at white institutions. African-American students often see these institutions as hostile environments wherein white students and faculty perceived them as ''special admits'' and beneficiaries of affirmative action programs. Hostile communication from white faculty and students, patronizing attitudes and behaviors by administrators, and the exclusion of African-American contributions to the curriculum are said to interfere with efforts to create a positive learning atmosphere. Moreover, when African-American students form their own support groups, their efforts are frequently discouraged by university officials. Hence, African-American students are kept from pursuing the very activities that might protect them and enhance their potential to remain in college.

Financial assistance also plays an important role in attrition among African-American college students. African-American students are far more likely than whites to receive financial aid to attend college, because of their parents' lower average incomes compared to whites. However, African-American students often get financial-aid packages that combine loans and work study along with grants. This debt burden, coupled with the students' comparatively lower income and their fears of not being able to repay the loans, leads more African-American students to drop out of college.

The majority of African-American students are presently enrolled at predominantly white institutions. It is at these institutions that strong networks and support systems need to be in place to ensure the progression of African-American students from matriculation to graduation. These colleges and universities must aggressively implement any strategy that will enhance the commitment of African-American students to their institutions.

SELECTED BIBLIOGRAPHY

James E. Blackwell, ''Strategies for Improving the Status of Blacks in Higher Education,'' *Planning and Change* 14, no. 1 (1983): 56–73; Patricia H. Cross and Helen S. Astin, ''Factors Affecting Black Students' Persistence in College,'' in Gail E. Thomas, Ed., *Black Students in Higher Education: Conditions and Experiences in the 1970s* (1981); Chalsa M. Loo and Garry Rolison, ''Alienation of Ethnic Minority Students at a Predominantly White University,'' *Journal of Higher Education* 57, no. 1 (1986): 58–

77; Donald H. Smith, "Social and Academic Environments of Black Students on White Campuses," *Journal of Negro Education* 50, no. 3 (1981): 299–306.

                                                                    MARY F. TOLIVER

AYERS v. FORDICE, 112 S. Ct. 27272 (1992). On 26 June 1992, the U.S. Supreme Court, in an eight-to-one decision, concluded that Mississippi had not met its obligation to dismantle its dual racial system of higher education and thereby had violated the U.S. Constitution and the Civil Rights Act of 1964.* From 1964 to 1969, the U.S. Department of Health, Education, and Welfare (HEW) did little to enforce the antidiscrimination clause of Title VI of the 1964 Civil Rights Act. HEW attempted to encourage segregating states to dismantle their segregated systems of higher education, a benign posture. But the ruling in the 1973 case that began as *Kenneth Adams et al. v. Elliot L. Richardson et al.** (Richardson was then secretary of HEW) was that those states that maintained dual systems of segregated higher education were in violation of Title VI. The ten segregating states included Mississippi and collectively became known as the "Adams states." These states were sent letters by HEW requesting that they devise statewide plans to desegregate. Mississippi's plan was rejected in 1973 by HEW as being unsatisfactory because it would not have brought the state into compliance with Title VI. HEW concluded that the plan did not go far enough in the areas of student recruitment and enrollment, faculty hiring, elimination of unnecessary program duplication, and institutional funding practices to ensure that "a student's choice of institution or campus henceforth will be based on something other than racial criteria."

In 1981, the Board of Trustees initiated a volunteer effort to dismantle the state's dual system by issuing mission statements that identified the specific purpose for each of the state's eight universities. The result was that there would be three major categories of universities in Mississippi: comprehensive universities (the University of Mississippi, Mississippi State University, and the University of Southern Mississippi), all of which were exclusively white in prior years; an urban university (Jackson State University),* that was previously all African-American; and regional universities (Alcorn State University* and Mississippi Valley State University*), which were previously all African-American, along with Delta State University and the Mississippi University for Women, which were previously all white. According to the Board of Trustees' plan, the comprehensive universities were to have the greatest resources and program offerings to support research, doctoral degree offerings, and leadership roles in certain disciplines. The sole urban university was to have a smaller research role, a limited degree mission, and a specific focus on urban studies and setting. The regional universities were to focus primarily on undergraduate education; they were not established on geographical factors at all. In spite of this "mission classification" effort in 1985, more than 99 percent of Mississippi's white college students were attending the universities that had been established exclusively for whites, while 71 percent of Mississippi's African-

American college students were attending universities that were originally founded exclusively for African-Americans.

In January 1975, on behalf of his son and other African-American college students, Jake Ayers, Sr., filed a lawsuit in federal court. His claim was that Mississippi was operating a dual system of higher education, one for African-Americans and one for whites. By maintaining these racially segregated systems, plaintiffs contended, the state violated the Fifth, Ninth, Thirteenth, and Four-teenth Amendments of the Constitution and Title VI of the Civil Rights Act of 1964.

The *Ayers v. Fordice* case has implications for eighteen other states that have operated *de jure* separate institutions of higher education. The primary legal issue in this case is whether Mississippi had met its affirmative duty to dismantle its dual system of racially segregated institutions of higher education. Both the U.S. District Court and the 5th U.S. Circuit Court of Appeals acknowledged that Mississippi has this constitutional requirement. Moreover, each of the lower courts concluded that Mississippi had discharged its duties, as it had adopted a set of racially neutral policies for operating its eight universities, making it possible for all students to choose and attend any one of those universities. The U.S. Supreme Court, however, held the state to a higher standard by examining its new policies and practices relative to those that facilitated and/or perpetuated the dual system prior to 1954.

The Supreme Court held that the lower courts did not examine Mississippi's duties in the proper light. The Court adjudged that Mississippi was in violation of the Constitution and the 1964 Civil Rights Act to the extent that it had not met its affirmative obligation to dismantle its racially segregated system of higher education. The Court vacated the 5th Circuit Court of Appeals ruling, and the case was remanded back to the Circuit Court for remedial proceedings.

The Supreme Court acknowledged that Mississippi cannot be discharged from its constitutional obligation to dismantle its dual system of higher education until its policies and practices are no longer traceable to its prior de jure segregated system. The Court reasoned that the establishment of racially neutral policies alone is insufficient if they do not eliminate vestiges of segregation in higher ed-ucation. The Court examined four significant sets of policies and practices: cur-rent admissions policies and whether they perpetuate the state's former de jure dual system, the present widespread program duplication and whether it perpetu-ates a dual system, and the state's efforts to dismantle this dual system and whether those efforts actually serve to perpetuate segregation in state universities. After examining each set of policies, the Court concluded that each set is rooted in the state's prior effort to operate a segregated system of higher education.

SELECTED BIBLIOGRAPHY

Ayers v. Allen (Ayers I, 674 F. Supp. 1532, 1529 (N.D. Miss, 1987); *Ayers v. Allen (Ayers* III), 914 F. 2d 676 (Stu cir. 1990); *Clarion-Ledger*, 27 June 1992; Robert Davis, ''*United States v. Fordice*,'' *Mississippi Law Journal* 62 (1992); *Meredith v. Fair*, 305 F. 2d 343, 361 (5th Cir. 1962); *Harvard Law Review* 106 (1992).

LARRY LEFLORE

B

BAKER, GWENDOLYN CALVERT (31 December 1931, Ann Arbor, Michigan). A university professor and administrator, association director, and UNICEF official, Baker was born in Ann Arbor, Michigan, the eldest of the five children of Viola (Lee) and Burgess Calvert. She married as a college freshman, had three children, and then completed her education. She received her B.A. degree in 1964, M.A. degree in 1968, and Ph.D. degree in 1972 from the University of Michigan. The topic of her dissertation was multiethnic education and teacher training.

Baker taught in the Ann Arbor Public Schools for four years and then at the University of Michigan in various ranks from 1969 to 1976, when she became the university's affirmative action officer. As an educator and author, Baker helped develop the field of multicultural education. The second edition of her book, *Planning and Organizing for Multicultural Instruction*, was published by Addison Wesley in 1993.

Baker served as Chief of Minorities and Women's Programs at the National Institute of Education in Washington, D.C., from 1978 to 1984. There she helped fund multicultural education projects on both local and regional levels and helped train women and minorities as program reviewers. In 1981 Baker joined the Bank Street College of Education in New York City, serving as dean and vice president of Graduate and Children's Programs. She was appointed executive secretary of the Young Women's Christian Association in 1984. Her accomplishments included the development of a national logo and the reorganization of the national office and its administrative procedures. Baker served in her spare time on the New York City School Board from 1986 to 1991, the last year as its president. In 1991 she was named Outstanding Alumna by the University of Michigan.

Baker was appointed as Chief Executive Officer of the United States Committee for UNICEF in 1993. She also serves on the board of the Greater New York Savings Bank and as vice president of Independent Sector, an umbrella organization for private nonprofit groups.

SELECTED BIBLIOGRAPHY
Christa Brelin and William C. Matney, eds., *Who's Who among Black Americans, 1992–1993* (1992).

ELIZABETH L. IHLE

BALDWIN, MARIA LOUISE (13 September, 1856–9 January, 1922). Educator and community activist, Baldwin was the first African-American female school administrator in the state of Massachusetts and New England. She attended the Allston Grammar School and the Cambridge Latin High School in Cambridge, Massachusetts, graduating in 1874, and received her teacher education from the Cambridge Teachers' Training School in 1875. Although Baldwin wanted to teach in the Cambridge public schools, she was not hired because of her race. In response to her letter of application for a teaching position, a member of the school committee suggested that she would be of more service to African-American children in the South. Therefore, Ms. Baldwin taught for two years in the Chestertown, Maryland, public schools. The members of the African-American community in Cambridge protested to the Cambridge school committee; and in the fall of 1882, Maria Baldwin was appointed to a teaching position as a primary grade teacher at the Agassiz elementary school on Sacramento Street, near Harvard University.

From 1882 to 1889, Baldwin taught grades one through seven and, in the fall of 1889, was selected as principal of the Agassiz School. When the Cambridge school committee considered her candidacy for the position, there was again hesitation on the part of some members because of Baldwin's race. Alice Longfellow, the daughter of poet Henry Wadsworth Longfellow, intervened on her behalf, and Baldwin was selected for the position. She supervised twelve teachers and a student body of 500, 98 percent of whom were white. While she was principal, she also taught the eighth-grade history and English classes. Her teaching ability, sense of fairness, and concern for her students were admired by parents and members of the Cambridge community. During her forty-year career at the Agassiz School she taught many of the children of the Harvard University professors who lived in the area of the school. One of her most famous pupils was the poet Edward Estlin Cummings, better known as e. e. cummings.

Under Baldwin's leadership, a new school was designed to replace the old building; the architectural plans for the new building incorporated many of Ms. Baldwin's ideas, such as open-air classrooms, an assembly hall, and a science museum. In 1916, when this building was completed, she was appointed master of the new Agassiz School, one of only two women holding such a position in Cambridge at the time. Baldwin established innovative educational programs, including new teaching approaches to mathematics and science and school nurse services; she was also the first administrator to establish a parent-teacher group in Cambridge.

Maria Baldwin was active in the civic life of Cambridge and Boston. She was a member of the Twentieth Century Club, the Boston Ethical Society, the Cantabridgian Club, and the Robert Gould Shaw House Association. Baldwin was a respected contemporary of other African-American Bostonians such as William Monroe Trotter and Josephine St. Pierre Ruffin. Ms. Baldwin helped to organize the League of Women for Community Service, an African-American women's civic club in Boston, and served as president for many years. She was also active in other African-American civic organizations such as the Banneker Club and the Women's Era Club, Boston, organized by Josephine St. Pierre Ruffin. Maria Baldwin conducted weekly literary club meetings in her home for young African-American college students. Among the Harvard students who visited with her was W. E. B. Du Bois.* Baldwin was respected and admired as an outstanding public speaker and lecturer by other Bostonians of that time such as Charles W. Eliot, president emeritus of Harvard University, Thomas Wentworth Higginson, Julia Ward Howe, and Elizabeth Cary Agassiz. In 1897, she gave the annual Washington's birthday memorial address at the Brooklyn Institute of Arts and Sciences in New York, the first woman ever to present an address to this organization. The topic of her speech was the life and work of Harriet Beecher Stowe.

While addressing the members of the Council of the Robert Gould Shaw House Association at the Copley Plaza Hotel, Boston, on 9 January 1922, she collapsed; she died shortly thereafter. Funeral services were held at the Arlington Street Church, and her ashes were buried in the Forest Lawn cemetery, Boston. The Agassiz School assembly hall was named Baldwin Hall in her honor. Though the original school building was later demolished, some of the original assembly hall woodwork was incorporated into the newly constructed school, in a library and media center dedicated to Baldwin's memory. The Cambridge Historical Commission has designated the home where Maria Baldwin and her family lived from 1894 to 1906 as a historical landmark site on the Cambridge Black Heritage Trail.

SELECTED BIBLIOGRAPHY

Maria Louise Baldwin, "The Changing Ideal of Progress," *Southern Workman* (January 1900); Benjamin Brawley, *Negro Builders of America* (1937); William E. B. Du Bois, "Tribute to Maria L. Baldwin," *The Crisis* (April 1922): 248–49; Edward T. James, *Notable American Women, 1607–1950*, vol. 1 (1971): 86–87; Rayford W. Logan, *Dictionary of American Negro Biography* (1972); Dorothy B. Porter, "Maria L. Baldwin, (1856–1922)" *Journal of Negro Education* 21 (Winter 1952): 94–96; "Honors for a Cambridge Teacher," *Cambridge Chronicle* (6 March 1897); "Miss Baldwin's Lecture," *Cambridge Chronicle*, (24 July 1897); "Pay Tribute to Negro Teacher," *Boston Herald* 18 March 1922).

                                        BRENDA BERNADINE BELL–BROWN

BANKS, JAMES A. (24 September 1941, Lee County, Arkansas). James Banks is a professor of education and the director of the Center for Multicultural Education at the University of Washington, Seattle. He received a B.E. degree from Chicago State University (1964) and an M.A. (1967) and Ph.D. (1969)

from Michigan State University, both in the areas of social science and education. Within social studies education, Banks has served as a public school teacher, consultant, lecturer, and textbook editor. He is presently an internationally recognized scholar in both multicultural–multiethnic and social studies education.

Preparation for participatory democracy, civic responsibility, reflective decision-making, critical thinking, and the study of social problems are themes that run through Banks's writings and discussions. His critiques of the exclusive employment of Western traditional scholarship, which he views as Eurocentric, sexist, and narrow, have been widely hailed. He maintains in much of his work that technology, demographics, and changing attitudes have permanently influenced human interactions while creating demands for societal change. As a consequence, schools must prepare students for a rapidly changing world where international cooperation and cultural pluralism are desirable. Banks also advocates education for freedom, democracy, justice, empowerment, and the acceptance of cultural differences.

As a multicultural-multiethnic educator, Banks has been at the forefront of a movement to reform the curriculum from kindergarten through higher education. Rejecting tokenist models, he advocates a complete multicultural curriculum that opposes separatism and divisiveness, legitimates all peoples and cultures, and promotes equity, shared values, and the possibility for humankind to exist harmoniously.

Dr. Banks has authored or edited eighteen books, the most recent being the *Handbook of Multicultural Education* (1995), a landmark collection of scholarship which he compiled with associate editor Cherry A. McGee Banks of the University of Washington-Bothell. Other publications to Banks's credit include *Teaching Strategies for Ethnic Studies* (1975), *Teaching Strategies for the Social Studies* (1975), *Curriculum Guidelines for Multicultural Education* (1976), *Multicultural Education: Theory and Practice* (1981), and *An Introduction to Multicultural Education* (1994). Banks is also one of the authors of *The World Around Us* (1993), the widely accepted Macmillan/McGraw-Hill social studies program for students in grades K through 7. Additionally, Banks has written over one hundred articles on multicultural and multiethnic education which have been published in such esteemed scholarly journals as *Educational Researcher*, *Phi Delta Kappan*, *Harvard Education Review*, *Social Education*, *School Review*, *Educational Leadership*, *Journal of Negro Education*,* and *Educational Review*.

Banks served as president of the National Council for Social Studies in 1982 and was named Distinguished Scholar/Researcher on Minority Education (1986) by the American Education Research Association. In May 1993, he was awarded a special honorary doctorate of humane letters by Bank Street College of Education, in recognition of his accomplishments in multicultural and social studies education. Additionally, Banks has been the recipient of many distinguished fellowships, special appointments, visiting professorships, lectureships, and

scholarly awards. His biography appears in the *Dictionary of International Biography, Contemporary Authors, Leaders in Education, Men of Achievement, Who's Who in the West, Who's Who in America,* and *Who's Who in the World.*
SELECTED BIBLIOGRAPHY
"Dr. James A. Banks: Making a Difference," *UW News: For Parents of University of Washington Students* 6, no. 1 (Spring 1990); James A. Banks, "Multicultural Education: For Freedom's Sake," *Educational Leadership* (December 1991/January 1992): 32–36; "It's Up to Us," interview with James A. Banks, *Teaching Tolerance* (Fall 1992): 20–23.

WILLIAM H. WATKINS

BARBER-SCOTIA COLLEGE. Barber-Scotia College, Concord, North Carolina, is an accredited four-year, coeducational, liberal arts institution. Historically related to the Presbyterian Church (USA), Barber-Scotia College was founded in 1867 as Scotia Seminary, a preparatory school for young Negro women. For more than a generation, Scotia, as it was called, adhered to this program. Sensitivity to the demands of society and responsiveness to the needs of students brought significant changes in programs and policy—the 1916 expansion of curricula; the change in name to Scotia Women's College; the 1930 merger with Barber Memorial College, Anniston, Alabama; the 1932 adoption of the name Barber-Scotia College; and the change to coeducation in 1954. The student enrollment of the institution, although representing over twenty-five states, the U.S. Virgin Islands, and foreign countries, comes primarily from the Carolinas. The college offers B.S. and B.A. degrees in the following areas: biology, sociology, mathematics, management information science, communications/journalism, english, recreation administration, business administration, education, and medical technology.
SELECTED BIBLIOGRAPHY
National Association for Equal Opportunity in Higher Education, *Profiles of the Nation's Historically and Predominantly Black Colleges and Universities* (1993).

SAMUEL L. MYERS

BARNETT, MARGUERITE ROSS (21 May 1942, Charlottesville, Virginia–26 February 1992, Houston, Texas). Until her illness and untimely death from cancer, Marguerite Ross Barnett rose through the ranks of academia to become a national leader in higher education administration. She received her B.A. from Antioch College and her M.A. and Ph.D. in political science from the University of Chicago (1970). During the 1970s she taught political science at the University of Chicago, Princeton, and Howard* universities. At Howard, she chaired the Political Science Department. In 1983 she became the vice-chancellor for academic affairs at the City University of New York after having served as director of the Institute for Minority Education at Columbia University Teachers College. From 1983 to 1986 she was a chancellor at the University of Missouri, St. Louis, where she established the nationally acclaimed Bridge Program, which was named an outstanding public school initiative by the American Council on Education. In 1990 she became the first African-American president of the University of Houston. At Houston, she continued her commitment to public schools, creating the Texas Center for University-School Partnerships, a research and outreach program designed to assess and disseminate information on national school reform efforts.

The author and/or editor of five books and forty-nine articles, Barnett is renowned for her studies of race, public policy development, and African-American electoral politics. One of her books, a revision of her 1970 dissertation titled *The Politics of Cultural Nationalism in South India*, won the 1981 Political Science Association's Ethnic and Cultural Pluralism Award for the best scholarly work of the previous five years. Throughout her academic career, Barnett served on numerous educational boards including those of the National Student Loan Marketing Association, the American Council on Education, and the Council for the Advancement and Support of Education. She also served on the boards of several corporate and civic organizations in St. Louis and Houston. She received an honorary degree from Spelman College,* the Archibald F. Glover Memorial Award for Academic Leadership, the Missouri Black Legislative Caucus Award for Outstanding Achievement, and the Association of Black Women in Higher Education's award for Educational Excellence. In 1991, she was appointed by President George Bush to serve on the President's Commission on Environmental Quality, one of only two academic representatives on that commission.

Barnett's advice in her last years was noted in her obituary: "We can either be bystanders to a passing twenty-first century historical drama of heroic proportions or we can be leaders." She is survived by her husband, Walter King, her daughter, Amy Barnett, and her mother, Mary Eubanks.

SELECTED BIBLIOGRAPHY

Marguerite R. Barnett and James A. Hefner, *Public Policy for the Black Community* (1976); Marguerite R. Barnett, "The Congressional Black Caucus: Illusions and Realities of Power," in Michael Preston, Lenneal Henderson, and Paul Puryear, eds., *The New Black Politics* (1982); Marguerite R. Barnett, "The Strategic Debate over a Presidential Candidacy," *Political Science* (Summer 1983); Funeral Program for Marguerite R. Barnett, 2 March 1992, Union Baptist Church, Scottsville, Virginia.

LORENZO MORRIS

GEORGE BELL (1761, Virginia–1843, Washington, D.C.). George Bell was a pioneering advocate for public education for African-Americans in the nation's capital. Bell was born into slavery in Virginia; his freedom was purchased by his wife, Sophia Browning, whose freedom Bell purchased in turn with wages earned from his work as a carpenter in Washington, D.C.

Although Bell could neither read nor write, he recognized that education was essential for African-Americans. In 1804, the capital city government authorized public schools for white children; the first two schools were opened in 1806.

No provisions were made for the education of African-American children. Bell became a leading activist for this cause establishing in 1807 the first school for African-American children in southeastern Washington, D.C. Nichols Franklin and Moses Liverpool helped Bell build the one-story frame schoolhouse, which was named the Bell School. The school remained in operation for several years, but later closed because of funding problems. Bell organized other free African-Americans into the Resolute Beneficial Society, whose goal was to reopen the school. Their efforts proved successful when the 29 August 1818, issue of the *National Intelligencer* announced the reopening of the Bell School. The school had an average population of sixty-five to seventy students and offered classes in reading, writing, arithmetic, and English grammar. Evening classes were started in October 1818.

SELECTED BIBLIOGRAPHY

Letitia Woods Brown, *Free Negroes in the District of Columbia, 1790–1846* (1972); Rayford W. Logan and Michael R. Winston, *Dictionary of American Negro Biography* (1982).

WILLIAM R. CRUMPTON

BENEDICT COLLEGE. Located in Columbia, South Carolina, coeducational Benedict college offers an expanded and flexible curriculum. Its students pursue courses of study in the fields of business, government, social and health services, public and private school instruction, civic, cultural, religious, and scientific work. Benedict has twice been listed in *Money* magazine's ''College Guide'' among the top seven historically black colleges and universities nationally that offer the best value in American education. The college has also been recognized by the Knight Foundation for its commitment to high standards of quality in education and its distinguished record of providing educational opportunities to African-American students.

SELECTED BIBLIOGRAPHY

National Association for Equal Opportunity in Higher Education, *Profiles of the Nation's Historically and Predominantly Black Colleges and Universities* (1993).

SAMUEL L. MYERS

BENNETT COLLEGE. Bennett College is a four-year liberal arts college for women. Located in Greensboro, North Carolina, it was founded in 1873 as a coeducational institution and reorganized as a women's college in 1926. The college is affiliated with the United Methodist Church and is a member of the United Negro College Fund. Bennett offers the bachelor of arts, bachelor of sciences, and bachelor of arts and science in interdisciplinary studies degrees. Within the college's four academic disciplines—education, humanities, natural sciences, and social sciences—Bennett students can concentrate in one major area, combine two or more majors for a specialized career goal, or design non-traditional programs of study. The general education core of Bennett's liberal arts curriculum is designed to improve reading, writing, and reasoning skills while inspiring each student to develop her own identity. Innovations such as the Bennett Scholars Program, Special Services, dual-degree programs, and computer-assisted instruction contribute to a distinctive curriculum especially suited to the Bennett women who will shape and lead future generations.

SELECTED BIBLIOGRAPHY

National Association for Equal Opportunity in Higher Education, *Profiles of the Nation's Historically and Predominantly Black Colleges and Universities* (1993).

SAMUEL L. MYERS

BEREA COLLEGE. Founded in 1855, Berea College was initiated for the purpose of providing a high-quality liberal arts education within the context of the Christian faith. The college limits enrollment to 1,500 students, charges no tuition, and takes 80 percent of its students from the Southern Appalachia area and Kentucky. Berea was founded with a commitment to educating black and white students together, making it one of the first interracial colleges in the South. For many years, blacks comprised about half of Berea's student body, but their numbers fell to about 10 percent following the integration of other institutions of higher education.

Because no tuition is charged, the college depends upon endowment income and gifts from friends and alumni to meet its financial needs. In addition to carrying a full academic load, students work ten to fifteen hours per week in a labor program which permits them to earn at least a portion of their educational expenses. Some positions in the program relate to academic or career interests, and other enable students to follow a special interest such as positions in the crafts area, where students make fine furniture, brooms, woven items, and a variety of ceramic products.

Berea's Appalachian Center is the focus of the college's commitment to its region. In addition to offering academic courses, the center directs a variety of services and research programs for and about the region. The Hutchins Library houses the Weatherford-Hammond Appalachian Collection, one of the finest in the nation for Appalachian research; and the Appalachian Museum offers a variety of displays and special programs on the history and culture of the region.

The college also has an outstanding academic program. Bachelor of science degrees are offered in four areas—agriculture, business administration, technology and industrial arts, and nursing. Bachelor of arts degrees are offered in art, biology, chemistry, child and family studies, classical languages, economics, education, English, French, German, history, mathematics, music, philosophy, physical education, physics, political science, psychology, religion, sociology, Spanish, and theater. Approximately 25–30 percent of Berea's students go on to graduate school immediately after graduation, and about 55 percent of all students eventually earn a graduate degree.

ED FORD

BEREA COLLEGE v. KENTUCKY, 211 U.S. 26 (1908). In this decision, the U.S. Supreme Court upheld the Day Law, which made it illegal to teach white and African-American students in the same school. Passed by the Kentucky legislature earlier in 1904, the Day Law was enacted against Berea College,* the only school in the state involved in "racial coeducation," as integration was called during the period. As a private missionary school, Berea College also was the only school in the South still practicing "racial coeducation." Much to the chagrin of most Kentuckians, Berea had been integrated for nearly forty years. This decision meant that the state finally was able to force the college to segregate. The winds of racial change were blowing nationally as well as in the South. Following the Reconstruction period, the Supreme Court had upheld several cases legalizing racial segregation. They were based upon the philosophy inherent in the 1896 *Plessy v. Ferguson** case, that there were no civil rights violations if separate facilities were provided for African-Americans. With that precedent in mind, the Court proceeded to determine whether it could legally force a private institution to segregate. The *Berea College v. Kentucky* decision answered the question in the affirmative.

The case began in November 1903, when state legislator Carl Day visited the campus and was appalled by the "race mixing." Thus he introduced his bill, stating that it would "prevent contamination of white children in Kentucky." Calling for a fine of a hundred dollars a day for each day the law was broken and a fine against instructors, the bill became law on 15 July 1904. In response, Berea attorneys appealed the decision. In 1905, however, a Kentucky circuit court turned down the appeal, arguing that the law fell under the state's police powers, which had originally granted the school's charter; thus, the state could amend the charter. A year later, the court of appeals upheld the lower court decision. On 9 November 1908, the Supreme Court upheld the lower court decision, bringing missionary schools in line with the prevailing separate-but-equal philosophy.

Within the new perimeters and constraints of Jim Crow, Berea College continued to honor its commitment to African-American education. The college paid transportation costs and tuition for students to attend various African-American schools such as Fisk, Hampton, Tuskegee, and Wilberforce. To accommodate African-Americans in the lower grades, the college raised a sum of money to improve Berea's local African-American public school. However, its greatest project was establishing an African-American school, Lincoln Institute, in 1912. Located twenty-two miles east of Louisville, the new school never met the expectations of its founders. Considering Berea's earlier stellar commitment to educational equality, African-American alumni expected an African-American to be selected as principal of Lincoln Institute, but this did not occur. Then, considering Berea College's earlier unflinching commitment to the liberal arts, as much as to industrial education, it was surprising that Lincoln Institute was primarily an industrial school, one more indication of the southern white philosophy of African-American education. Finally, in 1950, the Day Law was amended, and African-American students returned to Berea College, after a forty-six-year absence.

SELECTED BIBLIOGRAPHY

Jacqueline G. Burnside, "Suspicion versus Faith: Negro Criticism of Berea College in the Nineteenth Century," *Register of Kentucky Historical Society* 83 (Summer 1985): 237–66; Richard Allen Heckman and Betty Jean Hall, "Berea College and the Day Law," *Register of Kentucky Historical Society* 66 (1968): 35–52; James M. McPherson, *The Abolitionist Legacy: From Reconstruction to the NAACP* (1973); George C. Wright, "The Founding of Lincoln Institute," *Filson Club History Quarterly* 49 (1975): 57–70.

LAWRENCE H. WILLIAMS

BERRY, MARY FRANCES (17 February 1938, Nashville, Tennessee). Mary Frances Berry was born to George Berry and Frances Southall in Nashville, Tennessee. She graduated from Pearl High School with honors in 1956. There, one teacher-mentor, Minerva Hawkins, awakened hopes in Berry that inspired determination to be academically excellent and to pursue a profession. Berry financed her own education and earned the B.A. and M.A. degrees (1961 and 1962) at Howard University* in Washington, D.C., as well as the Ph.D. degree in history (1966) and the J.D. degree (1970) at the University of Michigan in Ann Arbor.

Berry has developed a multifaceted career, achieving national distinction as a scholar-activist, educator, administrator, and public servant. Her scholarly writing includes over twenty articles and five books of which she is the sole author, *Black Resistance/White Law* (1971), *Military Necessity and Civil Rights Policy* (1977), *Stability, Security, and Continuity* (1978), *Why ERA Failed* (1986), and *The Politics of Parenthood* (1993), as well as *Long Memory* (1982), coauthored with John Blassingame. With her inimitable style of teaching legal history, which includes her unique incorporation of multicultural materials into traditional courses, Berry moved swiftly up the career ladder in academia. She has held faculty and/or administrative positions at Central Michigan University, Eastern Michigan University, the University of Michigan, the University of Maryland, the University of Colorado, Howard University, and the University of Pennsylvania. At the University of Maryland in College Park, she advanced from an assistant professorship to being the first director of Afro-American Studies and, by 1974, provost for Behavioral and Social Sciences, thereby becoming the highest-ranking African-American woman at College Park. In 1976, Berry became the first African-American woman to head a major research university when she was appointed chancellor (and professor of history and law) at the University of Colorado in Boulder. Taking a leave of absence in 1977, Berry achieved yet another first for African-American women by serving until 1980 as Assistant Secretary for Education, the nation's chief educational officer, in the Department of Health, Education, and Welfare. Since 1980, Berry's excellence in education has been recognized by her 1987 appointment as the University of Pennsylvania's first Geraldine Segal Professor of Social Thought and

Professor of History, her election to the presidency of the Organization of American Historians (1990–91), and her twenty honorary doctoral degrees.

SELECTED BIBLIOGRAPHY

Mary Frances Berry, "Deliberately Fraught with Difficulties," *Harvard Educational Review* 52 (November 1982): 462–66; Mary Frances Berry, "Twentieth-Century Black Women in Education," *Journal of Negro Education* 51 (summer 1982): 288–300; Dianne Pinderhughes, "Black Women and National Educational Policy," *Journal of Negro Education* 51 (summer 1982): 301–7; Alex Poinsette, "Colorado University's Chancellor," *Ebony* 30 (January 1977):58–60, 65–66; Barbara Reynolds, "The Woman the President Couldn't Fire," *Essence* 15 (October 1984): 12, 158; Carol Hobson Smith, "Black Female Achievers in Academe," *Journal of Negro Education* 51 (summer 1982): 323–27.

GENNA RAE MCNEIL

BETHUNE, MARY MCLEOD (10 July 1875, Mayesville, South Carolina–18 May 1955, Daytona Beach, Florida). A college founder-president, leader of women's organizations, federal administrator, and race leader during America's "separate-but-equal" era, Mary McLeod Bethune received her entire formal education in missionary institutions. As a girl, she attended for two or three years a small, rural Presbyterian school in the vicinity of her hometown; and from 1888 to 1894, she attended Scotia Seminary (now Barber-Scotia College*), where she completed the normal and scientific course. In 1894–95, she studied at the nondenominational Institute for Home and Foreign Missions in Chicago, now the Moody Bible Institute.

In 1904, Bethune established the Daytona Educational and Industrial Training School for Negro Girls, a school that existed for nineteen years as a single-gender institution. In 1918, its name was changed to the Daytona Normal and Industrial Institute, to reflect an increasing emphasis on teacher education. Founded without the support of a sponsoring agency or endowment, Bethune's school was considered one of the highest-quality African-American educational institutions in the state. In the 1920s, it became the coeducational Bethune–Cookman College,* operating under the auspices of the northern-based Methodist Episcopal Church. In the first half of the twentieth century, there existed neither a recognized girl's boarding school nor a college for African-Americans in Florida south of Daytona Beach. Bethune's school thus provided critical educational opportunities to thousands who otherwise would never have gone to school at all.

As president of the Florida State Teachers Association, in 1919 Bethune championed better teacher preparation, stricter professional standards for teachers, and greater sensitivity to teachers' status as civic role models. In 1923–24, as president of the National Association of Teachers in Colored Schools (NATCS),* she sought to make that organization the authoritative voice of African-Americans in all relevant educational matters both locally and nationally, thus paralleling its contemporary white counterpart, the National Education Association. Bethune's involvement with NATCS presaged key elements in her vision for the two major African-American women's organizations of her era: the National Association of Colored Women, where she served as president from 1924 to 1928; and the National Council of Negro Women, which she founded in 1935, serving as president until 1949.

From June 1935 to December 1942, Bethune continued as president of Bethune-Cookman College, though in a part-time capacity as necessitated by her position with the federal government. Toward the end of her presidency, World War II sent the school's enrollment spiralling downward, from 481 in 1940–41 to 155 in 1942–43. Although Bethune's plan to transform the institution into a "self-supporting, food-producing community" proved unsuccessful, she persevered in her desire to transform the school into a senior college. In the early 1940s, Bethune added an additional two years of study, and the college awarded its first bachelor of science degrees in August 1943.

Bethune was prominent in the Association for the Study of Afro-American Life and History,* the Commission on Interracial Cooperation and its successors, the Southern Conference on Human Welfare, and the Southern Conference Educational Fund. Working in the informal Federal Council of Negro Affairs, unofficially known as "the Black Cabinet," which she helped form in August 1936, Bethune originated and chaired both the first and second National Conference on the Problems of the Negro and Negro Youth sponsored by the National Youth Administration (NYA). Her most influential educational role, however, was as the NYA's chief African-American specialist during the Great Depression and into World War II. The NYA assisted young people between the ages of sixteen and twenty-four primarily through work-study programs in secondary schools and colleges, vocational training projects, and job placement. Bethune's responsibility was to promote equitable African-American participation in NYA component programs; her success in this endeavor was such that many African-Americans regarded her agency as more responsive to their needs than any other in Washington. Bethune administered a Special Fund for Higher Education through her own Division of Negro Affairs, making her the only African-American New Deal official directly allocating money.

During her lifetime Bethune received a dozen honorary degrees, the highest awards of Haiti and Liberia, and the NAACP's Spingarn Medal (1935). Since her death, she has continued to garner titan respect. She has been honored through the issuance of a commemorative postage stamp; designation of her homes in Florida and Washington, D.C., as national historical sites; and depiction in a bronze statue located in Washington, D.C.'s Lincoln Park. This statue captures not only Bethune's likeness but also that of two children beside her, thus reflecting Bethune's most singular career concern: educating and nurturing youth.

SELECTED BIBLIOGRAPHY
Rackham Holt, *Mary McLeod Bethune* (Garden City, NY: Doubleday, 1964); Carol O. Perkings, "The Pragmatic Idealism of Mary McLeod Bethune," *Sage* 2 (Fall 1988): 30–36.

ELAINE MOORE SMITH

BETHUNE–COOKMAN COLLEGE. Founded by Dr. Mary McLeod Bethune* in 1904, Bethune-Cookman College is a historically black, United Methodist Church-related college, in Daytona Beach, Florida, offering the baccalaureate degree. The institution's mission is to serve in the Christian tradition the educational, social, and cultural needs of its students and to develop in them the desire and capacity for continuous intellectual and professional growth and service to others. The college enrolls promising secondary school graduates from diverse social, economic, and educational backgrounds. Most of the students come from Florida; however, the college actively recruits students from the national and international communities. The college gives priority to teaching by continually adapting teaching techniques to meet student needs and by providing support programs for faculty development. Research, as a supplement to teaching, is encouraged in order to enhance knowledge and to meet the challenges of a changing world.

SELECTED BIBLIOGRAPHY
National Association for Equal Opportunity in Higher Education, *Profiles of the Nation's Historically and Predominantly Black Colleges and Universities* (1993).

SAMUEL L. MYERS

BLACK COLLEGIAN. Established in 1970, the *Black Collegian* is a career and self-development magazine targeted to African-American college students. It regularly features articles on college life, aspects of black history and culture, and profiles of black role models and exemplary programs for African-American college-going or college-bound students. As a source of educational and career information, the *Black Collegian* identifies and describes a wide variety of graduate school, internship, and co-op programs as well as job opportunities, along with information on how to qualify for these opportunities. The publication boasts a circulation of over one hundred thousand and is distributed to over eight hundred college campuses via career counseling and placement offices, selected academic departments, and student organizations. It has received many awards and honors and has consistently ranked high in surveys of the nation's best college/career publications.

D. KAMILI ANDERSON

BLACK ISSUES IN HIGHER EDUCATION **MAGAZINE**. The premiere edition of *Black Issues in Higher Education* was issued in March 1984 as an eight-page newsletter, under the direction of William E. Cox and Frank L. Matthews. It was the first publication devoted entirely to the concerns of blacks and other minorities in the field of education. *Black Issues* is currently published bimonthly, with an average of eighty-four pages per edition. The magazine is the national forum for the intellectual exchange of ideas and news stories on such issues as minority recruitment and retention, research topics, testing, and educational policy. The publication also regularly reports on minority participation in intercollegiate sports, curricula reform, litigation, and the educational status of African-Americans, Hispanics, Native Americans, and Asian Americans and other minorities. *Black Issues* is subscribed to and read by a multitude of professional and lay people who understand the relevance of minority education to the betterment of society as a whole.

Black Issues also provides the educational record of minority participation in higher education by publishing data on the number of degrees conferred to minority students by race at all postsecondary levels and disciplines. Special reports on leadership, graduate and professional education, science and engineering studies, community colleges, diversity, and women in higher education focus attention on important contemporary issues. Exclusive interviews are granted by prominent national leaders such as the secretary of education, key congressmen and senators, faculty leaders, and college presidents. Finally, the magazine provides its readers with an employment section that lists advertisements from colleges and universities across the nation, reaching over one hundred thousand readers each edition.

FRANK L. MATTHEWS

BLAKE, ELIAS, JR. (13 December, 1929, Brunswick, Georgia). A program evaluator, higher education policy researcher, college professor, college president, and consultant, Elias Blake, Jr., received a B.A. degree in history at Paine College* in 1951, an M.A. in education at Howard University* in 1954, and a Ph.D. in educational psychology at the University of Illinois (Urbana) in 1960. At the forefront for college accessibility for African-Americans for over a quarter of a century, Blake has championed the importance of sustaining the original mission and expanding the capacity of the historically black colleges and universities (HBCUs). From 1969 to 1977, Blake headed the Institute for Services to Education, Inc. (ISE), the first Washington-based agency to expressly involve HBCUs in the expanding array of federal student and institutional aid programs. From 1977 to 1981, he served as chair of the presidentially appointed National Advisory Committee on Black Higher Education and Black Colleges and Universities.

Instrumental in the development of the Upward Bound* program from its beginning as a pilot precollege program to a nationwide program, Blake based his design for the program on the work of the ISE. He served as the first Upward Bound grants officer for the southeastern region from 1967 to 1969.

Blake's work showing the major historical impact of the HBCUs on the education of African-Americans changed the nature of the policy debate on the role of these institutions in an integrated society. His research into the impact of HBCUs on the production of African-American physicians, Ph.Ds, federal officials, lawyers, and army officers provided the theoretical framework for the amicus curiae brief of the National Association for Equal Opportunity in Higher Education's appeal of the *Adams v. Richardson** case. Since 1993, Blake has served as the lead educational expert for the plaintiffs in the *Ayers v. Fordice** desegregation litigation in Mississippi, the first and only higher education desegregation case to go to the Supreme Court.

For ten years (1977–87), Blake was president of Clark College (now Clark Atlanta University*). During his administration Clark was expanded from a traditional liberal arts and teacher education institution to one that offers career fields such as business, mass communications, social work, and medical technology. His tenure saw the installation of a fully operational microcomputer and telecommunications network, a quadrupling of alumni contributions, and a doubling of the college's endowment. Clark's new fiscal strength was sufficient to anchor its 1988 merger with financially troubled Atlanta University. Blake moved on to Howard University in 1987, where he served until 1991 as director of the Division of Higher Education Policy Research.

Since 1991, Blake has served as an independent consultant to such organizations as the Presidential Board of Advisors on Historically Black Colleges and Universities, Central State University,* Winston-Salem State University, and the Black College Satellite Network. He also serves as president of the Benjamin E. Mays National Resource Center, an educational reform think tank that encourages more productive cooperation between educational institutions and private organizations.

SELECTED BIBLIOGRAPHY

Christa Brelin and William C. Matney, eds., *Who's Who among Black Americans, 1992–1993* (1992).

                                                                CAROL J. HOBSON SMITH

BOARDING SCHOOLS, AFRICAN-AMERICAN. The self-help tradition within African-American education historically has been strong. Even as they have struggled to improve and to reform public education, African-American parents and communities have looked to alternatives such as private, independent African-American boarding schools dedicated to the proper, complete, and comprehensive education of African-American youth. These schools have played an important but often overlooked role in providing critically needed educational facilities and opportunities.

In the late nineteenth and early twentieth centuries, in a context of racism and hostility toward educating African-Americans, boarding schools for African-American children developed rapidly throughout the South. Although historians have not focused on these institutions as topics of inquiry, it is clear that they were initiated as alternatives to and as supplements for the dilapidated public facilities typically provided for the education of black children and the stark absence of support for African-American schooling above the lower elementary grades. There were, for example, only sixty-four public high schools for African-American youth in the entire South in 1916, and boarding schools often made it possible for blacks to continue their education into the secondary and college level.

Many African-American boarding schools were established and supported by African-American or other religious denominations, including the Baptist, Roman Catholic, Colored (now Christian) Methodist Episcopal, African Methodist Episcopal, and Presbyterian churches. These schools served as feeder schools to the normal schools, seminaries, colleges, and universities operating under the auspices of these churches. Until the 1930s, numerous black colleges and universities maintained boarding schools on campus, as enrollment at these schools often ranged from the upper elementary grades through the college and professional studies levels. Even more numerous were the independent, unaffiliated African-American boarding schools that dotted the rural Black Belt. Though smaller and less prestigious than the university-supported schools, these institutions were equally important in providing education for African-Americans. Hampton Normal and Agricultural Institute in Virginia (now Hampton University*) and Tuskegee Normal and Industrial Institute (now Tuskegee University*) in Alabama were in a class by themselves; but each, particularly Tuskegee, served as a model for the boarding schools' industrial, agricultural, and teacher education-oriented curricula.

Many of the founders of African-American boarding schools, as learned men and women themselves, were aware of the need for enriched and strong academic training along with vocational skills. One of these visionaries, Haines Normal and Industrial Institute (Augusta, Georgia) founder Lucy Craft Laney,* is an example of this theme of self-help in action. At Haines, Laney developed a model for African-American boarding schools serving the academic, vocational, and social needs of black students and communities. Another boarding school founder, Dr. Laurence C. Jones,* was a 1907 graduate of the University of Iowa who had a longtime dream of moving to the South and working to improve educational opportunities for the black community. Influenced by the Tuskegee idea and a family history that emphasized the importance of industrial training—an uncle had founded the Woodstock Manual Labor Institute in Michigan in 1846—Jones started the Piney Woods Country Life School in 1909, serving African-American communities in Rankin and Simpson counties in Mississippi. One of the oldest existing African-American boarding schools, the Piney Woods School today continues to play a role in the African-American educational infrastructure as a leading member of the Association for African-American Boarding Schools, a six-member body representing both the legacy of earlier times and the continuing need for options and alternatives for black youth.

Other schools in the Association include: Southern Normal School in Brewton, Alabama; Saints Academy* in Lexington, Mississippi; Redemption Christian Academy in Troy, New York; Laurinburg Institute in Laurinburg, North

Carolina; and Pine Force Academy in Pine Force, Pennsylvania. Together with such contemporary organizations as the Council of Independent Black Institutions,* the Association of African-American Boarding Schools represents the ongoing commitment within African-American communities to deliver appropriate educational services to black youth in a context supportive of their full abilities and special talents.

SELECTED BIBLIOGRAPHY

Alferdteen B. Harrison, *Piney Woods School: An Oral History* (1982).

MICHAEL FULTZ

BOARD OF EDUCATION OF THE CITY SCHOOL DISTRICT OF NEW YORK et al. v. HARRIS et al., 622 F.2d 599 (1979). This case presents a narrow, but important, issue of statutory interpretation regarding discriminatory treatment of school employees. It concerns a school district's eligibility for federal financial assistance under the 1972 Emergency School Aid Act (ESAA). In 1972, the U.S. Congress passed the ESAA, providing federal financial assistance to aid elementary and secondary schools throughout the United States in the elimination of minority segregation and discrimination among students and faculty, the voluntary elimination of minority group isolation, and assisting schoolchildren in overcoming the educational disadvantages of minority group isolation. The act declared an educational institution ineligible for funding if, after the act, it had in effect any practice resulting in disproportionate demotion or dismissal of personnel from minority groups or engaging in discriminatory employment practices.

The Board of Education of the City School District of New York brought suit against the Department of Health, Education and Welfare (HEW) after the board's applications for ESAA assistance were denied. The board requested a final decision in its favor and that HEW be restrained from denying the board's applications for the reasons cited by HEW. The denial was based on statistical evidence, which resulted from a compliance investigation under Title VI of the Civil Rights Act of 1964* and showed teacher assignments that served to identify certain schools racially.

The board did not challenge the accuracy of the statistical evidence; however, it claimed that such evidence was the product of difficulties flowing from, among other factors, licensing requirements for teaching positions, a bilingual consent decree, and demographic changes in student population.

The district court remanded the case back to HEW for further consideration of the justifications for the statistical disparities or inconsistencies. On remand, HEW determined that such justifications did not adequately rebut the evidence of discrimination established by the statistics, and the district court upheld HEW's finding of ineligibility and denied relief. The board appealed on the contention that HEW was required to establish that the statistical disparities resulted from purposeful or intentional discrimination in the constitutional sense. The court of appeals affirmed the district court's decision, stating that "Congress intended to grant disqualification not only for purposeful discrimination but also for discrimination evidenced simply by an unjustified disparity in staff assignments.''

HEW argued that an agency is ineligible for ESAA funds if it has policies in practice that have a disparate impact on the schools, regardless of the intent. The board conceded that, if this was the applicable standard, the denial of funds was permissible. Thus, the issue before the Supreme Court was whether discriminatory impact or purposeful discrimination was the standard by which ineligibility was to be determined. The Supreme Court's primary concern was with the intent of Congress in passing this act.

Section 706 of the act sets forth the eligibility criteria for ESAA funding. It authorized grants to local educational agencies that are implementing a desegregation plan approved by a court or by HEW ''as adequate under title VI of the Civil Rights Act of 1964.'' The ineligibility provisions of section 706 stipulated that ineligibility comes about if the agency has in effect a practice that either (a) ''results in disproportionate demotion or dismissal of . . . personnel from minority groups'' or (b) ''otherwise [engages] in discrimination . . . in the hiring, promotion, or assignment of employees.''

The Court found that the first portion of the ineligibility criteria clearly spoke in terms of effect while the second portion, arguably, might have been said to, in the words of the Court, ''possess an overtone of intent.'' The portion relevant to this case was the second, regarding racial ''discrimination'' in the ''assignment of employees.'' The Court decided that the structure and text of the act, Congress's statements regarding the policy behind the act, and the legislative history of the act all point to impact or effect as governing both prongs of the ineligibility provision. On 28 November 1979, the Supreme Court held that discriminatory impact is the standard by which ineligibility under ESAA is to be measured, irrespective of whether or not it was purposeful discrimination.

This case was of considerable significance to the broader struggle of African-Americans to achieve equal educational opportunity because the factual discriminatory impact of a standard or policy is more easily established in a judicial context than is a motive of purposeful discrimination.

SELECTED BIBLIOGRAPHY

Civil Rights Act of 1964, Title VI, 42 U.S.C. s 2000d, et seq.; *Emergency School Aid Act* (''ESAA''), s706(d)(1,5), 20 U.S.C. (1976 Ed.) s1601 et seq., repealed effective 30 September, 1979, through passage of the Education Amendments Act of 1978, Pub.L. 95–561, Title VI, 92 Stat. 2252, et seq.; Spencer Rich, ''Senate Panel Approves Harris As New Secretary of HEW,'' *Washington Post*, 27 July 1979, A5.

BEVERLY BAKER-KELLY AND LAURA H. G. O'SULLIVAN

BOB JONES UNIVERSITY v. UNITED STATES, 461 U.S. 574 (1983). In this decision, the Supreme Court held that the Internal Revenue Service (IRS) could lawfully deny the university tax-exempt status under Section 501(c)(3) of the Internal Revenue Code and deny its supporters tax deductions for contributions under Section 170 of the code. Bob Jones University had, since its inception, refused to admit unmarried African-American students; by 1982, it admitted them only under social strictures against interracial association. In an eight-to-one decision, the Court sustained the IRS's interpretation of the code to require all tax-exempt entities to meet the standards of common-law charitable trusts, namely, that they confer a public benefit in a manner consistent with public policy. The Court also agreed that the IRS acted within its discretion in determining in 1970 that private educational institutions that discriminated on the basis of race did not meet that definition. In addition, the Court found that Congress had effectively ratified the IRS's position with respect to the status of racially discriminatory schools. The case was decided together with *Goldsboro Christian Schools, Inc. v. United States,* a case involving a private, white-only academy also denied tax-exempt status under the IRS policy. In both cases, the Court held that the religious nature of the two institutions did not define them as absolutely entitled to the favorable tax status under the code.

By the 1970s, numerous decisions in the federal courts had held that direct governmental financial assistance to racially discriminatory schools violated either the Constitution or the 1964 Civil Rights Act. Bob Jones University itself was denied scholarship loans by the Department of Health, Education, and Welfare in 1967. By 1974 the school was denied access to veteran's educational benefits. Without conceding that tax exemptions fell into the same category as actual monetary assistance, the IRS was persuaded by 1970 that there was sufficient legal basis to conclude that racial discrimination in private education was inconsistent with "public policy." The IRS promulgated a rule in 1970 that no schools or colleges having racially discriminatory admissions policies would any longer be accorded tax-exempt status under Section 501(c)(3). Of course, such an administrative decision is open to judicial challenge. Under the tax law, however, the only way to challenge an IRS ruling is first to pay the tax and then to sue in federal court for a refund. Bob Jones University attempted to avoid this procedure by bringing suit directly against IRS for a court order preventing the withdrawal of the university's tax-exempt status. When this failed, the university paid a tiny portion of its back FICA taxes and sued for a refund in order to challenge the IRS ruling.

The university won the first round of the suit, but lost in the court of appeals. When Bob Jones University, in 1981, asked the Supreme Court to take the case on its discretionary calendar (by petition for certiorari), the government did not resist. While insisting that the court of appeals had ruled correctly, the government agreed that the case was an important one and, as the IRS policy applied nationwide, a Supreme Court ruling would be useful. In late 1981, however, just before the government's brief would have been due, the newly installed administration abandoned the position the IRS had taken since 1970 and vowed to revise the regulations, at least until Congress might expressly readopt them as part of the tax Code. The government asked the Court to dismiss the case as moot. In the end, the Court permitted the government to realign and argue this case on the same side as Bob Jones University, but appointed an independent lawyer, William T. Coleman, Jr., to argue (successfully, as it transpired) in support of the decision of the court of appeals.

SELECTED BIBLIOGRAPHY

Bob Jones University v. Simon, 416 U.S. 725 (1974); *Bob Jones University v. United States*, 639 F.2d 147 (4th Cir. 1980); *Norwood v. Harrison*, 413 U.S. 455 (1973); *Green v. Kennedy*, 309 F. Supp. 1127 (D.D.C.), app. dism. *sub nom.*; *Cannon v. Green*, 398 U.S. 956 (1970); *Green v. Connally*, 330 F. Supp. 1150 (D.D.C.), affd *sub nom.*; *Coit v. Green*, 398 U.S. 956 (1970); *Bob Jones University v. Johnson*, 396 F. Supp. 597 (D.S.C. 1974), affd mem. 529 F.2d 514 (4th Cir. 1975); Lincoln Caplan, *The Tenth Justice: The Solicitor General and the Rule of Law* (1988).

MIRIAM R. EISENSTEIN

BOND, HORACE MANN (8 November 1904, Nashville, Tennessee–19 December 1972, Atlanta, Georgia). Historian of African-American education, educator, college president. Although Horace Mann Bond was destined to become, in 1945, the first African-American president of prestigious Lincoln University* in Pennsylvania, he is perhaps best known for his comprehensive and meticulously researched historical and sociological accounts of African-American education. Both *The Education of the Negro in the American Social Order* (1934) and *Negro Education in Alabama: A Study in Cotton and Steel* (1939) are considered classics in educational historiography. In addition, throughout his long and highly productive career, Bond published a number of discussions that demanded that American society recognize the intellectual abilities and accomplishments of African-Americans. Bond was particularly forceful in criticizing racially biased interpretations of intelligence tests, which conveyed the notion that African-Americans were inherently inferior and neglected to consider the influence of environmental factors—such as the paltry, discriminatory funding received by African-American schools in the South—on test scores.

As a child, Bond was considered a prodigy. Given the deplorable conditions of African-American schools in the South during his youth, he was fortunate to have acquired much of his elementary and secondary education in private schools associated with African-American colleges located near the churches where his father was the minister. In the fall of 1919, at the age of fourteen, Bond enrolled in Lincoln University, graduating cum laude in 1923. In the spring of 1924, Bond enrolled in the graduate program at the University of Chicago, receiving the M.A. degree in education in 1926 and the Ph.D. degree in 1936.

Bond was most productive during the 1924–39 period. Although he held a number of faculty and administrative positions during those years, in 1939, at the urging of officials of the Julius Rosenwald Fund,* a leading philanthropic organization of the period, Bond left his associate professorship at Fisk University* to become president of Fort Valley State College* in Georgia. In 1945, Bond returned to his alma mater, Lincoln, serving as president until 1957. A significant aspect of Bond's presidency at Lincoln was his attempt to foster strong ties between the university and the emerging independent nations of Africa.

It was not accidental that Bond's first published works directly rebuked allegations that African-Americans were marked by innate intellectual deficiencies and/or debilitating psychological traits. Not only was the new fad of mental measurement, strengthened by the U.S. Army's mass testing program during World War I, beginning to influence American public schooling, but Bond was also a prominent member of a new generation of African-American academics— college-educated "New Negroes" of the 1920s. Although the Harlem Renaissance has been generally discussed in terms of the literary, aesthetic, and nationalist values transforming African-American consciousness, the work of Horace Mann Bond, E. Franklin Frazier, Charles S. Johnson,* Howard Hale Long, and others point to a largely neglected aspect of this broad social movement: a self-assertive intellectualism based on a faith in self, a belief in social science as an avenue of racial uplift, and a belief in the capabilities of African-Americans rooted in the educational and occupational achievements of a growing African-American middle class. Bond, along with a number of this new cohort of African-American social scientists, published several articles in W. E. B. Du Bois's* journal, *The Crisis,* * and especially in the National Urban League's* monthly magazine, *Opportunity*, which sharply criticized intelligence tests for what would now be considered their cultural bias and for neglecting to take into account the obvious relationship between achievement and the environmental factors of growing up with restricted educational opportunities in the segregated South. He also opposed both classroom grouping practices and differentiated curricula based on biased test scores. Bond returned to these themes later in life, both in his distinguished 1957 Harvard lectures (published as *The Search for Talent*, 1959) and in his work *Black American Scholars: A Study of Their Beginnings* (1972).

SELECTED BIBLIOGRAPHY

Wayne J. Urban, *Black Scholar: Horace Mann Bond, 1904–1972* (1992); Michael Fultz, "A 'Quintessential American': Horace Mann Bond, 1924–1939," *Harvard Educational Review* 55, no. 4 (1985): 416–42; Roger Williams, *The Bonds: An American Family* (1971).

MICHAEL FULTZ

BOWIE STATE UNIVERSITY. Bowie State University, founded in 1865, is Maryland's oldest historically black university, among the oldest institutions of its kind in the country. The university is one of the eleven senior colleges and universities in the University of Maryland system. Undergraduates at Bowie State choose from twenty-seven majors in the departments of behavioral sciences and human services, business, economics, and public administration; communications, education and physical education; humanities and fine arts; history, politics and international studies; natural sciences, mathematics, computer science, and nursing or select the Dual Degree in Engineering offered with other area universities. Bowie State also has a strong graduate program offering the master of education in six areas: the master of arts in administrative management (business or public administration), counseling psychology, human resource development and organizational communications; and the master of science in computer science, management information systems, and nursing. Bowie State is home to the Adler-Dreikurs Institute of Human Relations, the Academy for Computer Training, the Family Life and Education Center, the Prince George's County (MD) Entrepreneurial Development Program, the Center for Alternative Dispute Resolution, and BSU-TV (regional cable television). As the state system's regional comprehensive university for south-central Maryland, Bowie State is an active partner with area business, industry, government, and public schools, providing many opportunities to be a part of the growth and development of the area.

SELECTED BIBLIOGRAPHY

National Association for Equal Opportunity in Higher Education, *Profiles of the Nation's Historically and Predominantly Black Colleges and Universities* (1993).

SAMUEL L. MYERS

BRANSON, HERMAN RUSSELL (14 August 1914, Pocahantas, Virginia–7 June 1995, Washington, D.C.). Herman Branson was a noted physicist and chemist who discovered the basic structure of protein and studied the chemistry of sickle cells. He earned a bachelor of science degree from the University of Pittsburgh and Virginia State University* and his Ph.D. from the University of Cincinnati. Branson's mathematical definition of the alpha helix, the basic structure of proteins, has been hailed as one of the most far-reaching accomplishments in the biological sciences. His contributions also include the first-time application of integral equation descriptions and the techniques of information theory to the study of living systems, as well as ground-breaking physiochemical studies of the sickle hemoglobinopathy.

His outstanding scientific career was complemented by his work as a university professor and administrator. He was on the faculties of Dillard University* and Howard University.* At Howard, where he began as a professor of mathematics, Branson established the second Ph.D. program in the history of the university and supervised many master's and doctoral students in scientific research. Branson became president of Central State University* in Ohio in 1968 and, in 1970, of Lincoln University* in Pennsylvania. At both institutions, he emphasized the importance of graduate study for African-American students. Branson was the founder of the National Association for Equal Opportunity in Higher Education (NAFEO), through which billions of dollars have been channelled to academic institutions in support of African-American education. At NAFEO, he played a major role in convincing the federal government to earmark financial support through Title III grants for historically black colleges in general and 1890 land-grant black colleges in particular.

Branson authored one hundred publications in the disciplines of physics, chemistry, mathematics, medicine, biology, and education. He was an active member of more than twenty national and international scientific, educational, and civic organizations and commissions, including the Corporation of the Massachusetts Institute of Technology, the Institute of Medicine of the National Research Council, and the Woodrow Wilson National Fellowship Foundation. He was the recipient of ten honorary degrees.

SELECTED BIBLIOGRAPHY

Christa Brelin and William C. Matney, Jr., eds., *Who's Who among Black Americans, 1992/1993* (1992); Program from the funeral services for Herman Branson.

WILLIAM R. CRUMPTON

BRIGGS v. ELLIOT, 132 F. Supp. 776 (E.D. S.C., 1955). This case marked the NAACP's initial, direct legal challenge to racial segregation in public schools, which challenged segregation in the Clarendon County, South Carolina, schools. In the first round of the litigation in *Briggs,* the lower courts applied the separate-but-equal doctrine of *Plessy v. Ferguson** and ordered that, though the county could maintain separate African-American schools, it had to improve them. When the case reached the Supreme Court, it was remanded on procedural grounds back to the lower courts; thus the larger challenge was avoided. The case was later won as a companion case to *Brown v. Board of Education of Topeka, Kansas.**

In all symbolic respects, the district court in *Briggs* acknowledged the *Brown* decision. It declared ''null and void'' all state laws requiring segregation of the races in its public schools and enjoined the state from refusing to admit a child to any school on the basis of race. At the same time, the court made clear what it viewed as the limits of the Supreme Court's decision and therefore the scope of its order. It decided that, although governmental power could not be used to enforce segregation, school integration was not required. Further, the district court ruled that if a state opens its schools to children of all races it does not violate the Constitution even though children of different races voluntarily attend different schools. The opinion reads, and was read, as a primer for white parents determined to find means to avoid sending their children to schools with African-Americans.

Even later, when courts began ordering relief in some school desegregation, the *Briggs v. Elliot* philosophy continued to define the parameters for judicial action in school desegregation cases. Thus, *Briggs* can be seen as a decision that *Brown* would be a symbolic, not a substantive, victory. The Supreme Court intended, through *Brown,* to send a message about what our society should aspire to in its treatment of African-Americans. It laid down not a rule of law but a moral imperative, enforceable by public sentiment and not court decrees. However, as *Briggs* made unequivocally clear, the Court was not ready to force whites to surrender racial entitlements closely related to their status as citizens.

SELECTED BIBLIOGRAPHY
Briggs v. Elliot, 132 F. Supp. 776 (E.D. S.C., 1955).

DERRICK A. BELL, JR.

BROOKS v. SCHOOL DISTRICT OF CITY OF MOBERLY, MISSOURI, 267 F.2d 733 (1959). Seven African-American schoolteachers were employed by the defendant school district to teach in its segregated school maintained for African-Americans during the 1954–55 school year and were not reemployed when the school system was integrated in the fall of 1955. The main issue in the case was whether plaintiffs met the burden of proving that the board of education's action in failing to renew their teaching contracts was a result of racial discrimination. Such discrimination, they asserted, was in violation of their rights under the equal protection clause of the Fourteenth Amendment to the Constitution; they asked for an injunction and damages. The trial court found that the plaintiffs had not met their burden of proving that the board's action in failing to renew their teaching contracts resulted from racial discrimination. The court of appeals found that the board had wide discretion as to the performance of its duties, including those relating to the employment of teachers, and agreed that the plaintiffs had failed in proving that the board's action was founded upon racial discrimination.

This case stands for the proposition that both the trial and appellate courts gave broad discretion to the decisions of the board of education—perhaps, too broad. The impact of this case was that integration was a double-edged sword that had a much greater impact than determining where one could sit in the classroom or on the bus. Though integration created equality in some spheres, it proved to be a tool to stifle progress in other areas.

SELECTED BIBLIOGRAPHY
Brooks v. School District of City of Moberly, Missouri, 267 F.2d 733 (1959).

BARBARA L. BERNIER

BROWN, CHARLOTTE HAWKINS (11 June 1883, Henderson, North Carolina–11 January 1961, Greensboro, North Carolina). An educator, a school and women's club founder, social worker, author, lecturer, orator, and religious leader, Charlotte Hawkins received her elementary education at the Alston Grammar School of Cambridge, Massachusetts, and graduated from the Cambridge English High School in 1900. In that year she changed her name from Lottie to Charlotte Eugenia.

With the support of mentor Alice Freeman Palmer, the second woman president of Wellesley College, Hawkins entered the State Normal School of Salem, Massachusetts, in 1900. In 1901 she left college, accepting an offer from the American Missionary Association (AMA)* to teach at their Bethany Institute in the rural community of Sedalia, North Carolina. Unfortunately, the school closed the next spring. Hawkins accepted the challenge to found a new school to replace Bethany Institute. She raised funds in Massachusetts, returned to Sedalia, and opened her school, the Alice Freeman Palmer Institute,* in a converted blacksmith's shop on 10 October 1902. When Palmer died later that year, Hawkins renamed her school the Alice Freeman Palmer Memorial Institute in honor of her friend and mentor. To support the school and maintain its growth, Hawkins traveled continuously and untiringly to raise funds. In 1907 the school was formally chartered.

In the early years the curriculum emphasized manual training and industrial education for rural living. But, by the mid-1930s, the focus changed to stress solid college preparatory academic offerings and cultural education. Palmer grew to become perhaps the nation's leading finishing and preparatory school for African-Americans. As the fame of Charlotte Hawkins Brown and the Palmer Memorial Institute spread, she became nationally known not only as an educator but also as a lecturer, social worker, and religious leader. Brown was president of Palmer Memorial Institute from 1901 until 1952 and continued as its finance director until 1955. Under her three successors, the school existed through the 1970–71 academic year.

Charlotte Hawkins married Edward Sumner Brown in 1911. The marriage failed because of career differences and ended in 1915. In 1923 she married again, this time to John Moses. That marriage lasted less than a year. She continued to use the surname ''Brown'' throughout her professional career.

In 1913, Brown became one of the founders of the North Carolina Federation of Negro Women's Clubs. This statewide group was part of a national organization of progressive African-American women's groups. Under her presidential leadership, which lasted more than twenty-one years, one of the federation's outstanding programs was the purchase and maintenance of the Efland Home for Wayward Girls. To ensure the preservation of such a facility in the future, Brown lobbied the North Carolina General Assembly and was successful in persuading them to appropriate $50,000 to establish a new facility for delinquent girls in Rocky Mount. Brown also organized the Girls and Young Adults Division of the Federation of Negro Women's Clubs in 1948 and developed a college scholarship fund that operated from 1956 to 1971. She also served as president of the North Carolina Teachers Association, was cofounder (with Mary McLeod Bethune*) of the National Council of Negro Women. Brown also served as vice president of the National Association of Colored Women's Clubs and was the founder of the Sedalia Singers. In recognition of her many educational and civic services she received numerous honorary degrees and awards. Among these were honorary doctorates from Lincoln University,* Wilberforce University,* Howard University,* and Tuskegee Institute.* She had the distinction of being honored by the North Carolina Board of Education in its Hall of Fame. She was the author of *Mammy: An Appeal of the Heart of the South* (1919) and *The Correct Thing to Do, to Say, to Wear* (1941). She aided in the founding of the *Negro Braille Magazine*. In honor of Brown's many achievements, the Charlotte Hawkins Brown Memorial State Historic Site was dedicated in November 1987. It is North Carolina's first state-funded historic site honoring the contributions of African-Americans or women.

SELECTED BIBLIOGRAPHY

Ruth Ann Stewart, "Charlotte Eugenia Hawkins Brown," in *Notable American Women: The Modern Period* (1980); Marsha C. Vick, "Charlotte Hawkins Brown," in *Notable Black American Women* (1992); Sandra N. Smith and Earle H. West, "Charlotte Hawkins Brown," in *Journal of Negro Education* 51 (Summer 1982). The most exhaustive collection of materials assembled on the life and career of Charlotte Hawkins Brown is with the Historic Sites Section of the Division of Archives and History in Raleigh, North Carolina. The Charlotte Hawkins Brown Papers are at the Schlesinger Library of Women, Radcliffe College, Cambridge, Massachusetts, and the Charlotte Hawkins Brown and Palmer Memorial Institute Papers are in the Holgate Library, Bennett College, Greensboro, North Carolina.

CHARLES W. WADELINGTON

BROWN v. BOARD OF EDUCATION OF TOPEKA, KANSAS, 347 U.S. 483 (1954) (*BROWN I*) and **BROWN v. BOARD OF EDUCATION OF TOPEKA, KANSAS,** 349 U.S. 294 (1955) (*BROWN II*). *Brown I* is the most significant ruling on race and equal educational opportunities in the history of the United States Supreme Court. In *Brown I* the Court held that the de jure segregation of students in public schools on the basis of race deprived minority children of equal educational opportunities in violation of the Equal Protection Clause of the Fourteenth Amendment. A year later, in *Brown II*, it set about the task of dismantling segregated school systems. The Court ordered the lower courts to require the defendant school districts to "make a prompt and reasonable start toward full compliance" (p. 300) to implement its mandates aimed at ending de jure segregation.

Brown I is commonly referred to as *Brown v. Board of Education, Topeka*, because the lead case was initiated there. Yet, it actually involved four class-action lawsuits brought on behalf of African-American students who were denied admission to schools attended by white children because of laws that either required or permitted racial segregation. In addition to Topeka, the other actions originated in Clarendon County (South Carolina), Prince Edward County* (Virginia), and New Castle County (Delaware). Segregation was permitted under state law in Kansas; it was required by both the state constitutions and statutory provisions in the other three locations. The Delaware suit was an appeal from a state court action; the remaining cases sought further review of federal court rulings.

All of the lower courts based their decisions to uphold de jure segregation on the pernicious "separate but equal" standard adopted by the Supreme Court's 1896 ruling in *Plessy v. Ferguson*,* which apparently originated almost fifty years earlier in a Massachusetts case, *Roberts v. City of Boston** (1850). The Court subsequently extended *Plessy* to public education in *Gong Lum v. Rice* (1927). Only in Delaware did the Court order the immediate admission of African-American students to schools previously attended exclusively by white children; it did so based on its finding that the schools where the white young-sters were in attendance were superior with respect to such factors as teacher training, pupil-teacher ratios, and physical plant facilities. Thus, even though each of the actions was premised on different facts and a variety of local con-ditions, they were consolidated on appeal in light of the common legal question they presented.

Oral arguments in *Brown I* were conducted originally in December 1952, but the Court was unable to reach a decision, seemingly because it was divided on the constitutionality of the "separate but equal" doctrine. Consequently, it heard a second round of arguments, focused largely on the circumstances relating to the adoption of the Fourteenth Amendment, over a three-day period in early December 1953. At long last, the Court ruled unanimously on 17 May 1954, striking down de jure segregation in public schools.

The Court briefly reviewed its rulings in *Sweatt v. Painter** and *McLaurin v. Oklahoma State Regents** (1950), companion cases that prohibited interschool and intraschool segregation, respectively, in higher education on the basis of tangible and intangible inequities. These cases were part of a successful long-term strategy adopted by the NAACP* aimed at ending segregation in education that culminated in *Brown*.

Applying the principles enunciated in *Sweatt* and *McLaurin* to elementary and secondary schools, the Court focused on the detrimental psychological effects of segregation on African-American students. Then, for the first time in its history, it relied on data from the social sciences and considered the deleterious effects of racial segregation in reaching its decision. The result was that, while stopping short of an outright reversal, the Court unequivocally repudiated *Plessy*'s denial of the fact that segregation led to feelings of inferiority among Af-rican-Americans. It went on to hold: "We conclude that in the field of public education the doctrine of 'separate but equal' has no place. Separate educational facilities are inherently unequal." As it was able to reach its decision on the basis of the equal protection clause of the Fourteenth Amendment, the Court found it unnecessary to consider whether segregation violated that amendment's due process clause.

In *Bolling v. Sharpe*, a companion case decided on the same day as *Brown I*, the Court, in an opinion authored by the Chief Justice, unanimously struck down the law calling for school segregation in the District of Columbia as unconstitutional. However, because the equal protection clause applies only to the states, the Court based its holding here on the due process clause of the Fifth Amendment.

Although a monumental decision, *Brown I* did not address remedies. Therefore, the Court concluded its ruling by ordering further oral arguments to consider appropriate relief. Given the need to fashion remedies stemming from its decision in *Brown I* and *Bolling*, in *Brown II* the Court invited the attorneys general from all of the states as well as from the federal government to present their views on the question of relief. In addition to the United States, the states of Arkansas, Florida, Maryland, North Carolina, Oklahoma, and Texas filed briefs and participated in the oral arguments along with the parties from *Bolling*. Just as in *Brown I*, the Court's short but unanimous opinion, published on May 31, 1955, was written by Chief Justice Warren.

Unfortunately, in *Brown II* the Court neither mandated an immediate end to nor set a time table for eradicating school segregation. Rather, because of the varied local problems presented by the cases, it remanded them to local courts with orders for its decrees to be effectuated in a "prompt and reasonable" fashion.

Clearly, *Brown I* and *Brown II* set the stage for a myriad of far-reaching changes in American society. Yet, as significant as these rulings are, questions about their meaning continue to be debated. For example, it is not clear whether *Brown I* focused primarily on issues of race or education; that is, although the Court relied heavily on data from the social sciences in *Brown I*, it subsequently struck down other forms of segregation without any references to its psychological effects. Equally uncertain is whether it guaranteed the rights of African-American students to be free from de jure segregation or whether it imposed on states the affirmative duty to ensure their right to attend integrated schools.

In *Brown I* and *Brown II* the Supreme Court perhaps simultaneously recognized its power and its limitations. It raised national consciousness by clearly and decisively striking down racial segregation in education as unconstitutional, but it accepted the inherent constraints on its ability to bring about change by leaving it to the political process, legislation, and subsequent litigation to complete the revolution that it helped to set in motion. By acting as cautiously as it did in this latter regard, the Court apparently hoped to set the stage for later developments that would provide equal opportunities in other walks of life such as interstate commerce, bus terminals, and public facilities. However, based on the massive resistance that ensued, the wisdom of this approach is questionable.

The Court in *Brown I* intentionally defined the issue narrowly. It adopted this approach because, except for the most stubborn and closed-minded, all people should have been able to understand the need for equal educational opportunities. Thus, taken together, *Brown I* and the limited scope of remedies it effectuated in *Brown II* represent a compromise that attempted to steer a middle course. On the one hand, the Court recognized that it could not permit the unacceptable status quo to remain in place indefinitely. On the other hand, it sought to avoid lecturing what it correctly perceived would be a recalcitrant and resentful South. An unfortunate consequence was that, in attempting to limit conflict by easing equality in, the Court's decisions inadvertently may have strengthened the resolve of opponents of its ruling, who heightened their resistance. If, as opponents of *Brown* might have asked, equal educational opportunities were as important as the Court (and others) maintained they were, then why did it not order an immediate end to segregated schooling? The struggles to implement *Brown* are ample witness to the defiance that it spawned.

The shortcomings of *Brown I* and *Brown II* notwithstanding, these rulings represent the dawn of a new era in American history, one dedicated to attaining equal opportunities for all Americans as evidenced by the Civil Rights movement that it helped to engender. Yet, as the four decades that have elapsed since *Brown I* have vividly illustrated, the struggle for justice and equality is far from over.

SELECTED BIBLIOGRAPHY

Bolling v. Sharpe, 347 U.S. 497 (1954); *Gong Lum v. Rice*, 275 U.S. 78 (1927); *McLaurin v. Oklahoma State Regents*, 339 U.S. 637 (1950); *Plessy v. Ferguson*, 163 U.S. 537 (1896); *Roberts v. City of Boston*, 59 Mass. 198, 5 Cush. 198 (1850); *Sweatt v. Painter*, 339 U.S. 629 (1950).

CHARLES J. RUSSO

BUREAU OF REFUGEES, FREEDMEN, AND ABANDONED LANDS.
The Bureau of Refugees, Freedmen, and Abandoned Lands, known popularly as the Freedmen's Bureau, was established by Congress on 3 March 1865. Conceived as a governmental response to the massive social and economic dislocation of the American Civil War, its task was threefold: to provide relief to the white and African-American refugees from the war; to address legal, economic, moral, and educational issues regarding African-Americans arising from emancipation; and to administer and dispose of the property confiscated from the former Confederate government and from disloyal southern whites.

Before the bureau was created, a welter of uncoordinated and occasionally conflicting private and governmental agencies attempted to deal with the problems of refugees and former slaves. Northern voluntary philanthropic organizations competed with one another and collided with Union Army and Treasury Department policies and personnel. These agencies delivered food, clothing, and medical supplies to refugee camps and plantations, established schools, and organized the labor of the freed slaves, among other tasks.

By 1863, abolitionist activists among the voluntary agencies began agitating Congress to establish an Emancipation Bureau. The intention was to make the problems and promises of emancipation a central responsibility of the federal government, to remove the former slaves—the freedmen—from the occasionally hostile and usually inconsistent control of the military, and to coordinate and support voluntary work among the freedmen.

The legislation creating the Freedmen's Bureau fell far short of the goals of the proposed Emancipation Bureau. By linking freedmen's affairs with the welfare of all southern refugees and the problems of abandoned property, the legislation effectively transformed the moral and political problems of emancipation into a technical problem equivalent to temporary war-related complications. It lodged the bureau in the War Department, where it was frequently staffed with military officers lacking any commitment to the interests of the freedmen. The legislation did direct the bureau to cooperate with the work of the voluntary agencies, but provided no funds for direct aid to the agencies.

Further, the actions of President Andrew Johnson left the bureau with inadequate means to carry out its mandate. Congress had expected the federal government to become the caretaker of thousands of acres of abandoned and confiscated lands in the South. It directed the Freedmen's Bureau to give the land in forty-acre allotments to loyal southern whites and the freed slaves and to fund its other activities through the sale and rental of any remaining property. Johnson's pardon of Confederates, however, beginning in May 1865, left the bureau with only a tiny fraction of the expected property and with uncertain tenure on much of the property remaining under its control. Johnson's action scuttled southern land reform and left the agency with inadequate funding. When Congress reauthorized the bureau in 1866, over Johnson's veto, it made only superficial improvements in its funding.

The bureau was headed by General Oliver Otis Howard, its first and only commissioner. He organized it along the lines of nineteenth-century military organizations, appointing military officers to supervise bureau activities in each southern state under military rule. These assistant commissioners, in turn, appointed subassistant commissioners and assistant subassistant commissioners to supervise the bureau's work in various regions of the South. Lower-level agents were frequently military personnel, though northern and southern civilians also served in such capacities. Turnover was always very high, especially as military men were mustered out, with resulting discontinuities and inconsistencies in the work of the bureau.

Because the dilemmas of white refugees were resolved relatively quickly after the end of hostilities and because, after Johnson's pardons, there was little abandoned property to control, freedmen's affairs became the bureau's primary obligation, focused on labor, justice, moral reform, and education. The bureau regularized and enforced labor contracts between white land-owners and African-American workers, seeking to mitigate the widespread fraud against the freedmen while assuring the reestablishment of the cotton economy. It developed a short-lived system of courts to adjudicate disputes between whites and African-Americans when the civil courts proved unwilling to deal justly with the freedmen. "Moral reform" was fostered through lectures on the virtues of hard work and fidelity to contracts, organizing temperance societies, and providing civil sanction for slave marriages and through other modes of "elevating" the freedmen.

The bureau was most successful in its contributions to southern African-American education. Under the leadership of its general superintendent of education, Rev. John Alvord, the Educational Division provided supervision and coordination to the nascent African-American school system developing in southern cities. State-level assistant superintendents assisted the northern freedmen's aid societies and missionary societies in organizing schools in smaller towns and on plantations, urging the freedmen to support the work by raising funds among themselves for property for schools and donating labor to build schoolhouses in return for northern teachers. The bureau expended over $5 million to assist in developing freedmen's schools, primarily through the instrumentality of the private aid societies—about a million dollars per year. It also published statistics in the Semi-Annual Report on Freedmen's Schools that were useful to the aid societies in their fund-raising efforts.

The American Civil War and Reconstruction constituted a virtual social revolution. Most immediately, they transformed southern labor relations and the economics of slavery and cast the former bondsmen into new social and economic roles. The foundations of earlier power relationships were destroyed, while the exact contours of new relationships were fluid. The freedmen—landless, impoverished, and defenseless—demanded and had the right to expect protection and assistance in their new situation. Yet the Bureau of Refugees, Freedmen, and Abandoned Lands was inadequate to the task. Lacking resources of all sorts—funds, adequate staff, agents committed to the work at hand, police powers in the form of a military presence to enforce its mandates—the bureau was further hampered by southern white intransigence and growing northern indifference to the plight of southern African-Americans.

After only four years of work, the bureau was ordered to wind up its labors in January 1869. Education and bounty offices were all that remained after that date, but with inadequate funding even those offices were sharply reduced. The final report of the Education Division was published in July 1870. The bureau itself expired in 1872, with few of its functions intact.

SELECTED BIBLIOGRAPHY

Donald G. Neiman, *To Set the Law in Motion: The Freedmen's Bureau and the Legal Rights of Blacks, 1865–1868* (1979); William S. McFeely, *Yankee Stepfather: General O. O. Howard and the Freedmen* (1968); Ronald E. Butchart, *Northern Whites, Southern Blacks, and Reconstruction: Freedmen's Education 1862–1875* (1980); George R. Bentley, *A History of the Freedmen's Bureau* (1955).

RONALD E. BUTCHART

BURROUGHS, NANNIE HELEN (2 May 1879, Orange, Virginia–20 May 1961, Washington, D.C.). Educator and school founder, Nannie Helen Burroughs was born on 2 May 1879, in Orange, Virginia. Her father died when Burroughs was a young child, and she and her mother moved to Washington, D.C., where Burroughs graduated from the M Street High School. Burroughs was instrumental in forming the Woman's Convention Auxiliary (WC) of the National Baptist Convention (NBC) in 1900. She served as corresponding secretary for the WC from 1900 until 1948, when she became president.

In 1900 Burroughs proposed to the new WC the idea of establishing a trade school for girls. Although the WC approved of the plan, the men of the NBC balked at the idea. If the school trained women to be missionaries, they might support it. But if it trained women to be breadwinners, the men would not find it acceptable. By 1905, the NBC agreed to the idea, and land was bought in Washington, D.C., in 1907. Ironically, after waiting all those years, Burroughs never did receive the financial support of the convention. Wanting to serve people of all faiths, she was unwilling to call the school a "Baptist" school, and the convention refused to offer any support. The school finally opened late in 1909, almost ten years after she initially proposed the idea.

The curriculum of the National Training School for Women and Girls reflected the dual goals of practical instruction for self-support and moral grounding for life. The school taught domestic science and clerical and secretarial skills and also taught nontraditional occupations for women such as printing, shoe repair, and barbering. Burroughs insisted on providing both liberal arts and vocational education, believing that "it is our duty to get both." She also emphasized training of spiritual character; the school was called "School of the Three Bs" for its emphasis on Bible, bath, and broom as tools for racial advancement.

By the end of the Progressive Era, Burroughs was working in two additional areas that mirrored the era's climate of social reform. First, she became involved in the fight to help African-American women workers. The vast majority of African-American women wage earners—as many as 90 percent—worked in farm or domestic work. One third of all domestic workers were African-American, mostly household servants, and seven out of eight of them were women. In 1920 Burroughs organized the National Association of Wage Earners to attract public attention to the plight of African-American women working outside the home.

Second, Burroughs worked to instill racial pride in young people. From 1920 to 1925 she was involved in the International Council of Women of Darker Races. This group hoped to broaden their own cultural knowledge and also to gain recognition for the study of women of color as an accepted field. The group advocated the teaching of African-American history and culture in all U.S. schools and proposed a course of study and textbooks for review by school boards across the country. By 1929, her own school required students to take an African-American history course, and Burroughs encouraged further study by sponsoring annual oratorical and writing contests based on aspects of African-American history. After 1953, the school focused exclusively on training women for missionary service. Burroughs remained president until her death in 1961.

Burroughs also was an active member of the National Association of Colored Women and the National Association for the Advancement of Colored People* and wrote extensively for the African-American press.

SELECTED BIBLIOGRAPHY

Evelyn Brooks Barnett, "Nannie Burroughs and the Education of Black Women," in Sharon Harley and Rosalyn Terborg-Penn, eds., *The Afro-American Woman* (1978); Paula Giddings, *When and Where I Enter: The Impact of Black Women on Race and Sex in America* (1984); Evelyn Rhodes Higginbotham, "Nannie Helen Burroughs," in D. Hine, E. Brown, and R. Terborg-Penn, eds., *Black Women in America* (1993); Evelyn Rhodes Higginbotham, "Religion, Politics, and Gender: The Leadership of Nannie Helen Burroughs," *Journal of Religious Thought* (Winter/Spring 1988); Gerda Lerner, *Black Women in White America* (1972); Victoria Wolcott, "National Training School for

Women and Girls,'' in D. Hine, E. Brown, and R. Terborg-Penn, eds., *Black Women in America* (1993). The Burroughs papers are located at the Library of Congress, Washington, D.C.

MARGARET A. NASH

BUSING. Busing as a means to transport children to school is not a controversial issue in the United States; it is an indelible part of American education. Compulsory attendance laws mandating school attendance by children began in 1852 in Massachusetts. Student transportation at public expense based on the distance a child lives from his or her public school dates back to 1869 in that same state. Busing became controversial in the mid-to-late 1960s as civil rights legislation gave enforcement powers to end de jure school desegregation, as mandated by the 1954 *Brown v. Board of Education of Topeka, Kansas** decision. Racially segregated housing patterns meant that children had to be transported to schools that were not within walking distance of their homes. As southern municipalities sought to evade their responsibility to desegregate schools, the political rhetoric of elected leaders and media manipulation transformed busing into a symbol for opposition to school racial integration. Labels such as ''forced busing'' and ''massive busing'' were coined as slogans by opponents of school desegregation. Two factors—the planned racial integration of schools and the removal of students from their neighborhoods for that purpose—contributed to the enormity of the controversy surrounding busing. School districts often contrived intricate diversionary tactics to avoid dismantling their dual school systems.

In the North the key tactic used by school boards to avoid school desegregation was their emphasis on de facto rather than de jure segregation. These boards argued that voluntary residential patterns, not state laws, caused most of the racially separate schools. Therefore they claimed no responsibility to desegregate. This rhetoric belied the evidence that gerrymandering had been school policy in many northern communities, such as Denver, Colorado. The only recourse remaining to African-American parents was to sue the school boards for overt discrimination. Successes came slowly.

Two important Supreme Court decisions related to desegregation/busing efforts were *Swann v. Charlotte-Mecklenburg Board of Education** (1971) in the South, and *Keyes v. School District No. 1** (1973) in the North. The *Swann* case established the transportation of students as a tool for desegregation. The *Keyes* case established the notion that the ''purpose or intent to segregate'' could be inferred from the actions of school officials and that therefore remedies were permissible to correct the harm that had been caused by those actions.

In the 1970s, busing was depicted by many opponents of integration as having a negative impact on education. However, the amount of busing that was devoted to school desegregation was relatively modest. A 1977 study by the U.S. Commission on Civil Rights cited the amount of busing for desegregation during the decade between 1966 and 1975 as affecting about 5 percent of all students.

The burden of busing for the purpose of desegregation fell disproportionately on African-American students, 9 percent of whom were bused to school, compared with only 3 percent of white students.

The antibusing phenomenon, fueled by the intransigence of racism, has had a significant influence on views of the media, social scientists, and legislators regarding busing as a remedy for school segregation. The media, for the most part, has tended to focus only on those communities where virulent opposition to busing existed and to ignore communities that successfully implemented desegregation plans. In the 1970s such prestigious social scientists as David Armor and James S. Coleman attacked the efficacy of school desegregation in terms of academic achievement (Armor, 1972) and white residential stability (Coleman, 1976). These attacks represented a significant departure for social scientists, whose work had been mostly supportive of civil rights concerns since the 1940s. The findings of Armor and Coleman gave "scientific" credence to desegregation opponents' belief that the "forced" desegregation social-change experiment was not working and must be stopped.

Politicians also used antibusing rhetoric to strengthen their support among whites opposed to integration. Presidents Richard Nixon, Gerald Ford, and Jimmy Carter used direct or indirect statements against busing during their campaigns or while holding office. Antibusing legislation was continually introduced by congressmen, often prior to or immediately following a desegregation order in the district they represented.

The combination of events within various segments of society resulted in the emergence of a number of beliefs and concerns that in general were not supported by fact. Many citizens believed that integration does not help the education of African-American children and that it harms the education of white children, that integrated schools are unsafe, that busing hampers a parent's ability to respond to school emergencies, and that it impedes students' participation in extracurricular activities (Orfield, 1978).

The changing mood of the country was reflected in *Milliken v. Bradley** (1974), which held that, absent constitutional violations by surrounding school districts or the state as a whole, desegregation plans must be implemented within the city limits. In *Milliken II* (1977), the Court emphasized an array of "educational components" considered necessary to balance the limited scope of integration possible with a plan confined to within city limits. The restrictive nature of *Milliken*, along with media manipulation of the issue, lack of support from legislators and the White House, and the continual policy debate in many communities, culminated in a cessation of the desegregation thrust that had reached its height in the early 1970s. Also, African-American parents became weary of one-way busing plans that put the burden of desegregation on their children. African-American children often were placed in segregated classrooms within ostensibly desegregated school buildings, to the dismay of their parents.

Since the late 1970s, school desegregation policy has been relatively dormant. Court strategies have moved to negotiated agreements, compensatory education programs, magnet schools, and instructional changes, because of the limited desegregation that would occur in most urban school districts because of continued residential segregation based on race and social class status.

SELECTED BIBLIOGRAPHY

David Armor, "The Evidence on Busing," *Public Interest* 28 (Summer 1972): 90–126; George Chambers, "Transportation of Students," in Harold E. Mitzel, ed., *Encyclopedia of Education Research* (1982); James S. Coleman, "Liberty and Equality in School Desegregation," *Social Policy* 6 (January/February 1976): 9–13; Gary Orfield, *Must We Bus: Segregated Schools and National Policy* (1978).

RONALD D. HENDERSON

C

CALHOUN v. LATIMER, 377 U.S. 263 (1964). In the fall of 1961, after years of foot-dragging, a reluctant court ordered an even more reluctant Atlanta school board to adopt a desegregation program, albeit one so gradual that it must be seen as a continuation of the city's efforts to resist integration. Under the plan, students would continue in their present, racially segregated assignments (although no longer in schools formally classified as "white" or "Negro") while a "top-down" integration plan was phased in. The plan would reach the first grade in 1970, sixteen years after the Supreme Court's decision in *Brown v. Board of Education of Topeka, Kansas.** In the meantime, students not otherwise subject to desegregation could request voluntary transfers to another school. A "careful screening of each applicant to determine his or her fitness to enter the school to which application [was] made," with transfers approved only for students passing a personality and aptitude test.

Two years into the plan, African-American parents represented by the NAACP* sued the school board on the grounds that the desegregation plan was too slow in dismantling the dual school system and too limited in its reach. They sought in *Calhoun v. Latimer* the reorganization of the district lines that funnelled African-American and white students to different schools in the first place and also asked that the top-down plan be accelerated to reach more quickly those younger students who might yet avoid the stigmatizing and bias-teaching taint of racial segregation in their education. The court of appeals disagreed. While striking down the testing and "suitability" requirements of formal transfers, the court found the plan adequate to achieve desegregation with "all deliberate speed." Despite statistics revealing that under the plan only 54 black students out of 396 applicants had gained transfers in a system with 116,000 students, the court virtually crowed: "The result to date is that there are eleven integrated school high schools in Atlanta."

The court's unwillingness to require more than token efforts and minimal speed to dismantle school systems that had separated the races for nearly a century was all too typical of desegregation cases. By 1974, after nearly two decades of desegregation and of white flight to private and suburban schools free of blacks, Atlanta's school district was 82 percent African-American (versus 32 percent in 1952). The virtual stagnation of progress led many African-American parents to question whether the goal of racial integration reflected their deeply held values or whether it was simply a tactic to obtain quality education for their children.

Lawyers for the local NAACP branch subsequently negotiated a settlement with the Atlanta school board that allowed this limited student desegregation in exchange for full desegregation of faculty and staff, including an African-American superintendent of schools. These lawyers, with some reason, believed that only by changing those who were in charge of the school system would they obtain any meaningful improvement for African-American students. Though thousands of African-American parents supported the agreement, and the federal court ultimately approved it, the national NAACP office and many other African-Americans were outraged, viewing the settlement as a pact with the devil. Legal Defense Fund (LDF) lawyers, representing a group of African-American Atlanta residents who opposed the settlement, appealed the district court order. After winning reversal on procedural grounds, the LDF urged interdistrict busing with the suburbs to achieve real integration. The appellate court ruled against them, holding that Atlanta had done all that was required to desegregate its schools. Plaintiffs were left with a plan that met their ideological requirements but promised little in the way of either actual integration of educational improvement for African-American children. The NAACP committed itself, both before and after *Brown*, to obtaining nothing less than racial integration in Atlanta.

SELECTED BIBLIOGRAPHY
Calhoun v. Latimer, 388 U.S. 263 (1964).

DERRICK A. BELL, Jr.

CALIVER, AMBROSE (1894, Saltville, Virginia–26, January 1962, Washington, D.C.). A government official and educator, Ambrose Caliver obtained his early education in the public schools of Virginia and Tennessee. He was awarded the B.A. degree from Knoxville College* (1915), the M.A. degree from the University of Wisconsin (1920), and the Ph.D. degree from Columbia University (1930). After serving as a high school administrator in Tennessee and Virginia from 1915 to 1917, he accepted a position as an instructor of manual arts at Fisk University* in 1917 and rose to the position of professor and academic dean, serving from 1927 to 1929.

Upon his appointment as Specialist in Negro Education in the U.S. Office of Education, Caliver became the first African-American to be classified at the professional level in the federal government service. His assignments extended over a wide range of educational programs, from the elementary through the secondary, college, and adult education levels. It was during this period that Caliver initiated and organized the National Conference on Fundamental Problems of Negro Education, the first such conference to focus on this topic in a national setting. He went on to serve as principal investigator for the National Survey of Higher Education of Negroes and as Senior Specialist for the Higher Education of Negroes.

Caliver's most distinctive contributions were in the field of adult education. In 1946 he became director of Project Literacy Education. He also served as chief of Adult Education and as executive director of the Literacy Commission in Washington, D.C. In 1955, he founded the National Commission on Adult Literacy of the Adult Education Association, an organization that sponsored study groups across the country to engage in what Caliver described as a mass approach to adult civic education.

In 1961, a few months before his death, Caliver was elected president of the Adult Education Association. In a posthumous tribute, the Association declared that "his wisdom, vision, perseverance and statesmanship have profoundly influenced the development and administration of adult education in community, state, and national affairs."

SELECTED BIBLIOGRAPHY

Ambrose Caliver, "Education of Negro Leaders," *Journal of Negro Education* 17 (1948): 240–48; Walter G. Daniel and John B. Holden, *Ambrose Caliver: Adult Educator and Civil Servant*; Theresa Wilkins, "Ambrose Caliver: Distinguished Civil Servant," *Journal of Negro Education* 31 (1962): 212–14.

WALTER G. DANIEL

CALVIN, VIRGINIA BROWN (16 June 1945, Lake Providence, Louisiana). In July 1993, Virginia Brown Calvin, Ed.D., was named superintendent of the South Bend Community School Corporation (South Bend, Indiana), making her both the first African-American and the first female chief executive in the corporation's history. The fifth largest school district in the state of Indiana, the South Bend Community School Corporation has an annual budget of approximately $120 million.

Before coming to South Bend in 1972, Calvin was a special education and elementary school teacher in Texas, New Mexico, and Mississippi. In 1973, Calvin earned her doctoral degree in early childhood education, counseling, and special education at Texas Women's University in Denton, Texas. In 1970, she completed her master's degree in elementary education and reading at New Mexico Highlands University in Las Vegas, New Mexico. She did her undergraduate work in elementary education at Alcorn State University* in Lorman, Mississippi.

Calvin has been affiliated with the South Bend Community School Corporation for twenty-two years. At the time of her appointment as superintendent of schools, she was serving as executive director of curriculum and instruction. During her years in that position, she launched an ambitious, multiyear "Valuing Diversity" program, involving all corporation employees and various community groups, the first of its kind in the state of Indiana and one of the first in the nation. She is probably best known, however, as the former principal of Muessel Elementary. During her ten years there (1982–92), the school earned national attention and acclaim. In 1988, Muessel was named both a National and a State Blue Ribbon School and, in April 1993, one of ''America's Best Elementary Schools'' by *Redbook Magazine*.

Calvin has been recognized on many occasions for her civic and educational contributions. In 1991, she was named Educator of the Year by both the Community Education Roundtable and the *Michiana Executive Journal*; in 1984, she was named Woman of the Year by the YWCA of South Bend. In 1982, she received a Mayor's Commendation for Outstanding Contributions to the Community of South Bend; in 1979, she was given a Governor's Certificate of Recognition from Governor Robert Orr.

Dr. Calvin and her husband Richmond Calvin, Ed.D., a full professor of education at Indiana University/South Bend, live in Granger, Indiana. They are the parents of two children, Brent and Shannon.

SELECTED BIBLIOGRAPHY

Christa Brelin and William C. Matney, eds., *Who's Who among Black Americans, 1992–1993* (1992).

MARY ELLEN HAMER

THE CATHOLIC CHURCH AND AFRICAN-AMERICAN EDUCATION. From its earliest days, the American Catholic Church was instrumental in providing education for African-Americans, even within the confines of slavery. Some of the organized efforts were the result of African-American Catholic initiative in the early years of the nineteenth century. After the slave rebellion in Santo Domingo (later known as Haiti), there was an influx of refugees from the island to the shores of the United States. They migrated to port cities along the eastern coast, with a majority finding a home in the French-speaking Catholic colony of Louisiana. These settlers and their descendants formed a nucleus for the historic breakthroughs in education that were to follow. Among those settling in Baltimore, Maryland, were several free, well-educated, French-speaking Catholic women.

One of these women was Elizabeth Lange, who settled in Baltimore in about 1817. Realizing the plight of poor African-American children, many of whom spoke French, Elizabeth Lange opened a school for them in her home, assisted by Madeleine Balas and Rosine Boegue. By 1829, with the help of a French priest, Jacques Joubert, the women established a religious community, which became known as the Oblate Sisters of Providence.*

In 1836, their school, St. Frances Academy,* opened as the only institution offering a secondary education for African-American females prior to the Civil War. Over the next several years, additional schools were founded in Baltimore, New Orleans, St. Louis, and other areas in the South.

One of the first women to join the Oblate Sisters of Providence was Maria Becraft, a free woman who had been educated in several of the privately run schools for free African-Americans in Washington, D.C. At the age of fifteen, Becraft started a school for African-American girls in the city's Georgetown section. In response to a request by the pastor of Holy Trinity Parish in Georgetown, she also conducted another school for African-American girls. She later joined the Oblate Sisters in Baltimore, leaving her school in the care of a former student, Ellen Simonds.

Another milestone in the struggle for African-American education in the 1800s was the establishment of the second permanent religious community of African-American women, the Sisters of the Holy Family,* in New Orleans in 1842. A priest, Father Etienne Rousselon, directed this congregation of sisters, founded by Henriette Delille and Juliette Gaudin, two freeborn women of color, who were committed to teaching and to the care of orphans, the ill, and the elderly. They opened St. Mary's Boarding Academy for Girls, an orphanage, and the Lafon Home for orphan boys. Thomy Lafon, a free well-educated African-American Catholic, was a former teacher and prominent businessman who became a major benefactor of the Holy Family congregation.

Marie Bernard Couvent, born in Guinea, West Africa, was brought to Santo Domingo, where she was enslaved. Eventually obtaining her freedom, she settled in New Orleans and married Gabriel Bernard Couvent, a free African-American man. In 1848, she founded a free school for orphans of color, donating property she had inherited from her husband for the school's construction. The Couvent School served 250 children, who were taught and cared for by an African-American lay faculty. After the Civil War, former students and teachers of the school were among the chief leaders in the movement to create an integrated public school system in New Orleans. The Couvent School was later renamed the Holy Redeemer School, and a public school was named in honor of Marie Couvent for her great contribution to education in New Orleans.

Following the Civil War, many religious groups began missionary work among the freedmen. The Catholic Church, itself a mission church, sought to preserve the faith of the relatively few African-American Catholics in the United States and to win converts among nonchurched and Protestant African-Americans. The Society of St. Joseph, formerly part of a community in England, became the first Roman Catholic clerical society of priests and brothers to devote themselves exclusively to ministry in the African-American community. One of the founders of this small congregation was an African-American, Charles Randolph Uncles, who in 1891 became the first African-American priest to be ordained in the United States.

The Josephites built schools and churches throughout the South, championing the cause of African-American clergy and working for equality in all areas of life. They established eighty-seven elementary schools and twenty-three high schools, staffed by African-American and white religious congregations. Many of these schools were built in poor rural communities where educational facilities were inadequate or nonexistent.

In addition to the efforts of religious communities, the role of laypersons was crucial to educational progress of the African-American community. Daniel Rudd, a former slave from Cincinnati, Ohio, organized delegates from all over the nation to convene five National Black Catholic Lay Congresses from 1899 to 1894. Education was the dominant theme of discussion by delegates at each Congress. One delegate, Dr. William S. Lofton, insisted upon the creation of a national Catholic institution to meet the educational needs of African-American youth. The Federated Colored Catholics, founded by prominent educator Thomas Wyatt Turner of Hampton Institute,* also pressured Catholic bishops for an educational institution that would respond to the issues raised by the Lay Congresses. In response to these calls for action, the Cardinal Gibbons Institute was founded in St. Inigoes, Maryland. The institute was administered by African-American Catholics Victor Daniel, formerly a professor at the Tuskegee Institute,* and his wife Constance. The institute was a secondary academic institution offering courses in industrial training subjects. Financial difficulties and school integration brought about its closing in 1967. Many other Catholic schools would later close for these same reasons.

Mother Katherine Drexel, founder of the Sisters of the Blessed Sacrament, established a network of educational facilities throughout the nation. The capstone of their achievements was the 1915 founding of Xavier University* in New Orleans, the only African-American Catholic university in America.

In Lafayette, Louisiana, in 1910, Eleanor Figaro, a graduate of St. Paul's School, gathered eighteen children in a shed and began the parish's first Catholic school for African-Americans. She later taught at Sacred Heart School for forty-two years and in 1949 became the first African-American woman to receive the papal honor, *Pro Ecclesia et Pontifice*.

Several other religious communities made valuable contributions to the education of African-Americans. Among these are: the Holy Ghost Fathers, the Society of the Divine Word, and the third group of African-American religious women, the Handmaids of the Most Pure Heart of Mary.* These dedicated efforts were accomplished with the commitment of the families and their communities.

Many Catholic elementary schools are still flourishing, and certain high schools continue in the tradition of instilling high moral values and providing quality education for African-Americans. This is accomplished in spite of often necessary closings of Catholic schools, especially in predominantly African-American communities. Some schools have attempted to solve their financial difficulties by consolidating, becoming coeducational, or serving larger regions.

SELECTED BIBLIOGRAPHY

Loretta M. Butler, *A History of Catholic Elementary Education of Negroes in the Diocese Lafayette, Louisiana*, Ph.D. diss., The Catholic University of America, Washington, D.C. (1963); Cyprian Davis, OSB, *The History of Black Catholics in the United States* (1990); Donald E. Devore and Joseph Logson, *Crescent City Schools* (1990); Elio Gasperetti, Marilyn Nickels, and Anthony Scally, *African Heritage in the Catholic Church* (1979); James Hennessey, *American Catholics: A History of the Roman Catholic Community in the United States* (1978); Rev. Peter Hogan, *Josephite History, The Josephite Harvest* (1992–93); Holy Family Sisters, *The Greatest Gift of All: A Pictorial Biography of Mother Henriette Delille, Foundress of the Sisters of the Holy Family* (1992); Grace H. Sherwood, *The Oblates' One Hundred and One Years* (1931); D. Spalding, ''The Negro Catholic Congresses,'' *Catholic Historical Review* (1969); U.S. Catholic Historian, *The Black Catholic Community* (1988) and *The Black Catholic Experience* (1986); Sr. M. Clare Warnagiris, *Maria Becraft and Black Catholic Education (1827–1832)*, master's thesis, Morgan State College, (1974).

LORETTA M. BUTLER

CENTRAL STATE UNIVERSITY. Central State, unique among Ohio's state-assisted universities in being predominantly African-American, originated as a separate department of Wilberforce University* in 1887. Central State began operating independently in 1947 and offers varied undergraduate programs through the colleges of arts and sciences, business administration, and education. In addition to traditional degree programs, a certificate program in African and Afro-American Studies and interdisciplinary programs in the allied health fields are available. Cooperative education is an option in many departments. New emphasis in Central State's curriculum has been placed on preparation for high-tech careers with majors in computer science (mathematics), computer information systems (business administration), and water resources management and a four-year degree program in manufacturing engineering. The sixty-acre main campus in rural Greene County has undergone a major rebuilding. Highlighting the new construction are the Paul Robeson Cultural and Performing Arts Center, a library/College of Education building, and the Galloway/Alumni Tower, an historic landmark reconstructed with funds donated by alumni and friends to remind Centralians of their proud heritage.

SELECTED BIBLIOGRAPHY

National Association for Equal Opportunity in Higher Education, *Profiles of the Nation's Historically and Predominantly Black Colleges and Universities* (1993).

SAMUEL L. MYERS

CHEEK, JAMES EDWARD (4 December 1932, Roanoke Rapids, North Carolina). James Cheek received his elementary and secondary education in Greensboro, his bachelor of arts degree from Shaw University* in 1955, his master of divinity degree from Colgate Rochester Divinity School, Rochester, New York, in 1958, and his doctor of philosophy degree in 1962 from Drew University, Madison, Wisconsin. He served as president of Shaw University from 1963 to 1969 and as president of Howard University* from 1 July 1969, to 30 June 1989. He was a presidential appointee on the Commission on Campus Unrest (the Scranton Commission) in 1970, where he eloquently articulated the needs, perceptions, and aspirations of African-Americans. Immediately before this appointment he served as Special Consultant to the President of the United States on Historically Black Colleges and Universities. He was also appointed chairman of the President's Board of Advisors on Historically Black

Colleges and Universities, from 1990 to 1993. He also received in 1983 the Presidential Medal of Freedom, the nation's highest civilian award.

Cheek's leadership is indicated by the extraordinary growth of Howard University both physically and programmatically during his two-decade presidency. Howard's total operating budget rose from $43 million in 1969 to $417 million at Cheek's retirement in 1989, a nearly 900 percent increase. During his administration, Howard gained twenty-eight buildings, nearly seven hundred faculty members, seventy-two academic programs (including sixteen Ph.D.s), over three thousand students, seven new schools, one million library volumes, and nearly $60 million in the book value of its endowment.

In fulfillment of his mission to address the social and economic problems affecting African-Americans, Cheek's administration saw the establishment of eleven major research centers, including the Institute for the Study of Educational Policy, the Center for Sickle Cell Disease, the Institute for Child Development and Family Life, and the Moorland-Spingarn Research Center.* In addition, the Howard University Press,* the WHMM-TV (Channel 32) public television station, and the commercial radio station WHUR (96.3 FM) were founded during his tenure as president.

In recognition of Cheek's outstanding educational achievements and leadership, nineteen universities have conferred honorary doctorates upon him.

Cheek is married to Celestine Juanita Williams of Newton Grove, North Carolina, and they have two children, James Edward, Jr., and Janet Elizabeth.
SELECTED BIBLIOGRAPHY
Special Report, "James Edward Cheek: Two Decades of Remarkable Accomplishments," *New Directions: The Howard University Magazine* 16, no. 3 (July 1989): 1–64; Patricia Fagin Scott, ed., *Institute for the Study of Educational Policy: Four Year Report, March 1974 to September 1978* (1978).

KENNETH S. TOLLETT

CHILDREN'S DEFENSE FUND. Located in Washington, D.C., the Children's Defense Fund (CDF) marks its inception to 1968, the year its founder, Marian Wright Edelman, moved from Mississippi to the nation's capital to set up an advance office of the Poor People's Campaign. This effort evolved into the Washington Research Project, Inc., and expanded to Cambridge, Massachusetts, in 1970, where Edelman was working with the Boston school desegregation efforts.

In 1973, CDF, as a private nonprofit organization supported by foundations, corporations, and individuals that received no government funds, began door-to-door research to uncover the reasons why the 1970 census had identified two million American children as truant. This research resulted in CDF's first published report, *Children out of School,* and the beginning of a 20-year history of advocacy, research, and public information efforts directed at policymakers, corporations, and the general public designed to advance the status of low-income, minority, and disabled children and their families.

CDF's advocacy has contributed to the success of federal legislation in education (e.g., Education for All Handicapped Children Act), child health (through the expansion of Medicaid coverage to poor children up to age eighteen), and child care and early childhood education (e.g., Child Development Block Grant and Head Start*). CDF also promotes adolescent pregnancy prevention, youth employment, improved foster care and adoption policies, and early childhood education using media campaigns, policy analyses, lobbying, and demonstration projects. CDF also publishes annually a report entitled *A Children's Defense Budget*, which examines the adequacy of proposed federal spending to support children. CDF maintains state offices in Minnesota, Ohio, and Texas and local projects in Marlboro County, South Carolina; the District of Columbia; Cleveland-Cuyahoga County, Ohio; and New York City.

SELECTED BIBLIOGRAPHY

George Kaplan, "Suppose They Gave an Intergenerational Conflict and Nobody Came," *Phi Delta Kappan* 72 (May 1991): K1–K12; Lawrence F. Rossow, "Administrative Discretion and Student Suspension," *Journal of Law and Education* 13 (July 1984): 417–40; David L. Martin, "Are Our Public Schools Really Ignoring the Very Children Who Need the Schools Most?" *American School Board Journal* 162 (March 1975): 52–54, 57.

DENISE A. ALSTON

CHILDRESS, RUFUS CHARLES (2 April 1867, Laurens County, South Carolina–26 December 1958, Little Rock, Arkansas). Rufus Childress was a pioneer Arkansas educator who served that state for more than a half-century as a classroom teacher, school principal, college professor, agent of the Julius Rosenwald Fund,* and assistant supervisor in the State Department of Education in the "separate but equal" era, often the first (or among the first) of his race in these positions. He was also a lifelong community activist and humanitarian, what was then known as a "race man," devoted to the betterment of his people.

Childress was born to a former slave woman in Laurens County, South Carolina. With his mother, father, and six brothers and sisters, he migrated to Arkansas, settling on a farm in Monroe County near Cotton Plant. He attended church schools established by the American Missionary Association* and completed high school requirements at Philander Smith College's* high school. He became the first classical philosophy degree graduate from Philander Smith on 6 June 1888. In 1889 he became the first African-American Arkansan to take and pass the civil service examination and was appointed railway mail clerk, a position which he held for five years. He then entered the field of education, teaching in the rural schools of Jackson and Monroe counties, moving from there to Pulaski County in 1909 as a rural school principal in what would later become Stephens School in an expanded Little Rock school district.

He served on the faculty of Philander Smith College in mathematics for twelve years, after which he held a position on its board of trustees for thirty years. In 1921 Childress was appointed as the agent of the Rosenwald Fund in

Arkansas and served in that capacity until 1932. Schools for African-Americans and for whites were built under his supervision. In 1932 he became Assistant State Supervisor for Negro Schools and for county training schools; the latter program operated under the auspices of the Slater Fund.* He also worked with teacher education programs funded by the Anna T. Jeanes Foundation.* He retired in 1946, after serving as director of extension work for teachers at Agricultural, Mechanical, and Normal College in Pine Bluff. Two schools were named for him, one in Nashville, Arkansas, and the other in Wynne, Arkansas; both institutions closed as a result of school desegregation. In the fall of 1970, Childress High School became Wynne Junior High School. Childress Hall at the University of Arkansas, Pine Bluff,* bears his name.

Childress was very civic-minded, always seeking to broaden educational, social, and economic opportunities for African-Americans in Arkansas. In 1898 he and his colleagues founded the Association for Teachers of Negro Youth of Arkansas, which became the parent organization of the Arkansas Teachers Association. His efforts obtained public library facilities for African-Americans in Little Rock. He founded or helped establish the Sunday School Movement, the first African-American Boy Scout troop in Arkansas (1927), the Congress of Colored Parents and Teachers of Arkansas (1928), the Urban League of Greater Little Rock (1937), and a branch of the Florence Crittenden Home for Unwed Mothers (1948).

Childress is interred in Fraternal Cemetery, Little Rock, Arkansas.

SELECTED BIBLIOGRAPHY

D. B. Gaines, *Racial Possibilities as Indicated by the Negroes of Arkansas* (1898); Thomas E. Patterson, *History of the Arkansas Teachers Association* (1981).

ROSELLA HUGHES BARDLEY

CHOICE IN EDUCATION, AFRICAN-AMERICANS AND. The promotion of choice in school selection is a reform issue that has gained popularity, ostensibly as a strategy for improving public schools. A variety of choice policies have been adopted by states and school districts around the country that are seeking to find ways to satisfy a public that has grown increasingly dissatisfied with the quality of public education. Though specific proposals vary in form and content, most policies call for an approach that grants parents, rather than school districts, the right to choose where their children will be educated. The primary difference among choice proposals is whether enrollment options are limited to public schools or include private schools as well.

Limiting choice to public schools generally involves eliminating or changing school enrollment policies that assign students to particular schools based upon neighborhood, race, or some other demographic criteria. Public school choice policies have been designed to open access to all schools within a school district, to schools in neighboring districts, and, in some cases, to schools in other states. In many cities, magnet schools have also been established in order to provide parents with some degree of choice relative to the theme or emphasis adopted by particular schools, such as arts education.

The inclusion of private schools in choice programs results in far more radical changes because it alters the method of allocating funds to schools. Instead of distributing funds to schools on a per-student basis (calculated by average daily attendance), these funds or some percentage of them are given directly to students (through their parents) in the form of a voucher that can be redeemed at any school participating in the program. Unlike the public school choice proposal, this proposal increases the total number of students eligible to participate in the program through the inclusion of private school students. In most cases, private schools participating in the programs are still allowed to charge tuition that exceeds the amount of the voucher; the parents simply apply the voucher toward the cost of school fees.

Advocates for choice often use the language of the marketplace to explain the reasoning behind choice proposals. They argue that a free-market approach to providing educational services would improve the entire system because such a policy would offer renewed incentives to both suppliers and consumers of education. Supporters of vouchers also contend that choice will produce greater diversity among schools as they develop ways of distinguishing themselves by appealing to the needs, tastes, and desires of different constituencies.

One major underlying assumption of both plans is that schools can be improved through competition. Choice advocates argue that by granting parents the right to choose which schools their children will attend, schools will have to find ways to attract students; otherwise, they will be forced to close because of low enrollment. Moreover, competition among schools, it is argued, will force schools of poor quality to improve and to become more accountable to those they serve. Similarly, parents will be compelled to become more informed about educational alternatives, or their children will be relegated to inferior schools. Parents of children who have a record of poor behavior or poor school performance will also be forced to change, lest they find their children unable to be admitted to schools of superior quality.

Few reform initiatives have encountered such pervasive support as school choice. It has been suggested that the reason for this appeal is the relation of school choice to the American ideals of liberty and personal freedom. Given its popularity and the potential for some variants of choice to alter fundamentally the nature of public education, a critical analysis of choice is essential.

A closer examination of choice reveals that it will not result in uniformly positive outcomes for all children. Though the appeal of choice typically rests on the notion that parents have the ultimate power to gain access to schools for children, in reality several factors preclude or limit this possibility. Under all choice plans, schools retain the ability to establish admissions criteria and to restrict access on that basis. Students with special needs, such as those who qualify for special education services that require additional resources, are less likely to be admitted to private schools unless the state is compelled to pay for services that exceed the amount of the voucher. Similarly, students with past records of poor school performance or poor behavior are also less likely to gain access to improved public or private schools, as none of the choice plans developed thus far have required that such students be served. Finally, parents who cannot supplement the allotted voucher amount for the full cost of tuition will be prohibited from enrolling their children in more expensive schools. Thus, poor and working-class children, especially children of color, will undoubtedly be excluded from certain educational settings on basically the same grounds as they are currently: normative standards established by institutions, special needs, records based on real or perceived judgements of academic and social incompetence, and economics.

This exclusion is especially likely for African-Americans, who overwhelmingly continue to send their children to public schools. Frustrated with schools that are too often unable to meet the needs of their children, some African-American parents have indicated that they find choice an attractive alternative. A survey conducted by the Joint Center for Political and Economic Studies found that 88 percent of African-Americans were in favor of educational choice plans that include public and private schools, with the highest support (95%) coming from families earning less than fifteen thousand dollars per year. Undoubtedly, much of this support stems from the perception that desegregation of public schools has not fundamentally altered the inequality in resources and patterns of differential treatment (manifested through placement in special education classes, suspension and expulsion rates, and inequitable ability grouping practices).

Although the possibility for establishing new schools exists, the issues of financial viability and prospects for overall accountability of the school to the parents and students must be considered. The financial viability of new schools will hinge upon their ability to operate successfully with the revenue generated by vouchers. Most private schools typically pay teachers salaries that are far lower than those paid in public schools. If the new schools are going to be able to attract and retain capable and qualified teachers, they will have to compete with the public schools or find ways to attract individuals whose motivation to teach is based on some factor other than monetary reward. Moreover, unless subsidized by a financially stable institution, new schools will be required to find innovative ways to cover operating expenses such as facilities maintenance, insurance, and security. Perhaps most important, African-Americans must consider whether or not choice will actually increase or improve the accountability of the schools their children attend. The primary source of accountability under most choice plans comes from the power of parents who ''vote with their feet.'' That is, parents who are dissatisfied with the way their children are being served at a particular school have the right to withdraw their children and take their vouchers with them. While such a prospect might seem to provide parents with a means of ensuring accountability, it assumes that alternatives are available and accessible. This, however, may not be the case. As most choice plans do not provide students with transportation to school, options regarding school selection are limited not only by school admissions policies but also by distance. Moreover, the availability of high-quality schools in many urban and rural areas may be limited; lack of transportation may thus be a major obstacle to obtaining a quality education.

What will happen to schools that are failing? If, as expected, choice will lead to a loss of students and consequently a loss of funding, improving such schools seems unlikely. Even with the knowledge that they must improve in order to retain students, without sufficient resources there is very little teachers and administrators can do to initiate reforms. The students left behind at these schools, either because their parents lack the necessary resources to enroll them in better schools or because no other school will accept them, will be locked into an even more retrenched situation. In short, the more likely outcome of choice seems to be the further decline of poor schools, rather than their improvement, as argued by proponents.

Since the 1954 *Brown v. Board of Education of Topeka, Kansas**decision and subsequent efforts to desegregate schools, middle-class parents, and white parents in particular, have moved away in large numbers from what were to have been integrated schools. Many have left for less-integrated private schools, while others have relocated from urban areas to predominantly white suburbs where the racial composition of neighborhoods makes desegregation unlikely. With the departure of the middle class, support for public schools in urban areas has waned as they have increasingly come to be seen as the schools of last resort. Only when public school systems have a monopoly as education providers has this not occurred. Choice eliminates that monopoly and provides yet another means for those with the resources and know-how to abandon inner-city schools. If taken to an extreme, it has the potential to undermine public education altogether. For those who might feel that such an outcome is warranted, consider the fact that almost every major civil rights issue since World War II has involved some question related to access to public education. This is more than just coincidence. Public education represents the only social benefit to which citizens and even noncitizens are entitled. If schools are privatized and responsibility for educating children is transferred from state government to individual citizens, one of the only levers that can be used to fight for equity and social justice will have been lost. At a time when disparities between rich and poor are growing, and the number of African-Americans in poverty is increasing, such a development would not only increasingly marginalize millions of African-Americans, it might also eliminate even the small possibility that education can serve as an avenue to individual and collective advancement.

SELECTED BIBLIOGRAPHY

Alexander Astin, ''Choice: Its Appeal May Be Illusory,'' *Sociology of Education* 65, no. 4 (October 1992); John Chubb and Terry Moe, *Politics, Markets and America's Schools*, Brookings Institute (1990); James Coleman, ''Some Points on Choice in Education,'' *Sociology of Education* 65, no. 4 (October 1992); John Coons and Stephen Sugarman,

Scholarships for Children, Institute of Governmental Studies (1992); "School Enrollment and Economic Characteristics of Students," U.S. Department of Commerce, Bureau of the Census, Current Population Reports, Series P-20, No. 404, October 1984; "Choice in California Education," *EdSource* (August 1993); William Gormley, *Privatization and Its Alternatives* (1991); James Guthrie, "School Choice: An Idea Whose Time Is (Slowly) Coming," *Educator* 8, no. 1 (Spring 1994); David Kirp, *Just Schools: The Idea of Racial Equality in American Education* (1982); G. McDougall, "Local Public Goods and Residential Property Values: Some Insights and Extensions," *National Tax Journal* 20 (1976): 436; Kenneth Meier, J. Stewart, and R. England, *Race, Class and Education: Second-Generation Discrimination* (1989); "The School Voucher Initiative," in the *Metro Educator*, Southwest Regional Laboratory, (September 1993); Joe Nathan, *Progress, Problems and Prospects with State Choice Plans*, U.S. Department of Education, Office of Planning, Budget, and Evaluation (1989); John Ogbu, *The Next Generation: An Ethnography of Education in an Urban Neighborhood* (1974); Margaret Plecki, "What Research Says about School Choice in the U.S.," *Educator* 8, no. 1 (Spring 1994); H. Rosen and D. Fullerton, "A Note on Local Tax Rates, Public Benefit Levels, and Property Values," *Journal of Political Economy* 85 (1977): 433; Timothy Sieber, "The Politics of Middle Class Success in an Inner-City Public School," *Journal of Education* 164, no. 1 (1982): 30–47.

PEDRO A. NOGUERA

CITIZENSHIP EDUCATION SCHOOLS. Beginning in the 1950s, the African-American residents of John's Island, a rural and, until the 1930s, isolated island located off the coast of South Carolina, developed a major adult literacy program that had long-term and widespread consequences for social change on the island and throughout the South. John's Island resident Alice Swine's concern for the intellectual growth of her fellow islanders caused her to convince Esau Jenkins, a prominent leader on the island, to advocate for such a program. Jenkins met with other individuals at Myles Horton's Highlander Folk School* in New Market, Tennessee. Out of these meetings, the leadership training program was developed to cultivate among the islanders "a better understanding of the nature of a democratic society."

In 1956, the first citizenship education school began operating in the rear of a small cooperative store owned by the John's Island Progressive Club. The school was headed by Septima Clark, a defiant former employee of the South Carolina school system, who had led a personal crusade against the oppression of the state's segregated system and had been fired for her beliefs and membership in the NAACP.* Clark approached her cousin, Bernice Robinson,* a Charleston beautician, to become the school's first teacher. The first citizenship class was modeled after a sewing circle. It consisted of four men and ten women whose skills in reading, writing, mathematics, and citizenship were developed within the context of sewing. This teaching method originated from Clark's earlier work with adult education and Robinson's innovative teaching techniques, specifically designed to be compatible with the students' culture and experiences, using folktales and examples from African-American history to make the material more relevant to their lives. Aware of her limited knowledge of teaching methods, Robinson continuously evaluated herself and the needs of her students. Initially, she used a third-grade curriculum, but soon learned that it did not meet the needs of her adult students. She then began allowing the students to develop their own curriculum; in her words, ''I started teaching them what they wanted to learn.'' The people indicated that they wanted to learn to write their own names, read the words of the state election laws, and fill out catalog order forms and money orders.

Robinson and her students utilized whatever materials were at hand. They used cardboard as writing paper and mimeographed copies of state election laws, social security requirements, and information about governmental agencies. In addition to teaching students to read and write, an equally important objective of the John's Island Citizenship Education School was its focus on empowering the people of that island. Robinson brought to her students' attention the more liberal political views of citizenship used at Highlander, and they began to talk about the uses of and need for power at the local, state, and national government levels.

By 1958, the John's Island Citizenship Education School boasted sixty students who had passed the ''illiteracy test'' required to vote in state elections. Because of its success, the John's Island model was emulated on the other South Carolina Sea Islands of Wadmalaw, Edisto, Daufuskie, and St. Helena.

In addition to registering new voters, islanders launched several community projects such as the Progressive Club, the Committee on Better Racial Assurance (COBRA), Rural Mission, Inc., the Local Community Improvement Association, and the Sea Island Comprehensive Health Care Corporation. These organizations played a major role in sponsoring the activities of the citizenship education schools. Funding was provided by the United Church of Christ's Marshall Field Foundation, under the administration of civil rights activist Andrew Young.

Under the Southern Christian Leadership Conference's direction, Clark, Robinson, and educational consultant Dorothy Cotton were instrumental in helping to incorporate the school's concepts into the SCLC's voter registration drive. The schools began to train community leaders as teachers and voter registration organizers. Classes were developed to teach strategies in political education. These classes centered on discussions of the processes of government and its lack of effectiveness in promoting social change. They also encouraged students to integrate their classroom learning into their community action efforts. The work of the citizenship education schools resulted in a large increase in the number of registered voters on the islands. Between 1954 and 1964, the number of registered voters in Charleston County grew from five thousand to slightly over fourteen thousand. A Highlander report for 1959–60 noted an estimated 300 percent increase since the 1956 election in the number of registered voters on John's Island alone.

Citizenship Education schools became crucial to the civil rights movement because they taught what the movement hoped to achieve and the skills that were necessary to accomplish those goals. Predictably, such schools came to be perceived as a major threat to the white power structure. Despite the many detours that were necessary to avoid retaliation from angry whites, citizenship education schools managed to train over ten thousand teachers between 1962 and 1966. At one point during this period, 195 classes were being held in eleven southern states, with a group of fifteen coordinators working from a central office in Atlanta, Georgia. Between 1962 and 1967, the schools were responsible for the registration of nearly seven hundred thousand African-American voters. Over the next twenty years, the success of their programs was proven by a manifold increase in the number of African-American elected officials.

In addition to training skilled teachers, citizenship education schools produced a number of grassroots leaders in the civil rights movement. They brought scholars such as Vincent Harding, John Henrik Clarke, and others in contact with grassroots activists like Fannie Lou Hamer and Hosea Williams. These gatherings helped to minimize elitism within the movement and the local community. The schools demonstrated that literacy teachers can evolve from within the community and that adult literacy is crucial to the development of grassroots political power. Moreover, they offered proof that for any movement to succeed there must be a strong, empowering literacy component, to help people liberate themselves and create vehicles for self-expression and autonomy.

SELECTED BIBLIOGRAPHY

Guy and Candie Carawan, *Ain't You Got a Right to the Tree of Life?* (1989); Septima Clark, *Ready from Within: Septima Clark and the Civil Rights Movement*, ed. Cynthia Stokes (1986); Shyrlee Dallard, *Ella Baker: A Leader behind the Scenes* (1990); David J. Garrow, *Bearing the Cross: Martin Luther King, Jr., and the Southern Christian Leadership Conference* (1986); Aimee Isgrig Horton, *The Highlander Folk School: A History of Its Major Programs, 1932–1961* (1971); Myles Horton, *The Long Haul* (1990); Bernice Robinson, speech on the Citizenship Education Schools delivered at the Septima Clark Center for Urban Literacy, Columbus, Ohio, (September, 1993).

LIZ PEAVY AND FRANCES JAMES-BROWN

CIVIL RIGHTS ACT OF 1964, 78 Stat. 241. On 2 July, 1964, Congress passed the Civil Rights Act of 1964 (Public Law 88–352), and President Lyndon Johnson signed it into law a few hours later. The act, which engendered "the longest filibuster in the history of the United States Senate," was the most comprehensive civil rights measure in American history. Initially sent to Congress on 19 June 1963, by President John F. Kennedy, the act was an attempt to ameliorate the multiple injustices suffered by African-Americans, including the continued denial of equal educational opportunity. Congress modified the original eight titles and expanded them to eleven.

Title I, Voting Rights, is designed to guarantee to all citizens the right to vote without discrimination based on race or color. Title II, Injunctive Relief against Discrimination in Places of Public Accommodation, prohibits discrimination on the grounds of race, color, religion, or national origin in specific places of public accommodation. Included are hotels and motels, theaters, and other places of amusement presenting sources of entertainment that move in interstate commerce and restaurants, lunch counters, and gasoline stations that sell food or goods that move in commerce or serve interstate travelers. Title III, Desegregation of Public Facilities, authorized the attorney general to intervene in pending actions in the federal courts seeking relief from discriminatory practices by state and local governmental units or officers. Title IV, Desegregation of Public Education, has two main purposes. First, it authorizes the Commissioner of Education to provide, upon application by local school authorities, technical assistance and financial aid to assist in dealing with problems incident to desegregation. Second, it authorizes the attorney general to institute suits seeking desegregation of public schools where the students or parents involved are unable to bring suit and where the attorney general considers that a suit would materially further the public policy favoring the most orderly achievement of desegregation in public education.

Title V, Commission on Civil Rights, makes the Commission on Civil Rights a permanent body and gives the commission new authority (a) to serve as a national clearinghouse for information concerning denials of the equal protection of the laws and (b) to investigate allegations as to patterns or practices of fraud or discrimination in Federal elections. Title VI, Non-Discrimination in Federally Assisted Programs, prohibits discrimination on the grounds of race, color, or national origin in connection with programs and activities receiving federal financial assistance and authorizes and directs the appropriate federal departments and agencies to take action to carry out this policy. Title VII, Equal Employment Opportunity, eliminates, through the utilization of formal and informal remedial procedures, discrimination in employment based on race, color, religion, sex, or national origin. The title authorizes the establishment of a federal Equal Employment Opportunity Commission and delegates to it the primary responsibility for preventing and eliminating unlawful employment practices as defined in the title. Title VIII, Registration and Voting Statistics, directs the secretary of commerce promptly to conduct a survey to compile registration and voting statistics in such geographic areas as may be recommended by the Commission on Civil Rights.

Title IX, Intervention and Procedure after Removal in Civil Rights Cases, provides guidelines related to court cases that have been remanded to the state court. It also allows the attorney general to intervene or become a party in federal court cases involving the denial of equal protection of the laws under the Fourteenth Amendment to the U.S. Constitution on account of race, color, religion, or national origin. Title X, Establishment of Community Relations Service, provides assistance to communities and persons therein in resolving disputes, disagreements, or difficulties relating to discriminatory practices based on race, color, or national origin. Title XI, Miscellaneous, contains three provisions: maintains the authority the attorney general has under existing law, authorizes appropriation to carry out provisions of the act, and provides that the invalidation of any portion of the act shall not affect the validity of the remainder of the act.

Although the 1964 act covered many areas of public life, it has been particularly instrumental in the field of education. For example, it required the Commissioner of Education to "conduct a survey" concerning the lack of equal educational opportunities for individuals of differing racial, religious, and ethnic groups, resulting in the publication of the *Equality of Educational Opportunity* report (commonly known as the Coleman Report*) in 1966. Amended as recently as 14 October 1992, the 1964 Civil Rights Act has been constantly used by African-Americans in the fight against discrimination; it has been particularly instrumental in the attempt to achieve equity in education.

SELECTED BIBLIOGRAPHY

Albert P. Blaustein and Robert L. Zangrando, eds., *Civil Rights and African-Americans: A Documentary History* (1968, 1991); "Civil Rights Act of 1964," *U.S. Code Congressional and Administrative News*, 88th Congress Second Session, vols. 1 and 2 (1964); Congressional Quarterly Service, *Congress and the Nation, 1945–1964, vol. 1, A Review of Government and Politics in the Postwar Years* (1965); "Significant Decisions in Labor Cases," *Monthly Labor Review* (February 1990); 52–54; Charles and Barbara Whalen, *The Longest Debate: A Legislative History of the 1964 Civil Rights Act* (1985).

JAMES E. NEWBY

CIVIL RIGHTS MOVEMENT, IMPACT OF, ON AFRICAN-AMERICAN EDUCATION. The Civil Rights Movement in the United States brought dramatic changes not only to the nation's black schools but also to the entire system of American education. However, many of the changes wrought were not always in tune with the perceived goals of that movement. The underlying assumption of civil rights leaders was that equal resources for African-American schools would be available only if African-Americans attended schools with whites. Little thought had been given to the impact that dismantling the dual school system would have on the larger African-American community and its schools, which had grown into important and vital institutions within the community.

For purposes of discussion, the modern Civil Rights Movement covers the years between the *Brown v. Board of Education of Topeka, Kansas** decision of 1954 and the assassination of Dr. Martin Luther King, Jr. However, the quest for equality and the quest for educational opportunity have been so intertwined in African-American history that it is difficult to separate the two distinct movements. Following the Civil War, the newly emancipated slaves knew the necessity of acquiring an education if they were to take advantage of and protect their newly acquired civil rights. The 1896 *Plessy v. Ferguson** decision had segregated with the force of law the very public school systems the freedmen had worked so hard to establish. Schools were always separate but seldom, if ever, were resources allocated on an equal basis. Aware of the conditions as early as the 1930s, the leadership of the National Association for the Advancement of Colored People* (NAACP) understood that the political environment was not conducive to a frontal assault on the *Plessy* decision. The organization's strategy was to make the courts confront the issue of the inequality of separate educational systems, first at the graduate and professional levels, without mounting a direct assault on the legality of "separate but equal."

In its efforts to equalize educational opportunity, the NAACP won a series of sweeping victories in the courts. In 1935, the Maryland Circuit Court of Appeals ruled in *Murray v. Maryland** that the University of Maryland had to admit Donald Murray because the state did not provide a law school for African-Americans. In 1938 in *Missouri ex rel Gaines v. Canada*,* the U.S. Supreme Court ruled that the state of Missouri had to admit Lloyd Gaines to the University School of Law or establish a law school for African-Americans. The impact of these court decisions made southern states reexamine their policy of granting out-of-state tuition to African-Americans seeking graduate and professional education.

The entry of the United States into World War II shifted the civil rights struggle to increasing job opportunities in the defense industries. In 1941, African-American labor leader A. Phillip Randolph threatened a massive protest march on Washington, D.C. if President Franklin Roosevelt did not issue an executive order banning discrimination in the government defense industry. When Roosevelt issued Executive Order 8802, it was a weaker version of what Randolph had advocated. The following year, the Congress of Racial Equality (CORE), an integrated group that used direct tactics, staged a sit-in Chicago to force a local restaurant to serve African-Americans. Although these direct-action tactics, the forerunners of the Civil Rights Movement, proved successful during the war years when the nation needed a united front at home, the NAACP turned once more to the courts as the key to eliminating the dual school system and the inferior education imposed on African-Americans. Through a series of decisions beginning in 1948, the Supreme Court issued rulings that brought *Plessy* under direct attack. The Court held in *Sipuel v. University of Oklahoma** that equal opportunity for college education must be made available for African-Americans. In 1950, the Court ruled in *Sweatt v. Painter* that even where a state had established a separate law school, it could not be inferior in facilities, program of study, or reputation. The court outlawed segregated graduate school education in *McLaurin v. Oklahoma State Regents of Higher Education*.*

These cases set the stage for a direct assault on segregated education in *Brown*. Combining four other cases, the NAACP's attorneys argued that segregation laws served to perpetuate slavery. The court agreed and unanimously ruled that the doctrine of "separate but equal" had no place in public education. Following the *Brown* decision, education became the central focus of "massive resistance" to integration efforts throughout the South. Although some border states proceeded to integrate their dual school systems, the lower South made every attempt to circumvent the new law of the land. One hundred southern congressmen issued the "Southern Manifesto" in 1956, pledging to resist the federal courts' purported abuse of judicial power by all legal means. White citizen's councils sprang up throughout the South, buttressed in their tactics by the Klu Klux Klan and an increase in racial violence, beatings, bombings, and killings.

In 1955 the Interstate Commerce Commission banned segregated buses and bus terminals in interstate travel. That same year Rosa Parks was arrested and the Montgomery bus boycott began, catapulting the Rev. Dr. Martin Luther King, Jr., to national prominence. While direct action was used to test the new ban on interstate commerce and to open up places of public accommodation, the Civil Rights Movement remained focused on the emotionally charged area of school integration. In 1955, when Autherine Lucy attempted to integrate the University of Alabama, whites rioted. In Mansfield, Texas, a white mob blocked the entrance of African-American students to an all-white public school. Incidents like these were repeated throughout the South and culminated in Little Rock, Arkansas, where President Eisenhower was forced to call on the National Guard after Governor Orval E. Faubus placed state troopers at the entrance of the school to block the entry of African-American students.

The African-American college students of the 1960s played a primary role in the Civil Rights Movement and, as a consequence, forged a direct link between the civil rights struggle and American higher education. The revival of the sit-ins and freedom rides would change the face of the old South. On 1 February 1960, four students staged a sit-in at the Woolworth's in Greensboro, North Carolina; by spring, the movement had spread throughout the South, engaging thousands of African-American college students. The Freedom Rides of 1961 brought national attention to the extreme violence directed toward both black and white civil rights workers. Despite these efforts, less than 8 percent of all black public school students were in integrated classes throughout the South. At the college level, integration scarcely existed. Court orders and federal troops were still required to force the admittance of one or two students in major southern state universities.

Southern members of Congress had been quite effective in preventing any new civil rights legislation from passing, including bills proposed in 1957 and 1960. However, strong pressure from civil rights groups, rampant racial violence, and the impact of the 1963 March on Washington resulted in President Lyndon B. Johnson urging Congress to pass the civil rights bill originally recommended by President Kennedy.

The 1964 Civil Rights Act,* which reaffirmed many of the provisions of the Civil Rights Act of 1875, became the most comprehensive civil rights legislation passed by Congress as a direct result of the Civil Rights Movement and had a tremendous impact on America's educational system. Title IV provided for federal assistance in desegregating public school systems; Title VI banned discrimination in federally assisted programs; and Title VII provided for equal employment opportunity. Discrimination based on race, color, religion, sex, or national origin was declared an unlawful employment practice. Through this and other civil rights legislation passed in the 1960s and early 1970s, Congress equipped the federal government with the enforcement arsenal necessary to promote equal opportunity. In 1965, President Johnson issued Executive Order 11246 (as amended), which outlined the government's antidiscrimination policy and prescribed specific affirmative efforts to recruit, employ, and promote groups that had heretofore been excluded and thereby overcome systemic discrimination. Despite these efforts, the U.S. Civil Rights Commission reported in 1973 that the federal civil rights enforcement effort was "inadequate" and proceeding "at a snail's pace."

The Civil Rights Movement ended in the late 1960s with the ascendancy of the Black Power movement and the assassination of Dr. Martin Luther King, Jr. Most legal barriers had been dismantled, but the material conditions concerning equal opportunity for African-Americans had not changed. Discrimination had taken on a new dimension, whereby covert discrimination could be hidden within the mantle of economic disparity. The gap between the haves and the have-nots began to widen, both between the races and within the African-American community. Those who were adequately prepared took advantage of new opportunities and began moving out of historically black neighborhoods and into middle-class suburban areas.

Integration has had a severe impact on the African-American community in general and on African-American educational institutions in particular. The quest for integration was based first on the assumption that unless whites and blacks actually shared the same physical facilities, African-Americans and their schools would not receive their fair share of educational resources. This assumption eventually went beyond calling for the elimination of legal barriers to the argument that all–black schools were inherently inferior. The emphasis on integration and the lack of strong, positive cultural identity led to the unintended assumption that black educational institutions were bereft of culture and quality and that, therefore, black leadership had little to bring to the negotiation table. As a consequence, many African-Americans accepted the closing of all–black schools or the downgrading of black high schools to elementary schools or to schools for slow learners. African-American teachers were often fired or given nonproductive assignments, and African-American principals were often demoted to assistant principals or even to maintenance workers.

The legislation that has had the most impact on educational access was not a civil rights bill, but the Higher Education Act of 1965 as amended in 1972. The education amendments of 1972 amended Title III to strengthen developing institutions and amended Title IV to provide student financial assistance. Title IV programs included Basic Educational Opportunity Grants, which went directly to students who applied to the U.S. Office of Education, and the Supplemental Educational Opportunity Grants, which were multiple-year grants awarded by colleges to students with financial need. Also included in Title IV was the college work-study program, which provided 80 to 100 percent of salary for the employment of students in financial need. Title IX and Title IV (part E) provided for insured student loan programs—the state and federal Guaranteed Student Loan Program and the National Direct Student Loan Program.

The impact of these federal higher education policies was to remove the financial barriers to equal educational opportunity for African-American students. Coupled with the Civil Rights Act of 1964, the Educational Amendments of 1972 provided for greater access for blacks to institutions of higher education. In the 1964–65 school year, African-American undergraduates were 6.5 percent of all college students. The percentage increased to 8.7 percent in 1974 and reached 10.2 percent in 1976, fairly close to the percentage of African-Americans in the population at that time.

Although the Civil Rights Movement was an effective agent of change in removing the legal barriers to access at all levels of education, it is not clear that the results—the destruction of African-American–controlled schools—was in the best interest of black students and educators and the black community in general. At the post-secondary level, the government's elimination of financial barriers had more of an impact in providing African-American students with greater access to college and graduate and professional schools than did the direct tactics of the Civil Rights Movement or federal civil rights legislation.

SELECTED BIBLIOGRAPHY

Taylor Branch, *Parting the Waters: America in the King Years 1954–63* (1988); John E. Fleming, *The Lengthening Shadow of Slavery* (1976); Institute for the Study of Educational Policy, *Equal Education Opportunity for Blacks in U.S. Higher Education, An Assessment* (1977); Richard Kluger, *Simple Justice: The History of Brown v. Board of Education and Black America's Struggle for Equality* (1976); Lorenzo Morris, *Elusive Equality: The Status of Black Americans in Higher Education* (1979).

JOHN E. FLEMING

CLAFLIN COLLEGE. Since 1869, Claflin College has been working to improve the lives of all people by offering quality education. Today, Claflin is a four-year liberal arts college in Orangeburg, South Carolina associated with the United Methodist Church, offering majors in art, biology, business administration, chemistry, education, English, health and physical education, mathematics, music education, religion and philosophy, and the social sciences. Two Methodist laymen from Massachusetts began the school with only a teacher training center and a technical training center. Claflin features many new buildings, including a new science center, a fine arts center, and a new health and physical education center, a big jump from the few buildings William and Lee Claflin had in 1869. Claflin's mission remains: to prepare students for a better life, not just for making a living.

SELECTED BIBLIOGRAPHY

National Association for Equal Opportunity in Higher Education, *Profiles of the Nation's Historically and Predominantly Black Colleges and Universities* (1993).

SAMUEL L. MYERS

CLARK, KENNETH BANCROFT (24 July 1914, Panama Canal Zone). Considered one of the preeminent African-American social scientists in the twentieth century, Kenneth Clark received his early education in the racially diverse setting of Harlem in the 1920s. In 1931, he was accepted to Howard University,* originally intending to become a medical doctor. However, after taking a psychology course, he began to gain a "systematic understanding of the complexities of human behavior and human interaction, . . . the seemingly intractable nature of racism, for example." He went on to receive a master's degree in psychology in 1936 and began teaching at Howard the following year. He later attended Columbia University where, as the first African-American doctoral candidate in psychology, he received the Ph.D. degree in 1940. Clark has received honorary degrees from various colleges and universities, including Johns Hopkins University and Princeton University.

In 1938, Clark married Mamie Phipps, a fellow psychology student at Howard, with whom he coauthored many articles concerning the nature of racism, particularly its effects on education. Their best-known study, conducted in 1947, showed the effects of internalized racism and racial segregation on pre–school-aged African-American children. When given the choice between playing with white dolls or black dolls, two thirds of the children preferred the white dolls. Results of this study were made available to the NAACP,* to be utilized in the organization's developing case against legalized segregation, which culminated in the 1954 *Brown v. Board of Education of Topeka, Kansas** decision. Clark was called in as an expert witness in three of the four cases consolidated under *Brown*. In one of his testimonies, he explained the damaging effects of segregated schooling as "a confusion in the child's own self-esteem—basic feelings of inferiority, conflict, confusion in his self-image, resentment and hostility toward himself."

In the early 1960s, Clark served as head of the federally funded Harlem Youth Opportunities Act (HARYOU), a reform program established to combat the problem of juvenile delinquency. In 1967, he founded the Metropolitan Applied Research Center (MARC), a nonprofit corporation comprised of social scientists and other professionals, based in Washington, D.C. In 1970, MARC designed for the District's school board a program that, like HARYOU, called for a concentration on reading skills, teacher evaluations based on student performance, and increased community involvement in the schools.

In 1975, Clark retired from teaching and, along with his family, founded the consulting firm Clark, Phipps, Clark and Harris, Inc. The firm advised corporations regarding racial policies and minority hiring programs and included among its clients some of the nation's largest employers. Clark capsulized his educational philosophy in a 1993 essay, *Unfinished Business: The Toll of Psychic Violence*, in which he commented: "We have not yet made education a process where by students are taught to respect the inalienable dignity of other human beings . . . [but] social sensitivity can be internalized as a genuine component of being educated. By encouraging and rewarding [such] behavior in our children, we will be protecting them from ignorance and cruelty."

SELECTED BIBLIOGRAPHY
Christa Brelin and William C. Matney, eds., *Who's Who among Black Americans, 1992–1993* (1992).

                                                                    TRACEY T. JONES

CLARK ATLANTA UNIVERSITY. Clark Atlanta University, incorporated on 1 July 1988, is a predominantly African-American, private, urban, coeducational institution of undergraduate, graduate, and professional education. Clark Atlanta University inherits the historical missions and achievements of its two parent institutions, Atlanta University and Clark College. Founded in 1865, Atlanta University in 1929 became an exclusively graduate and professional institution, the first with a predominantly African-American student body. Founded in 1869, Clark College was the first Methodist-affiliated college established to serve African-Americans. Each of these schools began modestly, but with a firm commitment to the highest standards of intellectual and responsible achievement. Thus, by 1888 Clark College had developed the independent Gammon Theological Seminary, and Atlanta University was providing African-American teachers and librarians throughout the South. Over the years, the program of Clark College evolved from one that concentrated on training teachers and ministers to a diversified panoply of disciplines in the social and natural sciences and the arts and humanities; Atlanta University developed schools of education, social work, library science, and business administration in addition to the several disciplines of the School of Arts and Sciences. Clark Atlanta University inherits also firm commitments shared by both its parent institutions. One such commitment is to close cooperation with its contiguous sister institutions in the Atlanta University Center. Another continued commitment is to serving the educational needs of students of diverse racial, national, and socioeconomic backgrounds.

SELECTED BIBLIOGRAPHY
National Association for Equal Opportunity in Higher Education, *Profiles of the Nation's Historically and Predominantly Black Colleges and Universities* (1993).

                                                                    SAMUEL L. MYERS

COBB, JEWELL PLUMMER (17 January 1924, Chicago, Illinois). Cell biologist and university administrator, Jewell Cobb was born and reared in an upper-class Chicago family. Her father, Frank V. Plummer, was a medical doctor, and her mother, Carriebel Cole Plummer, had been educated as a dancer at Sargeants, a physical education college affiliated with Harvard. An only child, Cobb attended public schools and spent summers in Michigan at the family's summer home. Family friends included historian Carter G. Woodson* and writer/librarian Arna Bontemps, anthropologist Allison Davis,* and YWCA director Alpha White.

Initially Cobb attended the University of Michigan, influenced by friends she had met during her summers in the state, but later transferred to Talladega

College,* where she graduated in 1944. She earned her master's and doctoral degrees in cell physiology from New York University in 1947 and 1950, respectively.

During the 1950s, Cobb taught at New York University and Hunter College and conducted research at the Cancer Research Foundation on the effects of cancer chemotherapy drugs on human tumors. She also did research on how melanin, a pigment in the skin, serves as a shield from ultraviolet rays. She became a faculty member at Sarah Lawrence College in 1960, and later dean. In 1969 she became dean and professor of zoology at Connecticut College, and in 1976 she became dean of Douglass College. In 1981, Cobb became president of California State University, Fullerton, helping the institution transform itself from a primarily commuter to a primarily residential facility.

In 1990 Cobb left Fullerton to become Trustee Professor at California State University, Los Angeles, and a principal investigator of the Access Center, a National Science Foundation grant that helps middle and high school teachers to develop innovative mathematics and science curricula. She also works with a consortium of six institutions to encourage more minority students to consider careers in science and engineering.

Cobb has received many awards, including numerous honorary doctorates. Buildings at Douglass College and California State University, Fullerton, are named for her.

SELECTED BIBLIOGRAPHY

Jewell Plummer Cobb, "Filters for Women in Science," *Annals of the New York Academy of Sciences* (1979).

ELIZABETH L. IHLE

COGNITIVE STYLE. Cognitive style theory suggests that individuals utilize different patterns in acquiring knowledge. "Cognitive" refers to the processes involved in the overall act of learning. It includes perception, judgment, values, and memory. "Style" implies that, as individuals, we employ personal characteristics in the acquisition of knowledge and, more often than not, approach a learning experience in ways that differ from those of other individuals.

Cognitive style is not an indication of one's level of intelligence, but a description of the unique strategies that learners employ in acquiring new information. Information is presented to us in various ways, sometimes through experiences that we initiate, as when we select a hobby or read a book, and sometimes through experiences initiated by other persons, as during classroom activities. Classroom experiences are intended to increase the knowledge of learners, and successful teachers vary the ways in which information is presented. Part of the time, teachers are lecturing to the entire class, and learners are expected to remain quiet and relatively inactive. At other times, when children are engaged in group activities or individual assignments, they are expected to be actively engaged. However, we now know that some children learn better in an active setting than they do in a quiet, inactive one, and that some learners prefer to work alone rather than in groups.

Research in psychology has informed us that the various styles of processing information are influenced by the environment in which one spends one's childhood. For example, differences in cognitive styles have been found between children who were confined to a playpen in infancy and those who were allowed to crawl about freely during these critical years of early development. Other studies reveal that acquisition of the sensorimotor skills necessary for crawling, standing, and walking provides children with some of their earliest exercises in cognition. Child development experts have also suggested that this important early learning period, from birth to the age of twenty-four months, is the time frame within which children develop a foundation for a later understanding of logical and mathematical concepts. The different experiences that children are encouraged to have during this early period of growth will influence how they process information and learn later in life.

Because of various individual cognitive styles, learners appear to have skills available to them under some circumstances that are not necessarily available to them at other times. Some skills seem available to them during out-of-school experiences (which are more under their control) that may not be available to them in the quiet settings of the classroom. Studies have identified approximately twelve different cognitive styles, but only a few will be described here, as examples that will lead to a better understanding of the theory and the identification of the cognitive style unique to African-Americans.

The two most common cognitive styles that have been defined and tested by psychologists are *field dependent* and *field independent*. These two styles are linked together in descriptions because they have somewhat opposite meanings. Persons who are more field independent are able to pick out objects whose surroundings might hide them from view. For example, field independent persons can easily see fruit on a vine or tree even though its color might not differ much from that of the leaves and branches. In other words, field independent persons are able to view obscured objects in such a manner that they seem independent from other parts of the scene. On the other hand, field dependent learners are less able to view objects as separate from the overall environment and would have greater difficulty viewing fruit as standing apart from the tree or surrounding foliage. Therefore, field dependent learners prefer that things remain in their total context to enable them to better understand the meaning of their individual parts. In social settings, the field dependent style prefers group interaction, while the field independent style prefers to interact with individuals or to work alone.

Reflectivity and *impulsivity* represent the second most studied pair of cognitive styles. Reflective style persons attempt to solve problems through patience and thought. They gain a great deal of success when correct answers are the primary goal. In some situations where time is a factor, reflective style persons will not be as successful as they would like. Impulsive style persons offer quick responses to the solution of problems despite the probability of a high error rate. When credit is given for speed, impulsive style persons will probably outscore reflective style persons.

Starting in the 1950s, various studies began to report that from infancy many African-American children demonstrate a sensory active cognitive style. African-American children, it was noted, tend to prefer learning environments that enable social interactions between pupils and teachers. The findings of this research reveal that classrooms that employ child-centered, cooperative learning methods are most compatible with this cognitive style.

SELECTED BIBLIOGRAPHY

Nancy Bayley, "Comparison of Mental and Motor Test Scores for Ages 1–15 Months by Sex, Gender, Birth Order, Geographic Location and Education of Parents," *Child Development* 36 (1965): 379–411; M. W. Curti, E. B. Marshall, and M. Steggerda, "The Gesell Schedules Applied to 1, 2, and 3 Year Old Negro Infants of British West Indies," *Journal of Comparative Neurology* 20 (1935): 125; Marcelle Géber, "L'enfant africain occidentalisé et de niveau social superior en Uganda," *Courier* 8 (1958): 517–23; Nathan Kogan, *Cognitive Style in Infancy and Early Childhood* (1976); Harry Morgan, "Assessment of Students' Behavioral Interactions during On-Task Classroom Activities," *Perceptual and Motor Skills* 70 (1990): 563–69; Benjamin Pasamanick, "A Comparative Study of the Behavior Development of Negro Infants," *Journal of Genetic Psychology* 69 (1946): 3–44; J. R. Williams and R. B. Scott, "Growth and Development of Negro Infants: Motor Development and Its Relationship to Child Rearing Practices in Two Groups of Negro Infants," *Child Development* 24 (1953): 103–21.

HARRY MORGAN

COLE, JOHNNETTA B. (14 October 1936, Jacksonville, Florida). An anthropologist, feminist, educator, administrator, researcher, lecturer, African-American spokeswoman, and college president, Johnnetta Cole received the B.A. degree from Oberlin College* in 1957 and the M.A. and Ph.D. degrees from Northwestern University in 1959 and 1967, respectively. Cole became the first African-American woman to occupy the presidency of Spelman College* in 1987. Under her leadership, Spelman has become one of America's outstanding colleges and is recognized as the first historically black college to be named the number-one regional liberal arts college in the South in *U.S. News and World Report's* annual college issue.

Cole is the author of numerous publications including *Conversation: Straight Talk with America's Sister President* (1993), *Anthropology for the Nineties: Introductory Readings* (1988), *On Racism and Ethnocentrism* with Elizabeth H. Oaks (1985), and *Anthropology for the Eighties: Introductory Readings* (1982). She is the recipient of many academic and professional awards including the Sara Lee Corporation Frontrunner Award in the Humanities (1992), Key Honoree, Legal Defense Fund's Black Women of Achievement Award (1992), and the Achievement Award from the Association of University Women (1991). She has received honorary doctorates from numerous institutions,

including Bates College, Fisk University,* Princeton University, and Yale University.
SELECTED BIBLIOGRAPHY
Johnnetta B. Cole, *Conversations: Straight Talk with America's Sister President* (1993).
HARRIET HUNTER-BOYKIN

COLEMAN REPORT. The Coleman Report, published in 1966 as *Equality of Educational Opportunity*, was the response to Title IV, Section 402, of the Civil Rights Act of 1964,* which required the Commissioner of Education to "conduct a survey" concerning the lack of availability of equal educational opportunities for individuals because of race, color, religion, or national origin in public education at all levels. The survey was carried out by the National Center for Educational Statistics of the U.S. Office of Education and by private consultants and contractors. The report was named after James S. Coleman, who at the time was at Johns Hopkins University and had major responsibility for the design, administration, and analysis of the survey. Coleman and his colleagues focused on six racial and ethnic groups—"Negroes," Native Americans, Asian Americans, Puerto Ricans, Mexican Americans, and whites— relative to four major questions. The first question dealt with the extent to which the racial and ethnic groups were segregated from one another in the public schools. The second question asked whether the schools offered equal educational opportunities in terms of educational quality, as measured by several criteria such as the number of laboratories, textbooks, and libraries. The third major question focused on how much students learned, as measured by their performance on standardized achievement tests. The fourth dealt with possible relationships between students' achievement and the kinds of schools they attended.

Major findings of the report showed a relative lack of equal educational opportunity for minorities, particularly for African-Americans. The report found that, among minority groups, "Negroes" were by far the most segregated. Of all groups, however, white children were most segregated. With some exceptions—specifically, Asian Americans—the average minority student scored distinctly lower on standard achievement tests at every level than the average white student. Analyzing "school inputs"—facilities and curricula of the schools— accounted for relatively little variation in student achievement. The quality of teachers showed a stronger relationship to student achievement and was found to be more important for minority achievement than for that of the majority. An even stronger relationship was found between the educational backgrounds and aspirations of the other students in the school and the achievements of African-American and other minority students. However, the extent to which a student felt that he or she had some control over his or her own destiny had a stronger relationship to achievement than did all "school" factors taken together. African-Americans in schools with mostly white students had a greater sense of control. The Coleman Report was heralded as the most powerful social science case for school integration that had ever been made. Despite the massive number of critics the report engendered, it was one of the most significant research studies of the era. It inspired a plethora of research on equal educational opportunity, particularly for African-Americans, and set in motion ongoing debates over policy implications.

SELECTED BIBLIOGRAPHY

"Civil Rights Act of 1964," *U.S. Code Congressional and Administrative News*, 88th Congress, Second Session, vols. 1 and 2 (1964); James S. Coleman, "The Concept of Equality of Educational Opportunity," *Harvard Educational Review* 38 (1968): 7–22; James S. Coleman et al., *Equality of Educational Opportunity* (1966); James S. Coleman, "Statement of Dr. James S. Coleman," in *Hearing before the Select Committee on Educational Opportunity of the United States Senate, Part 1A* (1970); Editorial Board of the *Harvard Educational Review Equal Educational Opportunity* (monograph; expanded version of Winter 1968 special issue) (1969); James Edward Newby, "Equality of Educational Opportunity: Content Analysis of Six Selected Negro Authors, 1960–1970," Ed.D., diss., University of Southern California, 1974.

JAMES E. NEWBY

COMER, JAMES PIERPONT (25 September 1934, East Chicago, Indiana). A noted child psychiatrist and leader in the nation's school reform movement, James Comer is most noted for his work with the nationally recognized Yale Child Study Center School Development Program. Also known as the Comer Process,* this program began in 1968 with two predominantly African-American urban elementary schools in New Haven, Connecticut. Since that time, Comer's work has been implemented in over six hundred schools in the United States, and in Trinidad/Tobago. Calling attention to the need to address the mental health and psychosocial issues that have an impact on child development and achievement, Comer's philosophy of child-centered education has been at the forefront of school improvement initiatives for over two decades. African-American children, in particular, have benefitted from Comer's philosophy of education, in that it emphasizes the importance of parents and members of the community working in collaboration with schools to nurture positive self-concepts in children and healthy attitudes toward learning and achievement.

Comer's early family life experiences as the first of four children born to Maggie and Hugh Comer in East Chicago, Indiana, would later form the basis of his philosophy of educational policy and practice. He earned an A.B. degree in 1956 from Indiana University and an M.D. degree from Howard University* in 1960. In 1961; he enlisted for military service in the Public Health Service in Washington, D.C.

Comer became increasingly concerned about the mental health problems he observed in the African-American community, which he believed were brought on and exacerbated by the social conditions of that time. He relocated to Michigan, where he earned a Master's of Public Health from the University of Michigan in 1964. Later that year Comer began training in psychiatry at Yale University School of Medicine. He completed his training at the Hillcrest Children's Center in Washington, D.C., and in 1968 he was called back to Yale University to direct the School Development Program.

Comer's work has brought him acclaim in the areas of child development theory and school reform. He has lectured widely at colleges and universities and has received numerous awards from major organizations in education and the behavioral sciences. He serves as Maurice Falk Professor of Child Psychiatry at the Yale Child Study Center, Director of the School Development Program, and Associate Dean of the Yale School of Medicine. His major writings include: *Beyond Black and White, Black Child Care*, and *School Power: Implications of an Intervention Project. Maggie's American Dream: The Life and Times of a Black Family* was written to pay tribute to the life and legacy of his mother, the late Maggie Comer, who greatly inspired his life's work and ideology of educational practice. His book *Raising Black Children*, coauthored with noted psychiatrist Dr. Alvin Poussaint, provides an in-depth discussion of modes of parenting at various stages of child development and identifies practical approaches for raising African-American children in the context of racism and discrimination, past and present.

SELECTED BIBLIOGRAPHY

James Comer, *Maggie's American Dream: The Life and Times of a Black Family* (1988); James Comer, *School Power: Implications of an Intervention Project* (1980); *New York Times*, 24 January 1990, 13 June 1990, 12 August 1990: *Newsweek*, 2 October 1989; *Chronicle of Higher Education*, 11 April 1990.

VALERIE MAHOLMES

COMER PROCESS AND AFRICAN-AMERICAN EDUCATION. The Comer Process formally known as the School Development Program (SDP), was established in 1968 by James Comer* in two predominantly African-American elementary schools in New Haven, Connecticut, as a collaborative school intervention project between the Yale Child Study Center* and the New Haven Public School System. These schools had the poorest academic achievement and attendance results in the city as well as serious relationship problems among students, staff, and parents. Through the integration of child development principles and the cooperation of parents, staff, and members of the community, the SDP was able to guide the schools to become two of the highest-achieving elementary schools in the city. Since that time, the SDP has become one of the nation's leading school reform movements. The SDP employs preventive processes that address all aspects of a school's operations and allow the school to review its aims and methods and to identify problems in a "no-fault" atmosphere. Through collaborative decision-making strategies, the program develops creative ways of dealing with problems using the collective judgment of school officials and parents.

Using a child-centered educational approach, the School Development Program's mission is to emphasize child development, curriculum, instruction and assessment, human relations, organizational development, and social science research in a way that helps create supportive and nurturing school environments for children. Additionally, the program seeks to remain at the forefront of school reform by providing schools, school systems, and other educational stakeholders with training and consultation.

The first and most important mechanism of the SDP, the School Planning and Management Team (SPMT), is the governing body of Comer Process Schools. The SPMT is comprised of parents, staff, administrators, and student service support staff; in some middle and high schools, students are represented. The significance of this mechanism is based on the premise that school success is best generated when adults pool their collective wisdom and human resources and provide appropriate modelling for children. The SPMT carries out three critical operations. The first of these is the development of a comprehensive school plan, which contains specific goals and objectives addressing student development along six pathways: (a) cognitive, (b) language, (c) ethical, (d) physical, (e) psychological, and (f) social. Staff development is the second SPMT function. Appropriate and meaningful staff development activities are sponsored that are based on the needs and goals articulated at the building level by faculty and staff. In its third role, the SPMT uses the principles of action research to periodically assess and modify the programs specified in the comprehensive school plan. Because the SDP is a data-driven process, schools are encouraged to use school-level data to guide in the development of the comprehensive school plan and to inform their decision-making activities. Schools are also asked to conduct formative and summative assessments to document the SDP process and its anticipated outcomes.

The Students and Staff Support Team (SSST) (formerly called the Mental Health Team) is comprised of student support staff such as counselors, school psychologists, and school nurses. The purpose of this second SDP mechanism is to address global mental health issues such as crisis prevention and intervention and to address individual student issues such as inappropriate behavior and psychosocial functioning. The primary goal of the SSST is to focus on preventing problems rather than simply responding to them. The SSST fosters a synergistic relationship among student support staff, creating a caring and supportive school climate conducive to student growth, development, and achievement. A member of this team sits on the SPMT in order to communicate pertinent issues and concerns to be addressed by the governing body. The SSST meets weekly to consult with classroom teachers in developing strategies that prevent classroom related behavioral problems and to set up individualized programs for children with special needs.

The operation of the SSST has resulted in better coordination of student support services; a decrease in suspensions, retentions, and expulsions; and the development of preventive strategies employed in classrooms to help teachers manage student behaviors more effectively.

The third SDP mechanism, the Parents' Team (PT), utilizes a process that systematically establishes a home-school partnership. It serves to bridge the gap that may exist between the home and school, thereby fostering a climate of partnership and collegiality. A multilevel involvement process, the PT engages its members in school activities ranging from broad-based support to participation in decision-making activities. On the first and broadest level, as many parents as possible are invited to the school's social functions such as fashion shows, potluck suppers, and school plays. This allows parents to become acquainted with school staff in situations other than parent-teacher conferences centered on the disciplinary and achievement problems of their children. At the second level, parents are trained to become involved in day-to-day school activities such as working as a teacher's aide or in the main office. In this capacity, parents make positive contributions to the school, enabling them to develop collegial relationships with teachers and student support staff. These parents also serve as role models for other parents who might want to become involved and provide for the students a sense of continuity between home and school. At the very top level, fewer parents are involved. A parent is selected by their constituents to serve as a representative on the SPMT. At this level, parents have a significant voice in the school's decision-making process. This allows them to develop a sense of commitment to and ownership of the school's policies and initiatives.

Successful implementation of the SDP requires adherence to three principles, which guide the way each of the three mechanisms function. The principles are (a) no fault, a problem-solving approach creating an atmosphere of mutual respect and trust; (b) consensus, a decision-making process by which team members arrive at mutual agreement, avoiding "winner-loser" feelings and behaviors; and (c) collaboration, the involvement of all adult stakeholders in decision-making and carrying out agreed-upon plans and activities.

The School Development Program is operational in over six hundred elementary, middle, and high schools across the country and in Trinidad/Tobago. Leadership development programs are conducted several times a year by Yale Child Study Center staff to train process facilitators, principals, teachers, curriculum specialists, and research and evaluation personnel regarding the theories and principles of the program. Additionally, a number of research universities have adopted the SDP philosophy and have partnered with schools in SDP districts to educate preservice teachers regarding child development theory and to provide them with supervised experiences for service in inner-city areas. These school-university partnerships have encouraged the restructuring of teacher education programs and curricula in order to prepare new teachers to meet the challenges of educating children, particularly in urban areas.

SELECTED BIBLIOGRAPHY

James Comer, *Maggie's American-Dream: The Life and Times of a Black Family* (1988); James Comer, *School Power: Implications of an Intervention Project* (1980); James Comer, Norris Haynes, and Muriel Hamilton-Lee, "School Power: A Model for Improving Black Student Achievement," in W. D. Smith, E. W. Chunn, eds., *Black Education: A Quest for Equity and Excellence* (1989).

VALERIE MAHOLMES

COMMITTEE OF TWELVE FOR THE ADVANCEMENT OF THE INTERESTS OF THE NEGRO RACE. This body resulted from a conference of twenty-nine prominent African-Americans who met in a ''secret'' session in the meeting rooms of Carnegie Hall in New York City, 6 through 8 January 1904. Spearheaded by Booker T. Washington* and underwritten by philanthropist Andrew Carnegie, the conference had as its objective to set aside the differences between the ideologies of Booker T. Washington* and W. E. B. Du Bois* and address solutions to problems facing African-Americans in the areas of education, economics, voting rights, civil rights, and lynching. Although the conference was not wholly successful in realizing its main objective, the conferees unanimously adopted a resolution to establish a twelve-member Committee of Safety with the following directives: (a) to be a bureau of information on all subjects related to the race, (b) to seek to unify and bring into cooperation the actions of various organizations, and (c) to be a central bureau of communication among all parts and sections of the country.

Washington and Du Bois were made members of this committee. Along with civil rights leader Hugh M. Browne, they selected nine other members. In July 1904, the following nine men were named to the committee: Dr. I. B. Scott, H. T. Keating, Bishop George W. Clinton, journalist T. Thomas Fortune, Dr. C. E. Bently, politician Charles W. Anderson, National Baptist Convention president Dr. E. C. Morris, Howard University* professor Kelly Miller, and activist Archibald Grimké. Du Bois resigned from the committee four months later.

Funded by an annual contribution of $2,700 from Carnegie for about ten years, the Committee of Twelve seldom met as a body. Instead, its members corresponded with Washington and Browne. Some pamphlets were published by the committee. Among them were *Self-Help in Negro Education*, by Richard Robert Wright (1909); *Work of the Colored Law and Order League, Baltimore, Md.*, by James H. Waring (1908); and *Negro Banks in Mississippi*, by Charles Banks (1910).

In 1905, 1909, and 1910, the committee assisted African-American voters in Maryland both financially and politically to defeat the Poe Amendment, which was designed to disenfranchise African-Americans in the state. After 1910, the activities of the committee began to wane. In 1911, Washington ordered the balance of the Committee's funds to be used to underwrite the first edition of *The Negro Year Book.**

SELECTED BIBLIOGRAPHY

Booker Taliaferro Washington, *The Booker T. Washington Papers* (1971–1980); Booker T. Washington, Tuskegee, Alabama, 28 February 1911, to Hugh M. Browne, Cheyney, Pennsylvania, Committee of Twelve Correspondence, Box 38, Tuskegee Institute, Alabama.

DONALD FRANKLIN JOYCE

COMMONWEALTH OF PENNSYLVANIA v. BROWN, 270 F. 2d 782 (E.D., Pa. 1967). The series of cases surrounding Girard College, which began in 1958 and culminated with this decision, firmly established that state sponsorship or involvement with an educational institution that maintains discriminatory admissions practices and criteria violates the Constitution's call for equality.

Girard College in Philadelphia, Pennsylvania, as established by the will of Stephen Girard, admitted only poor white male orphans for its first one hundred and twenty-seven years. In 1954, several otherwise eligible poor African-American male orphans challenged Girard's admission policies on the basis that, as an institution overseen and administered by the City of Philadelphia and the Commonwealth of Pennsylvania, its indirect state involvement prohibited it from admitting only white applicants. The question of whether or not the now discriminatory intentions of Stephen Girard could be maintained and overseen by a state entity was finally adjudicated.

After having its admissions policies declared unconstitutional by the United States Supreme Court, Girard College, with the help of the City of Philadelphia, attempted to maintain the testator's intentions and design by separating the state from the school. This separation was caused by an earlier court decision ordering the state to remove itself from any involvement with Girard College if it wished to uphold the testamentary intentions. The only other option offered by the court was to obey the Fourteenth Amendment's demand on public institutions for equal treatment and opportunity and open the school to all poor male orphans residing in the Philadelphia area, regardless of race.

The U.S. District Court found that the city and state elected to pursue the first alternative in order to uphold the exclusionary desires of Stephen Girard. However, these attempts to fully dissociate Girard College from state supervision were not successful. In the state's appointment of private trustees, the court found language approving exclusionary admissions policies. The court also found evidence of indirect sanction of Girard College on the part of the state, such as having the private trustees report to the state Orphan's Court and presenting the trustees with certificates of appreciation. Given the history of direct association between the state and the college, the court found a significant connection between governmental policy and discriminatory admissions practices.

This case is significant because it obligated educational institutions to be completely separate from state or local governments if they maintained exclusionary admissions criteria. Institutions receiving even minimal governmental assistance were put on notice that partial disassociation from the state was not sufficient. Educational institutions that discriminate may not have any connections with the local government, whether in terms of overseeing, administering, monitoring, or financing the schools.

SELECTED BIBLIOGRAPHY

Commonwealth of Pennsylvania v. Brown, 260 F. Supp. 323 (1966); *Commonwealth of Pennsylvania v. Brown*, 392 F. 2nd 120 (1968); "Girard Is Upheld by Court on Race," *New York Times*, 1 March 1967; "Girard Will Faces New Test," *New York Times*, 27 January 1967, p. 4; Milton Myron Gordon, "The Girard College Case: Resolution and Social Significance," *Social Problems* 7, no. 1 (Summer 1959); "New Girard Appeal on Negro Is Filed," *New York Times*, 23 August 1967; "New Move in Girard Suit,"

New York Times, 7 March 1967, p. 6; "N.A.A.C.P. Suit Assailed," *New York Times*, 14 March 1967, p. 1; "U.S. Judge Widens Ruling on Girard: Makes Permanent Writ to Insure Negro Admission," *New York Times*, 6 July 1967.

BEVERLY BAKER-KELLY AND CHARLES B. ADAMS

COMMUNITY CONTROL OF SCHOOLS, AFRICAN-AMERICANS AND. Community control of schools refers to authority over a school's staff, curriculum, administration, and/or related governing bodies by recognized groups or individuals within the community. Community control differs from terms such as "parent involvement" or "community involvement." These terms suggest participation of individuals or members of the community in school activities but may not entail representation on school boards and other governing bodies. There have been few moments in history when African-Americans have exercised community control of schools. However, under certain circumstances African-Americans have controlled the curriculum, faculty, and/or administration of their community's schools.

During the pre–Civil War era when the majority of African-Americans were enslaved, the minimal education that African-Americans in slave states received was primarily through subterfuge. In the North, white philanthropists, inspired by the revolutionary ideals of the new republic that became the United States, began to establish independent schools in Boston and New York for free "African" (as they were then called) children.

The African Free School (AFS) in New York was established in 1789 by the Manumission Society to divert a growing number of free African-American children from the "slippery paths of vice." Throughout its history, the white trustees of AFS sought to teach free African-Americans industry and sobriety, virtues calculated to temper African-Americans' "uncivilized" behavior, purportedly learned during slavery. The gradual appearance, however, of a more sophisticated group of African-American leaders from other parts of the country created a new level of awareness in New York City's black population that whites had not anticipated.

By 1827 New York's African-American leaders had embraced the African Free Schools (another school had been added to accommodate an increase in school enrollment), although political issues involving the nation's black population made community leaders keenly aware of the content of the AFS curriculum. In 1832 a controversy over AFS principal Charles Andrews's advocacy of African-Americans recolonizing Africa led to his dismissal. Parents had begun pulling their children out of AFS in protest of Andrews' assertion that African-Americans who were unhappy with their status in the United States should leave the country. These developments marked a qualitative change in the African-American community's interest in the African Free Schools. Whereas in 1827 the Manumission Society and African-American community leaders had formed a partnership to boost student enrollment, by the 1830s the

African-American community had achieved enough cohesion to assert their collective interest in school administration and curricular policies.

In the years following 1832, African-American demands for community control of public schools, along with logistical problems tied to the rapid expansion of the African Free Schools, led the Manumission Society to drop its role in public schooling (which actually had been an attempt to ameliorate the condition of slaves) and instead focus on extending charity education to the poor. Overall, in asking for African-American teachers whose political views reflected the community at large, African-Americans in the early nineteenth century exhibited a keen awareness of the political role of education. Public education, for the African-American community, was not only a service provided by city officials but also a resource to be adapted to the needs of African-Americans.

In the wake of the Civil War, over three million enslaved African-Americans were declared free. For the most part, they were illiterate and lacked the skills necessary to support themselves. Various public and private funding sources collaborated during this period (including northern benevolent societies, the Bureau of Refugees, and the Freedmen's Bureau*) to plan the schooling of these newly freed African-Americans, with the intention of containing and controlling them. Even so, slaves and free persons of color had already begun to make plans for the systematic instruction of their illiterates. For instance, as early as 1861 an African-American teacher named Mary Peake* established a school in Fortress Monroe, Virginia. By 1800, seven hundred thousand African-American children were enrolled in school in ten Southern states; almost a million were enrolled by the turn of the century.

Some consider the momentous 1896 Supreme Court decision rendered in the *Plessy v. Ferguson** case to have been a serious blow to the educational efforts made for African-American children because it essentially legimated educational apartheid and bolstered the tradition of white supremacy. However, in terms of community control, the *Plessy* decision may have unintentionally served to keep intact African-Americans' ''control'' of their educational institutions.

Effective community schools that existed before the 1960s have largely been ignored by educators and historians interested in this period of African-American education. These segregated schools, though lacking financial resources and adequate facilities, often became models of community-controlled institutions, as white school boards showed little or no interest in the education of African-American children. It has been suggested that prior to 1940 America was a nation of small towns and rural areas, making transportation and communication limited (television had not been invented); people lived close together and close to where they worked. As a result, there was a great deal of interaction between parents and community authority figures such as teachers and administrators, enabling them to speak a ''common tongue.'' There existed an almost direct transfer of authority from the parents to school personnel because educators were thought of as surrogate parents. Under these circumstances, the school was a natural reflection of the African-American community's aspirations and ideals.

An example of this type of community control is evident in a case study of Caswell County Training School (CCTS), located in rural North Carolina. Here, African-American parents exercised control over school expenses and activities, and African-American principals made decisions about the curriculum. Although parents did not participate in school decision-making and teachers did little to facilitate parents' fundraising efforts, their combined forces created a situation in which the African-American community control of public schools up until the 1940s may be attributed to the legal separation between African-American and white schools, shared values between the community and school, and close interaction between school officials and the community.

African-American community control continued until the late 1960s in the South and into the late 1970s in the northern areas. Desegregation resulting from the 1954 *Brown v. Board of Education of Topeka, Kansas** decision, however, brought about at least three changes that systematically eroded African-Americans' community control of schools. First, integration took its greatest toll on African-American children by requiring that they attend schools outside their home environments. Amid predominantly white teachers and students, pupil-teacher relationships were strained for African-American students. Second, massive firings or reassignments of African-American teachers, principals, and administrators diluted the number of African-American personnel in control of curriculum. Third, as the traditional education role of African-American parents was dismantled, many were unsure how to interact with the predominantly white school system. These events in effect robbed African-Americans of the community control they had enjoyed historically.

Similar to the emerging black-nationalist consciousness that spearheaded early efforts at community control of schools among eighteenth-century blacks in the Northeast, the Civil Rights Movement of the 1960s inspired African-Americans to look for new ways to regain control of community institutions. Though the *Brown* decision ushered in an era of African-American political activity around the issue of desegregation that, at times, overshadowed the issue of community control, civil rights leaders were able to renew black America's faith in the grassroots political process. Thus, not all control was surrendered; some African-American parents continued to demand the power to control their local schools.

The most famous of these efforts was New York City's Ocean Hill–Brownsville school district where, in an effort to pilot a school decentralization plan, the board of education appointed a governing board equally composed of teachers, administrators, and African-American and Latino parents whose children attended school in the district. The governing board implemented several new policies, including a more expanded multicultural curriculum and its right to choose teachers and principals. However, not all of the changes were popular with teachers, some of whom were rumored to be discrediting the actions of the governing board behind closed doors.

In response to these rumors as well as to pressure from various board members and parents, several teachers were dismissed who supposedly did not support the board's initiatives. Despite pressure from outside constituencies to reverse its decision, the board refused to reinstate the teachers. In response, the United Federation of Teachers called a citywide strike. In the midst of the strike, a committed group of predominantly African-American teachers took the opportunity to infuse the curriculum with books by African-American and Latino authors. Eventually, under pressure from Jewish groups who claimed that the governing board was anti-Semitic (several of the dismissed teachers were Jewish), the New York City Board of Education suspended the Ocean Hill–Brownsville School Board. Although the Ocean Hill–Brownsville Governing Board was eventually dismantled, it played a key role in modeling future legislation that called for the decentralization of New York City's public schools.

African-American parents continue to seek the opportunity to have a voice in the schooling of their children. The success of James Comer's* School Development Program (SDP) (the Comer Process*) is reliable evidence of this phenomenon. In low-income, predominantly African-American neighborhoods, the SDP aims to recreate the shared value systems that once existed between African-American parents and school officials by reconfiguring school governance structures to include parental representation. Preliminary evaluations indicate that the SDP dramatically increases pupil attendance, academic achievement, and parental participation.

Other contemporary efforts by African-Americans to win back control of schools seem to be modelled after independent African-American schools and academies that have flourished in the South since the 1800s. The recent push to establish all-male academies staffed with African-American male teachers represents such an endeavor. The old academies, for the most part, were financed entirely by individuals and churches within the African-American community. In this way the community retained control of independent African-American educational institutions. Interestingly, this did not always mean that African-American independent schools displayed more innovative, multicultural curricula than schools controlled by whites. Many independent African-American institutions continue to employ a curriculum quite similar to their white-controlled counterparts. However, they employ African-American teachers, principals, and support personnel.

Given the ongoing predominance of negative images of African-American families in the mass media, particularly African-American parents' supposedly ineffectual role in education, it is important to present an accurate historical account of African-American efforts toward community control of their schools. Though African-Americans frequently sought to control the education their children received, in most cases these efforts have been systematically opposed (as in the case of the African Free Schools) or dismantled (e.g., the Ocean Hill–Brownsville Governing Board). But the work of James Comer and others demonstrates that African-Americans today continue to seek a strong, effective voice in their children's education.

SELECTED BIBLIOGRAPHY

C. Ascher, "School Programs for African-American Males . . . and Females," *Phi Delta Kappan* (1992): 777–82; J. E. Blackwell, *The Black Community: Diversity and Unity*, 2d ed. (1985); J. P. Comer, "Child Development and Education," *Journal of Negro Education* 58, no. 2 (1989): 125–39; R. W. Irvine and J. J. Irvine, "The Impact of the Desegregation Process on the Education of Black Students: Key Variables," *Journal of Negro Education* 52, no. 4 (1983): 410–23; R. Lowe and H. Kantor, "Considerations on Writing the History of Educational Reform in the 1960s," *Educational Theory* 39, no. 1 (1989): 1–9; J. D. Ratteray, "Independent Neighborhood Schools: A Framework for the Education of African-Americans," *Journal of Negro Education* 61, no. 2 (1992): 138–47; J. L. Rury, "The New York African Free School, 1827–1836: Conflict over Community Control of Black Education," *Phylon* 44, no. 3 (1983): 187–97; D. T. Slaughter-Defoe, "Parental Educational Choice: Some African-American Dilemmas," *Journal of Negro Education* 60, no. 3 (1991): 354–60; E. V. Walker, "Caswell County Training School, 1933–1969: Relationships between Community and School," *Harvard Educational Review* 63, no. 2 (1993): 161–83; C. V. Willie, A. M. Garibaldi, and W. L. Reed, eds., *The Education of African-Americans* (1991); M. Zimet, *Decentralization and School Effectiveness: A Case Study of the 1969 Decentralization Law in New York City* (1973).

LANCE MCCREADY

COMPENSATORY EDUCATION IN HIGHER EDUCATION, AFRICAN-AMERICANS AND. Compensatory education, broadly defined, includes most efforts that provide supplemental or alternate educational programs or services. Such efforts might take the form of cultural and instructional enrichment, remediation, or expanded access to educational opportunities for those previously denied them because of race, class, or gender. The term is generally associated with the elementary and secondary education initiatives that emerged in the 1960s. However, compensatory education also exists within higher education. It is generally downplayed because of its perceived incompatibility with higher education's primary role of producing superior scholarship and therefore is not easily identifiable.

For African-Americans the idea of compensatory education in higher education predates the popularized use of the term beginning in the 1960s. The meaning and scope of compensatory education over time have been guided more by circumstances, conditions, and events connected to the changing status of African-Americans than by a single pedagogical theory. Prior to the Civil War, for example, the number of African-Americans who received college degrees was negligible. By the end of the Civil War, the count was twenty-eight. Although the numbers were small, the achievement of these individuals was notable and established the point that, given the opportunity, African-Americans could compete at the best colleges of the day. With this backdrop, most post–Civil War efforts to provide college opportunities to greater numbers of former slaves embodied the concept of compensatory education. The chronology that follows traces key efforts and influences in college compensatory education and the African-American from the post–Civil War period to the present.

Compensatory education was inextricably linked to the African-American struggle for first-class citizenship, which began to occur systematically after Emancipation in 1863. Following the Civil War, the former slave class began to build a system of higher education that would reinforce their notions of freedom and social order. Several private African-American colleges were founded in the South by or with the help of the American Missionary Association,* the Freedman's Bureau,* and several religious benevolent societies and former slaves. In the midst of these efforts emerged the Hampton Normal and Industrial Institute,* in 1868, which became the "ideological antithesis" of the African-American higher education movement. Its founder, white educator Samuel Chapman Armstrong,* advocated educating the ex-slaves for a place in the existing social order of inequalities by teaching the "dignity of labor." A critical element of Armstrong's beliefs was that the freedmen were "culturally and morally deficient" and therefore "unfit" to participate fully in a "civilized" society. Booker T. Washington,* a former slave and one of Armstrong's distinguished students, further developed the Hampton model when he founded Tuskegee Normal and Industrial Institute (now Tuskegee University*) in 1881. Washington advocated the model's value in uplifting the masses of his race. The two institutes became known as the Hampton-Tuskegee Idea, or the Hampton Model.

As the Hampton–Tuskegee Idea gained increasing popularity among northern businessmen-philanthropists and southern whites, its critics among African-American leaders grew, as highlighted by the popularized "Washington–Du Bois debate." W. E. B. Du Bois* not only was critical of Washington's industrial education philosophy but was also distressed at the long-term implications of Washington's leadership and influence on the quality of higher education for African-American youth.

Public higher education for African-Americans came twenty-eight years after the Morrill Land Grant Act of 1862, which established state colleges for agricultural and technical programs. It was not until the second Morrill Act of 1890* that funding was to be "equally divided" between the already established white state institutions and the more recently created African-American state colleges (or normal schools). The distribution formula, however, was not fully enforced. Thus, at a time when a fragile system of higher education was being constructed, the Hampton-Tuskegee model and the second Morrill Act served to undermine compensatory education efforts. The resulting institutionalized higher educational inequalities grounded in Armstrong's cultural and moral deficit theories would continue to haunt African-Americans. The Supreme Court affirmed these inequities under the "separate but equal doctrine" in *Plessy v. Ferguson*,* a decision that stood for almost sixty years.

At the heart of the modern civil rights movement was the argument that the "separate but equal" doctrine had a debilitating effect on the quality of education received by African-American children and that desegregated educational environments were required to undo the harm. One week after the 1954 Supreme

Court decision in *Brown v. the Board of Education of Topeka, Kansas,** which overturned *Plessy*, it ruled in *Hawkins v. Board of Education** that the *Brown* decision also applied to higher education. Desegregation therefore became the primary compensatory strategy for both secondary and higher education. Change, however, was painfully slow.

Even though the *Brown* and *Hawkins* decisions set the stage for dramatic increases in the number of African-Americans in higher education, participation rates remained limited during the years prior to and immediately following the *Brown* and *Hawkins* decisions. Compensatory education efforts, therefore, continued to focus on the talented few. One such effort was the National Scholarship Service Fund for Negro Students (NSSFNS), which began in 1949. By 1954, it had successful placed approximately 2,300 African-American students in predominantly white colleges and universities, with scholarship aid totaling $450,000. Because these were among the top African-American students, little else was provided by way of academic support. Thus compensatory education efforts were largely defined as educational access for what Du Bois earlier had called the "talented tenth,"* that is, the elite among African-American students.

A major shift in compensatory education began to occur in the 1960s. Providing access to white institutions to the talented few diminished as an adequate strategy in the face of the growing pool of African-American high school graduates aspiring to attend college. The civil rights movement continued to gather momentum. The dramatic incidents of civil unrest in urban centers catalyzed a quick succession of public policy actions. In 1963, President John F. Kennedy signed into law the National Defense Education Act and the National Defense Student Loan and Workstudy Programs. President Lyndon Johnson enacted the Civil Rights Act of 1964,* the Economic Opportunity Act of 1964 (EOA), and the Higher Education Act of 1965 (HEA). President Johnson also authorized the establishment of the Office of Economic Opportunity (OEO), which spawned programs such as Upward Bound* (transferred in 1969 to HEA). These and other initiatives formed the core of federal policy generally associated with expanded educational opportunities for low-income and minority students. This kind of federal involvement fueled the growing optimism among young African-Americans and sparked increases in their college-going rates. Many of these students arrived at the campuses inadequately prepared. Most universities, however, were unprepared to accommodate these new students, who were said to have been culturally and academically "disadvantaged" (a variation of persistent cultural-deficit theories). As a result, two major compensatory education strategies emerged.

One of these strategies was federally funded categorical programs. Upward Bound and Educational Talent Search, the earlier programs, and subsequent HEA compensatory programs (legislatively known as "Trio") grew out of the need for colleges and universities to recruit and retain this new population of students. Other Trio programs and their date of HEA authorization include Student Support Services (1968), Educational Opportunity Centers (1972), Veterans

Upward Bound (1973), Ronald E. McNair Post-Baccalaureate Achievement (1986), and Upward Bound Math and Science (1991). Each program, in some way, focused on preparing capable but otherwise ''disadvantaged'' students for college entrance or retention. Trio programs have touched the lives of thousands of low-income and largely African-American students (an estimated 646,341 by 1993). Still, these programs reached only 10 percent of those identified as eligible students. An often neglected fact is that such programs have also served as models for a variety of college compensatory education efforts. For example, the Upward Bound model has spawned a number of discipline-specific (e.g., science, engineering) precollege or ''bridge'' programs. The Student Support Services model has been the prototype of various college retention initiatives, many of which benefit African-American students.

Another strategy for compensatory education was community colleges. A wide variety of two-year colleges began to emerge in the 1960s. Although they met a range of vocational/technical community needs, they also began to accommodate the increasing numbers of underprepared students seeking to attend four-year colleges. They did so just as many four-year colleges and universities began backing away from institutionalized compensatory efforts. Thousands of African-American and other students thought to be underprepared were able to pursue higher educational goals at community colleges. Some did so for specific nondegree skills. Others saw it as an alternate route leading to a college degree.

Because there remained a wide range of community colleges and because matriculation agreements were difficult to formulate and maintain, most students were unsuccessful in transferring from two-year to four-year institutions. As early as 1975 some very disturbing evidence began to appear. African-American students who began college at public community colleges substantially decreased their chances of earning a bachelor's degree. Today African-Americans remain overrepresented in urban community colleges and underrepresented in the rest of higher education. By necessity, urban community colleges have employed a variety of compensatory or alternative education strategies for their students. Miami-Dade Community College, Cuyahoga Community College, and City University of New York La Guardia Community represent the more successful institutions. Limited resources and support, however, continue to be barriers for most such colleges.

College compensatory education in the 1960s initially enjoyed a significant, though fragile, support base within the politically liberal segments of American society. The 1966 Coleman Report, *Equality of Educational Opportunity*,* however, opened the way for the critics of compensatory education. The report suggested that lower academic performance among African-American students was not simply the result of poor schooling but was also related to family environment. Critics used the report as a justification to minimize the significance of compensatory education.

Contemporary critics of compensatory education began to appear in 1968. Some attacks were program specific. In 1968, for example, Upward Bound warded off criticism of its curriculum by Gloria Joseph. The program's overall effectiveness was criticized in 1974 by a later-discredited Government Accounting Office study. Other attacks have been framed in more global terms, for example, Arthur Jensen's 1969 thesis that genetic differences explain the lower academic achievement among African-Americans. Genetic differences, according to Jensen, render compensatory education efforts all but futile. Although Jensen's study was later discredited, its initial impact shook the very foundation of compensatory education and its role in educating African-Americans. It also fueled the arguments of a growing conservative white backlash movement across the nation, which began attacking the "Great Society" programs as being inefficient and ineffective.

In the wake of an increasingly conservative political environment, many universities have recast their earlier compensatory education efforts as "developmental" or "retention" initiatives. A significant number of colleges and universities have integrated these initiatives with counseling and tutorial services. More sophisticated strategies have also included offering courses through academic departments, as well as learning resource centers, thereby integrating such efforts into the overall academic structures. At the same time, these universities have moved away from reliance on the long-standing cultural deficit theories in designing programs and curricula and instead have placed more emphasis on cultural differences in approaches to learning.

SELECTED BIBLIOGRAPHY

James D. Anderson, *The Education of Blacks in the South, 1860–1935* (1988); Alexander Astin, *Minorities in American Higher Education* (1982); Arthur M. Cohn and Florence B. Brawer, *The American Community College* (1989); James S. Coleman, *Equality of Educational Opportunity* (1966); K. Patricia Cross, ed., *Underprepared Learners* (1983); W. E. B. Du Bois, *The Souls of Black Folk* (1903); Laurence R. Marcus and Benjamin D. Stickney, *Race and Education: The Unending Controversy* (1981); John U. Ogbu, *Minority Education and Caste: The American System in Cross-Cultural Perspective* (1978); Richard C. Richardson, Jr., and Lois W. Bender, *Fostering Minority Access and Achievement in Higher Education* (1987); Gail E. Thomas, ed., *Black Students in Higher Education* (1981).

ROLAND B. SMITH, JR.

CONSENT DECREES. Court litigation has been one of the weapons in the struggle for educational equity. Through court challenges, African-Americans have been successful in their efforts to require the country and its institutions to abide by the laws of the land. Consent decrees have in many past instances represented the successful conclusion to court cases brought by African-Americans intent on securing equal educational rights. Consent decrees (also referred to as consent judgments) are agreements to which the parties have acquiesced and that a judge has entered as an order of the court. Once the judgment is entered, the defendant agrees to cease any alleged illegal activity; however, the defendant makes this agreement without admitting any wrongdoing. Thus, the consent decree is not quite a judicial sentence "but is in the nature of a solemn contract of agreement of the parties, made under the sanction of the court'' (*Black's Law Dictionary*). In fact, the consent decree has been referred to as a hybrid of a contract and a court order.

Judgments entered by consent of parties have been used in a variety of cases, such as those dealing with antitrust, alimony, child support, prison and mental hospital reform, and school desegregation. Although consent decrees are implemented frequently, the legal community is at odds in its support of consensual judgments. For example, some praise consent decrees on the grounds that they are assumed to save the courts and the litigants expenses and time, that they are more effectively implemented than decisions founded upon force, and that consent decrees allow parties to exercise full autonomy in the judicial process.

However, opponents of consent decrees take issue with each of these claims. For example, they argue that there is no empirical evidence to suggest that consent decrees are more cost-efficient and time-efficient than other forms of resolution (e.g., adjudication and contracts), particularly when postdecree litigation is not taken into account. Opponents also contest the claim that consent decrees have high rates of compliance. They cite numerous cases where court decrees are consistently violated and cases where the court has been unsuccessful in reprimanding noncompliance. Cases involving alimony, child support, prison and mental hospital reform, and school desegregation are common instances where there have been high rates of noncompliance. Finally, opponents argue that instead of increasing litigant autonomy, consent decrees actually allow the courts to control the parties.

Opposing legal views aside, consent decrees have been instrumental in the resolution of several important court cases involving African-Americans' educational rights. In one such case, *Martin Luther King Junior Elementary School Children et al. v. Ann Arbor School District Board,** the plaintiffs—eleven preschool and elementary schoolchildren who spoke ''Black English''—alleged that the Ann Arbor school district impeded their ''equal participation in instructional programs'' by not recognizing their special needs as speakers of the African-American vernacular. Specifically, the plaintiffs claimed that the school board was in violation of Section 1703(f) of the Equal Educational Opportunities Act. Judge Charles Joiner, the presiding judge, agreed that the teachers' and administrators' responses to children who spoke black English were in violation of the section. The court did not, however, determine a remedy for this situation. Instead, the court ordered a consent decree, in which the defendants were required to work with the plaintiffs to develop a remedy that would ''help teachers to recognize the home language of students and to use that knowledge in their attempts to teach reading skills and standard English.''

In a second case, *United States of America v. State of Louisiana*, the United States filed suit against Louisiana claiming that the state was ''illegally maintaining a dual college system based on race.'' In this case, a three-judge panel held that Louisiana was illegally operating a dual college system. Consequently, the district court ordered a consent decree, in which the state was instructed to develop a plan to remedy the dual college system. However, in line with the nature of consent decrees, the state was not required to admit guilt. For this particular consent decree, the district court retained jurisdiction over the case and set a date for the discussion of possible remedies to alleviate the dual system of education. However, the case was eventually passed to the Fifth Circuit for further litigation. The district court of the Eastern District of Louisiana subsequently ordered the merger of Louisiana State Law School and Southern University Law School. The court also ordered the consolidation of Louisiana's three boards of higher education. This decision effectively overturned the previous consent decree.

Consent decrees represent an important tool in African-Americans' struggle for educational equity and access. At a time in history where "the quest for social justice in America requires creative approaches to the enforcement of basic legal rights" (Anderson, 1983: 579), consent decrees are an effective alternative to costly, drawn-out court litigation. As the courts seek to diminish their activist role as agents of social change and reform, consent decrees are likely to become more common in cases involving educational rights. This trend will challenge educators, legislators, and the nation's courts to ensure that consent decrees are fairly negotiated and vigorously implemented. Otherwise the result may be to lessen or reverse the progress of African-Americans—and other excluded groups—toward educational equity, and thus full citizenship, in this nation.

SELECTED BIBLIOGRAPHY

Lloyd Anderson, "The Approval and Interpretation of Consent Decrees in Civil Rights Class Action Litigation," *University of Illinois Law Review*, no. 3 (1983): 579–632; Paul R. Diamond, "Constitutional Requirements," in Reginald Wilson, ed., *Race and Equity in Higher Education* (1982), pp. 104–37; *Kenneth Adams et al. v. Joseph A. Califano, Jr., Secretary of the Department of Health, Education, and Welfare et al.*, 430 F. Supp. 118; Gil Kujovich, "Equal Opportunity in Higher Education and the Black Public College: The Era of Separate But Equal," *Minnesota Law Review* 72, no. 29 (1987): 29–165; *Martin Luther King, Jr., Elementary School Children v. Ann Arbor School District*, 473 Federal Supplement 1371 (1979) U.S. District Court, Eastern District Michigan; Peggy Simpson, "Constitutional Crisis," *Ms.* (September 1989): 90–98; *United States of America v. State of Louisiana et al.*, 692 Federal Supplement 642 (1988) U.S. District Court, Eastern District Louisiana.

WALTER R. ALLEN AND DERRICK GILBERT

COOPER, ANNA JULIA (10 August 1858?, Raleigh, North Carolina–27 February 1964, Washington, D.C.). An educator, author, and feminist, Cooper struggled for over ninety years to improve the educational system of the United States for African-Americans. Anna Julia Haywood was born to the slave Hannah Stanley and the slave master George Washington Haywood. Entering St. Augustine Normal School and Collegiate Institute* in Raleigh, North Carolina, at nine years of age, Cooper began a life devoted to education. After graduation and several years of teaching at St. Augustine's, she married George A. C. Cooper of Nassau in 1877. He died in 1879, just two months after ordination in the Protestant Episcopal Church.

In 1881, at age twenty-one, Cooper entered Oberlin College* and was inspired to address the unheard voice of southern African-American women. After her 1884 graduation from Oberlin, she served one year as the head of the language department at Wilberforce College and two years as a teacher of math, Greek, and Latin at St. Augustine. In 1887, after receiving her M.A. degree from Oberlin, she joined the faculty of Washington, D.C.'s Preparatory High School for Colored Youth (which became the M Street High School in 1891).

As one of the leading educational activists of the period, Cooper received recognition as a leader in the movement to promote educational programs for African-American women. An internationally respected feminist, Cooper wrote *A Voice from the South by a Black Woman from the South*, in an effort to reveal the injustices and inequalities confronted by African-American women. In 1900 Anna Cooper was selected to serve as an official delegate, an executive committee member, and one of only two African-American women to address the first Pan-African Conference in London.

The following year, Cooper became the second African-American female principal of the M Street School. Under her influence, the reputation of this prestigious college preparatory school flourished. However, in 1906 the Washington, D.C., school board decided not to reappoint Cooper because she refused to support their move to weaken the curriculum for African-American youth. From 1906 to 1910, Cooper chaired the language department at Lincoln University* in Missouri. She returned to the M Street School in 1910; it became the Paul Laurence Dunbar High School* in 1916. During the summers of 1911 to 1917, she pursued graduate studies in Paris and at Columbia University. In 1925, at sixty-six years of age, she received the Ph.D. degree from the Sorbonne, becoming the fourth African-American woman to earn a Ph.D. degree.

While in her nineties, Cooper wrote two books, *Life and Writings of the Grimké Family* and *The Third Step*. She also lectured on the educational system's failure to confront racism, challenge gender-biased instruction, and initiate community-based instructional programs. When she died in Washington, D.C., at the age of 105, this distinguished educator, innovative administrator, feminist scholar, and author asked to be remembered simply as ''somebody's teacher on vacation.'' She is interred in the Hargett Cemetery in Raleigh, North Carolina.

SELECTED BIBLIOGRAPHY

Anna Julia Cooper, *A Voice from the South by a Black Woman from the South* (1892; reprinted 1988); Leona C. Gabel, *From Slavery to the Sorbonne and Beyond: The Life and Writings of Anna J. Cooper* (1982); Louise Daniel Hutchinson, *Anna J. Cooper, A Voice from the South* (1981); David W. H. Pellow, ''Anna 'Annie' J. Cooper: Educator, Scholar, Writer, Feminist, Pan-Africanist, Activist,'' in Jessie Carney Smith, ed., *Notable Black American Women* (1992).

ELIZABETH CLARK-LEWIS

COOPER v. AARON, 358 U.S. 1 (1958). In *Cooper v. Aaron*, the U.S. Supreme Court ruled that "the constitutional rights of children not to be discriminated against in school admission on grounds of race or color . . . can neither be nullified openly and directly by state legislators or state executives or judicial officers, nor nullified indirectly by them through evasive schemes for segregation whether attempted 'ingeniously or ingenuously.' " This ruling clearly rejected the Little Rock School Board's request for a two-and-one-half-year suspension of its court-approved desegregation program. The importance of the ruling necessitates a brief review of the case facts.

Following the Supreme Court's 1954 decision in *Brown v. Board of Education of Topeka, Kansas*,* the Little Rock School Board developed a desegregation plan. The plan, approved by a federal district court, called for a gradual desegregation of the school system, starting at the high school level with the transfer of nine African-American students in September 1957. The plan was stopped, however, when Governor Orval Faubus ordered the Arkansas National Guard to place Central High School off-limits to the nine students.* A federal district court, concluding that the governor's action had obstructed the court-approved desegregation plan, issued an injunction against any action that would preclude the African-American students from attending Central High. The students did enter the school on 23 September 1957. However, they were threatened and insulted by a large crowd that had formed around the school. To ensure the students' safety, President Dwight Eisenhower sent federal troops to the school. Eventually the troops were replaced by federalized National Guardsmen, who remained on the school grounds until the end of the school year.

The school board in February 1958 asked the federal district court to order a postponement of the desegregation plan. The board's reason was that a viable education program at the high school could not be maintained because of vocal and violent public hostility. The district court granted the board's request; however, the Eighth Circuit Court reversed the decision. The case was then appealed to the Supreme Court.

The primary issue addressed in *Cooper* was whether a state governor or legislature has a duty to obey federal court orders that rest on the Supreme Court's considered interpretation of the Constitution. The Court first described in detail the case facts and previous legal actions associated with the case. The key point developed by the Court was that numerous State of Arkansas officials had caused the public hostility against the admission of the nine students to Central High. Such action, the Court stated clearly, showed state efforts to resist the Court's ruling in *Brown*. The Court concluded that constitutional rights cannot be "sacrificed or yielded to the violence and disorder" caused by state officials. The Court reasoned that constitutional law clearly holds that no state official or agency shall deny any person equal protection of the law. The Court, in essence, reaffirmed the principle that justice delayed is justice denied.

While the Court disposed of the case in the first part of its decision, it believed that it also had to refute the State of Arkansas' premise that its officials were not bound by the Court's holding in *Brown*. Noting that Article VI of the Constitution makes the Constitution the "supreme Law of the Land" and precedent clearly states federal courts are responsible for interpreting the Constitution, the Court concluded that no "state legislator or executive or judicial officer can war against the Constitution without violating his undertaking to support it."

The *Cooper* decision was significant for African-American education because it clearly showed how adamant the Court was in its determination to reaffirm the *Brown* decision and remove racial segregation from the schools. As the Court stated at the end of the decision, its intent was to advance the constitutional ideal of equal justice as a "living truth." To underscore their unanimity in this ideal, all nine justices individually signed the decision, a practice that has happened only once in the Court's history.

SELECTED BIBLIOGRAPHY

Cooper v. Aaron, 358 U.S. 1 (1958).

BRUCE BEEZER

COPPIN, FANNY JACKSON (1837, Washington, D.C.–21 January 1913, Philadelphia). An educator, social activist, and missionary, Fanny Coppin was born a slave in Washington, D.C. Her maternal aunt, Sarah Orr Clark, purchased her freedom for $125. Soon after receiving her freedom, Fanny was sent to New Bedford, Massachusetts, to live with relatives. Seeking better educational opportunities, at the age of fourteen Fanny moved to Newport, Rhode Island. There she lived with the George Henry Calvert family for six years. During that time, she paid a tutor for private French lessons, received instruction in sewing, and attended the Rhode Island State Normal School at Bristol, completing the course with academic honors. However, it was at Oberlin College* in Ohio, from 1860 to 1865, that Coppin received the training that more fully prepared her for her life's work. She was first enrolled in the Ladies Department, but in 1861 she was registered as a member of the freshman class of the Collegiate Department. She became the first African-American student teacher in the Preparatory Department, and during her senior year she utilized her skills to organize an evening class to teach reading and writing to newly freed persons.

She graduated from Oberlin with a baccalaureate degree and joined the faculty of the Philadelphia Institute for Colored Youth, serving as head of the girls' department from 1869 to 1871 and as principal from 1871 to 1900. She was the first African-American woman to head such an institution. During her tenure as principal, Coppin introduced new curricula and fostered the development of innovative programs. Among them were the Teacher Training Program and the Industrial Division. The Industrial Division was the first trade school for African-Americans in the city of Philadelphia.

As a social activist, Coppin's influence extended to the larger community of Philadelphia. She was the first African-American female member of the Board of City Examiners for Clerical Officers, a member of the Board of Managers of the Home for the Aged and Infirm Colored People, and helped to organize the

Home for Girls and Women and the Colored Woman's Exchange. She gained national recognition because of her efforts to improve the quality of life for African-Americans. In 1897, she served as a vice president of the National Association of Colored Women, an organization that encouraged the development of self-help and social service programs.

Coppin was also very active in the missionary and outreach activities of the AME church, holding both local and national offices. She was a regular writer for the Women's Department of the *Christian Recorder*, the official newspaper of the AME church. It was at a fund-raising fair that she had organized for the *Recorder* that Fanny met her future husband, Levi Coppin. They were married in 1881.

Levi Coppin was elected a bishop of the AME Church in 1900 and assigned to the Fourteenth Episcopal District in Capetown, South Africa. Fanny Coppin arrived in Capetown on 2 November 1902, and began to structure educational programs for women and girls. The Fanny Jackson Coppin Girl's Hall at Wilberforce Institute in Capetown was so named in tribute to her educational and missionary work among the women.

It was apparent that Fanny Coppin's health was declining when she returned to the United States in 1904. During the last years of her life she wrote *Reminiscences of School Life, and Hints on Teaching*, an autobiographical look at her educational philosophy, teaching strategies, and efforts to educate African-Americans. In recognition of her accomplishments in the field of teacher education and her many years of service to African-Americans, the Colored Normal School in Baltimore, Maryland was renamed the Fanny Jackson Coppin Normal School in 1926 (today, Coppin State College*).

SELECTED BIBLIOGRAPHY

Fanny Jackson Coppin, *Reminiscences of School Life, and Hints on Teaching* (1913, reprint 1987); Linda Perkins, "Heed Life's Demands: The Educational Philosophy of Fanny Jackson Coppin," *Journal of Negro Education* 51, no. 3 (1982): 181–90; Linda Perkins, "Fanny Jackson Coppin," in Jessie Carney Smith, ed., *Notable Black American Women* (1992); *Philadelphia Tribune*, 30 March 1990.

CYNTHIA NEVERDON-MORTON

COPPIN STATE COLLEGE. Founded in 1900, Coppin State College, Baltimore, Maryland, is the only public senior college in the University of Maryland system. Coppin has the unique mission of focusing on the needs and aspirations of the people of the inner city, a constituency it has served since its inception. Through traditional liberal arts programs and through majors in such diverse areas as computer science, nursing, management science, criminal justice, early childhood and elementary education, special education, and physical education for the handicapped, the college has enabled its constituents to enter and participate fully in the broader U.S. culture. Coppin's position in the University of Maryland system will allow it to expand its existing dual-degree and certification programs with the university beyond the current ones in dentistry, engineering, pharmacy, and social work. The college serves as an intellectual and physical oasis in the urban environment, reaching out to the community via cooperative programs with the city schools and with area business and industry.

SELECTED BIBLIOGRAPHY

National Association for Equal Opportunity in Higher Education, *Profiles of the Nation's Historically and Predominantly Black Colleges and Universities* (1993).

SAMUEL L. MYERS

COUNCIL OF INDEPENDENT BLACK INSTITUTIONS. The Council of Independent Black Institutions (CIBI) is an umbrella organization for independent African-centered schools. Member schools are found in cities throughout the United States as well as the United Kingdom and West Africa. These schools enroll students at all levels, from prekindergarten through secondary. The heaviest concentrations, however, are at the elementary level. Organizational planning began during the April 1972 African-American Teachers Association Conference; the formal founding of CIBI as a national (and later international) organization took place later that year at a five-day meeting (29 June–3 July) in Frogmore, South Carolina. CIBI was formed to enable educators of African descent to share information, materials, and curriculum and to have material unity that would support the development of independent schools as alternatives to public schooling. However, CIBI member schools have ceased to define themselves as merely alternatives to public schools, envisioning themselves as providing authentic education for people of African descent through building and maintaining institutions for that purpose. The organization holds annual teacher-training institutes that attract teachers in public and private schools. It also sponsors an annual science exposition for children from various member schools. Every other year, it conducts its convention, where educators from CIBI schools and elsewhere meet to share information on curricula and other education-related matters and to elect and install new officers.

CIBI offers a speaker's bureau and an alumni association for graduates of member institutions. It also provides technical assistance to those operating or wishing to open independent African-centered schools or to any institution or group that serves children of African descent.

CIBI publishes a semiannual newsletter, *FUNDISHA! TEACH!*, which provides a forum for curriculum innovations, book reviews, news about member schools, and other features pertaining to people of African descent. It has also published African-centered curriculum materials that have been developed and used effectively over the years by teachers in CIBI institutions as well as in other schools. CIBI's social studies curriculum guide, *Positive Afrikan Images for Children*, published in 1990, is an example.

A number of individuals who figure prominently in contemporary African-centered education discourses have linkages to schools or organizations that are or have been CIBI members, including such notables as Carol D. Lee, founder of New Concept Development Center in Chicago; Hannibal Tirus Afrik, a founder of Shule ya Watoto in Chicago; Jacob Carruthers, associated with the Blyden

Institute, which operated in Chicago during the late 1970s and early 1980s; Agyei Akoto, director of NationHouse Positive Action Center in Washington, D.C.; historian Yosef ben-Jochannon, formerly a volunteer instructor at the Nyerere Education Institute in New Brunswick, New Jersey; Bernida Thompson, director of Roots Activity Learning Center in Washington, D.C.; and Imani Humphrey, founder and director of the Aisha Shule and the W. E. B. Du Bois Preparatory School in Detroit. Kasisi Jitu Weusi was the founding National Executive Director of CIBI.

SELECTED BIBLIOGRAPHY

A. Akoto, *Nationbuilding: Theory and Practice in Afrikan Centered Education* (1992); J. Churchville, "Freedom Library Day School," in Black Child Development Institute, ed., *Curriculum Approaches from a Black Perspective* (1973); Council of Independent Black Institutions, *Positive African Images for Children: The CIBI Social Studies Curriculum* (1990); K. J. Weusi, "CIBI: A Critical Evaluation," *Black News* 3, no. 18 (1977).

KOFI LOMOTEY AND MWALIMU J. SHUJAA

COUNCIL OF THE GREAT CITY SCHOOLS. Founded in 1961 in Chicago and now located in Washington, D.C., the Council of the Great City Schools is the only education organization in the United States that exclusively represents large urban school districts. It is a coalition composed of the nation's largest public school systems, with a leadership of the superintendents and a member of the board of education of each respective district comprising the council's board of directors.

The mission of the council is to improve education for America's 5.8 million inner-city school children, which it carries out through public and legislative advocacy as well as research and information exchange to highlight the achievements and confront the challenges and problems of big-city school systems. Urban schools educate many of the country's most culturally and ethnically diverse children—some 37 percent African-American, 32 percent Hispanic, and 22 percent Asian American. Children educated daily in the great city schools account for about 13.1 percent of the nation's public school enrollment.

In many of the nation's inner cities, the public schools operate within high concentrations of poverty, homelessness, crime, drug abuse, teen pregnancies, racial tension, and limited English proficiency. These realities are often further complicated by inequitable funding for urban schools. The council is in a unique position to expound on problems facing inner-city schools and to try to match those problems with possible solutions.

In its role to represent and serve America's urban schools, the council focuses national attention on the needs and challenges of urban schools and provides a coalition through which the largest school systems can more effectively communicate with each other to reach common goals. Amidst a background of cultural and ethnic diversity, the council extends beyond its membership to other national organizations, businesses, and government policymakers to arrive at solutions and serve as the voice for urban schoolchildren through the strength of alliance.

Adhering to the axiom, "There is strength in numbers," the council links its members' various departments through a network of liaisons, including public information, technology, vocational education, personnel, finance, research, legislation, special education, and curriculum. Such networking provides an effective alliance of special interests and common concerns on behalf of urban schoolchildren.

The organization's day-to-day operations are conducted by a central staff headquartered in Washington, D.C. The council is led by Dr. Michael Casserly, who was appointed executive director in March 1993 after serving as the council's associate director of legislation and research for more than fifteen years. As chief executive officer, Dr. Casserly, who holds a Ph.D. from the University of Maryland, is recognized as one of the key players in the nation's capital to shape federal policy. The Washington Almanac says, "Casserly is considered by many to be one of Washington's most effective education lobbyists . . . and fully committed to his constituency."

On behalf of the nation's urban schools, the organization represents their needs before Congress, the federal government, and the courts through its legislative unit. The council has been instrumental in securing federal funds for its member districts and initiating various legislative policies, such as the federal Magnet School Assistance Act, the Urban Schools of America (USA) Act, the Dropout Prevention Demonstration Act, and the Teacher Professional Development Act. It also convened the National Urban Education Summit that led to the development of the six National Urban Education Goals.

The council prepares reports and surveys focusing on urban school characteristics and issues through its research initiatives. It produced the first-ever report card on the quality of urban education with its report *National Urban Education Goals. Baseline Indicators 1990–91*. As the voice of urban education, the council disseminates news and information to the public and the nation's news media in its public advocacy role. It publishes the monthly newsletter *Urban Educator*, which has widespread circulation to the media, corporate foundations, congressional leaders, and White House and Department of Education officials, as well as its membership. The council is the chief news source for information on urban schools and serves as an information clearinghouse for its membership.

Through its special-projects function, the council holds two major conferences each year that are open to both members and nonmembers. The annual fall conference is held in a selected member city while the annual legislative policy conference is held in the nation's capital and features leading policymakers. The organization also conducts special forums focusing on emerging urban school concerns and issues.

The council is growing and expanding, opening its doors in 1993 to include the largest urban school district in each state. Heretofore, eligibility for council membership was limited to school districts located in cities with populations over 250,000 or with enrollments over 35,000 students. It has also forged an

alliance with deans of colleges of education and is strengthening its development efforts to increase private-sector support for the advancement of urban education.
SELECTED BIBLIOGRAPHY
Lawrence J. Haas, *Washington Almanac* (1992).

HENRY DUVALL

***THE CRISIS:* A RECORD OF THE DARKER RACES**. This monthly periodical was launched as the official publication of the National Association for the Advancement of Colored People (NAACP)* in November 1910. From its inception until 1934, it was edited by the NAACP's director of publicity and research, William Edward Burghardt (W. E. B.) Du Bois,* the organization's only African-American national officer at its founding. Through *The Crisis*, Du Bois exerted a strong influence upon black America, particularly among the rising urban, educated, middle-class, and professional group that would become the backbone of the NAACP and other African-American organizations of the period. He once remarked that the magazine's subscription list was "a sort of national directory of influential colored people and their sympathizers."

Du Bois wanted complete freedom in editing *The Crisis*, and he frequently battled the NAACP's board of directors to achieve this end. Toward the end of his editorship, he openly clashed with the board over issues of segregation and the need for a more comprehensive response to African-American's economic dislocation. As he later noted in his autobiography, "I knew the Negro problem better than any of the white members of the board, and at the same time I was the only colored man whom they could put their hands on to carry out the objects of the organization."

Du Bois made clear the editorial objectives of *The Crisis* from the very first issue. In his words, the publication was "to set forth those facts and arguments which show the danger of race prejudice, particularly as manifested today toward colored people. . . . it will first and foremost be a newspaper; it will record important happenings and movements in the world which bear on the great problem of inter-racial relations. . . . Second, it will be a review of opinion and literature. . . . Thirdly, it will publish a few short articles. Finally, its editorial page will stand for the rights of man, irrespective of color or race, for the highest ideals of American democracy."

Throughout Du Bois's twenty-four-year editorship, *The Crisis* provided readers with a comprehensive overview of news and opinion of interest to and affecting African-Americans. Though titles for the magazine's sections changed over time, the pattern was set in the inaugural issue. The "Along the Color Line" section presented tidbits of information on current events. Subdivided into headings such as "Politics," "Education," "The Church," "Social Uplift," "Organizations and Meetings," "Crime," "Foreign," and others, noteworthy news items in these areas ranged from two to twenty lines in length. Other standard features included the "Opinion" section, which surveyed reactions from the African-American and white press to various events; "The Burden," which highlighted gross injustices perpetrated against African-Americans, including lynchings and acts of discrimination; the "NAACP" page; and a book review section entitled "What to Read." In the magazine's "Editorial" section, Du Bois exercised his prerogative to comment on any subject that interested him. Beginning with its second issue, *The Crisis* also featured an "Educational Directory," which presented advertisements and other information from the nation's historically black colleges and universities. These items were eventually moved to a position of prominence at the front of the journal, right after the table of contents. In the May 1911 issue, the "Men of the Month" section first appeared, with brief profiles on newsworthy achievers, both men and women, mostly African-American, but some white. Beginning in 1912 and continuing through the 1920s, each July issue of *The Crisis* was designated the annual "Education Number" and featured pictures of current college graduates, along with data on African-American college enrollment and achievement.

During its first decade of publication, *The Crisis* was so great a success that for several years its notoriety rivalled that of its parent organization. Under Du Bois's firm hand and eloquent pen, circulation skyrocketed. From an initial print run of one thousand copies, its readership grew to fifteen thousand by July 1911. In May 1919, the average monthly circulation surpassed the hundred thousand mark. However, by the time of Du Bois's rather bitter and acrimonious departure from the editorship and from the NAACP itself in 1934, circulation had dropped precipitously, averaging only sixty-two thousand in 1920 and thirty thousand in 1930. Yet, for almost a quarter of a century, *The Crisis* was an aggressive, unflinching monthly periodical that both chronicled and shaped the African-American protest tradition.

From the departure of Du Bois as editor in 1934 until the present, *The Crisis* has continued its coverage of African-American life. His successors made innovations that resulted in a magazine with an expanded scope of coverage to include such topics as popular culture, media issues, and youth.

SELECTED BIBLIOGRAPHY

Elliot M. Rudwick, *W. E. B. Du Bois: Propagandist of the Negro Protest* (1969); "W. E. B. Du Bois in the Role of *Crisis* Editor," *Journal of Negro History* 43, no. 3 (July 1958): 214–40; Mary White Ovington, *The Walls Came Tumbling Down* (1947); Charles Flint Kellog, *NAACP*, vol. 1, 1909–20 (1976), 92–115; W. E. B. Du Bois, *The Autobiography of W. E. B. Du Bois* (1968); W. E. B. Du Bois, "Editing 'The Crisis,'" in John Henrik Clarke, Esther Jackson, Ernest Kaiser, and J. H. O'Dell, eds., *Black Titan: W. E. B. Du Bois (1970)*.

MICHAEL FULTZ

***CUMMING v. RICHMOND COUNTY BOARD OF EDUCATION*, 175 U.S. 528 (1899).** On 10 July 1897, the Richmond County Board of Education suspended, for "economic reasons," support to Ware High School, which served sixty African-American students. However, it continued to support the Tubman

High School for white girls and Richmond Academy for Boys (a high school for white boys). This action precipitated three African-American property owners and taxpayers (Cumming, Harper, and Ladeveze) of Richmond County, Georgia, to seek an injunction restraining the board from maintaining the existing high schools for white children and restraining county tax collector Charles S. Bohler from collecting taxes to support said schools. They claimed that the board had abused the discretion provided by the statute under which it proceeded, or "had acted in hostility to the colored race." The plaintiffs argued that this action violated the equal protection of the laws guaranteed by the Constitution. They also claimed that it was unconstitutional for the board to levy or for the tax collector to collect from them any taxes for benefits denied their children. The board claimed its action was caused not by hostility toward African-Americans but by a lack of funds, which required a choice between a high school for African-American students or four primary schools in the same building for about three hundred African-Americans. African-American high school students, the board argued, could pursue their education in three other "colored high schools" in the city of Augusta. Those schools—Payne Institute, Walker Baptist Institute, and Haines Normal and Industrial Institute—were private and under sectarian control.

The trial court sustained the demurrer of defendant Bohler and refused to grant an injunction against him. But it overruled the demurrer of the board of education and issued an order restraining the board from using "any funds or property . . . for the support, maintenance or operation of any white high school in the county until said Board shall provide or establish equal facilities in high school education . . . for such colored children of high school grade." However, the court suspended the order until the Georgia Supreme Court could review the case. That court reversed the decision of the trial court against the board and dismissed the plaintiff's petition. The Supreme Court affirmed its decision. In a unanimous decision, written by Justice John Harlan (the dissenter in *Plessy v. Ferguson**), the Court ruled that a school district may provide, without violating the Constitution, a high school education for white children but not for African-American children when the reason is lack of funds rather than hostility toward the black race. Federal interference with a state program of public education cannot be justified in the absence of a state's clear and unmistakable disregard for rights protected by the Constitution. The Court concluded that the board's action in closing the African-American high school for "economic reasons" while continuing to support white high schools was not a violation of the equal protection clause of the Fourteenth Amendment.

Cumming was the first case to reach the Supreme Court after its 1896 *Plessy* "separate-but-equal" decision. It laid the groundwork for state discretion in defining separate-but-equal and extended the legacy of racial segregation in education. Some scholars have pondered the possible outcomes had the plaintiffs challenged school segregation or insisted on equal support for African-American schools, rather than seeking an injunction to close the high school for whites.

SELECTED BIBLIOGRAPHY
Richard Bardolph, ed., *The Civil Rights Record: Black Americans and the Law, 1849–1970* (1970); Derrick A. Bell, Jr., *Race, Racism and American Law* (1973); "Comment," *Yale Law Journal* 9 (March 1900): 227–29; Mark V. Tushnet, *The NAACP's Legal Strategy against Segregated Education, 1925–1950* (1987).

JAMES E. NEWBY

D

DANIEL FAMILY. Few families in America can lay claim to the exceptional educational attainment and contributions of the Daniel family of Virginia. The family exemplifies African-Americans' strength and resolve to improve themselves and their race despite harsh adverse conditions in the larger society. Charles James Daniel (1845–1916) and Carrie Green Daniel (1866–1943), a husband-and-wife team of educators, were the quintessential education advocates and role models of their time, in terms of both educational attainment and vocational contributions. Born of free parents in the state of Virginia, the couple took advantage of all the schooling opportunities available to African-Americans at the time. Their eight children continued the parents' trek toward educational attainment: six of the eight completed bachelor's and graduate degrees, and five of the six earned Ph.D.'s.

Charles Daniel entered the Richmond Institute in 1871, graduating from its normal department in 1877 and from its academic department in 1878. He next studied law at Howard University* for one year before deciding to enter the teaching profession. He obtained a position as teacher and principal of a school in Danville, Virginia, in 1882, where he remained until 1888, when he assumed the position of secretary at the Virginia Normal and Collegiate Institute (now known as the Virginia State University*), a position he held for twenty-eight years. In recognition of his long and distinguished service to the institution, the gymnasium on the campus was given the name "Daniel Hall."

Carrie Daniel (nee Green) attended Wayland Seminary in Washington, D.C., and graduated from a normal course in 1886 as the ranking student in her class. Upon graduation, she returned to her hometown of Danville, Virginia, to teach at the Holbrook Street School; in 1889, she married her principal, Charles Daniel.

Vattel Elbert Daniel (1890–1971), the couple's first-born, attended the Virginia Normal and Industrial Institute and graduated as the valedictorian of the class of 1914 of Virginia Union University.* The University of Colorado awarded him the degree of master of arts, and he earned a Ph.D. in philosophy at the University of Chicago. He taught for two years at Armstrong High School in Richmond, Virginia, and after a stint of military service during World War I, taught at Wiley College in Marshall, Texas, where he became professor of sociology and dean of the college. It was largely through his leadership that Wiley College became the first historically black college west of the Mississippi River to receive an "A" rating from the Southern Association of Colleges and Secondary Schools.* In 1943, he left his position at Wiley College to become dean of the Graduate School at Alabama State College at Montgomery. Upon his retirement from Alabama State, he returned to Wiley College to serve as professor of sociology and cochairman of the Division of Social Studies until 1966. He died in 1971, at the age of 81.

Sadie Iola Daniel (1892–1975) was the second child and eldest daughter. She graduated as the valedictorian of her class at Virginia Normal. She then entered the Normal Department of Fisk University,* graduating summa cum laude after only two years and continuing to graduate magna cum laude with a bachelor of arts three years later. After one year as teacher and assistant principal of the Owensboro, Kentucky, Western High School, she accepted an appointment as one of the first African-American teachers in the Armstrong High and Normal School, in Richmond, Virginia, teaching English, psychology, and elementary school methods for seven years. She then was appointed to teach history at the Paul Laurence Dunbar High School* in Washington, D.C., and later was reassigned to the District's Miner Teachers College, where she rose through the academic ranks to become a professor of social studies and accepted many supervisory and administrative assignments, including a brief period as assistant dean of students. Through the years she continued professional study, earning a master's degree and certificate of advanced studies from Columbia University and a Ph.D. from New York University. Additionally, Sadie served many terms as alumni trustee and assistant secretary of the Fisk University board of trustees.

Charles James Daniel, Jr. (1894–1943), the third child, was interested in trade education and studied brick masonry at St. Paul College, Lawrenceville, Virginia. When past thirty years of age, he decided to return to school to pursue a standard high school education. He enrolled as a freshman at the Bluestone Harmony High and Industrial School in Keysville, Virginia, graduated, and continued his education at the Fayetteville (North Carolina) State Normal School. For many years, he was a rural school principal in Wake County, North Carolina, near Raleigh.

William Andrew Daniel (1895–1970), the fourth child, graduated as an honor student from the Virginia Normal and Industrial Institute and also from the academy of Virginia Union University. He received his bachelor of arts degree from Virginia Union in 1917. After teaching foreign languages for one year at Storer College* in West Virginia, he volunteered for military service during World War I and was selected for officer training. He was commissioned a second lieutenant in the United States Army and was later promoted to the rank of first lieutenant. After the war, William entered the University of Chicago, where he studied both social work and sociology and received both the master of arts and doctor of philosophy degrees in sociology. His doctoral dissertation was published as a book titled *The Education of Negro Ministers*. William was awarded the Harmony Foundation medal for social research in 1926.

Following his doctoral studies, he was employed by the Institute of Social and Religious Research as an associate director, and later by the American Missionary Association,* first as a research secretary and then as general secretary. Thereafter, he was employed by several federally sponsored agencies including the National War Labor Board. His last employment was as professor of sociology and dean-registrar of the Delaware State College, where he also served as interim president. He also served on the Board of Trustees of Talladega College* (Alabama) and Dillard University (Louisiana).

Carrie Ora Daniel (1898), the fifth child, was the last to graduate from the Virginia Normal and Industrial Institute. She was an honor student there and at Hartshorn College, where she completed an academic course two years later. Between studying at Virginia Union University and Fisk University, from which she received the bachelor of arts degree, cum laude, as an English major, she was a longtime English teacher, librarian, and guidance counselor at the Kimball West Virginia High School, and later a housewife. After a year teaching English at Dunbar Senior High, Kansas City, Kansas, she married and returned to West Virginia. She obtained a master's degree in education from Marshall College (West Virginia).

The sixth child, Robert Prentiss Daniel (1902–68), spent twenty years at Virginia Union University as student and teacher. He was the ranking student of his class throughout his collegiate career, was valedictorian and class secretary, and received the bachelor of arts degree. For twelve years after graduating, he was a teacher of mathematics and freshman English, and then became an instructor in education, rising through the ranks to become the director of the Division of Education and Psychology. Concurrently, he earned master of arts and doctor of philosophy degrees from Teachers College, Columbia University, with a major in educational psychology. Armed with his doctorate, he assumed a leadership position in higher education administration. In 1936, a month before his thirty-fourth birthday, he was installed as the second African-American president of Shaw University* (North Carolina). His tenure as president of Shaw was marked by the expansion of programs and facilities and a redefinition of institutional goals and objectives. In 1950, he left Shaw to return as president of Virginia State College, where he proceeded to diversify the college's curriculum and physical capacity to accommodate a growing student body.

Manilla Corrine Daniel (1899–1930) was the youngest daughter. She studied dressmaking and attended Hartshorn College and Pratt Institute in New York.

Walter Green Daniel the eighth and youngest child of the family, graduated magna cum laude from Virginia Union University in 1926 with a bachelor of arts degree. He went on to acquire the professional bachelor of education degree in 1927 and the master of arts in education from the University of Cincinnati in 1928. Teachers College awarded him the doctor of philosophy degree in June 1941. In 1950, Teachers College awarded him a fellowship in intergroup relations. In 1957–58, he participated in a postdoctoral program in the Department of Psychological Foundations and Services that included a six-week traveling seminar focusing on comparative educational systems in Communist and non-Communist countries. Walter's first full-time teaching position was as director of practice teaching at Winston Salem State Teachers College. He joined the faculty of the Department of Education at Howard University as an assistant professor in 1929, was promoted to associate professor in 1935, and professor in 1946. He was appointed University Librarian in 1935 and served in that capacity for eleven years. He resigned from Howard in 1951 to accept a position as specialist in higher education in the U.S. Office of Education. He later served a year as professor of education and psychology at Bowie State College,* four years at the William Sloane House International Center for the Greater New York City YMCA, and then to Virginia Union University as the director of the Division of Education and Psychology. In 1961 Walter was invited to return to Howard University to plan and develop a program for the preparation of elementary school teachers. He also designed a program leading to the degree of Master of Arts in Teaching (MAT) and a Prospective Teacher Fellowship Program for the Improvement of Classroom Teachers. In 1963, he was appointed editor-in-chief of the *Journal of Negro Education.** He retired from Howard University in 1970. Walter's professional writing has included approximately one hundred books, pamphlets, chapters, articles, editorials, and book reviews. He is a Fellow in Education of the American Association for the Advancement of Science.

SELECTED BIBLIOGRAPHY

Carroll Miller, "Editorial Comment, Walter Green Daniel: Editor, Teacher, Scholar, Educational Administrator, Community Leader," *Journal of Negro Education* 42, no. 2 (Spring 1973): 103–8; L. P. Jackson, "The Daniel Family of Virginia," *Negro History Bulletin* 11, no. 3 (December 1947): 51–58; Andrew Billingsley, *Black Families in White America* (1968).

                                                                           WILLIE T. HOWARD, Jr.

DAVIDSON, EDMONIA WHITE (20 July 1903–27 August 1992). A teacher at all levels of education from elementary through college, an educational researcher, author, program developer, social activist, and humanitarian, Edmonia Davidson was born in Nashville, Tennessee. She was the oldest of the eight children of George and Hortense Stone White. Upon graduating from the Nashville public schools, she received her B.A. from Howard University* (1933) and doctorate in Adult Education and Social Foundations of Education from Teachers College, Columbia University (1958). Her dissertation focused on the study of migrant workers along the east coast of the United States, reflecting what would become her lifelong concern about the poor in this country.

    Throughout her lifetime she sought to improve the life conditions of African-Americans. She stressed community development, insisting that prospective and in-service teachers know and understand the communities of their employment as a prerequisite to classroom success with students. For a number of years she worked with Dr. Charles S. Johnson,* Director of Social Sciences at Fisk University* (later, its first African-American president), on studies of cotton and tobacco tenancy in the South. She participated in the American Youth Commission study of African-American youth recorded in *Growing Up in the Black Belt* and in Swedish economist Gunnar Myrdal's classic study, *An American Dilemma.*

Davidson's teaching career began in the public schools of Tennessee. Later she taught at Fayetteville State Teachers College* in North Carolina; Alcorn College in Mississippi; Tennessee State University, Nashville; Southern University* in Baton Rouge, Louisiana; and Howard University, Washington, D.C. At Howard she organized the graduate program in adult education and retired as professor of education emerita in 1975. Following her retirement she directed Project Cope, which worked with single mothers in Washington, D.C., heads of households who lived in public housing.

During World War II, Davidson was program secretary in the college division of the YWCA's National Board, where she was responsible for programs for 325 local YWCAs and 400 YWCAs on college campuses. She was an active member of Delta Sigma Theta Sorority, the National Council of Negro Women, the Democratic Party, and the NAACP.*

SELECTED BIBLIOGRAPHY

Obituary, *Washington Post*, 1 September 1992, C-4; Funeral Program.

FAUSTINE C. JONES–WILSON

DAVIS, ALLISON (10 October 1902, Washington, D.C.–21 November 1983, Chicago, Illinois). A member of the University of Chicago faculty for over forty years, Davis began his academic career as a social anthropologist. In 1933 Davis, accompanied by his wife, Elizabeth Davis, moved to Mississippi, where he conducted a study of African-American society. This work, which became the source for two books (*Children of Bondage* with John Dollard and *Deep South* with Mary and Burleigh Gardner), explored the caste and class systems in urban and rural settings in the South. The study revealed the complexity of an African-American community that was just beginning to be recognized.

Davis completed a bachelor of arts degree at Williams College in 1924 and a master's degree in English at Harvard in 1925. Between 1925 and 1932, Davis taught English at Hampton Institute* in Virginia and was a research associate at the Institute for Human Relations at Yale University. In 1932, Davis returned to Harvard, where he received a master's degree in anthropology. After teaching at Dillard University, Davis completed his Ph.D. at the University of Chicago in 1931.

Hired as the first African-American professor at the University of Chicago, Davis continued the work that he had entered upon with his studies on African-American society. On the basis of his earlier work, Davis began an examination of how the variables of culture and class affect the educational achievement of students. In 1948, Harvard University asked Davis to deliver the Inglis Lectureship, the purpose of which was to examine problems in the field of education and to describe potential solutions. For Allison Davis, the problem was the influence of social class on learning, and his solution was a transformation of the schools as they were currently being operated. Davis showed that class status is a significant factor in individuals' scores on achievement and intelligence tests. He wrote, "It is apparent that at least part of the difference must be due to the nature of the material in the tests themselves" (*Social Class Influences upon Learning,* 1948: 45). Subsequently, Davis challenged the fundamental assumptions underlying the measurement of intelligence and the manner by which large numbers of students were being mislabeled. He became one of the earliest and strongest critics of intelligence testing and called for reform in testing strategies.

In 1966, Davis was appointed to the President's Commission on Civil Rights. He was named John Dewey Distinguished Service Professor of Education at the University of Chicago in 1970. In recognition of his work, Davis was elected the first Fellow in Education of the American Academy of Arts and Sciences. He died at the age of 81.

SELECTED BIBLIOGRAPHY

Allison Davis and John Dollard, *Children of Bondage: The Personality Development of Negro Youth in the Urban South* (1940); Allison Davis, Burleigh B. Gardner, and Mary R. Gardner, *Deep South: A Social Anthropological Study of Caste and Class* (1941); Allison Davis, *Social Class Influences upon Learning* (1948); Allison Davis, *Leadership, Love, and Aggression: How the Twig Is Bent* (1983).

MICHAEL R. HILLIS

DAVIS, HILDA ANDREA (24 May 1905, Washington, D.C.). A dean of women, professor of English, and mental health administrator, Davis earned a bachelor's degree magna cum laude in English and Latin from Howard University* in 1925, a master's in English from Radcliffe College in 1932, and a doctorate in human development from the University of Chicago in 1953. A nationally recognized leader in educational, women's, civic, and religious organizations, she has been an advocate for racial and sexual equality throughout the twentieth century.

For nearly twenty-six years, Davis was a professor and a voice for women's concerns in historically black institutions. She was director of girls' activities, teacher of English and Latin, and registrar at Palmer Memorial Institute,* Sedalia, North Carolina (1925–32); dean of women and assistant professor of English at Shaw University,* Raleigh, North Carolina (1932–36); and dean of women and professor of English at Talladega College,* Talladega, Alabama (1936–52). At Shaw and Talladega, she was, like most deans of women, the sole woman administrator in the president's cabinet.

In 1952, after sixteen years as dean of women at Talladega, Davis resigned in protest when the college's first African-American president, Arthur Douglass

Gray, sought to displace her through reassignment. She accepted an administrative post in the Delaware State Mental Health Department in Delaware City, remaining there until 1965, when she left to become the first African-American awarded a full-time faculty contract at the University of Delaware, Newark. Upon retiring from the university in 1970, she accepted a faculty appointment at Wilmington College in New Castle, Delaware. She retired from the college in 1977.

Coupled with Davis's service to institutions of higher learning has been a lifetime of involvement in progressive educational organizations. Among her most important efforts has been leadership in women's groups, such as the Association of Deans of Women and Advisors to Girls in Negro Schools.* She became the second elected president of this Association in 1938 following the death of its founder, Lucy Diggs Slowe.* Davis also served two terms as president of the National Association of College Women (1939–45 and 1957–61), the only person to be elected to the presidency for two nonconsecutive terms. An unwavering integrationist, Davis was among the earliest African-American members of the American Association of University Women and the National Association for Women in Education (formerly the National Association of Deans of Women).

For her contributions to higher education, Davis has garnered many honors, including induction into the Delaware Women's Hall of Fame (1986); the Medal of Distinction from the University of Delaware (1987); an honorary doctorate from Trinity College of Washington, D.C. (1989); and a citation for outstanding service from the Wilmington, Delaware, chapter of the Talladega College Alumni (1981). Scholarships and awards in her name have been established by the National Association for Women in Education, *SAGE: A Scholarly Journal on Black Women*, Wilmington College, and the National Association of University Women (formerly the National Association of College Women). Davis resides in Newark, Delaware, and continues her organizational work at the local and national level.

SELECTED BIBLIOGRAPHY

Patricia Bell-Scott, "Hilda Andrea Davis," in Darlene Clark Hine, ed., *Black Women in America: An Historical Encyclopedia* (1993); Patricia Bell-Scott, "Hilda Andrea Davis," in Jessie Carney Smith, ed., *Notable Black American Women* (1992); Hilda A. Davis, "Black Women in Higher Education: An Historical Perspective," *Spelman Messenger* (1990); Hilda A. Davis and Patricia Bell-Scott, "Association of Deans of Women and Advisors to Girls in Negro Schools," in Darlene Clark Hine, ed., *Black Women in America: An Historical Encyclopedia* (1993).

PATRICIA BELL-SCOTT

DAVIS v. COUNTY SCHOOL BOARD OF PRINCE EDWARD COUNTY, 103 F. Supp. 337 (1952), 347 U.S. 483 (1954). This lawsuit was filed on 23 May, 1951, by Spottswood Robinson, an attorney for the National Association for the Advancement of Colored People.* Plaintiffs in the case were 117 African-American students from segregated Moton High School, in Farmville, Virginia, the county seat of Prince Edward County.* The suit was named for the first student on the list of plaintiffs, Dorothy E. Davis, a ninth-grader at Moton in 1951. It was pursued in the aftermath of a student-initiated strike that had begun on 22 April 1951. The original goal of the strike was to achieve recognition of the need for adequate school facilities for African-American children. However, when NAACP attorneys appeared in Farmville in response to a letter from the striking students, they explained that they could not support the aim of separate educational facilities; they would, however, sue the county to obtain desegregated schools.

Davis was heard in U.S. District Court, in Richmond, Virginia, on 25 February 1952. On 7 May 1952, the three-judge bench agreed that, compared to the county's white school, Moton was inferior in terms of physical plant, curricula, and transportation. They stated that these deficiencies should be corrected, but ruled in favor of keeping Virginia schools racially separate. An appeal was filed with the Supreme Court on 12 July 1952. At the request of the Supreme Court, *Davis* and four other school segregation cases were consolidated. The first of these consolidated cases to be argued was *Brown v. Board of Education of Topeka, Kansas.**

When the ruling on the *Brown* case was announced on 17 May 1954, political leaders in Virginia enacted policies to block the desegregation of public schools. These policies, known as "massive resistance," gave the governor authority to block funding to any school that was ordered or otherwise attempted to desegregate. Under massive-resistance laws, Virginians could obtain tuition grants for children enrolled in private schools, thereby allowing them to avoid any school that might be desegregated. Subsequently, in the fall of 1958, public schools in Virginia's Norfolk, Charlottesville, and Warren counties were closed in defiance of desegregation orders. However, with the collapse of massive-resistance laws in January 1959, they all reopened in the spring.

Prince Edward County, Virginia, closed its public schools on 2 June 1959, as the *Davis* suit was being fought as part of *Brown,* at the federal rather than state level. The county's public schools remained closed until September 1964, when, under pressure from the Supreme Court, the county was forced to reinstate a system of public education for all its children.

SELECTED BIBLIOGRAPHY

Margaret Hale-Smith, "The Effect of Early Educational Disruption on the Belief Systems and Educational Practices of Adults," *Journal of Negro Education* (Spring 1993): 171–189; Bob Smith, *They Closed Their Schools: Prince Edward County, Virginia, 1951–1954* (1965).

MARGARET E. HALE-SMITH

DEVELOPMENTAL EDUCATION, AFRICAN-AMERICANS AND. Developmental education is a system of instructional strategies intended to correct students' academic shortcomings and maximize their potential for academic success. As known and practiced in institutions of higher education, developmental education is designed to assist underprepared college students to acquire the personal, social, and academic skills necessary for success in college. Underprepared students have been defined as "those whose skills, knowledge, and academic ability are significantly below those of the 'typical' student in the college or curriculum in which they are enrolled." Thus, underpreparedness is relative to the particular institution—its entrance standards, the expectations of its faculty, and the characteristics of its average student. With a growing enrollment of underprepared students, caused in part by relaxed standards for high school graduation and the entrance of nontraditional students (e.g., returning older students), colleges and universities throughout the country have instituted learning centers and tutorial programs to aid not only disadvantaged students, but students in general.

Unlike remedial education, which seeks to "remedy" or correct academic shortcomings, developmental education takes a holistic approach to correcting deficiencies by addressing not only the scholastic needs of students but also their psychosocial needs as related to academic deficiencies. This is done through diagnostic assessment, proper placement, appropriate instruction, guidance, and counseling. The actual structure in which developmental education is delivered may range from individual or group tutoring for regular college classes to basic skills courses (especially in English, mathematics, writing, and study skills) that may be required prior to taking freshman-level college courses.

While developmental education has been part of the history of higher education in the United States since the mid-1800s, it gained prominence in the mid-1960s and early 1970s, when civil rights laws provided greater access to higher education for African-Americans and other disenfranchised groups. According to "One-Third of a Nation," a 1988 report by the Commission on Minority Participation in Education and American Life, the percentage of African-American high school graduates under twenty-four years of age who were enrolled in or had completed one or more years of college rose from 39 percent to 48 percent between 1970 and 1975. For the most part, this growth took place in colleges and universities that were previously closed to the average African-American student. These colleges and universities, aided by federal funding and pressured by political considerations, opened their doors to a large population of African-American students.

Whereas the majority of African-American students who attended institutions of higher education prior to the 1960s had attended historically black colleges and universities (HBCUs), large numbers of them now attended prestigious white institutions of higher learning. These institutions were able to lure high achieving African-American students with scholarships made possible through government funds and foundations grants. This had a domino effect on recruitment efforts of other institutions of higher learning, as white state institutions who were also pressured to recruit African-American students vied with the

HBCUs for what was left of the college-bound African-American population. Again, the white institutions were able to attract large numbers of African-American students with scholarship offers, attractive campus facilities and special programs. With the exception of African-American students whose parents and supporters insisted that they attend black schools, the HBCUs were left to scout among the "at-risk" population to fill their classrooms, resulting in the recruitment of many students whose preparation for college, both academic and social, was inadequate to meet the standards of their respective institutions. Coupled with the open-admission policies adopted by many two-and four-year state institutions, this situation necessitated the establishment of support systems to assist in the retention of underprepared college students, many of whom were African-American.

Support systems provided by the various colleges and universities differed according to their commitment to the retention and graduation of underprepared students. Those institutions with little or no commitment to underprepared students offered no special support beyond what was available to all students. These institutions became "revolving doors" for many African-Americans students. Far more African-American students matriculated into these institutions than graduated. Those institutions with some degree of commitment to assisting underprepared students provided remedial and developmental programs.

According to a 1991 survey of 826 two- and four-year public and private institutions in the Southern Regional Education Board (SREB) states, over 90 percent of the public colleges and universities and 85 percent of all institutions had remedial/developmental programs. More than a third of the first-time freshmen were enrolled in at least one remedial course. College students who were African-American or Hispanic were much more likely to be enrolled in remedial/developmental courses than were students of any other race or ethnic group. Among all institutions, 53 percent of African-American first-time entering students were enrolled in at least one remedial reading, writing, or mathematics course. The remedial enrollment rates for African-American students ranged from 50 percent at private colleges to almost 60 percent at public liberal arts/comprehensive colleges. African-American students attending public liberal arts/comprehensive colleges were twice as likely as other racial/ethnic groups to be enrolled in a remedial/developmental course. At public doctoral/research institutions, this percentage increased to more than three times the rate of white students and to ten times the rate of Asian/Pacific Islanders. Even in private institutions, the remedial enrollment rate of African-American students was ten percentage points higher than the nearest race/ethnic group (nonresident aliens).

SELECTED BIBLIOGRAPHY

Allen B. Ballard, *The Education of Black Folk* (1973); J. S. Brubacher and R. Willis, *Higher Education in Transition: A History of American Colleges and Universities 1636–1976*, 3d ed. (1976); Commission on Minority Participation in Education and American Life, *One-Third of a Nation* (1988); Martha Maxwell, *Improving Student Learning Skills*

(1988); Southern Regional Education Board, *Issues in Higher Education*, SREB Report No. 25 (1991).

DOROTHY L. ALEXANDER

DILLARD UNIVERSITY. Dillard University is a private, coeducational, undergraduate, liberal arts college, related to the United Church of Christ and the United Methodist Church. The university is accredited by the Commission on Colleges of the Southern Association of Colleges and Schools* to award the baccalaureate level degree. It is also accredited by the Department of Education of Louisiana and listed by the University Senate of the United Methodist Church. Dillard is a member of the Association of American Colleges and the American Council on Education. The nursing program is accredited by the National League for Nursing. The curricula of each of the other divisions of instruction are approved by the concerned accrediting agency. The university is also approved by the Veterans Administration for training under the provisions of Public Laws 346, 16, and 550. Dillard offers a curriculum organized under the divisions of education, humanities, natural sciences, nursing, the social sciences, and business administration. Majors are offered in more than thirty areas. The university awards the bachelor of arts degree, the bachelor of science degree, and the bachelor of science in nursing degree. There are approximately one hundred institutional faculty members. Located in New Orleans, Louisiana, Dillard's physical facilities include some of the best in the region.

SELECTED BIBLIOGRAPHY

National Association for Equal Opportunity in Higher Education, *Profiles of the Nation's Historically and Predominantly Black Colleges and Universities* (1993).

SAMUEL L. MYERS

DRAKE, JOHN GIBBS ST. CLAIR (2 January 1911, Suffolk, Virginia–14 June 1990, Palo Alto, California). A sociologist, anthropologist, educator, and social activist, St. Clair Drake received a B.S. degree (with honors) from Hampton University* (Va.) in 1931; and the Ph.D. from the University of Chicago in 1948. Drake holds a central place in the formation of the African-American studies movement in the United States during the 1960s and 1970s; in 1969, he organized and developed one of the leading programs in the field at Stanford University, Palo Alto, California. A 1974 survey by James E. Conyers and Edgar G. Epps* placed Drake among the ten most important African-American sociologists for his contributions to the discipline.

Drake's academic career stretched over almost sixty years, beginning in 1932–35, when he was a secondary school teacher at Christiansburg Institute in Cambria, Virginia. He later taught on the college level at Dillard University,* New Orleans, 1935–46, and at Roosevelt University, Chicago, Illinois, 1946–58 and 1961–69, headed the Department of Sociology at the University of Ghana, 1958–61; and taught at Stanford University, where he served as professor of sociology and anthropology, chairperson of the African and Afro-American Studies Program, 1969–76, and professor emeritus to 1990.

A fervent social activist, Drake refused to serve in a segregated United States armed forces during World War II and instead joined the integrated merchant marines, where he served as a pharmacist's mate, first class. His duties included being in charge of X-ray statistical work. A Pan-Africanist in outlook, Drake's life and work emphasized a Third World and black perspective in understanding issues facing African peoples at home and abroad. Likewise, his career was spent in service to African peoples around the world. In addition to his teaching in Africa, he was an advisor to several African leaders during the postcolonial era, including Prime Minister Kwame Nkrumah of Ghana. In 1961, 1962, and 1964, he served on the training staff of the Peace Corps for Ghana. He also aided in the development of several organizations, which sought to promote the study of African and black life outside of the continent, including the American Society for African Culture and the American Negro Leadership Conference on Africa.

A productive scholar, Drake wrote eight books and dozens of articles, which explored the complex relationships among capitalism, nationalism, and race relations in the ancient and modern worlds. His three most significant books are *Churches and Voluntary Associations among Negroes in Chicago* (1940); *Black Metropolis: A Study of Negro Life in a Northern City*, written with Horace Cayton (1945; revised and enlarged, 1962, 1970), which has been called "a landmark of objective research and one of the best urban studies produced by American scholarship"; and *Black Folk Here and There* (1987), referred to by one critic as a major investigation of "the relation between anthropology and history."

Drake was the recipient of many honors for his work as a scholar and social reformer, including membership as an honorary fellow of the Royal Anthropological Society of Great Britain and Ireland. He was married to Elizabeth Dewey Johns, and they were the parents of two children, Sandra and Karl. Drake died of a heart attack at the age of 79 and was cremated in Palo Alto, California.

SELECTED BIBLIOGRAPHY

George Clement Bond, "A Social Portrait of John Gibbs St. Clair Drake: An American Anthropologist," *American Ethnologist* 5, no. 4 (November 1988): 762–81; James E. Conyers and Edgar G. Epps, "A Profile of Black Sociologists," in James E. Blackwell and Morris Janowitz, eds., *Black Sociologists: Historical and Contemporary Perspectives* (1974); St. Clair Drake, *The American Dream and the Negro. 100 Years of Freedom?* (1963); St. Clair Drake and Peter Omari, *Social Work in West Africa* (1963), *Race Relations in a Time of Rapid Social Change* (1966), *The Redemption of African and Black Religion* (1970), *Teaching Black: An Evaluation of Methods and Resources* (1971); Charles Moritz, ed., *Current Biography Yearbook 1990* (1990); James A. Page and Joe Min Roh, comp., *Selected Black American, African, and Caribbean Authors: A Bio-Bibliography* (1985); Anna Rothe, ed., *Current Biography 1964* (1947); "St. Clair Drake, 79, Scholar-Author, Dies," *Jet* 78, no. 13 9 July 1990): 53–54; Gloria Waite, "St. Clair

Drake,'' in Charles D. Lowery and John F. Marszalek, eds., *Encyclopedia of African American Civil Rights* (1992).

JULIUS E. THOMPSON

DROPOUTS, AFRICAN-AMERICAN STUDENTS AS. Approximately seven hundred thousand students drop out of high schools each year and another three hundred thousand are chronically truant; nationally, one of every four students entering the eighth grade will drop out before graduating. This ratio increases to two of four in the inner cities; dropout estimates for Native American, Hispanic, and African-American youth range from 35 to 85 percent. While the high school graduation rates of African-Americans have steadily improved over the last two decades, it is conservatively estimated that as many as 30 percent of eighteen-to twenty-four-year-old African-Americans are still not graduating from high school. Estimates of African-American dropouts should always be viewed as conservative because of the limitations of the methodologies used to calculate these data.

Gender differences are also evident in the dropout statistics. Of the primary reasons that African-American males dropped out of high school in 1979, disliking school was first (29%), followed by students having been expelled or suspended (18%) and their desire to work (12%). Twenty-one percent cited ''other'' reasons. For African-American females, 41 percent left school because of pregnancy, and 18 percent said they disliked school. Forty-one percent cited other reasons that included home responsibilities (8%), poor performance in school (5%), and having been previously expelled or suspended (5%). By way of comparison, white males' primary reasons for leaving school were disliking school (37%), their desire to work (15%), and having been expelled or suspended (9%). White females cited disliking school (27%), marriage (17%), and pregnancy (14%) as their major reasons for leaving.

Analyses by race, sex, and ethnicity show that school-related processes and economic reasons are key determinants of a student's propensity to drop out of school. However, it is ironic that economic reasons are cited as key factors influencing the decision by many poor and nonwhite students to drop out of school, because those young people who do will find it more difficult to obtain and keep jobs throughout their lives, given their lack of education and lower academic skills. According to recent census unemployment data, more than half of African-American high school graduates are unemployed, compared to approximately three fourths of African-American high school dropouts. However, less than 20 percent of white high school graduates were unemployed, compared to more than a third of white high school dropouts. These data, which show that even those African-Americans who are high school graduates have a very difficult time securing gainful employment after twelve years of schooling, suggest that there are fewer economic incentives for nonwhite students to stay in school.

Even though there are many dropout prevention programs across the country, a 1987 survey of more than one thousand programs by the U.S. General Accounting Office showed that only a slight majority of the students served by these programs are nonwhite. Approximately 34 percent of the youth served were black, 17 percent Hispanic, and 4 percent from other racial groups, while 45 percent were white. Males constituted about 54 percent of the students served. About three quarters (76%) were from poor families, with 67 percent from urban and 14 percent from rural areas. Fifty-nine percent were under sixteen years of age. This survey also showed that approximately three fourths of the youth in these programs were potential dropouts, and one fourth had dropped out at some time. Almost half of the programs (47%) were also targeted toward potential dropouts. Programs such as Urban League Street Academies and similar alternatives have been very successful in helping more students, especially African-Americans, to return to high school and complete their degrees during the 1970s and 1980s.

SELECTED BIBLIOGRAPHY

Children's Defense Fund, *Children out of School in America* (1974); Antoine M. Garibaldi and Melinda Bartley, "Black School Pushouts and Dropouts: Strategies for Reduction," in Willy DeMarcell and Eva Chunn, eds., *Black Education: A Quest for Equity and Excellence* (1990); Russell W. Rumberger, "High School Dropouts: A Review of Issues and Evidence," *Review of Educational Research* 57, no. 2 (Summer 1987); Russell W. Rumberger, "Dropping Out of High School: The Influence of Race, Sex and Family Background," *American Educational Research Journal* 20, no. 2 (Summer 1983).

ANTOINE M. GARIBALDI

DUAL SYSTEMS OF EDUCATION. In 1954, when the landmark *Brown v. Board of Education of Topeka, Kansas** decision was rendered, compulsory, de jure segregation of African-American and white schoolchildren was maintained in seventeen states (Alabama, Arkansas, Delaware, Florida, Georgia, Kentucky, Louisiana, Maryland, Mississippi, Missouri, North Carolina, Oklahoma, South Carolina, Tennessee, Texas, Virginia, and West Virginia) and the District of Columbia. In addition, laws in four other states (Arizona, Kansas, New Mexico, and Wyoming) permitted segregation in varying degrees. But even this list, of twenty-one states and the nation's capital, whose educational practices were outlawed as violating the equal protection clause of the Fourteenth Amendment to the Constitution (the Fifth Amendment in Washington, D.C.) underestimates the extent and the legacy of public school segregation in the United States: at least thirty-three states at one time or another legally mandated or permitted single-race educational facilities. Indiana repealed its permissive segregation legislation only in 1949, while Arizona required segregation at the grade-school level until 1951, when it was made optional. Moreover, as late as the 1940s and 1950s widespread segregation without legal sanction was openly flaunted in a number of prominent settings throughout the United States, most notably in some of the urban areas of Ohio and in southern Illinois and New Jersey, while officials in many large

metropolitan areas such as Chicago illegally gerrymandered school district boundaries and promoted redlining real estate practices so as to concentrate African-
American students in specific schools well into the 1960s. The establishment of
dual systems of education, separate and decidedly unequal, has, in fact, been part
of American's heritage from the colonial period onward.

Prior to the American Revolution and during the early years of the nineteenth
century, separate school facilities for African-American youth, often sponsored
by philanthropic societies, were typically the sole avenues for educational opportunity available in northern cities, when, indeed, any educational opportunities were provided at all. (Some private schooling also took place in individual
African-American homes, with the teacher paid by small tuition fees.) New York
City, in fact, along with a few other urban locales, developed a flourishing
system of African Free Schools sponsored by the Quaker-led American Manumission Society. Although by the 1840s and 1850s some of these separate
schools were merged into the then-fledgling common school systems of the
Northeast and Midwest, it was not uncommon for segregated schooling to continue. In 1850, in what is considered the first legal case of its kind, the Massachusetts Supreme Court upheld the regulatory powers of Boston's Primary
School Committee to segregate African-American children in separate schools.
Five-year-old Sarah Roberts had to pass several white schools on her way to
her assigned elementary school for blacks, and her father sued city authorities
on her behalf. Although lawyers for the family charged that officially segregated
schools stigmatized African-American children, that they were not equal, and
that they were not "common" schools, these arguments were to no avail. Thus,
the *Roberts v. City of Boston** case provided the first state-level precedent for
"separate-but-equal" education in the United States.

Education for African-Americans in the South, of course, had long been
banned, though before the early nineteenth century some slaves had been permitted a degree of literacy and arithmetic skills in order to enhance the economic
efficiency of the estate. With the harsh entrenchment of the plantation system
(due to rapid and profitable increases of cotton production), the rising threat of
slave rebellions, and the growth of the abolitionist movement and sectional hostilities between the North and the South, the years 1820–35 saw a wave of
draconian legislation sweep across the South, forcefully prohibiting the education and assembly of the slave population.

As W. E. B. Du Bois* and others have asserted, a mass movement among
African-Americans must be credited as primarily responsible for the creation of
public school systems in the South in the aftermath of the Civil War. The overwhelming desire among the ex-slaves for long-denied educational opportunities,
combined with their new voting rights, acted as political pressure upon delegates
at the various state Reconstruction conventions held in the late 1860s and resulted in unprecedented constitutions establishing the concept of universal education within the region. A telling pattern, however, emerged at all but two of
the conventions: that is, the delegates vigorously debated segregated versus

mixed schooling proposals but could come to no consensus. Black delegates were unalterably opposed to mandatory segregation, but seem to have been divided as to the advisability of mandatory integration. Equally telling, in the early 1860s, just prior to the passionate state Reconstruction debates, Congress passed legislation that unilaterally segregated schools in Washington, D.C. Congress, in fact, even went so far as to segregate the taxes paid by blacks and whites to support the separate schools.

Once the former Confederate states were readmitted to the Union, their "Redeemer" governments almost immediately curtailed educational expenditures and instituted school segregation legislation. Thus, it was during the period 1870–85 that segregated, dual systems of education were formally established in the former slaveholding states. But despite the fact that educational funding was decreased well below levels maintained during Reconstruction—expenditures in nine southern states, for example, dropped 21 percent between 1875 and 1880 alone—the separate schools during this fifteen-year period received roughly equal funds.

Beginning in the late 1880s, however, and continuing on a virtually uninterrupted upward slope into the 1940s, separate education in those southern states that maintained de jure segregation became maliciously unequal. As enrollments expanded within the new southern systems—white enrollments increased 106 percent in ten states between 1880 and 1895, while African-American enrollments increased by 59 percent over the same period—funds were diverted from African-American schools. As black communities were politically disfranchised during the period between 1890 and 1910, they were powerless to stop the educational disfranchisement that accompanied that trend.

A unique feature of the organized racial division of school funding was that whites in the "Black Belt" regions of the South—the former plantation areas, where African-Americans traditionally made up a majority of the population—benefitted far more than did whites living in the piedmont or hill counties, since there were simply more African-American children in the former areas, from whom intended funds could be diverted. As a result, poor white politicians in the 1890s such as Mississippi governor James Vardaman fomented a tremendous outpouring of racial animosity against African-Americans and African-American education that lasted well into the twentieth century: African-American education came to be viewed as an intolerable "burden" on white taxpayers, while absurd rationalizations took shape that African-American children were only capable of elementary-level studies or, at most, an industrial education to fit them for their future status as an exploited, unskilled working class. The 1911 Atlanta University report on the Negro Common School pointedly observed that African-American schools were worse off than they were two decades prior; as late as 1916 there were only sixty-four public high schools in the entire South for African-American youth.

Figures that indicate expenditures solely for instruction tend to underestimate the total scope of the differences between white and African-American schooling in the de jure segregated South, demonstrating only, in most cases, the discriminatory salaries paid to African-American teachers. Well into the 1930s and 1940s, substantial numbers of African-American youth attended rural one-and two-teacher "schools" that lacked desks, blackboards, sufficient textbooks, and other basic necessities of quality education. Five southern states in 1929–30 provided publicly funded transportation for 439,723 white students, 17 percent of their total enrollments, but transported only 4,970 black students, one half of 1 percent of those enrolled. Long distances to be travelled on foot to dilapidated, undersupplied facilities only compounded the disadvantages of short school terms, overcrowded conditions, lack of voice in control and administration, and other aspects of enforced inferiority perpetuated by dual systems.

Although there were few positive features of de jure segregated schooling in the South or of the often-illegal de facto patterns in the North, African-American teachers and other educators must be honored for their often valiant and persistent struggles on behalf of African-American youth. They fought a battle against social forces they could not defeat, but from the 1860s to the 1960s they created an African-American educational infrastructure that sought to uplift the race, connect school and community, and so nurture and sustain academic and social competence until such time as social change could occur.

The historical reality of dual systems of education—that is, of de jure segregated schooling—must not, however, be confused with the benefits or limitations of single-race institutions without state-imposed separation and consequent inequalities. The social, political, and economic context of the second half of the nineteenth century fostered the development of dual systems of schools for African-Americans that corresponded to their circumscribed, disfranchised role in society as a whole. It will be up to the American people as a whole and to organized, politically astute African-American communities in particular to determine the fate of single-race institutions in the future.

SELECTED BIBLIOGRAPHY

"A Critical Survey of the Negro Elementary School," *Journal of Negro Education* 1, no. 3 (1932); "The Courts and the Negro Separate School," *Journal of Negro Education* 4, no. 3 (1935); "The Availability of Education in the Negro Separate School," *Journal of Negro Education* 16, no. 3 (1947); Horace Mann Bond, *The Education of the Negro in the American Social Order* (1934; reprint, 1966); James D. Anderson, *The Education of Blacks in the South, 1860–1935* (1988); W. E. B. DuBois and Augustus G. Dill, eds., *The Common School and the Negro American* (Atlanta University Publication #16) (1911); Robert A. Margo, *Race and Schooling in the South, 1880–1950* (1990).

MICHAEL FULTZ

DU BOIS, WILLIAM EDWARD BURGHARDT (23 February 1868, Great Barrington, Massachusetts–27 August 1963, Accra, Ghana). W. E. B. Du Bois was a college professor, historian, sociologist, and one of the most influential African-American leaders in the movement for racial equality in the United States during the first half of the twentieth century. Born of African, French, and Dutch ancestry, Du Bois received B.A. degrees from Fisk University* in 1888 and Harvard University (cum laude) in 1890. He was the first African-American to receive a Ph.D. from Harvard, in 1895. He also studied at the University of Berlin. Upon returning to the United States, Du Bois taught Latin, Greek, German, and English at Wilberforce University* in Ohio.

In 1886 Du Bois married Nina Gomer and moved to Philadelphia, where he taught at the University of Pennsylvania. During his tenure there, he wrote *The Philadelphia Negro*, the first sociological study of urban African-Americans. This study and other studies written by Du Bois focused on areas of African-American life such as education, health, family life, crime, morality, and the church. From 1897 to 1910, Du Bois chaired the sociology program at Atlanta University (now Clark Atlanta University*).

Du Bois opposed the ideas of Booker T. Washington,* head of Tuskegee Institute (now Tuskegee University*) in Alabama, who believed that African-Americans would excel through manual labor and the trades rather than by intellectual, professional, or political advance. His response to Washington's philosophy was, "We shall hardly induce black men to believe that if their stomachs be full, it matters little about their brains." Unlike Washington, Du Bois asserted that African-Americans should speak out against racial bigotry. According to Du Bois, one method of eliminating prejudice was to encourage college-educated African-Americans to lead the way in a movement against discrimination. As he wrote in a collection of essays called *The Souls of Black Folk* (1903), "Work, culture, liberty,—all these we need, not singly but together, not successively but together each growing and aiding each."

In 1905, Du Bois organized the Niagara Movement* to fight racial discrimination in the United States. It existed until 1910, but failed to win the support of most African-Americans at that time. Later, this movement merged with a group of white liberals to form the National Association for the Advancement of Colored People (NAACP)* in 1909. This new interracial organization adopted many of the Niagara Movement's ideas and programs.

From 1910 to 1934, Du Bois was the founding editor of several periodicals, including the NAACP magazine *The Crisis*.* He left the NAACP in 1934 and returned to Atlanta University, where he taught history and economics. Du Bois served as a chief consultant on racism and imperialism at the founding convention of the United Nations in 1945. From 1944 to 1948, he rejoined the staff at the NAACP.

By 1948, Du Bois had become dissatisfied with the slow progress being made in race relations in the United States. He subsequently joined the Communist Party in 1961, hoping it would bring a solution to the problems of African-Americans, and later renounced his U.S. citizenship, moving to Ghana, where he died a Ghanaian citizen. Du Bois authored numerous books, among them *John Brown* (1909), *The Negro* (1915), *Darkwater: Voices from within the Veil* (1920), *Black Reconstruction in America* (1935), *Black Folk Then and Now* (1940), and *The Autobiography of W. E. B. Du Bois* (1968).

SELECTED BIBLIOGRAPHY
W. E. B.Bois, *The Souls of Black Folk* (1903); W. E. B. Du Bois, *The Autobiography of W. E. B. Du Bois* (1968); Ben Richardson and William A. Fahey, *Great Black Americans* (1976); Charles Flint Kellogg, *NAACP* (1967); Leon Litwack and August Meier, eds., *Black Leaders of the Nineteenth Century* (1982); Mark Stafford, *W. E. B. Du Bois* (1989).

CONSTANCE A. BURNS

(PAUL LAURENCE) DUNBAR HIGH SCHOOL OF WASHINGTON, D.C. In November 1870, by order of the Board of Trustees of Colored Schools of Washington and Georgetown, Paul Laurence Dunbar High School was chartered as the first high school for African-American youth in the United States. Named for the famous African-American antebellum poet and founded by Emma J. and A. E. Hutchins, a white abolitionist couple from New Hampshire, the school began in one room of the basement of the Fifteenth Street Presbyterian Church. Forty-five advanced pupils promoted from the city's African-American grammar schools comprised the school's premier class. Mrs. Hutchins served as the school's first teacher, while her husband was its first supervisor.

For almost half a century, Dunbar classes were held in various District of Columbia school buildings, including the Thaddeus Stevens School (1871); the Charles Sumner School,* later renamed the Myrtilla Miner School, where Dunbar's first graduating class of eleven students held their commencement exercises in 1877; and the M Street High School (1891). It was not until 1916 that a separate building just for Dunbar High was erected and opened. This building was demolished in 1977 to make way for a modern Dunbar campus, which reopened in April of that same year.

At its inception, Dunbar offered African-American students a classical education comprised mainly of traditional core subjects. Almost all of its early graduates went on to become teachers in the lower grades. Technical and business courses were added later. Contemporary features of Dunbar High include the Dunbar Pre-Engineering High School, a collaborative venture between the D.C. public schools and private industry.

The school's early principals included such distinguished African-American educators as Mary Jane Patterson, the first African-American woman college graduate in this country, and Richard T. Greener, the first African-American graduate of Harvard University. Its ninth principal, Anna Julia Cooper,* an African-American graduate of Oberlin College,* took the helm in 1901. Under her astute leadership, Dunbar was propelled to national recognition for its rigorous academic program.

Since 1870, more than twenty-five thousand young men and women have graduated from Washington's Dunbar High School. The roster of twentieth-century Dunbar alumni reads like a ''who's who'' of African-American achievers: the first African-American general (Benjamin O. Davis), the first African-American federal judge (William H. Hastie), the first African-American Cabinet member (Robert C. Weaver), the discoverer of blood plasma (Charles

Drew), and the first African-American senator since Reconstruction (Edward W. Brooke).

SELECTED BIBLIOGRAPHY

Mary Gibson Hundley, *The Dunbar Story (1870–1955)* (1965).

BARBARA DODSON WALKER

E

EDMONDS, RONALD R. (24 May 1935, Ypsilanti, Michigan–15 July 1983, East Lansing, Michigan). Remembered as the founder of the Effective Schools movement of the late 1970s and 1980s, Edmonds advocated a reform agenda for the nation's public schools based on the idea that all children can learn. Born and raised in Ypsilanti, Michigan, he received his bachelor's degree in American history from the University of Michigan–Ann Arbor and a master's degree in the same subject from Eastern Michigan University in his hometown.

Edmonds's commitment to educational equality drove both his scholarship and practice. He began his educational career as a high school teacher in Ann Arbor, Michigan, from 1964 to 1968. From 1970 to 1972, he served as assistant superintendent for the Michigan Department of Public Instruction. Returning to school to obtain a certificate of advanced study at the Harvard Graduate School of Education, he began the research that would evolve into a theory, and ultimately a movement, to successfully educate poor and minority children. To counter the increasingly conservative social and governmental policies of the time that blamed the child for his or her educability and minimized the accountability of school professionals, Edmonds sought to show that low-income children and children of color could be effectively taught. Moreover, he steadfastly asserted that the nation's public school system has an obligation to do so.

As acting director of Harvard's Center for Urban Studies from 1973 to 1977 and as a lecturer in education in the Graduate School of Education, Edmonds conducted an intensive investigation of public schools across the country whose records of success in educating poor and minority students were exemplary. He identified five factors that contributed to the effectiveness of these schools (style of leadership, instructional emphasis, school climate, teacher expectations, and measurement of students progress), and set about developing guidelines for maximizing and replicating their success that could be easily understood by both educators and the lay public.

When Edmonds left Harvard to assume the position of senior assistant for instruction in the New York City public schools, he launched the NYCPS School

Improvement Project. Initiated in June 1979, the goal of this project was to translate educational research findings into day-by-day professional educator behavior. The project emphasized early childhood education and demanded an end to social promotions common in elementary school, substituting instead a series of transitional classes for pupils who did not pass grades one through three. Grades four and seven thus became "gateways" through which pupils could advance only after a battery of standardized tests, which Edmonds advocated as valuable measures of performance for both students and administrators.

In 1981, Edmonds joined the faculty of Michigan State University (MSU) in East Lansing, where he served as professor of education, professor of urban affairs, and senior researcher in MSU's Institute for Research on Teaching. After a brief illness, Edmonds died in 1983 at the Ingham Medical Center in Lansing, Michigan. His passing was mourned by educators, policymakers, journalists, and community activists, who valued his dedication to the principle and realization of effective schooling for all children.

SELECTED BIBLIOGRAPHY

R. Brandt, "On School Improvement: A Conversation with Ronald Edmonds," *Educational Leadership* 40 (1983): 12–15; "Ronald Edmonds, 1935–1983: Silenced Voice for Children," *Social Policy* 14, no. 2 (Fall 1983): 5–6; "Ronald Edmonds Dies: Ex-City School Aide, 48," *New York Times*, 19 July 1983, B-6; *Social Policy*, Special Issue on School Effectiveness, Dedicated to Ronald R. Edmonds (Fall 1984); Charles V. Willie, "In Memoriam," *Harvard Graduate School of Education Bulletin* (October 1983): 4.

NATAKI H. GOODALL

EDMUNDS, HELEN GREY (3 December 1911, Lawrenceville, Virginia). An international educator, historian, and civic leader and activist, Edmunds was the first African-American woman to earn a Ph.D. in history at Ohio State University (1946). Edmunds completed her secondary education at St. Paul's High School (1929) and St. Paul's Junior College (1931). She received an A.B. degree at Morgan State University* in 1933 and an M.A. degree at Ohio State University (1938). She has received numerous awards and honorary degrees (L.H.D., Litt.D., and LL.D.) from universities in the United States, Africa, and Europe. Her major research interests have focused on African-American history particularly the history of African-American women in politics since 1900; U.S. history; and international relations.

Early in her college teaching career, Edmunds was a professor of Latin, Greek, and history at Virginia Theological Seminary and College, Lynchburg (1934–35) and instructor in history at St. Paul's College,* Lawrenceville, Virginia (1939–40). Subsequently, she began her long teaching and administrative career at North Carolina Central University,* Durham, serving as a professor of history at the undergraduate and graduate level (1941–77), and chairperson of the History Department (1963–64). While at North Carolina Central, Edmunds became the first African-American woman to head a graduate school of arts and science, serving as dean from 1964 to 1971. She has also served as visiting professor and scholar at universities such as the Massachusetts Institute of Technology (1984–85), Harvard University (1985–86), and the Radcliffe College Bunting Institute (1986–87).

Edmunds has made a significant contribution to the training and preparation of history professors and to the study of black history. In 1977, the Helen G. Edmunds Graduate Colloquium was established in her honor at North Carolina Central. She was also appointed by Governor James E. Holshouser to the North Carolina Historical Commission (1975–81). Edmunds has served as national chairperson for the Humanities Bicentennial celebration of the Association for the Study of Afro-American Life and History (1974–75).

Edmunds has also participated in many African-American civic and community organizations. She has served on the board of directors, advisory council and committees of the United Negro College Fund,* the Links, Inc., the NAACP Legal Defense Fund, the National Peace Corps Advisory Council, National Council of Negro Women, Inc. She has been a commencement speaker and lecturer on international relations and African-American history at almost a hundred universities and colleges as well as several urban school systems in North Carolina, Ohio, Maryland, and Michigan.

In 1970, Edmunds was appointed United States Alternate Delegate to the General Assembly of the United Nations by former President Richard M. Nixon. She has received recognition for both her academic excellence and her achievements in history and intercultural endeavors from the Colloquium Board of Directors, North Carolina Central University (1977). In April 1989, a classroom building was dedicated at North Carolina Central University, Durham, as the Helen G. Edmunds History and Social Sciences Building.

SELECTED BIBLIOGRAPHY

Etta Moten Barrett, "Helen G. Edmunds," in *Notable Black American Women* (1991); Frank W. Hale, Jr., "Helen G. Edmunds and Eternal Verities," in *They Came—They Conquered* (1983); Carroll L. Miller, "Profile: Dr. Helen Grey Edmunds," in *Role Model Blacks, Known, but Little Known: Role Models of Successful Blacks* (1982); Emily Wilson, "You Follow Me? Helen G. Edmunds," *Hope and Dignity: Older Black Women of the South* (1983).

BRENDA BERNADINE BELL-BROWN

EDWARDS, WILLIAM J. (12 September 1869, Snow Hill, Alabama–4 March 1950, Snow Hill). An educator, school founder, author, and social activist, Edwards was born to parents who were ex-slaves. His mother Martha died before he was a year old; and his father Jackson deserted him and his siblings soon after her death. Edwards' early life was one of sickness and dire poverty. A childhood illness left him with impaired vision and crippled. He was, however, able to receive treatment for these diseases and recovered by his later teenage years.

Edwards's earliest ambition was to receive an education. He learned of Tuskegee Institute,* founded by Booker T. Washington* in Tuskegee, Alabama, where students could work to pay for their education. He matriculated at Tuskegee in 1889, where he became profoundly influenced by Washington's philosophy of industrial education. Upon his graduation in 1893, he returned to his rural community and, with financial support from northern white philanthropists, founded Snow Hill Institute, the first major offshoot of Tuskegee Institute. Snow Hill featured a vigorous academic program and an industrial education department that taught rural citizens the skills that assisted them in overcoming the peonage-like conditions faced by African-Americans in the South. Based partly on Edwards's opposition to northern migration and partly on the overwhelming need for economic empowerment within the African-American community, the institute's community extension program emphasized the necessity of land tenure for African-American farmers and sharecroppers, some of whom received assistance in purchasing their own farms.

During the course of his fund-raising trips in the North, Edwards took summer courses at Harvard University. His educational philosophy began to turn toward a blend of industrial education and the academic focus stressed by scholars such as W. E. B. Du Bois.* This created problems with the northern philanthropists, who preferred the more accommodating ideology of industrial education espoused by Washington. These pressures, combined with his ill health, led to Edwards's retirement in 1924. From 1925 to 1944, Edwards worked with the Black Belt Improvement League, a group he organized to promote self-sufficiency and better living conditions for rural African-Americans.

SELECTED BIBLIOGRAPHY

William J. Edwards, *Twenty-Five Years in the Black Belt* (1918); Donald P. Stone, *Fallen Prince: William James Edwards, Black Education and the Quest for Afro-American Nationality* (1990); Booker T. Washington, ed., *Tuskegee and Its People* (1905).

DONALD P. STONE

EDWARD WATERS COLLEGE. Founded in 1866 as Brown Theological Institute, Edward Waters College is an open-admission, equal-opportunity institution and the oldest historically black institution of higher learning in the state of Florida. An accredited liberal arts coeducational institution, the four-year college is affiliated with the African Methodist Episcopal Church. Located in Jacksonville, cultural and financial hub of northern Florida, Edward Waters College affords its students many opportunities for career exploration as well as varied social and recreational activities. The mission of Edward Waters College, is to equip its students with those tools requisite for achieving upward social and economic mobility in today's society. The college has a special commitment to the implementation of programs designed to ensure an educational experience of the highest quality for all students with varying degrees of academic strengths and weaknesses and financial need.

SELECTED BIBLIOGRAPHY
National Association for Equal Opportunity in Higher Education, *Profiles of the Nation's Historically and Predominantly Black Colleges and Universities* (1993).

SAMUEL L. MYERS

EFFECTIVE SCHOOLS MOVEMENT. In his 1966 report *Equality of Educational Opportunity,** James Coleman concluded that poor health, poverty, dysfunctional home and community environments, drugs, and crime caused many urban minority students to be culturally deprived. Other researchers such as Daniel Moynihan and Arthur Jensen concluded that some students were not educable and that the school could do little to overcome the purported problems of the home, the community, and the genetic makeup of urban students. These researchers promoted the idea that school reform was wasted on the poor minority child. Moreover, intervention efforts for students with major differences in cognitive or linguistic styles were often tainted by racist and classist concepts. The standard approach taken by many educators was to attempt to remake poor minority students in the mold of white middle-class culture, ignoring the many positive aspects of these students' own culture that could contribute to their learning. The burden of learning was thus placed on the student without regard to his or her level of readiness, learning style, program preference, or expressed career goal. These assertions and approaches formed the basis for a school culture that expected little of poor minority children in school and society.

Out of this deficit model milieu emerged Ronald Edmonds,* an African-American educator, social scientist, and researcher, who was alarmed by the poor academic record of urban students of African-American heritage in particular. Edmonds rejected the cultural-deficit theory and argued an anthropological approach free of the ethnocentrism that he believed compromised compensatory programs. He designed a research model that challenged the traditional result of schooling for the urban poor and the findings of Coleman, Moynihan, and Jensen and earned him the title of founder of the effective schools movement. He noted that while most schools were failing in their efforts to educate the urban child, a few schools were defying the odds and were producing students whose academic achievements were on a par with their suburban peers. These schools found success with their students regardless of factors such as race, socioeconomic status, ethnicity, or gender. Edmonds studied these schools, seeking the reasons they were able to educate students effectively while others with similar demographics failed.

Edmonds believed that schools should proceed on the assumption that students have intellectual skills but, for some reason, the context of school does not trigger the use of these skills. African-American educators have a responsibility to provide all students—especially urban poor and minority students—with school experiences that will contribute to their success. In most instances, this requires a drastic change in pedagogic approach. Edmonds's research identified schooling practices and characteristics associated with measurable improvements in student achievement, attitude, and excellence in student behavior. He found that the effective schools in his study shared five correlates that contributed to their excellence: (a) strong leadership at the administrative level; (b) high expectations on the part of students and staff; (c) a safe and orderly climate for teaching and learning; (d) an emphasis on instruction ensures that the acquisition of basic and higher order skills takes precedence over all other school activities; and (e) frequent and consistent monitoring of student progress, which provides achievement data that can be used for evaluating program success.

Edmonds's research demonstrated the existence of schools that effectively taught poor and minority students, thus proving that all children can learn despite their social or economic level and ethnicity. Today, many school districts operate "effective school programs" and oftentimes the public, as well as the educators, espouse effective schools rhetoric.

SELECTED BIBLIOGRAPHY

Ronald Edmonds et al., "A Black Response to Christopher Jencks' Inequality and Certain Other Issues," *Harvard Educational Review* 43 (1973): 76–92; Christopher Jencks et al., *Inequality: A Reassessment of the Effect of Family and Schooling in America* (1972); Daniel P. Moynihan, *The Negro Family: The Case for National Action* (1965); Arthur R. Jensen, "How Much Can We Boost I.Q. and Scholastic Achievement?" 39, no. 4 (Winter 1969): 1–123; Barbara A. Sizemore, "Pitfalls and Promises of Effective Schools Research," *Journal of Negro Education* 54 (1985): 269–88; State of New York, Office of Education Performance Review, *School Factors Influencing Reading Achievement: A Case Study of Two Inner City Schools* (March 1974).

J. JEROME HARRIS

ELEMENTARY AND SECONDARY EDUCATION ACT OF 1965, Pub. L. No. 89–10, 20 U.S.C. § 2701–3386 (Supp. 1993) (originally enacted as Elementary and Secondary Act of 1965, Pub. L. No. 89–10, 79 Stat. 27 (1965). On 12 January, 1965, President Lyndon Baines Johnson sent a message on education to Congress, proposing significantly increased federal grants to improve the quality of education for all American youth. On the same day, Senator Wayne Morse (Ore.) introduced a bill that purported to implement the president's directives. On 8 March, a second bill was reported that was favored over the first. Congress declared a national policy to provide financial assistance to local agencies serving areas with a concentration of children from low-income families. The purpose of the bill was to expand and improve educational programs to meet the special educational needs of disadvantaged children.

Under the bill, the Commissioner of Education was authorized to apportion federal funds to state educational agencies for basic educational grants and special incentive grants. In turn, state agencies would allocate funds to local education agencies. Local agencies that served at least one hundred or more disadvantaged children between the ages of five and seventeen qualified for the grants. The commissioner was also required to develop plans for acquiring school library resources (books, periodicals, documents, audiovisual materials), textbooks, and printed material; providing educational services that were not available in sufficient quantity or quality; and developing model educational programs in elementary and secondary schools. Particular educational services designated for funding were the construction or leasing of facilities; acquisition of modern educational equipment; and the provision of guidance counseling, remedial instruction, media programming, and special services for students living in rural areas or isolated areas. The commissioner was further authorized to make grants to institutions of higher learning for educational research, surveys, and demonstrations; to disseminate information derived from educational research; and to finance cooperative arrangements to promote such activities.

The bill contained several general provisions. Most important, it limited the amount of federal payments and precluded federal control over a school's curriculum, programming, or selection of instructional materials. Although the second bill was approved on 11 April 1965, without amendments, it was subsequently amended seven times between 1965 and 1995. The significance of this legislation is that the executive and legislative branches of government recognized that children of low-income families had special educational needs. Federal and state interventions were needed to support adequate educational programs for those children.

SELECTED BIBLIOGRAPHY

S. REP. NO. 146, 89th Congr., 1st Sess. (1965), reprinted in 1965 *U.S. Code & Admin. News 574; H. REP. NO. 143, 89th Congr., 1st Sess.* (1965), reprinted in 1965 *U.S. Code Cong. & Admin. News 1446*; "Legislative History of the Elementary and Secondary Education Act of 1965," 1965 *U.S. Code Cong. & Admin. News 1446–1505*; "Elementary and Secondary Education," *111 Cong. Re. 1176* (1965); "Statement by the President, Following Senate Subcommittee Approval of the Education Bill," *1965 Pub. Papers* (1965): 365–66; "Recorded Remarks on the Message on Education," *1965 Pub. Papers* (1965): 33–34.

CYNTHIA R. MABRY

ELIZABETH CITY STATE UNIVERSITY. Elizabeth City State University in Elizabeth City, North Carolina, was founded in 1891 as a normal school and began operations in January 1892. Over the years the institution evolved into its present state. Since 1972, it has been a constituent institution of the sixteen-campus University of North Carolina system. The school, an undergraduate institution, with a graduate residence center through which graduate degrees may be earned, granted its first degrees in 1939, when it was known as Elizabeth City State Teachers College and was solely a teacher-training institution. Currently, it grants degrees in such fields as geology, physics, accounting, criminal justice, industrial technology, political science, music merchandising, computer science and middle-grades education.

SELECTED BIBLIOGRAPHY
National Association for Equal Opportunity in Higher Education, *Profiles of the Nation's Historically and Predominantly Black Colleges and Universities* (1993).
                                                              SAMUEL L. MYERS

EPPS, EDGAR G. (30 August 1929, Little Rock, Arkansas). Edgar G. Epps has served as the Marshall Field IV Professor of Urban Education at the University of Chicago since 1970. He has previously held faculty positions at Tuskegee University* (1967–70), the University of Michigan (1964–67), Florida A & M University* (1961–66), and Tennessee State University* (1958–61). In addition, he has been visiting professor at Harvard University, Carleton College, and the University of Wisconsin at Milwaukee. He was educated at Dunbar High School in Little Rock, Talladega College* in Alabama, Atlanta University,* and Washington State University, where he earned the Ph.D. degree in sociology.

His books include *Black Students in White Schools* (1972), *Race Relations: New Perspectives* (1973), *Cultural Pluralism* (1974), and *Black Consciousness, Identity and Achievement* (1975). *College in Black and White: African-American Students in Predominantly White and Historically Black Public Universities*, edited by Epps, Walter Allen, and Nesha Haniff, was published in 1991. *Restructuring the Schools: Problems and Prospects*, edited by Epps and John J. Lane, was published in 1992. Epps has also authored articles for several educational publications, including the *Journal of Negro Education** and the *Encyclopedia of Educational Research*.

Epps has been a member of the Chicago Board of Education (1974–80) and the board of directors of the Southern Education Foundation* (1976–86). He has also served on technical review panels for the Department of Education on projects involving the education of minority children. From 1993 to 1994 he was a member of the Southern Education Foundation's Task Force on Postsecondary Desegregation. He has also served as an expert witness in the *Knight v. Alabama* higher education desegregation case.

SELECTED BIBLIOGRAPHY
Christa Brelin and William C. Matney, eds., *Who's Who among Black Americans, 1992– 1993* (1992).
                                                    FAUSTINE C. JONES-WILSON

EQUAL SALARY SUITS. Acting at the insistence of the Maryland State Colored Teachers Association, on 8 December 1936, attorneys for the NAACP* filed suit in state court, charging that the board of education in Montgomery County, Maryland, discriminated against African-American teachers, paying them lower salaries than were paid to white teachers with equivalent credentials, solely on the basis of race. Seven months later, on 30 July 1937, just before a ruling favorable to the plaintiff, the board agreed to equalize all teacher salaries in the county within a two-year period. This case, *William Gibbs v. Board of*

Education, marked the beginning of the African-American teacher salary equal-ization movement of the 1930s and 1940s, a drive that displayed the newfound determination of African-American teachers and communities in the South to combat racial injustice in the provision of educational opportunities. Discrimi-natory salaries for African-American teachers and administrators were part and parcel of the long-standing and concerted action on the part of the segregation states to oppress African-American communities. Highly trained and competent African-American educators had been driven from the profession because of the low levels of remuneration. Moreover, in 1941 the NAACP estimated that $25 million in salaries was illegally denied to African-American teachers annually, funds that not only would have benefitted the teachers themselves but would have enhanced the prosperity and quality of life in black communities as a whole.

Salaries often characterized as hardly plow-hand wages were one of the most significant features of African-American education before World War II. In fact, given that for many years almost all public funds for African-American edu-cation in the South went exclusively for teacher salaries—to the neglect of needed instructional materials and building construction—it might be said that discriminatory salaries were a linchpin of the entire structure of the South's segregated system of schooling.

It is perhaps surprising to note that in the 1890s, just prior to the southern state disfranchisement movements that devastated African-American voting strength, the disparity between African-American and white average annual teacher salaries was actually smaller than it would be in the years after the turn of the century. That is, between 1890 and 1910, the discrepancy in salaries expanded considerably as political disfranchisement led to educational disfran-chisement. These disparities were reduced over the 25–30 years, but only mod-estly. According to one data source, in Florida, for example, the black/white teacher salary ratio fell from 93 percent in 1890 to 46 percent in 1910 before increasing to 47 percent in 1936; in Louisiana, the figures were 82 percent in 1890, 26 percent in 1910, and 43 percent in 1936. In Mississippi, on the other hand, the racial disparity in teacher salaries was greater in 1936 that it had been in 1910.

In general, the pattern for African-American teacher salaries was the same throughout the segregated South: African-American teachers in urban areas earned somewhat more than did those in rural areas, and teachers in rural areas in very small schools earned the lowest salaries of all. The effects of this dis-crimination were pervasive, given that the overwhelming majority of African-American teachers prior to World War II were concentrated in one-and two-teacher rural schools. Rarely within a segregating state did the salary of the highest paid African-American teacher equal that of the lowest-paid white teacher. Overall, by 1941, African-American teachers earned approximately 50 percent of the salary paid to comparable white teachers, and the racial gap in actual dollars (rather than as a percentage) was growing larger.

By 1946–47, some thirty-two equalization suits had been filed in twelve of the seventeen states that, along with the District of Columbia, mandated segregated schooling. Of these suits, twenty-three ended in victory for the African-American plaintiffs, and four were pending. Two of the most important of these suits were *Walter Mills v. Anne Arundel County School Board** and *Alston v. Norfolk School Board.** The *Mills* case, brought in Maryland in 1939, was the first of the black teacher salary cases to be filed in federal district court, charging that the discriminatory compensation was a violation of the equal protection clause of the Fourteenth Amendment. The *Alston* case was significant as the first and only equalization suit to reach the Supreme Court. Unlike *Mills*, the *Alston* case was initially dismissed by a federal district court judge in 1940 on the grounds that, by signing a contract to teach for the lower salary, Alston had waived his right to object. This opinion was overruled by the U.S. Circuit Court of Appeals, however, which commented in a strong and unequivocal decision: "That an unconstitutional discrimination is set forth in these paragraphs hardly admits of argument . . . This is as clear a discrimination on the ground of race as could well be imagined." Later in that year, the Supreme Court refused to hear the school board's appeal of the case.

As Thurgood Marshall,* who served as the NAACP attorney in several of these cases noted, there was often "bitter opposition" to the African-American teacher salary equalization movement among southern white school authorities, adding that "intimidation, chicanery, and trickery of almost every form have been encountered." Moreover, there were a variety of legal difficulties. For example, because education is a state and local public function in the United States, it was legally necessary to file separate equalization lawsuits in each city or county in which discriminatory practices were to be challenged. Thus, the scope of the litigation movement was daunting. Also, it was difficult to argue against racial differentials in salaries when the city or county did not maintain a formal salary schedule; each contract was said by the school board to be individually negotiated, and the salary itself to be the result of "mutual bargaining." In court, white school authorities crafted a number of duplicitous arguments: that African-Americans had a lower cost of living and thus the salary differentials represented different lifestyles; that African-American teachers did not perform the same duties as white teachers and therefore their services were not worth as much; that there was an oversupply of African-American teachers so that the market forces of supply and demand "naturally" necessitated lower salaries; and that the differentials were based not on the race of the teachers but on differences in the schools in which they taught. Regarding these latter two arguments, the district court in a Nashville, Tennessee, case observed that a cost-conscious school board should then be obliged to hire African-American teachers to work in white schools. As Nashville had never done so, the judge ruled in behalf of the African-American plaintiffs.

Such maneuvers on the part of school authorities were, of course, aspects of the southern resistance that Marshall noted. It was not uncommon for southern school boards to fire individual plaintiffs, selected teacher activists, or other African-American educators not connected with particular cases. Melvin Alston became the plaintiff in the famous case bearing his name only after Ms. Aline Black, the original plaintiff, was fired by the Norfolk school board. After an equalization lawsuit was filed in Prince George's County, Maryland, none of the contracts of probationary African-American teachers were renewed. In Birmingham, Alabama, the complainant was reclassified under the Selective Service Act and inducted into the armed services. Several of the black state teachers' associations of the period provided transition funds for fired teachers—in one instance, when Ocala County, Florida, teacher N. W. Griffith was discharged in retaliation for filing an equalization lawsuit, he was subsequently elected president of the state's African-American teachers' group.

Several cities and counties established complex teacher rating systems that either undermined the financial benefits of victorious lawsuits or forestalled the filing of a lawsuit. Although a federal court ruled in *Susie Morris v. Little Rock School Board* that the school board's rating system perpetuated discriminatory salaries, courts in other states approved such mechanisms, even those that included subjective factors that white school authorities used specifically to limit African-American teachers' wages.

Thus, by 1950, although the African-American teachers' salary movement had made important strides, full salary equalization in the South had yet to be attained. The NAACP had established significant legal precedents, and African-American teachers and communities had displayed courage and perseverance, but the scope of the problem was too broad, and racist southern resistance was still too strong.

SELECTED BIBLIOGRAPHY

Thurgood Marshall, "Teachers' Salary Cases," in Florence Murray, ed., *The Negro Handbook, 1946–47* (1947), 40–50; National Association for the Advancement of Colored People, *Teachers Salaries in Black and White* (1941); "Legal Efforts to Equalize Salaries of White and Negro Teachers," in Jesse P. Guzman, ed., *Negro Year Book* (1947), 62–67; Ada Coleman, "The Salary Equalization Movement," *Journal of Negro Education* 16, no. 2 (Spring 1947): 235–41; Mark V. Tushnet, *The NAACP's Legal Strategy against Segregated Education, 1925–1950* (1987).

MICHAEL FULTZ

F

FAIR HOUSING ACT OF 1968, EDUCATIONAL IMPLICATIONS OF THE. Drawing on the reports of various commissions on urban housing and civil disorder, including President Johnson's Commission on Urban Housing and the Kerner Commission, Congress enacted Title VIII of the Civil Rights Act of 1968, also referred to as the Fair Housing Act. Senator Walter Mondale and Representative Emanuel Cuellar were the original sponsors of the legislation in the Senate and the House of Representatives, respectively. The Fair Housing Act prohibits discrimination based on race, color, religion, sex, and natural origin in the sale or rental of most housing. The law does not prohibit discrimination by homeowners in the sale or rental of single-family dwellings. However, the act does cover activities of all segments of the real estate industry, including real estate brokers, builders, apartment owners, sellers, and mortgage lenders and extends as well to federally owned and operated dwellings and dwellings provided by federally insured loans and grants. The act prohibits a wide variety of discriminatory activities on the bases of race, color, religion, sex, or national origin including refusal to sell or rent a dwelling; discrimination in the terms, conditions, or privileges of the sale or rental of a dwelling; indicating a preference or discrimination in advertising; and denial of a loan for purchasing, constructing, or improving a dwelling.

The Fair Housing Act also prohibits such forms of discrimination as "blockbusting," which means convincing owners to sell property on the grounds that minorities are about to move into a neighborhood. The law also forbids "steering," a practice of directing a racial, ethnic, or religious group into a neighborhood in which members of the same group already live.

The Fair Housing Act has been criticized for failing to eliminate or, at a minimum, to make inroads into ending housing segregation. The main criticism of the Fair Housing Act has centered on the difficulty of identifying and proving that a defendant has violated the federal housing law. Real estate agents, owners, lenders, and builders rarely reveal their discriminatory actions, leaving most individuals unaware of unlawful discrimination. Moreover, the act primarily relies on private persons to seek enforcement of the rights protected under the legislation. Prior to 1988, the act provided for only limited relief, consisting of actual damages and up to $1,000 in punitive damages. Further, the Department of Housing and Urban Development (HUD), which is charged with the overall administration of the Fair Housing Act, was given insufficient power to enforce the law. When HUD has found discrimination, its attempts to conciliate a resolution have been unsuccessful in the majority of cases. According to a 1988 study, 4,658 housing discrimination complaints were filed with HUD; only 214 of these were conciliated to a resolution by HUD itself. There were 908 successful conciliations reached by state and local housing bodies, for a total of only 1,123 successful conciliations out of 4,658 complaints filed.

Though progress in housing has undoubtedly been achieved for a minority of African-Americans who have achieved middle-class economic status, residential segregation for most African-Americans continues today, especially in urban areas. In 1991, for example, the majority (57%) of African-American households with children under eighteen were raising their children in the nation's inner cities; 45 percent of these households were located in poor neighborhoods. African-Americans who live in segregated neighborhoods experience inferior employment opportunities and are significantly underserved by inadequate education, health care, law enforcement, and other government services.

The Fair Housing Act has been a disappointment in terms of enhancing the integration of America's schools. Today, as in 1968 when the Fair Housing Act was passed, U.S. society is marked by racially separate school systems and residential neighborhoods.

SELECTED BIBLIOGRAPHY

Robert Harding, "Housing Discrimination as a Basis for Interdistrict School Desegregation Remedies," *Yale Law Journal* 3 (1983); Willis Hawley, *Effective School Desegregation* (1981); James Kushner, "Apartheid in America: An Historical and Legal Analysis of Contemporary Racial Residential Segregation in the United States," *Howard Law Journal* 22 (1979); Julius Menacker, "Public Housing Policy and School Segregation," *Education Law Reporter* 50 (1989); Gary Orfield and Carole Ashkinaze, *The Closing Door* (1991); Jeanne Woodward, *Housing America's Children in 1991* (1993).

JOSEPH R. MCKINNEY

FAMILY INFLUENCE ON SCHOOLING, AFRICAN-AMERICAN. African-American families have a long-standing commitment to the education of their children. The testimony of former slaves reveals such a strong desire for literacy and book learning that they learned to read, write, and spell through subterfuge. Even though slaves were not afforded opportunities to learn, the slavemaster's legal and customary repression of literacy betrayed the master's fear of the slaves' capacity and desire for book learning.

Following the Civil War, African-American families saw education as the key to literacy, which they hoped would in turn assure African-American children a life of freedom and prosperity. Fearless in the face of poverty and discrimination and sustained by a distinctive orientation toward learning, during Reconstruction African-American parents in the South (at times in cooperation with the Freedmen's Bureau*) built a free school system. At the time, white landlords, tenants, and laborers who held racist beliefs about blacks' abilities were forced to recognize African-Americans' deep-rooted belief in education.

Prior to the 1950s, African-American children were primarily educated in their own segregated communities, where they experienced a shared value system among schools, families, and churches. The *Brown v. Board of Education of Topeka, Kansas** decision of 1954, however, changed these relationships. Lawyers and lawmakers involved with the *Brown* case took African-Americans' demands for equal citizenship (and therefore equal access to traditionally white schools) as a cue to attack the cohesive systems of education African-Americans had established in their own communities. For the first time, African-American families and the educational institutions they helped to build were judged in relation to educational institutions in the white community and found to be of lower quality. African-American families were indirectly implicated as ineffective supporters of their children's educational pursuits. As a result, masses of black students were called upon to integrate predominantly white school districts, and a significant portion of African-American children were henceforth schooled outside their home communities. As court-mandated integration began to take effect, African-American families struggled to provide school support for their children in communities that were unfamiliar with the culture of African-Americans. In the face of integration, many African-American parents felt alienated from their children's new, predominantly white schools.

The Moynihan report on the African-American family and the Coleman Report* on equal education opportunity issued by the U.S. government in 1966 continued the theme of placing the blame of African-American children's overall poor academic achievement on their families. Moynihan concluded that African-American families were failing to instill positive orientations toward achievement in their children. He reported that the ''fundamental problem'' confronting African-American communities was a ''crumbling'' family structure that failed to supply African-American youth with appropriate achievement orientations and in so failing perpetuated a cycle of poverty and disadvantage in them and their offspring.

Moynihan's thesis, linking lower rates of occupational attainment among African-American to deficiencies in their families, rather than in society and its institutions, received abundant support. Much of the report seemed to reflect the increasingly popular perception that African-American families and schools were oppositional rather than interdependent. Even before the Moynihan report, Kenneth Clark's* *Dark Ghetto*, first published in 1965, reported the findings of New York's HARYOU project (a compensatory education program) and placed the blame for black children's poor academic achievement on their schoolteachers' low expectations.

Much of the current research on African-American families' influence on the schooling of African-American children has taken issue with the negative assumptions propagated by the Moynihan report and has moved away from a pathological view of African-American families. Researchers interested in African-American families' influence on schooling and academic achievement have focused on the quality of parent-child interactions within the home as embedded within a broader sociocultural and community context. Several examples illustrate that African-American families' desire to provide their children with quality education has not waned. Rather, the institutional barriers faced by African-American families make it more difficult for them to participate in the schooling process.

Parents generally have their most direct impact on academic achievement during children's preadolescent years, when they help foster the necessary cognitive socialization that has been shown to influence academic achievement. African-American parents who effectively tutor their children and encourage verbalizations offer the best preparation for schooling. Not all parents, however, possess the time, energy, confidence, or knowledge to tutor their children. In this case, overall parental support, a future time orientation, and a belief in an education ethic despite evidence of discrimination in the workplace are crucial to African-American children's success in schools. Research on parental attitudes indicates that African-American parents' beliefs about schooling and learning have a causal influence on their children's developing achievement attitudes and behaviors. Additionally, African-American students' locus of control, resiliency, people orientation, and other personality factors mediate the home environment and other contextual factors.

The Moynihan report purported that female-headed households, by virtue of being single-parent environments, negatively affected African-American children's school performance. Subsequent research on African-American families suggests, however, that although two parents offer greater financial stability, they do not guarantee a supportive home environment for learning. Both single-parent and two-parent home environments can positively support the academic achievement of African-American children.

What seems to have the greatest impact on African-American families' ability to foster academic achievement are what Uri Bronfenbrenner terms ''macrosystemic forces'' such as racism, classism, and sexism that indirectly affect African-American parents' ability to provide a nurturing home environment. Poverty and economic loss, for example, have been shown to diminish African-American parents' capacity for supportive, consistent, involved parenting by causing psychological distress that impacts their behavior toward children. Additionally, the historical mistreatment of African-Americans serves as the foundation for contemporary racist institutional practices such as job ceilings.

The power and pervasiveness of macrosystemic forces underscore the need for African-American families to utilize extended family networks such as grandparents, relatives, churches, and other community supports that play an important role in mediating the systemic oppression of African-Americans. The rise of single-parent families coupled with skyrocketing unemployment rates in the African-American community have already caused scores of African-American grandparents to assist their sons and daughters by taking grandchildren into their homes.

Overall, in order for African-American children to thrive in schools, their schools, and communities will need to provide their families with the kind of support that is reminiscent of preintegration America, where large numbers of African-American families and schools were bonded through shared value systems in small, close-knit communities. James Comer's* School Development Program (SDP)* is an example of such an effort. Through the implementation of jointly run (parents, teachers, and administrators) school planning and management teams, principles of shared community responsibility and no-blame problem solving, and a comprehensive school plan, SDP aims to transform predominantly African-American, low-income schools into learning, caring communities where all adults feel respected and all children feel valued and motivated to learn and achieve.

Although African-American families have historically valued schooling for their children, the desegregation process and resultant community restructuring have taken away much of the proximal influence these families traditionally had on schooling. Racism, economic pressures, and the rise of female-headed African-American households have stirred debate among researchers as to the ability of economically disadvantaged African-American families to provide their children with nurturing home environments that support cognitive growth and subsequent school success. Extended family networks such as African-American grandparents continue to play an important role mediating the negative effects of macrosystemic forces. Despite the negative images set forth by the Moynihan report, evidence across disciplines implicates institutional barriers rather than "crumbling" African-American families as the primary problem plaguing African-American students.

SELECTED BIBLIOGRAPHY

W. R. Allen, "Race, Family Setting and Adolescent Achievement Orientation," *Journal of Negro Education* (1978); J. D. Anderson, *The Education of Blacks in the South, 1860–1935* (1988); J. Bempechat, *Fostering High Achievement in African-American Children: Home, School, and Public Policy Influences* (1992); P. J. Bowman and C. Howard, "Race-related Socialization, Motivation, and Academic Achievement: A Study of Black Youths in Three-Generation Families," *Journal of American Academy of Child Psychiatry* 24, no. 2 (1985): 134–41; U. Bronfenbrenner, "Alienation and the Four Worlds of Childhood," *Phi Delta Kappan* 67 (1986): 430–36; R. L. Calabrese, "The Public School: A Source of Alienation for Minority Parents," *Journal of Negro Education* 59, no. 2 (1990): 148–54; D. Y. Ford, "Black Students' Achievement Orientation as a Function of Perceived Family Achievement Orientation and Demographic Variables," *Journal of Negro Education* 62, no. 7 (1993): 47–66; S. T. Johnson, "Extra-school Factors in Achievement, Attainment, and Aspiration among Junior and Senior High School-Age African-American Youth," *Journal of Negro Education* 61, no. 1 (1992): 99–119; H. P.

McAdoo, "Family Values and Outcomes for Children," *Journal of Negro Education* 60, no. 3 (1991): 361–65; V. C. McLoyd, "The Impact of Economic Hardship on Black Families and Children: Psychological Distress, Parenting, and Socioemotional Development," *Child Development* 61 (1990): 311–46; Daniel P. Moynihan, *The Negro Family: The Case for National Action* (1965); Arthur R. Jensen, S. Prom–Jackson, S. T. Johnson, and M. B. Wallace, "Home Environment, Talented Minority Youth, and School Achievement," *Journal of Negro Education* 56, no. 1 (1987): 11–121; D. T. Slaughter and E. G. Epps, "The Home Environment and Academic Achievement of Black American Children and Youth: An Overview," *Journal of Negro Education* 56, no. 1 (1987): 3–20; R. Strom, P. Collinsworth, S. Strom, D. Griswold, and P. Strom, "Grandparent Education for Black Families," *Journal of Negro Education* 61, no. 4 (1992): 554–69; E. V. Walker, "Caswell County Training School, 1933–1969: Relationships between Community and School," *Harvard Educational Review* 63, no. 2 (1993): 161–83; K. R. Wilson and W. R. Allen, "Explaining the Educational Attainment of Young Black Adults: Critical Familial and Extra-Familial Influences," *Journal of Negro Education* 86, no. 1 (1987): 64–76.

LANCE MCCREADY

FAYETTEVILLE STATE UNIVERSITY. Fayetteville State University in Fayetteville, North Carolina, has been a constituent institution of the University of North Carolina system since 1972. It was originally established as the Howard School in 1867, the second-oldest state-supported institution in North Carolina and one of the oldest teacher education institutions in the South. FSU has grown from a one-building school to a campus of 40 buildings and 156 acres. In 1939, the Howard School became Fayetteville State Teachers College, marking the beginning of a four-year curriculum. In 1963, FSU began a program in liberal arts and now offers baccalaureate degrees in over thirty disciplines; associate degrees in twenty-five disciplines; master's degrees in business administration, educational administration and supervision, elementary education, psychology, special education, biology, history, political science, and sociology; and masters of arts in teaching degrees in history, mathematics, and biology. FSU's teacher education programs are fully accredited by the National Council for Accreditation of Teacher Education, and the institution as a whole is fully accredited by the Southern Association of Colleges and Schools.*

SELECTED BIBLIOGRAPHY

National Association for Equal Opportunity in Higher Education, *Profiles of the Nation's Historically and Predominantly Black Colleges and Universities* (1993).

SAMUEL L. MYERS

FISK UNIVERSITY. Fisk University in Nashville, Tennessee, was incorporated under the laws of the state of Tennessee on 22 August 1867. Its purpose was the education and training of young men and women, irrespective of color. The Fisk Jubilee Singers, students who traveled in the United States and Europe from 1871 to 1878 earning money for the college through their recitals, built the Fisk tradition in music and art, and it was they who introduced to the world

African-American spiritual music as an American art form. The institution now offers undergraduate degrees in twenty-one major areas of study and master's degree in four fields of study.

Recognition by agencies and organizations has assured Fisk a ranking position among America's foremost liberal arts colleges. In 1930, Fisk became the first historically black college to gain full accreditation by the Southern Association of Colleges and Schools.* It was also the first such institution to be placed on the approved lists of the Association of American Universities (1933) and the American Association of University Women (1948). The department of chemistry is on the approved list of the American Chemical Society. In the fall of 1952, Fisk was granted a charter for the establishment of a chapter of the Phi Beta Kappa Honor Society, Delta of Tennessee. Fisk holds memberships in the National Association of Schools of Music, the American Association of Schools of Music, and the American Association of Colleges for Teacher Education.

SELECTED BIBLIOGRAPHY

National Association for Equal Opportunity in Higher Education, *Profiles of the Nation's Historically and Predominantly Black Colleges and Universities* (1993).

SAMUEL L. MYERS

FLORIDA A & M UNIVERSITY. Florida Agricultural and Mechanical University, a coeducational land-grant institution, was founded in Tallahassee, Florida, in 1887. It was designated a land-grant institution in 1891 and became a university in 1953. FAMU is a four-year public institution, offering undergraduate and graduate programs to meet the needs of a diverse student population. Although historically black, the university seeks qualified students from all racial, ethnic, religious, and national groups. The university is comprised of 419 acres, with physical facilities valued at $119 million, a student enrollment of more than 8,500, and a faculty and staff of nearly 1,100. Academic components consist of twelve schools and colleges of arts and sciences: education, engineering sciences, technology and agriculture, and pharmacy and pharmaceutical sciences; FAMU/Florida State University College of Engineering; and schools of allied health sciences, architecture, business and industry, general studies, journalism, media and graphic arts, nursing, graduate studies, and research in continuing education. Current graduate degree offerings include master of agriculture, M.S. in architecture, master of applied social sciences, M.S. in school/community psychology, master of education, M.S. in education, M.B.A., M.S. in agricultural education, M.S. in pharmaceutical sciences, Ph.D. in chemical engineering, and Ph.D. in mechanical engineering.

SELECTED BIBLIOGRAPHY

National Association for Equal Opportunity in Higher Education, *Profiles of the Nation's Historically and Predominantly Black Colleges and Universities* (1993).

SAMUEL L. MYERS

FLORIDA MEMORIAL COLLEGE. Founded in 1879, Florida Memorial
College is an undergraduate, coeducational, historically black college affiliated
with the Baptist Church. The college is proud of its 116-year religious heritage
and is one of the oldest academic centers in Florida. Located in Miami, its
spacious and attractive campus spreads over seventy-five acres. Unique to Florida Memorial is its airway science program, which leads to rewarding careers
in the aviation field. The college offers bachelor of arts and bachelor of science
degrees through five academic divisions. Degree programs include accounting,
air traffic control, airway computer science, airway science management, aviation flight management, biology, business, data processing, business administration and hospitality management, computer science, criminal justice, elementary
education, English and modern foreign languages, mathematics and preengineering, medical technology, physical education, psychology, religion and philosophy, political science, and public administration.
SELECTED BIBLIOGRAPHY
National Association for Equal Opportunity in Higher Education, *Profiles of the Nation's
Historically and Predominantly Black Colleges and Universities* (1993).

SAMUEL L. MYERS

FORT VALLEY STATE COLLEGE. Fort Valley State College in Fort
Valley, Georgia, is a four-year, public liberal arts and 1890 land-grant institution
centrally located in the Georgia Peach Belt. Founded in 1895, the Fort Valley
Normal and Industrial School merged with the Forsyth State Teachers and Agricultural College in 1939 to become Fort Valley State College. Pursuant to its
mission and in addition to its land-grant function, the college offers a comprehensive curriculum that includes over forty undergraduate majors and five graduate programs. Among its newer degree offerings are those in computer science,
ornamental horticulture, agricultural economics, veterinary science, agribusiness,
criminal justice, electronic engineering technology, mass communications, and
commercial design. One of the three postsecondary institutions in Georgia previously provided for blacks only, Fort Valley State College's program outreach
is international and is supported by a strengthening grant funded by the U.S.
Agency for International Development that supports project activities in Africa
and in the Caribbean.
SELECTED BIBLIOGRAPHY
National Association for Equal Opportunity in Higher Education, *Profiles of the Nation's
Historically and Predominantly Black Colleges and Universities* (1993).

SAMUEL L. MYERS

FOSTER, LUTHER HILTON (21 March 1913, Lawrenceville, Virginia–27
November 1994, Atlanta, Georgia). Luther Foster served as president of Tuskegee Institute (now Tuskegee University*) from 1953 to 1981. Prior to becom-

ing president, he was the business manager at Tuskegee from 1941 to 1953. His forty-year tenure at Tuskegee was longer than that of any of the previous three presidents. The length of his presidency was second only to that of Booker T. Washington.* Foster grew up in Lawrenceville, Virginia, and on the campus of Virginia State College (now University)* in Petersburg. He was the son of the late Luther Hilton Foster, Sr., and Daisy Poole Foster. He followed in the career footsteps of his father, who was the business manager and later the president of Virginia State College.

Foster received his first B.S. degree from Virginia State College in 1932 and a second B.S. degree from Hampton Institute* in 1934. He earned his M.B.A. degree from Harvard University in 1936 and the M.A. (1941) and Ph.D. (1951) degrees from the University of Chicago. Foster started his professional career as a budget officer at Howard University* in 1936. He left Howard in 1940 and accepted the position of business manager at Tuskegee in 1941, He remained in this position for twelve years under the leadership of President Frederick D. Patterson.* It was Patterson who recommended Foster to become Tuskegee's fourth president in 1953.

Foster assumed the presidency of Tuskegee Institute on 1 June 1953. His leadership came at a crucial period in the history of Tuskegee Institute. The era of philanthropy was being transformed, as reflected by the declining number of individual and organizational donors who had, since the Washington era, provided substantial support for Tuskegee's continued development. With his expertise in fiscal affairs and organizational skills, Foster was able to lead the school over many hurdles toward continuing growth and prominence. Under his leadership, many new funding strategies were devised. Academic instruction was concentrated in six areas: the college of arts and sciences and the schools of applied sciences, education, engineering, nursing, and veterinary medicine. All were fully accredited under Foster's administration. Community outreach was strengthened through the development and expansion of a human resource center, extension programs, and a residential Job Corps center. The Foster era also witnessed an increase in student enrollment, from 2,482 in 1967 to 3,736 in 1981. The teaching faculty was increased to 320 members, with a support staff of 989. Several new buildings were constructed in the latter years of his tenure. Foster retired on 1 August 1981.

Foster held positions on several important commissions, councils, and boards including president, United Negro College Fund* (1961–63); member, Presidents' Advisory Commission on International Education (1962–68); trustee, College Retirement Equities Fund (1965–84); member, President's Task Force on Priorities in Higher Education (1969–70); and member, National Advisory Committee on Black Higher Education.

Foster died in Atlanta in 1994 while returning to his home in Alexandria, Virginia. He was cremated, and his remains were interred in the Tuskegee University Cemetery.

SELECTED BIBLIOGRAPHY
Luther H. Foster Papers, Tuskegee University Archives, *Centennial Tribute to President Luther H. Foster* (11 April 1981); *Ten Years of Leadership* (6 April 1963); *Annual Report of the President 1981* (December 1981).

EDWIN HAMILTON

FRANCISCAN HANDMAIDS OF THE MOST PURE HEART OF MARY.

This order of African-American nuns, the third in the nation, was founded in 1916 by Elizabeth Barbara Williams (1860–1931), a black woman, and the Reverend Ignatius Lissner, a French member of the Society of African Missions. The congregation was originally established to provide African-American teachers for African-American children attending the society's schools in Savannah, Georgia. A 1915 bill before the state legislature threatened to outlaw the instruction of African-American children by white teachers. To save the schools, which were staffed by white Franciscan Sisters, Father Lissner obtained permission to establish a new religious order of African-American nuns. Williams was working at Trinity College in Washington, D.C., when she heard about plans for the new congregation. Earlier, she had been a member of a small Franciscan congregation in Louisiana and had served with the Oblate Sisters of Providence.* In October 1916, she received the habit, took the name Mother Mary Theodore, and joined Father Lissner in his efforts.

Ironically, the proposed Georgia bill did not pass. The white nuns remained at two of the schools, and the Handmaids of Mary taught at the third. Over the next seven years, the Handmaids faced extreme poverty, racial and religious discrimination, and scarcity of members. To meet their financial needs, they ran a laundry business, but it met with little success. When the opportunity came to relocate the order to New York City to operate the first Catholic nursery school in Harlem, the Handmaids readily accepted, opening the St. Benedict Day Nursery in 1923. St Benedict was primarily a custodial program serving mostly children from extremely poor families. Over time, it expanded to provide a more comprehensive education, and the Handmaids established a primary school (St. Mary's) to accommodate its graduates.

From 1926 to 1936, the Handmaids taught at St. Benedict the Moor School, a Catholic school serving African-Americans who lived in downtown Manhattan. They also staffed the St. Aloysius School, which opened in 1941 serving grades one through eight and provided after-school care for girls whose mothers worked at night. In the 1950s, they were again called upon to provide teachers for Catholic schools in the South, teaching at the Christ the King School and St. Thomas School in High Point and Wilmington, North Carolina, respectively (elementary schools), and the St. Cyprian School (a preschool) in Georgetown, South Carolina. In the 1970s, they established St. Elizabeth's Elementary School in Kingston, Jamaica.

Their numbers dwindled to fewer than forty members, the Handmaids are presently at work in New York City, where they provide tutoring and pastoral services in various Catholic parish schools. They also run two nurseries, a summer camp on Staten Island, and a senior citizens program. Their mission continues to be one of developing within black students a sense of pride and self-respect and within white students an appreciation and acceptance of people of color.

SELECTED BIBLIOGRAPHY

"Who Are These Handmaids?," brochure comp. and ed. by A Handmaid of Mary, n.p., n.d.; "The 65th Anniversary," manuscript by the Franciscan Handmaids of Mary; Rector, T.A., "Black Nuns as Educators," *Journal of Negro Education* (1982).

THERESA RECTOR

FRANKLIN, JOHN HOPE (2 January 1915, Rentiesville, Oklahoma). A historian, professor, writer, and civil rights activist, John Hope Franklin was born the son of a lawyer in the all-black town of Rentiesville. After receiving his B.A. degree in history from Fisk University* in 1936, Franklin proceeded to Harvard for his graduate work where he received his masters degree in history in 1939. Before receiving his Ph.D. degree in history from Harvard in 1949, Franklin had taught at Fisk (1936–37) and at St. Augustine's College* at Raleigh, North Carolina (1939–43). During his career, he has held professorships in history at North Carolina College (now North Carolina Central University*) from 1943 to 1947; Howard University* (1949–56); Brooklyn College (1956–64); Cambridge University, England (1962–63); University of Chicago (1964–82); and Duke University (1982–85). He has been visiting professor at Cornell, Harvard, and the universities of Hawaii, Wisconsin, and California at Berkeley. He has served as chairman of the history departments at Brooklyn College (1956–64), an event that made the front page of the *New York Times*, and at the University of Chicago (1967–70).

Franklin's more than fifty-year-long career has had a lasting impact on society as well as on the world of academics. In 1949, he was an expert witness in the *Lyman Johnson v. The University of Kentucky* case that successfully challenged Kentucky's segregated graduate education system and won Johnson's admittance to the university. The 1954 *Brown v. Board of Education** school desegregation case defense team, headed by Thurgood Marshall,* benefitted from the historical research provided by Franklin. He has served as president of the American Historical Association (1979), the Southern Historical Association (1970), Phi Beta Kappa (1973–76), and the Organization of American Historians (1975). He was also a member of the Fulbright Board for seven years and served for three years as its chairman.

A prolific writer, Franklin's most notable publication is *From Slavery to Freedom: A History of American Negroes* (1947), currently in its seventh edition. As an internationally recognized historian whose emphasis is on southern American history, Franklin has been instrumental in having African-American history included in the academic curriculum of educational institutions. Other books he has published are: *The Free Negro in North Carolina 1790–1860* (1943); *The*

Militant South 1800–1860 (1956); *Reconstruction after the Civil War* (1961); *The Emancipation Proclamation* (1963); *A Southern Odyssey: Travelers in the Antebellum North* (1976); *Racial Equality in America* (1976); *George Washington Williams: A Biography* (1985); *Race and History: Selected Essays 1938– 1988* (1990); and *The Color Line: Legacy for the Twenty-First Century* (1993). One testament to his enduring scholarship is that most of the books he authored, coauthored, and edited are still in print today.

SELECTED BIBLIOGRAPHY

John Hope Franklin, "A Life of Learning," in Henry Louis Gates, Jr., ed., *Bearing Witness: Selections from African-American Autobiography in the Twentieth Century* (1991); Hal May and James G. Lesniak, eds., *Contemporary Authors, New Revision Series*, vol. 26 (1988); James J. Podesta, "John Hope Franklin," in Barbara Carlisle Bigelow, ed., *Contemporary Black Biography*, vol. 5 (1994).

SHARON D. JOHNSON AND EDWIN HAMILTON

FRAZIER v. BOARD OF TRUSTEES, 134 F. Supp. 589 (1955). This decision represented a significant victory for African-American students denied admission to colleges and universities on the basis of admission policies that admitted whites only. The case involved three young African-Americans who were residents of North Carolina and graduates of an accredited high school in that state, who initiated suit to enjoin the University of North Carolina's Board of Trustees from denying qualified African-American applicants admission to the consolidated undergraduate schools of the university on the basis of race. Plaintiffs filed this class suit before a U.S. District Court to challenge the constitutionality of the university's admission policy, which admitted to the university only African-Americans who desired to pursue graduate or professional degrees not offered at African-American colleges in the state, but denied African-Americans admission to the University of North Carolina's undergraduate schools. The district court found in plaintiffs' favor and rejected the university's admission policy, which was enacted under the authority vested in the university's board of trustees by the state. The court held the university's policy unconstitutional and declared that segregation in educational facilities on the college level could not be upheld even if the university's board of trustees was "clothed with authority and acting under the law of the state."

The court issued a judgment and an injunctive order against the board of trustees to enjoin the university from excluding the plaintiffs, and all future African-American applicants, from entrance to the University of North Carolina's undergraduate schools solely on the basis of race. Through an analysis of the Supreme Court's ruling in *Brown v. Board of Education of Topeka, Kansas,** which prohibited the segregation of children in lower public schools under the equal protection clause of the Fourteenth Amendment, the court ruled that the same equal protection clause also applied to institutions of higher education. The court supported its contention by stating, "There is nothing in the quoted statement of the court in *Brown v. Board of Education* to suggest that the reasoning does not apply with equal force to colleges as to primary schools. Indeed, it is fair to say that they apply with greater force to students of mature age in the concluding years of their formal education as they are about to engage in the serious business of adult life.'' The court corroborated its viewpoint by citing another Supreme Court case, *Sweatt v. Painter*,* in which graduate schools of law that adhered to policies of racial segregation were also found to promote inequality.

Coming in the aftermath of *Brown v. Board of Education of Topeka, Kansas*, which related primarily to primary public school education, *Frazier v. Board of Trustees* had a comparable significance for African-Americans in public institutions of higher learning.

SELECTED BIBLIOGRAPHY

"College Integration Urged," *New York Times*, 16 December 1955, p. 18; "Three Negroes at U. of N.C.," *New York Times*, 20 September 1955, p. 35; "Three Negroes Enter University of N.C.: Undergraduates Matriculate under U.S. Court Order—State Will Appeal," *New York Times*, 16 September 1955, p. 25; "Test at North Carolina," *New York Times*, 13 September 1956; p. 73; "U.S. Court Backs Three Negro Students," *New York Times*, 11 September 1955, p. 70; U.S. Commission on Civil Rights, *Equal Protection of the Laws in Public Higher Education* (1957).

BEVERLY BAKER–KELLY AND DIANNA NIXON

FREEDMEN'S AID SOCIETIES AND AFRICAN-AMERICAN EDUCA-TION. The freedmen's aid societies were organizations created during and immediately following the American Civil War to provide emergency relief and education to southern slaves as they escaped from plantations or were freed by force of arms or, after the Emancipation Proclamation (1 January 1863), were freed from slavery by presidential decree. The relief included food supplies, clothing, medicine and medical aid, assistance in reestablishing agricultural production, and teachers and books to begin educating the freed people. As the most urgent physical needs were met and a degree of normalcy reestablished in the South, the aid societies increasingly focused their efforts on supplying teachers and establishing schools for the freedmen throughout the southern states.

Two types of freedmen's aid societies developed during and immediately following the war. There were, on the one hand, ecclesiastical societies representing virtually every major Christian denomination. Some of these church organizations absorbed the freedmen's work within existing missionary efforts, as was the case with the Congregationalist-dominated American Missionary Association (AMA),* the American Baptist Home Mission Society, and the United Presbyterians. Others created special committees or societies within their churches dedicated specifically to the freedmen's work, including the Methodist Episcopal Freedmen's Aid Society, the Presbyterian Committee on Missions for Freedmen, the Protestant Episcopal Church's Commission of Home Missions to Colored People, and committees within nearly all the Friends' Yearly Meetings. The Roman Catholic Church joined the Protestant denominations with a very small, belated effort. Competing with the ecclesiastical societies were secular, ad hoc voluntary societies. These groups organized in the major cities of the North and began their work before any of the ecclesiastical organizations with the exception of the AMA. The more successful of them were supported by scores of auxiliary or branch societies in smaller cities and towns. These included the New England Freedmen's Aid Society, founded earliest and operating longest of the secular aid societies; the National Freedmen's Relief Association, centered in New York; the Pennsylvania Freedmen's Relief Association; and the Northwestern Freedmen's Aid Commission, with headquarters in Chicago. The secular organizations worked to reduce competition and needless duplication by affiliating in coordinating bodies, culminating in the American Freedmen's Union Commission in early 1866. The ecclesiastical groups, actuated in part by denominational rivalry and proselytism, remained aloof from the Union Commission.

The American Missionary Association, a venerable organization with firm abolitionist antecedents, was the first to respond with aid for the freed slaves, sending workers and supplies to northern Virginia in late 1861. The AMA was followed quickly into the South by the secular societies that began to organize in early 1862, working initially on the Sea Islands of South Carolina and extending their reach as Union forces moved into the Confederacy. Almost simultaneously committees of Friends across the North mobilized, working in the District of Columbia, Virginia, and the interior border states. During the remainder of the war other voluntary groups organized, and denomination groups turned their attention to freedmen's aid.

By 1866 over fifty freedmen's aid societies were sending teachers into all the southern and border states. In their first decade of work, the freedmen's aid societies expended nearly $7 million dollars, most of it for teachers, schools, and school supplies. In that same period, over five-thousand northerners, black and white, traveled into the South to teach, many giving their lives to the cause of southern African-American education. The aid societies established elementary schools in all the cities and larger towns in the South and began, on a small scale, to reach into larger plantations and towns. They extended their work to secondary schools and teacher education by the later 1860s. Most of the schools were intended to be integrated, though few white children attended them. The federal government provided aid to the freedmen's aid societies, though the level of aid was miserly and short-lived. Government assistance came initially from the Union Army and other agencies and, after the war, more efficiently from the Bureau of Refugees, Freedmen, and Abandoned Lands,* or the Freedmen's Bureau, as it was more commonly known. The Freedmen's Bureau provided buildings for schools, transportation for teachers, minimal financial assistance to the aid societies, and some level of protection against the occasionally violent opposition to African-American education. It also attempted to provide coordination among the competing groups, though it was never even-handed in those efforts. Its chief officers favored the missionary societies over the secular organizations, leaning particularly toward the AMA. In the first few years of freedmen's aid, the secular organizations raised more money and sent more teachers into the South than did the ecclesiastical organizations. Thereafter, however, the organizational advantages of established churches, the natural limits of volunteerism, and perhaps the northern supporters' uneasiness with the greater racial liberalism of the secular groups, began to eclipse the work of the voluntary societies. As the southern state governments began organizing public school systems, absorbing the elementary schools established by the aid societies, the secular societies began fading away, while the ecclesiastical societies shifted their focus to secondary education, teacher training, and higher schooling for freedmen in the South, turning their more prominent schools into academies, colleges and universities.

The South did not have a tradition of public education prior to the Civil War and had violently opposed any education for African-Americans. The work of the freedmen's aid societies, then, was important in three ways. First, the elementary schools built by the aid societies throughout the larger population centers provided the foundations of a public school system upon which the reconstruction state governments built. Second, the aid societies established the principle of access to formal education by African-Americans, even though they were unsuccessful in their commitment to integrated schools. Finally, they were crucial in building and supporting the institutions that would become most of the historically black colleges and universities of the South and were thus indispensable to the century-long struggle to protect and extend southern African-American schooling.

SELECTED BIBLIOGRAPHY

Ronald E. Butchart, *Northern Whites, Southern Blacks, and Reconstruction: Freedmen's Education, 1862–1875* (1980); James M. McPherson, *The Struggle for Equality: Abolitionists and the Negro in the Civil War and Reconstruction* (1964); Joe M. Richardson, *Christian Reconstruction: The American Missionary Association and Southern Blacks, 1861–1890* (1986); G. K. Eggleston, "The Work of the Relief Societies during the Civil War," *Journal of Negro History* 14 (1929): 272–99; Julius H. Parmelee, "Freedmen's Aid Societies, 1861–1871," in Thomas Jesse Jones, ed., *Negro Education: A Study of the Private and Higher Schools for Colored People in the U.S.* (1917).

RONALD E. BUTCHART

FREEDOM SCHOOLS, MISSISSIPPI. The Freedom Schools were independent alternative educational institutions established and operated in the state of Mississippi by the Student Nonviolent Coordinating Committee (SNCC) during and after its 1964 Freedom Summer project. Forty-one such schools were created to provide African-American Mississippians of all ages with new educational experiences and avenues for political and community advancement during a turbulent era of social change. Sponsored by the Council of Federated Organizations (COFO), a coalition of civil rights groups formed in 1962 to coordinate voter registration in the South, Freedom Summer was envisioned as a massive invasion of Mississippi by SNCC and northern white student volunteers for the purpose of raising the nation's awareness of racial discrimination in the South and drawing federal intervention to alleviate oppressive conditions of southern African-Americans. Mississippi was generally viewed by civil rights activists as the strongest bastion of white racism and resistance to desegregation. In 1964, led by SNCC field coordinator Robert Moses, approximately one thousand young people journeyed to Mississippi to work in the local projects that formed the Freedom Summer campaign.

The lessons learned from SNCC's previous attempts to coordinate voter registration efforts in Mississippi pointed to the need for a campaign centered on encouraging poorly educated African-American Mississippians to participate in the establishment of alternative political and educational institutions. The idea of the Freedom Schools was the brainchild of SNCC worker Charles Cobb, who maintained that the state-controlled educational system of the time prevented African-Americans from achieving social and economic equality. Cobb envisioned the Freedom Schools as filling an intellectual vacuum in the lives of African-American Mississippians, arguing that the schools could be used to train the next generation of civil rights workers.

In March 1964, COFO and the National Council of Churches sponsored a conference in New York City to develop a Freedom School curriculum, with input from prominent civil rights activists and educators such as Ella Baker, Septima Clark, and Myles Horton.* The conference yielded a curriculum that rejected traditional authoritarian teaching practices. It included at its core not merely the normal academic subjects but also a focus on black history, contemporary issues, leadership development, the history of the African-American liberation and civil rights movements, and the development of political skills. Other "special interest" subjects proposed to be covered in Freedom School coursework were foreign languages, higher mathematics, art, drama, typing, and journalism. Additionally, students would be expected to work on projects such as community newspapers, a statewide student conference, and local political organizing and voter registration efforts. While the bulk of the curriculum focused on students between the ages of fourteen and eighteen, an evening adult school component was also designed. Staughton Lynd, a professor then teaching at Spelman College, was chosen to be the director for the Freedom Schools.

Forty-one Freedom Schools, staffed by 280 African-American and white summer volunteers, were established in Mississippi during the summer of 1964. Classes were held in churches, private homes, and backyards. African-American Mississippians' response to the schools was greater than expected. SNCC had envisioned a statewide enrollment of about one thousand students, but over twice that number enrolled and attended classes. Freedom School teachers found themselves overwhelmed with students from all age groups. The response was greatest in communities such as Hattiesburg, where there had been previous civil rights activities, but Freedom Schools were also successful in smaller rural areas where little progress had been made.

Many of the Freedom School volunteers left at the end of the summer of 1964, and new, smaller Freedom School programs began in the fall. The impetus of these new Freedom Schools was primarily political, and their programs and objectives were influenced by the burgeoning black-power movement. The formerly integrated summer programs became less receptive to the use of white volunteers. The schools evolved into training grounds for a more politically radical grassroots movement. By the summer of 1965, the Freedom Schools were largely an organizing tool for direct political action within the civil rights movement.

The Freedom Schools project was an innovative idea that took advantage of African-Americans' historical commitment to education. Although support came from many people and organizations, the successes of SNCC's Freedom Schools were primarily the result of African-American Mississippians' determination to uplift themselves. The schools profoundly and permanently affected the lives of many of their students, giving them both confidence and new political awareness and proving that an alternative school system could be effectively created with the explicit aim of combating social injustices. They became models for the development of alternative, community-based schools and tutorial projects throughout the country.

SELECTED BIBLIOGRAPHY

"Freedom Schools Mississippi," in Clayborne Carson, ed., *The Student Voice 1960–1965* (1990); Clayborne Carson, *In Struggle: SNCC and Black Awakening of the 1960s* (1981); Doug McAdam, *Freedom Summer* (1988); Daniel Perlstein, "Teaching Freedom: SNCC and the Creation of the Mississippi Freedom Schools," *History of Education Quarterly* 30 (Fall 1990): 297–324; Mary Aickln Rothschild, "The Volunteers and the Freedom Schools," *History of Education Quarterly* 22 (Winter 1982): 401–20.

JULIE BURNETT NICHOLS

FREEMAN v. PITTS, 503 U.S. 467 (1992). In *Freeman v. Pitts*, the Dekalb County (Georgia) School District in metropolitan Atlanta sought final dismissal of federal judicial supervision that began under a desegregation order in 1969. The U.S. District Court for the Northern District of Georgia found that the school system had achieved unitary status regarding student assignments, transportation, physical facilities, and extracurricular activities, but that vestiges of a dual system of racially segregated schools remained in teacher and principal assignments, resource allocation, and the quality of education. The district court released Dekalb County schools from judicial control in those areas that had been found unitary. The 11th Circuit Court of Appeals reversed, holding that federal courts should retain full judicial control until the formerly segregated school system achieves unitary status in all areas concurrently for several years. The U.S. Supreme Court agreed to review the case. *Freeman v. Pitts* presented the Court with the issue of whether federal courts may incrementally terminate judicial supervision before full compliance with the desegregation order has been achieved or whether all relevant areas must be satisfied concurrently before termination of judicial oversight.

The Supreme Court reversed the decision of the court of appeals, holding that federal courts may relinquish control of school systems incrementally before full compliance with the mandates of desegregation had been achieved. Regarding resegregation, federal courts may decide not to order further remedies in student assignments despite racial imbalances, where such imbalances are not proximately traceable to constitutional violations. The Court stated that: "racial balance is not to be achieved for its own sake" and "where resegregation is a product not of state action but of private choices, it does not have constitutional implications." The Court restated its pronouncement in *Board of Education v. Dowell*, that judicial supervision was intended only as a temporary measure and that the ultimate objective was to return control to local authorities.

Although the Court restated its approval of the areas identified in *Green v. County School Board** as an appropriate basis for evaluating progress toward unitary status (student assignments, faculty, staff, transportation, extracurricular activities, and facilities), the Court noted that the *Green* factors need not be a rigid framework. Federal courts may exercise their discretion to determine whether other areas, such as the quality of education, should also be considered to evaluate progress toward unitary status. The Court also articulated a set of factors that federal courts must consider prior to partial withdrawal of judicial supervision. To exercise discretionary withdrawal federal courts must consider whether there is full and satisfactory compliance in the area to be withdrawn, the possibility of interconnectedness between the withdrawn area and areas not yet in compliance, and good-faith commitment to the whole of the court's decree and the constitutional mandate.

The Court's decision in *Freeman v. Pitts* represented a significant victory for defendant schools, generally making it easier for schools to be released from federal judicial supervision. But the majority opinion in *Freeman v. Pitts* also provides some additional opportunities for plaintiffs in future litigation because of the Court's permissive expansion of the *Green* factors and the Court's articulation of explicit factors that federal district courts must consider before exercising any discretionary withdrawal of judicial supervision.

SELECTED BIBLIOGRAPHY

Board of Education v. Dowell, 498 U.S. 237 (1991); *Freeman v. Pitts*, 503 U.S. 467 (1992); *Green v. County School Board*, 391 U.S. 430 (1968).

JOHN DAYTON

FUTRELL, MARY HATWOOD (24 May, 1940, Alta Vista, Virginia). An educator, administrator, professor, and teacher's union leader, Mary Futrell received a B.A. from Virginia State College (now University)* in 1962 and an M.A. and Ed.D. from George Washington University in 1962 and 1992, respectively. She served an unprecedented six years as president of the National Education Association (NEA), from 1983 to 1989. At NEA, Futrell introduced educational reform initiatives related to issues of dropouts, shared decision-making, student tracking, and teacher shortages. She created outreach efforts with business education organizations and parent groups in support of quality education while she designed and implemented a $15 million endowment fund for the National Foundation for Improvement of Education.

Futrell has traveled extensively at home and abroad in her quest to focus attention on the quality of education. In 1993, she was elected president of Education International in Brussels, Belgium. Her selection was based partly on her extensive experience in nonprofit organizational management, as well as her oratorical ability and lobbying skills. As chair of the U.S. Committee for UNICEF's Education Committee, she spearheaded efforts to create a stronger network for informing the public of its programs and services to help Third World nations. She has also a member of the National Board for Professional Teaching Standards.

In honor of her contributions to education, Futrell has been the recipient of Wayne State University's Distinguished Educator Award (1989), the National Association for Bilingual Education's Outstanding Achievement award (1989), and the Teachers College of Columbia University's Medal for Distinguished Service in Education. For her work as a social activist, the government of New Zealand honored her with its John F. Kennedy Human Rights Award (1989). Additionally, *Ms.* magazine named her the outstanding black business and professional person for 1984 and cited her as one of the "100 Most Influential Blacks in America" in 1985, 1986, 1987, 1988 and 1989. *Ladies Home Journal* named Futrell one of the country's "100 Top Women" in 1984 and 1988. In 1982, she was appointed to the Education Commission of the States by former Virginia Governor Charles Robb. She was also appointed to the Advisory Committee of the Virginia Conference of Libraries and Information and on Ethics in Politics by Virginia Governor Douglas Wilder. Governor Balilies also named her to his Israel–Virginia Commission. Futrell has received honorary doctorates from the University of Lowell Eastern Michigan, George Washington, Virginia State, Kent State, North Carolina Central,* Wilberforce,* and Xavier* universities, and Spelman,* Bridgewater State (Massachusetts), and Lynchburg colleges.

SELECTED BIBLIOGRAPHY

Mary Hatwood Futrell, *Educational Choice* (1991); Mary Hatwood Futrell, *Career Summary* (1992); Doyle Watts, *Four Educators Comment on the Redesign of NCATE* (1986).

HARRIET HUNTER-BOYKIN

G

GENDER DIFFERENCES AND AFRICAN-AMERICAN EDUCATION.
As in many other areas in American life, education for African-Americans has not been free from racism and sexism. Historically, African-Americans have been excluded from equal participation in literally every sphere of the dominant society and denied access to authority because of race, class, and gender biases. During the long period of exclusion of African-Americans from the public sphere, black women shared the experience of racial oppression with black men. Moreover, the patterning of sex roles in a white, male-dominated society provided a detrimental impact on African-American males and females in the American educational enterprise. African-American women, because of their membership in two subordinate groups that lack access to authority and resources in society, are in structural opposition to a dominant racial and a dominant gender group. In each subordinate group, they share potential common interests with group comembers, African-American men on the one hand and white women on the other. In the past, both white and black women were excluded from positions of authority and prestige that had been reserved for men, placing them structurally in the same subordinate group. Yet, because of racism, African-American women also have occupied a subordinate structural position to white women in society. Thus, white women have wielded greater power and garnered more respect than African-American men and far more than African-American women, a unique privilege of women of the dominant group. Moreover, the black woman's issues and experiences in literally every area of American life have been quite different from those of African-American males and white females.

Prior to the nineteenth century, the prevailing thought was that a good education for a woman of any color consisted of teaching her to read and write. The major role of a woman was that of wife and mother. Unlike white women, however, African-American women had no real status in the teaching profession until the late nineteenth century, at which time they became a major force in the segregated educational system of the South. After 1900, the ranks of African-

American female teachers increased as more black women were educated and as more jobs became available, particularly in the rural South. By 1920, there were over 100 African-American institutions of higher learning to which women were admitted. At least three of these were exclusively for black women: Scotia Academy (later Barber–Scotia College*), Spelman,* and Bennett.* Although these schools were frequently compared to white women's colleges such as Wellesley, Vassar, and Smith, their curricula were quite different. The majority of courses taught in the African-American institutions were designed to meet the practical needs of the black community as opposed to providing a classical education. Moreover, African-American women who could pursue an education were trained as teachers and homemakers.

Similarly, an obvious gender differentiation is evident in the relative educational levels of African-American males and females. Formerly, sociological studies of African-American communities showed that black women had higher literacy rates and more years of schooling than black men. However, this distinction was primarily related to differences in societal role expectations and individual aspirations, which were linked to the prevailing economic conditions for African-Americans. From the late 1800s to the early 1900s, the options available to educated African-Americans who were interested in careers in education were quite limited. Racism and sexism were factors in determining where African-American males and especially African-American females could work. Many black institutions of higher learning had white presidents, a high proportion of white male and female faculty, a few black male teachers, and a very small number of black females. African-American women fortunate enough to acquire teaching positions were usually found teaching in rural schools and were paid less than white teachers (male or female) and African-American males.

In the rural South in the 1940s, African-American men aspired to gain a level of independence through working their own farms or learning a skilled trade such as bricklaying, plastering, or painting, skills that were generally transmitted from father to son. In contrast, African-American women were offered higher education so that they could become schoolteachers and thereby ''get out of the white folks' kitchen,'' as domestic work was the only other job possibility for black females. The black liberation movement resulted in the passage of such federal laws as the Civil Rights Act of 1964* and the Voting Rights Act of 1965,* statutes that began to break down barriers in many American institutions. Education, participation in public life, and job opportunities became more accessible to African-Americans.

However, as African-Americans began to participate in the wider society, they moved into a public arena that was sharply characterized by gender inequality. This situation, together with male domination of the African-American movement, signaled a significant differentiation in the participation of African-American men and women in the public sphere, as well as in higher education. In 1966, more African-American women than men had college degrees; 5.2

percent of the men and 6.1 percent of the women had completed four or more years of college. However, although African-American women were enrolled in college in somewhat greater proportions than African-American men, the latter were more likely to obtain graduate degrees beyond the master's level than the women.

Over the years, African-American women have consistently moved into the teaching profession, predominating as teachers in African-American elementary and secondary schools. Likewise, at the kindergarten and elementary levels, women hold most of the administrative positions. Males, however, have continued to predominate in the administrative and management positions of secondary and higher education. According to the National Education Association, about 15 percent of the nation's 1.4 million elementary school teachers are male, and about 45 percent of the 979,000 secondary teachers are male. Beyond the junior high school level, women hold very few policymaking and managerial positions. The majority of high schools have male principals; the majority of school boards, state departments of education, superintendencies, and other secondary and administrative positions are held by males. In a similar manner, white women have been the primary benefactors of affirmative action and have secured a major foothold in the white, male-dominated academic enterprise. At the college and university levels, though the number of African-American women in the ranks of tenured professors and in the administrative positions of dean and chairpersons is showing a significant decline, the number of white females is increasing. The absence of African-American women at the top levels of academic administration is obvious not only in predominantly white schools, but in historically black schools as well.

Regardless of the length of their contracts, African-American women earn less money and tenure than their white female counterparts. Moreover, in academia, white women are reaping more benefits from affirmative action, while African-American women continue to be burdened by race, gender, and class discrimination. As a general rule, the pattern of relations between blacks and whites in education continues to be dictated and defined by race. African-American churches and colleges have been virtually the only American institutions with significant African-American leadership, but these positions of authority have been reserved almost exclusively for African-American males. In mainstream institutions, white males and females are more inclined to hire or promote a white female over either an African-American male or an African-American female. According to Equal Employment Opportunity Commission statistics for 1991, white women comprised 27.5 percent of the full-time faculty in the nation's institutions of higher education, and African-American women only 2.2 percent. As related to salary, white women earned a median $40,254 on 11-to 12-month faculty contracts as opposed to a median $38,712 for African-American female faculty. In terms of rank, white women comprised 24.5 percent of the associate professors contrasted with 1.7 percent for African-American women. Of instructors, white women represented 40.7 percent, compared with

3.7 percent for African-American women. Pertaining to tenure, 88.2 percent of the white female faculty are tenured as contrasted with only 6.6 percent of African-American females. Aside from racial biases, gender differences in America's educational institutions are apparent and dramatic. Although women represent 54 percent of all students enrolled in college, they comprise only about 27 percent of the faculty. In 1988, 296 women headed colleges nationwide, 38 or 1.2 percent of whom were women of color.

These data are reflective of continuing gender issues and concerns of African-American women in American higher education. Serious concerns continue to exist relative to recognition and acceptance of their scholarship, as well as in relation to equitable compensation. The dynamics of gender discrimination in wages, along with those of race, place African-American women at a double disadvantage.

SELECTED BIBLIOGRAPHY

D. Clark Hine, "Opportunity and Fulfillment: Sex, Race and Class in Health Care Education," in *Black Women in United States History*, vol. 2 (1990), pp. 219–30; B. Collier–Thomas, "The Impact of Black Women in Education: An Historical Overview," *Journal of Negro Education* 51, no. 3 (1982): 173–80; D. Lewis, "A Response to Inequality: Black Women, Racism, and Sexism," in *Black Women in United States History*, vol. 2 (1982), pp. 383–405; *Black Enterprise*, March, May 1991; *Black Issues in Higher Education*, 11 and 25 March, 22 April, 1 and 15 July 1993.

LUETHEL TATE GREEN

GENERAL EDUCATION BOARD (GEB). Incorporated by an act of Congress on 12 January 1903, the General Education Board was a philanthropic organization founded in 1902 with a one-million-dollar donation from industrialist John D. Rockefeller, Sr. Its goal was the promotion of education in the United States without distinction by race, sex, or creed. From 1902 until it ceased operations in 1960, the GEB awarded $325 million dollars in grants to various educational efforts across the nation, particularly in the South. Of this amount, approximately $63 million went toward improving the education of African-Americans.

The GEB was empowered by its charter to establish or endow public schools, industrial/technical schools, normal or teacher training schools, high schools, and institutions of higher learning (including medical schools and college libraries). In cooperation with state and local governments, the board also provided financial support for teachers and supervisors in African-American schools in the rural South. To achieve these goals, the GEB worked with and supplemented the income of other philanthropic organizations such as the Anna T. Jeanes Fund* (the administration of which the board eventually took over), the Peabody and Slater funds, and the Southern Education Board.

Despite its efforts to fund all schools equitably, the GEB did relatively little to help change the Jim Crow social and educational policies of the South. Rather, board officials worked with southern leaders and existing policies based on local conditions and considerations, which included segregated schooling. To gather baseline data on the state of education in the South, particularly that of African-American southerners in rural areas, GEB agents travelled throughout the region collecting information on white and African-American schools, teachers, and students. Their surveys noted that the public elementary school system in the South, while segregated and inequitable, was adequate; however, the region lacked a well-organized secondary school system to supply teachers to the elementary schools and provide additional training.

Based on these findings, the GEB decided that the best approach to improving public education in the South would be to first improve the overall economic station of white and African-American southerners. As farming was the major source of income in the region and the foundation of the tax base that provided money for schools, GEB funds were directed toward establishing demonstration agricultural projects that greatly increased the crop yields of southern farmers, African-American and white. The GEB also supported the improvement of rural teaching in African-American schools by contributing additional funds to state-run normal schools for African-Americans and to the training of African-American elementary and secondary school principals.

One GEB program involved providing ''master'' teachers for rural African-American school districts. In many cases, the role of these master teachers, most of whom were northern whites sympathetic to the plight of African-Americans, evolved into one of supervising and training teachers and assisting county school superintendents in charge of African-American schools. Substantial GEB financial support for southern education was devoted to the creation of public high schools for African-Americans. However, because white southerners neither expected nor wanted African-Americans to attend high school, these schools were called ''training institutes'' instead.

The GEB was also influential in improving higher education for African-Americans, especially medical education. The Board contributed generously to the United Negro College Fund. During the 1930s, over forty African-American colleges and universities received GEB grants to build libraries and train librarians. GEB funds were given to the Howard University* Medical School and to the Meharry Medical College.* Additionally, a special relationship was worked out with the Medical College of Virginia to give refresher courses to African-American doctors; a similar arrangement was made with the St. Philip Hospital School of Nursing to train African-American nurses. The GEB tried unsuccessfully to convince the leadership of the historically black colleges to work cooperatively to avoid duplication of curriculum, but the strong sense of independence at these institutions proved difficult to overcome. In 1924 the GEB began to award fellowships to African-Americans. The board fellows list reads like a who's who of African-Americans, including teachers, artists, scientists and doctors.

Beginning in 1941, the GEB's American Youth Commission (established in 1935) published a series of seven studies dealing with African-American youth and the effects on their personalities of living in a segregated society. One of these reports, *Children of Bondage*, helped influence the Supreme Court justices' ruling in the 1954 *Brown v. Board of Education** case. In 1958, two years before the GEB ceased functioning, it organized a conference at Vanderbilt University's School of Divinity to bring African-American and white ministers together to discuss desegregation.

SELECTED BIBLIOGRAPHY

Raymond Fosdick, *Adventure in Giving: The Story of the General Education Board* (1962).

PETER A. SOLA

GIFTED AND TALENTED PROGRAMS, AFRICAN-AMERICANS IN. The most significant legislation for gifted education is the Jacob K. Javits Gifted and Talented Students Act of 1988. The act provides financial assistance to state and local educational agencies and gives highest priority to students who are racial minorities, economically disadvantaged, limited English proficient, and handicapped. Despite the stellar efforts of this legislation, there continues to be an underrepresentation of African-American students in gifted programs. For example, the U.S. Department of Education reported in its twelfth annual report to Congress in 1990 that African-American males are placed disproportionately in special education programs, more than any other racial and ethnic group. African-American males in particular are more liable than white males to be in classes for the mentally retarded, and one half as likely to be in gifted programs. Nationally, though approximately 16 percent of the total school population is African-American, they comprise only 8 percent of gifted programs. Several reasons help to explain the relative absence of African-Americans in gifted programs, including definitions of giftedness, identification practices, inadequate teacher preparation, and a lack of parent involvement in the educational process.

There is little consensus regarding how best to define the term "gifted." The federal government has proposed four definitions of gifted and talented students since 1970: Generally, the term "gifted and talented children" applies to those children who have outstanding intellectual ability or creative talent, the development of which requires special activities or services not ordinarily provided by local educational agencies. This definition also encompasses those children identified by professionally qualified persons as being capable of high performance and as having demonstrated and/or potential ability in any one of the following areas, singly or in combination: general intellectual ability, specific academic aptitude (grades in a particular subject area), creative or productive thinking, leadership ability, ability in the visual or performing arts, and psychomotor ability—and who by reason thereof require services or activities not ordinarily provided by the school.

Numerous definitions of gifted exist; however, the 1978 federal definition is the chief definition utilized by most states. The majority of states use some modification of the federal definition, and no states reflect the new and contemporary theories of Sternberg and Gardner. Cassidy and Hossler also found that thirty states (60%) had made no revisions of their definitions in a decade, and only fifteen states had made revisions in the last five years.

Norm-referenced intelligence or achievement tests are often the sole or primary assessment instruments used by school districts to determine placement in gifted programs. Most states rely primarily on standardized, norm-referenced tests to identify gifted students, including those from economically and racially diverse groups. Less often are multidimensional, multimodal assessment strategies utilized, even though numerous researchers have emphasized the importance of these strategies for identifying underrepresented student populations for gifted programs. Such holistic assessment strategies as culturally sensitive tests (also referred to as culturally neutral and culturally fair), parent nominations, self-nominations, portfolio and performance-based assessments, and creativity checklists, for example, along with learning-style assessments, appear to be promising practices. Nonetheless, the IQ score or percentile consistently is most frequently attached to giftedness identification practices, and high IQ scores (typically 130 or higher) predominate in most definitions and identification/ placement practices. Several researchers have noted differences in learning styles among African-American and white students. These differences have numerous implications for both giftedness identification and teaching practices. The extent to which students are global versus analytic learners, visual versus auditory, very mobile versus less mobile, less peer-oriented versus more peer-oriented, for example, will affect their learning, achievement, motivation, and school performance.

Few teachers have received extensive and continuous training in multicultural education or cultural diversity. This lack of experience often makes it difficult to understand the ways in which African-Americans and other culturally diverse students manifest their talents and abilities. The findings that African-American students tend to be concrete rather than abstract thinkers, to prefer individual rather than group learning experiences, and to be global rather than analytic thinkers are in contrast to the teaching and testing methods of most teachers and schools. Teachers who recognize and accept such differences are more likely to identify gifted African-American students than those who perceive such differences as deficits and as culturally and educationally irrelevant.

While the most prevalent method of recommending students for placement consideration in gifted programs is to ask for teacher feedback, this method tends to be ineffective as far as African-American students are concerned. Teachers frequently emphasize such behaviors as cooperation, answering correctly, punctuality, and neatness when identifying gifted students; however, these are not necessarily the characteristics of gifted African-American learners.

Many African-American parents are concerned that teachers and schools may not acknowledge the giftedness that resides within the minority student population. These parents are often apprehensive that school personnel may view them negatively or pathologically because of possible differential economic backgrounds, family values, educational levels, and occupations. There also exists much distrust of teachers among African-American parents, particularly those parents who are aware of the underrepresentation of African-American youth in gifted education programs. These concerns cause African-American parents to fear that their children will not be recognized as gifted, but rather as deviant and as troublemakers. For parent involvement to be effective, its definition must be clearer among parents and educators and based on assumptions about parents, families, and communities that are dynamic and positive.

The identification and placement of African-American students in gifted programs pose challenges to educators. However, promising practices exist in the literature and research regarding strategies to identify and place African-American learners in gifted programs. Educators must begin to focus on contemporary theories and definitions of giftedness that acknowledge the importance of context, capitalize on strengths, and compensate for weaknesses. Equally important, such perspectives do not support the current practice of relying almost solely on standardized, norm-referenced tests to identify gifted learners.

Identification and assessment must be fair and equitable, which includes (a) defensibility—procedures should be based on the best available research and recommendations; (b) advocacy—identification should be designed in the best interests of all students, and students should not be harmed by the process; (c) equity—procedures should guarantee that no one is overlooked and that the civil rights of students are protected; strategies should be specified for identifying the economically disadvantaged gifted; cutoff scores should be avoided because they are the most common way that economically disadvantaged students are discriminated against; (d) pluralism—the broadest defensible definition of giftedness should be used; (e) comprehensiveness—as many gifted learners as possible should be identified and served; and (f) pragmatism—whenever possible, procedures should allow for the modification and the use of instruments and resources on hand; requires flexibility, user-friendliness, and inclusiveness-orientation. Teachers must receive extensive and substantive preparation to work more effectively with gifted students, in particular, with those from culturally diverse backgrounds. A major component of this training is multicultural and cross-cultural training. Ultimately, such preparation should lead to more knowledge about these students and increased referrals for their identification and placement in gifted programs.

Additionally, efforts must increase relative to recruiting and retaining African-American teachers in gifted education. Less than 6 percent of all teachers in public schools are African-American, and even fewer (1.2 percent) are African-American males. These teachers are in a unique position to serve as mentors and role models to gifted African-American learners. They are in an important position of instilling values and goals in African-American learners who may be discouraged or disinterested in school.

Tapping the talents and potentials of all children requires a broadened vision of giftedness that reflects the understanding that talent and creativity may vary markedly depending upon cultural, ethnic, economic, and linguistic back-grounds. Accordingly, professionals in education must necessarily ensure that programs for able learners are inclusive rather than exclusive and that minority students, economically disadvantaged students, underachievers, and other non-traditional students have an equal opportunity to learn and achieve in a nurturing and least-restrictive educational environment.

SELECTED BIBLIOGRAPHY

J. A. Alamprese and W. J. Erlanger, *No Gifted Wasted: Effective Strategies for Educating Highly Able, Disadvantaged Students in Mathematics and Science*, vol. 1 (1989); J. Cox, N. Daniel, and B. Boston, *Educating Able Learners* (1985); R. Dunn and S. A. Griggs, "Research on the Learning Style Characteristics of Selected Racial and Ethnic Groups," *Reading, Writing, and Learning Disabilities*, vol. 6 (1990), pp. 261–80; Education Commission of the States, "A Close Look at the Shortage of Minority Teachers," *Education Week* (May 1989), p. 29; D. Y. Ford, "Determinants of Underachievement as Perceived by Gifted, Above-Average, and Average Black Students," *Roeper Review* 14, no. 3 (1992): 130–36; S. E. Richert, "Identification of Gifted Students in the United States: The need for pluralistic Assessment," *Roeper Review* 8, no. 2 (1985): 68–72; F. B. Tuttle, Jr., L. A. Becker, and J. A. Sousa, *Characteristics and Identification of Gifted and Talented Students*, 3d ed. (1988); U.S. Commissioner of Education, *Education of the Gifted and Talented: Report to the Congress of the United States by the U.S. Commissioner of Education* (1982).

DONNA Y. FORD

GORDON, EDMUND W. (13 June 1921, Goldsboro, North Carolina). Edmund W. Gordon's distinguished career spans professional practice, scholarly life as a minister, clinical and counseling psychologist, research scientist, author, editor, and professor. Gordon received his elementary and secondary education in the segregated public schools of Goldsboro. He completed the bachelor of science degree in zoology at Howard University* and the bachelor of divinity degree in social ethics from Howard's Graduate School of Divinity. He earned the master of arts degree in social psychology from the American University and the doctor of education degree in child development and guidance from Teachers College, Columbia University.

Gordon began his career in 1945 as an assistant to the Reverend James H. Robinson at the Presbyterian Church of the Master in Harlem, New York, where he pioneered the street youth-worker model as a response to violence among the city's youth. He was subsequently a parish psychologist in the Department of Pediatric Psychology at the Jewish Hospital of Brooklyn, research director for the for Head Start,* and cofounder (with his wife) of the Harriet Tubman Clinic for children in New York City. He has held appointments at several of the nation's leading universities including Yeshiva, Harvard, Columbia, and Yale universities, and City College of New York. At Yeshiva, he served as chairperson of the Department of Special Education and subsequently as chairperson of the Department of Educational Psychology. At Columbia's Teachers College, he served as chairperson of the Department of Guidance, Director of the Division of Health Services, Sciences and Education, and director of the Institute for Urban and Minority Education. He ultimately rose to hold the Richard March Hoe Professorship in Psychology and Education.

Gordon's scholarship is documented in his authorship of more than 100 articles and book chapters and in ten books and monographs authored or edited by him. He served for five years as editor of the *American Journal of Orthopsychiatry* and for three years as editor of the annual *Review of Research in Education*. He is best known for his research on diverse human characteristics and pedagogy and on the education of lower-class populations. His book, *Compensatory Education: Preschool through College*, continues to be regarded as the classic work in its field.

At the time of his 1991 retirement from Yale, in addition to his professorship in psychology, Gordon served as professor in the Institute for Social and Policy Studies, professor of Child Psychology in the Yale Child Study Center,* and professor of epidemiology and public health. He currently serves as distinguished professor of psychology at the City College of New York and of educational psychology at CUNY Graduate Center, where he is the director of the Institute for Research on the African Diaspora in the Americas and the Caribbean. He is also currently the John M. Musser Professor of Psychology Emeritus at Yale University, and a member of the board of the Educational Testing Service.

Gordon has been recognized as a preeminent member of his discipline and his profession. In 1978, he was elected to membership in the National Academy of Education. He served for four years as secretary and treasurer of the Academy. Dr. Gordon holds the honor of having been elected as a Fellow of the American Psychological Association, Fellow and Life Member of the American Orthopsychiatric Association, Fellow and Life Member of the American Association for the Advancement of Science, and Fellow and Life Member of the American Psychological Society. He has been awarded honorary degrees from Yale, Yeshiva, and Brown universities, and from the Bank Street College.

SELECTED BIBLIOGRAPHY
Christa Brelin and William C. Matney, eds., *Who's Who in Black America, 1992–1993* (1992).

CHARLES A. ASBURY

GOSS v. BOARD OF EDUCATION OF KNOXVILLE, TENNESSEE, 373 U.S. 683 (1963). On 11 December 1959, lawyers for seventeen African-American children and their guardians filed a class action suit against Tennessee public school authorities. The students sought admission to Tennessee public schools on a racially unsegregated basis. The school administrators admitted that compulsory racial segregation had been the practice and custom throughout the public elementary and secondary schools since 1870. In an attempt to integrate

Tennessee schools, school authorities submitted a desegregation plan to rezone school districts and to set up a transfer plan. The transfer policy allowed a rezoned student to transfer back to a segregated school if she were in the racial minority at her newly assigned school.

The trial court and the court of appeals approved the transfer provisions. However, the U.S. Supreme Court concluded that the transfer provisions were unconstitutional because they bolstered segregation; moreover, the Court held that racial classifications for transfers between schools violated the Equal Protection Clause of the Fourteenth Amendment. Additionally, because the transfers were solely based on racial classifications and did not allow a student to transfer from a segregated school to a desegregated school, the Court ruled that they constituted state-imposed segregation.

The significance of the *Goss* case is that the Tennessee school board was prohibited from implementing desegregation plans containing certain provisions, such as transfer programs that effectively perpetuated racial segregation and attempted to circumvent the desegregation laws. After the Supreme Court rendered its opinion in *Goss*, the court of appeals reversed its decision and nullified transfer programs. Consequently, school authorities in other states were forced to rescind their transfer policies.

SELECTED BIBLIOGRAPHY

Goss v. Board of Education of the City of Knoxville, 186 F. Supp. 559 (E.D. Tenn. 1960); *Goss v. Board of Education of the City of Knoxville*, 301 F. 2d 164 (6th Cir. 1962); *Goss v. Board of Education of the City of Knoxville*, 319 F. 2d 523 (6th Cir. 1962); *Goss v. Board of Education of the City of Knoxville*, 319 F. 2d 851 (6th Cir. 1963); R. Pride and J. Woodard, *The Burden of Busing: The Politics of Desegregation in Nashville, Tennessee* (1985).

                                                      CYNTHIA R. MABRY

GRADUATE EDUCATION AND AFRICAN-AMERICANS. Graduate education is defined as postbaccalaureate study for master's, professional, or doctoral degrees. Edward A. Bouchet, who received the Ph.D. in physics from Yale University in 1876, is reported to be the first African-American to be awarded the doctoral degree by an American university. Records indicate that it was not until the early 1920s that African-American women began earning doctorates, when Eva B. Dykes was awarded a doctorate in English from Radcliffe, Sadie T. Mossell received a doctorate in economics from the University of Pennsylvania, and Georgiana Simpson earned a doctorate in German from the University of Chicago. Howard University,* an historically black institution founded in 1867, is credited with producing the first African-American female lawyer, Charlotte E. Ray, in 1872.

It has been acknowledged that a multitude of factors contributes to successful completion of graduate study. These factors include motivation, aspiration, socioeconomic status, undergraduate preparation, interaction with faculty, campus environment, and avenues available to finance education, along with on-campus and off-campus support mechanisms. A 1985 College Board study, *Equality and Excellence: The Educational Status of Black Americans*, revealed that the tendency of African-Americans to concentrate in education, humanities, and social sciences in undergraduate and graduate degree programs reflects their early preparation and achievement, as well as their parental education. The College Board recommended that African-Americans select undergraduate and graduate majors in other fields such as biology, computer sciences, physical sciences, and the like in order to enhance their equality of preparation in an increasingly global and technological society.

In the period from 1970 to 1990, African-Americans represented about 12 percent of the U.S. population, but never earned as much as 10 percent of graduate, professional, or doctoral degrees. Enrollment of African-Americans in graduate programs was approximately 68,000 in 1970 and decreased slightly to 66,000 in 1980. Enrollment decreased further to 61,000 in 1982, increasing to 67,000 in 1984, 76,000 in 1988, and 89,000 in 1991. Enrollment declines in the early 1980s have been attributed to the economy, reduced financial aid, and the overall changing tone of the nation.

Data from the National Center for Education Statistics reveal that 20,345 African-Americans were awarded master's degrees in 1976, representing 6.6 percent of the total degrees awarded that year. Almost half of those degrees (12,434) were in education. The next most popular disciplines were public affairs and services, with 1,615 graduates, and business and management, with 1,549 graduates. In 1979, the number of master's degrees awarded to African-Americans decreased to 19,393, about a thousand less than in 1976, representing 6.5 percent of the total degrees awarded. Concentrations in education, though decreased by almost 2,000 enrollees, continued to dominate, with 10,825 of the master's degree recipients in 1979.

In 1981, the number of African-Americans receiving master's degrees decreased further to 17,133, representing 5.8 percent of the total master's degrees awarded. Education degrees in 1981 declined to 8,645, while degrees in business and management increased slightly over the 1976 figures. Decreases occurred in architecture and environmental design, from 195 in 1976 to 122 in 1981; in biological sciences, from 215 in 1976 to 171 in 1981; and in social sciences, from 883 in 1976 to 615 in 1981.

By the late 1980s, education had lost its popularity as a discipline for master's degree study. In 1987, only 5,250 of the 13,867 African-Americans who earned master's degrees did so in education; this represents less than half of those who had earned such degrees a little more than a decade earlier. Master's degrees in social science also decreased by about half in the late 1980s, from 883 in 1976 to 416 in 1987. There were increases in engineering, 419 in 1987 compared with 233 in 1976; in health professions, 856 in 1987 compared with 622 in 1976; and in business, 2,810 in 1987 compared with 1,549 in 1976. Many analysts welcomed this shift in discipline interest as necessary to counter the disproportionate concentration of majors in education, social sciences, and the humanities that had prevailed from the 1970s.

In the twenty-year period from 1969–70 to 1988–89, master's degrees awarded in the United States increased by close to 50 percent. From 1983–84 to 1988–89, there was close to an 8 percent increase in the overall number of master's degrees awarded, but the number of master's degrees awarded African-Americans decreased steadily from 1976. In that year, 20,346 such degrees were earned by African-Americans, but in 1987 only 13,867 master's degrees were awarded them. A slight increase was noted in 1989, when 14,076 African-Americans were awarded master's degrees, and in 1990–91, when 16,136 such degrees were earned by this population.

In 1976, a total of 2,694 African-Americans earned first professional degrees, representing 4.3 percent of the total degrees awarded. The three largest degree-granting fields were law (1,519 graduates), medicine (708 graduates), and theology (206 graduates). At the lower end of degree-granting fields were less than forty graduates in optometry and chiropractic medicine combined. In 1979, there was a slight increase in the number of degrees awarded but a decrease in the percentage of the total; 2,836 African-Americans earned first professional degrees, representing 4.1 percent of the total degrees awarded. In 1981, a total of 2,931 African-Americans earned first professional degrees in the same top areas as 1976: law, medicine, and theology. Also in 1981, there were further decreases in optometry and chiropractic medicine degrees.

From 1969–70 to 1988–89, professional degrees doubled in the general U.S. population, from 35,000 to 71,000. These degrees peaked in the 1984–85 academic year, with 75,000 persons receiving such awards. Increases were also noted in the number of African-Americans who received first professional degrees from 1976 to 1985. In 1989, there was a slight decline (from 3,420 in 1987 to 3,101 in 1989). In 1990–91, a total of 3,575 African-Americans earned first professional degrees.

The number of African-Americans earning doctoral degrees (Ph.D. or Ed.D) increased only slightly from 1976 (1,213) to 1981 (1,265). African-Americans earned 669 doctorates in education in 1976, decreasing slightly to 614 in 1981. This population increased doctorates earned in biological sciences, health professions, and psychology during this period. There were decreases in agriculture and natural resources, from 18 doctorates in 1976 to 15 doctorates in 1981; decreases in social sciences, from 117 in 1976 to 100 in 1981; and decreases in physical sciences, from 41 in 1976 to 32 in 1981.

The number of African-Americans earning doctorates declined during most of the years from 1979 to 1988. From the 1,056 doctorates awarded in 1979, 811 doctorates were awarded in 1989. By 1989, the most popular disciplines studied by African-Americans earning doctorates were, not surprisingly, education (389 graduates), social science (163 graduates), and humanities (72 graduates). Several sources report increases in graduate, professional, and doctoral degrees earned by African-American women in the late 1980s and early 1990s.

In 1991, more African-American women (630) earned doctorates than did African-American men (582).

Census data gathered in 1990 revealed that 7.2 percent of all Americans had attained a graduate or professional degree. That included 7.7 percent of all whites, but less than 4 percent of African-Americans. It is interesting to note that while 1,056 African-Americans were earning doctorates in 1979, nearly five thousand non–U.S. citizens earned doctorates. By 1989, the number of non–U.S. citizens earning doctorates had doubled to 8,195. By 1991, there was a slight increase in the number of African-Americans earning doctorates; 1,212 of the 37,451 doctoral degree recipients were African-Americans, representing a 3.1 percent increase.

The role of historically black colleges and universities (HBCUs) in producing undergraduates for careers and graduate schools cannot be minimized. The availability of mentoring relationships, a nurturing environment, availability of remedial instruction, and less reliance on standardized examinations for admissions have been viewed as strengths of HBCUs. HBCUs conferred 4,568 of the 20,345 master's degrees awarded to African-Americans in 1976–77; this number declined to 2,392 degrees of the total degrees conferred on African-Americans in 1989–90. Master's degrees awarded by HBCUs declined by a significant percentage from 1976 to 1990. In the same period, women consistently earned more master's degrees than men from HBCUs. The number of first professional degrees conferred on African-Americans by HBCUs increased slightly in the early 1980s, but data from the National Center for Education Statistics reveal that, in the 1976–77 year, 552 African-American students earned first professional degrees from HBCUs, the same number of students who earned first professional degrees in 1989–90. Fewer doctoral degrees are conferred by HBCUs. In the 1976–77 academic year, 35 of the 1,213 African-Americans earned doctoral degrees from HBCUs. By 1989–90, this number had increased to about 12 percent of the total number of doctorates awarded. From 1988 to 1990, more females earned doctorates from HBCUs than did males.

Data from the National Center for Educational Statistics indicate that enrollment in graduate programs by African-Americans and in first professional degree programs increased by a significant percentage in 1991. To maintain and expand this increase in participation in graduate education in the twenty-first century for African-Americans, some proponents have averred a need to build effective pipelines from secondary education to undergraduate and graduate education; secure more federal funding for graduate and professional education at HBCUs; develop more mathematics and science enhancement programs in elementary and secondary schools to prepare future teachers and scientists; and increase federal funds allocated to the Pell Grants, scholarships, fellowships, and college work-study programs. The need for more African-Americans as faculty, staff, and support persons to serve as role models, teachers, and mentors of African-Americans and others of color also has been affirmed.

SELECTED BIBLIOGRAPHY
Lerone Bennett, Jr., *Before the Mayflower: A History of the Negro in America 1619–1962* (1962); Deborah J. Carter and Reginald Wilson, *Ninth Annual Status Report 1990 on Minorities in Higher Education* (1991); College Entrance Examination Board, *Equality and Excellence: The Educational Status of Black Americans* (1985); *Chronicle of Higher Education*, Almanac, 40, no. 1 (25 August, 1993); John A. Gyrmes and Irene Baden Harwarth, *Historical Trends: State Education Facts 1969 to 1989* (1992); Charlene M. Hoffman, Thomas D. Synder, and Bill Sonnenberg, National Center for Education Statistics, *Historically Black Colleges and Universities. 1976–90*, U.S. Department of Education, Office of Educational Research and Improvement (1992); Harvey G. Neufeldt and Leo McGee, eds., *Education of the African-American Adult: An Historical Overview* (1990); Delores H. Thurgood and Joanne M. Weinman, *Summary Report 1989: Doctorate Recipients from United States Universities* (1990); Reginald Wilson and Deborah J. Carter, *Eighth Annual Status Report on Minorities in Higher Education* (1989).

MICHELLE R. HOWARD–VITAL

GRAMBLING STATE UNIVERSITY. Grambling State University, founded by Charles P. Adams in 1901, is a multipurpose, state-supported, coeducational institution located in Grambling, Louisiana. The guiding principles of the University embrace the motto that "Everybody Is Somebody." Its degree-granting academic units include the colleges of liberal arts, science and technology, education, and business; the schools of nursing and social work; and the division of graduate studies. Preliminary training is available for medicine, law, and dentistry. Opportunities for cooperative education are also provided in some colleges and schools, and noncredit continuing education programs are available to the citizens of Grambling and northern Louisiana. New emphasis in Grambling's graduate school curriculum has been placed on the Ed.D. in developmental education, a unique offering in Louisiana. With an enrollment of more than seven thousand, Grambling is small enough to provide its students with individual attention and concern and large enough to offer them choices from a wide spectrum of curricular experiences. The university is fully accredited by the Southern Association of Colleges and Schools* and the National Council for Accreditation of Teacher Education.

SELECTED BIBLIOGRAPHY
National Association for Equal Opportunity in Higher Education, *Profiles of the Nation's Historically and Predominantly Black Colleges and Universities* (1993).

SAMUEL L. MYERS

GREEK-LETTER ORGANIZATIONS AND AFRICAN-AMERICAN EDUCATION. The forerunner of present-day African-American Greek-letter organizations is Sigma Pi Phi Fraternity, founded in 1904 in Philadelphia. Sigma Pi Phi differed from later organizations in that it was an elite group of male college graduates who were involved in professional activities in their communities. It was strictly a graduate fraternity and admitted into its membership "only those who had made places for themselves in their communities through useful service.'' The declared purpose was to form a brotherhood that would unite a select group of African-American men of superior education who were congenial, tolerant, and hospitable. During the first two decades of the twentieth century, eight African-American undergraduate Greek-letter organizations were founded on college and university campuses. Graduate membership gradually developed, and graduate chapters were established throughout the country and abroad.

Alpha Phi Alpha Fraternity was founded in 1906 at Cornell University in Ithaca, New York; Kappa Alpha Psi at Indiana University in 1911; Omega Psi Phi in 1911 at Howard University* in Washington, D.C. (the first African-American Greek-letter fraternity to be established on a black college campus); Phi Beta Sigma followed in 1914 at Howard University. Analogous to these fraternities were the undergraduate sororities formed during the same period. Alpha Kappa Alpha, the first of this group, was founded at Howard University in 1908; Delta Sigma Theta was founded on the same campus in 1913. In 1920, Zeta Phi Beta was founded at Howard University under the auspices of Phi Beta Sigma fraternity. This Sigma-Zeta bond is the only constitutionally sanctioned brother/sister relationship within the realm of African-American Greek-letter organizations. Sigma Gamma Rho Sorority was established in 1924 at Butler University, Indianapolis, Indiana. In 1930, these eight Greek-letter organizations met to form an alliance known as the National Pan-Hellenic Council to consider problems of mutual interest. This affiliation has continued through the years.

Although each organization is unique, encouraging scholastic achievement is an ongoing commitment common to all. Innumerable programs and projects to support education for African-American youth attest to the widespread belief among African-American Greek-letter groups that education is critical for self-advancement and for improving the human condition. In the early 1920s, sororities such as Alpha Kappa Alpha and Delta Sigma Theta established scholarship funds to provide assistance to their members who otherwise would not have been able to remain in school. They also began to provide grants for foreign study, making it possible for members to study abroad at schools such as the University of Berlin, Oxford University, the University of London, and the University of Paris. Until 1964, Zeta Phi Beta focused most of its activities on housing and juvenile delinquency projects, including providing vocational guidance clinics. In 1965, however, the sorority expanded its goals to form a national project under the title, "Welfare, Education, and Health Services," to concentrate on education, poverty, and health programs. In 1923, Alpha Kappa Alpha focused on vocational guidance as a national program to help students identify their areas of interest and ability and to help them qualify for entrance into professions and trades. These programs affected thousands of youth over several years; but as guidance and counseling services became the norm in public schools, the sorority began to emphasize other issues.

In 1922, Kappa Alpha Psi fraternity initiated a national program of vocational guidance known as the Guide Right Program, a year-round project to assist

African-American high school youth in selecting careers. In addition to career guidance, the program assisted young people in obtaining employment. In 1925, the fraternity established a national scholarship fund to emphasize development of leadership among its undergraduates and encourage high school youth to attend college. The success of its scholarship fund led to the establishment of a research loan fund, to provide loans to deserving undergraduate males who aspired to engage in postgraduate research.

Concern for the education of black children and youth in the South was demonstrated by two noteworthy projects by African-American Greek sororities. The first project, the Summer School for Rural Negro Teachers, was a project undertaken by members of Alpha Kappa Alpha Sorority, who believed that improving the training of the teachers of African-Americans in rural southern communities could help these teachers inspire their students with the determination to improve their condition. The Summer School project was launched in the summer of 1934 at Saints Industrial School* in Lexington, Mississippi. A curriculum was developed which met acceptance by the state board of education, allowing teachers to receive academic credits upon completion of the coursework. A demonstration school with classes from kindergarten to high schools was established, attended by children from Saints School. Teachers in the summer school were assigned to regular teaching periods, for which they received credit in methods and practice teaching courses. The project met with overwhelming success, creating an awareness within the sorority of the appalling health conditions among rural African-Americans in the South. The sorority then shifted its focus to finding ways to alleviate at least some of the substandard conditions that were so detrimental to the welfare of African-Americans.

The second project of note for African-American children in the South during the late 1930s was initiated by Delta Sigma Theta sorority. Known as the National Library Project, it began in Franklin County, North Carolina, and was later carried to communities in western Georgia, providing books for African-American children in areas where libraries were inadequate or absent. Most Southern schools for blacks had very meager library facilities, if any; the few available books were often outdated hand-me-downs from the white schools. In addition, African-Americans were generally not permitted to use public libraries in the South during that time. The library project ended in 1956, as nationwide efforts to extend library facilities and services met with increasing success throughout the country.

In 1932, Alpha Kappa Alpha launched the Mississippi Health Project, which served more than fifteen thousand residents of the Mississippi Delta area until 1942. The program received both national and international acclaim in such publications as *Survey Graphic*, *Reader's Digest*, and the *Journal of Public Health*.

In addition to their traditional activity of awarding scholarships, African-American fraternities and sororities employ other diverse strategies as incentives for achieving academic excellence. Many sponsor writing contests and other scholastic competitions that seek out and encourage African-American high school youth. Since the 1980s, black fraternities have intensified their efforts to work with the African-American male. Phi Beta Sigma, Alpha Phi Alpha, Kappa Alpha Psi, and Omega Psi Phi all sponsor activities for African-American male youth that include mentoring, leadership training, and academic assistance.

African-American Greek-letter organizations also work in collaboration with charitable organizations such as the March of Dimes in prevention and awareness campaigns against teenage pregnancy. The United Negro College Fund* has been a major recipient of funds donated by African-American Greek-letter organizations. Several black fraternities and sororities have begun to established endowed chairs at historically black colleges and universities; others, like the Alpha Kappa Alpha sorority, have created nonprofit educational foundations that award scholarships, grants, research fellowships, and foreign travel grants.

SELECTED BIBLIOGRAPHY

William L. Crump and Rodger Wilson, *The Story of Kappa Alpha Psi: A History of the Beginning and Development of a College Greek Letter Organization 1911–1971* (1972); Marjorie H. Parker, *Alpha Kappa Alpha Sorority: Sixty Years of Service* (1966); Marjorie H. Parker, *Alpha Kappa Alpha in the Eye of the Beholder* (1979); Mary Elizabeth Vroman, *Delta Sigma Theta: The First Fifty Years* (1965); Charles H. Wesley, *History of Sigma Pi Phi* (1954); *The Archon* 40 (Spring–Summer 1990); *The Archon* 41 (Spring–Summer 1991); "Omega Psi Phi," *Ebony* 47 (March 1992); 112–14; "Phi Beta Sigma," *Ebony* 48 (March 1992); 54–56.

ERMA GLASCO DAVIS

GREEN v. COUNTY SCHOOL BOARD OF NEW KENT COUNTY, VIRGINIA, 391 U.S. 1689 (1968). The Supreme Court's ruling in this case virtually brought to an end the practice of adopting "freedom of choice" plans as a means of redressing systemic school segregation. New Kent County, located in rural eastern Virginia, had a population of some 4,500 in the mid-1960s, about half of whom were African-American. There was no residential segregation in the county. The county educational system consisted of two schools, New Kent, a white combined elementary/high school on the east side of town and a similar facility, George W. Watkins, on the west side, for African-Americans. The school district enrolled approximately 1,300 pupils, of whom 740 were African-American. There were no attendance zones, as each school served the entire county; twenty-one buses traveled overlapping routes to transport students to these segregated schools. In order to remain eligible for federal financial assistance, the district adopted a "freedom of choice" plan in 1965 to promote school desegregation. Yet, in the plan's first three years of operation, no white children attended Watkins and, although 115 African-American students enrolled in New Kent in 1967, 85 percent of the town's African-American youngsters continued to attend Watkins. Consequently, parents of the county's African-American students brought suit in 1965, challenging the continued maintenance of a racially segregated school system.

On 27 May 1968, a unanimous Supreme Court, in an opinion authored by Justice William Brennan, ruled in favor of the African-American parents. It ordered New Kent County to terminate its freedom of choice plan as it had failed to put an end to its racially segregated school system. However, the Court stopped short of striking down all use of freedom of choice plans to end segregation. Rather, it held that the adoption of such a plan in a school district with a history of racial segregation was not an end in itself if it offered little realistic hope that desegregation would take place. The Court reasoned that whether a freedom of choice plan constituted adequate compliance with a district's responsibility to end racial segregation could be determined in light of six factors that continue to be used as benchmarks in cases dealing with racial segregation in the schools: the composition of the student body, faculty, staff, transportation, extracurricular activities, and facilities. It ruled that because fourteen years had passed since its monumental decision in *Brown v. Board of Education of Topeka, Kansas** and many school districts continued to operate segregated school systems, the time for talk was over. Thus, *Green* marked the turning point in the battle against segregated schooling as the Supreme Court decreed that in order for a school district to meet its duty to end racial segregation, it was required to do more than merely formulate desegregation plans. The Court concluded that a segregated school district must take affirmative, realistic, and effective steps to convert promptly to a desegregated system.

SELECTED BIBLIOGRAPHY

Green v. County School Board of New Kent County, Virginia, 391 U.S. 1689 (1968).

CHARLES J. RUSSO

H

HALL, PRIMUS (29 February 1756, Boston, Massachusetts–22 March 1842, Boston) The son of Prince Hall, the founder of the first black Masonic order, Primus Hall was a soapboiler, soldier, and recognized leader in the African-American community of Boston. As a baby, he was given to Ezra Trask to be taught the trade of shoemaker with the understanding that he was to be free at the age of twenty-one. When it was determined by a physician that this occupation did not suit him, he worked as a farmer and truckman. At the age of nineteen, he enlisted in the army and served during the American Revolutionary War. Married more than once, Hall was the father of seven children. He was very active in the African Masonic Lodge begun by his father.

In 1798, the first separate school for African-American children in Boston was opened in Primus Hall's home. Elisha Sylvester and, later, two Harvard students were employed as teachers. In 1800, a petition for a school for African-American children was presented by the African-American community to the city of Boston, but was refused. By 1806, the school was moved to the basement of the church built by African-American preacher Thomas Paul. Not only did Primus Hall provide a place for the first separate school in Boston for African-American children, he was instrumental in raising funds from African-American seamen and the community to help support the school, which continued until 1835. Besides inspiring Boston's African-Americans to pursue justice and quality in education, the school offered them opportunities for employment and economic growth, which in turn provided funds for future generations of African-American Bostonians to pursue higher education.

SELECTED BIBLIOGRAPHY

Robert Ewell Greene, *Black Defenders of America, 1775–1973* (1974); Sidney Kaplan and Emma Nogrady Kaplan, *The Black Presence in the Era of the American Revolution* (1989); William C. Nell, *The Colored Patriots of the American Revolution* (1986); Charles H. Wesley, *Prince Hall, Life and Legacy* (1977); Arthur O. White, "The Black Leadership Class and Education in Antebellum Boston," *The Journal of Negro Education*

42 (Fall 1973): 506–10; George W. Williams, *History of the Negro Race in America, 1619–1880* (1968).

                                                                    SHARON D. JOHNSON

HAMPTON UNIVERSITY. Founded in 1868 in Hampton, Virginia, by General Samuel Chapman Armstrong,* Hampton University (formerly Hampton Normal and Agricultural Institute) historically has been in the forefront of the African-American educational enterprise. An historically black college, it is Virginia's only coeducational, nondenominational, four-year private college. Its diverse student population of over 5,700 includes some fourth-generation Hamptonians. The student-faculty ratio at Hampton is approximately sixteen to one. Its unique offerings include forty-one undergraduate degree programs in areas such as airway science, architecture, engineering, radio, television and print journalism, communications disorders, computer science, and marine science; bachelor's and MBA degree programs in business; bachelor's and master's degree programs in nursing; and a Ph.D. degree program in physics.

Hampton's strength can be found in the example it sets. Some twenty-eight schools and institutions have been outgrowths of Hampton. Its alumni have founded ten institutions, including Tuskegee University,* St. Paul's College,* and Bowling Green Academy.

SELECTED BIBLIOGRAPHY

National Association for Equal Opportunity in Higher Education, *Profiles of the Nation's Historically and Predominantly Black Colleges and Universities* (1993).

                                                                    SAMUEL L. MYERS

HANSBERRY, WILLIAM LEO (25 February 1894, Gloster, Mississippi–3 November 1965, Washington, D.C.). William Leo Hansberry, a pioneer historian of Africa, was the son of Harriet Pauline Bailey and Eldon Hayes Hansberry. His father, a professor at Alcorn A & M College* in Mississippi, had a personal library that stimulated the son's interest in ancient history and inspired him to pursue history as a career. While studying at Atlanta University (now Clark Atlanta University*), Hansberry learned about ancient and medieval African kingdoms and societies from reading W. E. B. Du Bois's* book, *The Negro* (1916). Upon transferring to Harvard University, he studied anthropology and archaeology (Harvard did not offer courses on Africa at the time) and immersed himself in the extensive reference works on ancient Africa at that institution's libraries. Hansberry received his B.S. and M.A. degrees from Harvard in 1921 and 1931, respectively. In 1922, he joined the faculty of Howard University,* where he introduced the first courses in African history and culture in the United States and possibly the world.

Hansberry pursued postgraduate study at the University of Chicago and Oxford University, but met with challenges in pursuing a doctorate in his primary area of interest, ancient African history, when he and his advisors realized that he knew more about it than anyone else in the country. Hansberry was also acutely aware that his ideas were at odds with prevailing notions about Africa's past. Indeed, he was most active during a period when Africa was subjected to European colonial rule justified by negative stereotypes, including the myth that Africa had no history. Because of his race, Hansberry was denied membership on several archaeological expeditions led by prominent white archaeologists. Moreover, several of his colleagues ridiculed his efforts as professionally unsound and without foundation in fact.

By the 1950s, African studies had begun to gain acceptance at American universities and foundations. In 1953, the fifty-nine-year-old Hansberry received a Fulbright Research Award that allowed him to study and conduct field work in Egypt, Sudan, and Ethiopia. While he was in Africa, Howard University established such a program, although campus politics prevented him from playing a meaningful role in it. Consequently, Hansberry taught an African civilization course in 1957 at the New School for Social Research in New York.

Hansberry's interest in Africa extended beyond the university. In 1927, he read a paper at the Fourth Pan-African Congress in New York. In 1934 he, Malaku Bayen (the first Ethiopian student at Howard University), and William Steen (one of Hansberry's African-American students) helped organize the Ethiopian Research Council. The council served as an information center and coordinating body for contributions to Ethiopia during the Italo-Ethiopian War. After the defeat of the Italians in 1941, Hansberry helped to recruit African-Americans who served in Ethiopia with distinction as teachers, journalists, pilots, and technicians. Hansberry's greatest contribution, however, was as a teacher, lecturer, and mentor of study and social groups. Some of his former students even formed "Hansberry clubs" in the Caribbean and Africa.

Hansberry published a number of articles on Africa, and two volumes of his lectures and essays (*Pillars in Ethiopian History*, 1974, and *Africa and Africans As Seen by Classical Writers*, 1977) were published after his death. These publications confirm Hansberry's commitment to the reinterpretation of the history of African peoples. His works foreshadowed the current controversies over Egyptian influence on ancient Greek culture, the need for reorientation of curricula and publications to include African peoples and their cultures, and the goal of a humane approach to the study of cultures. Hansberry's papers are held by his family in Washington, D.C. A smaller collection is deposited at the Moorland–Spingarn Research Center* at Howard University. A significant amount of materials pertaining to Hansberry is included in the papers of his former student, William S. Steen, whose collection is also deposited at Howard University.

SELECTED BIBLIOGRAPHY

Nnamdi Azikiwe, "Eulogy on William Leo Hansberry," *Negro History Bulletin* 27 (1965); Williston H. Lofton, "William Leo Hansberry: The Man and His Mission," *Freedomways* 1, no. 2 (1966); Raymond J. Smyke, "William Leo Hansberry: Tribute to a Heretic," *Africa Report* (1965); James Spady, "Dr. William Leo Hansberry: The Legacy of an African Hunter," *A Current Bibliography on African Affairs* 3, no. 10 (1972); "A Tribute to the Memory of Professor William Leo Hansberry," Department of History, Howard University (1972); Joseph E. Harris, "The Unveiling of a Pioneer," *A Tribute to the Memory of Professor William Leo Hansberry*, Department of History, Howard University (1972); "William Leo Hansberry and Ancient African History," Department of History, Howard University (1913–73); Rayford W. Logan and Michael R. Winston, eds., *Dictionary of American Negro Biography* (1982).

JOSEPH E. HARRIS

HARRIS, PATRICIA ROBERTS (31 May 1924, Matton, Illinois–23 March 1985, Washington, D.C.). Harris was a lawyer, teacher, diplomat, cabinet secretary, and business leader. She was the daughter of Hildren, a Pullman car waiter, and Bert Fitzgerald Roberts, and she was married to William B. Harris, an administrative judge. She received the A.B. degree (summa cum laude) in 1945 from Howard University* and the Doctor of Law degree from George Washington University in 1960. After obtaining the A.B. degree, Harris continued her education at the University of Chicago, studying industrial relations and working as the program director of the Young Women's Christian Association (YWCA) for two years. Returning to Washington, D.C., she became involved in civil rights and social work for over a decade. She served as assistant director of the American Council on Human Rights and as executive director of Delta Sigma Theta, an African-American sorority.

After earning her law degree, Harris worked as a trial attorney with the U.S. Department of Justice for one year and then accepted the associate dean and lecturer positions in the School of Law at Howard University. In 1963 President John F. Kennedy appointed her as cochair of the National Women's Committee for Civil Rights. Harris was the first African-American woman to hold both diplomatic rank and cabinet appointments. President Lyndon B. Johnson appointed her as U.S. Ambassador to Luxembourg from 1965 to 1967, and President Jimmy Carter appointed her as secretary to two cabinet posts, Housing and Urban Development from 1977 to 1979 and Health, Education and Welfare from 1979 to 1981. After serving as ambassador, she returned to Howard University to teach and became the dean of the School of Law in 1969. After two months as dean she left to join a Washington, D.C., law firm. In 1971 she became the first African-American woman to be appointed as a director of a major business corporation, the International Business Machines Corporation (IBM). After an unsuccessful race for mayor of Washington, D.C., in 1982, she became a law professor at George Washington University.

Harris was a long-standing advocate for minorities and the poor. As cochair of the National Women's Committee for Civil Rights, she helped to develop ways to broaden communication among races and sought support from various women's groups for the civil rights bill that was before Congress. While serving in her cabinet positions, she devoted her efforts to expanding federal social programs during periods of budget cutting. She spent her life paving the way for women in public service, particularly African-American women. On 23 March 1985, Harris died of cancer at George Washington University Hospital. She was buried in Rock Creek Cemetery in Washington, D.C.

SELECTED BIBLIOGRAPHY

Helen G. Edmonds, *Black Faces in High Places: Negroes in Government* (1971); Charles D. Lowery and John F. Marszalek, *Encyclopedia of African-American Civil Rights from Emancipation to the Present* (1992); Dianne M. Pinderhughes, "Black Women and National Educational Policy," *Journal of Negro Education* 51, no. 3 (1992); *Washington Post*, 24 March 1985, A-1, A-10.

PATRICIA HALL HARRIS

HARRIS–STOWE STATE COLLEGE. Harris–Stowe State College in St. Louis, Missouri, was founded in 1857 as the first teacher-education institution west of the Mississippi. The college became a member of the state of Missouri system of higher education in 1979. Throughout its years of existence, Harris–Stowe has retained its reputation for its outstanding degree programs and the quality and accomplishments of its graduates. The college is presently organized for two main purposes: (1) the formation of teachers through accredited, four-year teacher education programs and (2) the development of nonteaching urban education specialists through a unique and innovative four-year degree program especially designed for this new professional. In addition, it provides three categories of academic support programs that serve to supplement and enrich the regular four-year degree programs. These ancillary programs are the Subject-Matter Minors Program, the Developmental Program, and the Title IV Special Support Services Program.

SELECTED BIBLIOGRAPHY

National Association for Equal Opportunity in Higher Education, *Profiles of the Nation's Historically and Predominantly Black Colleges and Universities* (1993).

SAMUEL L. MYERS

HAWKINS v. BOARD OF CONTROL, 350 U.S. 413 (1956). This case established that states must integrate their systems of higher education without delay, in light of the *Brown v. Board of Education of Topeka, Kansas** decision mandating integration of public school systems, despite language in *Brown* that suggested that such integration could be performed over a period of time. In 1949, Virgil Hawkins, an African-American, applied to law school at the University of Florida, a state institution that was maintained exclusively for whites. He was denied admission because of his race and the availability of law facilities at Florida Agricultural and Mechanical College (now University),* a college reserved for African-Americans. In 1952, the Florida Supreme Court upheld his denial of admission under the doctrine of *Plessy v. Ferguson** (1896), which required that a tax-supported facility provide equal but not necessarily identical educational opportunities to students of different races.

In 1954, the U.S. Supreme Court directed the Florida supreme court to reconsider its decision in light of the *Brown* desegregation decisions. The Florida supreme court held that while the state was obligated to admit African-Americans to white institutions, it was not required to do so immediately. Instead, the state supreme court would have allowed the state to delay the admission of African-Americans to the University of Florida to allow the state to make necessary changes and adjustments to its existing system. The court based this delay on language in *Brown v. Board of Education of Topeka, Kansas* (II) (1955), which noted that full implementation of desegregation in public elementary and secondary schools could be delayed to address logistical and legal problems caused by such a change. Thus, the court held that the state was not obligated to admit Mr. Hawkins "to its Law School *immediately*, or at any particular time in the future."

In 1955, the Supreme Court reversed the Florida supreme court and required that Mr. Hawkins be admitted immediately to the University of Florida's law school. The Court limited its implementation language in *Brown* and held that graduate programs did not "present the problems of public elementary and secondary schools." Accordingly, there was "no reason for delay," and Mr. Hawkins was "entitled to prompt admission under the rules and regulations applicable to" white applicants.

SELECTED BIBLIOGRAPHY

Brown v. Board of Education, 347 U.S. 483 (1954); *Brown v. Board of Education* (II), 349 U.S. 294 (1955); *Sweatt v. Painter*, 339 U.S. 629 (1950); *Sipuel v. Board of Regents of University of Oklahoma*, 332 U.S. 631 (1948).

BEVERLY BAKER–KELLY AND J. GABRIEL EDMOND

HEAD START. Project Head Start is a federally funded program that provides educational, medical, and social service support to disadvantaged preschool children and their families. It was launched during the summer of 1965 as part of President Lyndon Johnson's "War on Poverty." Head Start was established under the Economic Opportunity Act of 1964, Title II, Urban and Rural Community Action Programs (Public Law 88–452) and administered through the newly created Office of Economic Opportunity (OEO).

In 1964, President Johnson's chief general in the war on poverty, OEO Director Sargent Shriver, commissioned a report on poverty in the United States from OEO's research division. The findings of that report indicated that of the nations's thirty million poor people, nearly half were children, and most of them were under the age of twelve. Shriver concluded that a comprehensive war against poverty would have to include a program for children. In December 1964, an interdisciplinary panel was established to consider the kinds of programs potentially effective in increasing achievement and opportunities for the poor. This group targeted the preschool population for as benefitting most from assistance. The comprehensive scope of Head Start was determined by the committee's very composition: early childhood educators, physicians, research and clinical psychologists, a college president, a dean of a college of education, an associate dean of social work, and a professor of nursing. On February 19, 1965, the panel's report was released. "Recommendations for a Head Start Program by a Panel of Experts" outlined a comprehensive preschool program that involved activities generally associated with the fields of health, social services, and education. The term "Head Start" was coined because, it was argued, if disadvantaged children were to profit from what the schools had to offer and catch up with middle-class children, they need a head start. Head Start was based on the presumption that an early childhood program providing comprehensive child development services could begin to break the poverty cycle at its earliest stages.

The Planning Committee report included seven program objectives, the first of which was to improve the physical health of the children. Children were to receive pediatric and neurological physical measurements; an assessment of nutrition, vision, hearing, and speech; and selected tests for tuberculosis, anemia, and kidney disease, all associated with poverty. Head Start would help children receive necessary immunizations and follow-up treatment. Dental examinations were also provided. Other objectives specified improving the mental processes and skills of children with particular attention to conceptual and verbal skills and establishing patterns and expectations of success for children that would create a climate of confidence for future learning efforts. The report also made frequent references to the importance of parental involvement in the program as classroom aides and volunteers.

The Johnson administration immediately announced a nationwide, eight-week summer Head Start program with a budget of $18 million serving 100,000 children. By May 1965, the budget had risen to $150 million and over half a million children were to be enrolled. Also, President Johnson announced that $150 million had been budgeted for 1966 to put Head Start on a year-round basis. In the summer of 1965, 561,359 children were enrolled in 11,069 centers around the country. The following year, 575,000 children were served in the summer, and 171,000 had been served in full-year programs. Funding for Head Start programs was allocated directly to community programs based on a competitive grant approach. Communities were encouraged to develop programs that reflect the most effective use of resources available to them. State education agencies were not involved in the process.

In 1967, Shriver outlined the following series of six basic steps that must be taken by school systems throughout the country if Head Start children were to get an even chance: reduce pupil-teacher ratios, increase use of teacher aides, offer tutorial assistance, serve hot meals, encourage participation by parents in actual school situations, and provide social services to poor families. According to the OEO guidelines of 1967, the following rules and regulations applied to all Head Start programs: Federal assistance was not to exceed 80 percent of the total program cost; 90 percent of the enrolled Head Start students had to meet the poverty guidelines; programs had to comply with conditions of Title IV of the Civil Rights Act of 1964*; a Central Policy Advisory Committee was to be developed, and at least 50 percent of its members had to consist of Head Start parents; parental involvement was continually stressed and emphasized; a medical director was required for all programs; a career development program was required in order to upgrade personnel as well as to provide staff incentives; and transportation was required for all children living beyond walking distance. It was strongly recommended that one hot meal and a snack were to be a part of the daily program.

Through the years, Head Start has continued to receive support from all the presidents and their administrations. The support included institutionalizing the Head Start program by moving it to the Department of Health, Education, and Welfare and administering it through the Office of Child Development. In 1972, Congress mandated that at least 10 percent of the national Head Start enrollment consist of children with disabilities. May 14, 1975, was designated National Head Start Day to honor the program's tenth anniversary. During the first ten years, Head Start had served more than five million children and their families. By 1975, 350,000 children participated in Head Start programs in 9,400 centers in more than 1,200 communities.

In 1978, Head Start served 19.6 percent of all eligible youngsters. Of Head Start's 363,000 children in full-year programs and 26,000 in summer programs, slightly over half were African-American children; about 25 percent were white children; 19 percent were Spanish-speaking; and the remainder Native Americans, Asian-Americans, and children from other ethnic minorities. Head Start also received special praise for enrolling 38,121 handicapped preschoolers in 1978, 13 percent of its total enrollment. The education of preschoolers with disabilities was financed by PL 94–142* and PL 21–230. Since 1982, only year-round (nine-month) programs have been offered. In 1989, approximately 452,000 children were enrolled in Head Start Programs. In 1992, Head Start's budget of over $2 billion was supported under the Administration for Children, Youth and Families of the Department of Health and Human Services.

SELECTED BIBLIOGRAPHY

Organization for Economic Co-Operation and Development (OECD), *Educational Policy and Planning: Compensatory Education Programmes in the United States* (1980); J. L. Hymes, Jr., *Early Childhood Education: The Year in Review: A Look at 1975* (1975); J. L. Hymes, Jr., *Early Childhood Education: The Year in Review: A Look at 1978* (1978); J. L. Hymes, Jr., *Early Childhood Education: The Year in Review: A Look at 1979* (1979); J. S. Payne, C. D. Mercer, R. A. Payne, and R. G. Davison, *Head Start: A Tragicomedy with Epilogue* (1973); V. Washington and U. J. Oyemade, *Project Head Start: Past, Present and Future Trends in the Context of Family Needs* (1987); E. Zigler and S. Muenchow, *Head Start: The Inside Story of American's Most Successful Educational Experiment* (1992).

FLORENCE MARGARET NEWELL

HIGHLANDER FOLK SCHOOL. Located on 105 acres in New Market, Tennessee, the Highlander Folk School was cofounded in 1932 by educational innovator Myles Horton* and Don West. They based their ideas for the school on the model of the Danish folk schools. Highlander's early programs during the 1930s and 1940s focused on worker education. Labor unions from across the South sent their members to Highlander to attend one-to five-week sessions at which they learned how to write, publish, and distribute newsletters and promotional materials; improve public-speaking and negotiating skills; and strengthen union activities. Highlander also offered courses on labor history, economics, and theories of social change.

Horton was often at odds with union leadership because of the school's bold stance on racial discrimination and segregation. African-American students were welcomed at Highlander in open violation of the state of Tennessee's Jim Crow law prohibiting blacks and whites from eating together or staying overnight under the same roof. In 1940, Horton informed all unions that Highlander would no longer accept students from unions that discriminated against African-Americans. Despite these efforts, the school failed to attract a significant number of blacks until the late 1940s, when it shifted its focus from working with the organized labor movement to working with the emerging civil rights movement.

In 1953, one year prior to the historic *Brown v. Board of Education of Topeka, Kansas** decision, the Highlander Folk School held a series of workshops with black and white community leaders from across the South to discuss issues related to public school integration. At these meetings, an alliance was forged to launch a major adult literacy and voting rights project in the Sea Islands located off the coast of South Carolina. The effort was spearheaded by Septima P. Clark,* an African-American educator and activist from Charleston, South Carolina, who was a former Highlander student. In 1957, the first "citizenship education school"* was established at Highlander for the purpose of enhancing the literacy skills of poor African-Americans in rural southern areas. Based on the success of the first school, additional schools were organized in twelve southern states. Thousands of African-Americans learned to read and were subsequently registered to vote as a result of these efforts.

As civil rights protests escalated in the late 1950s and early 1960s, the Highlander Folk School increased its involvement in that movement. Frequent visitors to the school included notable African-American activists such as Rosa Parks, Martin Luther King, Jr., and Andrew Young. As the school's role grew more prominent, white segregationists mounted an assault against what they perceived as a "communist training ground." In 1962, the state ordered Highlander closed and confiscated its property. However, such action had been anticipated by Highlander officials. In 1961, they had secured a charter creating another institution, the Highlander Research and Education Center, through which Highlander faculty and staff could continue to work as part of the civil rights movement. By the 1970s, however, their focus shifted to addressing the problems of the Appalachian region such as strip-mining, land and mineral ownership, and the occupational and environmental hazards of the mining industry. In this capacity, the Highlander Research and Education Center continues to serve as a catalyst and resource for social change through popular education for community development.

SELECTED BIBLIOGRAPHY

Frank Adams and Myles Horton, *Unearthing the Seeds of Fire: The Idea for Highlander* (1975); John M. Glen, *Highlander: No Ordinary School* (1988); Aimee I. Horton, *The Highlander Folk School: A History of Its Major Programs, 1932–1961* (1989).

EDWIN HAMILTON

HILLIARD, ASA G., III (22 August 1933, Galveston, Texas). A nationally recognized forensic psychologist, Asa Hilliard has served as an expert witness in several landmark federal cases on test validity and bias. He also has participated in the development of national assessment systems for professional educators and developmental assessments of young children and infants. Throughout his career, Hilliard has served as a consultant with numerous school districts, universities, government agencies, and private corporations. Several of his programs have become national models for valid assessment, teacher training, and curriculum equity.

Hilliard began his educational career in the Denver (Colorado) public schools. His B.A. (1955), M.A. (1961), and Ed.D. (1963) degrees were each earned from the University of Denver, where he also taught in the College of Education and in the Philosophy Colloquium of the Centennial Scholars Honors Program. Hilliard served for eighteen years on the faculty of San Francisco State University, where he was department chair for two years and the dean of education for eight years. From 1967 to 1970, he served as a consultant to the Monrovia Consolidated School System and was superintendent of schools for Monrovia, Liberia. He joined the faculty at Georgia State University in 1980, where he is currently the Fuller E. Callaway Professor of Urban Education.

Hilliard is a founding member of the Association for the Study of Classical African Civilizations and served as that organization's first vice president. He cofounded the annual National Conference on Infusion of African, African-American Content in School Curriculum and has conducted many ancient African history study tours to Egypt. He is the recipient of many awards, including the Presidential Decoration from the Republic of Liberia as Knight Commander of the Humane Order of African Redemption; the Morehouse College* Candle in the Dark Award in Education; the National Alliance of Black School Educators'* Distinguished Educator Award; the Association of Teacher Educators' Distinguished Leadership Award; and the New York Society of Clinical Psychologists' Martin Luther King, Jr., Award for Outstanding Research, Scholarly Achievement and Humanitarian Service. He has authored and edited numerous articles, technical papers, and books on testing, teaching strategies, public policy, cultural style, child growth and development, and African history.

SELECTED BIBLIOGRAPHY

Alan Backler and Sybil Eakin, eds., "Success for Every Child in Every School," in *Every Child Can Succeed: Readings for School Improvement* (1993); Leslie Williams and Doris Pronin Fromberg, eds., "African Influences in Ancient Contributions to Child Care and Early Education (Prior to A.D. 1750)," in *Encyclopedia of Early Childhood Education* (1992); Asa G. Hilliard III, ed., *Testing African-American Students* (1991); Asa G. Hilliard III, "Alternatives to I.Q. Testing: An Approach to the Identification of 'Gifted' Minority Children," in *Final Report, California State Department of Education, Special Education Support Unit* (1976).

JACQUELINE K. REED

HOBSON v. HANSEN (I & II), 269 F. Supp. 401 (1967). On 17 May 1954, the U.S. Supreme Court, in *Brown v. Board of Education of Topeka, Kansas,** declared the end of segregation in public schools under the equal protection clause of the Fourteenth Amendment. Following *Brown* and the companion case for the District of Columbia, *Bolling v. Sharpe*, which declared the end to legal segregation in the public schools, the D.C. Board of Education immediately implemented its desegregation plan to comply with the Supreme Court's decision.

In 1955, reports concerning serious educational retardation and poor standardized test scores of tenth-grade students brought quick administrative action. Dr. Carl F. Hansen, then assistant superintendent (later named superintendent) in charge of senior high schools, chaired the committee that developed a track system for curriculum. The board approved the plan for tenth-grade classes that year. In 1957, the track system was extended to the eleventh and twelfth grades; by 1959, it became operational system-wide.

The track system, with four academic levels, was based on the belief that students have different levels of academic ability, requiring a curriculum to meet these diverse achievement levels. The Honors track, with highly selective admission, was for the gifted and superior students. The Regular track was for those students who were above average and capable of college preparatory work. The General track was for students with normal achievement levels who planned to seek employment immediately after graduation. The Basic track served those students who were classified as academically retarded.

The track system, as it actually operated, became the basis for a court suit decided in June 1967. *Hobson v. Hansen* presented the basic question of whether or not the District's superintendent of schools and the board of education, in the performance of their duties, unconstitutionally deprived African-American and poor students of their right to equal educational opportunity comparable to that of the city's white or more affluent students. Judge Skelly Wright concluded that they did.

Judge Wright decided that the track system "had the tendency of resegregating the races within the individual school" (p. 411). Though the population characteristics in the public schools illustrated the low number of white students, administrative remedies had not been achieved as long as those white students attended 85 percent to 100 percent white schools. The use of "optional zones" simply afforded those white students living in predominantly African-American neighborhoods the opportunity to transfer to majority white educational facilities.

Furthermore, the court found that the racial composition of the student body tended to be reflected in the faculties of 90 out of 109 predominantly black schools in the District of Columbia. In 1962–63 and 1966–67, there were no African-American principals or assistant principals in schools that were more than two thirds white. African-American and poor facilities were overcrowded as compared to the underutilization of many white facilities. The court said that the track system, in violation of the plaintiff's constitutional rights, had the effect of separating the more affluent and academically prepared white pupil from the less-prepared African-American pupil. The court also found a correlation between track placement and family income. The standardized tests used to place pupils tended to favor the white and more affluent students. Intertrack movement by African-American pupils tended to be downward.

The court ordered: (1) termination of the track system, (2) development of a plan for pupil assignment, (3) development of a busing plan to relieve overcrowded schools, (4) abolishment of optional zones, (5) faculty integration, and (6) a teacher assignment plan filed with the court. Following the decree, the board voted not to appeal the decision, and Superintendent Hansen resigned. However, one board member did appeal the decision, but it was upheld in *Smuck v. Hobson.*

In 1970, the original plaintiffs returned to court in attempts to gain further relief based upon budget expenditures. Judge Wright, in *Hobson II,* found that per-pupil expenditures for teachers' salaries and benefits were significantly higher west of Rock Creek Park (which runs north-south and divides the more affluent white section from the rest of the city). The court concluded that the city's predominantly black schools did not enjoy the 27 percent advantage in per-pupil expenditures received by the predominantly white schools west of the Park. The court ordered that per-pupil expenditures on the elementary level should not deviate more than plus or minus 5 percent from the mean. The defendants were ordered to file annually with the court sufficient information to prove compliance with the order for equalization of per-pupil expenditures. Following completion of construction of new facilities in majority African-American areas and several years of substantial compliance, the court suspended the reporting requirements of its decree.

Hobson I was significant in that it declared ability grouping based on race to be unconstitutional; it also led to the creation of the elected D.C. Board of Education. *Hobson II* made per-pupil expenditures an additional basis for achieving equal educational opportunity.

SELECTED BIBLIOGRAPHY

George D. Strayer, *The Report of a Survey of the Public Schools of the District of Columbia, Washington, D.C.* (1949); A. Harry Passow, *Toward Creating a Model Urban*

School System: A Study of the Washington, D.C., Public Schools (1967); Joel S. Berke, *Answers to Inequity* (1974).

JULIUS W. HOBSON, JR.

HOLMES v. DANNER, 191 F. Supp. 394 (M.D. Ga., 1961). In this decision, a U.S. district court issued an injunction to enjoin officials at the University of Georgia from refusing to consider African-American applicants for admission to a state-funded institution of higher learning. The court held that four academically qualified African-American applicants had been denied admission to the University of Georgia under a tactic to exclude them solely on the basis of their race. By contrast, the court found that white students had been admitted even though they had not fulfilled admission requirements demanded of African-American applicants.

At trial, plaintiffs asked the court to determine whether the university, a public, tax-supported educational institution of the state, could deny African-Americans admission solely on the basis of race. In making its determination, the court reviewed the General Appropriations Act of 1956 and held that the maintenance of separate schools and colleges for African-Americans and whites was a condition precedent to the state's appropriation of funds to public universities. The court found that university officials were bound by the mandates of this act in order to receive funding. The court also reasoned that the administrative remedies provided to African-American applicants by university officials were inadequate, as the administrative officials to whom appeals were made were not free to admit African-Americans to the university under the General Appropriations Act of 1956. Furthermore, the court held that administrative remedies enacted by the state to respond to the plaintiffs' appeals were also inadequate, as administrative officials were not required to respond to appeals within any prescribed period of time. The court concluded that plaintiffs could possibly graduate from another college before securing final administrative action from the University of Georgia. Moreover, the court ruled that although the university had the primary right to establish admission requirements and to determine if applicants were qualified for admission, the court had the power to forbid admission policies that denied African-Americans due-process rights and equal protection of the law. In accordance with its ruling, the court issued a decree that plaintiffs were to be enrolled in the university.

On 9 January 1961, the governor of the state of Georgia issued a public statement averring that all funds appropriated to the university under the General Appropriations Act were to be cut off on the following day, as the court had entered its order on 6 January, directing admission to the plaintiffs by 11 January 1961. Plaintiffs sought a temporary restraining order to inhibit state officials from refusing to furnish funds to the university. The court granted plaintiffs' motion for a preliminary injunction based on its conclusion that plaintiffs and the other 7,500 students enrolled at the university would suffer irreparable harm to their constitutional rights if the state's refusal to appropriate funds should force the university to close.

Plaintiffs were then admitted and enrolled at the university on 11 January 1961. That evening, after violent demonstrations, the university's president suspended the plaintiffs from the university ''in order to protect all students.'' The court, however, ordered that the students' suspension be lifted, as the law-enforcement agencies of the state could adequately maintain law and order at the university. The court enjoined the university from suspending or withdrawing the plaintiffs from the university and declared that neither could the constitutional rights of the plaintiffs be sacrificed to violence and disorder nor could the lawful orders of the court thereby be frustrated. Consequently, this decision represented a significant step in breaking down barriers for African-Americans in obtaining full access to state-maintained institutions of higher learning.

SELECTED BIBLIOGRAPHY

Atlanta Constitution, 5 January 1960, p. 1, 10; 19 March, 1960, p. 5; 29 November 1960, p. 1; ''Georgia Unit Voting System Aired,'' *Christian Science Monitor*, 20 April 1959, p. 13; ''Retreat in Georgia,'' *Newsweek*, 30 January 1961, p. 51; *Southern School News*, February 1960, pp. 1–2; March 1960, p. 15; May 1960, pp. 1–2; February 1961, pp. 1, 8–11.

BEVERLY BAKER-KELLY AND DIANNA NIXON

HOME ECONOMICS AND AFRICAN-AMERICAN EDUCATION. The definition of home economics for many African-Americans is nebulous. It has meant, to many, an area that is for women to study and for only those who are interested in serving and cooking. It is to this day difficult to have people, especially African-Americans, understand that ''home economics is a synergistic study of the social, psychological, and physical needs of human beings throughout their life span.'' The early names used for the academic discipline of home economics include ''domestic art,'' ''domestic science,'' and ''domestic economy.'' Domestic science was a term used for food courses, while domestic art was used for courses dealing with clothing. During the 1920s, these terms at African-American institutions were replaced by the term home economics.

During the 1890s, a survey was made focusing on the conditions and educational facilities of Negroes in the South under the auspices of the John F. Slater Trust Fund,* by Elizabeth Hobson and Archibald Hopkins. Their report revealed that little was being done to teach the masses of African-Americans the elements of decent living. It appears that this was the beginning of extension home economics education for African-Americans on a wide scale in the South. The report recommended ''that trained pious, intelligent women teachers be sent into all congested districts to teach the women and girls the homely arts of cooking and sewing, of nursing, homemaking and house keeping. Hobson and Hopkins also observed that ''these women in a single generation had lost the skills which had made the cooks and seamstresses of the slavery period so celebrated.'' They further noted that efforts to teach the domestic arts were being met with opposition from both African-Americans and whites. "Introduction of industrial instruction into the colored schools of Norfolk was at first regarded as a doubtful experiment and started between two barriers of prejudice. The Negroes resented it, believing they were to be returned to slavery. The whites resented everything in the way of education for the Negro, and looked with suspicion upon the whites who advocated it. Further, they refused to accept as social equals those who taught the Negroes." Notwithstanding, the Norfolk experiment was successful. The growth in industrial and home economics instruction was immense, and within a period of less than ten years it included four thousand pupils and seventeen paid and thirty-two volunteer teachers as leaders in an area that included seven counties and five large towns in Virginia.

Early African-American pioneers of domestic science (home economics) in the latter part of the nineteenth and the twentieth century include Ellen Olga Paige of Florida A & M University*; Julia Page Davis of Fort Valley State College*; Mary L. Dotson of Tuskegee Institute (now University)* and Mary Lee McCrary of Langston University.* These educators made great contributions to the field of home economics in predominantly black institutions and communities across the country.

Home economics programs for African-Americans beyond elementary and high school originated at the Hampton Institute (now University)* in Virginia during the 1870s. The school dormitory was used as a home economics "practice house" long before the discipline had acquired educational significance. The program was headed by Elizabeth Hyde, who followed the development of the field through attending the national meetings of home economics societies. It emphasized the practice of the social graces, sanitation, aesthetics through harmonious color combinations, and laundry work.

Booker T. Washington,* a graduate of Hampton, applied many of the ideas he had learned at Hampton to the establishment of Tuskegee Institute, where home economics and domestic science studies flourished. Mary Dotson, a 1900 graduate of Tuskegee, studied chemistry in the academic department and applied it to her cooking lessons. After having completed classes at the Chautaugua Summer School in New York in such disciplines as chemistry, physiology, bacteriology, and cooking demonstrations, she returned to Tuskegee to teach cooking. One third of Tuskegee's student enrollment was young women, and all of the women in its day school studied cooking because Washington stressed its fundamental importance. Other courses taught to them were plain sewing, dressmaking, millinery, laundry, general housekeeping, and a special course on the preparation of foods for the sick. Special attention was also given to the arrangement of the table for different meals and to table manners in general.

The home economics courses offered at Hampton and Tuskegee set the precedents for courses at other historically black educational institutions that later developed into full-fledged academic curricula. Presently, home economics at African-American colleges has evolved from domestic training for women to professional training for both men and women in the areas of family and child development, textile clothing, fashion merchandising management dietetics, food and nutrition, consumer studies, home arts, and ecological studies.

SELECTED BIBLIOGRAPHY

Kathyrn A. Wadsworth and Anne C. Keast, "Home Economics as Students Define It," *Journal of Home Economics* 68, no. 1 (1976): 31–33; Emma S. Jacobs, "Pioneering in Home Economics among the Negroes of Tidewater, Virginia," *Journal of Home Economics* 21, no. 1 (1929): 85; Carrie A. Lyford, "Elizabeth Hyde," *Journal of Home Economics* 21, no. 1 (1929): 13; Mary L. Dotson, "A Story of a Teacher of Cooking" (reprint 1971); Max Bennett Thrasher, *Tuskegee—Its Story and Its Work* (1901).

BERTHA N. HARRISON AND LINA R. GODFREY

HORTON, MYLES (9 July 1905, Savannah, Tennessee–19 January 1990). Humanitarian, visionary, and educator, Myles Horton founded the Highlander Folk School* in Tennessee in 1932. Horton was guided in his work by principles and feelings of love and common humanity, believing in people's capacity to govern themselves and helping them grow so they would be able to do so. He inspired and encouraged his students to move toward personal and civic freedom. His philosophy was that poor and working-class adults should learn to take charge of their lives and circumstances and that nothing meaningful would happen for such people until they threw off their dependence and acted for themselves.

Initially, the focus of Horton's work was on training union organizers for the Congress of Industrial Organizations (CIO), but in the 1950s and 1960s, Highlander trained both African-Americans and whites for civil rights activism. Among workshop participants at the school were African-American civil rights leaders Martin Luther King, Jr., Rosa Parks, Andrew Young, Julian Bond, and Stokeley Carmichael. In the racially segregated South, Highlander Folk School was one of the few places where blacks and whites could meet together in common rooms for common purposes. Despite harassment by the state of Tennessee, including governors, the Ku Klux Klan, and other power-holders of the region, Horton never backed away from his mission to help the poor and oppressed empower themselves. He spent more than fifty years working with people to bring about educational change in three ways: as important in itself, to develop social leadership, and as a means to the attainment of social and economic justice.

Many people from around the world have studied at Highlander and have returned to their countries to create residential centers that deal with social issues as well as to use alternative and unconventional educational methods modeled after Highlander. Many of these educators became involved in the International Adult Education Association. They have spread Horton's vision and adapted his goals to empower oppressed citizens in Third World countries.

SELECTED BIBLIOGRAPHY
John M. Glen, *Highlander: No Ordinary School, 1933–1962* (1988); Myles Horton, with
Judith Kohl and Herbert Kohl, *The Long Haul* (1990).

TRACEY T. JONES

HOUSTON, CHARLES HAMILTON (3 September 1895, Washington, D.C.–
22 April 1950, Washington, D.C.). Charles Hamilton Houston, a lawyer and
educator, was born in the District of Columbia to William LePre Houston, a
lawyer and part-time law teacher, and Mary Ethel Hamilton, a hairdresser and
former teacher. Houston was reared in Washington, D.C., and attended the District's public schools. A Phi Beta Kappa graduate of Amherst College (B.A.,
1915) and an honor graduate of Harvard Law School (LL.B., 1922; S.J.D.,
1923), he became the first African-American editor of the *Harvard Law Review*.
Houston returned to Washington, D.C., in 1924. In that year he joined his father
as a partner in the firm of Houston and Houston, began teaching at Howard
University's* Law School, and married Margaret Gladys Moran.

Houston became the first full-time, salaried special counsel of the National
Association for the Advancement of Colored People* (1935–40), and planned
that organization's campaign against racial segregation in public schools that
culminated in the Supreme Court's 1954 *Brown v. Board of Education of Topeka, Kansas** and *Bolling v. Sharpe* decisions. As a litigator, his arguments
before the Supreme Court established critical legal precedents for racial justice
in education (*Missouri ex rel Gaines v. Canada**), employment (*Steele v. Louisville & Nashville Railroad*), and housing (*Hurd v. Hodge*). He was also the
teacher and mentor of Thurgood Marshall,* who would later become the first
African-American Supreme Court justice.

Houston's historical significance can be attributed not only to his civil rights
work but also to his success as an educator and dean. From 1924 to 1935,
Charles Houston devoted extensive time and attention to improving legal education at Howard University's School of Law. His far-reaching influence as a
faculty member and vice-dean of Howard University's Law School—from 1929
to 1935 its chief administrative officer—is based on Houston's leadership of a
remarkable transformation of that institution from an unaccredited evening
school to a highly respected, fully accredited law school with a mission of racial
advancement.

Howard's uniqueness derived from training requirements that included rigorous traditional courses, exposure to outstanding lawyers, and a curriculum that
focused on the institution's commitment to civil rights advocacy. Houston propounded a philosophy of "social engineering" by which he challenged students
to use the law for fundamental social change and African-American advancement. Houston was a demanding teacher who insisted upon unqualified excellence but was remembered by students as fair and accessible. Building upon the
foundation laid by Houston, Howard Law School later offered, under President

James Nabrit, the first course in civil rights and became virtually a laboratory for the practical study of civil rights issues.

Houston succumbed to a heart attack in Washington, D.C., at the age of 54. He was survived by Henrietta Williams Houston, whom he married in 1937 following his divorce from Margaret Houston; a six-year-old son, Charles, Jr.; and his father. Funeral services for Houston were held on 26 April 1950, at the Rankin Chapel of Howard University. He is interred in Lincoln Memorial Cemetery, just outside of the District in Suitland, Maryland.

SELECTED BIBLIOGRAPHY

Conrad Harper, "Houston, Charles H.," in Rayford Logan and Michael R. Winston, eds., *Dictionary of American Negro Biography* (1982); Charles Houston, "The Need for Negro Lawyers," *Journal of Negro Education* 4 (January 1935): 49–52; Richard Kluger, *Simple Justice* (1976); Rayford W. Logan, *Howard University* (1969); Genna Rae McNeil, *Groundwork: Charles Hamilton Houston and the Struggle for Civil Rights* (1983); Genna Rae McNeil, "To Meet the Group Needs: The Transformation of Howard University School of Law, 1920–1935," in Vincent P. Franklin and James Anderson, eds., *New Perspectives on Black Educational History* (1978); Spottswood Robinson and William H. Hastie, "No Tea for the Feeble: Two Perspectives on Charles Hamilton Houston," *Howard Law Journal* 20, no. 1 (1977): 1–9.

GENNA RAE MCNEIL

HOWARD UNIVERSITY. Howard University in Washington, D.C., is the only truly comprehensive university in the United States that has a predominantly African-American constituency. It embraces persons of all colors, religions, creeds, and a majority of national origins. Founded as a private university in 1867 by an act of the U.S. Congress, the university is named after General Oliver Otis Howard, commissioner of the Bureau of Refugees, Freedmen, and Abandoned Lands (the Freedmen's Bureau). The university has been coeducational as well as multiracial from its first year of operations. Today, the university consists of sixteen fully accredited schools and colleges, and its faculty includes the largest concentration of African-American scholars and Ph.D.'s at any single institution of higher education. About twelve thousand students were enrolled at the university in academic year 1992, representing every state and nearly 110 foreign countries. Since its founding, the university has grown from a single frame building to a main campus of more than eighty-nine acres, a twenty-two-acre West Campus on which the School of Law is located, a twenty-two-acre School of Divinity campus, and a 108-acre tract of land in Beltsville, Maryland, used for research in physical and biological sciences. The university is ranked as a level-one research institution by the Carnegie Foundation. The schools and colleges of the university are supported by fourteen research centers and four research institutes, and students may choose programs from nearly 125 areas of academic concentration to pursue bachelor's, master's, and doctoral or professional degrees. Howard's facilities include a state-of-the-art undergraduate library; specialized collections in a library system that has 1.8 million bound volumes; a comprehensive laser chemistry laboratory; a modern 500-bed hospital; a commercial radio station, WHUR-FM; and a public television station, WHMM. Howard University has awarded approximately 72,200 degrees and diplomas to date.

SELECTED BIBLIOGRAPHY

National Association for Equal Opportunity in Higher Education, *Profiles of the Nation's Historically and Predominantly Black Colleges and Universities* (1993).

SAMUEL L. MYERS

HOWARD UNIVERSITY PRESS. As early as 1882, studies and monographs were issued sporadically under the Howard University Press imprint. However, this was essentially a printing function, with the required editorial, production, and marketing functions carried out independently by various departments, centers, or individuals at Howard. As a scholarly publishing entity, the press was formally established in 1972 by the University's board of trustees. Since then, it has published 150 books focusing on the arts, education, literature (including some fiction), ethics, social, economic and political development, medicine, human relations, religious studies, intercultural communications, and foreign affairs. In addition, three scholarly journals—the *Journal of Negro Education,** the *Journal of Religious Thought,* and the *Howard Journal of Communications*—are published under the auspices of the Howard University Press.

As the only publishing house in North America owned and operated by a historically black institution of higher learning, Howard University Press has a special charge. Its commitment to the historic mission of its parent entity involves publishing scholarly books and periodicals that contribute to solutions for human and social problems in the United States and throughout the world. Priority is given to publishing those works that serve to increase the knowledge, understanding, and appreciation of the contributions and interests of African-Americans, other U.S. minorities, and black people throughout the world.

University presses function as important, and generally subsidized, branches of their parent institutions. Unlike commercial publishers whose operations are geared toward earning profits for shareholders, their primary objective is to advance knowledge by disseminating the results of scholarly inquiry. Howard University Press operations follow this pattern; thus, in 1979, after rigorous scrutiny, the press was admitted to the Association of American University Presses. However, like the university that spawned it, the press has extended itself well beyond the usual parameters of activity to include programs aimed at increasing the number of African-Americans and other minorities in the book publishing industry. Its principal effort in this regard is the Howard University Press Book Publishing Institute.

Launched in 1980 with the help of a grant from Time, Incorporated, the Institute is an annual summer program designed to acquaint students with the basics of the book publishing process. This intensive five-week course provides an overview of editing, copy writing, book marketing, design, and production processes via hands-on workshops, classroom sessions, and site tours. It is one of only four such programs offered in the United States, the only one sponsored by a university press, and the only one with a priority goal of increasing minority participation in the book publishing industry. That industry has provided significant support to the press's efforts by making financial and scholarship contributions to the institute and by donating time and lecturers to the program. Individuals from more than fifty colleges and universities throughout the nation have successfully completed the course, and several institute graduates have gone on to careers in publishing and related fields.

Howard University Press titles and authors have received numerous awards and honors from academic and publishing associations, as well as favorable reviews in both the general and the scholarly media. Press titles have been designated as supplemental texts for courses at 160 different colleges and universities in thirty-five states, the District of Columbia, the Virgin Islands, and Canada. The Press has copublished books with the National Archives of the United States and with publishing entities in the United Kingdom and Nigeria.
SELECTED BIBLIOGRAPHY
Howard University Press, "Howard U. President Launches First Black University Press in U.S." (1974); Donald Franklin Joyce, *Gatekeepers of Black Culture: Black-owned Book Publishing in the United States, 1817–1981* (1983).

D. KAMILI ANDERSON

HYPERACTIVITY AND THE AFRICAN-AMERICAN STUDENT. Hyperactivity is a behavioral condition that presents serious challenges for the academic performance of African-American students, especially those from low socioeconomic backgrounds who are more at risk of placement in special education classes for children diagnosed as having learning disorders. Because hyperactivity has been found to occur in males at least four times more frequently than it does in females, this puts African-American male students, who are disproportionately represented in special education classes, at heightened risk.

Classified as a heterogeneous Attention-Deficit Disorder (ADD), hyperactivity most frequently develops during infancy or early childhood. It is characterized by inattention, impulsiveness, restlessness, daydreaming, and excessive levels of activity and aggressiveness. Hyperactive children experience a high level of distractibility that negatively affects their ability to perform to their full academic potential. Several etiological theories have been put forth to explain the causes of hyperactivity. These theories associate the condition with neurological damage, biochemical imbalance, and environmental factors. Some research suggests that familial, environmental, and societal factors exacerbate symptoms in hyperactive children. A growing body of knowledge suggests that a considerable amount of hyperactive behavior may have a genetic base; that is, research indicates significant genetic influence on the development of temperamental characteristics and conduct behavior. However, it is generally agreed that hyperactivity is not the result of general intellectual retardation, severe language delay, or emotional disturbance.

While hyperactive children are described as having minimal neurological damage, the evidence linking hyperactive behavior to brain dysfunction is circumstantial and speculative. Hyperactive children frequently do not exhibit generalized and/or severe learning problems across the range of intellectual functioning. Much controversy has surrounded assertions that hyperactivity is due to biochemical or metabolic imbalances within the bodies of children. In effect, these theorists maintain that toxic effects associated with certain food substances, notably certain food colorings, additives, refined sugar, and vitamins, cause or exacerbate the symptoms recognized as hyperactivity. However, research on dietary modifications has been inconclusive.

Negative early parent-child relationships have been associated with hyperactivity and other problem behaviors. Studies highlighting the relationship between the effects of family disorganization and hyperactivity found that learning-disabled ADD children frequently came from families characterized by a significant amount of psychosocial stressors such as marital separation, illness, alcoholism, drug addiction, and child abuse (sexual, physical, and emotional). Disruptions in prenatal and postnatal responsiveness to the infant have been found to prevent the process of attachment between child and parent/caregiver and place the child at risk of hyperactive behavior. Hyperactivity may also stem from the child's own difficulty in modulating or regulating his or her arousal level to meet situational demands. Early parental behavior may exacerbate this problem.

The high costs of accurately assessing hyperactivity, including screening for allergies and other metabolic disorders and evaluations of intelligence, achievement, and emotional status, often preclude the use of such tests. This further disadvantages African-American and other American children of color, who are three times more likely than their white counterparts to live in low-income families. Minority children are also more likely to be confronted by many of the conditions that have been associated with or identified as causative factors in hyperactivity. Additionally, in many instances the more kinetic learning styles of children of color are misinterpreted as symptomatic of hyperactivity. Such children are penalized by being placed in inappropriate special education settings such as classes for the mentally retarded or emotionally disturbed. It is important that children not be categorized as hyperactive when in fact their behavior may be related to their ethnic or cultural orientation, rather than to the presence of a disability.

SELECTED BIBLIOGRAPHY

R. Goldberg, *Coping with Attention-Deficit Disorder throughout the Life Cycle* (1991); H. D. Grotevant, R. G. McRoy, and V. Y. Jenkins, *Emotionally Disturbed, Adopted Adolescents: Early Patterns of Family Adaption Process* (1988); W. L. Heward and M. D. Orlansky, *Exceptional Children*, 3d ed. (1988); S. A. Kirk, J. J. Gallagher, and N. J. Anastasion, *Educating Exceptional Children* (1993).

SYLVIA WALKER AND ADA VINCENT

I

IDEOLOGICAL ORIGINS OF AFRICAN-AMERICAN EDUCATION: COTTON MATHER'S *THE NEGRO CHRISTIANIZED*. Cotton Mather (1663–1728), Puritan minister of Boston and the most influential thinker in the American colonies around the turn of the seventeenth century, wrote probably the earliest comprehensive rationale for a separate and unequal kind of education for African-Americans. Mather's work, *The Negro Christianized (TNC)* (1706), a seminal document for understanding the origin and character of African-American education, lays out a program for training black slaves in Christianity as a means of saving their souls while making them more dedicated servants to their masters. The document resulted from over twelve years of Mather's personal experiences in having provided Christian education to blacks, including his own slaves. His earlier work, *Rules for the Society of Negroes* (1693), had established a meeting structure for blacks to receive the rudiments of religious training while adhering to controls on their behavior in the interest of their masters. The central tenets of the *TNC* program—that God has decreed a hierarchy among people in which some must be subservient; that people must be obedient to their superiors and reconciled to their lot, even if mean and servile; and that the Puritans were chosen people, nearer than others to God, and therefore best able to intercede on behalf of "strangers" such as the enslaved Africans—all derive from "A Modell of Christian Charity" (1630), John Winthrop's founding sermon for the New England social order.

TNC embodied a proposal, which Mather supported with four arguments, addressed to the slave-owning ruling class of New England. Mather argued first that masters, as God's servants, must comply with God's command in their treatment of their black servants and seek to bring them also into God's service. Despite their slave status, he contended that blacks should not be discounted as human beings. He rejected the notion abroad in the society of his day that blacks did not have rational souls and therefore nothing should be done for them. For Mather, the blacks' capacity to reason was proved because, among other things, some of them had already been vastly improved by education, thus confirming their humanness.

Second, growing from his enlarged definition of family, which held that members of one's household are members of one's family, Mather argued that masters had a special duty, in tending the souls of their households, to care for the souls of their slaves. Those content to leave a part of their families heathen he considered unworthy to be called Christians.

Third, Mather insisted that masters have an obligation of Christian compassion to improve the condition of the slaves who served and enriched them. Mather made clear the limited goals he assumed for the education of blacks based on his and the New England Puritans' assumption that blacks' servile status resulted from Divine Will. Though he believed the status of blacks must unavoidably be abject and servile in this world, he maintained that something could and should be done for their souls in the world to come.

Fourth, Mather argued that in addition to the spiritual rewards that would follow Christian training for their slaves, masters would also have the benefit of tangible material gains. Blacks who were made children of God, he wrote, became happier, more obedient, and dutiful servants, content with the meager material allowances that their masters might permit them, and content to await their reward in Heaven. Mather's vision of the Heaven to which blacks could look forward—where servants meet their masters—retains an echo of their earthly servility.

Mather anticipated slaveholders' objections to his program, such as doubts that blacks could benefit from Christian education and fears that Christian training would lead to blacks being baptized and thereby entitled to manumission, which would cause masters the loss of their slave property. He argued that the greater the task of teaching blacks and saving their souls, the greater would be the triumph of success. He also insisted that the masters' fears were groundless because no existing laws would free baptized slaves, and in any case slaveholders were free to establish whatever legal protections they wished.

The basic texts for instruction in Mather's program were a "shorter" catechism for those blacks considered less capable and a "larger" catechism for the more capable. Masters who could not personally instruct their slaves in the catechism were to hire others to do so, such as children or English servants of the family. On plantations with many black slaves, teachers could be hired for this purpose, or catechized overseers could perform the instruction; in any case, the endeavor was always to be supervised by the master. To ensure that this religious training would not interfere with work, such training was to take place on Sundays. Mather further recommended that black slaves be given appropriate rewards and privileges as incentives for good progress in their training. "Conferences" of blacks were to be held to instill in them "Admonitions of Piety" to motivate and shape the direction of their Christian training.

Mather argued that the black slaves were to be taught special prayers, simple at first, and more advanced as they progressed in instruction. The difference between the simple and more advanced prayers made it clear that the blacks' progress in religious training was linked to their learning to become increasingly accommodating servants. Similarly, the special Christian training for blacks outlined in Mather's shorter and larger catechisms showed an increasingly strong teaching that blacks' own sinfulness moved God's wrath to place them in so base a condition that only the "Great Savior," Jesus Christ, could end their misery. Moreover, they were taught that their "Savior" was the master who had bought them to serve God and make them God's children. This is among the ways Mather projected the master as both like God and connected with God. He thus established the master as the blacks' intermediary for salvation, with the master and the master's voice becoming expressions of God's will. When the blacks attained sufficient understanding, their religious instruction was to be extended to include introduction to the Ten Commandments, memorization of scriptural passages, and familiarization with a shortened version of the Apostle's Creed, all of which Mather paraphrased or interpreted for blacks in ways that would promote obedience and faithful servitude.

Retrospective assessments of Mather's *TNC* tend to characterize it as more an instrument of charity toward the black slaves than a tool of indoctrination and control for Mather's New England ruling class. Certainly, both Mather's program and his arguments for Christianizing blacks caused anxiety among masters for their slave investments. However, the clear thrust of *TNC* assumed and supported the propriety of slavery and the socio-religious assumptions of Mather's New England society, as outlined, for example, in Winthrop's founding sermon.

One practical function of Mather's program was to educate blacks to their perpetually marginalized but important role in the New England socio-religious hierarchy. The blacks' marginalized role buttressed the assumptions of the socio-religious order because the "stranger" was a required fixture in Puritan consciousness that helped to confirm the individual's or community's status in God's grace. With the introduction of blacks to early American society, color became a visible and permanent barrier between "we" and "they" and thus presented a clear dividing line for both superior godliness and social status. Therefore, however much the colonists fell short of their religious or social ideals, they could always see themselves favorably compared to the black "others," who were permanently "defective," both in God's gift of grace and in their likeness to His image.

Given the conceptual boundaries of Mather's theocratic order, his prescriptions for the education of blacks have, inevitably, more to do with bolstering the socio-religious hierarchy of the time than enlightening blacks. Nonetheless, by the evidence of Mather's 1693 *Rules for the Society of Negroes*, he might well have made the earliest formal efforts to hold classes for blacks in the American colonies. Whatever the shortcomings of *The Negro Christianized*, its publication remains a defining moment in the history of African-American education in New England and, eventually, the rest of the country.

SELECTED BIBLIOGRAPHY

Andrew Delbanco, *The Puritan Ordeal* (1989); Lorenzo J. Greene, *The Negro in Colonial New England* (1968); Winthrop D. Jordan, *White Over Black: American Attitudes Toward the Negro, 1550–1812* (1969); Cotton Mather, *Diary of Cotton Mather* (1957); Cotton

Mather, "The Negro Christianized: An Essay to Excite and Assist That Good Work, the Instruction of Negro-Servants in Christianity" (1706), in American Antiquarian Society, ed., *Early American Imprints, 1639–1800* (1981–82); Cotton Mather, "Rules for the Society of Negroes" ([1693] 1706), in American Antiquarian Society, ed., *Early American Imprints, 1639–1800* (1981–82); Dana D. Nelson, *The World in Black and White: Reading "Race" in American Literature, 1638–1867* (1992); John Winthrop, "A Modell of Christian Charity," in *Collections of the Massachusetts Historical Society*, vol. 7 (1838).

S. GARRETT MCDOWELL

INDEPENDENT SCHOOLS AND THE EDUCATION OF AFRICAN-AMERICANS. Three traditions of independent education have significantly influenced the education of African-Americans. Religious-based education, particularly that provided by Catholic and Lutheran schools, has been of continuing significance. These schools have tended to be neighborhood- or community-based, and many non-Catholics and Lutherans have utilized their facilities to considerable advantage. A second tradition is represented by the continuing efforts of African-Americans themselves to erect and sustain appropriate schools for their children. The philosophical orientation, academic mission, and financial status of these schools vary considerably, but they share an emphasis on the need for educational independence and self-reliance within African-American communities. Finally, a third, newer tradition is reflected in the attendance of African-Americans at private elite elementary and secondary schools. This tradition gained momentum during the Civil Rights Movement* of the 1960s. Taken together, less than 20 percent of the school-age population experiences private schools, as the majority of African-American children attend public schools. However, the attending population is highly competitive for college and is generally regarded as targeted for key leadership roles both within African-American communities and American society generally.

The literature that addresses African-Americans and private schools has primarily developed since 1950. Between 1950 and 1976, the emphasis was on the impact of the *Brown v. Board of Education of Topeka, Kansas** decision of 1954, which declared segregation in public education unconstitutional. *Brown* had implications for African-Americans in private schools as well. Concerns were expressed in a number of documents that, rather than encouraging integration, the decision had exactly the opposite effect. Because of "white flight"* from mandated desegregation in the South, there were disturbing trends toward resegregation of public schools. White families and communities were establishing private academies throughout the South to avoid having to send their children to public schools with African-American children.

Both African-Americans and whites have been aware of the trend toward creating private schools as vehicles for maintaining segregation. A 1984 study of the impact of Catholic schools* on racial integration in Chicago and Cleveland found that public elementary and secondary schools were highly segregated, but that parochial high schools were less segregated than public ones. However, results as to whether private schooling fostered school segregation were inconclusive. The study deemphasizes racial attitudes as precipitating white flight, instead stressing the de facto consequences of parochial schooling for the progress of school desegregation.

In contrast to the attitudes of administrators in the emerging southern, white academies, some administrators in established private schools, aware of the mandate for public school desegregation, showed an early and continuing interest in desegregating their schools. By 1969, reports were published describing the experiences of African-American students in some independent schools. By the late 1970s, legislation supported desegregation of private schools.

Educational focus on African-Americans and private schools soon included comparisons between public and parochial schools, especially as to benefits to lower-income and minority pupils. The focus began around 1967, soon after the timing of the first Coleman report* on equal educational opportunity and continued steadily through 1981, culminating in the production of a Coleman study that compared and contrasted public and parochial secondary schools. A lively debate was stimulated by Coleman's assertion that private schools produce greater cognitive outcomes and are more racially desegregated than public schools.

The comparative perspective continues to be of considerable interest to educators. General public dissatisfaction with the achievements of public school students probably contributes most to the increase in comparative studies of private versus public education. Thus, although initially most attention focused on desegregation issues in relation to African-Americans and private schools, later the focus emphasized their educational value, as well as the potentially special contributions of predominantly black independent schools to African-Americans. Apart from Coleman and colleagues, others have issued research reports summarizing the educational value to African-Americans of private schools. Research-related literature supportive of African-American independent schools also increased during the 1980s.

Critics of the role of desegregated independent schools, particularly private elite schools, in the lives of African-American youth have appraised the ability of those institutions to affirm African-American children's social competence and identity development. Research suggests that socioeconomic status differences between African-American and mainstream white student populations may exacerbate racial tensions because of social status-linked attitudes toward minorities. Since the mid-1980s, these reports have been buttressed by some direct accounts of students' experiences. Early exposure to such attitudes, however, may constitute excellent preparation for life in contemporary corporate America, particularly if children's experiences are buffered and mediated by supportive parents and school personnel. Additionally, public experimentation with choice options and the increasing overall cultural and social diversity of independent schools are newer trends impacting these school communities. Both trends could mitigate against the deleterious effects of any particular school community. First, African-American families in the twenty-first century will have allies with similar, if not identical concerns; second, the increments in educational options permit greater attention to the needs of individual children.

The shift in overall focus from debates surrounding desegregation to the relationship between the proper education of African-Americans and independent schools is important. Contemporary emphasis is appropriately placed on the meaning of the educational experiences provided for African-American students and their families. Familial socioeconomic status and school racial and ethnic composition are thus independent or intervening factors that may impact students' experiences within differing school communities.

SELECTED BIBLIOGRAPHY

Carol Ascher, "Black Students and Private Schooling," *Urban Review* 18 (1986); Virgil Blum, "Private Education in the Inner City," *Phi Delta Kappan* 66 (May 1985); Charles Clofeler, "School Desegregation, 'Tipping,' and Private School Enrollment," *Journal of Human Resources* 11 (Winter 1976); James S. Coleman, *Equality of Educational Opportunity* (1966); James S. Coleman and Thomas Hoffer, *Public and Private High Schools* (1987); Marva Collins, *Marva Collins Way* (1982); Peter Cookson, Jr., and Caroline H. Persell, *Preparing for Power: America's Elite Boarding Schools* (1985); George Cunningham, "Nonpublic School Alternatives to Busing: Attitudes and Characteristics," *Urban Education* 15 (April 1981); Michael Giles, "The Impact of Busing on White Flight," *Social Science Quarterly* 55 (September 1974); Christopher Jencks, "Is the Public School Obsolete?" *Public Interest* no. 2 (1966); Sylvester Monroe, "Diversity Comes to Elite Prep Schools," *Emerge* (October 1993); Edwin J. Nichols, *Teaching Mathematics*, vol. 1, *Culture, Motivation, History and Classroom Management* (1986); Joan D. Ratteray, *Access to Quality: Private Schools in Chicago's Inner City* (1986); Diana T. Slaughter and Deborah J. Johnson, eds., *Visible Now: Blacks in Private Schools* (1988); Barbara Schneider and Roger Shouse, "Children of Color in Independent Schools: An Analysis of the Eighth-Grade Cohort from the National Educational Longitudinal Study of 1988," *Journal of Negro Education* 61, no. 2 (1992); Richard Zweigenhaft and G. William Domhoff, *Blacks in the White Establishment? A Study of Race and Class in America* (1991).

DIANA T. SLAUGHTER-DEFOE AND TYRONE FORMAN

INSTITUTIONAL RACISM AND THE EDUCATION OF AFRICAN-AMERICANS. Racism has been defined as racial bias, or the prejudice or irrational belief that the differences in human character and ability are attributable to the superiority or inferiority of a given race of people. Race, so used, refers to a human population that is distinguishable, more or less distinctly, on the basis of certain genetically transmitted characteristics.

Regarding the process of education, however, it is probably not very useful to define racism attitudinally, in terms of mental acceptance or conviction, or even in terms of intent, as any one of these may or may not influence the educational process. It is probably much more useful to define racism behaviorally because behavior is clearly influential upon the educative process. Thus, from a behavioral perspective, individual racism is an action taken by one person toward another that produces negative results or effects because the other person is identified with a given racial group. Examples of individual racism, much less frequently seen in late twentieth-century America than during earlier periods, would include denial of voting rights or such overt acts of violence as slapping, kicking, bombing, lynching, or other cruelties.

Similarly, institutional racism involves those actions taken by an institution or social system that cause negative outcomes for members of certain groups and ensures the continuation of privilege for members of another group. Again, utilizing the power to effect negative consequences on members of other racial groups, as opposed to simply having the intention of doing so, represents the significant factor in institutional racism. Thus, institutional racism is frequently perpetrated unintentionally or even unknowingly. In the view of some researchers, because U.S. society provides no alternative institutions that could be utilized by antiracists wishing to avoid utilizing the existing institutions, all of which are permeated by racism, Americans are unable to extricate ourselves from the existing system, and are thus prevented from developing nonracist behaviors. Seen in this light, all Americans are unavoidably and inextricably involved in institutional racism. Given the turbulent and extremely painful history of the education of African-Americans, clearly the behavioral definition of institutional racism is meaningful to its consideration.

Because institutional racism pervades contemporary America, U.S. public policy and social arrangements perpetuate and exemplify institutional racism in innumerable ways. Examples directly affecting education include the escalating number of incidents of overt racial conflict being perpetrated against African-American students on predominantly white college campuses; the fact that curriculum materials and academic activities are heavily oriented toward the white middle class; educators' generally low expectations regarding the performance of African-American students; the extreme limitation of the numbers of African-American school personnel in supervisory, central office staff, and/or other key decision-making roles; the limitation of course offerings that are relevant to and/or reflective of African-American and other minority student cultures; and the understaffing and underfunding of programs that serve predominantly minority student populations.

By maintaining control of the major decision-making bodies, whites establish "rules of the game" in higher education (as at other levels) that are ostensibly egalitarian but that, in practical reality, reinforce an unequal class system that seriously limits educational opportunity for African-Americans. Limitations on African-American students can be seen in three highly significant areas: access to higher education (that is, the opportunity to enroll), distribution (the type of higher education institution attended by African-Americans as well as the fields of study in which they enroll or fail to enroll); and persistence (the opportunity to maintain continued enrollment that leads to the timely completion of the higher education program). For example, by screening all students seeking access to higher education through the use of norm-referenced tests of academic performance chosen by primarily upper-class, majority-group academic decision makers, students are allowed or denied access to private universities and major state colleges. Those thus screened out are funneled into community colleges whose enrollments, not surprisingly, are predominantly and disproportionately low-income African-American and Hispanic. Within community colleges, this social-class tracking continues by way of these institutions' emphases on vocational training programs and curricula.

It is not difficult to understand either how racism has become so thoroughly entrenched in America's educational and other institutions or how complex and seemingly intransigent a problem institutional racism has become for African-Americans. The subtlety of this type of racism in its contemporary form is such that it has now become "respectable," as it no longer appears in such blatant forms as lynching or denying voting rights. Having technically outlawed discrimination, though not having actually done away with it, most whites deny the existence of racism and subscribe to the widely held myth of enormous African-American socioeconomic progress, rationalizing that racial inequality is due to the moral failings of African-Americans, rather than to their own institutional acts of racism.

SELECTED BIBLIOGRAPHY

Nan Artman et al., "Racism and Higher Education: Toward a Theory and Practice of Organizing," in Tom and Susan Isgar, eds., *Racism and Higher Education* (1969); Paul Finkelman, ed., "Series Introduction" and "Introduction" in *Race, Law, and American History, 1700–1990: The Struggle for Equal Education, Part I* (1992); David Theo Goldberg, ed., "Introduction," in *Anatomy of Racism* (1990); Manning Marable, *The Crisis of Color and Democracy: Essays on Race, Class and Power* (1992); Lucius Outlaw, "Toward a Critical Theory of 'Race,' " in David Theo Goldberg, ed., *Anatomy of Racism* (1990); Monte Piliawsky, *Exit 13: Oppression & Racism in Academia* (1982); Howard Schuman, Charlotte Steeh, and Lawrence Bobo, *Racial Attitudes in America: Trends and Interpretations* (1985); William E. Sedlacek and Glenwood C. Brooks, Jr., *Racism in American Education: A Model for Change* (1976); David Steinberg, "Racism in American: Definition and Analysis," in Tom and Susan Isgar, eds., *Racism and Higher Education* (1969); Charles Vert Willie, *The Sociology of Urban Education* (1978).

EVONNE PARKER JONES

INTERCULTURAL EDUCATION. The concept of intercultural education was a precursor of the modern multicultural education* movement. The idea originated during the 1930s, when a group of educators and social scientists saw the need for organized pedagogical efforts aimed at teaching white children about the diversity of cultures in the United States and the contributions of various racial, ethnic, and religious groups to American society. An early attempt to create such a climate of interracial and interethnic understanding and help ease the racial ignorance of the majority population was undertaken by the Service Bureau for Intercultural Education (SBIE). Created in 1934 with support from the Rosenwald Fund,* the bureau employed Rachel Davis Du Bois, one

of the earliest developers of intercultural education, to develop intercultural curricular materials for elementary and secondary schoolchildren. By the end of
World War II, race relations issues began to take on heightened urgency.

The SBIE was guided by a philosophy that embraced democracy as its guiding
concept and progressive education as its vehicle. It was an adherent of three
internationally embraced concepts that were supportive of better human relations: democracy as a way of life, the Judeo-Christian religious heritage, and
scientific findings. The chairman of the board of directors was William Heard
Kilpatrick, then professor emeritus in philosophy at Teachers College, Columbia
University. Kilpatrick was a disciple of John Dewey and was president of the
John Dewey Society. He became editor of the society's 1947 yearbook, which
became *Intercultural Attitudes in the Making*, a reflection of his overlapping
interests and concerns. Board members included such top educators as Ernest
Melby, later dean of the School of Education at New York University, and such
notables as Frank Trager, who influenced the programs of many Jewish organizations. Three groups of theorists were influential in defining intercultural education following World War II: social reconstructionists such as Harold Hand,
George Counts, and Theodore Brameld, who felt that curriculum content should
be grounded in social realities; child-centered, needs-oriented theorists such as
Kilpatrick, Harold Alberty, and V. T. Thayer, who emphasized the wants and
interests of learners as a basis for selection of curriculum content; and values-
clarification theorists like Boyd Bode and H. Gordon Hullfish, who believed that
progressive education was at the crossroads and who therefore favored a value-
laden curriculum content.

William Van Til and other SBIE leaders felt that their job was to develop,
try out, and disseminate promising practices that could be used in schools. These
included "creating a democratic atmosphere in schools, permeating the curriculum with intercultural content, using the insights of group dynamics, and learning through both the study of and direct experience in communities." SBIE
developed many publications, among them books for a series to be published
by Harper, a clearinghouse of materials from a variety of intercultural sources,
yearbooks, and staff-written articles.

The SBIE conducted many intercultural workshops across the nation, training
college professors, public school teachers, curriculum theorists, and others. It
stressed the idea that "education and social action were one and inseparable if
America was to have a fighting chance of achieving democratic human relations
among people of varied backgrounds." As race-relations issues took on heightened urgency, other organizations with missions similar to that of the SBIE
emerged. The American Council on Race Relations and the Institute for American Democracy were two such groups. The philosophy of these associations
was that all Americans were entitled to equal treatment under the law, regardless
of race or ethnicity. By 1947, funding had levelled off for SBIE. As universities
began to include intercultural education in their curricula, the need for SBIE
was further reduced. That year, the SBIE's board accepted Dean Ernest Melby's

offer to absorb the organization into his School of Education at New York University.

SELECTED BIBLIOGRAPHY
William Van Til, *My Way of Looking at It* (1983).

PETER A. SOLA

J

JACKSON STATE UNIVERSITY. Founded in 1877 and located in Jackson, Mississippi, Jackson State University is the designated urban university of the state's university system. It has five schools: education, science and technology, liberal arts, business, and the graduate school. These schools offer forty baccalaureate, thirty-three master's, nine specializations in education, and four doctoral degree programs, including the only doctorate in early childhood education and the only doctorate in environmental science in the state of Mississippi and among the nation's historically and predominantly black colleges and universities. JSU is fully accredited by the Southern Association of Colleges and Schools.*

SELECTED BIBLIOGRAPHY

National Association for Equal Opportunity in Higher Education, *Profiles of the Nation's Historically and Predominantly Black Colleges and Universities* (1993).

SAMUEL L. MYERS

JARVIS CHRISTIAN COLLEGE. Jarvis Christian College, an accredited private, coeducational church-related college, is located one mile east of Hawkins, Texas. Since its founding in 1912, the college has maintained a tradition of high academic expectations and achievement in an intensely personalized environment. As a college of liberal arts, Jarvis encourages the development of abilities that carry one through life; communication, imagination, reason, and understanding. The curriculum provides flexibility and variety, and all students have the opportunity to develop a program of study that will enhance their career potential as well as develop their intellectual capabilities. Over 60 percent of the students are from Texas. The remaining students are from twenty-two other states and the District of Columbia. The multiracial faculty of more than forty full-time members includes outstanding scholars in every field, and 50 percent hold an earned doctorate degree in the subject matter areas of their primary teaching assignments. Jarvis offers sixteen majors/specializations and nineteen minors/specializations within four academic divisions: business administration,

education, science and mathematics, and humanities and social science. The
Division of General Studies is assigned the responsibility for the general edu-
cation curriculum, which all students must complete. An Advanced Summer
Enrichment Program (ASEP) that offers six credit hours of instruction empha-
sizing communications and mathematics is also offered by the college.
SELECTED BIBLIOGRAPHY
National Association for Equal Opportunity in Higher Education, *Profiles of the Nation's
Historically and Predominantly Black Colleges and Universities* (1993).

SAMUEL L. MYERS

JEANES FOUNDATION. The Negro Rural School Fund, which later became
known as the Anna T. Jeanes Fund, was the first fund established for the sole
purpose of improving rural public education for African-American children in
the South. It was founded in 1907 in Philadelphia by Anna Thomas Jeanes, a
wealthy Quaker woman, who donated one million dollars to create the fund. Its
goal of educating rural African-American children was accomplished by em-
ploying the most dedicated, experienced, and talented teachers from the black
schools, then providing them with the funds and training to become "master
teachers." The "Jeanes Teachers," later called the "Jeanes Supervisors," operated on a countywide basis in over fifteen southern states, visiting each small
rural town to provide various types of educational assistance. This assistance
often included developing curriculum, introducing new subjects, acting as principals and superintendents, and training teachers.

The Jeanes teachers were much more than just school supervisors, and their
impact extended far beyond the educational arena. Living by the motto, "the
next needed thing," they strove to achieve their goal of improving the overall
quality of life for the entire African-American community. This meant serving
as community advocates, raising funds to build new schools, and doing whatever
else was necessary to assist people in poor communities. They played an essential role in the overall educational, economic, cultural, and social development
for countless rural communities throughout the South. Their success led to the
Jeanes philosophy and system of supervising teachers being incorporated into
many of the educational systems in Africa, Asia, the Caribbean, and South
America.

The Jeanes Fund was also unique because it was one of the first white philanthropic organizations in which African-Americans had real power and authority. Anna T. Jeanes entrusted Booker T. Washington* of Tuskegee Institute*
and Hollis Frissell, president of Hampton Institute,* to oversee the initial one-
million-dollar donation. Washington, who was also the chair of the board of
trustees of the fund, was one of several prominent African-Americans involved
in its operation. In 1937, the Jeanes Foundation, along with the George Peabody
Foundation,* the John F. Slater Fund,* and the Virginia Randolph Fund, merged
into the Southern Education Foundation (SEF).*

SELECTED BIBLIOGRAPHY
James Anderson, *The Education of Blacks in the South 1860–1935* (1988); Horace Mann Bond, *The Education of the Negro in the American Order* (1934); Georgia Association of Jeanes Curriculum Directors, *Jeanes Supervision in the Georgia Schools: A Guiding Light in Education* (1975); Lance Jones, *The Jeanes Teacher in the United States 1908–1933* (1933); NASC History Writing Committee/Southern Education Foundation, *The Jeanes Story: A Chapter in the History of American Education* (1979).

VERNON F. CLARKE

JOHNSON, CHARLES SPURGEON (24 July 1893, Bristol, Virginia–27 October 1956). Charles Spurgeon Johnson was born in Bristol, Virginia, on the Tennessee border, the eldest of six children of Charles Henry and Winifred Branch Johnson. He received his B.A. degree from Virginia Union University* (1916) and the Ph.D. degree from the University of Chicago (1918). Johnson's career ranged from director of research for the Chicago Urban League and the National Urban League* and founder and editor of *Opportunity* magazine, to becoming the first African-American president of Fisk University.*

A leading race theorist, social scientist, educator, and educational administrator, Johnson shaped sociological theory and research on race relations by using scientific objectivity, personal documents, and statistical data. By utilizing these methodologies, he marshalled significant information on racial contacts, competition, conflict, and accommodation as a pragmatic approach to altering interracial behaviors and attitudes. His first significant publication, *The Negro in Chicago: A Study of Race Relations and a Race Riot* (1919), cited poor living conditions and unemployment of African-Americans as factors that exacerbated racial prejudices that ostensibly led to the riot. Other early works include *Ebony and Topaz* (1927), *Negro in American Civilization: A Study of Negro Life and Race Relations in the Light of Social Research* (1930), and *Economic Status of the Negro* (1933). In the late 1930s, Johnson focused on the economics of the South through the lives of cotton pickers in the *Shadow of the Plantation* (1934) and through the lives of college graduates in *The Negro College Graduate* (1938). In the 1940s, his publications correlated the conditions of the southern environment with the low level of educational attainment of African-Americans. In his *Statistical Atlas of Southern Counties* and *Growing Up in the Black Belt*, both published in 1941, Johnson proved that African-Americans in urban and industrial counties had higher educational levels than those residing in rural areas. *Growing Up in the Black Belt*, which linked the personality development of southern rural black youth to a social environment with racial implications, was prepared for the American Youth Commission. It became the infrastructure of a comprehensive educational plan for rural areas under the auspices of the Council on Rural Education. During World War II, Johnson continued his examination of race relations in three works: *To Stem the Tide* (1943), *Culture and the Educational Process* (1943), and *Into the Main Stream* (1947).

Johnson's documentation of race relations in the United States made him one of the nation's leading authorities in this area. He was asked by Swedish econ-

omist Gunnar Myrdal to prepare the memorandum on segregation for Myrdal's study of American race relations, *The American Dilemma*. The memorandum was late reworked and published by Johnson as *Patterns of Segregation* (1943).
SELECTED BIBLIOGRAPHY
Ernest W. Burgess, Elmer A. Carter, and Clarence H. Faust, "Charles Spurgeon Johnson: Social Scientist, Editor, and Educational Statesman," *Phylon* 17 (1956): 317–25; "Charles S. Johnson," *Sociology and Social Research* 42 (March–April 1958): 54–60; "Charles Spurgeon Johnson," *New York Times*, 9 June 1971, p. 1; "Charles Spurgeon Johnson," in *Biographical Dictionary of American Educators* (1978); Rayford Logan and Michael R. Winston, eds., *Dictionary of American Negro Biography* (1982); "Obituary, Charles Spurgeon Johnson," *New York Times*, 28 October 1956.

BEVERLY W. JONES

JOHNSON, MORDECAI WYATT (12 January 1890, Paris, Tennessee–10 September 1976, Washington, D.C.). A university president and clergyman, Johnson was the son of the Reverend Wyatt Johnson and Carolyn Freeman Johnson. After completing his grammar school education, he was enrolled in Nashville's Academy of Roger Williams University in 1903. When the school was destroyed by fire in 1905, Johnson completed the term at the Howe Institute in Memphis. In the fall of 1905, he entered the preparatory department of Atlanta Baptist College (later Morehouse College*), where he completed his high school studies. During his college years, from 1907 to 1911, he was strongly influenced by Atlanta president John Hope, Dean Samuel Howard Archer, and Professor Benjamin Brawley, from whom he learned a mastery of language and a deep respect for learning in the service of others. A leading student at the college, Johnson played varsity football and tennis, was on the debating team, and sang in the glee club and chorus. In recognition of his outstanding academic record, he was appointed to the faculty, where he taught history, economics, and English for two years. He also served as acting dean of the college for the 1911–12 academic year.

During the summers of 1912 and 1913, Johnson studied at the University of Chicago and received a second bachelor of arts degree in 1913. From 1913 to 1916, he matriculated at the Rochester Theological Seminary, graduating with the degree of Bachelor of Divinity in 1916. As a theologist, Johnson's most important intellectual influence was Walter Rauschenbusch, whose doctrine of the "social gospel" was aimed at placing Christianity in the service of social and economic reform. While at Rochester, Johnson was pastor of the Second Baptist Church in Mumford, New York. In 1916, he married Anna Ethelyn Gardner of Augusta, Georgia. They had three sons and two daughters.

From 1916 to 1917, Johnson was a secretary of the International Committee of the YMCA, working in the southwestern field. A year later, he became pastor of the First Baptist Church of Charleston, West Virginia, and established a reputation as a brilliant orator and community organizer. In Charleston he organized the Rochdale Cooperative Cash Grocery and the Charleston Branch of

the National Association for the Advancement of Colored People (NAACP).*
From 1921 to 1922 he was on leave from his church to study at Harvard University, where he received the Master of Sacred Theology degree in 1922. A
year later he was awarded an honorary Doctor of Divinity degree by Howard
University* in recognition of his application of religion to social problems.

In June 1926, Johnson was selected to be the first African-American president
of Howard University. His place in history is secured by the record of his
transformation of Howard during his thirty-four-year tenure. His appointment
as president was regarded nationally as a test of whether, in the context of a
segregated society, an African-American president could succeed in leading a
high-profile university, since all of the leading black colleges and universities
at the time—Fisk,* Hampton,* Spelman,* Shaw,* Morgan,* Talladega,* and
Lincoln*—had white presidents. During most of Johnson's administration,
Howard trained 48 percent of the nation's black physicians, 49 percent of the
black dentists, and 96 percent of the black lawyers. The academic quality of
Howard was therefore of national significance.

In the 1920s, Howard's instructional facilities were inadequate, library and
laboratory development were substandard, and its faculty was poorly paid. The
most serious problem was the uncertainty of continuing federal support, as there
was no statutory authority for the annual appropriations made by Congress since
1879. Only two of the university's schools and colleges were accredited (liberal
arts and dentistry). The situation in the colleges of law, medicine, and engineering was acute. On 13 December 1928, Congress amended Howard's 1867
charter to provide for annual appropriations. In recognition of this landmark
change, Johnson was awarded the Spingarn Medal of the NAACP.

Despite a reputation for strong, even authoritarian leadership, Mordecai Johnson was a champion of academic freedom. During the McCarthy era, he publicly
fought all efforts by the Federal Bureau of Investigation and Congressional
committees to interfere with outspoken Howard faculty. Among the nation's
university presidents, Johnson was also the outstanding spokesman for countries
then under the colonial domination of Britain, France, Belgium, and Holland.
During his tenure, Howard also attracted foreign students from more than ninety
countries. He articulated the view that Howard was providing progressive leadership, not only for black Americans, but for Africa, Asia, and the Caribbean
as well, at a time when the Soviet Union and the United States competed for
allegiance from nonaligned countries. Mordecai Johnson was the central figure
in the development of Howard into a major American university. He retired at
the age of seventy in June 1960.

Mordecai W. Johnson was honored by Liberia and Ethiopia in recognition of
his leadership in education and also received ten honorary degrees. In 1973 the
Howard University administration building was named in his honor. He died in
his sleep on 10 September 1976. The funeral service was held in Andrew Rankin
Memorial Chapel at Howard on 14 September 1976, followed by interment in
Lincoln Memorial Cemetery. The most complete collection of material for the

study of his administration at Howard is in the Moorland-Spingarn Research Center* at Howard University. Obituaries were published in the *Washington Post* (11 September 1976) and the *New York Times* (12 September 1976).

SELECTED BIBLIOGRAPHY

Benjamin G. Brawley, "Mordecai W. Johnson," in *Negro Builders and Heroes* (1937); Edwin R. Embree, "Lord High Chancellor," in *13 against the Odds* (1945); Michael R. Winston, ed., *Education for Freedom: The Leadership of Mordecai Wyatt Johnson, Howard University, 1926–1960* (1976); Broadus N. Butler, "Mordecai Wyatt Johnson: A Model of Leadership in Higher Education," *Howard University Magazine* (January 1977), pp. 28–33; Benjamin E. Mays, "The Relevance of Mordecai Wyatt Johnson for Our Times," *The Inaugural Address in the Mordecai Wyatt Johnson Lecture Series* (1978); James P. Johnson, Janet L. Sims, and Gail A. Kostinko, *Mordecai Wyatt Johnson: A Bibliography of His Years at Howard 1926–1960* (1976).

MICHAEL R. WINSTON

JOHNSON, SYLVIA T. (27 November 1937, Chicago, Illinois). A noted researcher and statistician, Sylvia Johnson's elementary education took place at the Francis W. Parker School in Chicago. Following four years at Hyde Park High School, she completed her studies at Howard University with an A.B. degree in mathematics. She then went on to receive an M.S. in student personnel work in higher education from Southern Illinois University and a Ph.D. degree in educational measurement and statistics from the University of Iowa. In 1974, she joined the Howard University* faculty, where she currently serves as graduate professor and area coordinator of research methodology and statistics in the School of Education and as editor-in-chief of the *Journal of Negro Education*.* She has also served as chair of the school's Department of Psychoeducational Studies and as a senior fellow at Howard University's Institute for the Study of Educational Policy.

Johnson's primary area of study has been measurement-related research, particularly examining test bias, minority group achievement, and the social-motivational context of assessment. The author of over thirty publications in the area of educational testing and research, she has written extensively on a number of related topics, such as the evaluation of SAT items, validity and bias in teacher certification testing, self-concept in children, and academic achievement and career choice among talented minority youth. She has participated in numerous research efforts targeting educational trends among low-income minority groups. As the principal investigator in the 1984 A Better Chance*–Ford Foundation study, *Science and Mathematics Career Choice among Talented Minority Youth*, she authored several articles and papers based on this work.

Johnson has made a variety of contributions in the public sector. In 1961, she was the plaintiff in the first Fair Employment Practices case in the state of Illinois, resulting in revisions to the law that gave African-Americans increased access to professional and technical/clerical positions in public schools and colleges (from which they had previously been barred). As an outcome of that work, she helped develop a motivational scale for predicting college and career achievement among African-Americans. She has also evaluated a program, sponsored by the Education Department of the NAACP* aimed at increasing the Scholastic Aptitude Test Scores of low-income African-American high school students. In 1986, she wrote a background paper for the National Research Council on the status of African-Americans, entitled *Extra School Factors in Achievement, Attainment, and Aspiration.*

Johnson is a trustee of the College Board and chairs the Design and Analysis Committee for the National Assessment of Educational Progress (NAEP). She has also served on the Technical Advisory Committee for the National Adult Literacy Survey. She was elected a fellow of the American Psychological Association and has been appointed to the National Board on Assessment of the National Academy of Sciences, National Research Council. She has presented lectures at the University of California at Berkeley and Jackson State University and has testified before congressional committees on a number of educational issues. With husband Howard N. Johnson, Sylvia Johnson is the cofounder of the JoAnne Katherine Johnson Foundation, which promotes educational activities related to bone marrow donations as well as nontraditional means of furthering scientific and mathematic achievement among high school and college students. In 1990, in collaboration with her sister, Henrice Taylor, Johnson recruited over seven thousand African-American donors for national marrow donor registries, where only a handful of African-Americans previously had been listed.

SELECTED BIBLIOGRAPHY

S. T. Johnson, "Review of the Sequential Assessment of Mathematics Inventories: Standardized Inventory," in J. J. Kramer and J. D. Coneley, eds., *The Eleventh Mental Measurements Yearbook* (1992); S. T. Johnson and M. B. Wallace, "Characteristics of SAT Quantitative Items Showing Improvement after Coaching among Black Students from Low-Income Families: An Exploratory Study," *Journal of Educational Measurement* 26 (1986): 133–45; S. T. Johnson and S. Prom-Jackson, "Career Choice in Science and Mathematics-Related Areas among Talented Minority Youth," in A. O. Harrison, ed., *Eleventh Conference on Empirical Research in Black Psychology* (1988), pp. 32–51; S. T. Johnson, "Test Bias by Arthur Jensen: A Critical Review," *Journal of Negro Education* 49 (1981): 253–62; S. T. Johnson, *The Measurement Mystique* (1979).

MARGO OKAZAWA-REY

JONES, LAURENCE C. (21 November 1882, St. Joseph, Missouri–13 July 1975, Piney Woods, Mississippi). Founder of the Piney Woods Country Life School in Rankin County, Mississippi, in 1909, Missouri-born Laurence Jones attended elementary school in St. Joseph, moved to Iowa at the age of sixteen, and became the first African-American student to graduate from Marshalltown High School in 1903. He graduated from the University of Iowa with a Bachelor of Philosophy degree in 1907. Jones frequently credited his family for his educational achievements. His father, a hotel porter, was an ex-slave who had served in the U.S. Army after the Civil War. His mother, born free in Wisconsin, was a seamstress. An uncle, Prior Foster, founded the Manual Labor Institute in Addison, Michigan, in 1848. Upon graduating from college, Jones went south with the intent of helping African-Americans. From 1907 to 1909, he served as director of the academic department and taught biology at Utica Institute, an African-American school in Mississippi. In 1909, on land and in an old cabin deeded to him by an ex-slave, and with only three students, Jones opened the Piney Woods School in Rankin County, Mississippi.

A racial moderate, Jones subscribed to the philosophy of accommodation advanced by Booker T. Washington* rather than to the more confrontational beliefs of W. E. B. Du Bois.* While Jones's relations with Washington were cordial, he never relied on Tuskegee as a prime source of teachers as did other African-American southern school founders. He also recruited in the Midwest for his teaching staff, persuading a number of African-American college graduates to leave Iowa and join him in his educational endeavors in Mississippi. Jones quickly gained local white support for his school, organizing his first board of trustees with two local African-Americans, two northern whites, and three southern whites. He relied upon contacts from his adopted state of Iowa to solicit donations of supplies and money and reached supporters through a monthly newsletter, the *Pine Torch*, first printed in May 1911.

By 1915, the Piney Woods School had reached an enrollment of 205 students, nearly half of whom boarded on campus. The school offered eight elementary grades and manual training in carpentry, blacksmithing, and sewing. A Piney Woods education addressed the problems of rural life through extension services such as farmer's conferences. George Washington Carver, the renowned African-American scientist from Tuskegee, frequently visited to provide demonstrations for local farmers. Formal teacher training was added to the curriculum in 1918; junior college training for teachers started in 1931. As well, from 1929 to 1950, Piney Woods provided the only educational program for blind African-American students in the United States.

Jones retired in 1974, after serving sixty-five years as principal of Piney Woods. He described the early history of his school in two autobiographies: *Up through Difficulties* (1913) and *Piney Woods and Its Story* (1933). The Piney Woods School is presently a private coeducational boarding school, with over three hundred students enrolled in prekindergarten to grade twelve.

SELECTED BIBLIOGRAPHY

Alferdteen Harrison, *Piney Woods School: An Oral History* (1982); Leslie Harper Purcell, *Miracle in Mississippi: Laurence C. Jones of Piney Woods* (1956); George A. Sewell, *Mississippi Black History Markers* (1977).

ARNOLD COOPER

JONES, THOMAS JESSE (4 August 1873, Anglesey, North Wales–5 January 1950, New York, N.Y.) An 1884 immigrant to the United States, Thomas Jesse Jones received a B.A. from Marietta College (1897), followed by an M.A.

(1899) and Ph.D. (1904) in sociology from Columbia University. Additionally, he studied at Union Theological Seminary, where he received the Bachelor of Divinity degree (1900). As a young man, Jones early formulated some distinctive ideas about race and class. In his view, immigrants and people of color would require extensive training in character building, religion, democracy, and morality to attain what he called the "Anglo-Saxon ideal." While yet a graduate student, Jones began teaching citizenship in the settlement houses in New York's immigrant neighborhoods. These experiences provided the foundations of the controversial concepts of social evolutionism and social studies education that he would later join to his views on race relations and racial development.

Beyond his extensive activities in immigration and social studies education, Jones is better known for his impact on African and African-American education. In 1902, Jones joined the faculty of Hampton Institute (now University),* serving as a professor, research director, and chaplain until 1909. At Hampton, Jones developed curricula for African-American and Native American students. A strong advocate of the "Hampton–Tuskegee" philosophy of racial accommodationism with an emphasis on vocational training for blacks, Jones's now-famous *Social Studies in the Hampton Curriculum* (1906) resonated with themes of responsible citizenship, patience, and piety. He also conducted the largest study ever undertaken on the education of blacks in America, entitled *Negro Education*, the results of which were published in 1917. During World War I, Jones was commissioned by the national YMCA to study the plight of black soldiers in Europe.

Though he was eulogized as a "champion of minorities" by the *New York Times* upon his death in 1950, African-American scholar and civil rights activist W. E. B. Du Bois,* consistently critical of Jones throughout his career, referred to him as "that evil genius of the Negro race." The emergent social studies community applauded Jones's work, however, and despite the criticisms of Du Bois and others, he gained prominence as a researcher and administrator. In 1916, he was invited to chair the Phelps–Stokes Fund's* influential Committee on the Social Studies, a subgroup of its larger Committee on the Reorganization of Secondary Education. He subsequently was appointed educational director of the Phelps–Stokes Fund in 1917, a position he held until 1946. At Phelps–Stokes, Jones conducted studies and administered funding that greatly influenced church missionary and corporate philanthropic organizations involved in educational programs for African-Americans in both the United States and sub-Saharan Africa.

SELECTED BIBLIOGRAPHY

Stephen T. Correia, For Their Own Good: An Historical Analysis of the Educational Thought of Thomas Jesse Jones, Ph.D. diss., Pennsylvania State University (1993); William H. Watkins, "W. E. B. Du Bois vs. Thomas Jesse Jones: The Forgotten Skirmishes," *Journal of the Midwest History of Education Society* 18 (1990); W. E. B. Du Bois, "Thomas Jesse Jones," *Crisis* 22, no. 6 (October 1921): 252–56; Kenneth King,

Pan-Africanism and Education: A Study of Race Philanthropy and Education in the
Southern States of America and East Africa (1971).

WILLIAM H. WATKINS

JOURNAL OF NEGRO EDUCATION: A HOWARD UNIVERSITY
QUARTERLY REVIEW OF ISSUES INCIDENT TO THE EDUCATION OF
BLACK PEOPLE. The Journal of Negro Education (JNE), a refereed scholarly
periodical, was founded at Howard University* in 1932. It is one of the oldest
continuously published periodicals by and about blacks. At the time of its inception, there was no publication that systematically or comprehensively addressed the enormous problems that characterized the education of blacks in the
United States and elsewhere. The mainstream educational journals only occasionally published articles or studies pertaining to black education, and no other
publication by African-Americans focused specifically on this area. There was
thus an urgent and critical need for a scholarly journal that would identify and
define the problems, provide a forum for analysis and solutions, and serve as a
vehicle for sharing statistics and research on a national basis. Consequently, the
Journal was launched with a threefold mission: first, to stimulate the collection
and facilitate the dissemination of facts about the education of black people;
second, to present discussions involving critical appraisals of the proposals and
practices relating to the education of black people; and third, to stimulate and
sponsor investigations of issues incident to the education of black people.

Under the leadership of Dr. Charles H. Thompson* for the first thirty-one
years of its existence, the Journal of Negro Education played a pivotal activist
role in documenting the condition of black schools and exploring the implications of segregated education. Working in concert with Howard president Mordecai W. Johnson* and former Howard Law School dean-turned-NAACP chief
counsel Charles Hamilton Houston,* Thompson saw to it that the Journal became a vehicle for documenting and promoting the desegregation efforts spearheaded by the NAACP* and other civil rights organizations. Some of the
groundbreaking research studies used to argue Brown v. Board of Education of
Topeka, Kansas* and other desegregation cases were published in the JNE. For
example, Howard Hale Long's 1935 yearbook article "Some Psychogenic Hazards of Segregated Education of Negroes" and its conclusions of gnarled personality development wrought by racial isolation foreshadowed the debate that
would later rock behavioral science and the national social order. Thompson
himself argued forcefully against Jim Crow educational policies and highlighted
the accomplishments and dilemmas of blacks in education in his over 100 articles and editorials published in the Journal.

In subsequent years, headed later by editors-in-chief Walter G. Daniel, Earle
West (acting editor), Charles A. Martin, Faustine C. Jones–Wilson, and Sylvia
T. Johnson,* the JNE continues to serve as an invaluable chronicle of almost
every development in black education of any consequence. Experts and researchers in education, sociology, history, and other fields—including such

noted authorities as W. E. B. Du Bois,* Charles S. Johnson,* Ralph Bunche, Horace Mann Bond,* Benjamin E. Mays,* E. Franklin Frazier, Dwight O. W. Holmes, Doxie Wilkerson,* Kenneth Clark,* Barbara Shade, James Banks,* Geneva Gay, James Comer,* Edmund W. Gordon,* and others—have contributed significant articles to the *Journal's* pages. Special features published in the *Journal* have included regular reports on African-American college enrollments, listings of doctoral research on blacks, book and media reviews, and news and announcements in education. The *Journal's* summer issues, which are annually devoted to presenting a comprehensive overview of a pressing concern, have addressed a wide range of timely topics including the Courts and "the Negro separate school" (1935), "Negro Higher and Professional Education" (1948), "The Negro Voter in the South" (1957), "African Education South of the Sahara" (1961), and "Education and Civil Rights" (1965), as well as various focuses on Black Studies (1970), black women in education (1982), international education (1987), and Africentrism and multiculturalism (1991).

Though edited and published under the sponsorship of the faculty of the Department (now School) of Education at Howard and (until 1992) its Bureau of Educational Research, the *Journal* is not now and has never been merely a local organ of Howard University. Its board, contributors, and content have consistently reflected the international scope of interest in educational issues affecting people of African descent and other people of color throughout the world.

SELECTED BIBLIOGRAPHY

Richard Kluger, *Simple Justice: The History of Brown v. Board of Education and Black America's Struggle for Equality* (1977); Aaron B. Stills and Fay Flanagan, "Charles H. Thompson's Journal: To Protect and to Serve," *Journal of Teacher Education* 3, no. 1 (1990): 65–69; Charles H. Thompson, "Editorial Comment: Why a Journal of Negro Education?" *Journal of Negro Education* 1, no. 1 (1932): 1–4; Stephen J. Wright, "Editorial Comment: Charles H. Thompson—Founder and Seminal Editor-in-Chief of the Journal of Negro Education," *Journal of Negro Education* 48 no. 4 (1979): 447–48.

D. KAMILI ANDERSON

K

KELLEY v. METROPOLITAN COUNTY BOARD OF EDUCATION OF
NASHVILLE AND DAVIDSON COUNTY, TENNESSEE, 836 F.2d 986 (6th
Cir. 1987), cert. denied, 487 U.S. 1206 (1988). Disputes over the validity of the
state of Tennessee's refusal for over thirty years to take affirmative steps to
eliminate segregation in the public schools, including sharing in the costs of
implementing desegregation plans, came to a head in the 1988 *Kelley v. Metropolitan County Board of Education of Nashville and Davidson County, Tennessee* case. At the time of the *Kelley* decision, several courts had ordered states
to share in the costs of desegregation and compensatory education programs.
Kelley, however, represented a setback to desegregation efforts. In it, the Sixth
Circuit Court of Appeals overturned a Tennessee federal district court's order
mandating the state to assume 60 percent of the costs of the combined city of
Nashville and Davidson County (Metropolitan Nashville) school district's desegregation program. The Sixth Circuit ruled that the state could successfully
raise the defense of "sovereign immunity" via the Eleventh Amendment to the
Constitution and thereby avoid financial liability for the Nashville desegregation
program.

The dismantling of the segregated schools of Nashville, Tennessee, was a
slow and painful process characterized by delay, open hostility, and ultimately
moved along only by the courage and persistence of African-American parents
and the federal judiciary. The state of Tennessee and the local Nashville school
system engaged in numerous legal tactics and evasive actions to obstruct the
progress of school desegregation in Nashville. The state took the position as
early as 1955 that it would not get involved with school desegregation, leaving
to local communities the full responsibility of eliminating vestiges of de jure
segregation.

State-enforced segregation of the races in public schools was mandated by
the Tennessee constitution at the time the *Brown v. Board of Education of
Topeka, Kansas** decision was handed down by the Supreme Court in 1954.
Additionally, three Tennessee statutes prohibited interracial schools and the

teaching of interracial classes. Anyone violating the law was subject to criminal penalties. In 1955, a class-action lawsuit was filed against the board of education of the city of Nashville to enforce the Supreme Court's decision in *Brown*, which declared an end to the judicially approved "separate but equal" laws and policies practiced by many states. In 1956, the Tennessee Supreme Court struck down the state's constitutional segregation provisions in *Roy v. Brittain*, but twenty-two years and four constitutional conventions would pass before the state finally removed the "separate but equal" provision from its constitution.

In 1957, the federal district court approved a desegregation plan for grade one but ordered the Nashville school board to develop a plan for all grades. The board submitted a parental preference voluntary desegregation plan to be implemented on a grade-a-year basis. In 1958, a federal district court judge struck down the board's proposed plan as unconstitutional. In 1960, a separate but parallel class action complaint was filed against Davidson County, which surrounded Nashville, with the goal of ending that county's segregated school system. In 1963, after the city of Nashville and Davidson County merged into a metropolitan government, the two desegregation cases were consolidated by agreement of the parties. In 1969, the plaintiffs were granted a restraining order against the board prohibiting it from purchasing any more new school sites and building new schools in an effort to maintain a dual school system.

In 1971, Judge L. Clure Morton rejected the Metropolitan Nashville board's school desegregation proposal as a token effort and entered a comprehensive order designed to integrate public schools in the city and surrounding county. The court's far-reaching plan included geographic school zone changes and, most significantly in terms of immediate impact on Nashville and Davidson County, the judge ordered that over thirteen thousand more students be transported by bus in the 1971–72 school year than had been bused the previous year. The court's order included a majority-to-minority (suburbs to inner city) transfer policy. From 1971 to 1980, the court entertained literally hundreds of motions, reports, and letters as it directed the desegregation of the Metropolitan Nashville schools. During this period, these schools experienced significant white flight.*

In 1980, the district court approved another board plan calling for, inter alia, insulating the elementary schools from the plan and limiting busing. The Sixth Circuit reversed, holding that it was fundamental error to drop the elementary schools from the desegregation plan. In a clear break with previous administrations, the Reagan-administration Justice Department filed an amicus brief with the Supreme Court in an effort to overturn the Sixth Circuit's ruling and reinstate the decision of the district-court. The Justice Department brief was aimed at eliminating mandatory busing as an available remedy for desegregation.

In 1981, the state of Tennessee and state officials were joined as defendants in the case. The Metropolitan Nashville board sought an order requiring the state to participate in and provide funds to assist it in implementing the court-ordered desegregation plan. By 1982, the Metropolitan Nashville school district was spending six million dollars per year to carry out the plan. In 1985, district court judge Wiseman ordered the state to pay 60 percent of the costs of the desegregation plan. Judge Wiseman found that the state had done nothing to facilitate the desegregation process. He noted that when the case began, racial segregation was constitutionally and statutorily mandated in Tennessee. In 1987, the Sixth Circuit reversed Judge Wiseman and held that the Eleventh Amendment constituted an absolute bar to the state being sued by its own political subdivisions, including the Metropolitan Nashville schools. The Supreme Court refused to review the case.

SELECTED BIBLIOGRAPHY

Brown v. Board of Education, 347 U.S. 483 (1954); Education Week 23 (January 1985): 10; Kelley v. Board of Education, 270 F.2d 209 (6th Cir.)., cert. denied, 361 U.S. 924 (1959); Kelley v. Metropolitan Board of Education, 463 F.2d 732 (6th Cir.), cert. denied, 409 U.S. 1001 (1972); Kelley v. Metropolitan Board of Education, 615 F. Supp. 1139 (D.C. Tenn 1985); Jack Peltason, Fifty-eight Lonely Men: Southern Federal Judges and School Desegregation (1971); Roy v. Brittain, 297 S.W.2d 72 (1956).

JOSEPH R. MCKINNEY

KENTUCKY STATE UNIVERSITY. Kentucky State University in Frankfurt, Kentucky, in its second century of educational service, is a coeducational liberal studies university with a multicultural and racially balanced student body. One of Kentucky's two 1890 land-grant institutions,* KSU's role within Kentucky's public higher educational system is to excel as a small university. Indeed, KSU has the lowest student-faculty ratio of any school in the Kentucky higher education system. It offers extensive community education programs and a cooperative extension program. Its Graduate Center offers a master's degree program in public administration. KSU also houses the Whitney M. Young, Jr., College of Leadership Studies. Central to KSU's twenty-six baccalaureate programs are the university's liberal studies requirements, mandated with the goal of providing students with the intellectual tools necessary in today's world. Its "Great Books Program" allows students to study classic works of literature, history, philosophy, mathematics, and science in seminars and tutorials. KSU offers predentistry, prelaw, premedicine, preengineering, preoptometry and preveterinary medicine programs as well as ten occupation-oriented associate degree programs. KSU is accredited by the Southern Association of Colleges and Schools* and has accredited social work, teacher education, nursing, and music programs.

SELECTED BIBLIOGRAPHY

National Association for Equal Opportunity in Higher Education, Profiles of the Nation's Historically and Predominantly Black Colleges and Universities (1993).

SAMUEL L. MYERS

KEYES v. SCHOOL DISTRICT NO. 1, 413 U.S. 189 (1972). This case, which arose from African-American parents' complaints about the Denver, Colorado, school system, was the first occasion for the Supreme Court to consider racial segregation in public school education outside the South. Until Keyes, racism had been considered a uniquely southern phenomenon. In Denver and other nonsouthern cities, no laws or formal policies prevented African-American and white children from attending school together. The blatant segregation that existed nonetheless was alleged to be the result of neither government engineering nor private racism but the natural, economically driven tendency of separation of the races by neighborhood.

As *Keyes* travelled to the high court, few had reason to be optimistic that the African-American parents would prevail. Though the district court had found that the school system for almost a decade had manipulated attendance zones and school location sites to segregate the city's African-American students in one particular neighborhood (affecting 37% of Denver's total black student population), the Supreme Court was expected to reverse the lower courts' decisions. It was thus with some surprise and even greater relief that Justice Brennan's majority opinion was received. Not only did the Court affirm the lower court's ruling, it went even further in holding Denver responsible for segregation throughout the entire city. Both the district court and the appellate court had ruled that the fact that Denver intentionally segregated students in one part of the city was not proof that it had discriminated in other areas and did not require the schools to undertake "all-out" desegregation that would include the almost totally African-American schools in the center of the city. The Supreme Court disagreed and held that if a school board has discriminated in one part of the school system, the whole system must be desegregated unless the board can prove that the current condition of racial separation is in no way the result of its intentional segregation.

As is often the case, what was hailed as a victory bore the seeds of eventual defeat. The *Keyes* requirement that the plaintiffs demonstrate that segregation was the result of discriminatory state action severely limited the potential for court-ordered desegregation in northern school districts. From then on, judicial relief would be given only in cases of de jure segregation—that is, segregation that resulted from private sources such as housing patterns and racially changing neighborhoods. Inner-city black neighborhoods that produce inner-city black schools would not be touched, and white suburbs would keep their white schools. African-American children would attend predominantly black public schools, supposedly secure in their knowledge that it was not government action but "private" white preference that was to blame for their isolation.

The concept of state action, however, is manipulable and provides a convenient excuse for judicial inaction in those cases where, for whatever reasons, the court is unwilling to intervene. Since *Keyes*, the Supreme Court has refused to require desegregation of all–African-American inner-city schools that result from white flight* to the suburbs. A more sympathetic, less fearful Court could easily find state action. Public schools are kept open with public money, which is in itself sufficient reason to find state actions regardless of another state involvement in segregating students. As Justice Douglas recognized in his concurring opinion, white neighborhoods and hence white schools exist because the government permitted and even encouraged their development, first by enforcing "whites only" restrictive covenants and now through the manner in which it disperses loans (red-lining), sites housing developments, and enforces zoning regulations, to name only a few examples.

Unwilling to lay down a rule that would mandate levels of desegregation whites would not tolerate (a point later reached with court-ordered busing), the Court, in *Keyes*, narrowed the legal violation it would acknowledge. Because it could not envision acceptance of desegregation in every school where African-American students were segregated—which would cover virtually every school in the United States and required unmatched levels of busing between school districts and their suburbs—the Court found it both expedient and morally acceptable to draw the line at those cases where plaintiffs could prove the state had acted wrongfully. Thus, while the Court spoke of an absolute right of African-American children to be free from discrimination in their school assignments, the standards of proof required as a prerequisite to that relief severely circumscribed entitlement to that "absolute right."

SELECTED BIBLIOGRAPHY

Keyes v. School District No. 1, 413 U.S. 189.

                                                                DERRICK A. BELL, JR.

KNOXVILLE COLLEGE. Knoxville College in Knoxville, Tennessee, is a four-year coeducational college that was founded in 1875 by the United Presbyterian Church of North America. Its accreditation by the Southern Association of Colleges and Schools* was reaffirmed in 1979. Since its inception, the college has been open to students of diverse backgrounds and cultures. The records of its graduates attest to Knoxville College's ability to challenge and stimulate students of demonstrated academic abilities and to assist others to overcome deficiencies in their preparation for college. Two of its graduates have had distinguished careers as college presidents: Dr. Richard V. Moore of Bethune–Cookman College* and Dr. Herman B. Smith, Jr., of Jackson State University.*

SELECTED BIBLIOGRAPHY

National Association for Equal Opportunity in Higher Education, *Profiles of the Nation's Historically and Predominantly Black Colleges and Universities* (1993).

                                                                SAMUEL L. MYERS

L

LADNER, JOYCE A. (12 October 1943, Hattiesburg, Mississippi). Veteran civil rights activist, educator, university administrator, sociologist, and author, Joyce Ladner is the third of nine children. She attended school in her home town of Hattiesburg. During the 1960s, as both a high school and a college student, Ladner participated in marches and demonstrations throughout the South protesting racial segregation. The summer before she earned her B.A. in sociology from Tougaloo College* in 1964, she was active in helping to organize the 1963 Poor People's March on Washington, one of the largest civil rights demonstrations in U.S. history. She went on to earn both her master's and doctoral degrees in sociology from Washington University in 1966 and 1968, respectively.

Ladner has consistently advocated through her research, service, teaching, and writing for improved race relations, gender equity, and child welfare services. Some of her published work includes *Tomorrow's Tomorrow: The Black Woman* (1977), *The Death of White Sociology* (1973), *Mixed Families: Adopting across Racial Boundaries* (1977, with Peter Edelman), and *Adolescence and Poverty: Challenges for the 1990s* (1991, with J. Quint and J. Musick). She has also contributed chapters to more than twenty books and written many articles for scholarly and popular publication. She has held professorships at Hunter College and the University Center of the City University of New York, and for nine years she was professor of sociology in the School of Social Work at Howard University.* Ladner later served as vice president for academic affairs at Howard (1990–94) and as its interim president during academic year 1994–95.

SELECTED BIBLIOGRAPHY

Fred Powledge, *We Shall Overcome: Heroes of the Civil Rights Movement* (1993).

PORTIA SHIELDS

LAND-GRANT COLLEGES AND UNIVERSITIES, AFRICAN AMERICAN. The land-grant system of higher education grew out of a reform movement that swept the nation and the world prior to the 1860s. This movement was based, in part, on the belief that modern society needed skilled factory workers and scientific farmers. It culminated in the United States with the passage of the Morrill Act of 1862, which granted each state and territory thirty thousand acres of public land for each congressman and senator, with the proceeds from the sale of those lands to be used to support and maintain "at least one college where the leading object shall be, without excluding other scientific and classical studies, and military tactics, to teach such branches of learning as related to agriculture and the mechanic arts." Another important legislative mandate that was designed to support the Morrill Act was the Hatch Act of 1887. This act provided the first federal funds to assist in establishing and maintaining a system of agricultural experiment stations as an integral part of land-grant colleges.

Because the Morrill Act was passed during the midst of the Civil War, it did not apply to the eleven Confederate states, nor did it benefit African-American education at that time. However, by 1871 most southern states were recipients of Morrill Act funds. Three of these southern states provided a portion of their funds to African-American institutions. For example, Mississippi's Alcorn University* was created with land-grant funds in 1871 but did not acquire official land-grant status until 1878. One third of Virginia's land-grant funds were allocated to Hampton Institute (now University)* in 1872. Hampton served as Virginia's sole black land-grant college until 1920, when publicly-supported Virginia State College (now University)* was designated. South Carolina shared a fraction of its land-grant funds with historically black Claflin College* from 1879 through 1896 until South Carolina State College (now University)* was designated.

A key provision in the 1890 amendment to the Morrill Act* mandated the inclusion of African-American institutions, thus providing the framework for the creation of the nation's seventeen historically black land-grant colleges. These seventeen institutions are located in sixteen states, mostly in the South (one per state, with the exception of Alabama). All are publicly controlled and supported, with the exception of Tuskegee University.* All of the original names of the land-grant institution have been changed over the years to reflect an expanded mission. Their contemporary names, locations, and dates of founding are as follows: Alabama A & M University,* Huntsville (1875); Alcorn State University,* Lorman, Mississippi (1871); University of Arkansas of Pine Bluff,* Pine Bluff (1873); Delaware State College,* Dover (1891); Florida A & M University,* Tallahassee (1887); Fort Valley State College,* Fort Valley, Georgia (1895); Kentucky State University,* Frankfort (1886); Langston University,* Langston, Oklahoma (1897); Lincoln University,* Jefferson City, Missouri (1866); University of Maryland Eastern Shore,* Princess Ann (1886); North Carolina A & T State University,* Greensboro (1891); Prairie View A & M University,* Prairie View, Texas (1876); South Carolina State University,* Orangeburg (1872); Southern University and A & M College,* Baton Rouge, Louisiana (1880); Tennessee State University,* Nashville (1909); Tuskegee

University,* Tuskegee, Alabama (1881); and Virginia State University,* Petersburg (1882).

The early survival of the nation's historically black land-grant colleges is due largely to the commitment and creativity of the leaders within these institutions. Prior to 1967, the federal government's meager and inconsistent financial support made it extremely difficult for these colleges to carry out the research and extension work of the land-grant mission. Since the 1960s, traditional academic content areas at historically black land-grant colleges have been expanded to include engineering, science programs, military science, liberal arts, and graduate programs. Continuing education centers and international programs also have been added. Subsequent legislation enacted by Congress in 1972, 1977, and 1983 significantly increased funding for research and extension for the black land-grant colleges to compensate for decades of neglect.

SELECTED BIBLIOGRAPHY

Bennie B. Mayberry, ed., *Development of Research at Historically Black Land-Grant Institutions* (1977); National Association of State Universities and Land-Grant Colleges, *Leadership and Learning: An Interpretive History of Historically Black Land-Grant Colleges and Universities* (n.d., circa 1993); Allen Nevins, *The Origins of the Land-Grant Colleges and State Universities* (1962); Wayne D. Rasmussen, *Taking the University to the People: Seventy-Five Years of Extension* (1989); Peter H. Schuck, "Black Land-Grant Colleges: Discrimination as Public Policy," *Saturday Review*, 24 June 1972, 46–48.

EDWIN HAMILTON

LANE COLLEGE. Lane College was founded in 1882 in northeast Jackson, Mississippi by the Colored (now Christian) Methodist Episcopal Church as the C.M.E. High School. The school was renamed Lane College in 1895. The campus occupies approximately fifteen acres. The college's mission is to help its students acquire a basic understanding of humanities, social sciences, and natural sciences while they obtain an in-depth knowledge in one of the major disciplines. The program of instruction is organized into five major divisions: general studies, humanities, natural and physical sciences, social sciences, and education. The college awards the bachelor of arts and bachelor of science degrees. Pre-professional training is offered in medicine, dentistry, nursing, and law. Developmental programs are available in reading, English, and Mathematics. In addition to the traditional liberal arts, majors are offered in business, communications, elementary education, and health and physical education. Cooperative majors are available in computer science and engineering.

SELECTED BIBLIOGRAPHY

National Association for Equal Opportunity in Higher Education, *Profiles of the Nation's Historically and Predominantly Black Colleges and Universities* (1993).

SAMUEL L. MYERS

LANEY, LUCY CRAFT (13 April 1854, Macon, Georgia–23 October 1933, Augusta, Georgia). An educator, clubwoman, community organizer, and civic leader, she received a certificate of graduation from Atlanta University* in 1873. She also studied at the University of Chicago, Tuskegee Institute,* Columbia University, and Hampton Institute (now University).* Laney was the first woman to be awarded an honorary degree from Atlanta University* (1898) and Lincoln University* (1904). She was presented with honorary master of arts degrees by South Carolina State College (now University)* in 1925 and by Howard University* in 1930.

A gifted teacher and a brilliant administrator, Laney was widely acknowledged by her contemporaries as the most outstanding African-American female educator in America. Laney believed that good kindergartens and primary schools were critical to the progress of her people, that women were by nature the best teachers of the young, and that the major responsibility for uplifting the race was the burden of educated African-American women. Between 1873 and 1883, she taught in schools in Milledgeville, Macon, Augusta, and Savannah, Georgia. In the late 1870s, she was a major leader in the educational movement that culminated in the establishment of the first public high school for African-Americans in Georgia. She was also the founder and first principal of Haines Industrial Institute (1886–1933) and organizer of the Augusta Colored Hospital and the nurse's training school (1892) that evolved into the Lamar Training School. In 1890, she established the first kindergarten in the city of Augusta, one of the first to open in the South.

Laney was instrumental in securing improved public schools, sanitation, and other municipal services in Augusta's African-American community. She was a founding member of the Georgia State Teacher's Association, which elected her secretary in 1882 and in 1922 she was made honorary president of the Georgia Federation of Colored Women's Clubs. Laney was an active member of the Southeastern Federation of Colored Women's Clubs and was a major figure in regional and national politics and activities of the YWCA. She chaired the "colored section" of the Interracial Commission of Augusta and served on the National Interracial Commission of the Presbyterian Church. An eloquent speaker, Laney was popular on the lecture circuit between 1879 and 1930. She was nominated for the William E. Harmon Award for Distinguished Achievement among Negroes in 1928, 1929, and 1930.

SELECTED BIBLIOGRAPHY

Benjamin Brawley, *Negro Builders and Heroes* (1937; reprint 1965); Sadie Iola Daniel, *Women Builders* (1931; reprint 1970); A. C. Griggs, "Lucy Craft Laney," *Journal of Negro History* 19, no.1 (January 1934): 97–102; Mary White Ovington, *Portraits in Color* (1927); June O. Patton, "Laney, Lucy Craft (1854–1933)," in Darlene Clark Hine, ed., *Black Women in America* (1993).

JUNE O. PATTON

LANGSTON, F. JOHN MERCER (14 December 1829, Louisa County, Virginia–1897, Washington, D.C.) An attorney, educator, and college president, John Mercer Langston was a staunch promoter of civil rights for African-

Americans and fought tirelessly in the arenas of education, politics, and law. Throughout his life, he fought against discrimination and encouraged African-Americans to demand equal rights. He was the son of Ralph Quarles, a white plantation owner, and Lucy Langston, who was of Native American and African descent. He received a B.A. degree in 1849 and an M.A. in 1852 from Oberlin College.* He also received private instruction in law and was admitted to the bar in Ohio in 1854. While in Ohio, he served as secretary for the state board of education.

Langston played an instrumental role in the education of African-Americans after the Civil War. He served as an inspector general in the Freedmen's Bureau* from 1868 to 1869. Between 1870 and 1875, he served as dean of the Law School, vice president, and acting president of Howard University.* From 1885 to 1887, he was president of Virginia Normal and Collegiate Institute (now Virginia State University).

Langston opposed Booker T. Washington's* educational philosophy and championed the cause of expanded educational and occupational opportunities for African-Americans. In 1888, he won a highly contested election for the 4th congressional district in Virginia, becoming the first African-American from Virginia to serve in the House of Representatives. He served on the Education Committee, where he drew up legislation providing for a National Industrial University for Colored Youth.

In addition to being an educator and politician, Langston was also active in the antislavery movement. He was a speaker and official in the State Convention of Colored Citizens of Ohio, the Ohio Anti-Slavery League, and the American Anti-Slavery Society. In 1877 he was appointed minister and consul-general to Haiti and charge d'affaires to Santa Domingo, serving in this position until 1885. Langston was interested in the educational, economic, and political conditions of Haiti and recommended improvement in trade relations between Haiti and the United States.

SELECTED BIBLIOGRAPHY

John Mercer Langston, *From the Virginia Plantation to the Nation's Capitol* (1894; reprint 1969); Rayford W. Logan and Michael R. Winston, eds., *Dictionary of American Negro Biography* (1982); Charles Lowery and John Marszalek, eds., *Encyclopedia of African-American Civil Rights* (1992).

VALINDA W. LITTLEFIELD

LEARNING ISSUES INCIDENT TO THE ACHIEVEMENT OF AFRICAN-AMERICANS. Historically and traditionally, education has been held in high esteem by African-Americans. This faith in the importance of education rests in the belief that knowledge is power and that education is an important vehicle for upward mobility. Despite the importance of education in the African-American community, a significant portion of African-Americans do not complete high school and many do not pursue higher education. Further, African-Americans are overrepresented among underachievers and underrepresented in programs for gifted and talented students. Several issues hinder the ability of and opportunities for African-Americans to manifest their potential and to achieve in educational settings. These issues relate to learning styles, teaching styles, teacher expectations, irrelevant curriculum and instruction, and inadequate and inappropriate assessment practices.

Learning styles generally are defined as the processes by which individuals make sense out of information. Every person has a preferred learning style, and research has shown that many aspects of learning style have a cultural/ethnic basis. For example, auditory learners use their ears and voices as the primary modes for learning because they prefer to hear and discuss what they are learning with others. Visual learners learn best by reading and viewing pictures and diagrams. Kinesthetic learners gain better understanding of the subject when than they are physically involved making products, acting out situations, carrying out experiments, and thus being active rather than passive learners. African-American learners have been identified by several researchers as kinesthetic, field-dependent learners.

Teaching style, that set of attitudes and actions that open a formal and informal world of learning to students, also influences the learning experiences and educational outcomes of African-American students. It is a subtle force that influences students' access to learning and teaching by establishing perimeters around acceptable learning procedures, processes, and products. Teaching, like learning, is never done in exactly the same way by any two individuals, and teachers generally prefer to teach the way they learn best. For the most part, students' learning styles should match teachers' teaching styles if students are to achieve optimally in school. When there is a mismatch, poor achievement may result. Given that the learning styles of African-Americans are often different from those of whites (Dunn et al., 1989) and given that most teachers are white, such a mismatch is likely to occur. Consequently, many educators and concerned others have called for efforts aimed at increasing the number of African-Americans in the teaching profession.

Teacher expectations have been shown to be strongly related to student achievement and performance. Negative teacher expectations result in low student motivation and poor performance. This phenomenon is often referred to as a self-fulfilling prophecy,* defined as a false or groundless expectation that comes true simply because it has been expected. When teachers communicate to students that their expectations are low, students tend to perform at low levels and lose faith in their ability to perform at higher levels. This communication can be either subtle and indirect or blatant and direct. Subtle messages take the form of nonverbal cues, while blatant and direct messages tend to be verbal or written. Both cases, when negative, are especially detrimental to the achievement and motivation of African-Americans, who are often marginalized in American school classrooms.

Testing and assessment are other important issues that affect the learning of African-Americans. U.S. public schools currently administer over 150 million standardized tests of achievement, competency, and basic and advanced skills per year (an average of 2.5 tests per student per year). Many of these tests have been shown to be biased relative to language differences or to be based on questions that reflect the experiences and facts of the dominant culture. Too often, the "correct" answers on these tests favor middle-class values and highly verbal students. The tests likewise fail to access accurately and adequately the skills, abilities, and strengths of African-American learners, such that these students do not receive the educational opportunities and experiences they need to achieve optimally.

The U.S. educational process, particularly relative to curriculum and instruction, ignores the contributions of African-Americans to world civilization and is full of negative perceptions of African-American and other nonwhite cultures. Perhaps most detrimental academically to African-American children is the reluctance of U.S. educators to broaden the cultural base of pedagogy and curricula. Black History Month notwithstanding, African-Americans must often wait until high school and sometimes college to learn about black heroes and heroines and to gain an understanding of the contributions of blacks to world history. Though increased cultural awareness of black heroes and heroines has been shown to enhance the self-concept and identity of African-American students, its effect on academic performance and outcomes has yet to be completely understood. Many forces threaten to impede the success of African-Americans in educational settings. However, increased sensitivity to their needs and proactive efforts can increase the academic success of African-American students.

SELECTED BIBLIOGRAPHY

R. Dunn, J. Beaudry, and A. Klavas, "Survey of Research on Learning Styles," *Educational Leadership* 47, no. 6 (1989): 50–57; S. T. Johnson, W. T. Starnes, D. Gregory, and A. Blaylock, "Program of Assessment, Diagnosis and Instruction (PADI): Identifying and Nurturing Potentially Gifted and Talented Minority Students," *Journal of Negro Education* 24 (1985): 416–30; D. M. Neill and N. J. Medina, "Standardized Testing: Harmful to Educational Health," *Phi Delta Kappan* 70, no. 9 (1989): 688–797.

DONNA Y. FORD

LEE v. MACON COUNTY BOARD OF EDUCATION, CA, 604-E (M.D. Ala., 1964). On 13 August 1963, Judge Frank M. Johnson, Jr., of the Federal District Court of the Middle District of Alabama ordered the Macon County Board of Education to begin desegregating its public schools immediately, under the 1955 Alabama School Placement Law. In September 1963, Detroit Lee, a citizen of Tuskegee, Alabama, with school-age children, submitted a petition along with six other sets of parents to the Macon board, asking for desegregation of all city and county public schools. The board did not reply to the petition; consequently, Lee sought and secured the assistance of the Tuskegee Civic Association (TCA) to file a desegregation suit against the board. In January 1963, the TCA's attorney, Fred D. Gray, filed a complaint, *Anthony T. Lee et al. v. Macon County Board of Education*, on behalf of sixteen African-American children. The purpose of this class-action suit was to obtain a permanent injunction against the

Macon County Board of Education to enjoin it from continuing the policy and practice of operating a segregated school system. The board voted to accept the court decision and to open the Tuskegee High school on a desegregated basis on 2 September, 1963.

Of the original sixteen plaintiffs, only four were admitted, along with nine new transfers. Anthony Lee, the lead plaintiff of the original group, was among those admitted. Plans for the 2 September opening were circumvented by an order from Governor George Wallace to delay the opening for one week. Wallace sent one hundred state troopers to Tuskegee High School to enforce his order. The thirteen black students arrived by school bus on opening day but were not allowed to get out of the bus. After a one-week delay, the school was opened with 275 white students and the thirteen African-American students. However, after one week of desegregation, white parents withdrew all of their children from school. One black student was expelled. Most of the white students enrolled in the newly established private white Macon Academy or in segregated schools in other countries. Because Tuskegee High had an enrollment of only the remaining twelve black students, its accreditation was revoked and the state board of education ordered it closed at the end of the first semester. The black students applied for transfers to schools in nearby Notasulga and Shorter. Six were assigned to each school. The Shorter school accepted the black students without incident, but Mayor James Rea of Notasulga blocked the entrance of the six black students assigned to his town's high school, Macon County High, claiming that the school had to be closed because of its violation of a hastily enacted fire ordinance. Judge Johnson promptly overruled the validity of the fire ordinance and ordered the students admitted. After a few months, the building containing classes for the African-American students burned down and the county board reassigned them back to the all-black high school in Tuskegee. Federal judges again intervened, ordering Macon County High to find space for the African-American students in another building.

The "Tuskegee Twelve" completed the 1963–64 academic year in the two formerly all-white county high schools. Three of them graduated from the Macon County High School in May 1964. The 1964–65 school year witnessed the reopening of Tuskegee High School with fourteen black students and a majority of white students. Enrollment at the school remained stable until the fall of 1966, when African-American students became the majority due to an increase in transfers by white students, all of whom withdrew within the next two years. By the end of the decade, Macon County High School was the only integrated school in the county. White flight* did not occur in Notasulga because it is the only town in Macon County with a substantial white majority population. Conversely, Macon County was 86 percent black; with the continuing exodus of white students, a predominantly African-American school enrollment prevailed.

In 1967, Judge Johnson expanded *Lee v. Macon* to make it a statewide school desegregation order. Gradually, the suit brought about peaceful desegregation in most public schools and junior colleges in Alabama.

SELECTED BIBLIOGRAPHY
Jessie P. Guzman, *Crusade for Civic Democracy: The Story of the Tuskegee Civic Association, 1941–1970* (1984); Robert J. Norrell, *Reaping the Whirlwind: The Civil Rights Movement in Tuskegee* (1985); Tuskegee Civic Association, *TCA Yesterday, Today and Tomorrow* (1988).

EDWIN HAMILTON

LEGAL EDUCATION AND AFRICAN-AMERICANS. Prior to the 1954 *Brown v. Board of Education of Topeka, Kansas** decision, African-Americans sought equal footing in their access to legal education and the legal profession. Until modern times, lawyers were trained through apprentice programs, in which aspiring students studied under legal masters. Historically, African-Americans were excluded from this practice because white lawyers would not accept African-Americans as apprentices. With the abolishment of the apprentice programs, African-Americans who sought entrance to white legal institutions faced insurmountable discriminatory practices. Although Harvard University produced the first African-American law school graduate, George Ruffen, in 1869, most white institutions excluded African-Americans. Those institutions, primarily in the North, that did not exclude African-Americans admitted only a few and only on a token basis.

As a result of discriminatory practices, African-Americans seeking a legal education faced four basic problems. Southern African-Americans invariably had to travel to the North, where tokenism limited the opportunities for legal scholarship. African-Americans who successfully completed law school had great difficulty in finding work; and many African-Americans simply could not pass the bar in many states. Although these problems were significant, lack of financial resources also plagued an overwhelming number of African-Americans who wanted to study law.

The practice of excluding African-Americans from southern universities and admitting token numbers in northern universities continued as late as 1935. The "separate but equal" standard set by *Plessy v. Ferguson** (1896) began the tradition of racial separation in public education and was the method used to keep African-Americans from obtaining legal education. In October 1935, the Maryland Court of Appeals ordered the University of Maryland Law School to admit Donald G. Murray because separate law schools for African-Americans did not exist in Maryland. If the state could have furnished "equal treatment" in legal training by providing Murray with a scholarship to attend an out-of-state school or if a separate school solely for African-Americans had existed in Maryland, the court would have ruled differently.

Another phenomenon, the concept of separate-but-equal law schools, emerged out of the Supreme Court's decision in *Missouri ex rel Gaines v. Canada** (1938), in which state-assisted schools were required to admit African-Americans when separate African-American institutions did not exist. This practice continued until the 1950 *Sweatt v. Painter** decision, which required the

University of Texas to admit African-American students even though a separate
law school was established for them. Sweatt's argument was that the newly
formed law school was indeed "separate" but definitely not "equal" to the
legal education he would receive at Texas University.

Southern states that established African-American law schools did so with
little funding; therefore, it was widely assumed that these newly formed institutions could never be equal to white law institutions. Howard University's*
law school, established in 1869, twenty-seven years before the separate-but-
equal doctrine became law, bore the heaviest responsibility for training a significant percentage of the nation's African-American lawyers. By the 1960s,
proponents of legal education realized that an increase in the number of African-
American lawyers was greatly needed. Many legal institutions devised special
programs aimed at helping African-American students. Debates over a fail-proof
method centered around lowering admissions standards for special admissions
and establishing preparatory programs to increase the number of African-
Americans in law schools.

One program that made a tremendous impact was developed by the Council
on Legal Education Opportunity (CLEO). CLEO was formed in 1968 to assist
educationally and economically disadvantaged students to enter accredited law
institutions, thereby increasing the number of African-American attorneys who
eventually will represent clients who cannot afford quality legal representation
because of educational and economic restraints. It offers summer institutes to
prospective law students and annual monetary fellowships to students who complete the CLEO program and attend law school.

As a result of the many programs aimed at helping African-Americans, the
1970s marked an increase in minority student enrollment in law schools. Many
whites, however, felt that preferential admissions policies and special programs
were unconstitutional and sought legal action to rid higher education institutions
of minority admissions programs. The first test case for the validity of minority
preferential treatment in admissions policies of law schools was *DeFunis v.
Odegaard* (1974). DeFunis applied for the University of Washington Law
School twice and was denied admission. He claimed that these denials constituted unlawful discrimination against white males. At the trial level, the court
sided with DeFunis and ordered the university to admit him. The case went to
the state supreme court, where the decision was overturned. The court held the
decision moot, as DeFunis was attending another law school and would not
attend the University of Washington Law School even if he won the suit.

*Regents of the University of California v. Bakke** (1978) had far-reaching
significance for African-American law school entrants, as it presented another
challenge to the constitutionality of minority preference admissions programs.
Allen Bakke was denied admissions to the University of California at Davis
medical school in 1973 and 1974 because he did not meet the requirements
under general admissions. The university operated a special admissions program
for economically and/or educationally disadvantaged students that reserved six-

teen out of one hundred seats for minority applicants. Bakke alleged that the special admissions process violated Title VI of the Federal Civil Rights Act. The Supreme Court held that the special program did violate Title VI, striking all quota programs, which in the past had enabled more African-Americans to enter graduate and law schools. The *Bakke* decision meant that federally funded institutions could not use race as an admissions criterion because the practice violates Title VI of the Civil Rights Act, although race could be taken into account.

The *DeFunis* and *Bakke* cases received enormous public attention because they challenged affirmative action. Neither decision, however, truly settled the question of whether special programs for African-Americans could survive to allow more access to the legal field.

According to American Bar Association (ABA) reports, African-American enrollment in 142 ABA-approved legal institutions increased in the 1980s. From 1978 to 1979 there were 5,350 African-American law students, while from 1984 to 1985 the numbers grew to 5,955, 4.74 percent of the total enrollment in all law schools. If this number is compared to the total number of law students, 121,606, in 1978–79 and 125,698 in 1984–85, the increase in African-American enrollment seems quite small.

The 1980s brought a series of protests by African-Americans concerning the disproportionate representation of blacks on the faculties of predominantly white law schools. In December 1982, African-American students at Harvard Law School demanded to have more tenured African-Americans and women on the Harvard Law School faculty. Students believed legal education would be served best by the inclusion of faculty with a variety of perspectives. The administration responded by reporting that one minority person was committed to the faculty for the 1983–84 fall semester. During this time, Harvard had an 11 percent African-American enrollment and two African-American faculty members.

If simply for the reasons noted above, there are concrete arguments for embracing the value of African-American law schools. Historically African-American legal institutions meet a very important need by admitting students who ordinarily may not be accepted by other schools. Additionally, students can more freely express ideas and can focus on legal problems that face African-Americans without persecution from others. Most important, minority schools have a history of supporting the African-American students academically as well as emotionally.

As issues in the legal arena began to slightly improve, 1991 brought back a familiar, upsetting twist to the issue of African-Americans and legal education. A Georgetown University law student, Timothy McGuire, in a student publication compared the aptitude test scores and grade point averages of African-American and white students. McGuire, who worked as a clerk in the admissions office, had illegally reviewed the records of African-American applicants and claimed that, on the average, minority applicants scored lower than white applicants. Once again, affirmative action and selection policies that give special consideration to African-Americans became an issue.

In September 1992, the Department of Education declared that the fourteen-year-old policy at the University of California at Berkeley that helped minority candidates gain admission to the school violated federal law. The policy was that African-Americans would only compete against African-Americans for placement in the law school and Hispanics would only compete against Hispanics, just as whites would compete against whites. Berkeley had used the admission procedures to maintain racial diversity on campus. As a result, the school entered into a voluntary conciliatory agreement that promised the school would not base its admissions decisions "solely on race, color or national origin."

Although there was a slight drop in law school enrollments nationwide in 1993, the number of minority students increased. A survey released by the American Bar Association (ABA) showed a 9.6 percent jump in the number of minority students enrolled in accredited juris doctor programs. There were 21,266 minority students enrolled as compared to 19,410 in 1992. African-Americans represented 40.9 percent of the total minority law school population. The numbers clearly indicate that although law school populations are becoming more diverse, change for African-Americans is coming very slowly. According to the Law School Admission Council, African-Americans, more than any other minority group, tend to wait longer to apply to law school. The primary reasons for this delay tend to be the lack of funds and the desire to explore other options.

SELECTED BIBLIOGRAPHY

Daniel Bernstine, *An Empirical Study of the University of Wisconsin Law School Special Admissions Program: A Progress Report* (1981); *Brown v. Board of Education*, 347 U.S. 483 (1954); *Christian Science Monitor* 24 (December 1982); Abraham Davis, *Blacks in the Federal Judiciary: Neutral Arbitrators or Judicial Activists?* (1989); *Missouri ex rel. Gaines v. Canada, Registrar of the University of Missouri et al.*, 305 U.S. 337 (1938); Allen Sindler, *Bakke, DeFunis, and Minority Admissions: The Quest for Equal Opportunity* (1978).

DENISE ANITA BALTIMORE

LEMOYNE–OWEN COLLEGE. LeMoyne–Owen College, an institution rich in tradition and very much a part of city life in Memphis, Tennessee, is the product of the 1968 merger of LeMoyne and Owen colleges, two institutions that trace their histories back to the nineteenth century. This private, four-year, coeducational, urban residential liberal arts college offers the bachelor of arts, bachelor of business administration, and bachelor of science degrees. A charter member of the United Negro College Fund,* the college is fully accredited by the Southern Association of Colleges and Schools.* With eighteen major fields of study available, LeMoyne–Owen has particular strengths in biology (pre–health professions), computer science, teacher education, social work, English, political science, and business administration (accounting and entrepreneurial studies). Its core curriculum provides students with a holistic and integrated approach to the study of basic skills and the liberal arts and sciences. The Division of Lifelong Learning at Lemoyne–Owen offers part-time undergraduate degree and credit-bearing programs and innovative continuing education programs in evening and weekend formats and also administers two summer sessions.

SELECTED BIBLIOGRAPHY

National Association for Equal Opportunity in Higher Education, *Profiles of the Nation's Historically and Predominantly Black Colleges and Universities* (1993).

SAMUEL L. MYERS

LIBRARIES AND LIBRARIANS, AFRICAN-AMERICAN. The story of African-American librarianship begins at Hampton Institute (now University).* As the Board of Education for Librarianship noted in its 1924–25 annual report, for the "proper development of library work for Negroes in the south, there should be preparation of Negro librarians in that environment." To this end, the Hampton Library School was founded at Hampton in September 1925 by a grant from the Carnegie Corporation. At that time there was only one other accredited library school in the south, Emory University Library School in Atlanta, Georgia, but that institution did not admit African-Americans. In its fourteen-year history, Hampton Library School graduated almost two hundred librarians, including a class of twenty-one graduating with the B.S. degree in Library Science. The school closed in June 1939 because of lack of financial support.

Another library school primarily created to train African-American librarians is the School of Library and Information Science at North Carolina Central University.* This school was authorized by the North Carolina state legislature in 1939, when that body amended the charter of the university, formerly known as the North Carolina College for Negroes. The Department of Library Science was established in the fall of 1939. In 1941, the School of Library Science was organized as a professional school. This school, which began offering a master's degree program in 1950, awarded its first degree in 1951. The school was accredited by the American Library Association in 1975. In 1984, it was renamed the School of Library and Information Sciences.

Founded in 1941 with the support of the Carnegie Corporation, the Atlanta University (now Clark Atlanta University*) School of Library Service was designed to replace the defunct Hampton Library School. In 1943, the school was fully accredited by the American Library Association to offer the B.S. and L.S. degrees and in 1949, the graduate program leading to a master's degree was initiated. The Atlanta school offered specialization in five areas of librarianship: college library service, school library service, public library service (general), public library service for children and young people, and reference and cataloging. Its graduate professional program emphasized the content of books and the basic concepts of knowledge, the field of communications, and the administrative and functional aspects of school, college, and public library service. The program also provided experience in the use of research methods and prepared teachers to give instruction in undergraduate courses in library service. The instructional program was supplemented by supervised field work done in college, university, public, and school libraries in Atlanta.

African-American book collections are located in every region of the nation, including state, public, and university libraries, along with collection in archives throughout the county. Some of the smaller collection include the James Weldon Johnson Memorial Collection at Yale, the Charles Blockson Collection at Temple University, and the Carter G. Woodson* Library of the Chicago Public Library system. Tuskegee University* houses the Booker T. Washington* Collection and the George Washington Carver Collection. In 1936, the Atlanta University Library began the formation of its Negro Collection with the purchase of the archives of the *Atlanta Independent* covering the years 1904–28. In 1942, the Harold Jacksman Collection of Contemporary Negro Life was added. The university's subsequent purchase of the Henry Slaughter Collection enhanced the prestige of the Negro Collection. In 1952, another collection, the Lincoln Collection, was added. These various collections were overseen by librarian Lawrence D. Reddick.

Among the larger African-American history collections are the Moorland-Spingarn Research Center* at Howard University,* the Schomburg Center for Research in Black Culture in New York City, the Fisk University* Library, and the Atlanta University Library. Founded in 1914, the Moorland–Spingarn Research Center at Howard University is one of the largest and most comprehensive collections of books, periodicals, manuscripts, sheet music, oral history interviews, photographs, artifacts, and memorabilia by and about African-Americans. Dorothy Porter Wesley, who served as its curator from 1930 to 1973, devoted her life to developing the Moorland Foundation. The collection was established in 1873 with the acquisition of the Tappan Antislavery Collection. The Jesse Moorland* Collection was added in 1914, and the Arthur Spingarn* acquisition was added in 1946. After Wesley's retirement, the university recognized her achievements with the dedication of the Dorothy B. Porter Room, which now houses the Howard University Museum. In 1973, the Moorland Foundation was renamed the Moorland–Spingarn Research Center.

The Schomburg Center for Research in Black Culture, part of the New York Public Library, opened in 1925, when the Division of Negro Literature, History and Prints was established at the 135th Street Branch Library. In 1926, African-American bibliofile Arthur A. Schomburg's collection was purchased and, in 1932, Schomburg came to the library as curator. After his death in 1938, the Negro Division was renamed in his honor. Jean Blackwell Hutson joined the Schomburg Center staff in 1936 and began to publicize the collection. She also supervised the filming of the Schomburg Catalog by the G. K. Hall Company. In 1972, the collection was transferred to the Research Libraries of the New York Public Library and renamed the Schomburg Center for Research in Black Culture.

Along with pioneers such as Wesley, Hutson, and Virginia Lacy Jones, several other African-American librarians/bibliophiles have made significant contributions to the field. Some of these include Daniel Alexander Murray, assistant librarian at the Library of Congress in 1880; Edward Christopher Williams, the first professionally trained African-American librarian, who was employed at the Western Reserve University's Adelbert College; Virginia Proctor Powell Florence, the first professionally trained African-American librarian to graduate from the Pittsburgh Carnegie Library School; and Sadie Peterson Delaney, who started the library at Tuskegee Institute Veteran's Hospital and began her pioneering work in bibliotherapy. Eliza Atkins Gleason, the first dean of Atlanta University's School of Library Science, was also the first African-American to obtain a Ph.D. in librarianship. Clara Stanton Jones was the first African-American and the first woman appointed director of the Detroit Public Library and the first African-American president of the American Library Association (ALA).

At the 1970 midwinter meeting of the American Library Association, the African-American members decided that the association was not adequately responding to the needs of African-American professionals and that a caucus would give them a chance to take better control of their professional destinies. The ALA Black Caucus had two initial goals: (a) that its Statement of Concern be read as a matter of record and (b) that a resolution to council be made to censure and bring sanctions against libraries and/or librarians that provided services to segregated schools. Since its inception, the ALA Black Caucus has provided scholarship support to library students at the University of Maryland School of Library and Information Services, aided the Library of Congress Black Employees Association in its efforts to eliminate discrimination, and provided support for African-American and Chicano employees at the Los Angeles County Public Library System. The caucus has also worked with the NAACP* in gathering information on libraries in segregated southern academies and has instituted an exchange of librarians between the U.S. and Africa. Other caucus activities include publishing a quarterly newsletter and sponsorship of workshops and conferences designed to promote and develop African-American librarianship. In 1988, at a midwinter membership meeting in Chicago, a group of Black Caucus members developed a strategy to address major issues confronting African-American librarianship, including organizational structure, membership services, and the role of African-American librarians in American society. The resulting mission statement set forth the following goals: "to serve as an advocate for the development, promotion, and improvement of library services and resources to the nation's African-American community; and to provide leadership for the recruitment and professional development of African-American librarians."

Issues of racial and ethnic diversity remain to be fully addressed by the library profession. Statistics compiled by the Association for Library and Information Science Education (ALISE) show that the field fails to attract minority entrants.

During academic year 1981–82, African-Americans accounted for 4 percent of all graduates from ALA–accredited library schools; by 1994, the number had declined to 3.2 percent of the total. Several strategies have been proposed to increase the numbers of minority librarians, including cooperative hiring efforts, enhanced financial incentives for students, and more aggressive recruitment of students, beginning as early as junior high school. It has been suggested that if only 10 percent of library science educators and librarians worked to mentor only one new minority entrant a year, the results would alter the demographics of the profession forever.

The 1990s have brought significant strides in the field of African-American librarianship. September 1992 marked the first national conference on African-American librarians. This conference, titled "Culture Keepers: Enlightening and Empowering Our Communities," was held in Columbus, Ohio. A follow-up, "Culture Keepers II: Unity Through Diversity," was held in Milwaukee in August 1994. "Culture Keepers III: Making Global Connections" is scheduled for 1997. Congressman Major Owens (D-NY), himself a librarian-turned-politician, noted at the opening session of the first conference that such meetings represent ambitious and expansionist thinking. He further urged African-American librarians to resolve to become culture keepers not only for African-Americans but also for Africans throughout the diaspora and in Africa. In June 1995 the ALA Black Caucus celebrated its twenty-fifth anniversary with a gala reception and benefit for the E. J. Josey Scholarship Fund to aid African-Americans pursuing a library science degree. Moving toward the twenty-first century, the ALA Black Caucus has developed a strategic planning committee to recognize the goals already accomplished and to plan for the future, including administrative/organizational, professional, and financial development, along with advocacy/outreach programs.

SELECTED BIBLIOGRAPHY

Thomas C. Battle, "Moorland-Spingarn Research Center, Howard University," *Library Quarterly* 58 (April 1988): 144–45: Jean Blackwell Hutson, "The Schomburg Center for Research in Black Culture," in Elinor DesVerney Sinnette, W. Paul Coates, and Thomas C. Battle, eds., *Black Bibliophiles and Collectors: Preservers of Black History* (1990); Casper LeRoy Jordan and E. J. Josey, "A Chronology of Events in Black Librarianship," in E. J. Josey and Ann Allen Schockley, eds., *Handbook of Black Librarianship* (1977), pp. 15–24; Kathleen de la Pena McCook and Paula Geist, "Diversity Deferred: Where Are the Minority Librarians?" *Library Journal* 118 (November 1993): 35–39; Jessie Carney Smith, *Black Academic Libraries and Research Collections: An Historical Survey.* (1977); S. L. Smith, "The Passing of the Hampton Library School," *Journal of Negro Education* 9 (January 1940): 51–58.

JANET SIMS–WOOD

LIDDELL v. MISSOURI, 731 F.2d 1294 (8th Cir. 1984), cert. denied, 469 U.S. 816 (1984). This case is commonly known as "the St. Louis desegregation case." More than twelve years after African-American parents brought suit to integrate the public schools of the city of St. Louis, Missouri, the Eighth Circuit

Court of Appeals upheld a settlement agreement between the city school district and twenty-three suburban school corporations. The facts and issues in the case must be viewed in the context of its long history, caused by the parties' propensity to appeal almost all of the decisions of the federal district court. In February 1972, *Liddell* was filed as a class action, alleging racial segregation in the St. Louis city schools in violation of the Fourteenth Amendment of the Constitution. After the federal district judge denied a motion by the St. Louis City Board of Education to join the state of Missouri and St. Louis County (containing the suburban school districts) as codefendants, the original parties entered into a modest consent agreement. This agreement called for an increase in the number of minority teachers and included a pledge by the board of education to attempt to implement racial balance in the city schools.

In 1977, the district court permitted the NAACP,* the City of St. Louis, two white citizens' groups, and the United States to intervene as plaintiffs in the case. The court also added the state of Missouri, the state board of education, and the state's commissioner of education as defendants. The court ordered a trial to determine whether the St. Louis city schools were unconstitutionally segregated. The district court ruled in favor of the defendants, finding no constitutional violation, and declared that, through its neighborhood school policy, the local board of education had achieved a unitary system in accord with the Supreme Court's 1954 *Brown v. Board of Education of Topeka, Kansas** decision.

In 1980, the Eighth Circuit Court of Appeals reversed the district court in *Adams v. United States* (1980), holding that the St. Louis City Board of Education and the state were jointly liable for the establishment and maintenance of a racially segregated school system within the city of St. Louis. The appeals court pointed out that the Missouri state constitution had mandated separate schools for "white and colored" children through 1976 and ruled that the state had failed to set in motion a timely desegregation plan after the *Brown* decision. Subsequently, the district court ordered the establishment of a mandatory desegregation plan for the city schools, with funding for its implementation shared equally between the city board of education and the state. The desegregation plan provided for transferring and exchanging students between the city and suburban schools, as well as the establishment of magnet schools and integrative programs. In 1982, however, the state filed suit, alleging that it was not financially responsible for certain desegregation costs. Simultaneously, the city's board of education and other plaintiffs sought the consolidation of the city and suburban county schools into one unified school district, arguing that the suburban defendants had also unconstitutionally acted to cause the racial imbalance in St. Louis's inner city. At this stage of the proceedings, the appeals court made it clear that interdistrict desegregation plans involving suburban school districts (like that ordered by the district court) would be sustained only if evidence established constitutional wrongdoing on the part of the suburban schools. Thus, the court reminded the litigants of the Supreme Court's holding in *Milliken v. Bradley** (1974), in which the high court struck down a Detroit desegregation plan because the plaintiffs had failed to prove interdistrict (city and suburban) discrimination.

Given the standoff between the city schools and the state, and the position taken by the appeals court, the district court relied on an innovative approach to involve the parties in the framing of a final settlement agreement. The court revealed a mandatory interdistrict desegregation plan that it would impose in the event the suburban schools were found to have engaged in purposeful discrimination. The plan established one unified school district. The court then scheduled hearings to determine whether the suburban school districts had committed constitutional violations. Shortly before the hearings were to begin, the city school district and all twenty-three suburban school districts agreed to a voluntary interdistrict desegregation plan. The plan required each suburban school district to accept voluntary African-American city transfers. In an effort to attract white students to the inner-city schools and improve curricular offerings in all city schools, the plan provided for the development and expansion of magnet schools and the overall improvement of the quality of education in the city schools.

In 1984, the state of Missouri, relying on the *Milliken I* decision, appealed the order approving the interdistrict settlement plan. It was this case, argued before the Eighth Circuit, that distinguished *Lidell* from other school desegregation litigation. The court held that the plan approved by the district court justly required the state to pay the full cost of interdistrict transfer, despite the state's contention that the interdistrict remedy was inappropriate as no interdistrict violation was ever legally demonstrated. The court found that the state's reliance on the *Milliken* case was misplaced because of the gravity and duration of the state's constitutional violation. The court also upheld orders requiring the state to pay the entire capital and operating costs of the magnet schools in the city, payment for one half of the costs for capital improvements, and payment for compensatory and remedial programs related to quality educational improvements in the city's segregated schools. The Supreme Court denied review of the case in October of 1984.

The primary significance of *Liddell* lies in the fact that the court approved a plan that allowed the parties to employ a number of flexible voluntary devices such as magnet schools, choice, and special programs with more resources while requiring the state to financially underwrite much of the plan. Many civil rights activists, who generally opposed magnet school desegregation programs, applauded the decision as offering an alternative to court-ordered busing to achieve a unitary school district.

SELECTED BIBLIOGRAPHY

Adams v. United States, 620 F.2d 1277 (8th Cir. 1980), cert. denied, 449 U.S. 826 (1980); *Brown v. Board of Education*, 347 U.S. 483 (1954); *Liddell v. State of Missouri*, 567 F. Supp. 1037 (E.D. Mo. 1983); *Liddell v. Board of Education*, 677 F.2d 626 (8th Cir.

1982), cert. denied, 459 U.S. 877 (1983); *Los Angeles Daily Journal*, 17 August 1983, p. 4; Rosemary Salomone, *Equal Education under Law* (1986).

JOSEPH R. MCKINNEY

LINCOLN UNIVERSITY OF MISSOURI. Located on fifty-two acres on the southeast corner of Jefferson City, Missouri, Lincoln University is a land-grant, comprehensive, multipurpose institution of higher education, offering associate, baccalaureate, and master's degrees. It was founded by members of the 62nd and the 65th U.S. Colored Infantry units as Lincoln Institute in 1866. Lincoln has a rich heritage and history of service to Missouri and the nation. Since 1954, it has moved forward with the process of racial integration and today stands as one of America's effective models of multicultural higher education. Approximately 151 full-time faculty members and a complement of adjunct faculty members provide instruction in the fifty-five degree programs (forty-four undergraduate and eleven graduate). The institution is recognized for its quality academic programs; its off-campus and continuing education services for government and other full-time workers and for incarcerated person; and its work with less-developed countries through the United States Agency for International Development. In 1983, the National Trust for Historic Preservation designated seven buildings on the Lincoln University campus as an historic district. Lincoln University is accredited by the North Central Association of Colleges and Schools, and its teacher education programs are accredited by the National Council for Accreditation of Teacher Education. Its nursing program is accredited by the National League of Nursing, and its music education program is accredited by the National Association of Schools of Music.

SELECTED BIBLIOGRAPHY

National Association for Equal Opportunity in Higher Education, *Profiles of the Nation's Historically and Predominantly Black Colleges and Universities* (1993).

SAMUEL L. MYERS

LINCOLN UNIVERSITY OF PENNSYLVANIA. Lincoln University in Chester County, Pennsylvania, was chartered in 1854 as America's first college for students of African descent. It is known for its diverse and distinguished faculty, its multinational and multiethnic student body, and its innovative, globally inclusive curriculum anchored in the African-American experience. Originally an all-male college, Lincoln graduated its first woman in 1953 and became fully coeducational in 1965. Today, it is a state-related, predominantly liberal arts institution. During its first one hundred years, graduates of this small university made up 20 percent of the African-American physicians and over 10 percent of the African-American attorneys in the United States. Its alumni include two African heads of state; government ministers and other officials in at least fourteen African countries; thirty-six college presidents; a dozen ambassadors from the United States, Africa, and the Caribbean; many federal, state, and municipal judges; several mayors and city managers; and noted professionals in virtually every field. In recent years, Lincoln has conferred almost half of the bachelor's degrees awarded in the sciences to African-Americans attending Pennsylvania institutions. It is also one of the country's leading producers of African-American undergraduate physics majors. Over 80 percent of its science graduates go on to graduate or professional schools.

SELECTED BIBLIOGRAPHY

National Association for Equal Opportunity in Higher Education, *Profiles of the Nation's Historically and Predominantly Black Colleges and Universities* (1993).

                                                                SAMUEL L. MYERS

LITTLE ROCK NINE. The Little Rock Nine is the name used to describe the nine African-American teenagers (six girls, three boys) who, in an effort to fulfill the promise of the 1954 *Brown v. Board of Education of Topeka, Kansas** decision, integrated all-white Central High School in Little Rock, Arkansas, in 1957. The individual students were Minnijean Brown, Elizabeth Eckford, Ernest Green, Thelma Mothershed, Melba Pattillo, Gloria Ray, Terrance Roberts, Jefferson Thomas, and Carlotta Walls.

In February 1956, lawyers for the National Association for the Advancement of Colored People (NAACP),* under the leadership of Thurgood Marshall* and Wiley Branton, Sr., and with the cooperation of newspaperwoman and Arkansas NAACP president Daisy Bates, failed in their efforts to get a federal district court ruling supporting the immediate integration of the state's public schools. The judge held that gradual integration was acceptable. Undaunted, Bates identified nine students who were willing and courageous enough to attempt integrating Little Rock's segregated white high school the following year. The students' initial efforts to register for school on 4 September 1957, were thwarted by Arkansas governor Orval Faubus, who called out the state's National Guard to prevent them from entering the school building, and by menacing, threatening whites who gathered at the scene. On 23 September, the nine tried again. This time, they were allowed to enter and attend some classes, but they had to be rushed out of the building before the end of the school day when an angry mob of whites stormed the school grounds seeking to harm them. Because these actions and those of the governor violated federal law as prescribed by the Supreme Court's ruling in *Brown*, President Dwight D. Eisenhower was forced to send in soldiers from the 101st Airborne Division to escort the Little Rock Nine back into Central High School on 25 September 1957. The soldiers remained at the school for several more weeks, but their numbers were gradually reduced until they were completely withdrawn in late November and the Arkansas National Guard was federalized to continue the vigil.

The 1957–58 school year was a stormy one for the Little Rock Nine and their families. The atmosphere at Central High was warlike. The nine faced almost continual harassment from their white counterparts at school, including taunts and insults as well as being pushed and hit. Some had acid thrown into their eyes; others had water, eggs, and soup dumped on their heads. Although at least one teacher and the girls' vice principal were fairminded in their treatment of Central's new African-American students, most of the teachers were unsympathetic and unsupportive. They turned a blind eye as the students suffered physical and verbal abuse and were restricted from participating in any of the school's extracurricular or other activities.

The Arkansas NAACP also came under attack for its efforts on behalf of the Little Rock Nine. Bates was fined one hundred dollars for refusing to supply information on the organization and its membership to city and state officials. She was repeatedly threatened and harassed. Her newspaper, the *Arkansas State Press*, was boycotted by its major advertisers, and her home was bombed.

The segregationists hoped that all nine students and their adult supporters would break under the sustained pressures of mistreatment they received in the integrated school setting. Their hopes were fueled when just before Christmas, one of the nine, Minnijean Brown, was suspended for retaliating against two white boys who were harassing her in the cafeteria. In February 1958, after several more such incidents, Brown was expelled. She subsequently received a scholarship to attend a private high school in New York. The remaining eight students suffered through the rest of the year, facing increasing pressures and occasionally befriended by a white student or two. On 27 May 1958, despite numerous death threats and other efforts to dispel his achievement and that of the black community that had supported him and the other members of the Little Rock Nine, Ernest Green graduated from Central High School, the first African-American to do so in the school's forty-nine-year history.

The remaining seven students expected to reenter Central High School in the fall of the following year, but Governor Faubus closed all of Little Rock's high schools in 1958 rather than continuing with integration efforts. The schools did not reopen at all that school year. Subsequently, two of the Little Rock Nine's families moved away. Others of the group went to live with supportive families and attend school in northern states, while some continued their studies through correspondence courses. Central High School reopened in September 1960 as an integrated building, but only two students from the original Little Rock Nine, Carlotta Walls and Jefferson Thomas, returned; both graduated from Central. All nine students eventually went on to become successful, contributing adults.

In 1958, the members of the Little Rock Nine received the NAACP's Spingarn Medal for their courage in breaking racial barriers. On 23 October 1987, then-Governor (later President) Bill Clinton hosted a historic reunion of the group in the mansion built by former Governor Faubus.

SELECTED BIBLIOGRAPHY

Melba Pattillo Beals, *Warriors Don't Cry* (1994); Willie Wofford, "Little Rock Nine Return to School Where Violence Erupted 30 Years Ago," *Jet* 73 (9 November 1987): 14; "Ebony Update: Ernest Green," *Ebony* 43 (December 1987): 72–76; "The Ernest Green Story," *Jet* 83 (25 January 1993): 14–17, 65.

FAUSTINE C. JONES–WILSON

LIVINGSTONE COLLEGE. Livingstone College, located in Salisbury, North Carolina, is an accredited four-year liberal arts institution founded in 1879. Named for the legendary explorer, missionary, and philanthropist David Livingstone, the college was conceived, founded, and nurtured by the African Methodist Episcopal Zion Church.* Its undergraduate College of Arts and Sciences offers nonsectarian academic programs leading to the B.A., B.S., and B.S.W. degrees. Its Hood Theological Seminary offers professional training for the ministry leading to the master of divinity and the master of religious education degrees.

SELECTED BIBLIOGRAPHY

National Association for Equal Opportunity in Higher Education, *Profiles of the Nation's Historically and Predominantly Black Colleges and Universities* (1993).

SAMUEL L. MYERS

LOCKE, ALAIN LEROY (13 September 1886, Philadelphia, Pennsylvania–9 June 1954, New York, N.Y.). A writer, critic, philosopher, scholar in the social sciences, and cultural mentor, Locke was educated at the Philadelphia School of Pedagogy. He received the B.A. degree (with honors) from Harvard University in 1907 and the B. Litt. in 1910 from Oxford University, which he attended as a Rhodes Scholar. He pursued graduate study at the University of Berlin (1910–11) and Harvard University (Ph.D., 1918).

Locke was associated with Howard University* for forty-one years, serving as an assistant professor (1912–17), professor of philosophy (1917–53), and chairman of the philosophy department (1918–53.) He was also an exchange professor at Fisk University* (1927–28), Inter-American Exchange Professor to Haiti in 1943; and a visiting professor at the University of Wisconsin (1945–46) and the New School for Social Research, 1947. As editor of *The New Negro*, the landmark collection of writing that helped bring about the Harlem Renaissance, Locke was a major force in the development of modern African-American literature and culture. *The New Negro*, published in 1925, forced critics to take African-American writing and writers seriously because of the high literary quality of the anthology.

Locke held membership in the International Institute of African Languages and Culture; the American Negro Academy;* the American Philosophical Association; the League of American Writers; the Conference on Science, Philosophy, and Religion; and the Society for Historical Research. He founded the Associates in Negro Folk Education, editing its "Bronze Booklet" series. Locke was also active in Phi Beta Kappa, Phi Beta Sigma, Theta Sigma, and Sigma Pi Phi; he was also a member of the Academie des Sciences Coloniales, Sociedad de Estudios Afro-Cubanos, and the National Order of Honor and Merit in Haiti. He was also was named to the Honor Roll of Race Relations in 1942.

SELECTED BIBLIOGRAPHY
Abraham Chapman, ed., *Black Voices: An Anthology of Afro-American Literature* (1968); "Afro-American Writers from the Harlem Renaissance to 1940," *Dictionary of Literary Biography*, vol. 51 (1987); Linda Metzger, ed., *Black Writers* (1989).

HAROLD O. ROBINSON

LOGAN, RAYFORD WHITTINGHAM (7 January 1897, Washington, D.C.–4 November 1982, Washington, D.C.). A history professor, educator, and civil rights activist, Logan received an A.B. degree from Williams College in 1917 (Phi Beta Kappa) and an M.A. (1932) and Ph.D. (1936) from Harvard University. A major pioneer among twentieth-century Afro-American historians, Logan was the author or editor of fourteen books and dozens of articles in a career that included service as professor and chairperson of three history departments (Virginia Union University,* 1925–30; Atlanta University,* 1933–38; and Howard University,* 1942–1964). At Howard, Logan also served as history professor, 1938–41; historian of the university, 1965–69; distinguished professor of history, 1971–72; and professor emeritus, 1972–82.

Logan's national and international interests in civil and human rights were expressed through his active participation as secretary of the Pan-African Congress in Paris (1921), London (1923), Lisbon (1923), and New York City (1927). He also served as the foreign affairs editor of the *Pittsburgh Courier* from 1945 to 1948 and was the paper's accredited correspondent at the establishment of the United Nations in San Francisco in 1945. His organizational service also included work as an accredited observer for the NAACP* at the U.N.'s General Assembly in Paris (1951–52); as a member of the United States Committee for UNESCO (1947–50); as director of the Association for the Study of Negro Life and History* and editor of the *Journal of Negro History*, 1950–51; and as a consultant to the U.S. Department of State on the Inter-American Affairs bureau.

Logan wrote widely on such concerns as colonialism in African, the nature of American relations with Haiti and the Dominican Republic, and African-American history. His three most important historical studies are *The Betrayal of the Negro* (1965), originally published in 1954 as *The Negro in American Life and Thought; The American Negro: Old World Background and New World Experience*, with Irving S. Cohen (1967, 1970); and *Howard University: The First Hundred Years, 1867–1967* (1969). His most important works as an editor are *Memoirs of a Monticello Slave* (1951); *W. E. B. Du Bois: A Profile* (1971); and the *Dictionary of American Negro Biography* with Michael R. Winston, (1983).

Logan was the recipient of many honors for his outstanding contributions to foreign and American letters and life, including Commander of the National Order of Honor and Merit of the Republic of Haiti, a Fulbright Research Fellow to France (1950–51), an honorary L.H.D. degree from Williams College in 1965, and LL.D. from Howard University in 1972, and the 65th Spingarn Medal award from the NAACP in 1980. In 1970, the Department of History at Howard University inaugurated a history lecture series in his honor.

He was married in 1927 to Ruth Robinson, who died on 30 June, 1966. Logan served in the U.S. Army, Infantry, during World War I, 1917–19, and received a discharge as a first lieutenant. He died of congestive heart failure at the age of 85 and was buried in Fort Lincoln Cemetery, Washington, D.C.

SELECTED BIBLIOGRAPHY

Genna Rae McNeil and Michael R. Winston, eds., *Historical Judgments Reconsidered: Selected Howard University Lectures in Honor of Rayford W. Logan* (1988); Linda Metzger, Hal May, Deborah A. Straub, and Susan M. Trosky, eds., *Black Writers: A Selection of Sketches from Contemporary Authors* (1989); *New York Times*, 6 November 1982; James A. Page and Joe Min Roh, comp., *Selected Black American, African, and Caribbean Authors: A Bibliography* (1985); Earl E. Thorpe, *Black Historians: A Critique* (1971); *Washington Post*, 7 November 1982; *Who's Who among Black Americans, 1975–76* (1976).

JULIUS E. THOMPSON

LOVE, RUTH BURNETT (22 April 1935, Lawton, Oklahoma). An educator and administrator, Love made a powerful impact on educational practices, policies, and procedures during her thirty-year career in public education. She received a B.A. degree in elementary education from San Jose State University in 1954, obtained an M.A. degree in guidance and counseling from San Francisco State University, and in 1969 earned a doctorate in human behavior from the United States International University.

Love was a teacher and counselor in the Oakland Unified School District from 1954 to 1959 and from 1961 to 1963. During the summer of 1958, she was a project coordinator in a girl's correctional institution in New Mexico. She was a Fulbright Exchange Teacher in Cheshire, England, in 1960 and a project director for Open Crossroads in Ghana, West Africa, in 1962. In 1963, Love moved to the California State Department of Education, where she served first as a consultant in the Bureau of Pupil Personnel Services and then as the Bureau Chief for Program Development in Compensatory Education. Many of the programs she developed there were used as national models.

In 1971, Love left California to direct the federal Right-to-Read Program in the U.S. Office of Education. She returned to Oakland to succeed Marcus Foster as superintendent in 1975, whereupon she introduced innovative programs and strategies that produced improved test results among that district's students; she also identified and attracted increased financial resources to improve the fiscal condition of the district. She realized similar achievements in the Chicago school system, where she served as the general superintendent from 1981 to 1984. She was the first African-American and the first woman to hold that position and was the highest-paid superintendent in the nation.

Love has received numerous awards, citations, and honorary doctorates. She has authored eleven books, including a series on career education entitled *Hello*

World (1973). Her articles have appeared in national and international journals and periodicals.

SELECTED BIBLIOGRAPHY

Nancy Arnez, "Selected Black Female Superintendents of Public School Systems," *Journal of Negro Education* 51 (Summer 1982): 309–17; Interview with Ruth Love, 26 June 1994; Ruth B. Love, "Let's Reward for Success, Not Failure," *Reading Teacher* 30 (October 1976): 4–6; Dianne Pinderhughes, "Ruth B. Love," in Jessie Carney Smith, ed., *Notable Black American Women* (1992); *Who's Who among Black Americans*, 6th ed. (1991).

EURADELL L. PATTERSON

LUCY et al. v. ADAMS, DEAN OF ADMISSIONS, UNIVERSITY OF AL-ABAMA, 350 U.S. 1 (1955). In 1955, Autherine Juanita Lucy and Polly Anne Myers brought a class action suit in a federal district court against William F. Adams, dean of admissions of the University of Alabama, to clarify their rights and to obtain an injunction because they were denied admission to the university "solely on account of their race or color." The district court, on 26 August 1955, ruled that "in conformity with the equal protection clause of the Four-teenth Amendment, plaintiffs and others similarly situated are entitled to equal advantages and opportunities available at the University of Alabama at the same time and upon the same terms and qualifications available to other residents and citizens of the State of Alabama." The court granted the injunction requested, but suspended it pending defendants' appeal to the court of appeals. Plaintiffs then asked the U.S. Supreme Court to vacate the district court's order granting suspension of the injunction.

Citing *Sipuel,* * *Sweatt,* * and *McLaurin* * in a per curiam opinion, the Supreme Court, on 19 October 1955, granted plaintiffs' request to reinstate the injunction but only to the extent that "it enjoins and restrains the respondent and others designated from denying these petitioners, Autherine J. Lucy and Polly Anne Myers, the right to enroll in the University of Alabama and pursue courses of study there." Thus, under federal court order, Autherine Lucy was admitted to the University of Alabama on 3 February 1956, but was driven from campus the following week by rioters. Myers, by then Mrs. Polly Myers Hudson, was denied admission because of "conduct and marital status." Citing fear for Lu-cy's safety and that of other students, the university suspended her.

A few weeks later, on 29 February, the district court judge ordered the university to reinstate her. After this order, the university's board of trustees "per-manently expelled" her for "defamatory" statements—specifically, her statements that the university had conspired in the riots that drove her from campus. Lucy's petition to hold the university in contempt for the expulsion was denied by the district court judge on 18 January 1957. It was over six years before another African-American student, Vivian Malone, was admitted to the University of Alabama after Governor George Wallace stood in the schoolhouse door to prevent her and James Hood's entrance. In 1965, Vivian Malone (now Jones) became the first African-American to graduate from that university.

Following a speaking engagement at the University of Alabama in 1988, professors urged Lucy, by then Mrs. Autherine Lucy Foster, to reapply. The university board rescinded her expulsion, and Mrs. Foster, a school teacher in Birmingham, enrolled in a master's degree program in January 1989. In May 1992, the university awarded her a master's degree in elementary education and awarded her daughter Grazia an undergraduate degree in corporate finance the same day. The university also announced a $25,000 endowed scholarship in Mrs. Foster's name. Today, over 8 percent of the University of Alabama's students are African-Americans.

SELECTED BIBLIOGRAPHY

"36 Years after the Hate, Black Student Triumphs," *New York Times*, 26 April 1992, p. 43; "Autherine Lucy Gets Her Master's—36 Years Ago, She Changed Alabama," *Seattle Post-Intelligencer*, 9 May 1992, p. A1; Thomas I. Emerson, David Haber, and Norman Dorsen, *Political and Civil Rights in the United States: A Collection of Legal and Related Materials* (1967); "Family Shares Victory of a Civil Rights Pioneer; College That Spurned Autherine Lucy in 1956 Grants Her a Degree, Gives Daughter Another," *Akron Beacon Journal*, 9 May 1992, p. A3; " 'Free Choice' Plan Is Likely to Come before Alabama Legislators in May," *Southern School News*, April 1957, p. 13; *Lucy et al. v. Adams et al.*, 134 F. Supp. 235 (1955), 224 F. Supp. 79 (1963); *New York Times*, 1 February 1956, p. L-64.

JAMES E. NEWBY

M

MANASSAS INDUSTRIAL SCHOOL FOR COLORED YOUTH, JENNIE DEAN AND THE (c. 1852, Sudley Springs, Virginia–3 May 1913, Catharpin, Virginia). Recognizing early the overwhelming need for a school where young African-American men and women could learn a marketable trade and become independent members of society, Jennie Dean established the Manassas Industrial School for Colored Youth in 1893. The school opened the following year with six students, a number that soon increased to seventy-five and included young women and men from Virginia, the District of Columbia, and at least ten other states.

The Manassas Industrial School, located in northern Virginia, provided instruction in English and arithmetic as well as blacksmithing, carpentry, shoe-making, farming, and other practical occupations for young men and classes in laundering, canning, cooking, and sewing for young women. A teacher training course was added later. Other activities included sports such as football, basketball, baseball, and tennis. Students also participated in the school's glee club, music classes, and prayer services.

Manassas Industrial operated as a private institution with an average yearly enrollment of 152 students for forty-four years until 1938, when it became a regional high school serving African-American students from Virginia's Prince William, Fairfax, Fauquier, and Rappahannock counties. From 1954 to 1959, the school served as the Prince William County High School for African-American students. During the 1958–59 school year, the county constructed a new facility on the site, which was appropriately named Jennie Dean High and Elementary School. This school was devoted to the education of black students until 1966, when it was integrated.

SELECTED BIBLIOGRAPHY

Stephen Johnson Lewis, *Undaunted Faith . . . The Life Story of Jennie Dean* (1942).

CHALMERS ARCHER, JR.

MARSHALL, THURGOOD (2 July 1908, Baltimore, Maryland–24 January 1993, Washington, D.C.; interred, Arlington National Cemetery). The grandson of a slave and son of a dining-car waiter and a teacher, Thurgood Marshall was the first African-American to serve on the U.S. Supreme Court. A product of segregated public schools, Marshall received his undergraduate degree with honors from Lincoln University* of Pennsylvania in 1930. He graduated first in his law school class at Howard University* in 1933.

Marshall began his legal career in private practice in Baltimore and, given his deep commitment to its goals, worked closely with the local branch of the National Association for the Advancement of Colored People (NAACP).* In 1936, Marshall accepted an invitation from the NAACP's staff counsel, Charles Hamilton Houston,* to join its national staff. When Houston left the NAACP in 1938, Marshall took charge of its Legal Defense and Education Fund. He became the organization's Special Counsel in May 1939, and until 1945 he was the only attorney on staff with substantial courtroom duties. Marshall remained with the NAACP until he became a member of the federal bench. The principle architect of the NAACP strategy that succeeded in toppling de jure segregation, Marshall was victorious in twenty-nine of the thirty-two cases he argued before the Supreme Court. Among his many accomplishments as the leading civil rights attorney of his time, Marshall is perhaps most remembered for his role in *Brown v. Board of Education of Topeka, Kansas* (1954).*

Marshall was nominated to serve on the prestigious U.S. Court of Appeals for the Second Circuit by President John F. Kennedy on 23 September 1961, but his confirmation (by a margin of fifty-four to sixteen) was delayed until 11 September 1962, due to opposition from southern senators. President Lyndon B. Johnson selected Marshall as Solicitor General of the United States in July 1965, and his appointment was ratified in less than a month. President Johnson nominated him to the Supreme Court in June 1967 and, despite ongoing petty resistance from southern senators, Marshall was confirmed on 30 August 1967, by a vote of sixty-nine to eleven.

Marshall authored Supreme Court opinions on a wide array of issues including antitrust legislation, criminal law, federal jurisdiction, the rights of minorities, and, of course, desegregation. His most significant contributions are in the area of constitutional law, where, as a champion of the underprivileged, he adopted what can only be described as a decidedly liberal perspective. An activist member of the liberal majority during his early years on the Court, Marshall found himself in the minority by the time of his 1991 retirement, as the Court adopted an increasingly conservative perspective. In fact, he was not above risking the wrath of his colleagues while in pursuit of justice, as exemplified in the opening line of his final opinion on the Court, a dissent in a case involving the death penalty, where Marshall wrote that "Power, not reason, is the new currency of this Court's decision-making" (*Payne v. Tennessee*, p. 2619, 1991). Thus, in stirring dissents during his later years on the Court, combined with earlier opinions, he expressed his persuasive powers to their fullest, rounding out his career as a champion for those who have long been overlooked by society.

SELECTED BIBLIOGRAPHY

Brown v. Board of Education, 347 U.S. 483 (1954); Ramsey Clark, "Thurgood Marshall," in Leon Friedman, ed., *The Justices of the United States Supreme Court: Their Lives and Opinions*, vol. 5 (1978); Roger Goldman with David Gallen, *Thurgood Marshall: Justice for All* (1992); Richard Kluger, *Simple Justice: The History of Brown v. Board of Education and Black America's Struggle for Equality* (1976); *New York Times*, 25, 26, 28, and 29 January 1993; *Payne v. Tennessee*, 111 S. Ct. 2597 (1991); Carl T. Rowan, *Dream Makers, Dream Breakers: The World of Justice Thurgood Marshall* (1993); Mark V. Tushnet, *Making Civil Rights Law: Thurgood Marshall and the Supreme Court, 1936–1961* (1994).

CHARLES J. RUSSO AND J. JOHN HARRIS III

MARTIN LUTHER KING JUNIOR ELEMENTARY SCHOOL CHILDREN v. ANN ARBOR SCHOOL DISTRICT BOARD, 473 F. Supp. 1371 (E.D. Mich. 1979). This case involved fifteen students at the Martin Luther King Junior Elementary School in Ann Arbor, Michigan, who resided with their parents at the Green Road Housing Project. They spoke "Black English," a dialect, in their homes and community. Each student had experienced reading difficulties. School officials asserted that "Black English" created an impediment to their equal participation in the school's instructional program. The students and their parents sued the Ann Arbor School District Board, the Michigan State Board of Education, teachers, and administrators ("the boards") for failure to take appropriate action to overcome the students' language barrier.

The Michigan district court ruled that the language difference between "Black English" and standard English was not a barrier in and of itself. Indeed, no barrier in communications or understanding existed between the African-American students and their teachers and classmates. A barrier that made it difficult for the students to learn to read was created, however, when Ann Arbor teachers taught those students just as they taught other students, without taking "Black English" into account to help the students switch from their home language to standard English. The problem was compounded by the fact that students were not receiving parental support for learning to read at home and that certain sounds in the English language are difficult to make. Moreover, the court concluded that teachers who treated "Black English" as an inferior language caused a psychological barrier against the student's ability to learn to read and use standard English by interjecting a conflict between what the students were taught in school and what they perceived as acceptable speech in their community.

The court ruled that the boards had violated the Equal Educational Opportunities Act of 1974, 20 U.S.C. § 1703(f) (1974). The act provided that "No state shall deny equal educational opportunity to an individual on account of his or her race, color, sex, of national origin, by . . . the failure of an educational agency to take appropriate action to overcome language barriers that impede equal participation by its students in instructional programs." In the court's opinion, the boards had an obligation to take appropriate action to overcome the language barrier by helping teachers recognize the problem, to provide the teachers with knowledge about "Black English," and to train the teachers to use that knowledge to teach the students to read. The court decided that the students' inability to master reading skills hindered their equal participation in the schools' instructional program. Ultimately, the boards' failure to develop a program to assist the teachers to consider the home language in teaching standard English contributed to the students' reading deficiencies and resulted in racial implications. Therefore, the court ordered the board to submit a plan of rational and logical steps to eliminate the language barrier.

The significance of this case was apparent in the court's lengthy decision, in which it stated that "the [students] have attempted to put before this court one of the most important and pervasive problems facing modern urban America—the problem of why 'Johnnie Can't Read.' . . . Full integration and equal opportunity require much more [than integrating housing and busing students] and one of the matters requiring more attention is the teaching of the young [African-American children] to read standard English."

SELECTED BIBLIOGRAPHY

Middleton, *Educators Differ: Black English Goes to Court*, 66 A.B.A.J. 1062 (1980); Note, "Black English and Equal Educational Opportunity," *Michigan Law Review* 79 (1980); 279–98.

CYNTHIA R. MABRY

MARY HOLMES COLLEGE. In 1892, the Board of Missions for Freedmen of the Presbyterian Church in the U.S.A. told Rev. Mead Holmes and his daughter, Mary Emile Holmes, to go south and establish a college for the "daughters of the colored race." First built in 1892 in Jackson, Mississippi, Mary Holmes Seminary was named after Mary Holmes's mother. Three years later, the entire school was destroyed by fire. The people of West Point, Mississippi, donated about twenty acres of land to the school, and a huge brick hall was soon erected. The school took students from poverty-stricken homes and, along with a strong emphasis on Bible teaching, gave them instruction in music and in more practical subjects such as cooking and sewing. For many years, training in nursing was also provided. On 1 January 1900, less than a year after again being destroyed by fire, Mary Holmes Seminary "No. 3" was dedicated by Holmes and her family and friends.

In 1932, Mary Holmes became coeducational and organized its first college department, with the primary purpose of training young people to become teachers. In 1959, the high school, which had evolved over the decades, was closed and the institution took on its current form as a two-year college. In 1965, the school made possible the launch of the Head Start* program in Mississippi by training volunteers to staff what was then considered a controversial educational activity. For many years the school operated the only rural transportation service in its home county, and in the 1960s Mary Holmes was the scene of pilot projects to develop catfish farming and legal services for the poor.

Today, Mary Holmes College in West Point, Mississippi, is a fully accredited private two-year coeducational college of liberal arts, career studies, and science. Students are not required to have an ACT or SAT score for admission and are almost always the first in their families to continue their education beyond high school. Over 95 percent of students receive substantial financial aid. Over 65 percent of graduates go on to four-year colleges and universities. Students can follow their choice among twenty-one areas of concentration to earn an associate of arts or associate of science degree. The college also offers a certificate in cosmetology. The newest addition to the campus is a 23,000-square-foot Learning Resources Center, housing a library, classrooms, computer labs, and a fully equipped media center.

SELECTED BIBLIOGRAPHY

Daily Times Leader, 27 September 1992, P.T-10; Mary Holmes Archives, West Point, Mississippi.

EDGAR W. HARRIS

MATHEMATICS EDUCATION, AFRICAN-AMERICANS AND. Mathematics is fundamental to the curricula of elementary, secondary, and postsecondary education. The teaching and learning of mathematics at these levels are the primary concerns in the field of mathematics education. Understanding the nature and development of the mathematical abilities of the general populace is central to the comprehensive goals of the field. There is a growing national crisis regarding the education of students in mathematics. The crisis is particularly acute for African-Americans and other racial/ethnic groups whose mathematics education has tended to be impoverished. This crisis has not only received increased attention from those in the field of mathematics education but has drawn the attention of other scholars who are interested in the issues of teaching and learning. Among others, these scholars include psychologists as well as pure and applied mathematicians. They share an interest in identifying experiences that would maximize students' mathematics learning. Appropriately, African-Americans have been a target population for efforts addressing these issues.

A number of factors influence the mathematical orientation of African-American students, factors that fall within the affective, cultural, and cognitive domains. These factors influence the participation and achievement of African-Americans in mathematics such that this population is underrepresented in advanced mathematics and science-related coursework and careers, as compared to their counterparts from other racial/ethnic groups.

Although African-American children enter school in kindergarten prepared to succeed in mathematics and certainly as prepared as any of their peers, they fall behind in their level of participation in mathematics over the years. It is well established that too few African-American secondary and postsecondary students are enrolling in and completing the more advanced mathematics courses such as algebra I, geometry, algebra II, trigonometry and precalculus. Records of African-American students' low enrollment in such elective courses date far back. In 1984, it was reported that the percentage of African-American students taking advanced mathematics courses, though increasing slightly between 1977 and 1980, remained smaller than corresponding percentages for students in other racial/ethnic groups. Research has found that half of the students taking mathematics courses in the United States leave the mathematics pipeline yearly. Alarmingly, this dropout rate is far greater for African-Americans.

The data spanning the past fifteen to twenty years show increased participation of African-American students in mathematics. However, improving rates of participation will require educational researchers to examine and directly address the underlying factors that contribute to the trends in enrollment patterns for African-Americans and other underrepresented groups in mathematics. Studies of African-American students' achievements in mathematics have been approached by examining both current and longitudinal performance data. The literature abounds with data that show minimal gains in mathematics achievement for African-American students. Although national assessment studies show that African-American students, particularly those at ages nine and thirteen, have made significant gains in mathematics achievement across the five mathematics assessment, these students (as a group) continue to rank in the lower percentiles.

Demographic factors and data present yet another dimension of the fundamental problems regarding African-American students' achievement in mathematics. If current trends of participation and achievement continue, coupled with the ensuing demographic forces, there will be few racial/ethnic role models as educators in mathematics classrooms with whom students can identify, resulting in a self-perpetuating cycle of underrepresentation. Traditional teaching and assessment practices seem to do very little to promote mathematics learning for the majority of African-American students. Careful identification and analysis of these and other concerns are needed to effectively prevent the continuation of underserved and underrepresented groups in mathematics classrooms. Much research has been conducted that points to achievement differences between African-Americans and other racial/ethnic groups. However, research other than comparison studies focusing strictly on African-Americans is necessary.

Through comprehensive educational reform, efforts to turn the tides of students' achievement in mathematics have been made. In particular, the nation presently is experiencing perhaps the most extensive reform movement in mathematics education ever known. One organization leading the reform efforts in mathematics education is the National Council of Teachers of Mathematics (NCTM). Founded in 1920, NCTM presently consists of one hundred thousand institutions and individual educators interested in promoting the goals of the mathematics education community. Two affiliates of NCTM that are strong advocates of reform are the National Council of Supervisors of Mathematics (NCSM) and the Benjamin Banneker Association (BBA), a group whose purpose is to directly address the mathematics education needs of African-Americans. The Mathematical Association of America (MAA) lends strong support to the reform efforts through its program, Strengthening Underrepresented Minority Mathematics Achievement (SUMMA). Some other organizations supporting reform efforts include the Special Interest Group/Research in Mathematics Education (SIG/RME) of the American Educational Research Association (AERA); the National Research Council (NRC) and its constituent, the Mathematical Sciences Education Board (MSEB).

Rapid technological advancements in our society are causing all sectors (educational, governmental, and business) to rethink the kinds of mathematics necessary for the society of today and tomorrow. Numerous documents have been published strongly recommending that school mathematics be meaningful, that it move beyond rote skills and computation, and that it be taught to all students. The most influential documents in the area of mathematics reform are two that are collectively referred to as the NCTM Standards. The NCTM published the *Curriculum and Evaluation Standards for School Mathematics* in 1989, the *Professional Standards for Teaching Mathematics* in 1991, and the *Assessment Standards for School Mathematics* in 1995. In these documents, school mathematics is considered to extend far beyond rote learning and drill. Emphasis is placed on mathematical problem solving, communication, reasoning, and connections in learning environments. Students' mathematical thinking and discussion about relevant mathematics are promoted. In the learning process, students gather and create knowledge from active participation in meaningful mathematics.

The Research Advisory Committee of the NCTM (1989) and independent researchers have advocated the systematic examination of mathematics learning among African-American students. Examples of efforts that directly or indirectly affect the mathematics learning of African-American students follow. A practical school-reform project entitled, Quantitative Understanding: Amplifying Student Achievement and Reasoning (QUASAR) began in 1989 to promote mathematics learning for economically disadvantaged students in the middle grades. Two of the six national sites served predominantly African-American student populations. A second project, Equity 2000, had as its primary goal the systemic change of schools and school districts throughout the nation. Emphases were placed on the elimination of tracking and improving the communication between educators and students. More recently, the National Science Foundation (NSF) has funded numerous Urban and Statewide Systemic Initiative Projects to encourage coordinated systemic efforts designed to promote and implement effective mathematics and science education for larger populations of students. Two examples of teacher-enhancement projects are Project IMPACT (Increasing the Mathematical Power of All Children) and the Atlanta Math Project (AMP). Both programs worked to implement mathematics reform for various populations through improving mathematics instruction at the elementary and middle-grade levels. An example of a curriculum project is the Connected Mathematics Project

(CMP), which developed a complete mathematics curriculum for the middle grades.

School policy and practice guide the views and actions of educators, who continue to be responsible for maintaining the low-level placement of African-Americans and other underrepresented groups in mathematics. Far too many African-American students have historically been tracked into general mathematics courses by standardized tests. They have been marginalized by the testing process and given various designations by educators, such as "culturally disadvantaged," "at-risk students," and/or "underachievers," classifications that go hand-in-hand with educators' minimal expectations for these learners. Extensive modification is needed in the areas of curricula, instruction, staffing, advising, tracking, and assessment if African-American students are to succeed in school mathematics.

SELECTED BIBLIOGRAPHY

C. Anick, T. Carpenter, and C. Smith, "Minorities and Mathematics: Results from the National Assessment of Educational Progress," *Mathematics Teacher* 74 (1981): 560–66; P. F. Campbell and C. Langrall, "Research into Practice: Making Equity a Reality in Classrooms," *Arithmetic Teacher* 41 (1993): 110–13; J. T. Fey, "Mathematics Education," in H. E. Mitzel, ed., *Encyclopedia of Educational Research* (1982); B. D. Hawkins, "Math: The Great Equalizer—Equity 2000 and QUASAR—Improving Minority Standing in Gatekeeper Courses," *Black Issues in Higher Education* (20 May 1993); 38–41; L. Humphreys, "Trends in Levels of Academic Achievement of Blacks and Other Minorities," *Intelligence* 12 (1988): 231–60; M. L. Johnson, "Blacks in Mathematics: A Status Report," *Journal for Research in Mathematics Education* 15 (1984): 145–53; J. Kilpatrick, "A History of Research in Mathematics Education," in D. A. Grouws, ed., *Handbook of Research on Mathematics Teaching and Learning* (1992); B. L. Madison, *A Challenge of Numbers: People in the Mathematical Sciences* (1990); L. A. Steen, "Mathematics for All Americans," in T. J. Cooney and C. H. Hirsch, eds., *Teaching and Learning Mathematics in the 1990s* (1990); L. V. Stiff, "African-American Students and the Promise of the Curriculum and Evaluation Standards," in T. J. Cooney and C. H. Hirsch, eds., *Teaching and Learning Mathematics in the 1990s* (1990); G. E. Thomas, "Cultivating the Interest of Women and Minorities in High School Mathematics and Science," *Science Education* 70 (1986); 31–43.

MICHAELE F. CHAPPELL AND DEBORAH H. NAJEE-ULLAH

MAYS, BENJAMIN ELIJAH (1 August 1894, Epworth, South Carolina–28 March 1984, Atlanta, Georgia). A college president, theologian, educator, and civil rights activist, Mays received an A.B. degree (with honors) from Bates College in 1920 (Phi Beta Kappa member) and an M.A. (1925) and Ph.D. (1935) from the University of Chicago. A major figure among mid-century American religious leaders, Mays combined a Baptist, deeply religious orientation and service record with a tremendous commitment to advancing African-American higher education, while also seeking to reform a segregated society.

His early career demonstrated these interdisciplinary interests. Between 1921 and 1924, he worked as a professor of mathematics at Morehouse College,* while also serving as pastor of Atlanta's Shiloh Baptist Church. His work with

African-American youth continued in 1925, when he assumed a teaching post as an instructor of English at South Carolina State College. From 1928 to 1930, he served as the National Student Secretary of the YMCA's African-American branch. During the early 1930s, Mays directed the first modern research study of the black church in America, for the New York City-based Institute of Social and Religious Research. Together with Joseph William Nicholson, he published *The Negro's Church* in 1933. Mays became a national spokesperson on black religious and higher educational interests when he was appointed in 1934 to the faculty of Howard University,* serving as dean of the School of Religion until 1940. He became president of Morehouse College in 1940, where he served until his retirement in 1967, continuing as president emeritus until 1984.

Mays contributed eight books to American letters, mostly on religious subjects; however, as a columnist for the *Pittsburgh Courier* from 1946 through the civil rights era, he wrote on a host of other concerns, such as civil rights, segregation, education, and world peace. His essays and articles also appeared widely in such publications as *The Crisis*,* the *Christian Century, Missions*, the *Negro Digest*, and the *Journal of Negro Education*.* Other books by Mays are *The Negro's God as Reflected in His Literature* (1938, 1969) and *Born to Rebel: An Autobiography* (1971, 1986).

Mays is especially remembered for his leadership at Morehouse and for his impact upon thousands of the school's alumni, including Martin Luther King, Jr., Andrew Young, and Julian Bond, among others. Few Americans have received the range of honors bestowed upon Mays during his lifetime, for his services in the areas of race relations, religious life, education and civic affairs. A highlight of his career came in 1969, when he was elected to the Atlanta Board of Education. Mays was chosen board president in 1971 and 1974 and served on the board until 1981. Between 1945 and 1984, he received at least forty-five honorary doctorates from American colleges and universities in the humanities, law, and divinity. He died of heart failure at the age of 89 and was buried in the Southview Cemetery, Atlanta, Georgia. His papers are deposited in the Howard University Library.

SELECTED BIBLIOGRAPHY

Lerone Bennett, Jr., "Benjamin Elijah Mays: The Last of the Great Schoolmasters," *Ebony* 33, no. 2 (December 1977): 72–80; "Biographical Sketch, Benjamin Elijah Mays," *Journal of Religious Thought* 32, no. 1 (Spring–Summer 1975): 132–38; Octavia B. Knight, "Benjamin Elijah Mays," in John F. Ohles, ed., *Biographical Dictionary of American Educators*, vol. 2 (1978); *New York Times*, 29 March 1984; Anna Rothe, ed., *Current Biography 1945* (1945); Leonard Ray Teel, "Benjamin Mays: Teaching by Example, Leading through Will," *Change* 14, no. 7 (October 1982): 14–22; Thomas Wilock, "Benjamin Elijah Mays, 1894–1984," in Linda Metzger, Hal May, Deborah A. Straub, and Susan M. Troskey, eds., *Black Writers: A Selection of Sketches from Contemporary Authors* (1989); *Washington Post*, 29 March 1984.

JULIUS E. THOMPSON

MCALLISTER, JANE ELLEN (24 October 1899, Vicksburg, Mississippi). In 1929, Jane Ellen McAllister was the first African-American woman to earn the

Ph.D. in education from Teachers College, Columbia University. Prior to that she received her A.B. degree with honors from Talladega College* in 1919 and her M.A. from the University of Michigan in 1921. McAllister began her teaching career in the summer of 1919, teaching Latin and mathematics at Emerson College in Mobile, Alabama, and at Straight University in New Orleans. In September of that year, she secured a permanent teaching position at Southern University.* Five years later, in 1926, she took a leave of absence from Southern to pursue doctoral work in education at Teachers College, Columbia University. Her dissertation, completed in the spring of 1928, was based on her experiences in Louisiana. As she wrote in that document, "Poorly prepared teachers teach poorly prepared students to be poorly prepared teachers." For the next forty years at HBCUs throughout the South (Virginia State College,* Grambling State University,* Southern University,* Fisk University,* and Miner Teachers College*), McAllister worked to upgrade teacher education programs for African-American teachers. Commenting later, she stated that this allowed African-American teachers "to carry back (to their schools) the legitimate hope that they can raise the level of aspiration and educate children—disadvantaged, deprived and made different by culture—for newly emerging, nondiscriminatory jobs."

After twenty-five years at Miner Teachers College in Washington, D.C., McAllister returned to her native Mississippi in 1951. For the next eighteen years, she gave her considerable skill and talent to developing programs that broadened the scope and the vision of the Jackson State College* faculty and students. With grants initially from the Southern Education Foundation* and later the Marshall Field and Ford foundations, McAllister initiated the televised lecture course on "Great Ideas in Antiquity" (Greek drama lectures were relayed by satellite to Jackson State, Tougaloo College,* Southern University, and Grambling College). By the end of the 1960s, she succeeded in shaping the kind of intellectual climate in which programs including a college enrichment program for promising high school students, project enrichment in service workshops for teachers, the National Science Foundation Summer Institutes for Teachers, and a freshman curriculum project could all flourish and grow.

McAllister is the author of more than twenty articles in scholarly publications and has received numerous awards and appointments, including being chosen Dean's Scholar, Columbia University (1949), and an observer to the White House Conference on Education (1955). A lecture series and a women's dormitory at Jackson State University are both named in her honor.

SELECTED BIBLIOGRAPHY

David Rae Morris, "My Mind to Me a Kingdom Is," master's thesis, University of Minnesota (1992); George Sewell, "Jane Ellen McAllister, Pioneer in Black Education," in *Mississippi Black History Makers* (1984); W. Winona Burns, "Jane Ellen McAllister: First Black Woman to Earn the Doctorate in Education in the World," *Sunbelt Magazine* (August 1980); Cynthia Parsons and W. Bruce Welch, "Mississippi Beehive College Puts Life in Negro Teacher Education," *American Education* (December 1967–January

1968); McAllister Papers, Manuscript Collection, Sampson Library, Jackson State University, Jackson, Mississippi.

BETTYE J. GARDNER

MCKENZIE, FLORETTA DUKES (19 August 1935, Lakeland, Florida). Floretta Dukes McKenzie, educator, administrator, entrepreneur, and consultant, was born to Martin W. and Ruth J. Dukes. She earned a bachelor's of science degree in history from the District of Columbia Teachers College in 1956 and continued her studies at Howard University,* where she received a master of arts degree in 1957. In 1984, McKenzie received the Ed.D. from George Washington University. After McKenzie completed her studies at Howard University, she taught in Baltimore, Maryland, from 1957 to 1967, until she became the District of Columbia Public Schools system's (DCPS) assistant superintendent from 1969 to 1974.

Between 1967 and 1979, McKenzie served as the director of the DCPS Opportunity Project for Education Now, assistant to the superintendent, acting deputy superintendent for instruction, special assistant to the superintendent for administration of school units and educational programs, deputy superintendent of educational programs and services, and acting superintendent. In 1974, McKenzie was the area assistant superintendent for the Montgomery County Public Schools. From 1977 to 1981, she was the assistant deputy superintendent of the Maryland Department of Education, deputy superintendent of schools in Montgomery County Public Schools, chief administrator and deputy commissioner of the Bureau of School Improvement, chief administrator of fifteen federal education discretionary programs and initiatives of the United States Department of Education, and the deputy assistant secretary in the Office of School Improvement. She also was a U.S. delegate to UNESCO, representing the Department of Education at the Twenty-first General Conference in Belgrade, Yugoslavia, and the Third Conference of Ministers of Education in Sofia, Bulgaria.

In July 1981, McKenzie established a partnership of local businesses, major corporations, foundations, and trade associations called the McKenzie Group, Inc., an educational consulting firm that offers direct assistance and services to both private and public organizations. Some of the McKenzie Group's clients are the Anchorage (Alaska) Public Schools System, Atlanta (Georgia) Public Schools, Broward County (Florida) Public School System, Chester–Upland School District, Durham (North Carolina) Public School System, McGraw–Hill Publishing Company, RJR Nabisco Foundation, Michigan State Department of Education, and the Joint Center for Political Studies.

McKenzie's talent and commitment to education have been recognized extensively throughout her career. She is the recipient of numerous honors and awards, including honorary doctorates from Georgetown University in 1986, Catholic University in 1985, Columbia University Teacher's College in 1987, and Trinity College in 1982. She also has received a doctorate of law from

Williams College in 1983, the District of Columbia Woman of the Year Award in 1983, and the (Washington, D.C.) Mayor's Distinguished Public Service Award in 1973. In 1992, she became the first African-American and female elected to the Marriott Hotel corporation board.

McKenzie has served on a number of professional organizations, including the American Association of School Administration, the National Urban League,* Gamma Theta Upsilon, Phi Alpha Theta, and Phi Delta Kappa; is an honorary life member of the Maryland Parent-Teachers Association; and has served on the board of trustees at George Washington University and the board of directors for the National Geographic Society, Potomac Electric Power Company, World Book, Acacia Life Insurance, Delta Sigma Theta, Inc., and Riggs National Bank.

SELECTED BIBLIOGRAPHY

Christa Berlin, ed., *Who's Who among Black Americans* (1994/95); "Biographical Sketch of Floretta Dukes McKenzie" (dated 1967 to present).

                                                            TENITA SHERRELL PHILYAW

MCLAURIN v. OKLAHOMA STATE REGENTS FOR HIGHER EDUCATION ET AL., 339 U.S. 637 (1950). In 1948, George W. McLaurin, an African-American citizen of Oklahoma with a master's degree, applied for admission to the University of Oklahoma to pursue studies leading to a doctorate in education and was denied admission solely because of his race, in accordance with Oklahoma statutes. McLaurin filed a complaint in a federal district court requesting injunctive relief, alleging that the action of the school officials and the statutes upon which they based their denial deprived him of the equal protection of the laws. The court, citing the *Gaines** (1938) and *Sipuel** (1948) decisions, held that the state had to provide McLaurin with the education sought "as soon as it provided that education for applicants of any other group." It also ruled that the Oklahoma statutes were unconstitutional, but, assuming that the state would follow the constitutional mandate, the court refused to grant the injunction requested.

Following this decision, the Oklahoma legislature amended the law to permit admission of African-Americans to colleges attended by whites, "upon a segregated basis," provided that those institutions offered courses not available in the schools attended by African-Americans. Consequently, McLaurin was admitted and segregated within the institution. He was required, under the most favorable circumstances, to occupy a special seat in the classroom and a designated table in both the library and the cafeteria. He filed a motion to modify the order and judgment of the district court, but the court held that "such treatment did not violate the provisions of the Fourteenth Amendment" and denied the motion. He then appealed to the U.S. Supreme Court.

After considering the question "whether a state may, after admitting a student to graduate instruction in its state university, afford him different treatment from other students solely because of his race," the Supreme Court concluded that the conditions under which McLaurin had been forced to receive his education deprived him of his right to the equal protection of the laws. In a unanimous opinion delivered by Chief Justice Vinson, the Court held that "Appellant having been admitted to a state-supported graduate school, must receive the same treatment at the hands of the state as students of other races." It reasoned that such restrictions "impair and inhibit his ability to study, to engage in discussions and exchange views with other students, and, in general to learn his profession." Although McLaurin was a fifty-four-year-old applicant, the Court further asserted that he was by virtue of his degree to become a leader and trainer of others and that those who will come under his influence will be directly affected by the education he receives. Their own education "will necessarily suffer to the extent that his training is unequal to that of his classmates. State-imposed restrictions which produce such inequalities cannot be sustained."

McLaurin attended the University of Oklahoma along with his wife, who also became a student. Because of failing health, McLaurin unfortunately did not complete his doctoral program. This case repudiated the 1908 *Berea College** decision prohibiting voluntary interracial association. The impact of intangible factors—his ability to engage in discussions and exchange views with other students—considered by the Court, became an important facet of the 1954 *Brown** decision.

SELECTED BIBLIOGRAPHY

Berea College v. Kentucky, 211 U.S. 45 (1908); *Brown et al. v. Board of Education of Topeka et al.*, 347 U.S. 483 (1954); George Lynn Cross, *Blacks in White Colleges: Oklahoma's Landmark Cases* (1975); Richard Kluger, *Simple Justice: The History of Brown v. Board of Education and Black America's Struggle for Equality* (1976); Irving Lefberg, "Chief Justice Vinson and the Politics of Desegregation," *Emory Law Journal* 24 (1975): 243–312; Loren Miller, *The Petitioners: The Story of the Supreme Court of the United States and the Negro* (1966); Mark V. Tushnet, *The NAACP's Legal Strategy against Segregated Education, 1925–1950* (1987).

JAMES E. NEWBY

MCLEAN, MABLE PARKER (19 March 1922, Moore County, North Carolina). Mable Parker McLean is currently serving her second term as the president of Barber-Scotia College,* having been asked in 1994 to return to that position out of retirement. She previously served the college for fourteen years as its first woman president from 1974 to 1988. She attended the public schools of Virginia and North Carolina and completed her undergraduate education at Barber-Scotia and Johnson C. Smith University.* She did graduate work at Howard University* and postgraduate studies at Northwestern University and the Catholic University of America.

McLean is known internationally as a member of the Middle East Exploration Study Seminar for Women Educators, a member of the President's Study of Educational Concerns of Haiti, and a participant in the President's Exchange Conference on African and American Universities for blacks in Bellaglo, Italy.

McLean has served at every level of education from nursery school assistant director to college president. She served at Johnson C. Smith University in the Department of Elementary Education for two years, was a demonstration teacher for one year at Bowie State University,* and worked as a public school teacher in North Carolina for ten years. She served for seventeen years at Barber-Scotia College as faculty, department chairperson, and academic dean. In 1994, Mc-Lean was asked to return to the presidency of Barber-Scotia.

McLean is the recipient of numerous honors and awards and of honorary degrees from seven U.S. colleges and universities. She is also a member and elder of the John Hall Presbyterian Church (USA); Order of the Eastern Star; the Links, Inc.; and Alpha Kappa Alpha Sorority, Inc.

SELECTED BIBLIOGRAPHY

Harold O. Robinson, *A History of African-Americans in Cabarrus County, North Carolina* (1992).

                                                              ALICE STEELE–ROBINSON

MEDICAL EDUCATION AND AFRICAN-AMERICANS. Medical education for African-Americans began before the Civil War, when David Peck Jones graduated from Rust Medical School in 1847. The first female African-American graduate of record, Rebecca Lee Crumpter, followed seventeen years later, completing her medical training at the New England Medical College (now Boston University). From that time through the 1950s and 1960s, virtually all African-American physicians graduated from either the Howard University* Medical School, established in 1868, or Meharry Medical Center,* which began preparing physicians in 1876. These two schools remain institutional leaders in graduating African-American physicians. Sometime later in the 1870s, several institutions located mainly in the South, including Flint Medical College in New Orleans, Leonard Medical in Raleigh, Knoxville Medical College in Knoxville, and the National University in Louisville, trained African-American physicians. These schools, which required limited academic credentials and hospital affiliation, were designated in the 1910 *Flexner Report* as inferior and were soon after dissolved. Subsequent civil rights legislation improved prospects for the medical education of African-Americans at universities throughout the United States; by 1975, historically white institutions (HWUs) were graduating 80 percent of African-American physicians. The year 1974 evidenced the highest African-American medical school enrollment (7.5%) ever seen in the United States; despite affirmative action programs and strengthened enforcement of civil rights ordinances, the combined percentage of underrepresented minorities has neither risen nor been equalled since. Underrepresented minorities include African-Americans, Native Americans, Mexican Americans, and mainland Puerto Ricans.

African-Americans remain underrepresented in medicine; their proportion of physicians is less than their proportion of the population. In 1992, even though African-Americans constituted 12.1 percent of the population and 9.5 percent of the population aged 20 to 29 who completed four or more years of college, they comprised only 5.9 percent of the graduating physicians, down 2.3 percent from a year prior. Whites, on the other hand, comprise 80 percent of the U.S. population and 76.4 percent of the nation's medical doctors. A total of 850 medical degrees were awarded to African-Americans in 1992 as compared with 15,365 for whites.

According to a 1992 student survey by the American Association of Medical Colleges (AAMC), African-American medical school graduates are more likely to practice in neglected inner cities where concentrations of disadvantaged populations are greatest. Therefore, in addition to providing health care to underserved groups, African-American physicians are among the few positive role models in the poorest neighborhoods to encourage young people to prepare for a medical career. Given the growing proportion of African-Americans among the nation's school-aged children, the significance of this community presence cannot be overestimated.

Who are the African-Americans who are seeking and obtaining medical degrees? In what fields do they practice? How likely are African-Americans to be medical educators? What efforts are in place to expand the pool of African-Americans qualified for medical study? In 1992, only 7 percent of African-Americans or 4,638 students were enrolled in medical schools in the United States. This figure includes 1,954 men and 2,684 women, 37 more women than were enrolled in 1991 and 241 more than were enrolled a decade before. There were 2,917 African-American applications, an increase of almost 10 percent over the previous year. Again, however, less than half were accepted; and only 1,203 African-Americans, including 470 men and 733 women, began their medical training in 1992. Each year, the majority of the nonmatriculants cite financial reasons for abandoning their plans to pursue a medical degree.

Although 37 percent of African-American applicants in the 1991–92 entering class reported a family income of at least $30,000, 26.2 reported incomes of $16,000 or less. The mean indebtedness of medical student seniors in 1992 was $55,497 for all programs. Data specific to African-Americans were unavailable; but for all underrepresented minorities, the overall mean debt burden was greater ($58,737) for programs totalling 4, 5, and 6 or more years. Notwithstanding the financial burden of a medical education, the graduation rate for African-American medical students is high, approximately 90 percent.

In general, retention rates for African-Americans are lower than other groups in medical school. In 1990–91, for example, 13 percent of African-American first-year students were required to repeat the academic year, and 4 percent repeated from all other classes. This figure is higher than that of any other underrepresented minority group and substantially higher than the 2.4 percent white repeating rate. The mean GPA for African-American female and male medical school matriculants in 1992 was 3.0 percent and 2.99 respectively, lower than whites and all other underrepresented minority groups. The same pattern holds for mean Medical College Admissions Test (MCAT) scores for African-Americans in each subject tested.

Upon graduation, African-Americans are more likely to select salaried clinical practice in the northeast or southern parts of the U.S. and are less likely to envision full-time academic careers. Instead, they specialize in primary care fields such as family practice, internal medicine, obstetrics and gynecology, and pediatrics. According to AAMC student data, in 1990, 16.6 African-American male and 14 percent of African-American female graduates (compared with 1.4 percent of whites) failed to secure their first choice of specialty placement in graduate medical education through the National Resident Matching Program.

In the decade between 1980 and 1990, underrepresented minority faculty increased from 835 to 1,325 or 2.7 percent of all faculty in 1980 to 3.3 percent in 1990. In 1991, African-Americans numbered 1,748 faculty in the nation's medical institutions, with only a combined 19 percent (314 faculty) on the faculties at Howard, Meharry, and the Morehouse College* School of Medicine, the latter of which was established in 1975. The remainder are distributed throughout the predominantly white medical schools. African-American females comprise only a little more than half of the number of African-American male teaching faculty (1,097 male and 651 females). Published AAMC data in 1993 reveal that whites are 82 percent of male medical school faculty and 77 percent of female faculty, with black males comprising 1.9 of all male faculty and black females comprising 3.7 percent of all female faculty in medical schools.

Regarding the ranking distribution, AAMC identified African-Americans as 1 percent of the professors, 1.9 percent of the associate professors, 2.9 percent of assistant professors, and 4.8 percent of the instructors. African-American faculty are 2 percent of all medical school faculty, 1.3 percent of all the Ph.D. medical school faculty, and 1.2 percent of all M.D./Ph.D. or M.D./other degree medical school faculty.

African-American males in clinical teaching outnumber African-American females in all specialty teaching categories, are most represented in internal medicine and obstetrics and gynecology, and represent equal numbers in psychiatry and surgery. Female African-American M.D. specialty areas of greatest concentration are internal medicine, pediatrics, and psychiatry, in respective order of association. African-American males in basic science or preclinical training are teaching in greatest numbers in physiology, pathology basic, and microbiology departments. African-American female basic science instructors are teaching in greatest numbers in pharmacy and pathology basic departments. Despite a 17.1 percent decline in the total number of doctoral awards since 1975, the number of Ph.D.s awarded to African-Americans in the life sciences increased by approximately 12 percent between 1991 and 1992.

In order to improve the participation of underrepresented minorities in medical education, remedies must be found to ameliorate the effects of poverty, racism, and educational disadvantage that plague at least half of the African-American school age population. In 1969, AAMC established its Office of Minority Affairs and instituted minority-focused initiatives to address these barriers to successful medical training focusing on academic deficiencies, admissions criteria, and institutional commitment. At the same time, federal funding sources such as the Health Education Assistance Loan, Stafford Student Loan, and Health Professions Student Loan programs were established to ease the financial strain of obtaining a medical degree. Ninety-one percent of senior underrepresented minority students as opposed to 76 percent of all senior medical students in 1992 indicated they received loans for medical school. In addition, these underrepresented minority students entered medical school with a mean premedical debt of $8,755.

Acknowledging that, to be of the most benefit, efforts at educational remedy must begin earlier than the high school years, many medical schools are collaborating with local elementary schools to improve the quality of science instruction and provide science enrichment activities. Through a national funding source, Health Careers Opportunity Program (HCOP) sponsored from the Division of Disadvantaged Health Services Administration, universities in general and medical schools in particular have designed an array of exciting science programs to interest students in careers in health professions.

In 1990, AAMC initiated Project 3000 by 2000, a program whose goal is to enter three thousand underrepresented minority medical students into medical training by the year 2000. Most accredited medical schools have also established offices of minority affairs with counseling and tutorial components, some of which are designed specifically for African-American medical students. HCOP also funds many medical schools' science courses and learning and study-skills programs. Recent innovations such as offering courses for students in the summer or spreading the required medical curriculum over five years rather than four may promote successful medical study for those students who may need extra time. Individual and small group tutorials are also available in the majority of U.S. medical schools.

Insufficient federal or privately supported opportunities to fund medical training for African-Americans remain a deterrent to increasing their representation in medical education institutions. Academic support for African-Americans who have experienced educational disadvantage is also required.

SELECTED BIBLIOGRAPHY

American Association of Medical Colleges, Facts: Applicants, Matriculants and Graduates, prepared by the Section from Student Services 20 October 1992); Paul Jolly and Dorothea M. Hudley, eds., *AAMC Data Book Statistical Information Related to Medical Education* (January 1992); American Association of Medical Colleges, *Minority Students in Medical Education*, Division of Minority Health, Education and Prevention (December 1991); American Association of Medical Colleges, *Participation of Women and Minorities on US Medical School Faculties 1980–1990*, Faculty Roster System (1991); *Summary Report: 1990 Doctorate Recipients from United States Universities*, National

Academic Press (1991); American Association of Medical Colleges, *Trends Plus: U.S. Medical School Applicants, Matriculants, Graduates, 1992*, Division of Minority Health, Education and Prevention (May 1993).

PORTIA SHIELDS

MEHARRY MEDICAL COLLEGE. Meharry Medical College in Nashville, Tennessee, has been cited as a "national resource" by the Robert Wood Johnson Foundation for its role in educating minority health professionals. It has trained close to a third of the African-American physicians and dentists practicing in the United States today. Meharry graduates constitute about 40 percent of the African-American faculty at U.S. medical schools and about 25 percent of the African-American faculty in U.S. dental schools. Meharrians serve as health care providers in forty-eight states and twenty-two foreign countries. Founded in 1876 as the Medical Department of Central Tennessee College, with the mission of educating health professionals for the African-American population, Meharry became an independent medical college in 1915. In 1886 the Department of Dentistry was established and in 1910 George Hubbard Hospital, the major clinical teaching facility, was opened. Today, Meharry operates schools of medicine, dentistry, graduate studies, and allied health professions as well as the teaching/research West Basic Sciences Center, Community Mental Health Center, Comprehensive Health Services Center, International Health Sciences Center, and Hubbard Hospital. The provision of primary care, particularly in medically undeserved areas, is a special emphasis, as is biomedical research into areas of concern to undeserved populations. A World Health Organization Center now operates within its international unit.

SAMUEL L. MYERS

MEREDITH v. FAIR, 305 F.2d 343 (5th Cir. 1962). In this case, the U.S. Court of Appeals of the Fifth Circuit held that the University of Mississippi denied James H. Meredith, an African-American student, admission to the university solely because of his race. Meredith filed his suit as a class action and alleged that the defendants were pursuing a state policy, practice, and custom "of maintaining and operating separate state institutions of higher learning for the white and Negro citizens of Mississippi." The court of appeals agreed. Reversing a district court decision denying Meredith relief, the court of appeals held that "[a] full review of the record leads . . . inescapably to the conclusion that from the moment the defendants discovered Meredith was a Negro they engaged in a carefully calculated campaign of delay, harassment, and masterly inactivity" to deny Meredith an opportunity to study at the university merely because of his race. Indeed, the court found that the university's stated reasons for denying Meredith admission—lack of alumni certificates, insufficiency of transfer credits, the applicant's alleged false voting registration, bad character, and character as a troublemaker—were pretextual and demonstrated the university's "determined policy of discrimination." As the court explained, the university's claims impugning Meredith's character and integrity were "frivolous." Moreover, "[t]he hard fact to get around is that no person known to be a Negro has ever attended the University." Accordingly, the court remanded the case to the district court with instructions that an injunction be issued enjoining the University of Mississippi from refusing to admit Meredith. As a result of Meredith's entry to "Ole Miss," other state universities were forced to reexamine their segregated admissions policies and to begin to open opportunities in higher education for African-American students.

SELECTED BIBLIOGRAPHY

Meredith v. Fair, 305 F.2d 343 (5th Cir. 1962).

LISA STARK

MERRITT, EMMA FRANCES GRAYSON (11 January 1860, Dumfries, Virginia–8 June 1933, Washington, D.C.). Emma Merritt was an educator, lecturer, social worker, and community volunteer. An innovative educator, she updated teaching methodology in the District of Columbia schools by developing a primary department for African-American students and adopting modern methods of instruction for the department. Her accomplishments included the establishment of demonstration schools to improve teacher capability and teaching techniques. She was the first to group students uniformly to improve teaching and learning environments. Before system administrators made any provision for silent reading in the curriculum, she introduced the concept to her pupils. She conducted a correspondence school by frequently communicating with former students who had acquired teaching positions in the rural South to keep them up-to-date with modern ideas in education. She started the first summer school and established the first kindergarten for African-American students.

Merritt's initial school attendance was at Ebenezer African Methodist Episcopal Church; she then went on to Old M Street High School, where she graduated in 1875. She received collegiate normal preparation at Howard University* from 1883 to 1887. She then studied at Columbia University from 1887 to 1890. She returned to Howard to study mathematics from 1889 to 1892 and to Columbia University from 1895 to 1898 to study psychology, child study, and sociology. Between 1898 and 1901, she studied mathematics, psychology, child study, and primary methods at the Cook County Normal School in Chicago, Illinois. She graduated from the Washington, D.C., Phoebe Hearst Training School in 1901 and was a student at the Berlitz School of Languages in 1913, where she received credit for extension courses and coursework taken at Columbia University. In 1925 she was granted an honorary degree of master of arts from Howard University. Her teaching career in Washington, D.C., began at the Stevens School* as a first grade teacher in 1875; she became principal of the Banneker Elementary School in 1887 and of the Garnet School in 1896. In 1898 she was promoted to primary instructor and director of grades 1–4. The year 1926 was the high point of her career, when she became supervising principal of the "colored" school system, Divisions 10 and 11.

SELECTED BIBLIOGRAPHY
Gerri Bates, "Emma Frances Grayson Merritt," in Jessie Carney Smith, ed., *Notable Black American Women* (1992); Gerri Bates, "Emma Frances Grayson Merritt," in Darlene Clark Hine, ed., *Black Women in America* (1993); Jane R. Caulton, "Innovative D.C. Teacher Started Family Tradition," *Washington Times*, 8 February 1990, B1, 4; Omelia Robinson, "Contributions of Black American Academic Women to American Higher Education," diss., Wayne State University, 1978, 128–29; Estelle Taylor, "Emma Frances Grayson Merritt: Pioneer in Negro Education," *Negro History Bulletin* 38 (1975): 434–35.

GERRI BATES

MILES COLLEGE. Founded in 1905 by the Christian Methodist Episcopal Church, Miles College is a coeducational, historically black institution, encompassing twenty-five acres in the western section of Birmingham, Alabama. Miles College operates under five academic divisions: education, humanities, social sciences, business and economics, and natural science and mathematics. There are several support programs, including three tutorial programs and student support services. Miles offers academic majors in thirteen areas: accounting, biology, business administration, chemistry, communications, elementary education, English, language arts education, mathematics, mathematics education, political science, social science, education, and social work. A member of the National Collegiate Athletic Association (NCAA) Division II and the Southern Intercollegiate Athletic Conference (SIAC), Miles College offers competitive teams in football, basketball, baseball, volleyball, and track and field. In both educational and community service, Miles College is noted for its commitment to providing educational opportunities for young people who may otherwise be denied a college education.

SELECTED BIBLIOGRAPHY
National Association for Equal Opportunity in Higher Education, *Profiles of the Nation's Historically and Predominantly Black Colleges and Universities* (1993).

SAMUEL L. MYERS

MILLER, CARROLL LEE LIVERPOOL (20 August 1909, Washington, D.C.). Carroll Miller received his B.A. degree (magna cum laude) from Howard University in 1929 and his M.A. degree and Ed.D. from Columbia University in 1930 and 1952, respectively. As an educator and an administrator, Miller realized early the challenge of sustaining the educational interest of youth with potential, and for that purpose he advocated reform and reassessment of the effectiveness of the educational process at all levels. He taught at Miles Memorial College* from 1930 to 1931, when he became a member of the faculty of Howard University,* rising to the rank of full professor of education by 1957. At Howard, Miller served as a departmental chair from 1961 to 1968, as associate dean of the College of Liberal Arts from 1961 to 1964, as acting dean of the Graduate School from 1964 to 1966, and as dean of the Graduate School from 1966 to 1974. He served as a distinguished professor of higher education from 1974 to 1988, at the end of which period he was designated professor emeritus. For his remarkable career, he was awarded in 1990 the Howard University Alumni Achievement Award, the highest award that institution gives to its distinguished alumni.

Though retired, Miller continues to serve Howard University as a consultant to its School of Social Work and as a member of the advisory board for its School of Continuing Education. Since 1984, he has been the chairman of the Charles H. Thompson Lecture–Colloquium committee, which sponsors an annual lecture on African-American education. A frequent contributor to the *Journal of Negro Education** since the 1930s, Miller has also served on its editorial board. He holds memberships and serves on the advisory boards and boards of directors of numerous educational and religious organizations in the greater Washington, D.C. area and nationally.

SELECTED BIBLIOGRAPHY

Christa Brelin and William C. Matney, eds., *Who's Who in Black America, 1992–1993* (1992); "Miller, Carroll Lee," vertical file, Howardiana Collection, Moorland-Spingarn Research Center, Howard University: Washington, D.C.; vita and resume of Carroll L. Miller.

ESME BHAN

MILLIKEN v. BRADLEY, 418 U.S. 717 (1974) (Milliken I); 433 U.S. 267 (1977) (Milliken II). *Milliken v. Bradley I* and *Milliken v. Bradley II* both addressed the scope and limits of the authority of the federal courts in the battle to end school segregation. *Milliken I* involved a suit filed in August 1970 by the NAACP,* parents, and students who sought to put an end to racial segregation in the public schools of Detroit, Michigan. Ruling in favor of the plaintiffs in *Milliken I*, the U.S. District Court for the Eastern District of Michigan ordered a multidistrict, area-wide desegregation remedy, including fifty-three suburban school districts, to end racial segregation in the Detroit public schools. It held that because the public schools in Detroit were unlawfully segregated and the proposed desegregation plans would make the city schools even more clearly a one-race system, it was necessary to go beyond district boundaries to fashion a remedy. The school board, superintendent, and governor, among others, appealed.

On 25 July 1974, a closely divided Supreme Court, in a 5–4 ruling, struck down the trial court's order in *Milliken I*. The majority reasoned that absent any findings that the affected suburban school districts failed to operate unitary school systems, or any claim or finding that their boundaries were established to foster racial segregation, or that they committed racial segregation, and absent any meaningful chance for them to present evidence or to be heard relative to the proposed interdistrict remedy or on the question of the constitutional violations, the district court acted impermissibly. Thus, the Court held that given the lack of evidence that the suburban districts engaged in illegal discrimination, the proposed interdistrict remedy could not be implemented. Accordingly, the trial court's ruling was reversed and remanded for the formulation of a deseg-regation plan consistent with the majority's opinion. The three dissenting opin-ions, joined by four justices, although based on slightly differing rationales, shared a common thread. They reasoned that since the state of Michigan played a part in establishing and maintaining the boundaries of the Detroit public school system, it had a duty to obviate racial discrimination even if it meant crossing district boundaries.

On remand in *Milliken II*, the federal trial court ordered a pupil-assignment plan limited to the Detroit public schools along with four remedial programs necessary to achieve desegregation. It found that because testing and counseling as administered in Detroit were infected with the discriminatory bias of a seg-regated school system, changes were necessary in those program areas; it also held that reading and in-service teacher training programs were necessary to assist in successfully implementing desegregation. Additionally, the court or-dered the state to share equally the cost with the Detroit Board of Education.

The Supreme Court agreed to hear the state of Michigan's appeal and, on 27 June 1977, unanimously upheld the trial court's decision. The Court addressed two issues. First, it ruled that, as the trial court acted on substantial evidence in the record when it ordered remedial relief to obviate the effects of de jure segregation, its finding had to be upheld, as it did not exceed the violation. Second, it held that the Eleventh (which protects states from financial liability based on the actions of public officials) and Tenth (which protects states from federal interference with their reserved powers, most notably education) Amend-ments notwithstanding, the lower court acted within the limits of its authority in ordering prospective compliance with its decree.

While *Milliken I* was the first major defeat for the NAACP and its supporters in the battle to end racial segregation, *Milliken II* represented a measure of vindication. Not only did *Milliken II* raise the issue of state financial responsi-bility for implementing a desegregation order, an approach adopted in the Su-preme Court's more recent ruling in *Missouri v. Jenkins*, 495 U.S. 33 (1990), but its reliance on remedial programs included elements of both equity and excellence to narrow gaps in achievement between African-American and white students.

SELECTED BIBLIOGRAPHY

Milliken v. Bradley I, 418 U.S. 717 (1974); *Milliken v. Bradley II*, 433 U.S. 267 (1977).

CHARLES J. RUSSO

MILLS v. BOARD OF EDUCATION OF ANNE ARUNDEL COUNTY, 30 F. Supp. 245 (E.D. Pa., 1939). This decision concerned a dispute over a dis-criminatory pay scale that existed between African-American and white public school teachers in Anne Arundel County, Maryland. In its decision, the court in effect extends the application of the Fourteenth Amendment (resurrected as an instrument for the protection of the African-American) to the state in its capacity as an employer. By granting the injunction, the court decided, in effect, that the county board must pay African-American teachers at least the minimum set for whites and may at no time pay them less than that which would be paid to white teachers of equal qualifications and experience.

In 1939, Walter Mills, principal of an African-American school in Anne Arundel County, sued the state board of education to equalize the salaries of Maryland's African-American and white public school teachers. Mills asked the court to declare the county's discriminatory pay-scale policy unconstitutional under the Fourteenth Amendment's due process and equal protection clauses. Historically, Maryland had laws that prescribed maximum teacher salaries for the various county boards of education, yet African-American teachers with professional qualifications and experience comparable to those of white teachers were paid roughly half that of their white counterparts. The state of Maryland had statutes that provided for minimum teacher salaries that were supposedly based on professional qualifications and years of experience. As a practical matter, only white teachers were employed in white schools and only African-American teachers in African-American schools in Anne Arundel County. Generally, the minimum pay scales in 1939 in Maryland counties were set at $765 per year for African-American teachers and $1250 per year for white teachers. Mills charged that these statutes were discriminatory on their face and should be declared unconstitutional. However, Mills's initial suit was dismissed and not decided on the merits because the County Board of Education was not included as a defendant.

After Mills's first case, Maryland passed statutes that established new state minimum salaries for white teachers, supposedly based on experience and preparation. However, these statutes increased the minimum salary for white teachers, while having no effect on the minimum salary for teachers in African-American schools. These statutes were offered as the first of several defenses to Mills's accusations of discrimination; however, they failed to address his accusations because white teachers' salaries were calculated on a yearly schedule, while African-American teachers' salaries were determined on a monthly basis. This fact had significance because the school year for African-American students was considerably shorter than that of white students. As a result of the shorter school year, the school board concluded that African-American teachers were justifiably paid less than white teachers.

Next, the defendants offered as their second defense another Maryland statute, which extended the school term for African-American students and as a consequence increased the African-American teachers' salaries by increasing the number of months worked. The defendants claimed that this statute did not apply only to African-American teachers; rather, it applied to all teachers, whether black or white. This statute indirectly increased the salaries of African-American teachers; however, it also failed to address the alleged discriminatory practices because it only affected pay scales at African-American schools, at which only black teachers were employed.

Although uniform standards were used to rate both black and white teachers, great disparities existed statewide in the minimum pay scales. The court said that practical application of these statutes did not necessarily require actual racial discrimination in practice, but instead ruled that the statutes did not allow the boards to discriminate. Furthermore, the court decided it was entirely permissible for the boards to use "full discretion" in determining actual salaries for particular teachers, provided the discrimination was not based solely on race. The court did hold, however, that Mills had been unconstitutionally discriminated against in his profession by the county school board and that he was entitled to an injunction against the continuation of such discrimination to the extent that it was based solely on the grounds of race. The court also held that the board would not be enjoined from paying Mills or his African-American colleagues less than any white teacher or principal filling an equivalent position in the county public schools because the board would be allowed some discretion in determining actual teacher salaries. In effect, the court acknowledged the discrimination but did very little to curtail such practices. The court made it clear that it did not decide whether the state minimum salary statute was unconstitutional on its face, because it said the county practice, rather than the "mere terms of the statute," prejudiced Mills. The court added that if the county continued to observe the "minimum state statute for salaries for white teachers, it [was] difficult to see how it would have legal justification for paying [African-American] teachers less than the minimum for white teachers of similar standard professional qualifications and experience, as such discrimination would seem to be based solely on race or color."

This decision represented a first step in overcoming overtly racial discrepancies in the compensation of African-American educators. In the aftermath of *Mills*, public officials had to devise less obvious policies to maintain racial apartheid in public education. In some sense, the legacy of *Mills* was not fulfilled until *Board of Education v. Harris** 584 F.2d 576 (1979), in which the discriminatory impact of a standard was deemed sufficient to invalidate that policy, precluding the necessity for demonstrating that the original purpose or intent of the standard was discriminatory.

SELECTED BIBLIOGRAPHY

Mills v. Lowndes et al., 26 F. Supp. 792, 801 (1939); National Education Association, *Programs for Equal Pay for Equal Work* (1939), p. 24ff; National Education Association, *Minimum Salary Laws for Teachers* (1937); "Recent Cases," *Harvard Law Review* 53 (1940): 669–71; U.S. Constitution, Amendment 14, Section 1; Doxey A. Wilkerson, *Special Problems of Negro Education*, Staff Study No. 12, Advisory Committee on Education (1939).

BEVERLY BAKER–KELLY AND TERENCE COLES

MISEDUCATION. Miseducation is a term coined by African-American educator and historian Carter G. Woodson* in the mid-1930s to describe the prevailing theories, practices, and outcomes of educational efforts provided for

African-Americans. Woodson described miseducation as an educational process that systematically socializes African-Americans to adopt and value European, especially Anglo-Saxon, beliefs, customs, and behaviors as well as knowledge base. He asserted that, either explicitly or implicitly, this process simultaneously forces African-Americans to abide the inferior status assigned to them in the larger society and accept second-class economic, social, and political standing in their communities—the very same communities they have been trained to despise, degrade, condemn, and, ultimately, reject—as their only legitimate place. Woodson's ideas were based on his assessments of his own formal education experiences as a secondary school and college teacher and of his associations with prominent educators and influential philanthropists involved in the matter of educating African-Americans. His scathing critique of African-American education was offered at a time when the effects of the Great Depression forced many African-American intellectual leaders to question and reevaluate their values and many areas of their life experiences and when Woodson and his contemporaries were less optimistic about the promise of African-American education, in both historically black and white universities, based on their views of its shortcomings and failures.

In Woodson's view, miseducation results in two major outcomes. First, he noted that formal schooling, with its Eurocentric focus, teaches students about civilization and life in general from the perspectives of Europeans and European-Americans. This emphasis on only white people's accomplishments and achievements suppresses and distorts those of other races of peoples, particularly African-Americans. Consequently, African-Americans who are educated to know and respect only European and European-American knowledge, history, culture, and worldviews remain ignorant of and disrespect those of their own people. Thus, Woodson pointed out, formally educated African-Americans might know what is presented as U.S. history without knowing about the myriad contributions made by people of African descent to the development of this nation. This situation, he believed, results in their internalizing the inferiority imputed to them, hating themselves, or warding off their feelings of inferiority by assuming a sense of superiority relative to the masses of black people. Second, Woodson maintained that miseducation results in African-Americans being trained first and foremost to serve the needs and satisfy the aspirations of white society. Examples of this are seen in the emphasis placed on recruiting young African-American men for college sports without an accompanying genuine commitment to their college education and in the ways many schools and teachers instill African-American students with the belief that they cannot hope to succeed as scientists or great thinkers. Such emphasis and training, Woodson theorized, renders African-Americans incapable of gaining or using the knowledge, skills, talents, and expertise necessary to enable them to be self-sufficient, to build and strengthen their own communities and generally improve their lives.

Whereas Woodson promoted the improvement of the quality rather than quantity of education, he did not propose different educations for black and whites.

He believed, however, that a true education for African-Americans would not be controlled by others or teach them to serve their oppressors. Instead, it would be controlled by African-Americans and would accomplish the following: It would equip African-Americans to earn a living; it would also allow them to manifest actively their authentic selves shaped by both their traditional African cultures and histories and the social, political, and economic conditions in the United States; finally, it would help African-Americans develop into valuable, contributing members of their communities who will be empowered to shape its positive development.

SELECTED BIBLIOGRAPHY

Carter G. Woodson, *Mis-Education of the Negro* (1933; reprint 1977); *Mind of the Negro as Reflected in Letters Written during the Crisis* (1926); *Education of the Negro Prior to 1861* (1915); John Hope Franklin, "The Place of Carter G. Woodson in American Historiography," *Negro History Bulletin* 13 (May 1950): 174–76; Thelma D. Perry, "The Bulletin—A Concept of Education," *Negro History Bulletin* 34 (October 1971): 124–26; Charles H. Thompson, "An Unusual Personal Experience with Carter G. Woodson," *Negro History Bulletin* 13 (May 1950): 185; W. E. B. Du Bois, "A Portrait of Carter G. Woodson," *Masses and Mainstream* 3 (June 1950): 19–25.

MARGO OKAZAWA-REY

MISSISSIPPI INDUSTRIAL COLLEGE. Mississippi Industrial College was established in 1905 as Mississippi Industrial Negro College in Holly Springs, Mississippi, by Bishop Elias Cottrell under the auspices of the Colored Methodist Episcopal Church (presently the Christian Methodist Episcopal Church [CME]). Ownership and control of the institution was vested in a board of trustees elected by the Mississippi CME Conference, whose membership was its sole source of financial support. The college served the African-American community in rural Holly Springs and surrounding Marshall County for over seventy-seven years before closing its doors in 1982 because of financial straits.

Founded to provide literacy and industrial training for African-Americans in the state of Mississippi, the college's stated mission was "to secure for its students the highest possible development in body, mind and spirit. This ideal governs the course of study. Discipline, Christian character, and service are the highest and chief end of training." A small, coeducational liberal arts college, Mississippi Industrial College originally had three academic departments: elementary, secondary/college preparatory, and industrial. By 1890, the college was offering bachelor of arts and bachelor of science degrees in the following areas: elementary education, mathematics, biology, social science, English, music education, business education, business administration, home economics, health and physical education, French, and religious education.

SELECTED BIBLIOGRAPHY

Andre G. Beaumont, ed., *Handbook for Recruiting at the Traditional Black Colleges* (1975); Daniel A. P. Murray Association, *The Murray Resource Directory to the Nation's Historically Black Colleges and Universities* (1993); Department of the Interior, *Negro Education: A Study of the Private and Higher Schools for Colored People in the United*

States, vol. 2 (1917); *Mississippi Industrial College Catalog 1976–1979* (1976); Charles H. Wilson, *Education for Negroes in Mississippi since 1910* (1974).

A. J. STOVALL

MISSISSIPPI VALLEY STATE UNIVERSITY. Founded in 1950, Mississippi Valley State University, located in Itta Bena in the heart of Mississippi, is the nation's youngest historically black public university. It annually offers more than seven hundred different courses and awards undergraduate degrees in twenty-one areas. A master's degree is offered in environmental health. The university also provides Mississippi's first nationally accredited art and environmental health programs. MVSU is also home to an Air Force ROTC detachment and has an outstanding marching band.
SELECTED BIBLIOGRAPHY
National Association for Equal Opportunity in Higher Education, *Profiles of the Nation's Historically and Predominantly Black Colleges and Universities* (1993).

SAMUEL L. MYERS

MISSOURI EX REL GAINES v. CANADA, 305 U.S. 337 (1938). W. E. B. Du Bois,* and later the National Association for the Advancement of Colored People (NAACP),* developed a systematic plan to dismantle the doctrine of ''separate but equal'' as the major barrier to equal access to educational opportunities. Carefully developing strategic plans, the NAACP sought its first test case in a border state where, it reasoned, resistance to racially integrated education would not be as great as in the deep South. That case came in 1935, when Donald Murray applied to the University of Maryland. Following the registrar's refusal to admit him, he filed a *Mandamus* suit against the university that alleged that his constitutional rights had been violated by the state of Maryland. The Maryland Circuit Court of Appeals directed the board of regents to the university to admit Murray, as the state did not provide a law school for African-Americans and provided only $200 (an insufficient sum) for out-of-state tuition.

Success in the *University of Maryland v. Murray** case encouraged the NAACP to sue on behalf of Lloyd Gaines, a graduate of Lincoln University* (Missouri). The NAACP filed the suit in 1936 in the Missouri Circuit Court and requested a *Mandamus* writ against the university's registrar. The court ruled against Gaines, and the NAACP eventually appealed the decision to the U.S. Supreme Court in *Missouri ex rel Gaines v. Canada*.

The Gaines case differed from the Murray case in that the state of Missouri had made a serious attempt to provide quality higher education for Negroes at Lincoln University. It was prepared to build a new law school there if need arose. To meet the immediate concerns of Gaines for a legal education, it offered him an out-of-state scholarship. In the Missouri case, the NAACP did not mount a frontal assault on the doctrine of ''separate-but-equal.'' Instead, it argued that the doctrine be equally enforced; if whites in Missouri were to have a law school, then the state, under *Plessy v. Ferguson** (1896), was obligated to provide one of equal status for African-Americans. The court ruled in a six-to-two decision that Missouri had to provide a law school for Gaines and other African-Americans or admit him to the white one. Gaines was ordered admitted to the University of Missouri School of Law in 1938; however, he disappeared before enrolling and was never heard from again.

The *Gaines* decision had enormous implications for the education of African-Americans throughout the country. The court had ruled that states could either provide substantially equal facilities or desegregate white ones. The NAACP and others reasoned that the same principle could then apply to elementary and high schools, wherever African-American students were denied equal facilities. The principle could be applied to all aspects of the dual educational system. While the *Gaines* case encouraged southerners to expand and create state-supported graduate and professional educational programs for African-Americans the decision formed one of the building blocks for the 1954 *Brown v. Board of Education of Topeka, Kansas** decision, in which the Supreme Court unanimously voted that segregated education was unconstitutional.

SELECTED BIBLIOGRAPHY
Albert P. Blaustein and Robert L. Zangrando, eds., *Civil Rights and the American Negro* (1968); Henry Allen Bullock, *A History of Negro Education in the South from 1619 to the Present* (1967); John P. Davis, ed., *The American Negro Reference Book* (1966); John E. Fleming, *The Lengthening Shadow of Slavery* (1976); Charles Flint Kellogg, *NAACP: A History of the National Association for the Advancement of Colored People* (1967); Richard Kluger, *Simple Justice* (1976); Rayford Logan, *The Betrayal of the Negro* (1965); Loren Miller, *The Petitioners: The Story of the Supreme Court of the United States and the Negro* (1966).

JOHN E. FLEMING AND EDNA C. DIGGS

MOORLAND, JESSE EDWARD (10 September 1863, Coldwater, Ohio–30 April 1940, New York, N.Y.). A YMCA administrator, university trustee, and clergyman, Moorland received a diploma in theology from Howard University* in 1891 and was subsequently ordained as a Congregational minister. He received honorary doctorates from Howard University in 1906 and from Oberlin College* in 1924.

Moorland first joined the YMCA as secretary of the African-American branch in Washington, D.C., and served from 1891 to 1893. In 1898 he accepted an appointment with the Colored Men's Department of the International Committee of the YMCA. Education and literacy were two areas that Moorland stressed during his twenty-five-year tenure in this post. He was also noted for conceptualizing training centers to improve staff development at local YMCAs.

Moorland joined the Howard University board of trustees in 1907, remaining until 1940. This was a period noted for the controversial efforts by several trustees to realign Howard's curriculum toward the industrial-education philosophy then in place at Hampton* and Tuskegee* institutes. In 1912, Moorland supported the efforts of prominent Howard scholars such as Kelly Miller and Alain L. Locke* to include instruction in African and African-American history in the school's curriculum.

In 1915, Moorland, with Carter G. Woodson* and J. A. Bigham, founded the Association for the Study of Negro Life and History,* an organization designed to promote black history and culture and to educate African-Americans, especially, about that history. He served as the organization's secretary-treasurer until disagreements over its management soured his relationship with Woodson and led to his removal in 1921.

Moorland's commitment to African and African-American scholarship is best evidenced by the donation he made to Howard University in 1914 of his personal collection of books, documents, photographs, and artifacts. Considered by experts at the time to be one of the largest collections of its kind, Moorland's gift was established by the Howard board of trustees in 1915 as the Moorland Foundation. Popularly called "the Negro Collection," the foundation became known as the Moorland–Spingarn Collection after the 1946 acquisition by the university of the Arthur B. Spingarn* Collection of Negro Authors. In 1973, the collection was renamed the Moorland–Spingarn Research Center.*

Jesse Moorland died in New York in April 1940 and is interred at Lincoln Memorial Cemetery in Suitland, Maryland.

SELECTED BIBLIOGRAPHY

Thomas C. Battle, "The Moorland–Spingarn Research Center," in *Dictionary of Literary Biography* 76 (1988); Jesse E. Moorland Papers, Moorland Spingarn Research Center, Howard University; Rayford W. Logan and Michael R. Winston, eds., *Dictionary of American Negro Biography* (1982); Howard University, *The Hilltop* 14 (May 1940): 2; Dorothy B. Porter, "A Library on the Negro," *American Scholar* 7 (Winter 1938); Elinor Des Verney Sinnette, W. Paul Coates, and Thomas C. Battle, *Black Bibliophiles and Collectors: Preservers of Black History* (1990).

THOMAS C. BATTLE

MOORLAND–SPINGARN RESEARCH CENTER. Located at Howard University* in Washington, D.C., the Moorland–Spingarn Research Center was established in 1915 by the Howard University Board of Trustees as the "Moorland Foundation, a Library of Negro Life," to house the collection of books, documents, photographs, and artifacts donated by Jesse E. Moorland* in 1914, documenting black history and culture. At the time, Moorland's collection was considered by experts to be the largest privately held collection of its kind, and Howard University became the first American university to develop a research collection whose materials focused solely upon the black experience. The Moorland Foundation was popularly called "The Negro Collection" and became known as the Moorland–Spingarn Collection in the years following the acquisition of the Arthur B. Spingarn Collection of Negro Authors in 1946. It was designated a research library in 1932 and became the Moorland–Spingarn Research Center (MSRC) in 1973.

Dorothy Burnett Porter (now Wesley) was appointed the collection's librarian in 1930 and served for forty-three years. Her remarkable tenure was noted for the great expansion of the collection's holdings, the improvement of its classification scheme, the preparation of an array of scholarly bibliographies, and the establishment of Moorland–Spingarn as an indispensable center of scholarship on black history and culture. Michael R. Winston* became director of the new research center when it was expanded and reorganized in 1973. His decade of leadership was marked by the redefinition of the MSRC's approach to archival documentation and the rapid expansion of its manuscript and archival holdings. Since 1986, Thomas C. Battle has continued the MSRC's mandate to develop as a comprehensive research facility documenting the worldwide experiences of people of African descent. It is one of the world's largest and most comprehensive centers documenting black history and culture. Its vast library and archival holdings are used by students and scholars from throughout the United States and the world. These materials contribute significantly to museum exhibitions, publications, video productions, and similar expressions of scholarly inquiry into Africana and related diaspora studies.

SELECTED BIBLIOGRAPHY

Thomas C. Battle, "The Moorland–Spingarn Research Center," in *Dictionary of Literary Biography* 76 (1988); Michael R. Winston, "Moorland-Spingarn Research Center: A Past Revisited, A Present Reclaimed," *New Directions* (Summer 1974); 20–25; Dorothy B. Porter, "A Library on the Negro," *American Scholar* 7 (Winter 1938): 115–17; Moorland Foundation, *The Arthur B. Spingarn Collection of Negro Authors* (1947); Elinor Des Verney Sinnette, W. Paul Coates, and Thomas C. Battle, *Black Bibliophiles and Collectors: Preservers of Black History* (1990).

THOMAS C. BATTLE

MOREHOUSE COLLEGE. Founded with the support of the Baptist Church, Morehouse College is a 126-year-old college for men located in Atlanta, Georgia. Morehouse is outstanding among predominantly black four-year colleges in the academic credentials of its student body, in the percentage of faculty with terminal degrees, and in the production of alumni who have pursued graduate study and become physicians, dentists, lawyers, and college presidents. The tradition of academic excellence and leadership is exemplified by the careers of such alumni as Martin Luther King, Jr., Lerone Bennett, Jr., Maynard Jackson, and Louis Sullivan.

A small, private institution renowned for its strong curriculum, Morehouse offers thirty-six liberal arts majors including computer science, religion, political science, business, and prelaw, premedicine and predentistry tracks, and the dual degree program in engineering and architecture. Qualified students may also participate in the honors program, the College's Phi Beta Kappa chapter, or the study-abroad program.

SELECTED BIBLIOGRAPHY
National Association for Equal Opportunity in Higher Education, *Profiles of the Nation's Historically and Predominantly Black Colleges and Universities* (1993).
                                                                    SAMUEL L. MYERS

MORGAN STATE UNIVERSITY. Located in northeast Baltimore, Maryland, Morgan State University is a comprehensive, urban-oriented institution with programs leading to undergraduate liberal arts, preprofessional, and professional degrees and master's and doctoral degrees emphasizing teaching, research, and public service. In recent years, the university has begun to significantly upgrade and expand its physical plant. The two latest additions to the campus inventory are a six-hundred-bed high-rise residence hall and a faculty to house the School of Engineering. Founded in 1867, Morgan has experienced strong growth in recent years as Maryland's public urban university. From 1988 to 1993, total enrollments grew by one third and full-time undergraduates by over 50 percent.

SELECTED BIBLIOGRAPHY
National Association for Equal Opportunity in Higher Education, *Profiles of the Nation's Historically and Predominantly Black Colleges and Universities* (1993).
                                                                    SAMUEL L. MYERS

MORGAN v. O'BRYANT, 671 F. 2d 23 (1st Cir.), cert. denied, 459 U.S. 827 (1992). This case, which was part of the ongoing Boston, Massachusetts, public school desegregation litigation, provides examples of both the hiring and the layoff remedies that courts have imposed to resolve educational inequities. In 1974, the District Court of Massachusetts found that Boston public school authorities had knowingly engaged in a policy of racial discrimination and intentionally maintained a dual school system segregated along racial lines. In addition to holding that pupil assignments were discriminatory, the court also found that school authorities discriminated in faculty hiring. To remedy the situation, the court ordered that one black teacher be hired for every white teacher until the percentage of black faculty teaching in Boston's public schools reached 20 percent, the approximate percentage of African-Americans in Boston at that time. The court also ordered affirmative recruitment efforts to continue until no less than 25 percent of the school system's faculty was African-American.

By early 1981, the percentage of African-American teachers in the Boston schools had reached 19.09 percent, but progress was threatened when the school system faced a budget crisis that ultimately required massive faculty layoffs. Because layoffs by reverse seniority (last hired, first fired)—as called for in the teachers' collective bargaining agreements—would have reduced black faculty to approximately 8 percent, the district court approved the school committee's plan to conduct race-based layoffs to maintain the existing percentage of newly hired African-American teachers. The Boston Teachers Union (BTU) and the

Boston Association of School Administrators and Supervisors (BASAS) appealed the decision, arguing that the district court's orders were not remedial and that they benefitted African-American teachers and administrators who were never shown to be the victims of hiring discrimination. The BTU and BASAS argued further that, even if the district court's orders were remedial, they constituted forbidden racial preferences.

In 1982, the First Circuit Court of Appeals upheld the district court's orders requiring the Boston schools to achieve a faculty that approximated the racial composition of the city's general population and also upheld the imposition of race-based layoffs. Emphasizing that the victims were the African-American school children, the appeals court reasoned that a racially balanced faculty vindicated minority students' constitutional right to attend school in a system free of the vestiges of past discrimination by providing them with role models and encouraging African-American students and parents to participate in the school community. Citing *Swann v. Charlotte–Mecklenburg Board of Education** (1971), the court stated that, once a court has found racial desegregation in a school case, race-conscious remedies not only are permitted but are required where "color-blind" approaches would be inadequate. The First Circuit, therefore, concluded that because race-based layoffs would protect the school committee's progress in hiring African-American teachers, the district court's orders were a reasonable response to the situation and did not constitute forbidden racial preferences.

SELECTED BIBLIOGRAPHY

"Race-Based Faculty Hiring and Layoff Remedies in School Desegregation Cases," *Harvard Law Review* 104, no. 8 (1991): 1917.

JOYCE WALKER-JONES

MORRILL ACT OF 1890. Known as the second Morrill Act, named after Vermont Senator Justin Smith Morrill, this legislation extended and refined the original groundbreaking federal-aid-to-education concept of the Morrill Act of 1862. The 1862 act was established to help higher education through giving federal lands to the states. Each state and territory received 30,000 acres of public land for each senator and representative in Congress; a total of 17,430,000 acres were turned over to the states. The proceeds were used by the states to endow and support state colleges for the teaching of agriculture and the mechanical arts for the "liberal and practical education of the industrial classes." These land-grant colleges* (A&M's) were a key impetus to the democratization of postsecondary education because they focused on the teaching of practical subjects, such as farming, home economics, engineering, and related fields as opposed to the classical subjects taught to those entering the learned professions.

In 1890, the second Morrill Act corrected several defects of the original, including the payment of an annual sum of money if states would "match" the federal appropriation. The most glaring omission of the original act was also "solved" by the 1890 revision, in its stipulation that no state would receive federal money if it did not admit to its land-grant colleges individuals of color. It further stipulated that the states could provide such an education in ''separate but equal'' institutions. By 1915, there were sixteen federally supported African-American land-grant institutions and seven state-run African-American normal schools and colleges.

PETER A. SOLA

MORRIS BROWN COLLEGE. A member of the Atlanta University Center, the world's largest educational complex serving African-American students, Morris Brown College in Atlanta, Georgia, is a private four-year liberal arts college offering more than fifty majors, including business administration, computer and social sciences, biology, chemistry, hospitality administration, and education. Founded in 1881 by the leaders of the African Methodist Episcopal Church, Morris Brown is fully accredited by the Southern Association of Colleges and Schools.* The cosmopolitan nature of the college is reflected in its student body, which represents thirty-eight states and thirty foreign countries or territories. The college has distinguished itself in the Intercollegiate National Mock Trial competitions and Model United Nations event, ranking it among some of the major universities in the country and the only private historically black college participating.

SELECTED BIBLIOGRAPHY

National Association for Equal Opportunity in Higher Education, *Profiles of the Nation's Historically and Predominantly Black Colleges and Universities* (1993).

SAMUEL L. MYERS

MORRIS COLLEGE. Founded in 1908, Morris College is a four-year coeducational liberal arts college located in Sumter, South Carolina. The college is owned and operated by the Baptist Educational and Missionary Convention of South Carolina and is fully accredited by the Commission on Colleges of the Southern Association of Colleges and Schools.* The college offers the bachelor of arts, the bachelor of fine arts, and the bachelor of science degrees. Course offerings are organized into six divisions: education, general studies, humanities, natural sciences and mathematics, business administration, and social sciences (including history and prelaw studies). Degrees are offered in criminal justice, English, history, liberal studies, political science/history, religious education, social studies, liberal–technical studies, sociology, fine arts, biology, business administration, mathematics, early childhood education, elementary education, community health, and recreation administration. An Army ROTC program is also included in the college's curriculum.

SELECTED BIBLIOGRAPHY

National Association for Equal Opportunity in Higher Education, *Profiles of the Nation's Historically and Predominantly Black Colleges and Universities* (1993).

SAMUEL L. MYERS

MOTEN, LUCY ELLA (1851–24 August 1933, Fauquier County, Virginia). An educator, administrator, and medical doctor, Moten graduated from Howard

University* in 1870. In 1876, she graduated from the Normal School in Salem, Massachusetts, and in 1883 graduated with honors from Spencerian Business College. She also pursued graduate study in education at New York University. Moten also spent time in Europe, and it was there that she got the idea of establishing a teacher's college for African-Americans based on the model of Christ's College in Cambridge, England.

Upon returning to America, Moten gained prominence as the founder and principal of Miner Normal School in Washington, D.C., which was in its day one of the top teaching institutions in America. For twenty-five years, Moten helped shape the school's faculty and student body as well as its campus. Under her tutelage, the faculty was strengthened, admissions standards were elevated, and the curriculum was extended to a two-year program. For four decades, Moten trained the majority of teachers employed in Washington, D.C.'s African-American schools. After she received her medical degree in 1897, she was also able to treat the medical needs of her students.

Moten's influence was not limited to Miner. She taught many summer teacher-training workshops throughout the South. Moten died as a result of being struck by a taxi in New York's Times Square at about age 82. She bequeathed more than $51,000 to her alma mater, Howard University. In 1954, the city of Washington, D.C. named an elementary school in her honor.

SELECTED BIBLIOGRAPHY

Tomika DePriest, "Lucy Ella Moten," in Darlene Clark Hine, ed., *Black Women in America* (1993); Thomasine Carruthers, "Lucy Ella Moten," *Journal of Negro History* (January 1934); Lillian Dabney, "Century of Public Schools of the District of Columbia," *Journal of Negro History* (April 1932).

                                                                      TOMIKA DEPRIEST

MOTON, ROBERT RUSSA (26 August 1867, Amelia County, Virginia–31 May 1940, Capahosic, Virginia). The son of Booker and Emily Brown Moton, Robert Russa Moton entered Hampton Institute (now University)* in 1885 and graduated in 1890. At Hampton, he was appointed assistant commandant for a year and in 1891 became commandant, a post he held for twenty-five years. He established a collaborative relationship with Booker T. Washington* of Tuskegee Institute (now University),* and the two men often travelled together on joint fund-raising tours for their respective institutions. Like Washington, Moton also established relationships with northern philanthropists, efforts that influenced his 1908 appointment as secretary of the Anna T. Jeanes Fund.*

Upon Washington's death in 1915, Moton became principal of Tuskegee Institute and served twenty years in that post. There, he worked to build a permanent financial base for the school and upgrade its curriculum. Tuskegee's endowment quadrupled during his tenure to nearly eight million dollars, and its academic curriculum was upgraded in 1925 to college level so that a baccalaureate degree could be offered. The vocational curriculum was also modified to reflect more modern business demands. Notwithstanding, the educational contributions of Robert Moton can hardly be separated from the work of Washington. As Washington's successor, Moton assumed the mantle of national race leadership and essentially ended the Washington–W. E. B. Du Bois* debate over African-American educational goals. Like Washington, Moton viewed racial progress as requiring optimism, hard work, self-improvement, and patience. In later years, Moton moved toward a more forthright and direct expression of anger and frustration with racial injustice. Again like Washington, Moton was able to enlist substantial financial help, primarily from northern philanthropists, to improve education for African-Americans in the South.

In 1930, Moton was sent to Haiti to study educational conditions. He urged American aid, but with less emphasis on a colonial approach and more emphasis on indigenous leadership. His views were presented in the *Report of the U.S. Commission on Education in Haiti* (1931). Moton was the author of three other books, *Racial Good Will* (1916), *Finding a Way Out* (1920), and *What the Negro Thinks* (1929).

Moton married Elizabeth Hunt Harris in 1905; she died a year later. In 1908, he married Jennie D. Booth, with whom he had five children. Upon retirement, he moved to his home, Holly Hall, in Capahosic, Virginia. He died on 31 May 1940.

SELECTED BIBLIOGRAPHY

Robert Russa Moton, *Finding a Way Out: An Autobiography* (1920; reprint 1969); William Hardin Hughes and Frederick D. Patterson, *Robert Russa Moton of Hampton and Tuskegee* (1956).

EARLE H. WEST

CLARA MUHAMMAD SCHOOLS. The Clara Muhammad schools were founded in 1975 in Chicago, Illinois, by Muslim American leader Imam W. Deen Mohammed. They were named in honor of his mother, the wife of Nation of Islam founder Elijah Muhammad, ''for her tireless efforts and unselfish commitment'' to education. Presently a system of twenty-six independent, full-time, elementary and secondary schools serving kindergarten through eighth grades, Clara Muhammad schools are located in virtually every major city where *masjid* (Islamic places of worship) exist in the continental United States; one school is located on the island of Bermuda. The Clara Muhammad schools are distinct from the University of Islam schools of the Nation of Islam in that their curricular focus reflects the spiritual and philosophical principles of the Qu'ran, which was the basis of the transition to the beliefs and practices of Al-Islam made by Imam Muhammad and his followers in 1975.

While the Clara Muhammad schools represent the only national system of Islamic schools in America, since their early beginnings they have served not only Muslims of all ethnic groups but the larger African-American community. They are open to all students regardless of race, religion, or national origin. Administered by a director of education who is the local resident *imam* or religious leader, each Clara Muhammad school is affiliated with a *masjid*. Although each school is autonomous, there exists a network of professional support, accreditation, and academic competition between schools. Promoting a philosophy of moral, human, and academic excellence, the schools teach a curriculum based on the universal educational principles of the Qur'an. These principles in turn promote a unique process that illuminates intelligence, presents knowledge in a practical, unified manner, and cultivates strength in morality and character. Further, Clara Muhammad schools address the identity crisis experienced by many African-American youngsters by seeking to instill in them a sense of clarity about their ethnic, spiritual, and human realities.

The curriculum at Clara Muhammad schools stresses the natural sciences and regards nature as the first textbook. The Arabic language is taught in all schools; in the more progressive schools, Spanish and French are also taught. The schools are coeducational; however, when students reach the second or third grade, classrooms are generally separated by sex. Uniforms are standard school policy. Parents are required to participate in the educational process. Students generally outperform their public school counterparts by one to two grade levels.

SELECTED BIBLIOGRAPHY

W. D. Mohammed, "Clara Muhammad Elementary and Secondary Schools," in W. D. Mohammed, *The Man and the Woman in Islam* (1976), pp. 48–52; Zakiyyah Muhammad, "Dilemmas of Islamic Education in America: Possible Alternatives," *Muslim Education Quarterly* 7, no. 4 (1990); Hakim M. Rashid and Zakiyyah Muhammad, "The Sister Clara Muhammad Schools: Pioneers in the Development of Islamic Education in America," 61, no. 2 (1992): 178–85.

ZAKIYYAH MUHAMMAD

MULTICULTURAL COUNSELING. The term "counseling" broadly refers to a professional arrangement whereby a counselor engages in an interactive relationship with a client in order to bring about therapeutic change. Ideally, such change should be positive, permanent, and congruent with the values, morals, and ethics of the counselee and the social structure in which he or she lives and operates. Multicultural counseling involves the application of accepted therapeutic skills and techniques to diverse groups of people while recognizing certain aspects of cultural difference such as race or ethnicity. "Multicultural counseling" and "cross-cultural counseling" are terms used alternately to describe the helping process when at least one party in the counseling dyad, usually the client, is culturally different from the other.

Some researchers believe that multicultural counseling must be holistic and must include critical social dimensions of a person's identity such as cultural group membership, historical phenomena, sociopolitical forces, and cultural context. They further assert that multicultural counseling must acknowledge and understand existing cultural differences and patterns of behavior such that a healthy, positive relationship can develop between counselor and client. From the point of view of the counselor, positive regard, awareness, patience, and acceptance of the client and the client's cultural world are essential to the therapeutic process. The counselor must demonstrate a genuine sensitivity to the needs of the client and respect for the client's ways no matter how different they may be from the counselor's. In response to these concerns, there has emerged a new type of counseling professional: the "culturally-skilled counselor." He or she uses strategies and techniques that are consistent with the client's life experiences and cultural values. A culturally skilled counseling professional is able to view each client as a unique individual while constantly being in touch with his or her own personal and cultural experiences as a person who happens to be a helping professional. The need to be culturally skilled has put the responsibility on counselors to examine their own cultural heritage, values, and biases and how they might affect clients from diverse backgrounds.

Likewise, the culturally different client must be committed to the therapeutic process for positive overall growth and development to take place. This may prove an extremely challenging task for a client who may already be encumbered with language, cultural, and adjustment difficulties. Often, such clients offer some resistance to acculturation. Assimilation into another culture or society may prove threatening and, to culturally different clients, may be equated with losing one's identify. Such thoughts and feelings may prevent these clients from receiving the full benefit of counseling intervention. Additionally, many cultures consider taboo any counseling relationship between two people, believing such an approach lacks any merit, significance, or implication for personal well-being. The culturally charged belief that "talk" therapy is of questionable benefit to clients can sabotage the effectiveness of the overall intervention process.

Many counselors agree that multicultural service delivery would benefit from less theory and more practical application for addressing client concerns in a culturally sensitive manner. If multicultural counseling is to continue evolving as a discipline, comprehensive approaches to service delivery must be developed, implemented, and evaluated. In the past two decades, African-American scholars have articulated the need for black or Afrocentric* psychology and have searched for ways to examine their experience based on their own cultural realities. A basic assumption of this approach is that any discipline seeking to understand the dynamics of African-American development must take into account the experiences that shape that development. As such, counseling strategies and techniques for African-Americans must be predicated on understanding African-American culture and the implications of this understanding for fostering optimal mental health.

Ultimately, multicultural counseling should complement rather than compete with traditional approaches to counseling. Its application must be understood as part of a perspective that seeks neither to invalidate or displace traditional theories, but rather to serve as an enriching addition to these theories and practices.

SELECTED BIBLIOGRAPHY

P. Arredondo, A. Psalti, and K. Cella, "The Woman Factor in Multicultural Counseling," *Counseling and Human Development* 25 (1993): 1–8; C. C. Lee, "Multicultural Counseling: New Directions for Counseling Professionals," *Virginia Counselors Journal* 17 (1989): 3–8; C. C. Lee, "Multicultural Counseling: New Perspectives for the 1990s and Beyond," *Counseling and Human Development* 23 (1991): 1–6; L. J. Myers et al., "Identity Development and Worldview: Toward an Optimal Conceptualization," *Journal of Counseling and Development* 70 (1991): 54–63; D. W. Sue et al., "Position paper: Cross-cultural Counseling Competencies," *Counseling Psychologist* 10 (1979): 45–52; C. E. Vontress, "An Existential Approach to Cross-Cultural Counseling," *Journal of Multicultural Counseling and Development* 16 (1988): 73–83.

CHRISTINE P. PHILLIPS

MULTICULTURAL EDUCATION, AFRICAN-AMERICANS AND. Multicultural education is a broad category of theories and practices that encompasses various ideological, theoretical, pedagogical, and political strands concerning the necessary and appropriate education in a demographically and culturally diverse society. Although popularized during the 1980s and early 1990s, this form of education is deeply rooted in the ethnic pride and women's movements that grew out of the civil rights and Black Power movements of the 1960s and that led to the development of ethnic studies and women's studies in colleges and universities across the country.

The major principle on which multicultural education rests is multiculturalism, which is ultimately concerned with creating a just society in which people of all cultures are equal contributors and beneficiaries along all the dimensions of life. However, the ideal of multiculturalism can only be achieved when there is a more complete understanding of all forms of oppression—including the structural inequality, domination, exploitation, and prejudice directed against groups of people because of race, class, gender, sexual orientation, religion, physical capabilities, and/or age—and when these forms are eliminated from this society. Having many different racial, ethnic, and cultural groups coexisting in the United States has not ensured equality or justice, despite the claims of Jewish English author Israel Zangwill and others who have argued for most of this century that these diverse groups should be blended together, as if in a melting pot, and that out of this blend a more superior culture could emerge. This melting-pot ideology suggests that various ethnic components can be mixed in such a way as to make them indistinguishable from one another, without necessarily favoring one or another of the components; nonetheless, it was based on the assumption that white Anglo-Saxon Protestant culture would remain the dominant, superior culture to which all others should be socialized and made indistinguishable from. Moreover, discussions of the American melting pot have only rarely included consideration of Native Americans, African-Americans, or Asian-Americans; indeed, they clearly enforced the politicization of race, ethnicity, and culture.

Multicultural education has been regarded by its proponents as a strategy for bringing about a multicultural society. Under its general rubric, however, lie many ideological, political, theoretical, and pedagogical principles, some of which are contradictory, even oppositional. Theorists have categorized the many perspectives on multicultural education into four dominant approaches: curriculum reform, achievement, intergroup education, and societal transformation. These categories are by no means simple or linear. Within each category are embedded several approaches, each with their own variations in conceptions, goals, and results; additionally there exist many overlaps between categories. All of the approaches attempt to answer questions about the purposes of education and the roles of schools in a pluralistic society and an interdependent world. All raise questions about how the socially constructed nature of knowledge will be discussed and understood and how the authentic voices, experiences, and perspectives of all people will be included in the curriculum. Some ask how the debt owed by Western civilization to Africa, Asia, and indigenous peoples around the world will be acknowledged, while still others focus on resolving issues pertaining to the victimization of marginalized groups by dominant ones. Still others look at both the content and process of education and schooling, as well as the power relationship between schools and the larger society, and assert the right to meaningful participation of all peoples in shaping the organization and function of this nation.

Multicultural education represents a fundamental challenge to the Western canon, in which the perspectives, experiences, values, accomplishments, and interests of upper-status European and European-American males have been consistently overrepresented. The curriculum reform approach attempts to change school and university curricula by adding the voices, experiences, and struggles of racial, cultural, and gender groups. This is often done in two ways. Most commonly, educators focus on significant figures and discrete cultural elements and characteristics or add concepts, perspectives, themes, and specific facts and information without changing the structure of the curriculum. Another approach is to add separate courses, such as in ethnic studies and women's studies, and immerse students in the content, often using methodologies that challenge and support them intellectually and emotionally.

The achievement approach assumes that the problem of schooling lies in marginalized students' failure to achieve academically as defined by the established goals of education. Within this approach, two primary schools of thought have merged. The cultural deprivation perspective, popularized in the 1960s and regaining popularity now, was challenged by the cultural difference paradigm. The change from both perspectives involves specific programs, such as bilingual education for immigrant students and math/science education for women, and teaching strategies, such as matching teaching and learning styles and incorporating the language and culture of African-American students.

The goal of intergroup education is to add information, knowledge, and methods that will teach students to form democratic intergroup attitudes and values. This is done primarily by assisting students to develop positive attitudes toward people who are different from themselves and enabling students from oppressed groups to understand their victimization and improve their self-concepts. The societal transformation approach, the most radical of the approaches, assumes that prejudice, discrimination, and intergroup conflict are systemic problems that function at both the institutional and the interpersonal levels and that affect whole groups of people by virtue of their social classification. The transformation paradigm is centered around the goals of changing individual attitudes and behaviors and reconfiguring asymmetrical power relations in economic, cultural, political, and social institutions. This means that knowledge, appreciation, and respect for different races, cultures, and genders must be coupled with a thorough understanding of the dynamics of oppression and a commitment to learning and devising activist strategies for effecting structural changes including the capitalist economic system.

Some African-American educators have been and/or are critical of multicultural education as it is most often presented. They have viewed the call for multicultural education as yet another massive effort to erode the historical and contemporary significance and impact of racism against African-Americans by including the experiences of other victimized groups that seem to equate one form of oppression with another, to thwart their attempts to organize Afrocentric* schools, and generally to divide the African-American community. Added to this, the entry of a new wave of immigrants to the United States from Southeast Asia, Latin America, Korea, and the Caribbean in the past thirty years has further challenged and confounded efforts to create and implement fully inclusive multicultural curricula and multicultural education programs in American schools. Other forms of structural inequality have also gained the attention of multiculturalists and shape the contemporary discourse of multicultural education. For example, people with disabilities have become a forceful voice in educating about able-bodyism; advocates for the elderly have unveiled the structural inequalities wrought by agism; Jewish people continue to organize curricula around the issue of anti-Semitism; and antisexist and antiheterosexist education advocates have gained a forum in these discussions.

SELECTED BIBLIOGRAPHY

Molefi Asante, *The Afrocentric Idea* (1987); James Banks, *Introduction to Multicultural Education* (1994); Patricia Hill Collins, *Black Feminist Thought: Knowledge, Consciousness, and the Politics of Empowerment* (1990); Manning Marable, *The Crisis of Color and Democracy: Essays on Race, Class, and Power* (1994); Liza Fiol–Matta and Mariam K. Chamberlain, *Women of Color and the Multicultural Curriculum: Transforming the College Classroom (With a Segment on Puerto Rican Studies)* (1994); Sonia Nieto, *Affirming Diversity: The Sociopolitical Context of Multicultural Education* (1992); Ron Takaki, *A Different Mirror: The Making of Multicultural America* (1993).

MARGO OKAZAWA–REY

N

NATIONAL ALLIANCE OF BLACK SCHOOL EDUCATORS (NABSE).
The National Alliance of Black School Educators is a coalition of over seven thousand African-American teachers and educational administrators dedicated to the affirmation of the inherent worth, dignity, and educability of African-Americans and to the eradication of problems that obstruct quality education for all children, particularly African-American children. Its origins can be traced to Chicago, Illinois, in 1970, when fifteen of the nation's black superintendents met at an ad hoc gathering called by Dr. Charles S. Moody, Sr. Out of that meeting, the National Alliance of Black School Superintendents was formed in 1971 under the leadership of East Orange, New Jersey, school superintendent Dr. Russell Jackson. The organization was reconstituted in 1973 as the National Alliance of Black School Educators, with Macon County, Alabama, superintendent Dr. Ulysses Byas as president.

NABSE provides a forum for African-American educators to exchange ideas and strategies aimed at improving educational opportunities for African-Americans, identifying and developing African-American professionals for educational leadership positions, and influencing public policy in education. In addition, the organization maintains a foundation that provides funding support for its educational development efforts (including a demonstration school project and the Charles D. Moody Research and Development Institute on African-American Education), publishes the *NABSE Journal*, and hosts annual conventions for its membership.

SELECTED BIBLIOGRAPHY

National Alliance of Black School Educators, Constitution and By-Laws (1992).

HUGH J. SCOTT

NATIONAL ASSOCIATION FOR THE ADVANCEMENT OF COLORED PEOPLE. The country's oldest and largest national civil rights organization, the National Association for the Advancement of Colored People (NAACP) was founded in New York City in 1909. Its founding members included a group of northern white liberals concerned about the oppression of African-Americans, among them writer William Walling, social worker Mary White Ovington, and Oswald Garrison Villard, grandson of abolitionist William Lloyd Garrison. These "new abolitionists," as they were later called, had invited members of the Niagara Movement,* led by activist scholar W. E. B. Du Bois,* to convene in order to plan a national campaign against the rising wave of anti–African-American violence and to work for an end to the legal disenfranchisement of African-Americans. A formal organization was established by 1910, with white attorney Moorefield Storey as president, Walling as chairman of the executive committee, and Du Bois as director of publicity and research. It is indicative of the conservatism of the racial equality movement of that era that Du Bois's presence on the executive committee was seen as radical, drawing strong criticism from many otherwise sympathetic northern whites (who tended to prefer the more accommodating philosophy of Booker T. Washington*) and even from some more conservative African-Americans.

The NAACP grew rapidly, however, and by 1913 had eleven branches and 1,100 members nationwide. This growth was due in large part to the efforts of Du Bois as editor of *The Crisis*,* the organization's official publication. The magazine's first issue appeared in November 1910; a thousand copies were sold. Circulation increased quickly, reaching one hundred thousand by 1919. *The Crisis* contained editorials, essays, and regular features on a variety of topics, all intended for the empowerment and uplift of African-Americans. The NAACP also attempted to appeal to the conscience of the nation through antilynching advertisements placed in prominent newspapers.

The NAACP received some financial support from member dues and subscriptions, but the bulk of its funding came from the northern philanthropic funds. One of these was the Garland Fund, founded in 1922 by industrial heir Charles Garland. The NAACP's relationship with this fund was strengthened by the presence of NAACP Secretary James Weldon Johnson as a member of the fund's board of directors. The Garland Fund provided support in 1925 for the establishment of a legal defense fund. It also financed research into improving education for southern blacks within the confines of the "separate-but-equal" doctrine mandated by *Plessy v. Ferguson*.* Results of this research were printed in the *Crisis* between 1926 and 1928, and helped shape the basis for the formulation of long-range plans regarding educational litigation.

The first lawsuits brought by the NAACP involved residential segregation and discrimination against African-Americans by the judicial system; they were argued by white attorneys such as Storey and NAACP chief counsel Arthur Spingarn.* This situation began to change, however, after the hiring in 1929 of accomplished African-American attorney Charles Hamilton Houston,* who had been instrumental in recruiting and training a new generation of African-American lawyers at Howard University.* One of Houston's proteges, Thurgood Marshall,* hired by the NAACP in 1936, would go on to become its most famous attorney and the nation's first African-American Supreme Court justice.

The NAACP's growing emphasis on litigation to advance educational opportunity put the organization somewhat at odds with the aims of the Garland Fund, which had as its primary focus the empowerment and solidarity of workers, African-American and white. In spite of the tension this caused, the fund continued to support the NAACP's litigation efforts. This support culminated in a 1930 grant of $100,000 (one-third the requested amount) to mount a broad-based litigation effort against segregation in the South. This litigation would encompass equalization of teacher salaries and more equitable allocation of funds between African-American and white schools and would set the tone for what was to become the NAACP's primary mission: the end of legal segregation in schools.

In order to attack the prevailing "separate-but-equal" doctrine, the NAACP's initial legal strategy was to file court cases at the higher education level. Equality of treatment could be said to exist when African-Americans and whites were provided substantially equal facilities even though they were separate. Inequality of educational resources was plainly apparent in southern universities because of the failure of those states to provide African-Americans with access to law schools, though such schools were available for whites. The NAACP launched a series of victorious lawsuits, beginning with *Donald Murray v. Maryland* (1936) and *Lloyd Gaines v. University of Missouri** (1938). In the latter case, the Supreme Court ruled that the university must provide Gaines with a legal education. In 1939, the legal department was incorporated as the NAACP Legal Defense and Educational Fund. Victories continued with *Sweatt v. Painter** (1947), a Texas case, and *McLaurin V. Oklahoma State Regents for Higher Education* (1950).

A decision was made to attack *Plessy* in its entirety, not just its "equal" clause, with respect to public elementary and secondary schools. In 1952, under the leadership of Special Counsel Thurgood Marshall, five public school segregation cases challenging the separate-but-equal concept reached the Supreme Court. Plaintiffs who sought equal educational opportunity filed cases in Clarendon County, South Carolina; Prince Edward County, Virginia; Topeka, Kansas; Wilmington, Delaware; and Washington, D.C. The five cases were consolidated in the Court's ruling; the historic decision *Brown v. Board of Education of Topeka, Kansas,** overturning the "separate-but-equal" doctrine in public education, was rendered on May 17, 1954, signalling the end of the era of legal segregation for African-Americans. In *Brown II* (1955) the Supreme Court ruled that its 1954 decision should be implemented with "all deliberate speed."

The South responded by alleging that states' rights were equal to those of the federal government; southern governors used policies of nullification, interposition, and massive resistance to fight the *Brown* decisions. NAACP leaders were forced to battle these governors at every step of their campaign to integrate public schools. The vitriolic resistance of southern whites to school integration was typified by Arkansas governor Orval Faubus's attempts to crush the 1957 Little Rock Central High School desegregation effort. Major resistance developed also in New Orleans, Charlotte, Boston, New York, and Detroit. Struggles to integrate institutions of higher education occurred in Alabama, Georgia, and Mississippi.

Meanwhile the NAACP's drive for freedom and equality expanded beyond education to other issues, including equal access to public accommodations. In 1955, local NAACP branch officials in Montgomery, Alabama, were involved in the bus boycott; and in 1958, the NAACP Youth Council began a campaign of sit-in demonstrations.* In this particular form of protest, influenced by theories of nonviolent civil disobedience espoused by Mahatma Ghandi, NAACP youths displayed the enormity of their convictions, as they withstood verbal harassment and physical assault from racist whites. In 1961, the NAACP Youth Division shifted its emphasis from passive resistance to direct action and selective buying in an effort to secure jobs for African-Americans. After the passage of the Civil Rights Act of 1964,* the NAACP became involved in testing public accommodations violations and accelerated its voter registration campaign in the south.

In 1967, Thurgood Marshall became the first African-American Supreme Court justice. In 1969 and 1970, the NAACP and its allies successfully fought off efforts to appoint presidential nominees Clement F. Haynsworth and G. Harrold Carswell as justices of the Supreme Court. In 1987 a similar effort defeated the nomination of Robert Bork. These were conservatives whose presence on the court could have contributed to a reversal of the judicial decisions that had provided increased equity for racial minorities.

In the continuing efforts toward integrated education, the NAACP filed cases and received court rulings regarding residential segregation patterns and consequent school segregation, as well as gerrymandering practices of local school boards. In the 1970s, courts generally ruled that these patterns of segregation resulted from state and local governmental actions and therefore were in violation of the law. These decisions included *Swann v. Charlotte–Mecklenburg** (1971) and *Keyes v. School District No. 1, Denver, Colorado** (1973). The NAACP's defeat in the 1974 *Milliken v. Bradley** case in Michigan was the outstanding exception to this general pattern.

In 1978, reacting to the Supreme Court's decision in the *Bakke* case regarding affirmative action relative to the admission of minority students, the NAACP held a conference to map new strategies for minority college admissions. In that same year the NAACP created the Academic, Cultural, Technological and Scientific Olympics (ACT-SO), to promote academic excellence among high school students. By 1992, about two hundred thousand African-American youth had been involved in this program.

The organization continues to launch voter registration drives, to file voting rights cases, to fight against proposed antibusing constitutional amendments, and to ban the awarding of tax-exempt status to universities that are racially segregated. The NAACP successfully campaigned for legislation designating Martin Luther King, Jr.'s birthday a national holiday, making King the first African-

American to be so recognized. In 1984, the NAACP and the National Urban League* joined forces to sponsor a national summit conference of the African-American family. In that same year, the organization launched SAT preparation clinics to assist African-American adolescents in improving their test scores. In 1987, in response to the critical decline in accreditation of African-American teachers, the NAACP devised a model test-preparation clinic for the National Teachers Examination. This experience is designed to help prospective teachers to pass the examination, which has become a licensing requirement in most states.

In the decade of the 1990s, the NAACP has been involved in diverse efforts to retain affirmative action and minority set-asides; to maximize the 1990 Census count of African-Americans; and to promote redrawing local, state, and congressional district lines based on 1990 census data. The organization also worked to convene two education summits to discuss and debate new priorities; to seek new and enlarged employment opportunities for African-Americans; to minimize the impact of the downsizing of armed forces on African-American personnel; and to affect U.S. foreign policy in South Africa and Haiti. For eighty-six years, the NAACP has sought to provide answers to the multiplicity of problems faced by African-Americans in the United States, particularly those related to education at all levels.

SELECTED BIBLIOGRAPHY

John Hope Franklin, *From Slavery to Freedom* (1947); Mark V. Tushnet, *The NAACP's Legal Strategy against Segregated Education, 1925–1950* (1987).

WAYSON R. JONES

NATIONAL ASSOCIATION OF TEACHERS IN COLORED SCHOOLS. In 1904, responding to a call issued by J. R. E. Lee, a respected professor of mathematics at Benedict College* in South Carolina, more than 125 African-American educators from fourteen states convened in Nashville, Tennessee, to organize "a distinctive National Negro Educational body." When the three-day meeting concluded, in a banquet at Fisk University,* the National Association of Teachers of Negro Youth had been born. In 1907, at its fourth annual meeting, NATNY merged with the National Association of Land-Grant Presidents to form the National Association of Teachers in Colored Schools (NACTS). In 1937, the organization again changed its name, to the American Teachers Association, the title it retained until 1966 when, as the nation's largest African-American educational organization, it merged with the National Education Association.

In retrospect, the founding of the NATCS was the culmination of two interwoven trends: the tortuously slow, criminally underfunded development of separate schooling for African-American youth in the post-Reconstruction South and the simultaneous growth of state associations of African-American teachers, starting in the late 1870s. By the time the NATCS was founded, African-American educators in thirteen of the seventeen southern states that mandated de jure segregated schools had established teacher associations, for the purposes of promoting self-help campaigns within local communities and demanding more and better public school facilities, higher teacher salaries, and improved professional preparation. Because these state associations were in most cases small and potentially at the mercy of white-controlled state governments, African-American educators hoped that a national association might strengthen their collective voice, synergistically combining individual efforts and race-based initiatives. As stated in the organization's first constitution, "The object of this Association shall be to harmonize and unite the agencies now at work for the elevation of the Negro people; to arouse a deeper educational interest among them; to encourage good citizenship; and to ascertain and publish statistics showing their educational status."

Membership in the NATCS, as in the state organizations, was comparatively meager well into the 1930s. This reflected the discriminatory treatment accorded African-American education in the South during this period and the institutional and local structures that systematically silenced any potential protest. African-American teachers were hired by white local officials, who also set their salary levels, and were ostensibly certified to teach by white state educational authorities. Denied adequate pedagogical school training in public high schools or colleges, isolated in dilapidated, crowded rural schools, grossly underpaid, and often forced to understate their true credentials in order to gain employment, African-American teachers during the first four decades of this century were in a precarious position, politically weak and socially vulnerable. Yet within this context the leadership of the NATCS (which included educators such as R. R. Wright,* president of Georgia State College; W. T. B. Williams, field agent for the Slater* and Jeanes* funds, N. B. Young, president of Florida A & M University*; John Gandy, president of Virginia State College* Mary McLeod Bethune,* president of Bethune–Cookman College,* among others) persisted in attempting to improve the educational and social conditions of African-Americans generally, and the professional qualifications and status of African-American teachers specifically.

In 1923, the association began to publish its *Bulletin*, providing African-American teachers with their own forum for articulating grievances and making suggestions for instructional improvement. In the mid-1920s, under the direction of a new, younger group of leaders—most prominently W. A. Robinson, supervisor of high schools in North Carolina's Division of Negro Education, and H. Council Trenholm, president of Alabama State Teachers College—the NATCS began the fight for what became its most important victory prior to the salary equalization battles of the early 1940s: accreditation of African-American high schools. Not only were African-American students from unaccredited schools ineligible to enter prestigious colleges, but the quality of secondary education in the few public facilities offered by southern states was often abysmal. Robinson's 1926 overview article in the *Bulletin* was the opening salvo in what became a five-year campaign. Joined by the Association of Colleges for

Negro Youth, the NATCS eventually persuaded the all-white regional accrediting agency, the Southern Association of Colleges and Secondary Schools,* to accredit African-American high schools and colleges. The NATCS also took the lead in the subsequent fight to have the states and the accrediting agencies maintain a single standard for accreditation, rather than allow local school officials to perpetuate lower standards of quality and accomplishment for African-American schools.

In addition to the accreditation drive, the NATCS was in the forefront among African-American organizations advocating the incorporation of black history and literature into the school curriculum. The association strongly promoted child and community health awareness, and projected as lasting vision of a socially conscious teacher, whose job extended beyond the classroom in an attempt to uplift both the school and the community. In sum, the NATCS must be credited with fostering an awareness of African-American educational hopes and desires and with keeping alive a subdued but notable protest tradition that made future gains possible. That the association could not accomplish more, and failed in its sustained attempts to establish a national headquarters in Washington, D.C., is more a testament to the social context of African-American education in hostile condition than a reflection on the drive and determination of that generation of African-American educators. As W. A. Robinson said in a 1950 speech to the American Teachers Association, "A generation of teachers and administrators is much too brief. Some of us realize that now. The best we can do in our time in the front lines is to have the courage and imagination to give our young charges a kind of education that builds into them moral and social stamina, a determination to be free Americans, and provides the strategy and skills for achieving those ends. Give them a sort of relentless dissatisfaction with things as they ought not to be and the will and courage to recognize and hate injustice." Such was the aspiration of at least one of the leaders of the National Association of Teachers in Colored Schools in assessing its unfinished legacy.

SELECTED BIBLIOGRAPHY

Thelma D. Perry, *History of the American Teachers Association* (1975); various issues of *The Bulletin*, the official organ for the National Association of Teachers in Colored Schools, vol. 1 (1923)–17 (1940).

                                                                MICHAEL FULTZ

NATIONAL BLACK CHILD DEVELOPMENT INSTITUTE. Founded in 1970, the National Black Child Development Institute (NBCDI) is a national, nonprofit organization dedicated to improving the quality of life for African-American children and youth. The principles that guide the institute's mission and goals include the right of every African-American child to live, learn, and grow in a safe environment; the responsibility of parents to become directly involved in the planning, implementation, and regulation of programs that affect their children; and the collective responsibility of individuals and the community to contribute human and financial resources to improve the lives of African-American children. NBCDI focuses primarily on issues and services that fall within four major areas: education, child care, health, and child welfare. NBCDI and its affiliates network, which consists of forty-two chapters nationwide, serves as a critical resource in these areas and continues to strengthen its base by providing direct services, public education programs, leadership training, and research for African-American children, youth, and families. NBCDI believes in the development and implementation of public policies that benefit our children and therefore closely monitors issues that affect African-American children on national, state, and local levels. The institute educates the public on these issues by publishing periodic reports and two quarterly newsletters, the *Black Child Advocate, Child Health Talk*, and *Black Flash* news alert, as well as convening annual conferences.

EVELYN K. MOORE

NATIONAL COALITION OF TITLE I/CHAPTER 1 PARENTS. The signing into law of Title I of the Elementary and Secondary Education Act of 1965* (ESEA) set into motion the birth of a major grassroots parent involvement on behalf of Title I children and for the rights of their parents. Title I, which was redesignated Chapter 1 in 1981 and reinstated as Title I in 1994, is the largest federal assistance program for local school districts. Funds provided through Chapter 1 are used to establish programs that address the educational needs of educationally deprived children living in poverty. Chapter 1 serves five million children in more than ninety-five thousand school districts. The success of Chapter 1 is often attributed to the program's emphasis on parental involvement.

In a 1964 report to the Office of Compensatory Education on child development, Secretary of Health, Education and Welfare Wilbur Cohen supported the concept of parental involvement in education. Title I was amended in 1966 to include a provision for community involvement. A program guide published in 1967 focused on comprehensive planning, including coordination with community groups. There was continued support for parental involvement in the 1968 Kerner Commission report, as well as from Education Commissioner Harold Howe in his statement on "Participation and Partnership." The National Advisory Council on the Education of Disadvantaged Children in 1971 recommended parent advisory councils at the local and district level as "essential in the planning, implementation and evaluation of local Title I programs."

A significant development in the formation of a national parent movement emerged in 1972 at a meeting sponsored by the National Advisory Council of the Education of Disadvantaged Children. This meeting focused on establishing a national conference for Title I parents similar to those held for Title I administrators. At the urging of William "Bill" Anderson (who became the founder of the National Coalition) and other supporters of Title I parents, a conference plan was designed.

In January 1973, fifty parents, whose expenses were paid by the National Advisory Council, attended this conference in Washington, D.C. Parents discussed the problems of parental participation in Title I and, at the end of the conference, formulated and passed several dozen resolutions regarding parental involvement in Title I. One of these resolutions called for the establishment of the National Coalition for ESEA Parents. In 1974, in St. Louis, Missouri, a consortium of public interest and civil rights groups, with the formal endorsement of the Office of Education, sponsored a national conference for Title I parents. At this conference a board of directors was formed, comprised of representatives from the HEW regions. This board of directors became the steering committee that developed the National Coalition of ESEA Title I Parents. When federal legislation changed the status of Title I to Chapter 1 in 1981, the name of the organization was changed to reflect this, and it became known as the National Coalition of ESEA Title I/Chapter 1 Parents (later, "ESEA" was dropped from the designation).

In the initial years, the coalition functioned as a small informal group of active Title I parents whose purpose focused on monitoring pending Title I legislation as well as helping other parents become more involved in the education of their children. The coalition received very little in contributions and worked from an office in Washington, D.C. provided by the NAACP* Legal Defense and Education Fund. Office assistance was provided by the Lawyer's Committee, and administrative training by the National Committee for Citizens in Education. Testimony was provided to Congress on the need for parent advisory councils and stronger provisions for community involvement in education, and an effort was made to keep Title I parents abreast of legislative development.

The visibility of the coalition increased in June 1976, when the Carnegie Corporation of New York awarded the organization a two-year grant of two hundred thousand dollars to establish the National Parent Center, the organization's headquarters. The center initially opened in Wilmington, Delaware, then relocated to Washington, D.C., in 1977. During the next fifteen years, the center became the major source of training, information, and resources for parents and school districts in the country. As the organization grew, its purpose was broadened to include building a network of parents, educators, and concerned citizens committed to advocacy of educational programs for disadvantaged children.

The success of the coalition has come from its ability to work with diverse educational and child advocacy organizations, as well as from the support of the Office of Compensatory Education. The coalition also has been able to sustain its basic operations financially without outside support. Its annual and regional training forums bring together grassroots parents, educators, organizational representatives, and federal decision makers to exchange ideas on ways to maximize educational opportunities for poor children. Major initiatives between the coalition and the National PTA, the Center for Law and Education, the Home and School Institute, the National Education Association, the National Council on Educating Black Children,* and the American Association for the

Advancement of Science have resulted in substantial gains and increased recognition for the role of parents in the education of children.

The coalition publishes a bimonthly newsletter and has published two parent
handbooks, *Organizing an Effective Parent Advisory Council* (which was the
major parent training handbook for parent councils in the late 1970s) and *Parents
in Transition* (a resource directory published in 1983 for parents). In addition, several resource-update newsletters continue to provide a review of the
wealth of information and resources for families, communities, and schools.
Since 1984, the coalition has awarded its annual Carl D. Perkins Student Financial Assistance Award. The award, named after deceased Congressman Perkins (D–KY) (who is considered to be the founder of Title I), provides financial
assistance to former Title I/Chapter 1 students enrolled in schools of higher
education.

As parental and family involvement takes a major role in educational reform
and as Title I/Chapter 1 changes to meet the challenges of this reform, the role
of national parent organizations will adapt accordingly. The coalition and other
parent organizations face challenges that include maintaining the advocacy and
decision-making roles of parents despite the federal tendency to reduce or eliminate parents' roles in decision making; establishing outside technical assistance
committees to aid in funding issues and expanding educational technology; ensuring that organizational leadership develops local organizing and networking
skills; and accommodating young, single-parent, and Hispanic families within
the governance structure of the organization. Above all, parent-focused organizations will need to work together at a deeper level to bring about the systemic
changes needed to address the educational deficiencies of poor children. The
need to work collaboratively at the local level will require a focus on human
relations skills and strategies that will help families, educators, and the community begin to build a trusting reciprocal relationship that increases responsibility and accountability for ensuring educational opportunities for children.

SELECTED BIBLIOGRAPHY

R. S. Browning, *The National Coalition for ESEA Title I Parents: Its History and Its
Future* (September 1974); National Advisory Council on the Education of Disadvantaged
Children, *Special Report on Parent Involvement* (1977); National Coalition of Title I/
Chapter I Parents, *Annual Report* (1976); National Coalition of Title I/Chapter I Parents,
Annual Report (1991–92).

ROBERT WITHERSPOON

NATIONAL COUNCIL FOR BLACK STUDIES, INC. The National Council for Black Studies, Inc. (NCBS) was founded in 1975 at the University of
North Carolina–Charlotte out of the substantial need for a national stabilizing
force in the developing discipline of Black Studies (see African-American Studies*). The roots of NCBS run deep in the evolutionary growth of the discipline
since the organization was formed only seven years after the establishment of
the first Black Studies program in the United States. NCBS is presently recog-

nized worldwide as a prime forum for internationally recognized scholars, educators, students, and community leaders and activists to share information, form networks, and promote the advancement of Black Studies as an integral and viable entity of educational systems.

The purposes of NCBS are numerous, and the scope of its functions is quite broad. As an organization that subscribes to the philosophy that education should engender academic excellence and social responsibility, NCBS steadfastly works to establish standards of excellence and provide development guidance for Black Studies programs in relevant educational institutions. The goals of NCBS are to facilitate, through consultations and other services, the recruitment of black scholars for all levels of teaching and research in universities and colleges; to develop multicultural education programs and materials for K–12 schools; to promote scholarly Afrocentric* research in all aspects of the African world experience; to increase and improve informational resources on Africana culture; and to provide professional advice to policy makers in education, government, and community development.

The organizational objectives, programs, and services of the NCBS are devoted to the educational well-being of people of African descent. Its resources include three major publications: *The Voice of Black Studies*, a quarterly newsletter; *The Afrocentric Scholar: The Journal of the National Council for Black Studies*; and *The Afrocentric Core Curriculum*, which is the model for Black Studies programmatic curricula. The Council's Progressive Scholars Resource Program furnished top-quality speakers, workshop leaders, and consultants on topics related to the African world experience. The Ella Baker/W. E. B. Du Bois* Africana Student Competition engages undergraduate and graduate Africana students in the development of scholastic essays, creative writings, and visual art works that examine critical issues and dilemmas facing African people. The council also provides Black Studies program review and consultation services and holds annual international, national, and regional meetings.

The contemporary reality confronting NCBS is the fact that a large number of faculty and administrators who work in the discipline of Black Studies primarily receive their training in the traditional academic disciplines, which at best only allow for an emphasis on or concentration in the relevant issues of the Africana experience. These professionals did not have the opportunity to receive credentialed training in Black Studies. Their dilemma is directly related to the developmental process of the discipline. Black Studies emerged as a new entity in education at the height of the social unrest that occurred in the United States during the 1960s. In response to students' (and their supporters') demands for curricula that would address the African-American experience, colleges and universities created Black Studies courses, programs, and departments by hiring staff who essentially had to train themselves in order to create and impart knowledge about the African and African-American experience. Not until the recently established doctoral program in Black Studies at Temple University did potential and current Black Studies professionals have a highly effective and direct means of further developing their knowledge base in the discipline.

During the past five years, NCBS has placed heavy emphasis on the creation and implementation of strategies to address the important matter of professional development in the discipline of Black Studies. In 1989, it opened the first of four subsequent Africana Studies scholar and administrative institutes. Funded by grants from the Ford Foundation, these institutes provide a range of academic and cultural activities designed to greatly enhance the professionalism of people who work in Black Studies or related fields. The lectures and other activities are conducted by some of the most prominent scholars and administrators in the discipline of Black Studies and the field of higher education. Participants are engaged in reflecting on their earlier learning, challenging the assumptions on which that learning is based, and holding up to scrutiny the frames of reference within which they have become accustomed to working. Both participants and lecturers are interactively absorbed in identifying the parameters of the discipline of Black Studies and, by so doing, advancing the discipline to its next logical level of development.

JACQUELINE E. WADE

NATIONAL COUNCIL ON EDUCATING BLACK CHILDREN. Founded in 1986 by the Honorable Augustus Hawkins, then a congressman from Los Angeles, California, the National Council on Educating Black Children (NCEBC) has as its mission "disseminating information to the network of organized groups responsible for educating African-American children with the goal of providing a vision for achieving excellence and equity for the highest quality of education for all children." As chairman of the House Committee on Education and Labor, Hawkins was concerned about all facets of the educational enterprise, particularly elementary and secondary education. There were many schools in his congressional district that did a poor job of educating African-American children; however, some schools did an outstanding job of educating similar populations. Through his work with the Council of Black Educators (COBA) in Los Angeles and his knowledge of research related to educating African-American children, Hawkins believed that a national effort could be initiated to address the issues of undereducating and/or miseducating this population.

On 26 February 1986, Hawkins convened a group of twenty African-American education advocates along with organizational representatives from the NAACP,* the National Urban League, the National Education Association, the American Federation of Teachers, the William Penn Foundation, the National Black Child Development Institute,* National Coalition of Chapter 1 Parents,* Delta Sigma Theta sorority, the National Council of Negro Women, and the National Association of Social Workers to discuss what could be done to salvage the education of African-American children. Those gathered at this meeting decided that the research on "effective schools"* undertaken by educator Ronald Edmonds* was very much in accordance with the concepts discussed within the group, and they agreed to adopt the five correlates of effective schools as the ideological foundation for a new organization, the NCEBC.

The first activity of this organization was a national invitational conference held in September 1986. The primary objective of the conference was to develop a plan of action encompassing the effective school correlates. Participants were divided into five areas of focus: parents, students, teachers, policymakers, and administrators. Each work group developed action items and activities related to its area of focus. By the end of the conference, the NCEBC's "Blueprint for Action" was developed and duplicated for participants, who left the conference with a charge to return to their communities, implement the "Blueprint," and form cooperative networks to maintain and expand its usage. Over the years, the "Blueprint for Action" has been revised, refined, and expanded; its dissemination and implementation remain the focus of the organization's mission. To date, more than a hundred thousand copies have been distributed throughout the nation. As a continuation of its efforts, the NCEBC also published *Educating Black Children: America's Challenge* (1987), a monograph focusing on issues pertinent to the successful education of African-American children.

NCEBC membership is currently distributed among six regional groupings (southeastern, northeastern, mid-Atlantic, midwestern, southwestern, and western). Each region has a director and sponsors regional and/or state conferences that support the goals of the national organization and serve as the primary mechanisms for dissemination of the "Blueprint." A unique feature of NCEBC is the collaboration that occurs among the individuals and organizations that comprise its membership. Community groups, parents, teachers, policymakers, administrators, and students work together without pay to inform and educate each other about the needs of African-American students. They solve problems and plan for more effective national, state, and local school policies, programs, and practices. As well, the regional councils work very actively in concert with local school districts and community organizations on major educational issues.

SELECTED BIBLIOGRAPHY

Dorothy S. Strickland and Eric Cooper, eds., *Educating Black Children: America's Challenge* (Washington, D.C.: Bureau of Educational Research, Howard University, 1987); *Minutes and Bylaws of NCEBC*.

FRANCENA D. CUMMINGS

NATIONAL TEACHERS EXAMINATION AND AFRICAN-AMERICAN EDUCATION. The National Teachers Examination, developed and administered by Educational Testing Services (ETS), is a battery of standardized tests that assess the academic achievement of college students entering or completing teacher education programs and advanced teacher candidates who have received additional training in specific fields. The NTE and its successor, the PRAXIS Series of professional assessments for beginning teachers, have been the primary assessment tools utilized in the United States since the 1940s. Though these tests cannot predict teacher effectiveness in the classroom, they are often used by states for that purpose. Thirty-five of the fifty states and the District of Columbia currently use the NTE or some similar test as a certification criterion. In some states, teacher candidates who fail the NTE (and/or some other teacher competency test) are prohibited from teaching until they pass the test; in others, licensed in-service teachers must pass the NTE and/or similar examination to retain their certification. The departments of education in each state using the NTE for credentialling purposes have very different qualifying or cutoff scores. The result is great variation in passing rates from one state to another. Additionally, each state that relies on the NTE results to certify its teachers is required by ETS to conduct independent content-validity studies. This results in wide variation among states.

The NTE consists of two parts: the Core Battery and the Specialty Area tests. The former has been of most concern to African-Americans. The Core Battery is administered three times yearly, and test-takers who fail to meet the cutoff score established by their respective state departments of education are allowed to retake the examination as often as desired. The Core Battery purports to represent the knowledge that is important to entry-level teachers; however, no consensus has been reached regarding the importance of the tests' content in the profession or among researchers. Its content appears to be taken from the curricula of teacher education programs rather than related to the competency of beginning teachers. Three tests comprise the NTE Core Battery: the General Knowledge examination, comprised of questions on literature and fine arts, mathematics, science, and social studies; the Communication Skills section, which measures listening, reading, and editing skills; and the Professional Knowledge section, which gauges test-takers' grasp of pedagogical and instructional aspects of teaching.

Minority teachers have been shown to fail the NTE in larger proportions than do white teachers. The 1992 ranges of those passing, derived from the seventeen user states, were 71 percent to 95 percent for whites, 15 percent to 50 percent for African-Americans, 39 percent to 65 percent for Hispanic Americans, 37 percent to 77 percent for Asian-Americans, and 20 percent to 70 percent for Native Americans. If the impact of competency testing continues unabated, combined with normal rates of attrition, researchers have warned that the African-American and other minority representation in the national teaching force could be reduced to less than 5 percent by the year 2000.

In 1986, the NAACP's* Education Department convened a blue-ribbon panel of African-American educators to address the decline in the number of African-American teachers. As a result of this meeting, the NAACP model for NTE Preparation Clinics was developed. Research indicated that there were many models for the preparation of teacher or school of education candidates at colleges and universities and in the private sector as well. Preparation clinics at colleges and universities and in the private sector tended to be one review class, two Saturdays or one session with other candidates, and the remaining sessions implemented by individuals through programmed material to be used at home. The NAACP model spans the eleven weeks preceding the administration of the NTE and requires one evening and one Saturday session weekly. Since 1990, the NAACP has established forty-three preparation clinics in six states.

Many instructional changes that occurred during the implementation of the NAACP model led developers to believe that African-Americans would begin to show marked improvement on the NTE. As confidence in the NAACP model grew, so did the news of PRAXIS, a three-part certification process designed by the ETS in 1992. It became apparent that PRAXIS was designed to replace the NTE within a period of undetermined years. For that reason, the PRAXIS Series, which includes the NTE, is under study by NAACP staff and consultants to determine what steps must be taken to enhance the pass rate of African-American teacher candidates.

SELECTED BIBLIOGRAPHY

American Association of Colleges for Teacher Education, *Minority Teacher Recruitment and Retention: A Call for Action* (1987); Beverly P. Cole, ''The Black Educator: An Endangered Species,'' *Journal of Negro Education* 55, no. 3 (1986): 328–29; Educational Testing Service, *A Guide to the NTE Core Battery Tests, Revised: General Knowledge, Communication Skills, Professional Knowledge* (1993); Educational Testing Service, *PRAXIS: Professional Assessments for Beginning Teachers* (1991); Asa Hilliard, III, and Barbara Sizemore, eds., *On Saving the African-American Child* (1984); G. Pritchy Smith, *Recruiting Minority Teachers* (1992); G. Pritchy Smith, *Report to the Education Seminar: NAACP* (1992); Task Force on Teaching as a Profession, Carnegie Forum on Education and the Economy, *A Nation Prepared: Teachers for the 21st Century* (1986).

MABEL LAKE MURRAY

NATIONAL URBAN LEAGUE, INC. The National Urban League, founded in 1910, is a nonprofit social service and civil rights organization. Headquartered in New York City, the League has 113 chartered affiliate branches located in thirty-four states and the District of Columbia. Each of these affiliates is incorporated in the state where it is located and has its own board of directors, whose membership reflects the diversity of the community.

The mission of the National Urban League is to assist African-Americans and other people of color in the achievement of social and economic equality. One of the main goals of the league is to fulfill the organization's overall mission through education using direct service and advocacy. In 1986, responding to well-documented research about the educational crisis confronting African-American and Latino students, the league launched its National Education Initiative, a program which had its origins in the organization's resolution on public education presented at its July 1985 delegate assembly. This five-year resolution (extended five more years in 1992) established education as a priority program area and called upon the National Urban League and its affiliates to develop programs to improve educational performance among African-American and Latino students through the mobilization of existing community resources. The major priority areas of the education initiative are parental involvement/

education, math and science education, coalition building, black history and culture, early childhood development, technological literacy, tutoring, enrichment, test review, guidance counseling, and mentoring. These program areas are formulated, coordinated, and monitored by the League's national office under the auspices of its education and career development and the employment and job skills training departments.

SELECTED BIBLIOGRAPHY

Alvin Toffler, "Civil Rights in the Third Wave," *The Urban League Review* (1983–84).

RENEE JEFFERSON

NEGRO HISTORY BULLETIN. The *Negro History Bulletin* was launched under the auspices of the Association for the Study of Negro (later Afro-American) Life and History* in October 1937. It was edited by Carter G. Woodson,* the association's founder, until his death in 1950. The *Bulletin* pioneered in demonstrating the need for black history instruction and curricula in U.S. elementary and secondary schools. For generations, crusading African-American teachers and librarians used the information provided in its pages as ammunition in their efforts to convince mainstream educational publishers to present positive, objective images of blacks in textbooks.

Through the *Negro History Bulletin*, Woodson strove to endow school-aged African-American children with an awareness, appreciation, and understanding of their history and culture. In announcing the forthcoming publication of the premier issue, he noted that the magazine's purpose was "to popularize Negro history lower down in the elementary school, to expose the children to an atmosphere charged not with propaganda, but with easily obtained and freely circulated information about the contributions of the Negro and his present status in the modern world." Nine monthly issues of the *Bulletin*, complete with lesson plans for subjects in black history, were published each year from October through June to coincide with the months public schools were in session. Issues were developed around such themes as blacks in art, science, and literature; blacks in Latin America and Europe; and blacks in the military.

Featured columns, authored by Woodson himself, included "Persons and Achievements to Be Remembered," "The Children's Page," "Books," and "Questions for Study." During World War II, Woodson also wrote several scathing editorials on racism in American life that were published in the *Bulletin*. Some issues featured plays, short stories, and essays on black history written by children. Most articles were well-illustrated with photographs.

After Woodson died, the editorship of the *Negro History Bulletin* was passed along to several prominent African-American scholars, including Rayford W. Logan,* Charles Wesley, and J. Rupert Picott. The *Bulletin*'s editorial focus changed during the 1960s and 1970s as the publication responded to the rising nationalism in Africa, the burgeoning black studies movement in American colleges and universities, and the greater inclusion of blacks and other nonwhites in school textbooks and other media. More and more, the classroom instructional units formerly published in the *Bulletin* were replaced by brief articles on various aspects of African-American life. The *Bulletin* temporarily suspended publication in 1987 with volume 50, numbers 1 and 2 (January–June 1987). It resumed publication on 15 May, 1994, with the release of volume 51, number 1 (December 1993). In its resurrected form, the *Negro History Bulletin* continues to provide information and guidance to educators and students.

SELECTED BIBLIOGRAPHY

Arvah E. Stickland, "Negro History Bulletin," in Walter C. Daniel, ed., *Black Journals of the United States* (1982), p. 287; Harrine Freeman, Secretary, Association for the Study of Afro-American Life and History, to Donald Franklin Joyce, 11 May, 1994; Jacqueline Goggin, *Carter G. Woodson: A Life in Black History* (1993); Donald Franklin Joyce, *Gatekeepers of Black Culture: Black-Owned Book Publishing in the United States, 1817–1981* (1983); "Notes," *Journal of Negro History* 22, no. 3 (July 1937): 402–3.

DONALD FRANKLIN JOYCE

NEGRO YEAR BOOK. Using funds obtained by Tuskegee Institute (now University)* president Booker T. Washington* from the Committee of Twelve,* the first edition of *The Negro Year Book* was published in 1912. It was the product of the Negro Year Book Publishing Company, an entity established at Tuskegee in 1910. This company, a partnership from 1910 until 1928, when it suffered financial reverses and Tuskegee assumed fiscal responsibility for it, had three founding members: Robert E. Park, who later chaired the University of Chicago's famed sociology department, was president; Emmett J. Scott, Washington's private secretary, was vice president; and Monroe N. Work,* head of Tuskegee's Department of Research and Records, was the publication's editor. From 1912 to 1952, *The Negro Year Book* was published in eleven editions. Work edited nine of them; Jessie Parkhurst Guzman, his assistant and successor, edited the tenth and eleventh editions.

The outgrowth of Work's activities as head of the Department of Research and Records, *The Negro Year Book* was the most comprehensive source of facts and statistics on African-Americans to appear in the first decades of the twentieth century. Compiled with vision and scrupulously edited, *The Negro Year Book* presented an array of facts and statistics on numerous aspects of black life under the headings of "Negro Progress," "The Race Problem," "The Negro World Distribution," "Governments," "Slavery," "Abolition," "The Church," and "Education."

Almost immediately after its first publication, *The Negro Year Book* became the reference of choice on all matters pertaining to blacks. Several of the nation's leading newspapers published sections of the *Year Book* annually. The research departments of the National Association for the Advancement of Colored People* and the National Urban League* used it frequently, as did many agencies of the federal government. All of the major libraries in the United States subscribed to it. Its circulation was worldwide. Today, the eleven editions of *The Negro Year Book* are classic reference tools on the conditions and achievements of people of African descent in the United States and throughout the African diaspora. They served as the models for many later comprehensive reference works.

SELECTED BIBLIOGRAPHY

Linda Elizabeth Hines, "A Black Sociologist in a Time of Trouble: Monroe Nathan Work, 1866–1945," master's thesis, Auburn University, 1972; Donald Franklin Joyce, *Gatekeepers of Black Culture: Black-Owned Book Publishing in the United States, 1817–1981* (1983); "Negro Year Book," *Tuskegee Student* 25 (May 1912): 6; Monroe N. Work, "An Autobiographical Sketch," 7 February 1940 (in the Monroe Nathan Work Papers, Tuskegee Institute Historical Collection, Tuskegee, Alabama); Monroe N. Work, ed., *Negro Year Book*, 1st ed. (1912).

DONALD FRANKLIN JOYCE

NEW DEAL, AFRICAN-AMERICAN EDUCATION IN THE. In October 1929, the stock market crash marked the beginning of the Great Depression in the United States. During the Depression decade African-Americans faced heightened job discrimination. Most African-Americans felt that Republican President Herbert Hoover had done very little to end the Depression; thus, in the election of 1932, they abandoned their support of the Republican Party. In 1936, for the first time, a majority of African-Americans voted for the Democratic presidential candidate, Franklin D. Roosevelt, and helped reelect him in subsequent elections.

Roosevelt called his program to address the problems caused by the Depression "the New Deal." During the New Deal era, a group of African-Americans advised Roosevelt on African-American problems. Called the "Black Cabinet," this group included such influential leaders as William H. Hastie, then-assistant solicitor in the Department of the Interior, and Mary McLeod Bethune,* founder of Bethune–Cookman College.* The Black Cabinet was instrumental in defining the New Deal for African-Americans. Its members' commitment to racial equality helped to make civil rights a New Deal concern.

The New Deal marked a major turning point in the fortunes of the nation's African-American citizens. Indeed, African-Americans gained some economic prosperity and achieved support for resolving many of the issues affecting them. Under the New Deal, the federal government imposed many business regulations and laws to assist the needy. These measures of reform, relief, and recovery aided African-Americans both substantively and symbolically. The Civilian Conservation Corps and the National Youth Administration (NYA), whose Negro Affairs division was headed by Bethune, provided a variety of vocational/trade, out-of-school, and work-study programs. African-American students from elementary to graduate school levels participated in and benefitted from many of these programs. The New Deal also brought about the desegregation of cafeterias, restrooms, and secretarial pools in the federal government. Thus, despite social disadvantages, African-American hopes and expectations for a better future increased during the Roosevelt era. Many affirmed, along with Bethune, that "we are on our way." Nonetheless, changes made during the New Deal were viewed by some African-Americans as minimal because, by the 1940s, the majority of blacks remained at the bottom of the American socioeconomic ladder.

SELECTED BIBLIOGRAPHY

Harvard Sitkoff, *A New Deal for Blacks, The Emergence of Civil Rights as a National Issue: The Depression Decade* (1978); E. Franklin Frazier, "Some Effects of the Depression on the Negro in Northern Cities," *Science and Society* 2 (Fall 1938): 489; Raymond Wolters, *Negroes and the Great Depression: The Problem of Economic Recovery* (1970); John P. Davis, "A Black Inventory of the New Deal," *Crisis* 42 (May 1935): 141–42; John P. Davis, "A Survey of Problems of the Negro under the New Deal," *Journal of Negro Education* 5 (January 1936): 10–11; Robert C. Weaver, "The New Deal and the Negro," *Opportunity* 13 (July 1935): 202.

CONSTANCE A. BURNS

NEW ORLEANS SCHOOL DESEGREGATION EXPERIENCE. The South's first experience with school desegregation occurred in New Orleans during Reconstruction. It began in 1868, when the Louisiana legislature amended the state constitution to require that all schools be open to all students, "without distinction of race, color or previous condition of servitude." It ended in 1877, when the Republican Party lost political control in both Louisiana and Washington, D.C., and the Democratic Party leadership wrote a new constitution that mandated segregation and separate schools for the African-American and white students of Louisiana.

During the nine years that de jure segregation was unconstitutional, twenty-six of the seventy-six schools in New Orleans were known to have racially mixed student bodies. Among the prominent African-American citizens who had been active in administrating the schools or who sent their children to them were the first African-American governor and lieutenant governor of Louisiana, P. B. S. Pinchback and Oscar Dunn, whose daughters were among the first students to test the desegregation laws by entering previously all-white schools. Approximately 10 percent of the thirty thousand students in New Orleans's public schools had schoolmates of a different race during this period. The city's racially mixed schools, its Grammar A primary schools and two of its three high schools, were generally the more advanced because they were attended by African-American students who had been educated in local private schools or northern boarding schools or at home. The majority of New Orleans schools during this period, however, remained de facto segregated.

When the desegregation laws passed the legislature in 1868, substantial opposition existed. Five lawsuits were known to have reached the local courts prior to a ruling on December 5, 1870, which upheld the existing law. In 1874, after four years of relatively peaceful acceptance of the integrated schools, there was a series of riots in which African-American students were physically removed from the schools and the city's superintendent of education was chased and violently beaten in the streets. Another form of opposition was evident in the dramatic rise of private school enrollment, beginning in 1869. In the first four years after the implementation of the desegregation law, private and parochial school attendance spiraled upward from two thousand in 1869 to seventeen thousand in 1872. At the same time, the number of private schools increased from ten to ninety-one.

New Orleans's school desegregation experience ended in 1877, when the Louisiana state government returned to Democratic Party rule. Segregated schools became the law of the state, thus concluding the nine-year desegregation experiment. Historians have published contradictory interpretations of this school desegregation experience. Prior to 1962, they primarily reported that the racial mixing never occurred. A later publication challenged this position by revealing the specifics of the school mixing and by explaining the emergence of the schools in terms of the circumstances in New Orleans during Reconstruction. Several researchers have continued to add to the historiography of these events, emphasizing the different roles various members of New Orleans' white and African-American communities had in establishing and sustaining the South's first school desegregation experience.

SELECTED BIBLIOGRAPHY

John W. Blassingame, *Black New Orleans: 1860–1880* (1973); Donald E. DeVore and Joseph Logsdon, *Crescent City Schools: Public Education in New Orleans, 1841–1991* (1991); Roger A. Fischer, *The Segregation Struggle in Louisiana, 1862–1877* (1974); Eric Foner, *Reconstruction: America's Unfinished Revolution* (1988); Nicholas Glass, "Mulatto Activism and Education: A New Look at the Desegregated Schools in New Orleans during Reconstruction," master's thesis, University of Wisconsin (1994); Louis Harlan, "Desegregation in New Orleans Public Schools during Reconstruction," *American Historical Review* 67 (April 1962): 663–75; T. H. Harris, *The Story of Public Education in Louisiana* (1924); Betty Porter, "The History of Negro Education in Louisiana," *Louisiana Historical Quarterly* 25, no. 3 (1942): 728–821; William P. Vaughn, *Schools for All: The Blacks and Public Education in the South, 1865–1877* (1874).

NICHOLAS GLASS

NIAGARA MOVEMENT. The Niagara Movement was a turn-of-the-century effort to promote racial justice and counteract the racially conservative philosophy of Tuskegee Institute's* Booker T. Washington,* who gained national attention when he outlined his proposal of racial accommodation at the Cotton States and International Exposition in Atlanta in 1895. Washington persistently enjoined African-Americans to work hard and accept the leadership of southern whites. In exchange for African-American acceptance of segregation, he asked that whites assist African-Americans in their quest for an education. The need for a more aggressive stand against racism and discrimination was urged by William Edward Burghardt Du Bois* and other African-American intelligentsia such as William Monroe Trotter, F. L. McGee, and C. C. Bentley. In July 1905, these men, along with twenty-five other African-American business and professional men, launched what became the Niagara Movement to counteract the pervasive influence of Washington and to serve as the voice of those who did not share his philosophy of accommodation.

Meeting at Fort Erie, Ontario, on the Canadian side of Niagara Falls, these men discussed a course of action. Du Bois was elected general secretary and provided the leadership in drafting a nineteen-point "Declaration of Principles," which addressed issues of freedom of speech, male suffrage, and an unfettered and unsubsidized press and called for the abolition of all caste distinctions based simply on race. Declining to condemn Washington outright, for fear of alienating potential white financial support, the Declaration of Principles nevertheless asserted a demand for those rights that the delegates believed were guaranteed by the Constitution. Seven committees were organized, including one on education, to carry out the Declaration of Principles. State branches were also organized to carry out the aims of the 1905 Conference. Washington immediately characterized the conference delegates as radicals. He began a systematic effort to infiltrate the movement, to isolate the leadership from the African-American community, especially the African-American press, and to convince influential whites not to lend their support.

Undaunted, the leaders of the Niagara Movement held a second meeting in August 1906 in Harper's Ferry, West Virginia. Meeting at Storer College,* the gathering paid homage to John Brown, who led blacks and whites in the 1859 attack against slavery. In an effort to fulfill the promise of emancipation, the group made five demands: the right to vote and all the privileges that go with it; an end to discrimination in places of public accommodations; the right to assemble; the legal enforcement of the law under the Fourteenth and Fifteenth Amendments; and equal education (not manual training) and opportunities for all. John Hope, chair of the education committee, recommended the publication of a booklet on conditions in Negro schools in the South, with the intention of influencing southern legislators and the interested public.

The Niagara Movement's third annual conference was held in Boston at Faneuil Hall in 1907. Shortly after this meeting, a major race riot occurred in Springfield, Illinois. Five thousand militiamen were called out to restore peace, but not before two African-Americans were lynched, four white men murdered, and numerous others injured. In spite of an ever-present crisis, the succeeding conferences were ineffective in impacting the growing tide of racism. The Boston meeting had been marred by a split between Du Bois and Trotter, which carried over into the fourth conference held at Oberlin, Ohio. The meeting was mostly talk and resulted in little concrete action. That the Niagara Movement was on the verge of collapse did not deter Washington from his relentless effort to destroy the organization. The fifth and final conference was held in Sea Isle City, New Jersey, in 1909 and was ignored generally by the African-American and the white press.

In spite of its lofty goals, the Niagara Movement failed to achieve the promise envisioned by Du Bois. Washington's consistent opposition to the movement in part explains the failure to attract white financial support. Even with the attainment of four hundred members, the movement was unable to meet its organizational expenses. The membership, pulled from the ranks of the "Talented Tenth,"* was somewhat alienated both socially and educationally from the masses. Even with these fundamental weaknesses, the goals of the movement were advanced for their era, which was dominated by Washington's accommodationist ideas.

The Niagara Movement made several significant achievements before its demise. The movement was the first national organization to demand for African-Americans the civil rights guaranteed to all Americans by the Constitution. Through a series of declarations, it helped educate African-Americans eventually to accept protest as an appropriate means to gain these rights, while informing the nation's majority that not all blacks were satisfied with the status quo in race relations. It laid the foundation for the creation of the National Association for the Advancement of Colored People,* an organization with which many of the leaders of the Niagara Movement aligned themselves. Du Bois, the most prominent of these, became the director of research and publications and the editor of the NAACP's monthly journal, *The Crisis.** The NAACP proved to be an effective organization in achieving the goals of the Niagara Movement, including ending legally enforced segregated education.

SELECTED BIBLIOGRAPHY

Herbert Aptheker, *A Documentary History of the Negro People in the United States* (1964); Francis L. Broderick, "The Gnawing Dilemma: Separatism and Integration, 1865–1925," in Nathan I. Huggins, Martin Kilson, and Daniel M. Fox, eds., *Key Issues in the Afro-American Experience* (1971); W. E. B. Du Bois, *The Souls of Black Folk*; Rayford W. Logan, *The Betrayal of the Negro: From Rutherford B. Hayes to Woodrow Wilson* (1965); Elliot M. Rudwick, *W. E. B. Du Bois: Propagandist of the Negro Protest* (1986).

                                                    JOHN E. FLEMING AND EDNA C. DIGGS

NORFOLK STATE UNIVERSITY. Norfolk State University, located on a 130-acre modern campus site in Norfolk, Virginia, is a fully accredited four-year coeducational urban institution. NSU is comprised of nine schools offering seven associate degree programs and fifty bachelor's and fifteen master's degree programs. Historically, this university's academic emphasis has been on the liberal arts, particularly the sciences, the high-technology disciplines, and research. NSU boasts a communications center with laboratories for teleconference downlinking, television and FM radio stations, a life-sciences center with a planetarium, a technology center, an ROTC/physical education and basketball arena complex, the Lyman B. Brooks Library, and a fine arts and music center. The school is a member of the Southern Association of Colleges and Schools* and adheres to the standards set forth by the State Council of Higher Education for Virginia. Its programs are nationally accredited by the American Corrective Therapy Association, National Accrediting Agency for Clinical Laboratory Scienccs, National League for Nursing, Council on Social Work Education, National Association of Schools of Music, American Medical Records Association, American Dietetics Association, American Psychological Association, Committee on Allied Health Education and Association, and American Assembly of Collegiate Schools of Business.

SELECTED BIBLIOGRAPHY

National Association for Equal Opportunity in Higher Education, *Profiles of the Nation's Historically and Predominantly Black Colleges and Universities* (1993).

SAMUEL L. MYERS

NORTH CAROLINA A&T STATE UNIVERSITY. Located in Greensboro, North Carolina, and founded in 1891, this public historically black institution is a state leader in the area of funded research, ranking third among the sixteen state universities. It leads the nation in the graduation of African-American engineers at the baccalaureate and master's degree levels. It also has one of two nationally accredited accounting programs at African-American universities in the nation, and it is one of only two schools of agriculture in North Carolina. Its teaching and research programs in animal science have been developed as a related activity to the University's School of Veterinary Medicine. North Carolina A & T's strength revolves around its academic programs, offered through seven schools and a college of arts and sciences. Its noted technology/engineering and high-technology thrust is built upon a strong liberal arts program and also includes nationally ranked programs in business, nursing, education, and agriculture. In March 1992, NCA&T became the first African-American university in North Carolina to be granted authority to plan and then launch Ph.D.'s in engineering.

SELECTED BIBLIOGRAPHY

National Association for Equal Opportunity in Higher Education, *Profiles of the Nation's Historically and Predominantly Black Colleges and Universities* (1993).

SAMUEL L. MYERS

NORTH CAROLINA CENTRAL UNIVERSITY. Founded by Dr. James E. Shepard* in 1910, North Carolina Central University in Durham became in 1925 the nation's first state-supported liberal arts college for African-Americans. Today, the university is a growing, comprehensive institution serving the entire state of North Carolina as one of the sixteen institutions of the University of North Carolina system. NCCU's African-American student enrollment is the second largest among North Carolina's forty-eight senior colleges and universities, and its white enrollment is larger than nine of the state's private senior colleges. The university enrolls more than five thousand students in the following five degree-recommending schools: the College of Arts and Sciences, the School of Business, the School of Education, the School of Law, and the School of Library and Information Sciences. A School of Graduate Studies coordinates advanced degree programs in business, education, the arts and sciences, and library and information sciences; and a University College conducts summer, evening, continuing education, and extension programs. NCCU's library collection of more than six hundred thousand volumes is the seventh largest in the state.

SELECTED BIBLIOGRAPHY

National Association for Equal Opportunity in Higher Education, *Profiles of the Nation's Historically and Predominantly Black Colleges and Universities* (1993).

SAMUEL L. MYERS

NURSING EDUCATION, AFRICAN-AMERICANS AND. The first three American nursing training schools were established in 1873. These early schools operated within hospitals, but in keeping with the ''Nightingale Tradition'' they enjoyed a degree of faculty autonomy and a separate funding apparatus and employed women as nurse supervisors. There were 15 hospital nurse training schools in 1880, and 431 twenty years later. The number of graduates increased from 157 to 3,456 within this time. The proliferation of nursing training schools continued, as hospitals gained increasing respectability and as a doubting public began to accept them as places of good care as opposed to dens of death. By 1926 there were 2,150 schools and 17,000 graduates. Virtually all of these schools excluded African-American women.

As the number of nursing training schools grew and nursing became another way out of domestic service for thousands of European immigrant and poor white women, African-American women chafed under the denial of opportunity to acquire this training. Mary Eliza Mahoney, an 1879 African-American graduate of the New England Hospital for Women and Children in Boston, was an exception to the rule of exclusion practiced by the vast majority of the hospital schools in the North and all such institutions in the South. Left with little alternative, African-Americans in the 1890s began to establish their own network of nursing schools and hospitals. In 1886, John D. Rockefeller contributed the funds for the establishment of a school of nursing at the Atlanta Baptist Seminary (now Spelman College*), a school for African-American women in Atlanta, Georgia. This was the first school of nursing within an academic institution in the country.

The earliest African-American hospital-based nursing schools were established by black physicians and as social service projects of black women's clubs. In 1891, Daniel Hale Williams, the famed surgeon, founded Provident Hospital and Nurse Training School in Chicago. In 1894, he was also instrumental in creating the Freedman's Hospital and Nurse Training School in Washington, D.C. Under the aegis of Booker T. Washington,* the Tuskegee Institute* School of Nurse Training in Tuskegee, Alabama, came into existence in 1892. In the same year, the Hampton Nurse Training School and Dixie Hospital in Hampton, Virginia, began accepting students.

In October 1896, the women of the Phyllis Wheatley Club founded the only African-American hospital and nursing training school in New Orleans, Louisiana. The Phyllis Wheatley Sanitarium and Training School for Nurses began rather inauspiciously in a private residence, consisting of seven beds and five patients. This institution was later renamed the Flint Goodridge Hospital and Nurse Training School. Finally, on October 4, 1897, Alonzo Clifton McClennan, an 1880 graduate of the Howard University* Medical School, founded the Hospital and Nursing Training School in Charleston, South Carolina. By 1920 there were thirty-six African-American nurse training schools.

By 1928, with some financial assistance from wealthy philanthropists, African-Americans had fashioned an extensive nursing training school network. However, black women desiring to proceed to the second step, that is, securing graduate education or specialization training, met considerable frustration. They were consistently denied admission to some of the county's leading graduate nursing programs. Upon her graduation from Teachers College, Columbia University, Estelle Massey Riddle became, in 1931, the first black nurse in America to earn a master of arts degree in nursing education. She then became the first African-American part-time instructor to serve on the staff of the Harlem Hospital nursing school, before moving on to become the educational director of Freedmen's Hospital in Washington, D.C.

African-American colleges were slow to develop collegiate degree programs in nursing education. As late as the mid-1930s, only one, Florida A & M University* in Tallahassee, boasted a baccalaureate nursing department. Howard University* in Washington, D.C., established a baccalaureate program as early as 1922, but it lasted only three years. Although short-lived, this was truly an amazing feat, considering that at the time only a handful of bachelor's degree programs existed for white women. Thus, Florida A & M had the longest continuous bachelor's degree program in nursing among African-American institutions. The situation was soon to change. In 1942, Dillard University* in New Orleans established a baccalaureate degree program. Following Dillard's lead, Hampton Institute* launched its baccalaureate program in 1944. Meharry Medical College* in Nashville, Tennessee, began offering bachelor's degrees in 1947. A year later Tuskegee Institute* in Alabama converted its hospital diploma school into a baccalaureate program. The major white philanthropic foundations, the General Education Board,* and the Julius Rosewald Fund* played a critical role in the black collegiate nursing-education movement.

The 1950s witnessed a flurry of activity, as several African-American colleges and universities created new baccalaureate nursing programs. The rising specter of integration propelled southern state governments to increase allocation for the development of separate black programs. Even more important, however, was the rise of massive federally funded health-care and education programs launched during World War II. In 1952, Prairie View College* in Texas initiated a baccalaureate program, followed the next year by North Carolina A&T University* in Greensboro, and in 1954 by Winston–Salem State University in North Carolina.

SELECTED BIBLIOGRAPHY
Darlene Clark Hine, *Black Women in White: Racial Conflict and Cooperation in the Nursing Profession, 1890–1950* (1989); Vanessa Northington Gamble, *The Black Community Hospital* (1989).

DARLENE CLARK HINE

O

OAKWOOD COLLEGE. Situated on a beautifully landscaped campus consisting of 1,185 acres, 105 comprising the main campus, Oakwood College is a four-year Christian institution of higher education that is owned and operated by the General Conference of Seventh-Day Adventists. Founded in 1896 in Huntsville, Alabama, and accredited by the Southern Association of Colleges and Schools* and the Seventh-Day Adventist Board of Regents, Oakwood offers the bachelor of arts and bachelor of science degrees as well as bachelor's degrees in business, social work, and general studies. It also offers several associate degree programs. Curricula are available in the natural sciences and mathematics, behavioral and social sciences, humanities, religion and theology, and applied sciences and education. Also offered are nursing and varied preprofessional curricula and one-and two-year courses, particularly in health sciences, engineering, and law.

SELECTED BIBLIOGRAPHY

National Association for Equal Opportunity in Higher Education, *Profiles of the Nation's Historically and Predominantly Black Colleges and Universities* (1993).

SAMUEL L. MYERS

OBERLIN COLLEGE. Founded in 1833, Oberlin College is an independent, coeducational liberal arts college that has long been dedicated to recruiting students from diverse backgrounds. Located twenty-five miles southwest of Cleveland, Ohio, Oberlin was the first college in the country to admit women, and one of the first to admit African-Americans. Women studied in the "Ladies Department" at Oberlin from the beginning, but in 1837 four women entered the regular college courses. Three of the four graduated in 1841, becoming the first women in America to receive bachelor's degrees. Oberlin began admitting African-American students in 1835. As a result of this decision, by 1900 nearly half of all the African-American college graduates in the country had graduated from Oberlin. In contrast, Harvard had graduated just eleven blacks by the turn of the century. This core of Oberlin-educated African-American men and women formed the first African-American professional class in the country. The importance of the decision to admit African-Americans to Oberlin is made even clearer when put into its historical context. In 1835, the state of Ohio was debating whether to allow African-Americans to attend elementary and secondary schools, and southern states were drafting stricter slave codes. For more than half a century after the first African-American received a bachelor's degree at Oberlin (in 1844), South Carolina and other states would declare it a crime to teach African-Americans to read or write.

Today, Oberlin's 440-acre campus provides outstanding facilities, modern scientific laboratories, a large computing center, a library unmatched in the depth and range of its resources, and the Allen Memorial Art Museum, one of the country's best college or university art museums. It academic program is comprised of two divisions: the College of Arts and Sciences and the Conservatory of Music. The two divisions share one campus, and many students take classes from both. Oberlin awards the bachelor of arts and the bachelor of music degrees; a five-year program leads to both degrees. Selected master's degrees are offered in the Conservatory. Among primarily undergraduate institutions, Oberlin ranks first for the number of graduates who go on to earn Ph.D. degrees; and its alumni include three Nobel laureates. Oberlin consistently receives high ratings in college guidebooks, including a five-star rating (the highest given) for academics in the 1993 *Fiske Guide to the Colleges*.

JANET DEGGES

OBLATE SISTERS OF PROVIDENCE. In 1829, with the aid of Father James Joubert, a Sulpician Father and refugee from the French Revolution, Mother Mary (nee Elizabeth Lange) founded the Oblate Sisters of Providence in Baltimore, Maryland. That year, she, along with four other French-speaking Afro-Caribbean refugees, Sister Mary Frances (nee Marie Balas), Sister Mary Rose (nee Rosine Boegue), and Sister Mary Theresa (nee Almaide Duchemin), became the first women of color in the United States to take the vows of the Catholic sisterhood. Dedicated to the spiritual education of all children of color, the Oblate Sisters established the first Black Catholic congregation in the United States. In 1845, Sister Mary Theresa left Baltimore and founded the Sisters Servants of the Immaculate Heart of Mary in Monroe, Michigan.

During the 1832 cholera epidemic, several members of the Oblate Sisters worked in the city almshouse hospital. The Sisters also took in boarders, many of whom were orphans, and opened a school. Despite their good deeds, their followers, many of whom were also Caribbean refugees, were forced to worship in the basement chapel of the church seminary and were buried in the segregated "colored" cemetery. Adequate funding was a constant problem for the Oblate Sisters, even though they made church vestments and did domestic work to survive. Church officials provided little spiritual guidance and even suggested that the Sisters disperse, hinting that they seek work as domestics in the homes of white families. Father Thaddeus Anwander, a Bavarian and Redemptorist priest, sympathized with the Sisters' plight and in 1847 received permission from his archbishop to attend to them. Under Father Anwander's leadership, enrollment of both boarders and day students increased, the number of Sisters doubled, and a school for boys was built. The construction of a new sanctuary enabled the Black Catholic congregation to attend, for the first time, a church that was their own.

During the Civil War era, public schools for African-American children did not exist, and money was scarce. However, Mother Mary and the Sisters persevered and were able to open a school for female war orphans. A building was bought from the Jesuits for the Oblate Sisters in exchange for the Oblates' washing and mending services at Baltimore's Loyola College. Free schools were established in Fells Point, Maryland, New Orleans, and Philadelphia, but some later closed due to a lack of resources. These ordeals continued until, reduced to utter poverty, the Oblates resorted to begging in Washington, D.C. Throughout each crisis, the Oblates did not give up their mission or their faith and, against all odds, continued to open schools across the United States.

By the 1900s, the Oblate Sisters had opened schools in Cuba. The Order served there for sixty-one years, until it was expelled by the Castro regime. They were aided in this mission by the involvement and cooperation of institutions of higher education. In 1924, the Sisters were allowed to attend summer school at Villanova, in order to further their own education. Classes were also taught at the motherhouse by members of the faculty of New Orleans's Xavier University.* In 1934, the new Reverend Mother, Mother Consuella Clifford, purchased property on Gun Road in Baltimore, where the present motherhouse was built. Today, the Oblate Sisters operate schools in Alabama, the Dominican Republic, Illinois, Maryland, New Jersey, New York, Pennsylvania, South Carolina, the District of Columbia, and Costa Rica.

SELECTED BIBLIOGRAPHY

Oblate Sisters of Providence, *Where He Leads Me I Will Follow*; Maria M. Lannon, *Mother Mary Elizabeth Lange: Life of Love and Service* (1976); Maria M. Lannon, *Response to Love* (Josephite Pastoral Center); M. A. Chineworth, *New Catholic Encyclopedia* (1967; reprint 1981).

DEVARA KOLOM BODOG

ORANGEBURG, SOUTH CAROLINA, MASSACRE. On 8 February 1968, thirty students on the campus of South Carolina State College,* a predominantly black college in Orangeburg, were shot by law enforcement officials. Three students were killed and twenty-seven others were wounded in what is known as the Orangeburg Massacre. Orangeburg was known for its peaceful handling of civil rights activities until students from South Carolina State and Claflin College,* led by John Stroman, organized unsuccessfully to force Harry E. Floyd to integrate All-Star Bowling Lanes, the only bowling alley in town. On 5 February 1968, the students attempted to stage a sit-in; several students were able to enter, but the chief of police ordered the bowling alley closed, as requested by the owner. The next night, larger groups of students returned and were met by law enforcement officers. General disorder resulted, and both male and female students were beaten. Twelve students who refused to leave the premises were arrested for trespassing.

On the following day, the students formulated a list of seven grievances and presented them to the city council. No agreement was reached. As the mood grew tense, Governor Robert McNair ordered National Guardsmen to the campus as reinforcements for the highway patrolmen already present. On the night of 8 February, students lit a bonfire at the periphery of the campus, close to the law-enforcement command post, which firefighters moved to extinguish. When one of the patrolmen guarding the firefighters was hit by a burning fencepost thrown into the fire, other police officers thought that the patrolman had been shot. They fired into the crowd of students, killing eighteen-year-old Samuel Hammond, Jr., seventeen-year-old Delano Middleton, and eighteen-year-old Henry Smith. Unarmed students were hit from all directions as they attempted to flee the scene. Ironically, the injured students were taken to a segregated hospital.

Governor McNair blamed the event on "black agitators," specifically Cleveland Sellars, a Student Nonviolent Coordinating Committee (SNCC) organizer. Sellars, who had been taken to the hospital for gunshot wounds, was arrested there. He was charged with various crimes, and later convicted of inciting to riot. Nine officers who participated in the shooting were charged by U.S. Attorney General Ramsey Clark with violating the civil rights of the murdered students. The officers were found not guilty by the South Carolina grand jury in federal court.

Two reporters, Jack Nelson and Jack Bass, discredited the governor's story by reporting an accurate account of the events. They later detailed the accounts in a book, *The Orangeburg Massacre*. Cleveland Sellars was pardoned twenty-three years after the Orangeburg Massacre by the South Carolina Probation, Pardon, and Parole Board. The court eventually ordered Harry Floyd to integrate All-Star Bowling Lanes.

SELECTED BIBLIOGRAPHY

John Bass and Jack Nelson, *The Orangeburg Massacre* (1984); "Troops Help Quell Carolina Outbreak," *New York Times*, 7 February, 1968, p. 27; "2 State College Negro Students Killed, 40 Others Wounded during Exchange of Gunfire between Police and Students," 8 February, 1968, p. 28; "3 students killed," *New York Times*, 10 February 1968, p. 23; Henry Hampton and Steve Fayer, *Voices of Freedom: An Oral History of the Civil Rights Movement from the 1950's through the 1980's* (1990).

NICOLE PETERS

P

PAINE COLLEGE. Paine College is a private four-year coeducational institution located in Augusta, Georgia. Established in 1882 by the Christian Methodist Episcopal Church and the United Methodist Church, Paine offers a sound liberal arts education. It is committed to timeless standards of instructional quality within a curriculum that responds to changing student needs. Majors are available in biology, business administration, chemistry, early childhood education, middle-grades education, music education, English, history, mass communications, mathematics, psychology, religion and philosophy, and sociology. Special programs include the preprofessional sciences program, cooperative education, Army ROTC, and the honors program. In keeping with advancing technology, Paine offers academic emphases in information systems and computer science.

SELECTED BIBLIOGRAPHY

National Association for Equal Opportunity in Higher Education, *Profiles of the Nation's Historically and Predominantly Black Colleges and Universities* (1993).

SAMUEL L. MYERS

PALMER MEMORIAL INSTITUTE. Located in Sedalia, North Carolina, the Alice Freeman Palmer Memorial Institute was founded in 1902 by Charlotte Hawkins Brown,* who for fifty years served as its president. The school was named in honor of educator Alice Freeman Palmer, Brown's friend and benefactor. From its beginnings, Palmer emphasized both academic and industrial education. The school also ran a farm that provided agricultural training for students who wished to become better farmers and that made it possible for students unable to pay tuition to work their way through school.

Palmer Memorial Institute was fully accredited by the Southern Association of Colleges and Secondary Schools (1922) at a time when very few African-American high schools had that distinction. By that time Charlotte Hawkins Brown was well on her way toward building Palmer into the only finishing school of its kind in America. It had evolved from a one-room school house into a well-known institution with a national reputation. At its height the campus consisted of over 250 acres of land with fourteen buildings. Starting in the late 1930s and early 1940s, after the school had abandoned an attempt to develop a junior college, Palmer limited its focus to college preparatory work. This was a very successful change, and by the end of the 1950s Palmer was a unique finishing and preparatory school with an enrollment of over two hundred students from all over the United States, the Caribbean, and Africa.

At its peak, over 90 percent of Palmer's graduating students attended college and 64 percent pursued postgraduate degrees. Several years after the death of Charlotte Hawkins Brown in 1961, the school began to decline, partly because of integration, which made it possible for African-Americans to be admitted to white public schools, and partly because of the increasing costs associated with a private school education. Because of this and other factors, Palmer experienced tremendous financial difficulties and was finally forced to close its doors after a disastrous fire destroyed the school's administrative and classroom building in 1971.

Nevertheless, the legacy of the school lives on. In 1983 the North Carolina General Assembly appropriated funds to develop the former Palmer Memorial Institute campus into a state historic site as a lasting memorial to Charlotte Hawkins Brown and the educational contributions of African-Americans to North Carolina. In November 1987 that effort became a reality, and today visitors to the memorial can view exhibits in a visitor center consisting of artifacts, memorabilia, and videos, which include photographs of Brown, Palmer Institute, and displays depicting African-American education from 1865 to 1971. There are also exhibits in Canary Cottage, Brown's home, which, when completed, will represent the home of the educator during the heyday (1935–45) of the institution. In addition, there will be panel displays explaining the restoration process for a period house. Future goals include development of an African-American resource center where scholars of all ages can discover the many contributions made by African-Americans to the history of North Carolina.

SELECTED BIBLIOGRAPHY

Griffith Davis, "Finishing School," *Ebony* (October 1947) 22–27; Lucinda Saunders, "An Idea that Grew into a Million," *Abbott's Monthly* (November 1930); Sandra N. Smith and Earle A. West, "Charlotte Hawkins Brown," *Journal of Negro Education* 51 (Summer 1982): 191–296. (The most exhaustive collection of materials assembled on the history of Palmer Memorial Institute are with the Historic Sites Section of the Division of Archives and History in Raleigh, North Carolina. Other prominent collections with primary source material include the Charlotte Hawkins Brown Papers, Schlesinger Library of Women, Radcliffe College, Cambridge, Massachusetts; Palmer Memorial Institute Papers, Holgate Library, Bennett College, Greensboro, North Carolina; and Palmer Memorial Institute Papers, Charlotte Hawkins Brown Memorial State Historic Site, Sedalia, North Carolina.)

CHARLES W. WADELINGTON

PASADENA CITY BOARD OF EDUCATION et al. v. SPANGLER et al., 427 U.S. 424 (1976). A district court's appropriate power to administer desegregation decrees has been an important judicial concern since the U.S. Supreme Court first considered it in *Brown II* (1955). *Green v. County School Board of New Kent County** (1968) and *Swann v. Charlotte–Mecklenburg Board of Education** (1971), as the present case, have pondered the issue. In 1968, several students and their parents brought a class action suit in the District court against the Pasadena, California, City Board of Education seeking an injunction for its unconstitutionally segregated high schools. The United States joined the students' suit under provisions of Title IX of the 1964 Civil Rights Act* and extended the complaint to other areas of the school system—the elementary schools, the junior high schools, and the special schools. In 1970, the district court ruled that the school board's policies and procedures violated the Fourteenth Amendment and ordered the board to submit a plan to correct the racial imbalance at all levels of the Pasadena Unified School District. In addition to provisions for the assignment of staff and the construction and location of facilities, the district court ordered that student assignment shall be such that "there shall be no school in the district, elementary or junior high or senior high school, with a majority of any minority students." The district court retained jurisdiction and school officials, having voted to comply and not to appeal, submitted their "Pasadena Plan," which the district court approved.

Four years later, successors to the original defendants—school officials—asked the district court for relief from the court's 1970 order, and the court denied their request. The Court of Appeals for the Ninth Circuit expressed reservations about some of the district court's action but affirmed its decision. Because of the importance of the case, the U.S. Supreme Court agreed to review it. The facts showed that the board of education complied with the plan and met the "no majority of any minority" requirement the initial year, 1970–71. However, during the following years, the school system had an increasing number of schools that were not in compliance with the requirement, because of "white flight"* and other population shifts unrelated to any segregative intent on the part of the school system. The district court judge had stated that the 1970 order "meant to me that at least during my lifetime there would be no majority of any minority in any school in Pasadena." This required school officials to make adjustments yearly to ensure compliance with the "no majority of any minority" requirement.

After determining that the intervention of the United States government in the case prevented the case from being moot, the Supreme Court focused on the question of whether the district court correctly denied the petitioners relief in 1974 when they sought to modify the "no majority" requirement. Citing *Swann v. Charlotte–Mecklenburg Board of Education** (1971), the Supreme Court stated that, "Neither school authorities nor districts are constitutionally required to make year-by-year adjustments of the racial composition of student bodies once the affirmative duty to desegregate them has been accomplished and racial discrimination through official action is eliminated from the system."

In its majority opinion delivered by Justice Rehnquist, the Court vacated the decision and remanded the case. Justice Thurgood Marshall,* joined by Justice Brennan, dissented. Justice Stevens took no part in the case. Justice Marshall argued that, at the time of the request to modify the court order, "racial discrimination through official action" had apparently not been eliminated from the Pasadena school system and that the system may not have achieved "unitary status in all respects such as the hiring and promoting of teachers and administrators." He asserted that, until a completely "unitary system" is established, a district court may act with broad discretion.

SELECTED BIBLIOGRAPHY

Paul R. Dimond, *Beyond Busing: Inside the Challenge to Urban Segregation* (1985); Annette B. Kolis, "Limiting Federal District Court Power after Successful Implementation of School Desegregation Orders," *Urban Law Annual* 13 (1977): 203–16; "Limitations of Federal School Desegregation Remedies," *Harvard Law Review* 90 (November 1976): 221–23; J. Harvie Wilkinson III, *From Brown to Bakke: The Supreme Court and School Integration 1954–1978* (1979).

JAMES E. NEWBY

PATTERSON, FREDERICK DOUGLASS (10 October 1901, Washington, D.C.–26 April 1988, New Rochelle, N.Y.) Frederick Patterson was the third president of Tuskegee Institute (now Tuskegee University*) (1935–53) and founder of the United Negro College Fund* in 1944. Patterson was the youngest of five children born to William R. Patterson and Mamie Brooks Patterson. He spent most of his childhood in various towns in Texas. He received his high school diploma from Prairie View Normal and Industrial Institute (now Prairie View A & M University*) in 1919. He earned both the doctor of veterinary medicine and master of science degrees from Iowa State College in 1923 and 1929 respectively. In 1932, he earned a Ph.D. degree from Cornell University. He was the recipient of thirteen honorary degrees, including degrees from New York University, Howard University,* Tuskegee Institute,* Morehouse College,* Atlanta University,* and St. Augustine College.* The Tuskegee Institute School of Veterinary Medicine honored Patterson in 1980 by naming a newly constructed building "Frederick Douglass Patterson Hall." Also in 1980, he was honored by Iowa State University as one of the recipients of the Distinguished Achievement Citation. Patterson was awarded the Presidential Medal of Freedom by President Ronald Reagan in 1987. He was awarded the NAACP's* Spingarn Medal posthumously in 1988.

Patterson began his professional career as a teacher at Virginia State College (now Virginia State University*) in 1923 and remained there for five years. He started his work at Tuskegee in the fall of 1928, teaching courses in veterinary science to nursing and agriculture students. In 1932, he was promoted to director of the School of Agriculture. In 1935, he was appointed president of Tuskegee Institute.

At Tuskegee, Patterson designed and implemented a number of innovative programs, including new degree program in commercial dietetics, installed in

1935. He implemented a scheme called the "5-Year Plan" in 1939 to allow students without money to work their way through Tuskegee. The Institute's commercial aviation program was launched in 1939, including the training of pilots and the building of a airport (Motion Field). The School of Veterinary Medicine was initiated in 1942, the first at an African-American institution. Graduate instruction was started at Tuskegee in 1943. The veterinary school was fully accredited in 1954. The School of Engineering was established in 1948.

The founding of the United Negro College Fund* was one of Patterson's most lasting contributions to African-American education. He was instrumental in bringing to the forefront the plight of a number of financially strapped African-American institutions of higher education such that they could collectively benefit from fundraising efforts.

Patterson retired from Tuskegee in 1953. His postretirement involvement included serving as head of the Phelps–Stokes Fund* (1953–70) and as founder and chairman of the board of the R. R. Moton* Memorial Institute (1958–88). He died of a heart attack on 26 April 1988, in New Rochelle, New York. Funeral services were held in New Rochelle on 29 April. A memorial and interment service was held at Tuskegee University on 4 May 1988. He was survived by his wife, Catherine, and a son, Frederick D. Patterson II.

SELECTED BIBLIOGRAPHY

Marita G. Goodson, ed., *Chronicles of Faith: The Autobiography of Frederick D. Patterson* (1991); Frederick D. Patterson Papers, Library of Congress, Tuskegee University Archives.

EDWIN HAMILTON

PAUL QUINN COLLEGE. Paul Quinn College was founded in Austin, Texas, in 1881 by a group of African Methodist Episcopal Church ministers. The college was moved to Waco, Texas, in 1887 and relocated to a 120-acre campus in Dallas, Texas, in 1990. It is presently a four-year, private, coeducational liberal arts college of sixteen buildings, including dormitories, a chapel, and a library. The college offers bachelor of arts, science, and applied science degrees in biology, business, computer and information sciences, elementary education, fine arts, health and physical education, history, mathematics, music, psychology, social work, and sociology. It is accredited by the Southern Association of Colleges and Schools,* the Council on Social Work Education, and the Texas Education Agency.

SELECTED BIBLIOGRAPHY

National Association for Equal Opportunity in Higher Education, *Profiles of the Nation's Historically and Predominantly Black Colleges and Universities* (1993).

SAMUEL L. MYERS

PAYNE, DANIEL ALEXANDER (24 February 1811–29 November 1893). Bishop of the African Methodist Episcopal Church, historian, former president of Wilberforce College,* and educator, Daniel Payne was born to London and

Martha Payne, free persons in Charleston, South Carolina. Daniel's parents died before he turned ten, leaving him to be raised by one of his relatives. He studied for two years at the Minor's Moralist Society School, a school run by free African-Americans, and the Lutheran Theological Seminary. He later studied under a private tutor who developed Payne's skill in mathematics, English, and French, Greek, and Latin. In 1826, he joined the Methodist Episcopal church, and two years later he began a successful private school for African-American children and adult slaves. The school had an ever-increasing curriculum, from the sciences to history. On 17 December 1834, the state legislature of South Carolina passed a law forbidding the teaching of slaves or free African-Americans to read or write. Payne subsequently closed his school and moved to Pennsylvania, swearing he would not return to Charleston until slavery was over.

In Pennsylvania, Payne studied theology at the Lutheran Theological Seminary. In 1837 he was licensed to preach, and two years later he was ordained a Lutheran minister by the Franckean Synod of the Lutheran Church. He temporarily became the pastor of the Presbyterian church in East Troy, N.Y., until he moved to Philadelphia and opened another school. Shortly afterward, Payne joined the African Methodist (AME) Church and was soon appointed to its traveling ministry. For the next few years he traveled around, establishing himself as one of the leading educators of both laymen and ministers in that denomination. In 1852 Payne was elected to the position of bishop. He utilized that position to increase the awareness and establishment of schools and historical and literary societies among African-Americans.

During his travels to promote the ideals and philosophies of the AME church, Bishop Payne met with President Lincoln and pleaded for the freeing of the slaves. On 10 March 1863, Payne purchased Wilberforce University for $10,000 and became the first president of an African-American institution of higher learning. He held this position for approximately sixteen years until his retirement.

After retiring from the presidency of Wilberforce, Payne established himself as a writer; some of his more notable works are *The History of the A.M.E. Church from 1816 to 1856* (1891), *Recollections of Seventy Years* (1888), and *A Treatise on Domestic Education* (1885).

SELECTED BIBLIOGRAPHY

Harry A. Ploski and James Williams, *The Negro Almanac: A Reference Work on the African-American* (1989); W. A. Low and Virgil A. Clift, *Encyclopedia of Black America* (1981); Rayford W. Logan and Michael R. Winston, *Dictionary of American Negro Biography* (1982); Dumas Malone, *Dictionary of American Biography* (1934).

                                                              EARL F. HILLIARD, Jr.

PAYTON, BENJAMIN FRANKLIN (27 December 1932, Orangeburg, South Carolina). The current president of Tuskegee University,* Benjamin Payton was appointed on 1 August 1981. He grew up in Orangeburg, South Carolina, in a family of nine children. He is the son of the late Reverend L. R. Payton and Sarah Payton; his father was a Baptist minister and farmer, and his mother was a schoolteacher. Payton attended college in his hometown and earned his B.A. degree (with honors) from South Carolina State College* in 1955. He earned the B.D. degree (1958) at Harvard University, the M.A. degree (1960) at Columbia University, and the Ph.D. degree (1963) at Yale University. Payton has been honored with six honorary degrees from Eastern Michigan University, Morris Brown College,* Benedict College,* Morgan State University,* Lehigh University, and the University of Maryland.

Payton's professional career began at Howard University* as an assistant professor and director of community services (1963–65). He joined the Protestant Council of the City of New York as Director, Office of Church and Race (1965–66), and was executive director of the Commission of Religion and Race and the Department of Social Justice of the National Council of Churches in the USA (1966–72). Payton was president of Benedict College* (1967–72), and program officer for education and public policy at the Ford Foundation (1972–81).

Payton's administrative goal at Tuskegee has been to build on the foundation of earlier leadership and ''to strengthen significantly Tuskegee's image and substance as a national and regional center of excellence.'' Over the years, specific academic programs have been reorganized and realigned to reflect Payton's administrative goal and strategic plan. Some selected new degree and reorganized programs include specialties in aerospace science, computer science, and psychology. The Department of Business was elevated to the School of Business. The departments of Engineering and Architecture were combined to form the School of Engineering and Architecture. A centralized Office of Computer Services and an Office of International Programs were established. The Kellogg Center for Continuing Education was established with a $10.5 million grant. Community outreach was expanded to include a variety of adult programs and precollege programs for high school students. A massive renovation of Tuskegee's aging buildings was undertaken in 1981, and renovations were made to Thrasher, Tompkins, and Huntington halls. The ''Chappie'' James Center was constructed at a cost of $18.5 million.

During Payton's tenure as president, the name of the school changed from Tuskegee Institute to Tuskegee University (1985). The school also saw its state appropriation rise from $1.4 million in 1982 to $3.6 million in 1992, while its endowment more than doubled from $14.9 million in 1981 to $37.3 million in 1991. Tuskegee's student enrollment in 1992 of 3,749 was reportedly the largest enrollment in its history.

Payton was married to Thelma Plane Payton, and they had two children, Mark and Deborah.

SELECTED BIBLIOGRAPHY

''A Ten-Year Report of the President, 1981–1991,'' *Tuskegee University Bulletin* 79, no. 2 (December 1991); Program from the inauguration services for President Benjamin

Franklin Payton at Tuskegee Institute 3 April, 1982); "Annual Report of the President, 1984," *Bulletin of Tuskegee Institute* 78, no. 2 (December 1984); "Annual Report of the President, 1992," *Tuskegee University Bulletin* 80, no. 1 (October 1992); "Annual Report of the President, 1993," *Tuskegee University Bulletin*, 81, no. 1 (October 1993); *Who's Who among Black Americans*, 5th ed. (1988).

EDWIN HAMILTON

PEABODY EDUCATION FUND. George Peabody, a businessman with connections in Boston, Baltimore, and London, established the Peabody Education Fund in 1867, with an initial gift of one million dollars, to be used to promote education in the southern states. Another million was soon added, and for forty-seven years the fund attempted to promote public education and teacher training in the former Confederate states, where the tradition had been private and pauper schools.

The fund's trustees, half distinguished northern men and half equally well-known southern men, selected Barnas Sears to be their agent. Successor to Horace Mann as Massachusetts school superintendent and president of Brown University, Sears was a respected educator and clergyman. From 1867 to 1880, he determined the policies and distributed the monies mainly by traveling extensively through the South, meeting with community leaders, urging the importance of public schools, and offering Peabody money if schools would be established that met the announced criteria. He required that such schools be free and under some form of public control and that the community itself raise three or four times the amount given by the fund. The long-range objective was to encourage the development of state systems of public education.

During the early years, it was common for Sears to stipulate that towns receiving aid should supply children of both races with schools. He did, however, acquiesce to separate schools for the races, believing that the embryonic public school system would be destroyed if racially mixed schools were required. The overriding assumption was that, in the long run, the best interests of all children required the development of a public school system rather than the continuation of a private system.

In many situations it was difficult for African-American communities to meet the fund's criteria. Thus, to prevent the fund from seeming to be for white children alone, Sears arranged for local agents of the Bureau of Refugees, Freedmen, and Abandoned Lands* (Freedmen's Bureau) to distribute the money and carry out the required supervision. Contributions to African-American schools reached 18 percent of Peabody distributions during 1868–69. Congressional appropriations to the Freedmen's Bureau ended in 1870, and thereafter aid to African-American schools was given in the same manner and on similar terms as to white schools. The proportion of such aid was generally in the range of 4 to 6 percent of total expenditures.

In 1875, the fund began a shift of emphasis from aiding common schools to encouraging teacher training. During this period, contributions to teacher training for African-Americans averaged about 18 percent of all fund contributions, and the proportion reached above 30 percent in some years. Regardless of race, aid for teacher education was mainly in the form of tuition payments assigned to specific schools as scholarships.

At first, scholarships were given for students to attend local normal schools. Soon, however, Sears decided that in order to upgrade teacher education it was desirable to encourage the establishment of a few regional schools that would offer a distinctly higher level of training. The Nashville (Tennessee) Normal-School was adopted as the regional model for training teachers at the collegiate level, and most of the increased aid went to that institution. Various states were assigned scholarship quotas to the Nashville school.

General Oliver Otis Howard was anxious to have the Peabody Fund adopt Howard University* as its central training school for African-Americans. Sears decided to restrict aid to southern schools that might eventually be incorporated into the state systems. Scholarship allocations on a sustaining basis were made to Hampton Institute,* Fisk University,* and Atlanta University* as well as to several normal schools of lower quality. However, no regional school was adopted for African-American students, and individual scholarship amounts were smaller than for white students.

As the first American educational foundation, the Peabody Education Fund influenced other philanthropists. The John F. Slater Fund* (1882), the Daniel Hand Educational Fund for Colored People (1888), the General Education Board* (1903), the Anna T. Jeanes Fund* for Negro Rural Schools (1907), and the Phelp–Stokes Fund* (1911) subsequently began to assist with the improvement of education in the southern states and particularly with the education of African-Americans.

Jabez Lamar Monroe Curry, a distinguished southerner, was Sears's successor as general agent for the Peabody Fund. By holding joint appointments to several other philanthropic boards, Curry brought the Peabody Fund into close collaboration with these other agencies and channelled contributions through them to African-American education. When the fund was dissolved in 1914, a final distribution of $350,000 was made to the Slater Fund ''for the industrial and scientific education of the Negro.'' The major beneficiary of the Peabody Fund at its close was the Nashville Normal School subsequently upgraded and renamed the George Peabody College for Teachers, making possible its role as the leading teacher-education institution of the South. However, until that institution integration in the 1950s, African-Americans did not benefit directly from this object of Peabody philanthropy.

Assessments of the significance of the Peabody Education Fund are mixed, and any evaluation must take into account the purposes of the fund. Following the Civil War and Reconstruction, the South was impoverished. Rejecting southern pleas for outright charitable gifts, the policies of the fund aimed at establishing a foothold for public school systems to replace the tradition of private schools. By making Peabody money conditional upon the schools being free and upon the community itself raising most of the money required to support schools and by requiring schools to be provided for all children even though racially separate, the trustees believed that the greatest long-range good for all citizens could be done. Having brought public opinion in the South to an acceptance of public schools, the fund turned its attention to upgrading teacher education in the belief that the permanency of public schools depended on improved teaching. In this way, the fund was doubtless a contributing factor to the advancement of all citizens in the South.

On the negative side, the policies of the fund meant that African-Americans received disproportionately less. Often, black communities could not raise matching funds. Public supervision was seldom possible, as many schools met in churches. Moreover, Sears naively underestimated southern white prejudice and viewed racially separate schools as a temporary expedient required to win support for public schools. In the end, he thought, both the law and Christian morality would see to it that the races received equal educational opportunity. Although history proved that assumption to be wrong, one must acknowledge that the Peabody Fund's role in the building of a public school system in the South was an accomplishment that made it possible for that region to recover from a devastating defeat in war and for all races to receive some benefit.

SELECTED BIBLIOGRAPHY

J. L. M. Curry Papers, Library of Congress; *Hamilton Fish Papers*, Library of Congress; J. L. M. Curry, *A Brief Sketch of George Peabody and a History of the Peabody Fund* (1969); Alvah Hovey, *Barnas Sears, a Christian Educator* (1902); Ullin W. Leavell, *Philanthropy in Negro Education* (1950; reprint 1970); *Proceedings of the Trustees of the Peabody Education Fund*, 6 vols. (1875–1916).

                                                                    EARLE H. WEST

PEAKE, MARY SMITH (KELSEY) (1823, Norfolk, Virginia–22 February 1862, Hampton, Virginia). A free woman of color at the beginning of the Civil War, Mary S. Peake was among the first in a slave state to openly educate newly emancipated African-Americans. Though she taught for fewer than six months and was not the most notable of educators, Peake's work and school have achieved symbolic importance in African-American education. Hers was one of the first southern schools for freed African-Americans to open in Hampton, Virginia.

The daughter of a free mulatto woman of Virginia and a Frenchman, Peake enjoyed unusual educational advantages for her time, place, and race. Sent to Alexandria, Virginia, for ten years of schooling, she received both literary education and training in needlework. She returned to Norfolk in 1839 to live with her mother and support herself as a dressmaker. There she met and married Thomas Peake, at that time serving in the merchant marine and later a leader in Hampton's African-American community. He brought Mary and her mother to Hampton, where Mary began teaching free and enslaved African-Americans. Teaching slaves was unlawful in Virginia, but it was tolerated by whites in

Hampton when pursued discreetly. Mary Peake's own stepfather became her student, as did other adult men who would become spokespersons for the region's newly emancipated African-Americans. Sometime prior to the Civil War, she contracted tuberculosis.

After Hampton was rebuilt by the former slaves and free blacks at the end of the Civil War, local African-American children requested that Mary Peake begin teaching again. Then, however, she could operate her school openly. Peake also initiated evening classes for African-American adults. To aid the school, the American Missionary Association* began contributing toward her salary in September 1861, making her the first teacher paid by a northern freedmen's aid society. Peake's school was among the earliest of what came to be known as "freedmen's schools," part of the effort to provide formal education to the freed people of the South. Peake retired from teaching in January 1862 and died of tuberculosis in Hampton in mid-February.

Mary S. Peake was only one of many southern African-American men and women who taught more or less secretly under slavery and continued into freedom; others taught much longer. Her school was not the first school opened under conditions of war-bought freedom, a claim long made. Anna Bell Davis opened an earlier school in Alexandria; Jane A. Deveaux and Simeon W. Beard in Georgia and George F. T. Cook and John F. Cook, among many others, in Washington, D.C., taught for as long before the war and for many years after the war. Peake's greater fame traces to her tie to the American Missionary Association, which published a brief and inaccurate biographical sketch as part of its campaign to promote freedmen's education. There was symbolic significance in her work, however, in that one of the first southern schools for freed African-Americans opened in Hampton where the first shipload of slaves arrived from Africa in 1619.

SELECTED BIBLIOGRAPHY

"Mary S. Peake," *American Missionary Magazine* 6 (April 1862): 83; Lewis C. Lockwood, *Mary S. Peake, The Colored Teacher at Fortress Monroe* (1863; reprint 1969); Robert Francis Engs, *Freedom's First Generation: Black Hampton, Virginia, 1861–1890* (1979); Ronald E. Butchart, *Northern Schools, Southern Blacks, and Reconstruction, 1862–1875* (1980).

RONALD E. BUTCHART

PENN NORMAL, INDUSTRIAL, AND AGRICULTURAL SCHOOL. Penn Normal, Industrial, and Agricultural School was established originally as the Penn School in 1865 on St. Helena Island, near Beaufort, South Carolina. It was one of few independent schools for the newly emancipated African-Americans in the South that survived Reconstruction without the support of a northern missionary organization, and the best-known of them. Its long history encompasses two conflicting visions of the proper education for southern African-Americans.

The Penn School was founded by Laura M. Towne, a white abolitionist from Philadelphia, and her lifetime companion, Ellen Murray. Towne's primary vision for the school was the social, cultural, and intellectual advancement of the freed-men. There was an emphasis on traditional academic curriculum and proscrip-tion of all corporal punishment, based on the belief that character and leadership were best developed through intellectual discipline and mutual respect. Towne and Murray also developed a teacher-training program in 1868. By 1870, teach-ers from the school were being employed throughout South Carolina, and it remained a significant source of the state's African-American teachers for many decades. From 1865 until Towne's death in 1901, Towne and Murray superin-tended the school and taught many of its classes, constant in their allegiance to Towne's original vision of rigorous academic training for the freedmen.

After Towne's death, the northern white trustees of the school rejected the academic emphasis Towne had pursued and embraced instead industrial edu-cation. The move to industrial education at the Penn School was signalled by the change in its name to Penn Normal, Industrial, and Agricultural School. Under the leadership of Rossa Belle Cooley, its new principal, the curriculum shifted sharply toward preparation for rural agricultural and domestic life. Teacher training remained a major part of the mission of the school, but the new focus of the school's mission altered the substance of the curriculum and shifted its ideology in a socially conservative direction.

Cooley headed the school from 1907 to her retirement in 1948, remaining at her post even longer than her predecessor. Under her leadership, the school became a model of industrial education and achieved a measure of national attention as an exemplar of enlightened African-American education. By World War II, its philosophy and focus were outmoded. Penn School then relinquished its educational mission to the public schools and became Penn Community Serv-ices, a community development program for the people of St. Helena Island.

SELECTED BIBLIOGRAPHY

James D. Anderson, *The Education of Blacks in the South, 1860–1935* (1988); Rupert S. Holland, ed., *Letters and Diary of Laura M. Towne, Written from the Sea Islands of South Carolina, 1862–1884* (1912); Elizabeth Jacoway, *Yankee Missionaries in the South: The Penn School Experiment* (1980); Gerald Robbins, "Laura Towne: White Pioneer in Negro Education, 1862–1901," *Journal of Education* 143 (April 1961): 40–54.

RONALD E. BUTCHART

PHELPS–STOKES FUND. The Phelps–Stokes Fund is a nonprofit foundation whose guiding motto is "Education for Human Development." The fund was established by the will of New York philanthropist Caroline Phelps Stokes in 1911 as a not-for-profit philanthropic organization with charter interests in the education of African-Americans, Native Americans, Africans, and poor whites. The Phelps–Stokes Fund was the first of its kind to commission studies and reports remarkable for their day. Its 1911 report, *Negro Education in the United States*, was the first scholarly study in the United States to focus attention on the inadequacy of racially segregated school systems. Correspondingly, its *Education in Africa* (1922) was the first comprehensive survey of education in Africa. Another Phelps–Stokes report, *The Problem of Indian Administration* (known as the Merian Report) (1928), is still considered the most far-reaching analysis of problems in Native American education.

Over the nearly eighty-three years of its history, the fund has carried out its mandate to improve educational opportunities for its target constituencies and to build bridges of international and interracial understanding. Its early relationship with Tuskegee Institute,* for example, laid the foundation for the establishment of the Booker T. Washington* Institute in Liberia. In 1934, the fund was instrumental in founding the South African Institute of Race Relations. The United Negro College Fund was guided in the 1950s by Dr. Frederick Patterson* while he was president of Phelps–Stokes. Throughout the 1960s and 1970s, the fund's work on historically African-American and Native American college campuses concentrated on the administrative and financial development of those institutions. In 1966, it created a separate, self-supporting affiliate, the African Student Aid Fund, to meet the needs for counseling, placement, and emergency financial assistance of African students studying at American institutions, as well as a program to place African refugees into two-year college degree and baccalaureate degree programs in various American universities. During the past two decades, Phelps–Stokes programs assisting Africans have facilitated faculty exchanges between American and African universities, seminars, conferences, and an International Exchange Program that bring African educators, government officials, businesspersons, and artists for short-term study tours to the United States.

The focus of the fund's domestic programs is presently centered around four programs: Education Policy and School Reform, the Phelps–Stokes Forum, International Development at the Historically Black Colleges and Universities, and the Anson Phelps–Stokes Institute and Center for Human Development. The aim of the Education Policy and School Reform program is to examine key educational policy issues and promote those policy and program options that are in the best interest of education for minority students. Senior Phelps–Stokes Fellows in this program conduct research and present their findings in the fund's publications and op-ed pieces and provide consultant advisory assistance on policy and program matters to school agencies. The fund's educational publications—*Dialogue*, the monthly newsletter on educational policy, and *Issues in Education and Policy and Practice*, the monograph series—are mailed to over two thousand educational policymakers and opinionmakers in the country. The Phelps–Stokes Forum is a public education initiative consisting of two series, African development and educational policy and school reform. The fund is also assisting a select number of historically black colleges and universities to develop international studies programs and curricula. The Anson Phelps–Stokes Institute and Center for Human Development provides administrative support to affiliate scholars and fledgling community educational and cultural organizations.

                                                    WILBERT LEMELLE

PHILANDER SMITH COLLEGE. Founded in 1877 by ex-slaves, Philander Smith is a four-year liberal arts, historically black Christian college affiliated with the United Methodist Church and the only United Negro College Fund* institution in Arkansas. The college which is located in Little Rock, Arkansas, offers the bachelor of arts degree, the bachelor of science degree in natural and physical science, and the bachelor of science degree in medical technology. Its curriculum is structured in five divisions: teacher education, humanities, business, science, and social sciences. It also offers preprofessional programs in dentistry, engineering, pharmacy, medicine, nursing, and the ministry. Extracurricular activities around campus include the Philander Smith College Collegiate Choir (which was recently ranked number one in the nation for the performance of African-American spirituals) and basketball, volleyball, and baseball teams for males and females. There are also Greek organizations on campus, a Student Government Association, The Student Christian Association, and a drama department.

SELECTED BIBLIOGRAPHY

National Association for Equal Opportunity in Higher Education, *Profiles of the Nation's Historically and Predominantly Black Colleges and Universities* (1993).

                                                    SAMUEL L. MYERS

PLAYER, WILLA (9 August 1909, Jackson, Mississippi). A linguist and college administrator, Willa Player was born in Jackson, Mississippi, the last of the three children of Clarence E. and Beatrice D. Player. The family moved in 1916 to Akron, Ohio, where Player received a public education and was, like the rest of her family, heavily involved in Methodist church activities. Following her high school graduation, she earned a bachelor of arts degree from Ohio Wesleyan University in 1929 and an M.A. the following year from Oberlin College.* She continued her studies in French at the University of Grenoble, France, and earned a Certificat d'Etudes in 1935. She did additional graduate work at the University of Chicago and the University of Wisconsin, Madison, and in 1948 earned a doctorate of education at Columbia University.

Player began her teaching career at Bennett College* in Greensboro, North Carolina, in 1930. The college had been founded as a coeducational institution in 1873 by the Methodists and did not become a college exclusively for women until 1926. Over the next twenty-five years, Player served the college in a variety of positions, finally being named college president in 1955. Her appointment made her the first African-American woman president of an African-American women's college, a post that she held for eleven years.

Player was well aware of the difficulties of being a woman and an African-American in the segregated South. While serving as Bennett's vice president, she wrote an article in 1947 about the discrimination that African-American women find in the southern job market and within their own communities and the need for African-American women to be prepared realistically for a segregated job market, for homemaking in the poorer sections of town, and for leadership within their own communities.

Throughout her life, Player has continued her many activities in the Methodist Church, serving as a member of the University Senate of the United Methodist Church in Nashville, Tennessee, and speaking at many church conferences. In 1962–63, she was president of the National Association of Schools and Colleges of the Methodist Church.

Player has received many honors throughout her distinguished lifetime. These include the Stepping Stone to Freedom Award for her contributions to the civil rights movement; the 1972 Superior Service Award and the Distinguished Service Award from the U.S. Department of Health, Education and Welfare; induction into the Ohio Women's Hall of Fame in Columbus; and several honorary doctorates.

SELECTED BIBLIOGRAPHY

Joan C. Elliot, "Willa B. Player (1909–): Educator, Government Official, Consultant," in Jessie Carney Smith, ed., *Notable Black American Women* (1992); Fenella MacFarlane, "Player, Willa B. (1909–)," in Darlene Clark Hine, ed., *Black Women in America: An Historical Encyclopedia* (1993).

ELIZABETH L. IHLE

PLESSY v. FERGUSON, 163 U.S. 537, 16 S. Ct. 1138; 41 L. Ed. 256 (1896). On 7 June 1892, Homer Adolph Plessy, an octoroon (⅞ white, ⅛ black), seated himself in a "whites-only" compartment of an East Louisiana Railroad line. He was challenged by the conductor, arrested, and charged with violating an 1890 Louisiana statute requiring segregation on trains within the state. Plessy took the case to court, charging that the statute violated his rights under the Thirteenth and Fourteenth amendments. Judge John J. Ferguson of the Criminal District Court for the Parish of Orleans and the Louisiana State Supreme Court ruled against Plessy. Plessy appealed his case to the U.S. Supreme Court.

The crux of the *Plessy* case was that the law requiring separate but equal accommodations on railroad cars was unconstitutional. If a physical distinction, skin color, could be used as a basis for segregation, then discrimination against persons with blond or red hair could also be considered reasonable and legal. By legally sanctioning segregation for some of its citizens, Louisiana implied that these citizens were inferior in the eyes of the law.

On 18 May 1896, the Supreme Court issued its decision. The Court ruled that segregation by race did not necessarily imply racial inferiority. It based its decision on the question of whether or not the statute of Louisiana was a "reasonable regulation." Delivering the opinion of the Court, Justice Henry Brown wrote that the question of reasonableness hinged on the degree to which the statute conformed "to the established usages, customs, and traditions of the people, and with a view to the promotion of their comfort, and the preservation of the public peace and good order" and that "Legislation is powerless to eradicate racial instincts or to abolish distinctions based upon physical differences, and the attempt to do so can only result in accentuating the difficulties of the present situation" Justice John Marshall Harlan, in a lone dissenting opinion, wrote in part that the "statute of Louisiana is inconsistent with the personal liberty of citizens, white and black, in the State, and hostile to both the spirit and the letter of the Constitution of the United States."

Until it was overturned by *Brown v. Board of Education of Topeka, Kansas** in 1954, the *Plessy* case made it lawful for nearly sixty more years to deny African-Americans equal protection under the law by forcing them to accept the notion of "separate-but-equal" accommodations in public and semipublic facilities, parks, waiting rooms, bus and railroad services, and the schooling of their children. Today, nearly 100 years later, the separate and unequal conditions of schooling for hundreds of thousands of African-American children may more nearly approximate the post-Reconstruction era of *Plessy* than the court-ordered desegregation era following *Brown*.

SELECTED BIBLIOGRAPHY

Robert Fairchild Cushman, *Cases in Constitutional Law* (1989); Jean West Mueller and Wynell Burroughs Schamel, "*Plessy v. Ferguson* Mandate," in *Social Education* (February 1989): 120–22.

KRINER CASH

POVERTY AND EDUCATION. Until the 1954 landmark decision of *Brown v. Board of Education of Topeka, Kansas*,* African-American and white children attended segregated schools that were purported to be "separate but equal." However, this historic decision disproved the notion that a segregated school system was "equal" for all students regardless of race. It further affirmed, based on the Fourteenth Amendment of the Constitution, that African-American children's right to equal protection was being systematically violated. Thus, the *Brown* decision set the precedent for all subsequent legislation with regard to education and race.

While the *Brown* decision proved to be a milestone in terms of desegregating public schools, it did not address the issue of poverty. It was not until the early 1960s that the United States focused on the significance of race and socioeconomic status with regard to education in a substantive way. The initial idea of a comprehensive assault on poverty (what later became commonly known as the "War on Poverty") was conceived by President John F. Kennedy in the early 1960s and implemented by his successor, President Lyndon B. Johnson. Prior to this period, the interest in poverty was not racially based. Many studies of that day concentrated on rural poverty, and the Kennedy Administration focused on poverty in Appalachia. The massive migration of southern African-Americans to northern cities during this time period helped the Kennedy/Johnson administration to refocus its attention. It was then that poverty emerged as an urban problem that most seriously affected African-Americans. In addition, the Civil Rights Movement and urban riots contributed to the redefinition of poverty.

On 23 November 1963, the day after the assassination of President Kennedy, President Lyndon B. Johnson instructed Walter Heller, chairperson of the Council of Economic Advisors, to continue designing a program to address the problems of poverty in this country. On 8 January 1964, in his State of the Union message, Johnson coined the phrase, "war on poverty." On 1 February, Sargent Shriver was appointed director of the newly established Office of Economic Opportunity (OEO), with a mandate to administer and implement the new antipoverty program. Subsequently Shriver, along with a planning committee that consisted of members from various branches of the federal government including the President's Committee on Juvenile Delinquency, drafted the Economic Opportunity Act.

The first battle the OEO encountered was establishing a definition of poverty. The OEO decided to adopt the definition created by Mollie Orshansky in the Social Security Administration's Office of Research and Statistics, as a tool for diagnosing poverty and measuring progress against it. This became known as the Orshansky Index. The Orshansky Index assumed that poor families spent approximately one third of their income on food. Thus, the poverty line was estimated to be three times the cost of the Department of Agriculture's low-cost budget for food, adjusted for family composition and rural-urban differences.

Having established an official definition of poverty, the OEO replicated the Mobilization for Youth Model, which was a comprehensive program in New York City organized to combat delinquency by elevating socioeconomically disadvantaged youth above structural and societal barriers to social mobility and self-sufficiency. Mobilization for Youth was very influential in the formulation of the multifaceted antipoverty program through the President's Committee on Juvenile Delinquency (later subsumed under the Office of Economic Opportunity), which adopted many of its ideas.

On 29 August, 1964, President Johnson signed into law the Economic Opportunity Act, a comprehensive piece of antipoverty legislation. In doing so, it became the "policy of the United States to eliminate the paradox of poverty in the midst of plenty in this Nation by opening to everyone the opportunity for education and training, the opportunity to work, and the opportunity to live in decency and dignity." This antipoverty legislation effort had a threefold purpose. First, it attempted to change the status of the socioeconomically disadvantaged by reinforcing their self-sufficiency through the expansion of education, training, and other related services. Second, it promoted and supported the participation of the poor in every aspect of the antipoverty programs, from planning to implementation. Third, it satisfied basic needs by expanding direct assistance to the poor through the provision of in-kind services, including health care, shelter, and nutrition. This combination of programs and services was designed to accomplish two things: (a) to provide a base of support for the current generation of poor people and (b) to build a ladder out of poverty for the next generation. To achieve its objectives, the Office of Economic Opportunity implemented various programs that concentrated on four major areas: juvenile delinquency, civil rights, job training, and education.

Although the United States made great strides in the 1960s and 1970s toward the provision of educational resources for African-Americans, the educational opportunities for African-Americans and whites are still not equal. Persistent and large disparities remain in the quality of education and the achievement outcomes for African-Americans and whites. For example, African-Americans, on average, continue to enter schools with substantial disadvantages in socio-economic backgrounds and tested achievement. Morever, because U.S. schools do not compensate for these disadvantages in background, most students leave these schools with the gap between African-Americans and whites not having been significantly closed. Early intervention compensatory education programs, such as Head Start,* were cited as having positive effects on the educational performance of African-American children.

Between 1976 and 1988, the higher education participation rate for African-American females decreased by 7.5 percent, while the participation rate for African-American males plummeted 17 percentage points during the same time period. The early 1990s (1990–93) saw an increase in enrollment of 12.3 percent for African-American undergraduates attending four-year institutions. While the trend of participation for African-Americans in higher education appears to be shifting, the factors cited in earlier studies are still pertinent. Minority students face a multiplicity of challenges when contemplating higher education, such as paying the bills for tuition, books, and living expenses while they study. Student aid, which can help alleviate this burden, may be inadequate or its existence may be unknown to certain students. Pell Grants, for example, can only be used to fund up to 60 percent of all postsecondary school expenses. While need-based federal aid, as well as other aid, has been available for years, it is conceivable that college costs, real or imagined, may be perceived by many low-income youth as exorbitant, which then discourages them from pursuing higher education. Over half of the high school graduates surveyed in the GAO study cited affordability, finances, and the need to work as reasons for not enrolling in college.

The continuing problems of unemployment for minority persons in urban areas, coupled with the general underrepresentation of minority persons in professional occupations, suggest that the usual incentives for pursuing higher education may be diminished. While several factors may have a negative impact on early school motivation, achievement, high school graduation rates, and college preparation, the single most significant influence on educational attainment is socioeconomic status. As the nation prepares for the future, its programs and policies must substantively address this reality.

SELECTED BIBLIOGRAPHY
James S. Coleman, *Equality and Achievement in Education* (1990); Economic Opportunity Act of 1964, Public Law 88–452, 78 Stat. 508; National Center for Children in Poverty School of Public Health, *Five Million Children: A Statistical Profile of Our Poorest Young Citizens* (1991); U.S. General Accounting Office, *Higher Education: Gaps in Parents' and Students' Knowledge of School Costs and Federal Aid* (1990); Gerald David Jaynes and Robin M. Williams, Jr., eds., *A Common Destiny: Blacks and American Society* (1989); Michael B. Katz, *The Undeserving Poor: From the War on Poverty to the War on Welfare* (1989); Business–Higher Education Forum, *Three Realities: Minority Life in the United States* (1990); U.S. Department of Commerce, "Money Income and Poverty Status of Families and Persons in the Current Population," *United States Bureau of the Census, Reports*, Series P-60, No. 125 (1979).

KIMBERLEY A. TURNER

PRAIRIE VIEW A&M UNIVERSITY. Prairie View A&M University in Prairie View, Texas, was founded in 1876 by the Texas legislature. A part of the Texas A&M University system, it is a statewide, public coeducational institution and a land-grant university authorized under the Morrill Act of 1890.* PVAMU has been designated by the constitution of the state of Texas as "an institution of the first class," serving a diverse ethnic and socioeconomic student population and providing education, research, and community service. A wide range of programs leading to the baccalaureate and master's degrees are offered. In addition to the graduate school, there are seven colleges: applied sciences and engineering technology, arts and sciences, Benjamin Banneker Honors College, business, education, engineering and architecture, and nursing. Cooperative education and Army, Navy, and Marine ROTC programs are available. The research thrust (with projects conducted for USDA, DOE, and NASA, among others) includes the Particle Detection Research Center (supporting Texas's Superconducting Super Collider), the Cooperative Agricultural Research Center, and affiliated with the Texas Agricultural Experiment Station and the Texas Engineering Experiment Station. The public service program includes a cooperative extension program, an international agribusiness program, and centers for economic and social research, thermal energy, and cooperative teacher education.

SELECTED BIBLIOGRAPHY
National Association for Equal Opportunity in Higher Education, *Profiles of the Nation's Historically and Predominantly Black Colleges and Universities* (1993).

SAMUEL L. MYERS

PREDOMINANTLY WHITE INSTITUTIONS, AFRICAN-AMERICANS IN. African-Americans have attended predominantly white colleges and universities since early in the nineteenth century. Beginning with the first known African-American student, Alexander Lucias Twilight, who graduated from Middlebury College in 1823, a slow but steady stream of African-Americans attended white colleges before and after the Civil War until the present day, when the majority of African-Americans attend predominantly white colleges and universities.

Until the conclusion of the Civil War and the ending of slavery in 1865, of course, those few free blacks who attended college did so in the rare northern white institutions that would admit them as students. These institutions, such as Oberlin,* Bowdoin, and Williams colleges, maintained a tradition of admitting a few African-Americans each year (often descendants of the same families) until well into the twentieth century. After the abolition of slavery, primary and secondary schools and some colleges were established for the freed men and women. The overwhelming majority of African-Americans, especially those who resided in the South, attended these schools under the strict racial segregation that obtained at the time.

A rare few African-American individuals served with distinction during those early years in white universities as teachers, students, and administrators. W. E. B. Du Bois* was the first black Ph.D. graduate of Harvard in 1896. Father Patrick F. Healy, S. J., was president of Georgetown University from 1873 to 1882. Dr. George Grant was made an instructor in Harvard's School of Dentistry in 1884. These individuals were the exception rather than the rule, as the vast majority of African-Americans attended the historically black colleges and universities (HBCUs) until the middle of the twentieth century. African-American athletes have always been accepted in predominantly white institutions much more readily than regularly admitted black students, because colleges, wanting to win athletic championships, discovered early on that African-Americans excelled in the two most lucrative college and professional sports, football and basketball. Some colleges, in the early part of the twentieth century, had more black athletes than regular black students. They generally received much better treatment, at least until their period of athletic eligibility expired. Graduation rates for African-American athletes were very low, and they began to improve only after the National Collegiate Athletic Association instituted what some considered arbitrary and controversial admissions standards, including a minimum 700 SAT score and a "C" average in academic subjects.

In 1940, of 330 African-American Ph.D.s in the United States, not one taught at a white college or university. Ninety percent of black students in 1941 attended HBCUs. The Julius Rosenwald Fund* of Chicago conducted a survey of predominantly white institutions in 1941 and found a total of two African-American faculty members, both of whom were working in nonteaching laboratory positions. In an effort to overcome this situation, the fund agreed to subsidize the salary of Allison Davis,* the eminent African-American sociologist, if the University of Chicago would agree to hire him. It did so in 1942. By June 1945, the fund noted, in a subsequent survey, the existence of fifteen black faculty members in white universities.

Five major factors changed this situation from one of virtual segregation to one of exponential increase in black students (and, to a lesser degree, black faculty) in predominantly white institutions: the World War II GI Bill, the *Brown v. Board of Education of Topeka, Kansas** decision, the Civil Rights Act of 1964,* the growth of community colleges, and federal Pell Grant legislation.

In 1944, President Franklin D. Roosevelt signed into law the Servicemen's Readjustment Act, more popularly known as the "G.I. Bill of Rights." Because the government was paying all costs, many white colleges opened their doors to African-American students for the first time. This resulted in the first surge of black student enrollment in predominantly white institutions and also served as an impetus for these institutions to hire African-American administrators, albeit mostly in marginal positions such as directors of minority affairs, affirmative action officers, and so forth. Over one million African-Americans served in the armed forces during World War II, and it is estimated that nearly 40 percent of them took advantage of either collegiate or vocational training.

The unanimous decision of the U.S. Supreme Court in the 1954 *Brown* case was responsible for the next increase in African-American enrollment in predominantly white institutions. Although the court's ruling was primarily about segregation in primary and secondary education, the impact of the decision impelled colleges and universities to gradually accelerate their enrollment of blacks.

The impact of *Brown* was bolstered by the growing civil rights movement of the 1950s and 1960s and by the demands of black student protestors and civil rights demonstrators. These forces gave impetus to President Lyndon B. Johnson to sign the Civil Rights Act of 1964,* which provided a legal basis for nondiscrimination in education and public life. Concurrent with this development was the explosive growth of community colleges. Between 1950 and 1975, the number of these institutions grew from 100 to 1,100. Because of their traditional open admissions policies, community colleges were most accessible to minorities, whose primary and secondary education often did not prepare them to compete successfully for entrance into selective four-year colleges. Thus, it is not surprising that currently 43 percent of African-American higher education enrollment in is these institutions, compared to 37 percent of white enrollment in similar institutions.

The next surge in black enrollment in white universities came in 1972, with the passage of Pell Grant legislation. These were federal Basic Opportunity Grants named for the legislation's sponsor, Senator Claiborne Pell. Such grants were awarded to students on the basis of financial need. Many African-American students whose family incomes were below the poverty line became eligible for them. Pell awards favored students at two-year institutions because of their lower tuition and thus favored the enrollment of African-American students in these colleges. As college tuition began to rise rapidly during the 1980s, these grants were supplemented with federal Stafford student loans. Student loan burdens increased as grants began to cover a smaller proportion of college tuition. This became a major disincentive to continuing college for many African-Americans, as those who persisted were faced after graduation with burdensome loan payments.

Finally, the *Adams v. Richardson** decision of 1973 was responsible for desegregating, although minimally, southern white colleges. When Judge John H. Pratt's order (in the U.S. District Court of Washington, D.C.) to dismantle ten previously segregated state higher education systems was upheld by the U.S. Court of Appeals in 1973, the affected states were required to file plans indicating how they would integrate the student bodies, faculties, and administrations of their public colleges and how they would "enhance" their historically black colleges. Since then, the states have moved with various degrees of compliance toward implementation of those plans. Nine other states were subsequently added to the *Adams* mandate. However, the NAACP Legal Defense Fund, which filed the original *Adams* lawsuit, maintained that "on virtually every measure [the] states have failed to meet their desegregation targets." Nevertheless, by 1982, African-American enrollment in predominantly white institutions in the South had increased to 9.4 percent, which represented approximately 63 percent of the total African-American enrollment in the nineteen affected states.

These forces have contributed to boosting the overall African-American enrollment in higher education and have resulted in 82 percent of the nation's 1,393,000 black students being enrolled in predominantly white colleges and universities. Although African-American enrollment has increased, degree attainment has stagnated and actually declined for African-American males at the associate's and master's degree levels. The number of Ph.D. degrees attained declined overall. The overall achievement rates for African-American students lags behind that of white students at predominantly white universities. Of the entering group of white students, 56 percent graduate after five years, compared to only 35 percent of African-American students.

The increasing enrollment of African-American students in white colleges and universities coincided with a downturn in the economy of the United States. This, combined with the lowered value of grant monies and the increasing burden of loans, made African-American students' progress in degree attainment tenuous at best. However, burdensome financial aid policies are not wholly responsible for this stagnation in degree attainment among African-American students. Equally significant are the declining state of race relations in colleges and universities, the increase in racial incidents on campuses, and the generally diminished learning environment of college classrooms. The increasing segregation of inner-city school systems, which produce a significant percentage of African-American college students, has led to increasing estrangement between African-Americans and whites once they reach the college campus. This is compounded by white student resentment over affirmative action policies, which they perceive as giving "unfair" advantage to minority students. Thus, the hostile climate on many campuses has been exacerbated by a politicized atmosphere that reflects the increasing conservatism of the country at large.

The graduate school performance of African-American students has shown three characteristics: lack of preparedness for majoring in scientific and technical fields, due to inadequate training in elementary and secondary school; inordinate representation in the field of education; and slower rates of graduate school completion because of a lack of financial resources. As a result, despite increased enrollment, African-American students are less likely to complete graduate degrees. This slowdown in graduate degree attainment, which does not portend well for the future growth in African-American professionals or the black professorate, is the result of several factors, including the rise in admissions scores required for entry into certain professional schools, the lack of financial aid and assistantships provided to African-American students, and the gradually declining efforts by predominantly white institutions to recruit African-American students.

The enrollment, retention, and graduation of African-American students are contingent upon six major factors: recruitment or outreach programs, flexibility in admissions requirements, availability of sound financial aid packages, favorable institutional climate, mentoring, and the attitudes of the African-American students themselves. Through innovative and exemplary programs, some universities have managed to boost the degree attainment and academic success of their African-American students to equal those of white students. The successes achieved by some of these programs illustrates that minority students can reach achievement and graduation rates comparable to those of white students, despite differentials in academic preparation in high school.

The shift in career choices of African-American students occurred as a result of desegregation and the resultant increased opportunity in fields other than teaching and social services. Yet, despite the near doubling in degrees awarded to blacks in engineering, for instance, African-Americans are still underrepresented in this field because they started from such a low numerical base. Education master's and doctorate degrees, where African-Americans previously were most represented, have plummeted 32.5 percent and 31 percent, respectively, since 1980.

Although the numbers of African-American faculty in predominantly white institutions have increased substantially since the 1941 Rosenwald Fund survey, they are still far from approaching parity. Although blacks are nearly 13 percent of the population, they account for barely 4.7 percent of college and university faculty; nearly half of this number teach in HBCUs. Thus, African-Americans represent only 2.2 percent of the faculty in predominantly white institutions.

Tenure rates for black and white faculty, despite a slight improvement for both, have consistently remained 10 points apart. Despite the myth that African-Americans with doctorates in science and engineering are eagerly sought after as hires for faculty positions, those with degrees in those fields are tenured at rates 15 percent below whites, even when matched for length of time in the field and research and scholarly productivity.

This vast underrepresentation and the lower rate of tenure for African-American faculty are due to the nature of the higher education enterprise. Faculty are probably the last of the true guilds, descended from their medieval origins: They pick their own apprentices (doctoral students) and in each discipline have the final say as to who is deemed worthy to enter their profession. Thus, they are a self-replicating profession, mostly immune from outside interference, and have tended to replicate themselves—white and male—successfully for many years.

The "experiment" of hiring African-American faculty to replace white faculty who were serving in the armed forces during World War II brought the first substantial number of African-Americans to white campuses. The introduction of Affirmative Action Order 11246 in 1965 and the passage of the Civil Rights Act of 1964, coupled with the *Adams* litigation, all brought pressure to bear on white colleges and universities, implying that they could lose federal funds if they continued to discriminate. These measures created the largest advancement in the hiring of minority faculty members. Both of these measures slowed perceptibly after the 1960s and 1970s, when it became evident that federal sanctions would not be applied. No university to date has lost funds for failure to hire minority faculty.

Despite these outside pressures, white faculty still control the selection of doctoral students and the hiring of faculty in institutions of higher education. Their philosophical disagreement over qualifications and "preferential" treatment for minorities is at the core of the argument over affirmative action, an argument that continues despite the factual historical record of discrimination and exclusion.

For the foreseeable future, the participation of African-Americans in higher education will occur primarily on the campuses of predominantly white universities and colleges. Therefore, efforts must be directed toward making these hospitable environments for African-American students, with meaningful and relevant curricula and a representative number of African-American faculty and administrators.

SELECTED BIBLIOGRAPHY

Allen B. Ballard, *The Education of Black Folk: The Afro-American Struggle for Knowledge in White America* (1973); James E. Blackwell, "Graduate and Professional Education for Blacks," in *The Education of African-Americans* vol. 2 (1990); Deborah J. Carter and Reginald Wilson, *Minorities in Higher Education: Tenth Annual Status Report* (1991); Deborah J. Carter and Reginald Wilson, *Minorities in Higher Education: Twelfth Annual Status Report* (1993); Manuel J. Justiz, Reginald Wilson, and Lars G. Bjork, eds., *Minorities in Higher Education* (1994); Ann S. Pruitt, ed., *In Pursuit of Equality in Higher Education* (1987); Walter R. Allen, Edgar G. Epps, and Nesha Z. Haniff, eds., *College in Black and White* (1991); Charles V. Willie, Antoine M. Garibaldi, and Wornie L. Reed, eds., *The Education of African-Americans*, vol. 2 (1990); Reginald Wilson, ed., *Race and Equality in Higher Education* (1982); Reginald Wilson and Sarah E. Melendez, *Minorities in Higher Education: Third Annual Status Report* (1984).

REGINALD WILSON

PREJUDICE AND RACISM, THEIR EFFECTS ON THE EDUCATION OF AFRICAN-AMERICANS. Prejudice and racism are two destructive forces that permeate the fabric of U.S. society and are manifested in virtually all of the nation's political, economic, and social arenas, with far-reaching consequences for both perpetrators and targets. Prejudice is a negative belief or hostile attitude toward a person based on that person's perceived or real membership in a particular social group. Prejudice is learned through messages transmitted from societal institutions such as family, school, and the media. These messages are prejudgments of others, based often on misinformation, limited information, or lies; once individuals have internalized these messages as the "truth," they are often resistant to evidence that may contradict it.

Prejudice is manifested through discriminatory practices at the individual and institutional levels. Individuals often act out their prejudices through language, avoidance mechanisms, and physical attacks. Institutionally, prejudice is manifested as the exclusion of individuals and groups from full political, economic, and social opportunities.

Racism is a systemic phenomenon that targets, exploits, and dehumanizes whole groups of people based on their racial characteristics for the purpose of amassing economic, political, and social benefits for the privileged group. The ideology of racism assists in maintaining social controls and provides rewards or punishment to individuals based on their racial category and, to a certain degree, on the extent to which they subscribe to established ideas, beliefs, and practices. This system is fundamentally based in asymmetrical power relations and is maintained and perpetuated largely by institutions and, to a lesser degree, by individuals.

In the United States, as well as in other places around the world influenced by Western European culture, racism is based on the ideology of white (often white male) supremacy and domination—the concept that all white people are superior to all peoples of color. Throughout modern history, attempts have been made to justify this ideology through the manipulation of theology, science, and psychology. Racist arguments, whether based in genetic, environmental, or cultural explanations, assert or imply that African-Americans are predetermined to be at the lower end, if not the bottom, of the societal hierarchy.

As a result of racism, African-Americans historically have been deemed intellectually inferior to whites and systematically denied equal access to and full participation in the U.S. educational system. In the southern states during the antebellum period, it was illegal to teach an enslaved African to read or to write. If found guilty of this charge, harsh punishment (even death) would be meted out to both the teacher and the slave. After the abolition of slavery, educational segregation between African-Americans and whites was strictly enforced as part of the Jim Crow laws, which were affirmed by the U.S. Supreme Court's 1896 *Plessy vs. Ferguson** decision upholding the concept of "separate but equal."

In addition to the law, pseudoscientific theories also were generated and used to justify racist educational practices and policies. Well-known scholars including nineteenth-century naturalist Louis Aggasiz and, more recently, Nobel Prize-winner William Shockley and University of California professor Arthur Jensen have argued the intellectual inferiority of African-Americans. These and other scholars have attempted to prove their theories by designing and utilizing methodologically flawed studies and by collecting data through culturally biased standardized assessment instruments such as the Stanford-Binet intelligence test. Because of pressure from African-Americans and liberal whites, the force of these genetic arguments subsided during the 1970s and 1980s. However, these arguments resurfaced forcefully in the 1990s, as educators and policymakers examined the underachievement of African-American and Latino children.

Most frequently prejudice and racism manifest in educational settings in more subtle and insidious forms, such as what psychiatrist Francis Cress Welsing refers to as inferiorization, negative labeling, and psychological attack. According to Welsing, inferiorization is the ''deliberate and systematic process utilized specifically by a racist society [white supremacist] . . . through all of its major and minor institutions, to mold specific peoples within that system into 'functional inferiors,' in spite of their true genetic potential for functioning.'' Through this process individuals are exposed to ''a stressful, negative and non-supportive social/environmental experience'' that leads to the evolution of a negative self-image and a loss of self-respect.

This process of psychological attack occurs within educational settings in numerous ways. African-American students are exposed primarily, if not solely, to Eurocentric curricula in which their voices, images, and interests are not fairly represented. They are disproportionately assigned to special education, general education, and vocational classes. They are subjected to corporal punishment and suspension more frequently than their white counterparts. Consequently, they drop out or are pushed out far more frequently. Many school officials and teachers continue to view African-American students as less intelligent than white students and maintain low expectations regarding their academic performance and ability. The predominantly white teachers in the nation's public schools, however well intentioned, bring their personal prejudices and biases into the classrooms, adversely affecting their treatment of students of color in general and African-American students in particular.

SELECTED BIBLIOGRAPHY

Gordon Allport, *The Nature of Prejudice* (1985); R. M. Baird, *Bigotry, Prejudice and Hatred: Definitions, Causes, and Solutions* (1992); Benjamin P. Bowser, *Black Male Adolescents: Parenting and Education in Community Context* (1991); L. A. Daniels, ''Targeting Black Boys for Failure,'' *Emerge* (May 1994); 58–61; C. Edelman, *The Economic Status of Black America: The State of Black America* (1989); J. T. Gibbs, *Young, Black, and Male in America: An Endangered Species* (1988); A. Hacker, *Two Nations: Black and White: Separate, Hostile, Unequal* (1992); F. Holmes, *Prejudice and Discrimination* (1970); J. Jones, *Prejudice and Racism* (1972); L. S. Robinson, ''Court Cases are Still Key,'' *Emerge* (May 1994).

SHARON E. MOORE

PRINCE EDWARD COUNTY, VIRGINIA. On 2 June 1959, public schools in Prince Edward County, Virginia, were closed by the county board of supervisors. This action was in defiance of the 1954 Supreme Court decision, *Brown v. Board of Education of Topeka, Kansas,** to desegregate public schools. It was also a culminating event in the protracted struggle for equal educational opportunities in the county.

The struggle began in 1951 with a lawsuit, *Davis v. Prince Edward County School Board,** filed by the NAACP* on behalf of African-American students from Moton High School. Moton High, located in the county seat of Farmville, Virginia, was built in 1939 to serve 180 African-American children. In 1951, when students walked out in protest, over four hundred individuals were enrolled at Moton. Although outbuildings had been provided to ease the cramped conditions, they were so poorly constructed that they were described as "tarpaper shacks." During the strike, students wrote to the NAACP asking for legal support to obtain a better facility. When attorneys Oliver Hill and Spottswood Robinson arrived in Farmville to meet with parents, students, and other members of the African-American community, they explained that the NAACP was no longer fighting for "separate but equal" educational facilities. There was general consensus that any action taken on behalf of the students would reflect the NAACP's goal of desegregated schools.

One month after *Davis* was filed in Richmond, Virginia, it was announced in Farmville that money for a new African-American high school would be available. In 1953, the new Moton High School was completed at a reported cost of $850,000. The building of a new school for African-Americans, however, did not resolve the problems in Prince Edward County. The lawsuit, which was denied at the state level, had been appealed in the U.S. Supreme Court, where it was added to other "separate but equal" cases being heard by the Court. When the Supreme Court announced its ruling in *Brown* in May 1954, it was announcing a ruling on the *Davis* case as well.

The Virginia General Assembly, looking for legal ways to circumvent the Supreme Court's orders, endorsed actions designed to thwart integration. Known as "massive resistance," the core of their efforts included the doctrine of "interposition" and thirteen bills known collectively as the "Stanley Plan," named for then Virginia governor Thomas B. Stanley. Interposition, a postbellum doctrine, supposedly permitted a state to interject its authority between itself and federal mandates. The Stanley Plan authorized the governor to close any school ordered to desegregate and also provided tuition grants for students who chose to attend private schools.

Staunch segregationists in Prince Edward County encouraged and supported attempts by their state legislature to fight school desegregation. Many helped organize the Prince Edward School Corporation, a vehicle used to collect funds to establish private schools for white children in the county. Although the massive resistance laws had been struck down by the courts in January 1959, thereby requiring those public schools closed by the governor to reopen, Prince Edward continued to resist by contesting the *Davis* case in the courts. In May 1959, the Federal Appeals Court ordered Prince Edward County to desegregate its high school by September 1959. On 2 June, 1959, the Prince Edward County Board of Supervisors announced that no funds would be available for the operation of public schools. This meant that only the 1,700 African-American students in the county would be without a means to obtain education, because the white children would be served by private schools established by the Prince Edward County School Foundation, formerly the Prince Edward County School Corporation described earlier.

During this time, under the leadership of Reverend L. Francis Griffin, president of the local NAACP chapter and Baptist minister in Farmville, the African-American community mobilized to serve their children. About sixty high school juniors and seniors left the county for Henderson, North Carolina, where they enrolled in the high school branch of Kittrell Junior College, an institution sponsored by the African Methodist Episcopal Church. The American Friends Service Committee, a Quaker organization, lent their support by locating families, generally in the North, with whom about sixty more students were placed.

By February 1960, Reverend Griffin established educational centers to provide basic skills for the children unable to leave. During the summers of 1961 and 1962, teachers from the Virginia Teacher's Association, an African-American teachers union, arrived to offer an intensive reading program. The American Federation of Teachers* also sponsored a similar summer program in 1963.

The closing of public schools in Prince Edward County and the plight of the children there had not escaped the attention of the Kennedy Administration. Although the White House did not become directly involved in providing assistance, it has been suggested that presidential concern was the catalyst for securing private donations of nearly one million dollars and the founding of the Prince Edward County Free School Association. Teachers from throughout the nation arrived in Prince Edward to volunteer their services in the Free Schools. There they followed the principles of nongraded teaching, a method pioneered by the Free School superintendent, Dr. Neil Sullivan, who had agreed to leave his post as superintendent of a Long Island, New York, public school system and lead the Free Schools for one year.

In September 1963, the Free Schools opened with an enrollment of approximately 1600 students. Three white children were included in that number. The Free Schools closed the following year when, under orders from the Supreme Court, Prince Edward County reinstated a system of public education. The enrollment in the public schools in September 1964 was nearly the same as that of the Free School.

SELECTED BIBLIOGRAPHY

Taylor Branch, *Parting the Waters: America in the King Years 1954–63* (1988); Margaret Hale–Smith, ''The Effect of Early Educational Disruption on the Belief Systems and Educational Practices of Adults: Another Look at the Prince Edward County School Closings,'' *Journal of Negro Education* 62 (Spring 1993); Richard Kluger, *Simple Jus-*

tice: The History of Brown v. Board of Education and Black America's Struggle for Equality (1975); Bob Smith, *They Closed Their Schools: Prince Edward County, Virginia, 1951–1964* (1965).

MARGARET E. HALE–SMITH

PROCTOR, SAMUEL DEWITT (13 July 1921, Norfolk, Virginia). A college president, educator, and clergyman, Proctor was educated at Virginia Union University* in Richmond, where he received an A.B. degree in 1942. He was awarded the B.D. degree from Crozer Theological Seminary in 1945 and received the Ph.D. degree from Boston University in 1950. Proctor also studied at the University of Pennsylvania (1944–45), and the Divinity School, Yale University (1945–46). His career has had a dual focus, with significant contributions made in the areas of religious work and higher education in the United States. Proctor became an ordained Baptist minister in 1943 and served as pastor of the Pond Street Church, Providence, R.I., from 1945 to 1959. During this same period he became a noted national educator and was professor of religion and ethics and dean of the School of Religion at Virginia Union University from 1949 to 1953. He served as vice president of that institution from 1953 to 1955, and as president from 1955 to 1960. In 1960, he became the youngest person ever appointed to the presidency of North Carolina A & T State University* and served in this office until 1964.

Proctor was very active in a number of religious, educational, and governmental programs during the 1960s and 1970s. He was associate director of the Peace Corps from 1962 to 1963 and worked closely with its program in Nigeria. From 1964 to 1965, he was the associate general secretary of the National Council of Churches. He worked in the federal government as director of the northeast region and as special assistant to the national director of the Office of Economic Opportunity, from 1965 to 1966. Between 1966 and 1968, he was president of the Institute for Service to Education and served as university dean for special projects at the University of Wisconsin, Madison, from 1968 to 1969. Proctor became a professor in the graduate school of education at Rutgers University in 1969, serving until 1984. He also served as the senior minister of the Abyssinian Baptist Church, New York City, beginning in 1972.

Proctor's activities have included service to many social, civic, and educational groups, and he has lectured extensively in the United States and other countries. He is the author of *The Young Negro in America, 1960–1980* (1966) and, with Theodore Roszak and Alexander Frazier, *A Man for Tomorrow's World* (1970). He is married to Bessie Louise Tate Proctor, and they are the parents of four sons. Proctor has received many national awards and honors, including over thirty honorary doctoral degrees.

SELECTED BIBLIOGRAPHY

William C. Matney, ed., *Who's Who among Black Americans* (1988); Ann Allen Shockley and Sue P. Chandler, comp., *Living Black American Authors* (1973); *Who's Who in America, 1984–85* (1984); Ethel L. Williams, *Biographical Directory of Negro Ministers* (1970).

JULIUS E. THOMPSON

PUBLIC LAW 94-142, THE EDUCATION FOR ALL HANDICAPPED CHILDREN ACT OF 1975. Public Law 94-142, the Education for All Handicapped Children Act, was approved by Congress in 1975 and signed into law by President Gerald Ford on 29 November. It was renamed the Individuals with Disabilities Education Act (IDEA) in 1990. Implementation of the law followed many years of legislative developments initiated and sustained by parents and advocates of children with disabilities. Prior to 1975, excessive numbers of these children were either unidentified, unserved, or inadequately served. Within the context of existing legislation, school systems blatantly excluded, isolated, or suspended these students, creating barriers to appropriate educational experiences. In addition to these barriers, African-American students with disabilities continued to be confronted with obstacles imposed by racism, neglect, and rejection. Implementation of the act has been instrumental in initiating some tremendous changes in the provision of special education services for all children with disabilities and has had a dramatic impact on regular education.

This historic federal law is grounded in the social and political developments of the 1950s and 1960s. Influenced by the efforts of the Civil Rights Movement to gain equal rights and opportunity for African-Americans, the objective of the act is to assure the right of students with disabilities to receive appropriate educational services. The Fourteenth Amendment to the Constitution and the Supreme Court's landmark decision in the case of *Brown v. Board of Education of Topeka, Kansas** (1954) provided the rationale used by parents and advocates in their pursuit of equal access to educational opportunity for individuals with disabilities.

The primary purpose of P.L. 94-142 is to assure that all children with disabilities have access to a "free appropriate public education which emphasizes special education and related services designed to meet their unique educational needs." Initially, the law specified services for individuals between the ages of three and twenty-one, regardless of type and severity of disability. Amendments to the law extended the age range to begin at birth. Another assurance of the law is protection of the rights of children with disabilities, and of their parents, at all stages of the special education process. The law established the parents' right to be informed and give consent prior to any evaluation or change in placement of their child. Parents have available a set of legal proceedings (due process) that may be used to appeal any findings and decisions that are incompatible with their beliefs.

The law also mandates that education occur in the least restrictive environment (LRE), one that most closely parallels that of nondisabled students. Prior to the implementation of the act, few children with disabilities were educated in the regular classroom with their nondisabled peers. This mandate reflects the intent of the law: total inclusion in public education in appropriate, normalized settings. The act encourages removal of the socioeconomic, cultural, and administrative obstacles to integration/inclusion. Also, in an effort to eliminate discriminatory testing (a factor in the overidentification of African-American students as having learning/behavior disorders), the act mandates the use of fair and accurate assessment procedures. The law requires development of an individualized education program (IEP) specifically designed to meet each child's needs. The IEP standardized educational programming by specifying content that must be included in each child's program. Although it is not a legally binding document, the IEP contains goals and objectives that, under ideal circumstances, have been agreed upon by both parents and educators. Further, P.L. 94-142 requires school divisions to encourage parents to actively participate in the decision-making and educational planning processes that have long-range implications for the education of their children.

A major impact of the act has been an increase in the number of children with disabilities who are being served in public education programs, with the majority receiving special education and related services in settings with non-disabled peers for at least part of the day.

Public Law 94-142 has been amended three times since 1975. The first set of amendments (1983) reinforced the original provisions of the law and extended research and transition services for secondary students. The second set of amendments, P.L. 99-457 (1986), improved services to preschoolers, and encouraged services for infants and toddlers (up to age two) with developmental disabilities. P.L. 99-457 reinforced the family's role in educational planning and replaced the IEP (for children up to five years old) with the Individual Family Service Plan (IFSP), which specifically addresses both the family's and child's needs for assistance.

In 1990, the act was amended a third time, with several significant changes. In this set of amendments, P.L. 101-476, the act was renamed the Individuals with Disabilities Education Act (IDEA) and its special education research, demonstration, and training programs were extended. Two objectives of IDEA are to increase opportunities for culturally diverse populations to participate fully in and benefit from the act and to increase the availability of transition services to disabled individuals as they complete their education.

Through implementation of this law, the federal government assures a free, appropriate education for African-Americans with disabilities, from birth to age twenty-one and entitles them to special education and related services. Although the intent of P.L. 94-142 is to assure equal educational opportunity, there has been considerable variation in the quality and scope of services provided. The influence of social, economic, and political inequities on implementation of the law is evident in the recurring problem of disproportionate representation of African-American children in special education categories that are viewed negatively by society. Although this law cannot be expected to singularly solve the deep-seated societal problems that serve as barriers to equal educational opportunity for African-Americans, it can be used as an instrument to help confront those barriers. IDEA and the other amendments to P.L. 94-142 reflect an attempt to address some of the concerns regarding the limited scope and quality of services provided African-Americans and other students from culturally diverse backgrounds.

Two concerns of African-American educators and parents revolve around the issues of testing and parental involvement. There is concern that even with the nondiscriminatory testing mandate, African-American students often are not accurately or fairly evaluated. Additionally, there is concern that the imbalance of power that exists in interactions between parents and educators operate to the disadvantage of parents, especially those who may be inadequately informed about or intimidated by special education regulations and guidelines. One approach to balancing these power relationships is through redefining and restructuring the participation of African-American parents in the special education assessment/placement process. Assisting parents to become more aware of their rights and encouraging them to exercise their due process rights have been suggested as approaches to address some of the issues and concerns of African-American educators and parents. In order for African-American students with disabilities to reap the greatest benefits from the act and its amendments, parents, educators, and other advocates of equal educational opportunity must continue to explore ways to increase the efficacy of the law.

SELECTED BIBLIOGRAPHY

S. R. Aleman, *Education of the Handicapped Act Amendments of 1990, P.L. 101–476: A Summary*, Congressional Research Service Report for Congress (1991); B. Harry, ''Restructuring the Participation of African-American Parents in Special Education,'' *Exceptional Children* 59, no. 2 (1992): 123–31; W. L. Heward and M. D. Orlansky, *Exceptional Children: An Introductory Survey of Special Education*, 4th ed., (1992); U.S. Department of Education, *Tenth Annual Report to Congress on the Implementation of the Education of the Handicapped Act*, Office of Special Education Programs (1988); U.S. Department of Education, *Thirteenth Annual Report to Congress on the Implementation of the Individuals with Disabilities Education Act*, Office of Special Education Programs (1991).

CHARLOTTE L. ORANGE

PUSHOUTS, AFRICAN-AMERICAN STUDENTS AS. The term ''pushouts'' has been coined to characterize the large numbers of students discharged from the educational system prior to receiving a high school diploma primarily through suspension, expulsion, or placement in special educational settings. Over the last two decades, a disproportionate number of pushouts have been African-Americans and other students of color.

This phenomenon was first identified in the late 1960s and early 1970s, when school systems were encountering problems associated with integration. Through secondary analyses of Office for Civil Rights data on suspensions and expulsions for the 1972–73 school year, the Children's Defense Fund (CDF)* found that of approximately twenty-four million students enrolled in the schools surveyed, almost thirty-seven thousand had been expelled and slightly more than ninety-three thousand had been suspended at least once, for an average of four days each. Students of color constituted only 38 percent of the total enrollment in this survey but accounted for 43 percent of the expulsions, 49 percent of the suspensions (with African-American students accounting for 47 percent of this total), and more than half of the 3.5 million school days lost by suspension. Moreover, students of color were suspended for an average of 4.3 days per suspension, compared to 3.5 days for white students. The finding signaled apparent inequities in the disciplinary systems of schools across the country and prompted administrators to investigate the causes and dispensation of suspensions and expulsions more closely.

As records were kept more consistently and school-system studies were conducted, concerned educators and citizens quickly recognized the severity and impact of suspensions on students' academic progress. Suspended students not only lost credit for missed school work but also missed valuable instruction time. Also, they generally were left unsupervised for the remainder of the day, with many parents never knowing that their children had been suspended from school. Consequently, these students were susceptible to becoming involved in acts that would result in misdemeanor charges, such as loitering, disorderly conduct, and minor acts of vandalism, thereby bringing them into contact with the juvenile justice system. Students suspended from school were also castigated by their peers and stigmatized or labeled as troublemakers by their teachers.

Incidences of suspensions cannot be separated from expulsions and dropout behavior because statistics clearly show that disciplinary problems are strongly related to the probability of students being expelled and a subsequent propensity to drop out. CDF's earlier analyses of the reasons for student suspensions are very similar to the infractions that lead to suspension in most schools today. In the CDF report, almost two thirds of all suspensions were administered for nonviolent offenses such as truancy, tardiness, and "class cutting." "Insubordination" was also a prevalent reason for suspension in CDF's study and included such offenses as classroom disturbance, disrespect for authority, use of profane or obscene language, or other similar violations of school rules, where the physical safety of students or teachers was not necessarily threatened.

To reduce the large number of students who were being pushed out of school through suspensions and expulsions, a variety of strategies and alternatives were developed in the 1960s and 1970s to better accommodate students who were experiencing academic and behavioral difficulties. Alternative schools such as Urban League Street Academies and other self-contained alternative schools, such as Free Schools, were established across the country. These latter institutions were private and not connected to local schools, used a variety of educational philosophies, had smaller enrollments, and attempted to provide students with a challenging academic environment that served students' social and behavioral as well as academic needs. Additionally, "in-school alternative, to suspension programs" were created and designed both to keep students in school, rather than suspending or expelling them, and to continue to provide them with the academic work they would have missed had they been suspended out of school. These programs were not only successful as educational innovations but also instrumental in helping teachers and administrators focus on the quantity of and reasons for suspensions and expulsions. Many students who otherwise might never have returned to school or graduated ultimately received their diplomas or General Equivalency Diplomas (GED).

The issue of pushouts is still a serious concern in many school districts, particularly for African-American students, despite the fact that only about 15 percent of these students aged sixteen to twenty-four had not graduated from high school compared to a rate of 27 percent in 1968, according to Census Bureau statistics. African-Americans still account for more than half of all students who are suspended or expelled and who drop out of urban school districts.

SELECTED BIBLIOGRAPHY

Children's Defense Fund, *School Suspensions: Are They Helping Children* (1975); Richard B. Chobot and Antoine Garibaldi, "In-School Alternatives to Suspension: A Description of Ten School District Programs," *Urban Review* 14 (1982): 317–36; Antoine M. Garibaldi, "In-School Alternatives to Suspension: Trendy Educational Innovations," *Urban Review* 11, no. 2 (1979): 97–103; Antoine M. Garibaldi, "Student Pushouts," in National Education Association, *Desegregation: Integration* (1980); Antoine Garibaldi, "In-School Suspension," in Daniel Safer, ed., *Alternative Educational Programs for Disruptive Youth* (1982); Antoine M. Garibaldi and Melinda Bartley, "Black School Pushouts and Dropouts: Strategies for Reduction," in Willy DeMarcell and Eva Chunn, eds., *Black Education: A Quest for Equity and Excellence* (1990).

ANTOINE M. GARIBALDI

PUTNAM, CAROLINE F. (29 July 1826–14 January 1917). Caroline F. Putnam founded the innovative Holley School for the freedmen of Lottsburg, Virginia, and generally assisted the African-American community in its economic, political, and social development. She devoted half a century to African-American community development, longer than any other northern white woman among the first generation of teachers of freedmen.

Putnam was born in Massachusetts; the exact place of her birth is not known. She spent her adolescence in Farmersville, New York. Nothing is known of Putnam's early education, but in 1848 she enrolled in Oberlin College as a second-year student. At Oberlin she met Sallie Holley, her lifelong companion, embraced Holley's Unitarianism, and was attracted to radical abolitionism. Putnam did not complete her studies at Oberlin, leaving the college in 1851 when Holley graduated. For the next decade Putnam worked for radical abolitionism as an assistant to Holley, who gained fame as an abolitionist lecturer. When the Civil War broke out, the two shifted their attention from abolition to aid for the freed slaves, raising funds and collecting clothing to assist the freedmen in their transition to freedom.

In November 1868, Putnam became more directly involved with the freedmen, moving to Lottsburg, Virginia, to establish a freedmen's school. Though named for Sallie Holley, the school was always Caroline Putnam's. She devised the curriculum, made innovations in pedagogy and policy, raised funds from northern friends, and taught in the school year-around. Holley joined her in 1870, but taught only intermittently.

The Holley School was notable for emphasizing a political curriculum and for adjusting the school to the needs of the African-American community. The curriculum stressed the historical struggle for African-American freedom. Putnam believed firmly in the academic potential of African-Americans, emphasized academic studies, and criticized industrial education unmercifully. A prolific correspondent, Putnam never wrote for publication. Caroline F. Putnam retired in 1903, after thirty-five years of schoolwork, but she remained in Lottsburg, superintending the school and assisting in the community until her death in 1917. Among the northern white women who assisted in establishing southern African-American education in the 1860s, only Laura M. Towne taught longer; none remained longer in the South. Putnam is interred in Lottsburg, near the school she founded.

SELECTED BIBLIOGRAPHY

John White Chadwick, ed., *A Life for Liberty: Anti-Slavery and Other Letters of Sallie Holley* (1899); Katherine Lydigsen Herbig, ''Friends for Freedom: The Lives and Careers of Sallie Holley and Caroline Putnam,'' Ph.D. diss., Claremont Graduate School (1977); Ronald E. Butchart, ''Caroline F. Putnam,'' in Maxine Seller, ed., *Women Educators in the United States* (1994), pp. 389–96.

RONALD E. BUTCHART

Q

QUARLES, BENJAMIN (23 January 1904, Boston, Massachusetts). A historian, educator, and biographer, Quarles received a B.A. degree from Shaw University, Raleigh, North Carolina, (1931), and an M.A. (1933) and Ph.D. (1940) from the University of Wisconsin, Madison. Among modern African-American historians, Quarles ranks as a pathfinder because of his major contributions to the field of African-American history. His academic career began at Shaw University* in 1934. In 1938, he began teaching at Dillard University, New Orleans, Louisiana, where he also served as dean from 1946 to 1953. He became a professor of history and chairperson of the department at Morgan State University* in 1953 and has served as professor emeritus since 1969.

Since 1948, Quarles has written and edited thirteen books and published twenty-three major articles in the field of history. His scholarship has emphasized the collective experience and the central role played by African-Americans in American history and their relationship to white American history. Some of his critics have complained that he often wrote without anger or harshness toward whites for their mistreatment of African-Americans in American history; yet others have praised him for his overall objectivity in writing about the past. Quarles' best-known works are *Frederick Douglass* (1948), *The Negro in the Civil War* (1953), *The Negro in the American Revolution* (1961), and *The Negro in the Making of America* (1964), an African-American history textbook that, by 1986, had a total circulation of 514,827. He is also the author of *Black Abolitionists* (1969), *Allies for Freedom: Blacks and John Brown* (1974), and *Black Mosaic: Essays in Afro-American History* (1988).

A civic-minded historian, Quarles has served many organizations during his career, including the Association for the Study of Afro-American Life and History* (member of the executive council, 1948–84), the American Antiquarian Society, Maryland Historical Society, and Maryland State Commission on Afro-American History and Culture, among many others. Many honors have been given to Quarles for his contributions to American scholarship and for his dedication as a teacher (over thirty-five years of service at historically black colleges and universities). He received a Guggenheim fellowship (1958–59); was an honorary consultant in American history at the Library of Congress (1970–71); and is the holder of seventeen honorary doctoral degrees from American universities, including Howard University,* the University of Pennsylvania, and Lincoln University* (Pennsylvania), among others. Quarles was married to Vera Bullock (deceased), and later to Ruth Brett, and they are the parents of two daughters, Roberta and Pamela.

SELECTED BIBLIOGRAPHY

Amos J. Beyan, "Benjamin Quarles," in Charles D. Lowery and John F. Marszalek, eds., *Encyclopedia of African-American Civil Rights: From Emancipation to the Present* (1992); August Meier, "Benjamin Quarles and the Historiography of Black America," *Civil War History* 26, no. 2 (June 1980): 101–16; August Meier and Elliott Rudwick, *Black History and the Historical Profession, 1915–1980* (1986); Linda Metzger, Hal May, Deborah A. Straub, and Susan M. Trosky, eds., *Black Writers: A Selection of Sketches from Contemporary Authors* (1989).

JULIUS E. THOMPSON

R

RACE/ETHNICITY. Historically, the dynamics of race, ethnicity, and racial formation in the United States have involved interrelated and contradictory patterns of assimilation, pluralism, and group subordination and solidarity. The terms *race* and *ethnicity* are often used interchangeably. Racial groups may include people of different ethnic backgrounds, and ethnic groups may include people with different racial characteristics and phenotypes.

The concept of race, which has no useful biological or genetic meaning, was developed by anthropologists more than two hundred years ago to describe the physical characteristics of people in the world. With the advent of European and Euro-American economic, political, and military domination of most of the world, whiteness has been socially constructed as the racially normative category. This construct has been dependent, in large part, on the maintenance of the concept of blackness as a nonnormative, alter-ego category. Racial stereotypes of African-Americans are rooted in this historically oppositional relationship, which has been used to justify and sustain white supremacy and privilege, suppress African-Americans, and stifle social-class antagonisms among poor white people, workers, and elites.

In 1903, African-American scholar-activist W. E. B. Du Bois* described the enduring, caste-like complexities of race as the problem of the "color line." He identified the inner conflict experienced by African-Americans as the result of society's normative contempt for blackness. Being black and American under conditions of white racial supremacy, DuBois maintained, forces people of African descent in the United States to experience themselves as "two warring souls in one dark body." Paradoxically, he also described this "double-consciousness" as a racial "gift." However, as E. Franklin Frazier notes in his description of the black bourgeoisie, this psychic duality has also led some African-Americans to abhor their racial identity, to refute their African heritage to gain economic and social privilege, and, if physically capable of doing so due to mixed ancestry, to abandon their blackness altogether by "passing" for white. Whether the racial identity of African-Americans should be characterized primarily by internalized self-hatred, low self-esteem, and accommodation to idealized white norms and values continues to be a matter of scholarly debate. A particularly ironic indicator of the changing but continuing social significance of race in the United States is that some whites now seek to be reclassified as black or Native American in order to qualify for affirmative action programs.

Ethnicity comes from the Greek word *ethnikos*, meaning "heathen," and came to mean "people" or "nation." It is not a single trait or a fixed category but a cluster of interrelated factors such as nationality, language, shared behavioral style, beliefs, values, racial characteristics (e.g., skin color and hair texture), religion, and socioeconomic status, which gives a group a sense of peoplehood. While ethnic identity or ethnic self-concept can endure across generations, even after emigration from another country, ethnic identification is a sociopsychological process that depends on self-identification and learned behavior. It is also a matter of choice that is influenced by changing societal perceptions.

Since the turn of the twentieth century, the assimilationist ideal of American society as a "melting pot" of ethnicities has been regarded as an inevitable and desirable societal goal. Nonetheless, many members of ethnic groups in the United States maintain a shared sense of cultural uniqueness or conscious "togetherness" based on their national origin. Noting that African-Americans have not advanced socially and economically following the pattern established by other American racial and ethnic groups, countervailing African-American intellectual traditions have maintained that achieving racial and cultural democracy requires not racial amalgamation and assimilation but group-affirming social action. They point out that historical cycles of racial and ethnic identity development and redefinition by African-Americans are exemplified by African-American resistance to slavery and involvement in political and cultural uplift activities culminating in the Harlem Renaissance, the Universal Negro Improvement Association led by Marcus Garvey, the Nation of Islam, the Civil Rights Movement, and the Black Power movement. Such movements have provided the masses of African-American people with alternative bases for developing a positive racial identity.

The particularity of the African-American experience has led some scholars to focus on the "fragility" of African-American ethnicity and racial identity. This fragility is thought to derive from cleavages within the African-American community and what sociologist Orlando Patterson terms "natal-alienation," or a form of institutionalized cultural marginality characterized by a loss of intergenerational and ancestral ties and historical group memory. Conversely, James A. Banks,* Geneva Gay, and William Cross, Jr., have contributed to a body of literature that defines racial or ethnic identity development as a dynamic, multifaceted process involving dimensions of both personal and reference group identity. Cross's psychosocial theory of racial identity development posits a five-stage development process wherein African-American racial identity surpasses the stage of internalization of white cultural norms and negative stereotypes to achieve positive racial identification and commitment.

Various explanations have been put forth to account for the relationship between race, ethnicity, social class, and the differential educational achievement of African-Americans. Educational theorizing has reflected extant social theories—from the spurious claims of nineteenth-century scientific racism to the assertions of Arthur Jensen, Richard Herrnstein, and Charles Murray regarding the purported genetic and intellectual inferiority of African-Americans in the 1960s and 1990s. Educational theorizing has also focused on issues of cultural difference and conflict that are believed to inhibit the academic attainment of African-American students. The multicultural education* movement that emerged in the United States during the 1980s attempts to address issues of inclusion of racial and ethnic minority groups in school practices, the curriculum, and the canon. However, one paradox of multiculturalism, some educators argue, is its failure to confront the historical and continuing effects of racism in education.

It is presently more commonly understood that African-American culture is incongruous with many aspects of mainstream schooling and European culture that reproduce racial subordination. Contemporary research with students of diverse ethnic and racial backgrounds has identified differences in students' cognitive styles and preferred learning modalities. It has also explored the degree of dissonance among these modalities, teacher expectations, and schooling practices and policies. Educators Janice Hale–Benson, Jacqueline Irvine, Etta Hollins, and others have focused analytical attention on ways that teachers can overcome this lack of cultural synchronization. Additionally, Gloria Ladson–Billings and William F. Tate have drawn upon the insights of critical race theorists such as Derrick Bell, Patricia J. Williams, Kimberle Crenshaw, Richard Delgado, and Mari Matsuda to offer an alternative theoretical account of persistent differences in educational opportunity and achievement of African-Americans. These approaches, which recognize the historically contingent nature of race, its social effects, and changing representations in curriculum and other school practices, differ markedly from the cultural-deficit theories that prevailed during the 1970s and 1980s. Current studies have also exhumed the implications of race and ethnicity for antiracist and African-centered curricular and pedagogical interventions as well as efforts to eliminate inequities in school funding, disciplinary practices, access to the curriculum, tracking, and assessment and to prepare teachers for increasing diversity.

Still, no consensus exists about the role of race, ethnicity, and culture in education, nor have educators reached agreement regarding how to interpret the behavior and attitudes of African-American students. Research by Signithia Fordham and John Ogbu suggests that because African-American students equate school success with "acting white," they reject school norms and values in order to maintain a somewhat specious and counterproductive racial identity. However, other interpretations emphasize that the collective autonomy African-American students seek to maintain is a rational response to hegemonic schooling that assaults their racial identity and undermines their dignity.

Race, ethnicity, social class, culture, and racial formation are important and recurring issues in the education of African-Americans. Like caste, racial and ethnic identifications have been used by U.S. policymakers to classify groups of people as inferior or superior and to meet the political needs and interests of the elite. Thus, for African-Americans, developing a healthy and positive racial or ethnic identity is necessarily transformational to overcome negative racial stereotypes and societal ascriptions of inferiority.

SELECTED BIBLIOGRAPHY

James A. Banks, "Ethnicity, Class, Cognitive, and Motivational Styles: Research and Teaching Implications," *Journal of Negro Education* 57 (1988): 452–66; Ruth Benedict, *Race: Science and Politics* (1959); A. Wade Boykin, "The Triple Quandary and the Schooling of Afro-American Children," in U. Neisser, ed., *The School Achievement of Minority Children* (1986); Alan Chase, *The Legacy of Malthus: The Social Costs of the New Scientific Racism* (1977); Rosalie Cohen, "Conceptual Styles, Culture Conflict and Nonverbal Tests of Intelligence," *American Anthropologist* 71 (1969): 828–56; William E. Cross, Jr., *Shades of Black: Diversity in African-American Identity* (1991); Harold Cruse, *The Crisis of the Negro Intellectual* (1967); W. E. B. Du Bois, *The Souls of Black Folk* (1961); Geneva Gay and Willie L. Baber, eds., *Expressively Black: The Cultural Basis of Ethnic Identity* (1987); Perry Gilmore, "Gimme Room': School Resistance, Attitude, and Access to Literacy," *Journal of Education*, 167 (1985): 111–28; Nathan Glazer and Daniel P. Moynihan, eds., *Ethnicity: Theory and Experience* (1975); Milton Gordon, *Assimilation in American Life: The Role of Race, Religion, and National Origins* (1964); Melville J. Herskovits, *The Myth of the Negro Past* (1958); Etta R. Hollins, Joyce E. King, and Warren C. Hayman, eds., *Teaching Diverse Populations: Formulating a Knowledge Base* (1994); Jacqueline J. Irvine, *Black Students and School Failure* (1990); Abram Kardiner and Lionel Ovesey, *The Mark of Oppression: Explorations in the Personality of the American Negro* (1951); Joyce E. King, "Dysconscious Racism: Ideology, Identity, and the Miseducation of Teachers," *Journal of Negro Education* 60 (1991): 133–46; Joyce E. King and Thomasyne L. Wilson, "Being the Soul-Freeing Substance: The Legacy of Hope in AfroHumanity," in Mwalimu J. Shujaa, ed., *Too Much Schooling, Too Little Education: A Paradox of Black Life in White Societies* (1994); Gloria Ladson–Billings and William F. Tate, "Toward a Critical Theory of Race in Education," paper presented at the annual meeting of the American Educational Research Association (1994); John Ogbu and Signithia Fordham, "Black Students' School Success: Coping with the Burden of 'Acting White,' " *Urban Review* 18 (1986): 176–206; Michael Omi and Howard Winant, *Racial Formation in the United States: From the 1960s to the 1980s* (1986); Orlando Patterson, *Slavery and Social Death: A Comparative Review* (1982); David Roediger, *The Wages of Whiteness: Race and the Making of the American Working Class* (1991); Barbara J. Shade, "Afro-American Cognitive Style: A Variable in School Success?" *Review of Educational Research* 52 (1982): 219–44; Susan Stodolsky and Gerald Lesser, "Learning Patterns of the Disadvantaged," *Harvard Educational Review* 37 (1967): 546–93; Beverly D. Tatum, "Talking about Race, Learning about Racism: The Application of Racial Identity Development Theory in the Classroom," *Harvard Educational Review* 62 (1992): 1–24; Patricia J. Williams, *The Alchemy of Race and Rights* (1991); Herman A. Witkin, "A Cognitive-Style Approach to Cross-Cultural Research," *International Journal of Psychology* 2 (1967): 237–38; Sylvia Wynter, "Rethinking 'Aesthetics': Notes towards a Deciphering Practice," in

M. Cham, ed., *Exiles: Essays on Caribbean Cinema* (1992); Alma H. Young, "Toward an Understanding of African-American Ethnicity," in Louis A. Castonell and William F. Pinar, eds., *Understanding Curriculum as Racial Text: Representations of Identity and Difference in Education* (1993).

JOYCE ELAINE KING

RACIAL ISOLATION IN THE PUBLIC SCHOOLS. The explosive race-related disturbances that occurred in various cities across the nation in the summer of 1967 were, in large part, the culmination of three hundred years of racism, leading to the conclusion, according to the Kerner Report, that America had moved toward two societies, one black, one white, separate and unequal. Because education is often thought of as a potential vehicle of upward mobility in American society, the 1967 race riots triggered a closer scrutiny of the pivotal 1967 report, *Racial Isolation in the Public Schools.*

On 17 November 1965, President Lyndon B. Johnson requested that the U.S. Commission on Civil Rights, under the direction of the Honorable John A. Hannah, determine the extent to which African-American students were receiving an inferior education as a result of racial isolation in the public schools. On 9 February 1967, the Commission submitted its report on race and education to the president. The study discussed the following areas: (a) the extent of racial isolation in the public schools and the extent of the disparity in educational achievement between white and black school children; (b) the factors that contribute to intensifying and perpetuating school segregation; (c) the relationship between racially isolated education and the outcomes of that education, and the impact of racial isolation on the attitudes and interracial associations of African-Americans and whites; and (d) the various programs that have been proposed or put into operation for remedying education disadvantage and relieving racial isolation in the schools.

The commission sought the services of experts, consultants, and organizations to assist its staff with the study. Papers were commissioned concerning a variety of subjects related to the problems of school desegregation. Conferences were held with school administrators and teachers. The commission held hearings and conducted investigations in numerous cities with parents, teachers, community leaders, and school officials. A special Advisory Committee on Race and Education, consisting of distinguished educators and students from across the nation, was also employed to assist the commission with the study. The commission also sought to obtain detailed information on a nationwide basis on each of the four areas of study. Through its survey *Equality of Educational Opportunity* (also known as the Coleman Report*), the U.S. Office of Education provided a nationwide database on student achievement and attitudes. All data collected were thoroughly examined by the commission staff with the assistance of experts and consultants.

On the strength of its findings, the commission made recommendations that provided a basis for action by government officials at all levels—action that would lead to educational policies that would fulfill for all American children, both black and white, the promise of equality of educational opportunity. Some of the major findings of the commission were that (a) racial isolation in the public schools was intense throughout the United States; (b) the high level of racial separation in city schools existed whether the city was large or small and whether located in the North or South; (c) racial isolation in the public schools had been consistently increasing; (d) the nation's metropolitan area populations were growing and were becoming increasingly separated by race and class—a separation reflected in the public schools; (e) racial and economic isolation between city and suburban school systems was reinforced by disparities of wealth and the manner in which schools were financed; (f) within cities, as within metropolitan areas, private industry and the government were responsible for the high degree of segregation; (g) in all central cities, as compared to their suburbs, private schools absorbed a disproportionately large segment of the white student population; nonwhites, however, whether in cities or suburbs, attended public schools almost exclusively; and (h) the policies and practices of city school systems had marked impact on the racial composition of schools.

The central fact that emerged from the commission's extensive investigation of racial isolation in American public schools was that African-American children "suffer serious harm when their education takes place in public schools which are racially segregated, whatever the source of such segregation may be." The study also pointed out that racial isolation in schools "has a significance different from the meaning that religious or ethnic separation may have had for other minority groups because the history of Negroes in the United States has been different from the history of all other minority groups." The report further explained that African-Americans, unlike other minority groups in this country, were first enslaved, later segregated by law, and, at the time of the report, "segregated and discriminated against by a combination of governmental and private action." African-Americans, the report continued, do not reside today in inner cities "as a result of the exercise of free choice," and the fact that African-American children attend racially isolated schools "is not an accident of fate wholly unconnected with deliberate segregation and other forms of discrimination." In light of this history, the report concluded, "the feelings of stigma generated in Negro children by attendance at racially isolated schools are realistic and cannot easily be overcome."

The commission further pointed out that the pattern of social and economic separation was well-established, self-perpetuating, and very difficult to reverse. However, in order to create a more just society, whereby both African-American and white children may be able to develop to their maximum potential, change is inevitable. Hence, the issue is not one of school choice, neighborhood schools, or busing students per se, but rather the elimination of segregated public education and the assurance of quality education for all students.

As a result of its study, the commission concluded that (a) there were "marked disparities in the outcomes of education" for black and white Americans; (b) there was a strong relationship between "the achievement and attitudes of a school child and the economic circumstances and education background of his [or her] family"; (c) the social class of a student's schoolmates—as measured by the economic circumstances and educational background of their families—also strongly influenced his [or her] achievement and attitudes"; (d) black students were "much more likely than white students to attend schools in which a majority of the students" were disadvantaged; (e) there were noticeable differences in the quality of schools that blacks attended as compared to those that whites attended; (f) the quality of teaching had "an important influence on the achievement of students, both advantaged and disadvantaged"; (g) the relationship between the quality of teaching and the achievement of black students was generally greater in schools that were primarily black than in schools that were primarily white; (h) there was also a relationship between "the racial composition of schools and the achievement and attitudes of most [black] students, which exists when all other factors are taken into account"; (i) "the effects of racial composition of schools are cumulative"; and (j) racial isolation in schools limits job opportunities for blacks.

The report concluded with essential principles that were deemed necessary for incorporation in new legislation that should come forth from Congress. It further explained that racial isolation in public schools was rigidly maintained throughout the United States and that African-American children suffered serious harm when their education takes place in racially segregated public schools. It also noted that we, as a nation, must commit ourselves to the establishment of equal educational opportunity for all children.

SELECTED BIBLIOGRAPHY

Brown v. Board of Education of Topeka, Kansas, 347 U.S. 483, 493 (1954); J. S. Coleman, E. Campbell, C. Hobson, J. McPartland, A. Mood, F. Weinfield, and R. York, Equality of Educational Opportunity (1966); Harold Horton, "Teaching African-American Children: The Legacy of Slavery," The New England Journal of Public Policy 10, no. 1 (1994) Otto Kerner, ed., The Kerner Report (1968); U.S. Commission on Civil Rights, Racial Isolation in the Public Schools, vol. 1 (1967).

HAROLD W. HORTON, SR.

REGENTS OF THE UNIVERSITY OF CALIFORNIA v. BAKKE, 438 U.S. 265 (1978). Few cases have captured the attention of the American public as did *Bakke*. Before the case was argued, the Supreme Court received more than fifty *amicus curiae* briefs on behalf of more than one hundred individuals and organizations who hoped the Court would provide a legal resolution to controversial issues on which there appeared to be no national consensus. The *Bakke* decision announced by the Supreme Court on 28 June 1978, entered a new area of law. It was the first Supreme Court decision that addressed the question of when voluntary measures intended to remedy the present effects of past discrimination may themselves take race into account. In *Bakke*, the Court addressed the legality of a medical school admissions program that set aside a fixed number of places for minorities.

The Medical School of the University of California at Davis opened in 1968 with an entering class of fifty students, which included three Asian-Americans but no African-Americans, Mexican-Americans, or Native Americans. Over the next two years, the faculty devised a special admissions program to increase the representation of "disadvantaged" students in each class. (The special admissions program operated with a separate committee, a majority of whom were members of minority groups.) In 1971, the size of the entering class was doubled, and sixteen of the one hundred places were set aside for students admitted through the special admissions program. Although the literature distributed by the school did not clearly indicate who qualified for consideration by the special committee, the application form asked candidates to indicate whether they wished to be considered as "economically and/or educationally disadvantaged." Candidates also were requested to indicate whether they wished to be considered as members of a "minority group," which the medical school apparently viewed as "blacks," "Chicanos," "Asians," and "American Indians."

Allan Bakke, a white male, applied for admission to the medical school in 1973 and again in 1974. In both years, he was rejected. Contending that his grades and test scores were better than those of the average student admitted under the special admissions program, Bakke sued the Regents of the University of California, claiming that the medical school admissions process had excluded him on the basis of race in violation of the California Constitution, the Equal Protection Clause, and Title VI of the Civil Rights Act of 1964* (which provides that no person shall be excluded from participating in any program receiving federal financial assistance on the ground of race or color). The trial court upheld Bakke's claim on all three grounds, and the California Supreme Court, which took the case directly from the trial court, agreed that the medical school had acted in violation of the federal Constitution and ordered that Bakke be admitted.

The Court's decision in *Bakke* consists of six separate opinions, two of which were supported by four justices. The swing vote was cast by Justice Lewis Powell. His separate opinion agreed with certain portions of the two major opinions while using entirely different reasoning to reach his conclusions. By a five-to-four majority, the Court ruled that state educational institutions could not set aside a specific number of slots for which only racial minorities could compete. Going in the opposite direction, the Court also ruled, five to four, that even absent a finding of past discrimination, race may be given some consideration in an admissions process as part of a school's exercise of First Amendment rights to create a diverse student body. In other words, the Court concluded that race may be *a* factor but not *the* factor in the admissions criteria of state universities. In a bitter dissenting opinion, Justice Thurgood Marshall* reminded his colleagues of the historic mistreatment of African-Americans and cited the need for the continuance of affirmative action programs as remedies for the effects of past and present discrimination. The three other dissenting justices (William Brennan, Byron White, and Harry Blackmun) also believed that both Title VI and the Fourteenth Amendment permit race-conscious affirmative action if the purpose is to remedy the lingering effects of "societal discrimination" against African-Americans and other minorities.

In several respects, the debate among the justices in *Bakke* mirrored the popular tensions on the problem of race preferences and scarce resources. A decade and a half after the *Bakke* decision, the intense national debate on affirmative action continues.

SELECTED BIBLIOGRAPHY

Timothy O'Neill, *Bakke and the Politics of Equality* (1978); U.S. Commission on Civil Rights, *Toward an Understanding of Bakke* (1979); "A Symposium: Regents of the University of California v. Bakke," *California Law Review* 67, no. 1 (1979).

JOYCE WALKER–JONES

RIDDICK v. SCHOOL BOARD OF THE CITY OF NORFOLK, 784 F.2d 521 (4th Cir. 1986). In 1984, a Virginia district court ruled that the Norfolk, Virginia, public schools could end court-mandated crosstown busing of elementary students for the purpose of desegregation. The court held that the neighborhood school plan adopted by the Norfolk School Board on 2 February 1983, did not discriminate against African-American students because of their race. Additionally, the court ruled that the plaintiffs had failed to show that the school board's student assignment plan was motivated by race. In 1986 the district court's decision was affirmed by the Fourth Circuit Court of Appeals. That same year, the plaintiffs attempted to get the U.S. Supreme Court to review the circuit court's findings; however, the Supreme Court refused to hear the case. The ruling of the Fourth Circuit Court of Appeals was left intact without approval of disapproval by the high court.

The ruling in *Riddick v. Norfolk School Board* may have a significantly negative impact on the education of African-American children. This ruling has left many African-American children in the city of Norfolk in racially isolated schools. As members of a global society, all children should be given the opportunity to socialize and interact with individuals across diverse racial, ethnic, and socioeconomic lines. The *Riddick* decision does not share this vision.

SELECTED BIBLIOGRAPHY

Riddick v. School Board of the City of Norfolk, 784 F.2d 521 (4th Cir. 1986); *Swann v. Charlotte–Mecklenburg Board of Education*, 402 U.S. 633 (1948).

VIVIAN W. IKPA

ROBERTS v. THE CITY OF BOSTON, 59 Mass. (Cush.) 198 (1849). The idea of separate schools for African-American children and white children was challenged in court for the first time when Benjamin F. Roberts sued the city of Boston following several attempts to enroll his five-year-old daughter Sarah in the city-supported primary school nearest her home. She was refused admission four times during 1847 and 1848, solely because of her color. The city of Boston supported 161 primary schools for children between the ages of four and seven years. Of these, two schools were established "for the exclusive use of colored children.'' Schools designated for ''colored children'' were more than twice the distance of the nearest primary schools attended by white children. All primary schools were under the immediate supervision of the Primary School Committee, which was accountable to the General School Committee. Regulations of the Primary School Committee required children to attend the nearest school, except children for whom ''special provision'' had been made.

Represented by Robert Morris, Jr., Boston's first African-American attorney, Roberts (who had established the city's first African-American–owned printing press), sued the city under the statute of 1845, c. 214, which provides that ''any child unlawfully excluded from public school instruction, in this commonwealth, shall recover damages.'' The court of common pleas rejected Roberts' claim, and he appealed to the Supreme Judicial Court of Massachusetts. Charles Sumner* (who joined Morris as cocounsel of the appeal) argued that under that laws and constitution of Massachusetts, ''all men, without distinction of color or race, are equal before the law.'' He argued that the legislature of Massachusetts did not make any distinction based on color or race in the establishment of public schools. Exclusion of African-American children from public schools open to white children was in the nature of ''caste'' and thus a ''violation of equality.'' He further argued that, although Massachusetts law gave the School Committee the authority to decide the ''qualifications'' of applicants, the committee must restrict such qualifications to age, sex, moral, and intellectual fitness; the committee could not consider race alone as a qualification or disqualification. The court, however, ruled against Roberts and refused to support the action. It reasoned that the general school committee of the city of Boston had power, under the laws and constitution of Massachusetts, to make provisions for the instruction of ''colored children'' in separate schools established exclusively for them and to exclude them from other schools. Suggesting that the schools for African-American children were equivalent to those for white children, the court concluded that the greater distance to the school for African-American children did not render the regulation in question unreasonable or illegal.

In 1855, the Massachusetts legislature responded to public opinion and wiped out the effects of *Roberts* in that state when it eliminated segregation in public schools. Nonetheless, *Roberts* became a precursor to *Plessy v. Ferguson** (1896), and raised issues argued over one hundred years later in *Brown v. Board of Education** (1954).

SELECTED BIBLIOGRAPHY

Derrick A. Bell, Jr., *Race, Racism, and American Law* (1973); Gerald Gillerman, ''Sarah Roberts, Charles Sumner, and the Idea of Equality,'' *Boston Bar Journal* 31, no. 5 (September–October 1987): 40–46; Charles Sumner, *Argument against the Constitutionality of Separate Colored Schools in the Case of Sarah C. Roberts v. the City of Boston* (1849).

JAMES E. NEWBY

ROBINSON, BERNICE V. (7 February 1914, Charleston, South Carolina–3 September 1994, Charleston, South Carolina). Bernice Robinson was the first teacher of the citizenship education schools established on the Sea Islands of South Carolina. These adult education centers were created to combat the unjust literacy tests African-Americans had to pass in order to vote in the South in the 1950s. Robinson's strategy for teaching adults went beyond the fundamentals of reading and writing to the politics of government. By getting black South Carolinians to think critically about the nature of their local governments, the American political process as a whole, and race- and class-based power imbalances, Robinson was able to motivate her students to change their perceptions of what they could and could not do to affect needed change in themselves and their communities. A recognized community leader, civil rights activist, and business woman, Robinson's contributions to the uplift of southern African-Americans have been recognized by the NAACP* (Distinguished Service Award for 25 Years of Service, 1977), the South Carolina Commission for Farm Workers (Service Award, 1975), the Charleston Citizens Committee (Certificate for Outstanding Service, 1977), the Avery Research Center (Black History Award, 1986), Hope Center (Recognition for Contributions to the Education of African-American People, 1993), and the Southern Bell Telephone Company (South Carolina's 1992 Honorary African-American Calendar).

SELECTED BIBLIOGRAPHY

Septima Clark, *Ready from Within: Septima Clark and the Civil Rights Movement* (1986); Guy Carawan and Candie Carawan, *Ain't You Got a Right to the Tree of Life?* (1989); Septima Clark, *Echo in My Soul* (1962).

LISA R. LOCKHART

ROSENWALD, JULIUS, AND THE JULIUS ROSENWALD FUND (12 August 1862, Springfield, Illinois–6 January 1932, Ravenia, Illinois). Capitalist/philanthropist and president of Sears Roebuck, Rosenwald donated millions of dollars to the African-American community by helping to build schools and libraries, contributing to the improvement of health care, and distributing funds for scholarships and grants. His philanthropic views were influenced by the writings of William H. Baldwin and Booker T. Washington.* He was a firm believer in the concept of self-help, not for the purpose of social equality but for individual uplift and the development of mutual trade between the races. Though his views reflected the separate-but-equal doctrine of the 1890s, he did support the role of government in promoting social welfare, predating the New Deal era's expansion of the federal government's role in assisting the individual.

Incorporated by Rosenwald in 1917, the Julius Rosenwald Fund was established on several philosophical concepts propounded by its founder: (a) that the generation whose labor contributed to the creation of wealth should also profit by it; (b) that donated money must be spent for immediate needs and not left to accumulate for the future; (c) that social services should, as far as possible, pay for themselves from the fees of beneficiaries; and (d) that the fund's donations be intended to stimulate public agencies in taking a larger share of responsibility for social welfare.

From 1917 to 1928, the fund operated under the direct control of Rosenwald and his family, assisted by Francis W. Shepardson and Alfred K. Stern. In 1920 a branch office was organized in Nashville, Tennessee, to assist in the construction of schools for rural African-Americans. On 1 January 1928, Edwin R. Embree became president of the fund, serving until its dissolution in 1948. During his tenure, over two hundred African-Americans scholars received fellowships ranging from one to seven thousand dollars for work on independent research projects approved by the fund's fifteen-member board. Charles Drew, Allison Davis,* Mordecai Johnson,* Horace Mann Bond,* Percy Julian, Ralph Bunche, James Weldon Johnson, W. E. B. Du Bois,* Arna Bontemps, and Langston Hughes were among the beneficiaries of this program.

Rosenwald's contribution to the building of schools for African-Americans in the South actually predated the creation of the fund when, in 1914, Booker T. Washington* requested and received help to fund an industrial training program for African-Americans. This ''Rosenwald School'' was the first of 4,977 such institutions constructed between 1914 and 1932. In order to qualify for the fund's donation of 15 percent of construction costs, a county needed the cooperation of African-American and white citizens and a commitment from county and state authorities to contribute the balance of funds and to incorporate the school into the existing county system. In 1936, the fund created a division of rural education comprised of several teacher education centers, whose purpose was to help supply the ''Rosenwald Schools'' with teachers.

The widespread lack of reading materials in rural schools prompted the fund to create a library services program, whose main goals included donating reading materials to rural schools, improving library facilities in African-American colleges, and encouraging the establishment of county library systems. From 1922 to 1948, rural schools received over half a million books, with the fund paying one third of the cost. The fund also supported African-American education by directly donating money to historically black colleges and universities.

The fund's health care improvement activities focused on two programs, the improvement of facilities and personnel for African-Americans and the distribution of medical services to persons of limited financial means. Though the fund tried to stimulate public and private interest, these efforts were hampered by segregation in the training of medical personnel. The fund also assisted in developing medical services for low-income people by trying to contain costs, operating services similar to contemporary health maintenance organizations.

Over its thirty-one-year history, the Julius Rosenwald Fund donated between sixty and seventy million dollars to educational, health, and social welfare programs. At least half of these funds supported programs that primarily benefitted African-Americans.

SELECTED BIBLIOGRAPHY
James Anderson, *Black Education in the South 1865–1935* (1989); Edwin Embree and Julia Waxman, *The Story of the Julius Rosenwald Fund: Investment in People* (1949); Morris Werner and Julius Rosenwald, *The Life of a Practical Humanitarian* (1939).

                                                                PETER A. SOLA

RUST COLLEGE. Rust College is a four-year, independently accredited liberal arts college, located in Holly Springs, Mississippi, a semirural area. The college campus and grounds consist of 125 acres of land with a physical plant valued at over twenty million dollars. It is the only four-year accredited predominantly black institution of higher learning located in northern Mississippi. In addition to national and regional accreditation and affiliations, Rust College is accredited by the Mississippi State Department of Education and has membership in the Mississippi Association of Independent Colleges. The college confers the bachelor of science/bachelor of arts degrees in business, social science, and mathematics, the humanities, mass communications, and education.

SELECTED BIBLIOGRAPHY
National Association for Equal Opportunity in Higher Education, *Profiles of the Nation's Historically and Predominantly Black Colleges and Universities* (1993).

                                                                SAMUEL L. MYERS

S

SABBATH SCHOOLS. African-Americans have had a longstanding commitment to education that predates the Civil War. Many underground educational activities were undertaken by slaves, despite the laws against teaching slaves to read enacted in most southern states prior to Emancipation. Following Emancipation, literate former slaves increased their educational activities, beginning a mass movement for African-American education. It was during this movement that native schools and Sabbath schools were established. Native schools were institutions developed, sustained, and staffed by ex-slaves without direct denominational affiliation, while the Sabbath schools were church-sponsored.

Sabbath schools provided classes in elementary education during weekends and evenings, enabling them to serve thousands of African-Americans who were unable to attend schools during the week. These Sabbath schools grew through the contributions of local African-American churches. The African Methodist Episcopal Church, the Consolidated American Baptist Missionary Convention, and other denominations established educational work as an auxiliary to their primary missions. As a result, fifty years after Emancipation more than 70 percent of African-Americans were literate.

Having been denied literacy, African-Americans developed a distinct social philosophy toward education. Literacy was viewed as a tool for social change and protection against economic exploitation. Education became an important tool for attaining economic and political power and developing racial pride. Sabbath schools, as independent schools, provided African-Americans a greater self-determination than white-dominated schools, affording them the opportunity to develop a philosophy of education without political compromise. Despite poverty and the lack of educational resources as compared to northern white schools, African-Americans overwhelmingly choose to send their children to African-American–controlled schools that were built, staffed, and supported through the resources of their communities. Tuition at Sabbath Schools was often charged on a graded scale, and subscription drives encouraged people to pledge money for the support of the schools.

SELECTED BIBLIOGRAPHY
James Anderson, *The Education of Blacks in the South, 1860–1935* (1988); A. M. Boylan, *Sunday School: The Formation of an American Institution, 1790–1880* (1985); H. A. Bullock, *A History of Negro Education in the South from 1619 to the Present* (1967); Ronald E. Butchart, *Northern Schools, Southern Blacks, and Reconstruction: Freedmen's Education, 1862–1875* (1980); Janet Duitsman Cornelius, *"When I Can Read My Title Clear": Literacy, Slavery, and Religion in the Antebellum South* (1991); V. P. Franklin, *They Rose and Fell Together: African American Educators and Community Leadership* (1990); Samuel L. Horst, *Education for Manhood: The Education of Blacks in Virginia during the Civil War* (1987); Clarence E. Walker, *A Rock in a Weary Land: The African Methodist Episcopal Church during the Civil War and Reconstruction* (1982); Carter G. Woodson, *The Education of the Negro Prior to 1861* (1968).

                                                              JULIE BURNETT NICHOLS

SAINT AUGUSTINE'S COLLEGE. Saint Augustine's College of Raleigh, North Carolina, founded in 1867, is closely associated with the Protestant Episcopal Church and seeks to develop the highest ethical and moral values in its students. The college offers degrees in thirty-eight distinct disciplines and emphasizes students' preparation for graduate studies and careers in the professions. The college recently began operating its own A.M. radio station, as well as a television and cable television stations. Its students come from the Carolinas, other states, and twenty foreign countries.

SELECTED BIBLIOGRAPHY
National Association for Equal Opportunity in Higher Education, *Profiles of the Nation's Historically and Predominantly Black Colleges and Universities* (1993).

                                                                SAMUEL L. MYERS

SAINT FRANCES ACADEMY. Established in 1828 by Mother Mary Elizabeth Lange, first mother superior of the Oblate Sisters of Providence,* St. Frances Academy of Baltimore, Maryland, is the oldest African-American institution of learning in the United States in continuous existence since its founding. The original purpose of the Academy was "to educate and train to virtue and industry colored female children in the city of Baltimore." It accommodated boarding and day students and, until 1926, served as an orphanage at various times. In the 1850s, the academy also operated a school for male students. In 1867, the sisterhood purchased a site for the school on Chase Street in Baltimore, where in 1871 a new building was erected. The building, designed by George Frederick Allen, designer of the Baltimore City Hall, is still the site of the Academy and is included on the National Register of Historic Places.

   The academy's curriculum included religious instruction and courses in English, French, arithmetic, geography, history, grammar, orthography, and writing. Students were also taught crafts such as sewing, embroidery, bead and lace work, music, and painting. The curriculum later came to include subjects such as algebra, science, biology and chemistry, world geography, typing and shorthand, foods and nutrition, and physical education. Although it was a parochial school, pupils of every religious denomination were accepted. Seen as a safe haven for the daughters of bourgeois African-American families, the academy received students from many states and from foreign countries as well. When schools were integrated after the *Brown v. Board of Education of Topeka, Kansas** decision of 1954, white students were enrolled.

Between 1853 and 1893, the Oblates initiated several educational programs in Baltimore. In 1863, the order operated a night school for adult African-American women. The convent school, which developed into the boarding academy, was discontinued in 1974; in September of that year, the institution reopened as the St. Frances–Charles A. Hall School, a coeducational high school. In 1991, the St. Frances–Charles A. Hall School was dissolved, and the academy again took the name St. Frances, continuing to operate as a coeducational institution.

SELECTED BIBLIOGRAPHY

Guinevere Spurlock, *A History of St. Frances Academy*, master's thesis, Morgan State University (1966).

JOSEPH T. DURHAM

SAINT PAUL'S COLLEGE. Saint Paul's College in Lawrenceville, Virginia, is a coeducational liberal arts institution affiliated with the Episcopal Church. It was founded in 1888. The college offers bachelor-level degrees in nineteen areas for students who plan to enter graduate school or the teaching profession or to pursue careers in business, criminology/law, environmental science, government, medicine, dentistry, social work, or theology. The college has been building upon its 105-year-old mission by tackling such regional issues as child care and single parenting through separate campus-based programs and adding an environmental science program to parallel an energy-related project. The main campus is on seventy-five acres bordering Lawrenceville; the remaining four hundred acres is former farm land with plans for future development. Several of its building include modern structures; three, including the stately Memorial Chapel, are listed on the National Register of Historic Places.

SELECTED BIBLIOGRAPHY

National Association for Equal Opportunity in Higher Education, *Profiles of the Nation's Historically and Predominantly Black Colleges and Universities* (1993).

SAMUEL L. MYERS

SAINTS INDUSTRIAL AND LITERARY SCHOOL. The names Arenia C. Mallory and Saints Industrial and Literary School (later, Saints Academy) can be thought of as synonymous. The school that Mallory built and headed from its earliest years grew to include a junior college division with a national reputation for its quality education and Christian principles. Although the school had been started a few years earlier when Arenia Mallory began her association, it flowered and grew to prominence under her direction.

Arenia Mallory originally had no plans to become an educator. Born on 28 December 1904, she spent her early years in Jacksonville, Illinois, in a well-to-do show-business family. She trained to become a concert pianist from early childhood, but during her late teenaged years, she became associated with and joined the Pentecostal Church of God in Christ. This association changed her life and created an estrangement from her family. The fundamentalist church taught strict obedience to the teaching of the Bible and forbade most show business, even any type of makeup. The church had only recently been organized by Charles Harrison Mason, an African-American, in the small rural southern town of Lexington, Mississippi. Charles Mason traveled throughout the country to spread the message of the church and garner converts to its teachings. During these travels he met Arenia Mallory at a tent revival and was greatly impressed with her.

Some of the early followers of Charles Mason felt the schools did not go far enough with regard to religious training and certainly not according to the religion practiced in the new church. One teacher began to teach the new church's doctrines in the public schools and was fired. This teacher then started a school in the local cotton-gin house based on the new church's religious teachings. The existence of the school pleased Charles Mason, who remembered Arenia Mallory's musical abilities and hired her as the school's music teacher.

Through the help of the fast-growing church and Mallory's evangelistic work for various groups, donations to the school dramatically increased. Subsequently, with the growth of the school's student body, Arenia Mallory organized a school choir and decided to use it as a means to raise funds. The group, which Mallory named the Harmonizers, was an immediate success. They became nationally famous, eventually singing at the White House. Arenia Mallory was the president of Saints Industrial and Literary School for nearly half a century and saw the school grow to national prominence, educating tens of thousands of students.

Saints, as it was affectionately called during her tenure, saw students arrive from almost every state in the union as well as Africa. For many years it was the only accredited high school for African-Americans in its area, and the only African-American school with a well-equipped library (furnished almost single-handedly by Mallory through national speaking engagements.) The school physical plant grew from its gin house beginning to become a beautiful campus with modern, well-equipped classrooms and dormitories valued at over a million dollars.

Arenia Mallory received many awards and tributes for her work at Saints Industrial and Literary School and Junior College. In 1936 she was awarded a master's degree in education by Jackson College, the leading African-American college in Mississippi. She was selected as one of the twelve outstanding women of America and earned a master's degree in administration from the University of Illinois. In 1952 she was selected to represent her church at the World Pentecostal Convention in London, England, and in 1955 she was chosen as a delegate to the tenth Celebration of the United Nations in San Francisco. Mallory was elected unanimously as vice president of the National Council of Women of the United States in 1956. She served as a vice president of the Mississippi State Teacher's Association and was a fellow of the Southern Conference on Human Relations.

Arenia Mallory received many similar awards during her lifetime, some that were unique in their day for a woman, and especially an African-American woman. But she often voiced the opinion that one of her greatest awards was having the doctor of laws degree conferred on her in 1950 by Bethune–Cookman College,* the school founded by her heroine, Mary McLeod Bethune.* This honor was superseded only by the thousands of letters and other acts of gratitude from the students to whom she had dedicated her life.

Shortly after the death of Arenia Mallory in May 1977, Saints School was closed and remained inoperational for ten years. But the school reopened for the 1993–94 school year with the addition of a new multimillion-dollar general-purpose building dedicated to Mallory's memory.

SELECTED BIBLIOGRAPHY

Dovie Marie Simmons and Olivia L. Martin, *Down behind the Sun: The Story of Arenia Cornelia Mallory* (1983).

ANSELM J. FINCH ARCHER

SAVANNAH STATE COLLEGE. Savannah State College was established in Savannah, Georgia, in 1890 as ''a school for the training and education of Negro youth.'' It was one of the first African-American public colleges established by the second Morrill Land Grant Act of 1890* and is the oldest of four state-assisted historically black colleges and universities. Called Georgia State College, it served as the state land-grant institution for African-Americans until 1947 when this status was transferred to Fort Valley State College.* The regents of the university system changed the name to Savannah State College in 1950.

The college is organized into the schools of business, humanities and social sciences, and sciences and technology. Fifty-one percent of the faculty hold the doctorate degree. The 165-acre campus, along the grassy marshlands of the Wilmington River, is one of natural beauty. The college is one of the leaders in the University System of Georgia, offering over thirty-six undergraduate degrees. Master's degrees in business administration, public affairs, and social work are offered in affiliation with Georgia Southern University; the college also offers Navy and Army ROTC programs. The college is listed as a historic landmark by the Georgia Historical Society.

SELECTED BIBLIOGRAPHY

National Association for Equal Opportunity in Higher Education, *Profiles of the Nation's Historically and Predominantly Black Colleges and Universities* (1993).

SAMUEL L. MYERS

SCHOOL SUPERINTENDENTS, AFRICAN-AMERICAN. The number of African-American superintendents, while small (estimated at about three-fourths of one percent of the total number of U.S. school superintendents), has increased significantly over the past twenty-five years. Prior to 1965, there were only four—Lillard Ashley in Boley, Oklahoma, appointed in 1956; Lorenzo R. Smith in Pembroke, Illinois, appointed in 1956; E. W. Warrior in Taft, Oklahoma, appointed in 1958; and Arthur Shropshire in Kinlock, Missouri, appointed in 1963—and their districts were small, predominantly rural school systems in the South and Southwest. After 1965, African American superintendents were in great demand in large urban areas serving mainly minority students. The surge of black consciousness and power in African-American communities literally pushed black educators into superintendencies and other key administrative positions previously denied them. In 1969, Ersel Watson became the first African-American educator to fill a superintendency in a large urban community with his appointment in Trenton, New Jersey. The following appointments soon followed: Marcus A. Foster in Oakland, California (1970); Hugh J. Scott* in Washington, D.C. (1970); Roland Patterson in Baltimore, Maryland (1971); Earl C. Jackson in Wilmington, Delaware (1972); Alonzo Crim in Atlanta, Georgia (1973); and Stanley Taylor in Newark, New Jersey (1973). Since then, more than 125 African-Americans have served or are serving as school superintendents in major U.S. cities, including Hartford, Boston, New York, Buffalo, Rochester, Newark, Philadelphia, Pittsburgh, Richmond, Durham, Miami, Birmingham, Dallas, Memphis, New Orleans, Detroit, Cleveland, Cincinnati, Minneapolis, Gary, Milwaukee, Kansas City (Missouri), and Portland.

African-American superintendents emerged during a period when the prestige of public education was very low. More often than not, they filled positions in school districts faced with the most demanding challenges, inheriting little that was worth preserving and much that needed to be changed. When they did obtain a superintendency, they were (and are today) often placed in school systems with large concentrations of African-American students from low-income families, declining student achievement test scores, insufficient funding support, and large-scale community unrest. Many of the urban school systems these superintendents inherited were viewed as reservoirs of unmet needs. Their districts were under increasing attack for not weeding out incompetence within their systems, for not finding suitable ways of rewarding those who excelled in their performance, and for not finding ways of programming learning experiences so that results could be related to methods employed. Moreover, disproportionately large numbers of African-American and other minority students in these systems were dropping out, and many of those who remained were merely passed along or pushed out, eventually finding their way into the world of work woefully deficient in job skills, marginally literate, and basically unemployable.

African-American superintendents exert considerable influence over the kind and content of education provided for a large number of African-American students. Simultaneously, African-American parents and communities have insisted that black superintendents respond to their demands for improving the life chances and educational lot of their youth. The challenge before African-

American superintendents is to be accepted as competent professionals by black communities and the general public alike. Race is rarely incidental to the assessment of their expertise and performance. Position survival and professional reputation are thus difficult for African-American superintendents to achieve and maintain. Although African-Americans impose greater demands upon them than were imposed upon their white predecessors, many whites are suspicious of their contacts with diverse groups and individuals in black communities.

Despite these challenges, African-American superintendents have made notable improvements both in the climate of the educational environment provided for African-American students and in their educational lot. However, they have not yet developed systems of education that, as former New York City and Atlanta school superintendent J. Jerome Harris notes, "mass-produce students who are able to shine and excel in the real world." Nonetheless, African-American superintendents may very well represent the last hope for thousands of African-American students that a quality education will ever be a reality.

SELECTED BIBLIOGRAPHY

College Entrance Examination Board, *Equality and Excellence: The Educational Status of Black Americans* (1985); J. Jerome Harris, "A Distinctive Application of Effective Schools Research," *Journal of Negro Education* 57 (1988): 292–306; Charles D. Moody, Sr., "The Black Superintendent," *National Scene* 54 no. 8 (1985): 10–11, 14; Hugh J. Scott, *The Black School Superintendent: Messiah or Scapegoat?* (1980); Hugh J. Scott, "Views of Black School Superintendents on Black Consciousness and Professionalism, *Journal of Negro Education* 59 (1990): 165–72; Task Force on Black Cultural and Academic Excellence, *Saving the African American Child* (1984).

HUGH J. SCOTT

SCIENCE EDUCATION, AFRICAN AMERICANS AND. Science careers are among those offering the highest economic and occupational benefits. The distinctions between the occupational attainment of African-Americans and that of whites has been partly attributed to African-Americans' underrepresentation in mathematics and sciences, where higher incomes are commanded. In 1988 African-Americans accounted for less than 3 percent of employed scientists and engineers.

The growth in the country's minority-group population drives the need for more effective inclusion in the technological mainstream, where most new jobs will require a college education or, at a minimum, proficiency with mathematical concepts and reasoning. The demand for people trained in mathematics and science may exceed supply by as much as 35 percent, for three demographic reasons. The supply of new workers is affected by a decline in the number of eighteen-year-olds as a percentage of the population, as well as a decline in the number of college freshmen majoring in science and engineering. Attrition among students in mathematics and science-based majors can occur because of changing student interests, inadequate preparation, and inferior mathematics achievement. This also reduces the number of adequately prepared entry-level workers in science-related fields.

The role of such variables as social class and gender in the pursuit of a career in science has not been well studied. In general, support exists for connecting social class with educational and occupational outcomes. Yet, social class variables may have less affect on career achievement for African-Americans than for whites. In one study, African-American scientists' families were found to have a mixed social class background, with similar levels of educational attainment but dissimilar levels of occupational attainment. African-American scientists' fathers were at least as well educated as white scientists' fathers. However, their occupational levels were of a lower status than those of white fathers. Mothers of both groups tended not to work outside the home; however, when employed, African-American scientists' mothers had jobs at higher salaries than white scientists' mothers. African-American scientists usually came from lower middle- or working-class families, challenging the common assumption that students from lower social classes who often attend poor quality schools are unable to undertake scientific careers. Measuring the social class level of African-Americans is fairly complex. In one large study, while social class did not consistently emerge as a predictor of degree completion for first-year science majors, related factors such as receiving multiple sources of financial aid were important predictors of persistence in engineering.

Among African-Americans in science-related majors, the ratio of males to females generally reflects that of the African-American student population as a whole. Comparison between women of different racial-ethnic groups shows little difference in the percentage who choose to study and pursue a career in science. However, this is not true for males; African-American males receive degrees in the sciences and mathematics at lower rates than white males. Efforts to explain gender and racial differences in students' involvement in science have included the role of middle-school experiences in stimulating (or discouraging) students' interest in science and mathematics. The dissimilarity between the participation rates for males and females in mathematics-based careers has received considerable attention. However, this same disparity among African-Americans has not been sufficiently studied. Failure to observe and understand intraethnic gender differences has the potential for attributing differences to gender that actually reflect race.

One might expect any differences in minority participation in science to be remedied by increased opportunities created by an increased minority presence in the population. However, such expectations do not apply in this situation. At the same time that there is increased demand in scientific professions and proportionally more ethnic group members, all levels of educational systems are experiencing severe difficulties in retaining and educating African-American students. Consequently, increasing the participation rates of African-Americans in the sciences will require complex and Herculean efforts.

Historically, African-Americans have had a role in science. There are innumerable examples of men and women who overcame whatever circumstances existed for them and made contributions to science. The current challenge is to ''place'' in science and technology, at a time when the chasm between the haves and the have-nots is greater than at any other and when the content of science is also rapidly changing. While everyone need not be computer programmers, scientists, or mathematicians, everyone must have the ability and opportunity to function in such a world. Even lower-skilled jobs are expected to require some technological knowledge.

Many children in poorer school districts will, at best, have access to computers in a ratio of thirty children to one computer. These same children will be expected to access technologically related opportunities (e.g., ability and aptitude assessments for college entry). Part of the challenge is to utilize the technically and scientifically competent, while providing opportunities for those whose exposure has been limited. A wide range of people with varying needs and skills must be included on the many different levels of science.

Finally, the costs associated with the production of scientists must be considered. These include costs associated with the purchase of manipulatives for prekindergarten children, providing sufficient computers for high school students, and training a cadre of elementary and secondary school teachers to employ the range of available tools, as well as support for young people selecting scientific majors in undergraduate and graduate schools. Along with the costs come challenges to creativity, for how to train and educate teachers for educating and developing diverse people, as well as how to tackle teaching and training in a world where effective solutions for social problems may be a prerequisite to effectively including African-Americans in any discipline.

Successfully engaging African-Americans in the sciences is important. At one level, enlarging opportunities and helping people acquire meaningful work are at stake. At another level, advancing the goals of the scientific community and competing in the international community depends on this inclusion.

SELECTED BIBLIOGRAPHY
B. J. Anderson, "Minorities and Mathematics: The New Frontier and Challenge of the Nineties," *Journal of Negro Education* 59, no. 3 (1990): 260–72; B. C. Clewell and B. Anderson, *Women of Color in Mathematics, Science and Engineering: A Review of the Literature* (1991); M. C. Linn and S. Pulos, "Aptitude and Experience Influences on Proportional Reasoning during Adolescence: Focus on Male–Female Differences," *Journal for Research in Education* 14, no. 1 (1983): 30–46; H. McAdoo, "Transgenerational Patterns of Upward Mobility in African-American Families," in H. McAdoo, ed., *Black Families* (1988); National Science Foundation, *Women and Minorities in Science and Engineering* (1990); J. Oakes, *Lost Talent: The Underparticipation of Women, Minorities, and Disabled Persons in Science* (1990); W. Pearson, Jr., *Black Scientists, White Society, and Colorless Science: A Study of Universalism in American Science* (1985); J. Pelham, *Factors Affecting Retention in Science-Based Curriculums at HBCUs* (1991); G. E. Thomas, "Black Students in U.S. Graduate and Professional Schools in the 1980s: A National and Institutional Assessment," *Harvard Educational Review* 57 (1987): 261–82; B. M. Vetter, *Recruiting Doctoral Scientists and Engineers for the Twenty-First Century* (1990).

JUDY PELHAM

SCOTT, GLORIA DEAN RANDLE (14 April 1938, Houston, Texas). A university president and administrator, Gloria Scott was born in Houston, Texas, the middle child of the five children of Freeman and Juanita Bell Randle. Two of her lifelong interests, education and the Girl Scouts, emerged in her childhood and adolescence. Her first-grade teacher inspired Scott to academic achievement and helped shape her lifelong commitment to education. Scott graduated as salutatorian from Jack Yates High School in 1955. Her adolescent activity as a Girl Scout foreshadowed her adult work with that organization.

Scott earned three degrees from Indiana University: a B.A. in zoology in 1959, an M.A. in zoology in 1960, and a Ph.D. in higher education in 1965. After finishing her formal education, she began a long series of higher education posts, first as a professor at Marian College in Indianapolis and then as dean of students at Knoxville College.* She joined North Carolina A & T* in 1967, setting up its Office of Institutional Research and Planning and serving as a teaching faculty member. She was on leave from 1973 to 1975, working in Washington with the National Institute of Education. During these years she served in a number of national posts with her sorority, Delta Sigma Theta. After returning to A & T for another year, she moved to Houston where she was professor of higher education at Texas Southern University and assistant to the president for research and planning. While there, she was elected to a three-year term as national president of the Girl Scouts. Under her administration the Girl Scouts endorsed the Equal Rights Amendment and funded state-and city-wide projects dealing with legislative internships, women's rights, and leadership training.

Atlanta was Scott's next destination, where she served for nine years as vice president of Clark College while teaching occasional courses at other universities, including Grambling State* and Bryn Mawr. In 1987 Scott was elected the second female president of Bennett College* in Greensboro, North Carolina. Bennett, one of two historically black women's colleges, has profited from Scott's leadership. She has reduced the college's deficit and increased enrollment. Over a third of the class of 1992 continued their education in graduate or professional schools.

Over the years Scott has been invited to serve on numerous boards and commissions. She chaired the board of trustees of Wilson College from 1979 to 1984 and was a member of the board of the American Association of Higher Education from 1982 to 1985 and cochair of the minority task force of the National Association of Independent Colleges and Universities from 1989 to 1992. She has received honorary degrees from Indiana University and Fairleigh Dickinson University. In 1959 Scott married Will Braxton Scott, who teaches sociology and social work at Bennett; they have no children.

SELECTED BIBLIOGRAPHY

Christa Brelin and William C. Matney, eds., *Who's Who among Black Americans, 1992– 1993* (1992).

ELIZABETH L. IHLE

SCOTT, HUGH JEROME (14 November 1933, Detroit, Michigan). Educator, administrator, and author, Hugh Scott was the recipient of the following degrees from Wayne State University in Detroit: bachelor of science in education (1956), master of science in education (1960), and an education specialist certificate in educational administration (1964). Scott received his doctorate in education from Michigan State University in 1966.

Scott is Dean of Programs in Education at Hunter College in New York City, a position he has held since 1975. Prior to the deanship, Scott was a professor of education at Howard University* in Washington, D.C., the city where earlier Scott made history by becoming, in 1970, the District of Columbia's first African-American superintendent of schools. He served as chief of the D.C. school system for three years (1970–73). Scott came to Washington, D.C., from Detroit, where he served the public schools there in posts ranging from elementary social studies teacher, through assistant superintendent in the system.

When it was published in 1980, Scott's landmark book *The Black School Superintendent: Messiah or Scapegoat?*, published by the Howard University Press,* was a pioneering study; its prophetic voice, vision, and insight positioned it also as the defining work to date on the trials and triumphs of African-American superintendents in the nation's urban centers. Scott's subsequent work, while broader in scope, continues to bear his unmistakable imprimatur of applied analysis and earnest counsel to practitioners, traits that have consistently marked his intellectual interests as reflected in the subjects he chooses and the audiences for which his work is focused.

SELECTED BIBLIOGRAPHY

Hugh J. Scott, "Beyond Racial Balance Remedies: School Desegregation for the 1980's," *New York University Education Quarterly* (Winter 1983); "Critical Leadership Mandates in Mainly Black Schools: Implications for School Performance and Achievement," in *Black Students: Psychosocial Issues and Academic Achievement* (1989); "The Quest for Equity: Imperatives for Administrators in Higher Education," in *Leadership, Equity, and School Effectiveness* (1990); "Views of Black School Superintendents on Black Consciousness and Professionalism," *Journal of Negro Education* (Winter 1990); "America 2000 and the Life Chances and Educational Lot of Black Americans," *NABSE Journal* (Fall 1992).

DAVID JULIAN HODGES

SELF-CONCEPT DEVELOPMENT AND EDUCATION, AFRICAN-AMERICAN. The academic self-concept of African-American students and its relationship to academic outcomes has been the subject of much discussion. Some suggest that African-American students report high levels of academic self-concept but produce low-quality academic work, indicating an inflated sense of academic competence. The status of African-American students' academic self-concept and its relationship to their academic performance may be linked to school climate factors, including teacher behavior and expectations, peer group influences, and students' general sense of well-being. Most discussions about self-concept ignore the social dynamics in schools, which may contribute to students' self-evaluation and school performance.

The perceived linearity, negative or positive, of the relationship between academic self-concept and achievement may not be valid, particularly in the case of African-American students whose experiences in and outside of school are often quite different from that of other children among whom many measures of self-concept are piloted and normed. The issues of instrumentation and validity as well as interpretation of data are also major issues of concern in any examination of the relationship between academic self-concept and achievement among African-American students.

Research on academic self-concept and achievement among African-American students has produced conflicting and sometimes contradictory findings. Many African-American students do not demonstrate low self-concepts as is widely believed. Studies by several researchers have shown that these students report high levels of positive self-concepts. However, the reported academic self-concepts are sometimes found to be incompatible with actual achievement. Lay and Wakstein (1985) reported that among African-American high school students high levels of academic self-concept depended less on actual performance than among white students. Brookover and Passalacqua (1982) reported a negative correlation between self-concept of academic ability and actual performance for some African-American students. They found that black students who attended predominantly black schools had a relatively high self-concept of academic ability but low performance scores. On the other hand, black students who attended predominantly white schools had a relatively low self-concept of academic ability but comparatively high performance scores. Brookover attributed these negative correlations between academic self-concept and performance among African-American students to the reference groups with which the two groups of students compared themselves. He concluded that the black students in predominantly black schools were exposed to lower academic competition from their peers and that their relatively low achievement was sufficient enough for them to judge themselves as academically strong, thus producing high scores on the measure of academic self-concept. African-American students in the predominantly white schools, he concluded, faced higher performance challenges from their peers and, using this higher academic standard as their reference, judged their own performance much more stringently, resulting in lower assessments of academic self-concept despite their relatively high academic performance.

While Brookover's findings are provocative and important, his conclusions may be incomplete and misleading. It may be argued that his explanation supports the stereotype that schools that are predominantly African-American have low academic performance standards and that students in these schools are usually low achievers. An alternative explanation may be exactly opposite to what Brookover speculated. In many predominantly black schools, there are committed, dedicated teachers who demand and expect high levels of performance from students. These teachers establish stringent performance criteria. Thus, students may be assessed more rigorously in these circumstances than they may be in other situations. These students may be made to feel that they are capable of achieving by teachers who continually reinforce their positive beliefs. Evidence suggests that, in some predominantly white schools, black students may be held to a lower standards of performance than their white peers because teachers believe that these African-American students are incapable of equally high achievement. In these settings black students may be assessed less stringently and may in fact be told in various ways that they possess limited achievement capabilities. This then may result in the high-performance, low self-concept dichotomy that Brookover observed.

Another explanation for the observed discrepancy between self-concept and performance reported by Brookover may be that in predominantly black schools, African-American students may feel good about themselves on other dimensions of self-concept, thus producing a ripple effect to the academic domains. However, actual performance may not be consistent unless there are well-focused efforts to also raise academic performance.

Significant enhancement of African-American students' academic self-concept and concomitant improvements in academic performance have been realized through the development of mechanisms that transform schools from insensitive, bureaucratic institutions to caring communities with high academic standards for all students. Several key school climate and program elements must be adopted in any effort to bridge the gap between self-concept and performance and to elevate both to acceptable levels among African-American students. These elements are (a) a caring, sensitive, and supportive environment; (b) individualized attention, (c) high expectations; (d) strong home-school linkages; (e) culturally sensitive curriculum and pedagogy; and (f) support mechanisms for children and adults.

SELECTED BIBLIOGRAPHY

J. Brophy, "Teacher Behavior and Its Effects," *Journal of Educational Psychology* 71 (1979): 733–50; J. Brophy, "Research on the Self-Fulfilling Prophecy and Teacher Expectations," *Journal of Educational Psychology* 75 (1983): 631–61; J. Brophy, "Teacher Influences on Student Achievement," *American Psychologist* 41 (1986): 1069–77; J. Brophy and T. Good, "Teacher's Communication of Differential Expectations for Children's Classroom Performance: Some Behavioral Data," *Journal of Educational Psychology* 61 (1970): 365–74; B. M. Byrne, "Self-Concept/Academic Achievement Relations: An Investigation of Dimensionality, Stability, and Causality," *Canadian Journal of Behavioral Science* 18 (1986): 173–86; D. S. Ford, "Self-Concept and Perception of School Students," *Journal of Negro Education* 54, no. 1 (1986): 82–88; R. Lay and J. Wakstein, "Race, Academic Achievement and Self-Concept of Ability," *Research in Higher Education* 22, no. 1 (1985): 43–64; N. M. Haynes and J. P. Comer, "The Effects of a School Development Program on Self-Concept," *Yale Journal of Biology and Medicine* 64, no. 4 (1990): 275–83; W. W. Purkey, *Self-Concept and School Achievement* (1970); R. Reasoner, "Enhancement of Self-Esteem in Children and Adolescents," *Family and Community Health* 6, no. 2 (1983): 51–64; R. Rosenthal, R. Baratz, and C. M. Hall, "Teaching Behavior Teacher Expectations and Gains in Pupils' Related Creativity," *Journal of Education Psychology* 124 (1974): 115–21; M. Rutter,

"School Effects on Pupil Progress: Research Findings and Policy Implications," *Child Development* 54 (1983): 1–29.

NORRIS M. HAYNES

SELF-ESTEEM DEVELOPMENT AND AFRICAN-AMERICAN EDU-CATION. Self-esteem is the conviction that one is competent to live and worthy of living. It is the sum total of the view an individual has of himself or herself. Some writers make a distinction between self-concept and self-esteem. Self-concept may be defined as a conscious, cognitive perception and evaluation by an individual of the self. Self-concept also implies a developing awareness of who and what one is. It refers to self-perceived physical characteristics, personality, skills, traits, roles, and social status.

Since the earliest empirical studies in the late 1930s, researchers have repeatedly reported that young African-American children have low self-esteem compared to white children. Many of these earlier studies assumed, or tried to show, a linear relationship between self-esteem and racial attitudes. A considerable number of studies have since reported contradictory findings and maintain that children's feelings of self-worth were not related to their assessment of their ethnic group. Several researchers have attempted to explain the elevated score of African-American children by investigating the effects or role of specific traits such as race, sex, socioeconomic status, and academic performance. These findings also contradicted the notion that group rejection could result in African-Americans hating themselves, a concept that has been widely accepted in lay and professional literature.

The development of self-attitudes of young African-American children has, for many years, been of great concern for African-American parents, psychologists, teachers, and sociologists. Like all children, African-American children's awareness of their individual existence and the perceptions of who and what they are result from the interaction with their environment and how they are viewed by significant others (parents, siblings, peers, teachers) within their environment. Black children growing up in America and proceeding through the socialization process have a double developmental task: First they learn and internalize the cultural norms and values of their own culture, and then they must incorporate the values of the dominant culture. These values usually are in conflict with African-American values and blatantly devalue those who are nonwhite.

Researchers who have begun to report more positive and accurate findings in terms of self-esteem among African-American children show that these children, based on the positive feedback from significant others in their environment, felt that they were competent and valued individuals. Their feelings of self-worth were not related to their evaluation of the status of their own ethnic group. Moreover, in a culturally supportive environment, African-American children have been shown to develop more positive attitudes toward their own ethnic group over a period of time.

Attributional style can be useful for understanding self-esteem among African-American students. Attributional style refers to the way students attribute causes to successful and unsuccessful life events. If African-American students feel that the cause(s) for a negative event resulted from internal (personal) traits or behavior, they exhibit the internal attributional style associated with low self-esteem. Conversely, students who attribute poor academic performance or other negative life experiences to external situations and circumstances are likely to have higher self-esteem.

SELECTED BIBLIOGRAPHY

J. A. Baldwin, "Theory and Research Concerning the Notion of Black Self-Hatred: A Review and Reinterpretation," *Journal of Black Psychology* 5 (1979): 51–77; F. Z. Belgrave, R. S. Johnson, and C. Carey, "Attributional Style and Its Relationship to Self-Esteem and Academic Performances in Black Students," *Journal of Black Psychology* 11 (1985): 49–56; W. E. B. Du Bois, *The Souls of Black Folk* (1903); M. P. McAdoo, "Racial Attitudes and Self-Concept of Young Black Children over Time," in H. P. McAdoo and J. L. McAdoo, eds., *Black Children: Social, Educational and Parental Environments* (1985); R. L. Taylor, "Psychosocial Development among Black Children and Youth: A Re-examination," *American Journal of Orthopsychiatry* 46 (1976): 4–19.

FRANCINE FULTON

SELF-FULFILLING PROPHECY. Generally, self-fulfilling prophecy refers to the phenomenon in which a person who holds a particular expectation that may or may not be based in reality acts in a way that generates outcomes that confirm the expectation. With regard to teaching practices and classroom interactions, the self-fulfilling prophecy usually refers to the dynamic whereby teachers' beliefs about the expectations of students' academic performance and overall behavior influence their treatment of these students. The students' responses are often congruent with this treatment, which confirms the teachers' beliefs or expectations; teachers then evaluate students accordingly. For example, a teacher who believes a student has the ability to learn will expect that student to learn and will provide the necessary instruction and attention. Given that kind of positive expectation and necessary attention, students are more likely to learn. Conversely, students are less likely to succeed if teachers expect them to fail. The term is typically applied when teachers expect failure and negative behavior from their students. A review of research literature suggests the following: (a) The self-fulfilling prophecy does exist. (b) It strongly influences, both negatively and positively, students' academic performance and overall behavior in schools. (c) Students of color in general, and African-American students in particular, are especially sensitive to its effects. (d) Teachers and school officials consistently transmit negative self-fulfilling prophecies to African-American and Latino students.

Several researchers have documented the influence of race on teachers' expectations of students' school performance. In a 1971 study of the self-fulfilling prophecy as a function of students' race, the teaching behaviors of white female tutors with African-American and white seventh-and eighth-grade students were investigated. The following behaviors were measured: teacher attention to student statements (subdivided into attention to requested statements and attention to spontaneous student statements); teacher encouragement of student statements, teacher elaboration of student statements, teacher ignoring of student statements, teacher praise of student statements, and teacher criticism of student statements. The results of the study showed a significant difference between African-American and white students in the amount of interaction each group received with white teachers. "Gifted" white students received significantly more attention than "gifted" black students; tutors requested more information from white students, more often ignored the statements of black students, praised black students less, and criticized black students more.

Stereotyping of black children as nonachievers occurs not only among white teachers but also among African-American teachers. A 1974 study investigated teacher expectation in an all-black school, with children in grades one through six and their teachers. Twenty percent of the children were identified beforehand as "bloomers," that is, as high achievers, and their names were submitted to the teachers. Teachers were then observed in their classrooms with all the students. It was documented that the teachers treated the bloomers more negatively than those without that identification. Findings from the studies cited here suggest that both black and white teachers have internalized beliefs about the inability of some black children to achieve academically, contributing to a self-fulfilling prophecy of school failure among these children.

The low expectations held by teachers and school officials regarding academic achievement and in-school behaviors of African-Americans are usually based on distorted and biased views of the values, norms, and practices of African-American culture and community and the inaccurate assessment of black students. African-American parents are stereotyped as lacking concern and commitment toward their children's education, which limits how and the extent to which teachers and school officials communicate with the parents. Similarly, students are stereotyped as more likely to deviate from established school standards and expectations, that is, to be troublemakers. Moreover, African-American students are often assumed to be intellectually inferior because of environmental or genetic deficits, or sometimes both. The setting and context in which learning occurs may also influence teacher expectations. Factors such as complexity of the classroom setting, ability grouping, ambiguity in student performance, and teachers' beliefs about their own ability to shape student performance all affect what teachers expect from their students.

SELECTED BIBLIOGRAPHY

J. B. Dusek, "Do Teachers Bias Children's Learning?" *Review of Education Research* 45, no. 4 (1975): 661–84; T. L. Good, "Research on Teacher Expectations," *Eric Research Document ED 249587* (1984); R. Rosenthal, R. Baratz, and C. M. Hall, "Teacher Behavior, Teacher Expectations and Gains in Pupil's Related Creativity," *Journal of Educational Psychology* 124 (1974): 115–21; R. C. Rubovits and M. L. Maehr, "Pygmalion Black and White," *Journal of Personality and Social Psychology* 19 (1971): 197–294; K. C. Smith, "Teacher Expectations and Minority Achievements: A Study of Black Students in Fairfax County," *Eric Research Document 307355* (1989).

NORRIS M. HAYNES

SELF-HELP TRADITION, AFRICAN-AMERICAN. The argument can be made that for as long as African-Americans have been in the United States, they have shown a remarkable propensity to engage in self-help activities. Therefore, the self-help tradition in education evident among African-Americans today is long-standing. As early as 1790, free African-Americans in several metropolitan areas established organizations whose expressed purpose was to further the cause of education.

With the abolition of slavery came African-Americans' quest for the formal education prohibited by slavery, and the pursuit of education became one of the driving forces within African-American communities. Although northern philanthropists and some compassionate southern whites assisted, the early education of African-Americans was, for the most part, dependent on their own efforts. A number of African-American organizations coalesced to participate significantly in the educational process within the African-American community. Chief among these self-help organizations were the African-American press, church, social and fraternal organizations, and literary organizations.

A great deal of the early focus on self-help was on educating southern African-Americans on how to live in urban areas. Numerous treatises have detailed the role of the Urban League affiliates and especially the African-American press in this regard. In particular, African-American newspapers and magazines provided their readers with instructions on appropriate dress, behavior, language, and the like. In providing such messages and others on the importance of education, the African-American press established the groundwork for self-help to flourish. Additionally, the African-American press prompted participation in self-elevation organizations by its coverage of self-help activities.

The African-American church contributed vastly to the education of African-Americans by making religious reading material readily available. In addition, black churches housed the earliest YMCAs for African-Americans, among the most important educational agencies in black communities. Most importantly, the African-American church served the ultimate self-help function in its establishment and financing of educational institutions at all levels. Its role in the development of African-American institutions of higher learning is legendary. Members of various religious denominations within African-American communities willingly raised funds to support the education of black America's future leadership.

African-American social organizations excelled in helping further education among African-Americans. For example, the Elks provided scholarships for youth and encouraged them to stay in school by sponsoring programs in Elk lodges throughout the country. African-American fraternities and sororities also actively promoted the education of black youth by providing numerous educational and informational projects for the African-American community. In addition to providing financial assistance, several fraternal organizations sponsored educational campaigns such as, "Go to High School—Go to College" and provided a traveling library to several southern states.

African-American literary, historical, and debate societies in large cities such as Philadelphia, New York, and Washington augmented the classroom education of African-Americans. Among the community-wide educational activities provided by the societies were lectures, exhibitions, and conferences.

Of special note was the establishment of the Association for the Study of Negro Life and History in 1915. This organization, later renamed the Association for the Study of Afro-American Life and History,* planned educational programs focusing on African-American history and culture and served as a catalyst for self-help activities related to the education of African-Americans. Many of the self-help activities conducted by organizations in the late 1800s and early 1900s survive to the present day. Various organizations develop and implement service and charitable projects of an educational nature. On a national level, the National Association for the Advancement of Colored People* and the National Urban League* improve the African-American community through community-wide educational activities. Some mention must also be made of the critical presence of African-American women among the thousands of self-help organizations that have existed through the years. It is no exaggeration to assert that self-help organizations would not have thrived were it not for African-American women.

Locally, many African-American churches sponsor educational fairs, provide tutors, and sponsor "Rites of Passage" programs for African-American children and adolescents. Also, numerous chapters of Boy Scouts, Girl Scouts, Camp Fire Boys and Girls, and Junior Achievement are found in African-American churches throughout the United States. All these groups help to expand the learning that takes place in formal settings. Local chapters of African-American sororities and fraternities have developed numerous educational self-help programs. These organizations have shown leadership in seeking and receiving funding from governmental and private organizations in order to improve the educational base within African-American communities. A number of these chapters have developed programs in such areas as drug abuse, teenage pregnancy, poverty, unemployment, health education, and crime prevention. In addition, these chapters have cooperated with other community groups to sponsor workshops, seminars, and conferences on issues of importance to African-American communities. In a similar vein, members of local chapters of organizations such as the National Coalition of 100 Black Women, the National Council of Negro Women, and Concerned Black Men serve as big brothers and sisters to numerous African-American youth. Through role modeling and mentoring, these groups expose African-American youth to a wide variety of training and opportunities. These chapters also provide financial support for many organizations, educational institutions, and programs.

Without a doubt, the status of black America has been and continues to be tremendously improved by the educational activities of its newspapers and its religious, social, and Greek-letter organizations.* As forces within society continue to make it necessary for African-Americans to organize in their own self-interest, it seems reasonable to conclude that such organizations will continue to provide leadership in many areas including education, and that self-help among African-Americans will continue well into the twenty-first century.

SELECTED BIBLIOGRAPHY

W. E. B. Du Bois, *Some Efforts of American Negroes for Their Own Social Betterment* (1898); Vincent P. Franklin, *The Education of Black Philadelphia: The Social and Educational History of a Minority Community, 1900–1950* (1979); Darlene Clark Hine, ed., *Black Women in America: An Historical Encyclopedia* (1993); Dorothy Porter, ''The Organized Educational Activities of Negro Literary Societies, 1828–1846,'' *Journal of Negro Education* (October 1939).

CAROLYN STROMAN

SELMA UNIVERSITY. Selma University in Selma, Alabama, opened its doors on 1 January 1878. Since its founding, it has been operated by the Alabama State Missionary Baptist Convention. Selma University is today a fully accredited, private coeducational Christian liberal arts college dedicated to the task of preparing students for useful and responsible living and for training Christian leaders. The school confers the following degrees: associate of arts, associate of science, associate in applied science, bachelor of arts, and bachelor of science. In addition, it offers a certificate and diploma program in Bible and theology. New degree programs have been developed to serve a student population reflecting the demographic, socioeconomic, and educational diversity found in central and ''Black Belt'' regions of Alabama as well as other states and foreign countries. Special academic programs and services in a supportive and Christian atmosphere provide the climate in which this purpose can be attained.

SELECTED BIBLIOGRAPHY

National Association for Equal Opportunity in Higher Education, *Profiles of the Nation's Historically and Predominantly Black Colleges and Universities* (1993).

SAMUEL L. MYERS

SERRANO v. PRIEST, 5 Cal. 3d 584 P.2d 1241 (1971). In 1968, the Western Center on Law and Poverty initiated a suit on behalf of taxpayers and their children who were public school students. The suit asked that California's school finance system be declared unconstitutional and that the court grant an injunctive relief requiring school officials to reallocate school finance funds. The trial court dismissed the action. This decision was upheld in the California Court of Appeals. In August 1971, the California State Supreme Court reversed the decision, handing down the landmark decision of *Serrano v. Priest*.

The basic theory of the case was that school finance systems based on local district wealth are "suspect classifications" requiring proof of "compelling state interest" in maintaining such finance systems. In the *Serrano case*, the court accepted education as a "fundamental interest" protected by the constitution and held that a statutory classification making the quality of a child's education dependent on the wealth of a school district is unconstitutional. The decision was based heavily on a newly emerging interpretation of "equal protection" of rights guaranteed under the Fourteenth Amendment to the U.S. Constitution. In short, school funding schemes based on the wealth of individual districts seriously impede equal educational opportunity for the children in poorer districts. The court could not find a compelling state interest to reinforce and maintain this kind of inequality.

Although the U.S. Supreme Court reversed the *Serrano* decision in a similar case, *San Antonio Independent School District v. Rodriguez*, in 1973, *Serrano v. Priest* has had the significant effect of having many state legislatures reexamine and in some cases reform state systems of educational finance for poorly funded districts.

SELECTED BIBLIOGRAPHY

Kern Alexander, *School Law* (1980); William R. Hazard, *Education and the Law*, 2d ed. (1978); Joseph T. Henke, "Financing Public Schools in California: The Aftermath of *Serrano v. Priest* and Proposition 13," *University of San Francisco Law Review* 21 (Fall 1986): 1–39; Jay D. Scribner et al., "School Finance Reform: The Aftermath of *Serrano v. Priest*," *Education and Urban Society* (February 1973): 133–47; William D. Valenti, *Law in the Schools* (1980).

KRINER CASH

SHAED SISTERS OF WASHINGTON, D.C. The five Shaed sisters of Washington comprise a family that contributed uniquely, substantially, and significantly to the public schools of the District of Columbia between 1922 and 1969. Most of this period was in the era of racially segregated education, a time when African-American educators made it their life's work to instruct African-American children well and hold them to standards of excellence, thereby positively influencing the capabilities of the young and the future of the race. These exemplary practitioners taught and served in supervisory positions in the elementary schools; each sister was recognized as being an educator who demanded from students the highest standards in productive education. Each of the sisters received numerous professional and personal honors for contributions to education and to the community. All five Shaed sisters possessed an unmistakable family physiognomy, but had variant personalities. All five were honor students and high achievers who demonstrated superior mental acuity, a proclivity for sharing their professional skills, wide-ranging interests, and general vibrancy.

The sisters and one brother, Gregory, a physician, were the children of Gregory W. Shaed, Sr., and Cenos Detwyler Shaed. Both parents were Florida natives who migrated to Washington, D.C., in 1900, seeking a life of increased significance and rewards. Mr. Shaed was one of the first African-Americans to qualify through the Civil Service examination for the position of "printer"—monotypist and linotypist—at the U.S. Government Printing Office, where he served from 1900 to 1939. Mrs. Shaed was a lifelong, prototypic homemaker. The two were highly literate at a time when most African-Americans were not, and they possessed total commitment to the importance of intellectual development. They established a supportive home environment of high expectations, which stimulated their offspring to educational achievement and community betterment.

Alice Evelyn Shaed (23 June 1902–24 July 1963), the eldest offspring, was born in Orlando, Florida, where her mother had returned for the birth of her first child. A high academic achiever, Alice graduated from Dunbar High School* in 1920 and attained the two-year teaching diploma from Miner Normal School in 1922. Later, without taking educational leave from her employment, Miss Shaed received a bachelor's degree from Howard University* in 1941 and a master of arts degree from Catholic University in 1946.

Alice Shaed began a forty-one year teaching career on 1 September 1922, in a first-grade classroom at Smothers Elementary School. Subsequently she taught at Wormley Elementary School and at Harrison School. Within ten years it became apparent that Miss Shaed was an exceptionally gifted teacher, and she attained the highest evaluation of "ES" (eminently superior), the rarely bestowed top annual rating in the public school system. At Harrison School she was regarded as being peerless as an intermediate-grades instructor, especially adroit in teaching the definitive arithmetic functions of long division, fractions, and decimals.

In recognition of this high quality of productive classroom teaching, Alice Shaed was selected to teach at the Morgan Demonstration School, an in-service, teacher-education facility of the public school system. From 1935 to 1945 her demonstration teaching for novice and faltering teachers became widely known. She was adept at showing them how to individualize and personalize the instruction of heterogeneous learners.

In 1945, Alice Shaed was appointed to the Department of Supervision and Instruction as a supervisor of intermediate grades. In 1957 she was promoted to the position of supervising director of this department for the entire school system, a position she held until her death in 1963. In this role she was generally acclaimed for providing effective, productive instructional supervision as a positive, helping, motivating service rather than as a negative, punitive, judgmental procedure. Alice Shaed was a frequent contributor to the professional journal *Mathematics Teacher*. Also, she served on major committees and represented the District of Columbia Public Schools at numerous regional and national conferences on the teaching of the new mathematics. On 17 May 1973, the Alice and Ernestine Shaed Elementary School was dedicated to honor these two sisters, the latter of whom died in 1970. It is the only public school in the District of Columbia named for two family members.

Ernestine Pamela Shaed (11 January 1904–11 April 1970), the second daughter, served as a peerless primary-grades teacher for forty-three years. An honor student, she graduated from Dunbar High School, then from the elementary two-year teacher education program at Miner Normal School in 1926. Her initial teaching appointment occurred in 1927 in Alexander Crummell Elementary School, where she earned an enviable reputation as a truly gifted teacher of reading. After three years at Crummell, she was transferred to the Lucretia Mott Elementary School, where she taught for the next forty years except for a brief period at Twining Elementary School. Her innovative, integrated methods of teaching reading were honed over many years to a legendary level of proficiency. In 1969, in recognition of her exceptional contribution to Mott School, Ernestine Shaed was honored as "Teacher of the Year." Ernestine Shaed was very effective as a teacher of prospective teachers. She served as a cooperating teacher for teacher education students at Howard University* and the D.C. Teachers College. She also served on numerous curriculum development committees in the public schools and frequently participated in in-service education programs. As indicated above, her exceptional pedagogical and community services were recognized and honored with those of her elder sister, Alice, by the naming of the Alice and Ernestine Shaed Elementary School on 17 May 1973.

Helen Virginia Shaed Waters (26 March 1906), the third daughter, was born in Washington, D.C. Her childhood interest and skills in the graphic arts led her to attend Armstrong Technical High School, from which she graduated as a high-achieving student in 1923. She graduated from Miner Normal College in 1925, then taught for one year in the public schools of Greenville, North Carolina. In 1926 she began her outstanding forty-year teaching career in the D.C. public schools, serving as a second-grade teacher at both Cook School (1926–28) and B. K. Bruce School (1928–31). Beginning in 1932 and for the next thirty-five years, Helen Shaed Waters taught intermediate grades 4, 5, or 6 in nine public schools and was recognized as an exceptionally gifted teacher. These schools were John J. Cook (1932–49); W. Scott Montgomery (1949–53); Leon Perry (1953–54); Petworth (1954–55); John Eaton School Reading Clinic (1955–58); Bancroft (1958–59); Bundy (1959–63); and River Terrace (1963–66). During her career she was honored as a model teacher, a master teacher, an eminently superior teacher, and as a demonstration teacher throughout the D.C. Public Schools system. She received special commendations for the consistent above-norms mastery of academic subjects that her classes attained regularly between the October and June citywide testing periods.

Prior to the time that the term "enrichment" became a regular part of pedagogical nomenclature and goals, Helen conducted a multiplicity of broadening experiences with her classes. Also, she participated in diverse extracurricular activities at all of the schools in which she taught. She did informal counseling with difficult pupils who were not being reached by other teachers. Her rewards have included having many of these students later return to credit her with the beginnings of their attainment in life. She vigorously supported the Parent

Teacher Association (PTA) programs and activities in each of the schools where she was employed. Helen studied further at the D.C. Teachers College, Howard University, and Syracuse University. She was noted for her storehouse of information and her precise diction. Her former pupils recall fondly Mrs. Waters' wide-ranging, interesting explanations of abstruse words and events. She has been an active member of St. George's Episcopal Church since the 1930s.

Dorothy Lee Louise Shaed Proctor (11 August 1910), the fifth child (and fourth daughter), was born in Washington, D.C. She graduated from Dunbar High School* as an outstanding student in 1927. In 1930 she graduated as the salutatorian from Miner Normal School and as a member of its three-year teacher certification program. Miner had expanded its pedagogic program from the original one-year program to a two-year course in 1897 and to a three-year course in 1926. Later she earned the B.A. degree (1937) and the M.S. degree (in clinical psychology, 1945) at Howard University. She pursued additional study at New York University, George Washington University, and D.C. Teachers College. Beginning with her initial appointment to teach the primary grades at Henry Smothers Elementary School in 1930, Dorothy taught and/or served as an administrator in various elementary schools until 1965: Henry Smothers School (1930–42); Briggs–Montgomery School (1942–45); Morgan demonstration School (1945–54); teaching principal at the Military Road School for the Trainable Retarded (1954–59); Brookland Elementary School (1957–59); and Powell Elementary School (1959–65). She served also as an elementary summer school principal in 1956 and 1957.

As was the case with her sisters, Dorothy was identified as a superior classroom teacher. Initially recognized as an outstanding teacher of developmental reading in the primary grades, she became equally renowned as an intermediate-grades teacher during the latter years of her service. Her social studies projects were particularly noteworthy. She worked also with prospective teachers in training at Catholic University, Miner Teachers College, and Dumbarton College. After retiring in 1965, Dorothy Shaed Proctor worked as a clinical psychologist in the Pupil Personnel Department of the public schools. From 1968 to 1972, she served with distinction in that capacity on both elementary and secondary school levels. Throughout her adult life, Dorothy was the most actively involved of the five Shaed sisters in a multiplicity of professional education organizations, philanthropic groups, fraternal organizations, and religious institutions. She received numerous awards and citations for her unstinting service.

Eunice Jane Shaed Newton (5 April 1913), the sixth and youngest child, was born in Washington, D.C. She graduated with honors from Dunbar High School in 1930; in 1934 she earned the bachelor of science in elementary education, summa cum laude, at Miner Teachers College, Washington, D.C. She earned the master of arts degree in 1938 from Teachers College, Columbia University (New York), and the doctor of education degree from the University of Pennsylvania in 1953. Her additional study was pursued at the University of Chicago

(1945, 1946), George Washington University Law Center, D.C. (1980–81), and American University, D.C. (1983).

Eunice began her teaching career in September 1934 at Anthony Bowen Elementary School. Although her service as a teacher in the D.C. public schools was for only thirteen years, and therefore the shortest tenure of the five Shaed sisters, her overall career in public education was the longest and most varied. She was employed forty-five years (1934–79) variously as a public school teacher, college professor, supervisor, department chairman, associate dean, director of elementary education, and other administrative positions at all levels of education—elementary, secondary, college, and university. After receiving her doctorate, Dr. Newton was employed as an adjunct professor at Miner Teachers College, Washington, D.C. From 1947 to 1956 she was employed in Raleigh, North Carolina, as an elementary and junior high school supervisor; from 1956 to 1962 she was director of college reading skills centers at Morgan State College,* Bennett College,* and North Carolina Central University;* served as visiting professor at the University of Pennsylvania Summer School, 1955–56; as national consultant for SRA and director of SRA Reading Institutes throughout the United States, 1956–62; and at Howard University, Washington, D.C., as associate dean, College of Liberal Arts, 1965–68; as director of elementary education, 1962–65; as chairman of the Department of Education, 1968–70; as visiting professor of comparative education, World Campus Afloat, spring semesters 1968 and 1972; as director, USOE Summer Teachers Institutes, NDEA, 1965; EPDA, 1970; as professor of education, 1962–79; and as director, Center for Academic Reinforcement, 1974–79.

Eunice Shaed Newton's ardent interest in the role of the language arts in academic achievement remained with her throughout her professional career. The critical importance of verbal communication in our symbolic/technological society became the dominant focus of her research, writing, and collateral activities. She has contributed to new knowledge through the publication of thirty-three refereed articles in national and international journals and a book. Following her retirement in 1979, Dr. Newton was a research fellow at the Moton Center for Independent Studies and a tutor in writing skills at the Howard University Law Center. She has continued to write and to serve as a consultant and board member of significant educational organizations.

Together, these five sisters have contributed 176 years of combined, cumulative services to the field of education, primarily in Washington, D.C.

CAROLYN HOLLOMAN TROUPE

SHAW UNIVERSITY. Shaw University, in Raleigh, North Carolina, was founded in 1865. It is the oldest historically black university in the South. In addition to the liberal arts and science offerings, the university features specialized degree programs in speech pathology and audiology, radio and television, adaptive physical education (pre-therapy), engineering, and computer studies. Its Division of International Studies offers a major in international relations with emphasis placed on Africa, the Caribbean, and the Middle East. Its Center for Alternative Programs of Education (CAPE) allows students an opportunity to pursue an academic degree through independent study, flexible course scheduling, and credit for prior learning experiences. CAPE Centers are located in several cities in North Carolina.

SELECTED BIBLIOGRAPHY

National Association for Equal Opportunity in Higher Education, *Profiles of the Nation's Historically and Predominantly Black Colleges and Universities* (1993).

SAMUEL L. MYERS

SHEPARD, JAMES EDWARD (3 November 1875, Raleigh, North Carolina– 6 October 1947, Durham, North Carolina). Educator and college founder, Shepard was the son of Reverend Augustus and Mrs. Harriet Whitted Shepard. He received his undergraduate and professional training at Shaw University.* When Shepard graduated from Shaw University's School of Pharmacy in 1894, he became one of North Carolina's first African-American pharmacists. However, his father's influence as a Baptist minister weighed heavily in his decision to accept an appointment as field superintendent of "work among Negroes" for the International Sunday School Association in Chicago, Illinois, with the southern region as his prime responsibility. Shepard worked directly with African-American churches to improve the literacy skills among the church leadership. He was also an active member of the Republican Party and in the late 1890s served as a member of the North Carolina state advisory board of the Republican conference. In 1897, Shepard was appointed chief clerk in the Recorder of Deeds Office in Washington, D.C., and one year later became the deputy collector of Internal Revenue in Raleigh, North Carolina.

In 1910, Shepard founded the National Religious Training School and Chautauqua in Durham, North Carolina. It was later renamed the National Training School. The school received support from numerous friends of its president, both African-American and white. The North Carolina General Assembly gave its support to the institution in 1923, and the name was changed again, this time to the Durham State Normal School. In 1925, Shepard's school became the North Carolina College for Negroes and the nation's first state-supported liberal arts college for Americans of African ancestry. In 1947, the name was changed once more to North Carolina College at Durham. In 1969, when it became a regional state university, it was renamed North Carolina Central University.* Presently, the university's main campus library is named as a memorial to Shepard, and his statue stands in front of the school's administration building. The city's African-American chapter of the Sertoma Club is also named in his honor, as well as a public middle school.

In addition to making his mark in religion and education, Shepard collaborated with a group of Durham's influential African-American businessmen to found the North Carolina Mutual Life Insurance Company (1898), Lincoln Hospital (1901), and Mechanics and Farmers Bank (1907).

SELECTED BIBLIOGRAPHY
Materials on file at the North Carolina Central University Archives, Durham, North Carolina.

                                                              WALTER M. BROWN

SHORTER COLLEGE. Shorter College, a two-year liberal arts coeducational institution, affiliated with the African Methodist Episcopal Church, was founded in Little Rock, Arkansas, in 1886. Shorter is accredited by the North Central Association of Colleges and Schools and serves a unique role in developmental education among the institutions of higher learning in Arkansas. For 100 years, the college has been committed to the mission that can be clearly seen in its original charter and the current mission statement. Five key elements identify that mission: (a) provide quality education in a Christian atmosphere, (b) provide opportunities to those who may be economically and/or educationally disadvantaged, (c) provide a liberal arts education leading to an A.A. degree or A.S. degree, (d) provide an open-door admission policy toward all ethnic groups, and (e) provide educational resources for community development.

SELECTED BIBLIOGRAPHY
National Association for Equal Opportunity in Higher Education, *Profiles of the Nation's Historically and Predominantly Black Colleges and Universities* (1993).

                                                              SAMUEL L. MYERS

SINGLETON v. JACKSON MUNICIPAL SEPARATE SCHOOL DISTRICT, 419 F.2d 1211 (5th Cir. 1970). In the wake of the systemic changes necessitated by the dismantling of dual school systems after *Brown v. Board of Education of Topeka, Kansas** and its progeny, further problems arose when segregated districts were ordered to consolidate to achieve unitary status. One of the more controversial aspects associated with these changes dealt with staff assignment policies and accompanying reductions in force necessary to implement faculty desegregation. Perhaps the best known, and certainly the most widely cited, of the federal cases on this subject is *Singleton v. Jackson Municipal Separate School District.* Decided shortly after, and in light of, the Supreme Court's rendered judgment in *Alexander v. Holmes County Board of Education** (1969), which sent the doctrine of "all deliberate speed" to its final resting place by mandating an immediate end to dual school systems, *Singleton* is remembered primarily for enunciating the guidelines applicable to reductions in force in the process of faculty desegregation.

At the heart of the first part of the Fifth Circuit's opinion in *Singleton* are three widely cited principles governing staff reductions pursuant to desegregation orders. The first mandated that, as school districts moved toward becoming unitary, the employment status of teachers and staff members who worked directly with students was to be determined without regard to race, color, or national origin. The second required that if a reduction in force made it necessary to dismiss or demote any school personnel, the individual(s) were to be selected from among all staff on the basis of objective and reasonable nondiscriminatory standards. Moreover, in the event of a dismissal or demotion, no position could be filled by a person of a different race, color, or national origin from the affected individual until qualified displaced staff members had the opportunity to fill the vacancy but failed to accept an offer to do so. The third principle maintained that, before any reductions in force could take place, a school board was required to develop, retain, and make available for public inspection non-racial criteria to be used in the selection of staff members to be dismissed or demoted. Consequently, while the Supreme Court refused to hear a further appeal on this part of *Singleton*, 396 U.S. 1032 (1970), rendering it binding precedent only in the Fifth Circuit, the opinion was widely relied upon because of the clarity of its guidelines.

The second part of *Singleton* discussed majority-to-majority transfer policies, transportation, school construction and site selection, and school attendance by students who lived outside the districts they attended. Subsequently, in *Carter v. West Feliciana Parish School Board*, the pupil desegregation section of the ruling was vacated and then reversed by the U.S. Supreme Court. The court, in a per curiam opinion, overturned the Fifth Circuit's decision on the basis that it misconstrued *Alexander* by improperly authorizing a deferral of student desegregation beyond 1 February 1990.

Singleton v. Jackson Municipal Separate School District occupies a central role in the battle against segregation by providing the ground rules regulating staff reductions pursuant to the implementation of court-ordered desegregation. Yet, it marked only a beginning, as its holding was limited to school systems operating under de jure segregation. Thus, it was left to later cases such as the 1986 ruling in *Wygant v. Jackson Board of Education*,* the only Supreme Court opinion to address the problem, to tackle the thorny question of reductions in force in school systems functioning under de facto segregation.

SELECTED BIBLIOGRAPHY

Singleton v. Jackson Municipal Separate School District, 419 F.2d 1211 (5th Cir. 1970).

CHARLES J. RUSSO

SIPUEL v. BOARD OF REGENTS OF THE UNIVERSITY OF OKLAHOMA et al., 332 U.S. 631 (1948).

At the time this case was filed, the state of Oklahoma segregated blacks and whites at all levels of education. In higher education, the state maintained the University of Oklahoma for whites and Langston University, which did not have a law school, for blacks. Instead of maintaining a separate law school, the state provided funds or scholarships for African-Americans to attend law schools open to them outside the state. In 1946, Ada Lois Sipuel Fisher, a twenty-two-year-old African-American graduate of Langston, applied for admission to the University of Oklahoma School of Law and was denied admission based on her race. Using her maiden name, Sipuel, she went into court. Relying upon the *Missouri ex rel Gaines v. Canada**

(1938) decision, she argued that the denial was contrary to the Fourteenth Amendment of the Constitution.

The District Court of Cleveland County, Oklahoma, awarded judgment to defendants, and the Supreme Court of Oklahoma affirmed. Affirming the reasoning and spirit of *Gaines*, the court stated that "the state must provide either a proper legal training for petitioner in the state, or admit the petitioner to the University Law School." The court, however, held that the state was not obligated to establish a separate law school unless African-Americans first requested it and that Sipuel failed to demand a separate school and admission to it. Distinguishing this case from *Gaines*, the court noted that Lloyd Gaines, upon advice, notified officials at Lincoln University* of his desire to attend law school, whereas Sipuel did not make known her "desire and availability" for legal education to Langston University officials. Thus, the Oklahoma Court concluded, "she has not brought herself within the rule of *Gaines*, and has wholly failed to establish any violation of the Fourteenth Amendment of the Federal Constitution."

The U.S. Supreme Court reviewed the case and reversed the judgment of the Oklahoma Supreme Court. The Court held in a unanimous, unsigned opinion that the state had to provide Sipuel with a legal education in a state institution "in conformity with the equal protection clause of the Fourteenth Amendment and provide it as soon as it does for applicants of any other group." It sent the case back to the state court for proceedings consistent with its ruling. The state court ordered defendants to enroll Sipuel in the University of Oklahoma School of Law until officials could establish a separate law school for African-Americans. The district court further ordered the Board of Regents not to enroll Sipuel in the University of Oklahoma if such a separate school was established.

The defendants responded by impetuously setting up a three-professor, ad hoc law school for African-Americans in a small, roped-off section in the state capitol. Sipuel refused to attend. To thwart the establishment of a separate law school, Sipuel went back to the U.S. Supreme Court under her married name, Fisher, and asked the Court to compel compliance with its mandate in *Sipuel*. She asserted that the Court had ordered her admission without any conditions.

With Justices Murphy and Rutledge dissenting, the Court found the state to be in compliance with mandate of the law and denied the request. The Court said that Sipuel, in her original case, as in the current petition, "did not present the issue whether a state might not satisfy the equal protection clause of the Fourteenth Amendment by establishing a separate law school for Negroes." This meant that the "separate-but-equal" rule, *Sipuel v. Board of Regents of the University of Oklahoma et al*, was still in effect. After the regents decided to close the ad hoc law school for "Negroes," however, the University of Oklahoma admitted Ada Lois Sipuel Fisher to its School of Law on 18 June 1949. She was graduated in 1951 and was admitted to the state bar. *Sipuel* showed significant inequality between African-American and white education and helped pave the road to *Brown v. Board of Education of Topeka, Kansas** (1954).

SELECTED BIBLIOGRAPHY

E. W. Brooke, Jr., "Notes and Comments," *Boston University Law Review* 28 (1948): 240–42; George Lynn Cross, *Blacks in White Colleges: Oklahoma's Landmark Cases* (1975); *Fisher v. Hurst, Chief Justice, et al.*, 333 U.S. 147 (1948); Richard Kluger, *Simple Justice: The History of Brown v. Board of Education and Black America's Struggle for Equality* (1976); Loren Miller, *The Petitioners: The Story of the Supreme Court of the United States and the Negro* (1966); Mark V. Tushnet, *The NAACP's Legal Strategy against Segregated Education, 1925–1950* (1987).

JAMES E. NEWBY

SISTERS OF THE HOLY FAMILY. Established in 1842, this Roman Catholic order of nuns has continuously provided educational and social services for blacks in the United States. They have also served in Central America since 1898, and in Africa since 1974. Although the Sisters' founding purpose was to teach and perform charitable work among slaves and needy free people of color in New Orleans, they have turned no one away because of race, color, or creed.

The force behind the founding was a young quadroon named Henriette Delille (1812–62, New Orleans), who was imbued from youth with a strong desire to serve God by dedicating her life to helping the "poorest of the poor" among her race. Because state law forbade the races to live together, she could not enter the white religious orders in New Orleans. She did not seek membership in the Oblate Sisters of Providence,* an African-American order founded in Baltimore, Maryland, in 1829, because she wished to serve in her native city.

Delille's dream of founding a religious community of African-American nuns was shared by two of her friends, Juliette Gaudin and Josephine Charles. The three had been inspired by a French missionary worker, Sister Ste. Marthe Fontiere, as early as 1825, to work among the indigent of their race. After two failed attempts to establish a religious community, the fulfillment of their dream finally was made possible with the assistance and support of Father Etienne Rousselon and Marie–Jean Aliquot, a French woman who had come to New Orleans to visit her sister, an Ursuline nun, but stayed on to work among the black Catholics of Louisiana. Ten years after its founding, another free woman of color, Susanne Navarre of Boston, Massachusetts, joined the order. It was not until after the end of the Civil War, however, when legal and class distinctions between free-born African-Americans (*gen de couleur libre*) and persons born in bondage had diminished, that a former slave, Chloe Preval, was accepted as a member of the congregation.

The founders began their mission with the teaching of religion and morals to free adults and slaves and catechism to children (slave and free), presenting sixty persons for first communion and confirmation every year. They also provided academic and religious instruction for young girls from free families of means. They took in boarders, sometimes accepting goods or service as pay.

They provided shelter and care for the sick, aged, poor, and orphaned children. Much of their early development was made possible by their inheritances, which they turned over to the congregation—gifts from friends and family and, in particular, the benevolence of philanthropist Thomy Lafon (1810–93), a free man of color in New Orleans.

In 1847, when the congregation's existence was threatened by Louisiana's Act 207, many of their friends, mainly from among the free people of color, joined them in forming the Association of the Holy Family to meet requirements of incorporation. They erected a new home for the aged, sick, and poor and dedicated it as the Hospice of the Holy Family in 1849, the first incorporated Catholic home for the aged in Louisiana. Today, after uninterrupted service, it is known as the Lafon Nursing Home of the Holy Family. By 1992, the year of the Congregation's 150th anniversary, the work of the founders had been carried on through 750 nuns. Their number peaked at 357 in 1964 and dropped to about 200 by 1993. Since their founding, the Sisters have taught at over fifty schools for African-Americans in Louisiana, Texas, Oklahoma, Florida, California, and Washington, D.C., and four schools in Belize, Central America. Three of the six schools established before 1900 are still in existence. St. Mary's Academy in New Orleans celebrated its 125th anniversary in 1992. This all-girls school took in boarders until 1978–79.

The most recent school established by the Sisters is the House of the Holy Family, started in 1990 as a memorial to the ideals of Mother Henriette Delille. Located in New Orleans, across from the Motherhouse, the school provides totally free education for sixty children, in grades 1–3, from among the poorest and homeless in the city. The children receive free books, uniforms, and a snack and a meal each day. The school is financed by the Sisters as teachers, the Holy Family Alumni Association, and charitable donations. The Sisters seek scholarships for graduates of this school to continue receiving a parochial education.

In addition to their teaching ministry, the Sisters operate the following institutions in New Orleans: St. John Berchmans Manor (opened in 1982), a 150-apartment complex for low-income elderly and the handicapped; Delille Inn (1987), a residence for senior citizens capable of independent living; Lafon Nursing Home (mentioned earlier), a 171-bed facility built in 1973; Lafon Child Development Center (opened in 1969 in the building that for sixty-one years had housed the Lafon Boys Home); and St. John Berchmans Child Development Center (established in 1977 on the site of the former St. John Berchmans Orphanage for Girls). They also serve as administrator at the St. Martin Manor and on the staffs of the Archdiocesan Christopher Homes, Inc., and the Flint–Goodridge Residence for Senior Citizens.

In the 1970s Sister Sylvia Thibodeaux of the Holy Family Sisters was permitted to join with Bishop P. E. Ekpu of Nigeria, West Africa, in establishing a religious order of indigenous women of that country. They founded the Sisters of the Sacred Heart, whose mission is to provide education and religious instruction in Nigeria. The Sisters of the Sacred Heart opened their first school in 1978 in Benin City.

Mother Henriette Delille continues to be a driving force behind the Sisters of the Holy Family. In 1988 the cause for her canonization to sainthood was presented in Rome by Archbishop Philip M. Hannan, who stated: "She worked with total dedication to the cause of evangelization and ministry to the black population. In doing so she made remarkable contributions which [benefitted] the people of all races in this Archdiocese." This is the legacy that has been accepted and passed on through the years by the Sisters of the Holy Family.

SELECTED BIBLIOGRAPHY

Peter W. Clark, ed., with Sister M. Boniface Adams, *The Greatest Gift of All* (1992; booklet commemorating the 150th anniversary of the Sisters of the Holy Family); Sister Audrey Marie Detiege, *Henriette Delille, Free Woman of Color* (1976); Sister M. Francis Borgia Hart, *Violets in the King's Garden: A History of the Sisters of the Holy Family of New Orleans* (1976); T. A. Rector, "Black Nuns as Educators," *Journal of Negro Education* (1982).

THERESA RECTOR

SIT-IN MOVEMENT. The "sit-in" technique evolved from the trade union sit-down strikes of the 1930s. In June of 1943, the Congress of Racial Equality (CORE) staged the first publicized sit-in demonstration for desegregation and fair treatment in the nation's history. Initially, sit-ins, lie-ins, wade-ins, teach-ins, jail-ins, and later freedom rides, were largely instigated and directed by CORE. In August of 1957, in Durham, North Carolina, the Reverend Douglas E. Moore, accompanied by students from North Carolina College (later North Carolina Central University*), led an unsuccessful sit-in at the white section of the Royal Ice Cream Company store.

In 1958, James Lawson and Glenn Smiley offered workshops on nonviolence in Nashville, Tennessee, and across the South. The workshops demonstrated, as the film *Eyes on the Prize* (1987) put it, that "nonviolence was not for the faint of heart. Participants had to sit quietly while other students, acting segregationists' roles, jeered, poked, and spat on them. Nonviolence required compassion, commitment, courage, and faith, but most importantly, it required discipline." Later, Dianne Nash, John Lewis, and others started an organization they called the Nashville Student Movement (NSM). Nash was elected head of the central committee. Using tactics learned in nonviolence workshops, the NSM sought to abolish segregation in Nashville, beginning with department store lunch counters. But on 1 February 1960, the "Greensboro Four" stole their thunder. Four black students—David Richmond, Franklin McCain, Ezell Blair, Jr., and Joseph McNeil—at North Carolina A & T College* sat at a local Woolworth's lunch counter until the store closed.

Students at other southern black colleges then shook the power structure of the African-American community, made direct action preeminent as a civil rights tactic, and accelerated the process of social change in race relations. They all but destroyed the barriers standing against the recognition of African-American's constitutional rights, and ultimately turned the African-American protest organizations toward a deep concern with the economic and social problems of the masses. Consequently, the American educational scene became the center of the sit-in and nonviolent protest movements. The sit-in movement spread to every state in the Deep South and several border states, involving more people than any other human rights movement in American history. Some seventy thousand African-American and white demonstrators staged over eight hundred sit-ins in more than a hundred cities. Some four thousand persons, mostly African-American students, underwent arrest, yet through their courage they convinced more people that direct mass action was the shortest, most effective route to their goal of desegregation. Their boldness, at times, seemed nothing short of alarming. The students and others solidified the common bond between them by singing such spirituals as "Oh, Freedom" and "We Shall Overcome" while working for recognition and respect.

In general, white southerners viewed the sit-in movement skeptically. However, student-generated sit-ins deflected press attention away from traditional African-American leadership's efforts to promote civil rights legislation. Students had developed the strategy of involving enough students to sustain sit-ins until segregation yielded. Meanwhile, the Student Nonviolent Coordinating Committee (SNCC) organized and spearheaded sit-ins at lunch counters, libraries, department stores, swimming pools, churches, movie theaters, state office buildings, and university administration buildings. The "jail-in" movement started in Rock Hill, South Carolina, on 6 February 1961, when students refused to pay fines and requested jail sentences. SNCC immediately urged a South-wide "Jail, No Bail" campaign. President John F. Kennedy encouraged the movement in an address of 25 September 1961, when he called for an end to discrimination in public places. Additionally, sit-ins helped bring about the passage of the Civil Rights Act of 1964.*

College student sit-ins swept the South. Arrests numbered in the thousands and brutality evidenced itself in scores of communities. Although the Deep South campaign ended in failure, these youths captured the imagination of the African-American community and, to a remarkable extent, of the whole nation. Retrospectively, the Southern Regional Council announced in September of 1961 that the sit-in movement had affected twenty states and more than a hundred cities in southern and border states with at least 141 students and fifty-eight faculty members expelled by college authorities; however, one or more establishments in 108 cities had been desegregated as a result of the sit-in movement. Gradually the sit-in movement slowed significantly. In 1966 SNCC changed its direction when Stokely Carmichael drew up his position paper calling for the exclusion of white members from SNCC and the adoption of a policy of "Black Power." Thence forth, SNCC spoke mainly the voice of Black Nationalism. Nonetheless, during the sixties, the Southern Christian Leadership

Conference (SCLC) and CORE organized "freedom rides" and sit-ins throughout the South, bringing an end to segregated bus lines and public conveniences.

The student movements for racial integration and for peace often moved in the same circles, even though the student movement for integration centered in the South and the peace movement centered in the North. When criticized for sitting-in, students responded with such tactics as placing full-page advertisements in newspapers. Sit-ins and concurrent demonstrations proved so conscience-raising that, by the summer of 1960, the status of African-Americans affected the forthcoming presidential campaign. The "road to revolution" had been paved by African-American population shifts from rural areas to the cities and from the South to the North and West; by Supreme Court decision on voting and school desegregation; by the refusal of Rosa Parks to move to the back of the bus; by the Montgomery bus boycott that followed and the emergence of Martin Luther King, Jr.; by the passage of the Civil Rights Act of 1957; and by the rise of national states in Africa, according to John Hope Franklin* and Alfred A. Moss.

The college students' sit-in movement symbolized change amid the continuity of African-American advancement, which in turn suggested the nature of changes yet to come. In like manner, the sit-in movement revolted against both segregation and the entrenched African American leadership by erupting in territory that the white South considered "safe" or in areas militant northern African-Americans considered "docile," in the words of Louis Lomax. This tactic permitted poorly educated African-American youths to "startle the world by the militancy of their inspired actions," Lomax continued. Conversely, the student sit-in movement caused lawmakers of the Deep South to resort to newer and more subtle racial legislation than the segregation statutes found so useful in the past, since the sit-ins could not be met by existing laws.

SELECTED BIBLIOGRAPHY

Louis Lomax, *The Negro Revolt* (1964); James Mencarelli and Steve Severin, *Protest3: Red, Black, Brown Experience in America* (1975); Martin Oppenheimer, "The Southern Sit-Ins: Intra-Group Relations and Community Conflict," *Phylon* 27 (Spring 1966): 20–26; Martin Oppenheimer, *The Genesis of the Southern Negro Student Movement (Sit-in Movement): A Study in Contemporary Negro Protest*, Ph.D. diss. University of Pennsylvania (1963); Howell Raines, *My Soul Is Rested* (1983); *Report of the National Advisory Commission On Civil Disorders* (1968); Juan Williams, *Eyes on the Prize* (1988).

LEE E. WILLIAMS II

SIZEMORE, BARBARA A. (17 December 1927, Chicago, Illinois). Educator and school superintendent Barbara Sizemore was born in Chicago, Illinois, on 17 December 1927, the daughter of Sylvester W. Laffoon and Delila Mae Alexander. She was married to Furman Sizemore and Jake Milliones (deceased) and has two children.

Sizemore graduated from Northwestern University, Evanston, Illinois, in 1947 with a B.A. in classical languages and in 1954 with an M.A. degree in elementary education. She received a Ph.D. degree in educational administration in 1979 from the University of Chicago. Sizemore was a teacher in the Chicago public school system; an elementary school principal; a high school principal; director of the Chicago Woodlawn Experimental Schools Project; and Coordinator for Proposal Development, Chicago Public Schools, from 1947 to 1972. She was associate secretary of the American Association of School Administrators (1972–73); superintendent of schools, District of Columbia Public Schools, Washington, D.C. (1973–75); and a self-employed educational consultant (1975–77). She became an associate professor in the Department of Black Community Education Research and Development at the University of Pittsburgh (1977–89), and interim chairperson (1985–86); she was appointed to full professor in 1989. In 1992, Sizemore became dean of the School of Education at DePaul University, in Chicago.

Sizemore's achievements in the field of education have been recognized many times. Her awards include the Danforth Fellowship (1965–67); staff associate, University of Chicago (1967–69); the Northwestern University Alumni Association Merit Award in 1974, the Pittsburgh United Nations Association Human Rights Award in 1985, and the African Heritage Studies Association Edward Blyden Award in 1992. She is also listed in a number of "who's who" directories and has received honorary degrees from Delaware State College, Central State University, and Baltimore College of the Bible.

Sizemore is an educator known for providing solutions to the problems of educating poor African-American inner-city children. Her publications include twenty-two book chapters, twenty-three journal articles, six book reviews, three pamphlets, two reports, and one book, *The Ruptured Diamond: A Case Study of the Politics of the Decentralization of the Public Schools of the District of Columbia, 1973–1976.*

SELECTED BIBLIOGRAPHY

Nancy L. Arnez, *The Besieged School Superintendent: A Case Study of School Superintendent–School Board Relations in Washington, D.C. 1973–1975* (1981); I. Cloyd, ed., *Who's Who among Black Americans* (1990–91); interview with Barbara Sizemore, biographee, dean, School of Education, DePaul University, 3 April 1993.

NANCY L. ARNEZ

SLATER FUND. In 1882, John F. Slater of Norwich, Connecticut, a wealthy manufacturer of cotton and woolen goods, gave one million dollars to establish the fund that would bear his name. Influenced by the work of the Peabody Education Fund,* Slater defined the purpose as "the uplifting of the lately emancipated population of the Southern States, and their posterity, by conferring upon them the blessings of Christian education." He envisioned "such education as shall tend to make them good men and good citizens—education in which the instruction of the mind in the common branches of secular learning shall be associated with training in just notions of duty toward God and man." Slater further suggested that provision be made for the "training of teachers from among the people requiring to be taught'' and warned that the fund should be used for the dissemination, rather than the advancement, of knowledge and as a help to those in need rather than going into the pockets of the rich.

The board of trustees selected Atticus G. Haygood, prominent minister from Georgia, as its first general agent. After travelling widely through the South to assess conditions and seek advice, Haygood recommended a policy that the fund would follow for several years. This policy provided aid to students in ''such schools as are best fitted to prepare young colored men and women to become useful to their race.'' The preferred schools were those that gave instruction in the trades and other manual occupations. Funds were also set aside to aid young men who were preparing for the practice of medicine among their people. Under this policy in 1885, as an example, amounts ranging from $500 to $2,000 were given for student aid to thirty colleges, including Leonard Medical School (Raleigh) and Meharry Medical College* (Nashville).

In 1891, upon the resignation of Haygood, J. L. M. Curry was added to the Slater Fund's board of trustees and made chairman of the education committee, in which capacity he also functioned as general agent. Curry was already general agent for the Peabody Education Fund and thus began the trend of cooperation and consolidation among the northern philanthropies that would continue for many years to follow. Curry found the policies of Haygood to have been too diffuse to accomplish significant results and therefore proposed to discontinue student aid and concentrate on helping a more limited number of schools to become firmly established.

In the 1892–93 academic year, the fund aided fifteen colleges with amounts ranging from $1,000 to $5,000 each for the payment of teacher salaries. Like Haygood, Curry found it necessary to travel and visit schools, since ''catalogs are deceptive, correspondence is unsatisfactory, and inspection of the school [is] essential.'' For the 1895–96 year, eleven colleges were aided with amounts ranging from $1,000 to $6,000 for salaries of teachers, most of whom taught industrial subjects. Consistent with the fund's preference for industrial education, Hampton* and Tuskegee* received much larger sums that other colleges. Replying to critics of this policy, Curry declared that this action ''is no adverse decision . . . as to the need of higher education, [for] few can be advocates of what tends to keep all Negroes mere hewers of wood and drawers of water.''

A policy change resulted from the appointment in 1907 of James Hardy Dillard as general agent. His surveys of the educational situation revealed that most students in the colleges and universities that received fund monies were at the high school level. He also found that most teachers in the common schools had not gone beyond the fifth grade. To address these two problems, Dillard conceived the idea of establishing central county training schools that would gradually develop into true high schools while also offering teacher training. By this means, more students would be prepared for college, the colleges could concentrate on truly college-level work, and teachers for the common schools would be better trained.

The new policy was first implemented in 1911–12, when four schools were assisted. To receive assistance as a county training school, schools had to (a) be a part of the public school system, (b) receive more from the state of county than from the fund, (c) offer more than eight years of schooling, and (d) move toward becoming full four-year high schools. Industrial training was also required as part of the curriculum. By 1926, 306 schools were being helped, 82 of which had the four-year high school course. Colleges were still receiving assistance, but in substantially reduced amounts, except for Hampton and Tuskegee. Other foundations, notably the Carnegie Corporation and the General Education Board,* cooperated with the county training school program by providing substantial amounts to be administered by the Slater Fund. Upon ending its work in 1914, the Peabody Education Fund transferred over $300,000 to the Slater Fund.

Dillard was succeeded as president of the fund by Arthur D. Wright in 1931. Wright, as Dillard before him, was also president of the Jeanes Fund*; in 1935 the Slater Fund began to support Jeanes teachers. Contributions to private colleges were gradually ended, and most money went to the county training schools. An unnamed benefactor gave the fund $20,000 annually to be used for theology fellowships during 1930–33. One recipient was Benjamin E. Mays,* for study at the University of Chicago. Contributions were also made to the *Journal of Negro History*. A total of twenty-nine "occasional papers" were published, including papers by James Weldon Johnson and Alain Locke.*

Although the founder had provided that the fund might be dissolved after thirty-three years, it continued its work until 1937, when it merged with the Jeanes Fund and the Virginia Randolph Fund to form the Southern Education Foundation.* Overall, from an initial gift of one million dollars, the fund contributed from its own resources and those of other foundations a total of around four million dollars in eighteen southern states. Colleges were helped toward financial stability, a strong impetus was given to the establishment of public high schools for black youth, and elementary school teachers were given better training. The fund has been criticized for favoring industrial education, but it never opposed higher and professional education; in fact, it assisted with the training of doctors and ministers. It was one of the first funds to elect an African-American to its board of trustees when, in 1931, C. C. Spaulding was elected. Evaluating the main emphasis of the fund, *The Crisis* reported that "in this way, more or less reluctant rural school authorities have been induced to give the beginning of high school training to Negro children in county districts," without which colleges could not exist.

SELECTED BIBLIOGRAPHY

John F. Slater Fund, *Proceedings and Reports* (1883–1936); Trustees of the John F. Slater Fund, *Occasional Papers*, Nos. 1–29 (1894–1935); John E. Fisher, *The John F. Slater Fund* (1986); "The Slater Fund," *The Crisis* 40 (June 1933): 131, 132.

EARLE H. WEST

SLAVERY, AFRICAN-AMERICAN EDUCATION DURING. Not long after the first Africans arrived in the English colony of Virginia in 1619, the colonists began to develop a system of legal restraints that would govern this peculiar institution, as slavery ran counter to English law. Virginia took the lead in distinguishing between African-American and white servants. These laws, systematically enacted throughout the South, became known as the slave codes.

In order to prevent slaves from entertaining any ideas of freedom, states passed restrictive legislation to discourage any attempt by whites to teach slaves to read or write. Many of these acts included monetary fines for any whites and corporal punishment for any free African-Americans caught teaching slaves to read and write. Slaves were not even to have access to the Bible. Southern whites knew the dangers involved if slaves became literate. The noted abolitionist Frederick Douglass reasoned that slaveholders feared literate slaves because education for slaves would sow discontent and lead to efforts to gain their freedom.

The slave system itself was the primary barrier to educational opportunities. Most slaves lived in rural areas on moderate-size plantations and farms. Less than 10 percent of all slaves lived in what could be classified as urban areas. The day-to-day existence of the slave was one of drudgery with little opportunity to develop skills. Only on the large plantations did there exist a division of labor and a demand for skilled craftsmen.

Life for most slaves was pretty much determined by the crops grown and the season of the year. Slaves generally rose before sunrise, prepared meals for the day's field labor, and worked until sunset. While the legal system prohibited formal education for slaves, the demands of the economic system precluded any such opportunities for most slaves.

That is not to say that there did not exist any form of learning within the slave quarters. The slave community remained a vibrant center for acquiring and passing on information. The ''slave grapevine'' was widely known for its ability to transmit information on the plantation, between plantations and even from state to state. Much of what slaves learned about abolitionist activities was transmitted over the slave grapevine.

The slave system did not prevent parents from teaching their children to survive in a hostile environment. Folktales and stories were used to pass community values on to the next generation. Children were taught religious principles quite different from the instruction of white ministers to obey their masters. The Bible had many parables that the slaves applied to their situation. The Old Testament, with its stories of the enslavement of the Israelites, found new meaning in the slave quarters, often manifested in slave songs. Songs were used to carry hidden messages. Slave preachers often used their sermons to inspire and encourage where otherwise no inspiration or encouragement existed.

Other types of learning existed for slaves on the larger plantations where economically efficient labor was required. In spite of the legal system and the alleged inferiority of the African race, some slaves were taught skills and allowed to acquire a high degree of knowledge. Domestic servants were comprised of coachmen, laundresses, seamstresses, cooks, footmen, butlers, housemaids, chambermaids, children's nurses, and personal servants. The day-to-day contact with slaveholders enhanced their knowledge and sometimes actually led to the slave being taught to read and write by a benevolent master or his children.

The peculiar institution also produced a number of skilled craftsmen and engineers, carpenters, blacksmiths, brickmakers, stonemasons, ironworkers, mechanics, cobblers, weavers, millers, and landscapers. Although many of these skilled craftsmen did not learn to read and write, they often learned elementary mathematics to carry out their jobs. Their jobs often gave them a measure of freedom through being "hired out" to other plantations and urban areas. Some slaveholders even permitted highly skilled and valued slaves to hire-out their own time, splitting their income with their masters.

A limited number of slaves were allowed to learn to read and write. For example, Lewis Clarke, a slave, was taught as a child to read and write by his white playmate. Caught writing by his mistress, he was threatened with dire punishment if he spelled another word. Another slave, Jamie Parker, convinced a freedman named Scipio to teach him the fundamentals of reading and writing. A slave patrol caught the two; Jamie was severely beaten by an overseer who could neither read nor write; Scipio was put to death.

Other slaves were mutilated for attempting to learn. The loss of a thumb or forefinger often served as a badge within the slave quarters symbolizing the valiant effort to acquire an education. The ability to read and write provided the slave with immeasurable status within the slave quarters. Despite the legal restrictions and severe sanctions imposed if caught learning to read and write, slaves had invested education with mystical qualities and felt that its acquisition was worth any amount of hardship. Slaveholders understood that educating their chattel would undermine and eventually destroy the very economic system they wished to perpetuate. Slavery was first and foremost then an economic system designed to maximize the productivity of the slaveholders' investment in human labor. Thus, slavery itself was the worst barrier preventing African-Americans from acquiring an education. It did not, however, keep slaves from wanting an education or understanding the value of learning. This overwhelming desire to learn manifested itself after the Civil War, when the newly emancipated slaves made great strides to overcome illiteracy.

The relationship between white Americans and free African-Americans was based on the white belief that blacks were inferior. Whites concluded that blacks were incapable of taking advantage of educational opportunities beyond the basic rudiments of learning. Therefore, during most of the pre–Civil War years, there was little or no effort to provide schools for blacks. In the South, there were no formal efforts to provide schools for the free blacks. While some urban centers had a large enough free black population to organize and support private schools, most free African-Americans went without an education.

Free African-Americans in cities such as Charleston, South Carolina, had a history of supporting schools. As early as 1810, the free people of color had organized the Minor Society to provide education for orphaned children. But the vast majority of free African-Americans had to do without instruction. Even the efforts to support formal learning were often curtailed by fear of slave insurrection influenced by the freemen. Often free African-American schools were closed. States passed laws prohibiting the distribution of abolitionist literature and even restricted the movement of free African-Americans in and out of the state.

The situation of African-Americans in the North was as much conditioned by race prejudice as it was in the South. Where schools existed, the notion of racially mixed schools was repugnant to most whites. Those communities that provided education for African-Americans established separate facilities for them. In New York, for example, the board of education spent an average of $1,600 for whites (including capital expenditures) for every dollar spent on blacks. Even when communities established tax-supported schools, often the African-American community had to resort to establishing private schools. African-Americans in the North were constantly faced with discrimination and segregation in the area of education. Only in Boston were they successful in integrating the schools, but not until 1855, after nine years of struggle.

During most of the pre–Civil War years, there were so few opportunities for college education that by 1861 there were only twenty-eight known African-American college graduates, and not all of these were educated within the United States. Oberlin College* in Ohio listed 245 African-Americans students enrolled prior to 1861, but only a few were in the college department, which graduated even fewer African-American students. Several colleges were established in Ohio and Pennsylvania for African-Americans prior to the Civil War. Wilberforce University,* for example, was started in 1856 by the Methodist Church to educate children of slaveholders. The school was temporarily closed during the Civil War when southern support abruptly ended. The college was sold to the African Methodist Episcopal Church in 1863 and became the first college owned and operated by an African-American institution.

The abolitionist/colonizationist movement provided some opportunities for African-Americans in the North to acquire an education. Advocates of colonization for free African-Americans also advocated education, the assumption being that they would immigrate to Africa. Despite their prejudice, the abolitionists did more to facilitate the education of African-Americans prior to 1861 than any other group. The New York Abolitionist Society supported the independent African Free School for forty-seven years. Middlebury College graduated the first African-American college graduate, Alexander Lucius Twilight, in 1822. Edward Jones graduated from Amherst College in 1826, but the college did not graduate another African-American until after the Civil War.

By the time of the Civil War, the American system of slavery in the South and race prejudice and discrimination in the North had effectively denied the four million slaves and five hundred thousand free African-Americans opportunities for learning. The overwhelmingly oppressive nature of slavery and race prejudice resulted in a minuscule number of African-Americans who could read and write by the time of the Civil War.

SELECTED BIBLIOGRAPHY

John W. Blassingame, *The Slave Community: Plantation Life in the Antebellum South* (1979); Henry Allen Bullock, *A History of Negro Education in the South from 1619 to the Present* (1967); John E. Fleming, *The Lengthening Shadow of Slavery: A Historical Justification for Affirmative Action for Blacks in Higher Education* (1976); Herbert Gutman, *The Black Family in Slavery and Freedom, 1750–1925* (1976); August Meier and Elliott M. Rudwick, *From Plantation to Ghetto* (1966).

JOHN E. FLEMING

SLOWE, LUCY DIGGS (4 July 1883, Berryville, Virginia–21 October 1937, Washington, D.C.). Educator, athlete, and women's suffragist, Slowe was orphaned at six years of age and reared by an aunt in Lexington, Virginia. She was educated in the public schools of Lexington and Baltimore, Maryland, and was a ranking graduate of the Colored High School of Baltimore. Slowe was the first woman to win a scholarship to Howard University* and the first woman from the Colored High School of Baltimore to attend Howard.

Slowe's precarious financial situation forced her to do clerical work during the school year and other jobs during the summer. At Howard she demonstrated the breadth of interest that was to characterize her later life. She served as vice president of Alpha Phi Literary Society, as first president of Alpha Chapter of Alpha Kappa Alpha Sorority (the first sorority for African-American women), and as president of the Women's Tennis Club. She sang in the first Howard University Choir under Lula Vere Childers and was also a poet and a writer. She graduated from Howard with a bachelor of arts degree and was valedictorian of the class of 1908.

After seven years as a teacher of English in the Colored High School of Baltimore, Slowe was appointed to the faculty of the Armstrong Technical High School of Washington, where she became the first assistant principal. Slowe then moved on to become the principal of Shaw Junior High School, the city's first junior high school for African-American students. In 1922, after three years at Shaw, she became the first dean of women at Howard University. During her public school career, Slowe continued her academic studies, receiving the degree of master of arts from Columbia University in 1915. This was also the period of her most active participation in competitive tennis, in which she won seventeen prize cups, retiring as women's champion.

Slowe's first appointment at Howard was to the position of associate professor of English, with the administrative duties of dean of women. One year later, she advanced to the rank of professor of English. Her accomplishments during her fifteen years as dean of women at Howard included the development of the women's campus, the organization of the Women's League (a clearinghouse for all women's problems), an annual Women's Dinner, an annual Christmas Candlelight Service, the Senior Mentor System, an annual Vocational Guidance

Conference, the Intersorority Council, the annual Weekend for the Training of Campus Leaders, and the appointment of residence hall directors who could qualify for faculty positions.

The interests of Dean Slowe were not limited to women at Howard but were gender-free and related to the major concerns of student, faculty, and staff in and outside the classroom and to community life in Washington and the nation. She was quite active in the national YWCA as a member of the National Board's Students Council and the Executive Board of the Division of College Work. Slowe became the sixth president of the College Alumnae Club, organized in 1910 by Mary Church Terrell,* and was a key organizer and first president of the National Association of College Women, founded in 1923. She was also one of the founders of the National Association of Deans of Women and Advisors to Girls in Negro Schools,* established in 1929.

Dean Slowe died on 21 October 1937, at her home in Washington, D.C. Funeral services were held at the Andrew Rankin Memorial Chapel on the Howard University campus, where a stained-glass window was installed and dedicated to her memory.

SELECTED BIBLIOGRAPHY

Dwight O. W. Holmes, "In Memoriam: Eulogy at the Obsequies of Lucy D. Slowe," 25 October 1937, Andrew Rankin Chapel of Howard University; Beatrice Walker ed., "A Collection of the Writings of Dean Lucy D. Slowe," *The Journal of the College Alumnae Club of Washington* (Memorial Edition) (January 1939): 8–22.

CARROLL L. MILLER

SOCIAL DARWINISM AND AFRICAN-AMERICAN EDUCATION. Social Darwinism is a loosely organized set of ideas about human society based on principles derived from the theory of evolution, as proposed by English scientist Charles Darwin in his *Origin of Species* in 1859. After extensive research, Darwin concluded that, over time, animals and plants changed and developed from their more primitive ancestors through continuous adaptation to new conditions. In the struggle for existence, those that adapted most successfully survived—a process termed "natural selection."

In an age that revered progress and science, others, most notably Herbert Spencer in England and William Graham Sumner in the United States, seized on Darwin's theories and applied them to the study of racial, social, and economic differences. "Social Darwinists" asserted that human beings were also evolving from a more primitive to a more advanced status, as exemplified by Victorian culture and classical art. By these standards, it seemed clear that some groups were inferior (Africans and other persons of color; the poor), while others were superior (northern Europeans; the rich; the well-educated), but since these differences were ordained by nature, nothing could or should be done to eradicate them. Life was a competitive struggle in which only the "fittest" among individuals and societies would be able to survive, aided by hard work and moral discipline. Social Darwinism, then, provided both a justification of widely held beliefs about race and class and an apparently scientific basis for the proper conduct of government and society.

Recognition of variations among peoples and attempts to explain them by legend, doctrine, or science have been part of human history since the first encounters between strangers. But for centuries, such contacts were limited and questions of race were not particularly urgent. However, the colonization of the New World by white Europeans placed them in direct and regular contact with darker-skinned native Americans and, more significantly, with the blacks they had imported from Africa as slaves. By the eighteenth century, both the theft of land and the enslavement of individuals were being justified on the grounds that native Americans and Africans were not only different but inferior. Even before the rise of Social Darwinism, the increasing wealth and success of the colonists were seen as proof that they were superior beings, intended by nature to rule and, if necessary, exploit others.

The industrial revolution of the nineteenth century produced hitherto undreamed of technological progress and enormous wealth, but it also created immense misery for those who worked in oppressive factories and lived in crowded slums. To Social Darwinists, however, if the poor were unable or unwilling to improve their situation, it was a sign that they were "unfit," not selected by nature to adapt. Government assistance of any sort was considered unreasonable: it would only prop up the weak, prolonging their agony while inhibiting the laws of natural progress toward a better society.

Social Darwinism provided a "scientific" rationale for untrammeled individualism and proclaimed financial gain as both the goal and symbol of salvation. Indeed, Spencerian philosophy can be viewed as the secular counterpart of religious ideas inherited from Calvin. But although the virtues of hard work and thrift were continually preached, along with their inevitable and just reward, the message was meant only for masters, not for slaves. To ensure that the distinction was clear, there were such convenient arrangements as the perpetuation of slavery, the prohibition against slaves owning property, and the ban on teaching slaves.

The impact of Social Darwinism on American thinking about such diverse issues as intelligence testing, immigration legislation, and segregation can hardly be overestimated. Indeed, Social Darwinist views were accepted more readily and more widely in America than in Great Britain; and, as one writer has noted, they have become part of the everyday assumptions that many Americans still carry around in their heads about how social life is and should be arranged. Although these ideas have a veneer of rationality, they have an irrational base and pernicious implications.

Later in the nineteenth century, Social Darwinism was given further "scientific" support by numerous efforts to measure skulls, in the belief that both intelligence and moral capacity were determined by the size of the brain. But the laboratory technicians who compared skulls, however objective they thought themselves to be, were captives of racist ideology; and their calculations (sometimes deliberately mishandled) inevitably resulted in ''proof'' that Caucasians were physically superior, native Americans and Mongolians in the middle, and Africans inferior. Another line of experimentation was undertaken by Sir Francis Galton (1822–1911), who compiled masses of data on upper-class Britons and concluded that intelligence and other desirable qualities were inherited. This led him to propose a movement, known as eugenics, to encourage the propagation of the ''best'' stock and to discourage (by sterilization, if necessary) the unfit from reproducing.

At the turn of the century, eugenics was eagerly adopted in the United States by people who were concerned about what they saw as growing threats to American society: immigrants from southern Europe and Asia, criminals and the feeble-minded, the poor, and especially black Americans who had formerly been slaves. A fundamental tenet of their philosophy was the belief that little or nothing could be done to improve the situation of these people by education, health care, employment opportunities, or decent housing. Although Social Darwinists had proclaimed that progress was inevitable, nature's pace (in weeding out the unfit) seemed too slow in the face of grave problems. Unabashed racists and liberal reformers alike, many of them leading scientists and politicians, believed that nature should be assisted by such measures as severe restrictions on immigration, segregation or sterilization of those deemed inadequate members of society, and the deportation of blacks to Africa.

What might be termed the triumph of Social Darwinism—and the means through which it most directly affected the education of African-Americans through most of the twentieth century—came with the development of intelligence testing. Its inventor, Alfred Binet, had only benign intentions for his simple test and its accompanying scale: the diagnosis and treatment of mental retardation in school children. But his work was brought to the United States and refined further by psychologists who were thoroughgoing eugenicists. They and their admirers believed that they could now offer incontrovertible, scientific evidence of the inherent inferiority of certain groups, particularly people of color.

The people who designed and administered the tests were far from being the ''objective'' scientists they claimed to be. Long before they had begun their research on testing, they were convinced that intelligence is a single, measurable entity; that it is almost entirely hereditary, its amount fixed at birth and incapable of being improved by subsequent experience or education; and (with Darwin) that individual variations should be arranged on a single scale, ascending from the primitive to the sophisticated. They were utterly blind to their own deeply held biases even while proclaiming their detachment.

It followed, then, that there were several problems with the tests themselves. For instance, many of the questions, drawn from middle-class life in the eastern United States, could not possibly be answered by individuals who did not share that experience, such as southern whites as well as blacks, or Italian immigrants. People whose reading ability was limited were similarly handicapped. Nevertheless, right answers were taken as marks of intelligence, while wrong or missing ones indicated stupidity. Not surprisingly, white middle-class children and adults tended to do better than "Slaves" or "Negroes," but this was repeatedly interpreted as evidence of high intelligence and inherent superiority, rather than of the more favorable background that equipped them for the tests. Conversely, unsatisfactory responses were said to indicate defective genes and led to designation as a moron or an imbecile.

In the light of the prevailing ideology, such factors as fear, a limited background, lack of familiarity with the material or the testing process, and an inability to read were simply not considered relevant, even when the psychologists' own research showed that better education resulted in better test scores. For instance, African-Americans who had moved north did better than whites who remained in the South—a sorry testimonial to the quality of schooling available to either race below the Mason-Dixon Line—and immigrants with longer periods of residence in the United States had higher scores than those who had arrived more recently.

The practice of intelligence testing received an enormous boost during World War I, when the president of the American Psychological Association persuaded the U.S. Army that he and his colleagues could quickly classify nearly two million army recruits. The army testing program not only provided immense amounts of data for later analysis, but appeared to demonstrate that IQ tests could successfully be given to large groups (Binet's original design was meant for one-to-one testing). Thus, although fierce debates were conducted regarding the merits of testing, an apparently insatiable demand had been created for numerous variations of standardized tests (that is, "scientifically" designed and administered, multiple-choice answers, machine scored). Educators attempting to cope with an increasing school population wanted to use the tests to assign students to appropriate classes; business and industry personnel managers, to assist with employment screening and job placement; government officials, to improve manpower training and allocation programs.

Today, there are numerous publishers of tests of all kinds, ranging from personality inventories and medical school admissions examinations to state licensing tests for barbers. The Educational Testing Service, one of the largest, supplies the well-known Scholastic Aptitude Test, used by many colleges and universities to help determine which applicants to admit. Designed by one of the psychologists who had worked in the World War I army testing program, the SAT initially (and for years afterwards) contained many of the same fundamental flaws, directly traceable to its heritage of Social Darwinist thought.

The selection of culturally biased questions is only one of the issues raised by critics of standardized testing. Some suggest, for instance, that relatively little can be learned about an individual's multifaceted intelligence by having him or her select "right" answers to a series of often ambiguously worded questions. By far the most important criticism, however, relates to the practice of using the results of a single test to label low-scoring students as retarded. As a result of this invidious process, countless millions of children and young people, many of them African-Americans, have been consigned to slower tracks, special education classes, or vocational programs that permanently limited their range of opportunities.

Herbert Spencer, the founder of Social Darwinism, coined a phrase that summarizes his philosophy, "survival of the fittest." This notion of dog-eat-dog competition is so deeply ingrained in the American consciousness that many people cannot imagine a society without winners and losers or recognize that the welfare of the community depends not on eliminating but on assisting the "unfit." In an educational system shot through with the vestiges of Social Darwinism, even well-meaning and conscientious teachers are likely to believe that some of their students are destined to fail and must therefore not be challenged academically. Others will be gratified to see their racist prejudices confirmed by statistics about the disproportionate numbers of African-Americans and Hispanics who perform poorly, fail courses, or drop out of school altogether.

Fortunately, many of the educational reforms that have been suggested or tried in the aftermath of *A Nation at Risk* (1983) are based on very different assumptions—for instance, that all children can learn and will learn if they are treated with respect and provided with the resources to make learning possible. There is also growing recognition of a multiplicity of talents, all valuable, but not all capable of assessment through the traditional tests, which focus on reading and mathematical ability.

Perhaps sometime during the twenty-first century, Social Darwinism will have been consigned to history, regarded only as a peculiar attempt to apply biological principles to all of life. To date, however, it has been responsible for an incalculable host of evils, and it is still dangerous (all the more, because so familiar) to the health and welfare of African-Americans and other minorities.

SELECTED BIBLIOGRAPHY

N. J. Block and Gerald Dworkin, eds., *The IQ Controversy: Critical Readings* (1976); Raymond E. Fancher, *The Intelligence Men* (1985); Howard Gardner, *Frames of Mind: The Theory of Multiple Intelligences* (1983); Thomas F. Gossett, *Race: The History of an Idea in America* (1963); Stephen Jay Gould, *The Mismeasure of Man* (1981); Richard Hofstadter, *Social Darwinism in American Thought* (1955); Paul L. Houts, ed., *The Myth of Measurability* (1977); Leon J. Kamin, *The Science and Politics of IQ* (1974); Daniel Seligman, *A Question of Intelligence: The IQ Debate in America* (1992); Bernard C. Watson, *Stupidity, Sloth and Public Policy: Social Darwinism Rides Again* (1973).

BERNARD C. WATSON

SOUTH CAROLINA STATE UNIVERSITY. Founded in 1896, South Carolina State University is a public coeducational, land-grant institution located in Orangeburg, South Carolina. The university offers more than sixty degree programs through the schools of arts and sciences, business, education, engineering technology, graduate studies, continuing education, home economics, and human services and is the only higher education institution in the state offering both the undergraduate and graduate degree programs in speech pathology and audiology as well as a doctoral program in educational administration (Ed.D.). Furthermore, the university has the distinction of producing the largest number of African-American Army officers through its ROTC program than any other institution of higher education in the United States. The university confers the B.A. and B.S., as well as the M.S. in education, nutritional sciences, and individual and family development; the M.Ed. and M.A.T.; and the M.A. in rehabilitation counseling and speech pathology. The university, proud of its history and traditions, continues its quest toward excellence in research, teaching, and public service.

SELECTED BIBLIOGRAPHY

National Association for Equal Opportunity in Higher Education, *Profiles of the Nation's Historically and Predominantly Black Colleges and Universities* (1993).

SAMUEL L. MYERS

SOUTHERN ASSOCIATION OF COLLEGES AND SCHOOLS. One of six regional accrediting associations in the United States, the Southern Association of Colleges and Schools was created by six southern colleges and universities in 1895. The association accredits more than twelve thousand public and private colleges and schools in eleven southern states—Alabama, Florida, Georgia, Louisiana, Mississippi, North Carolina, South Carolina, Tennessee, Texas, and Virginia—and in Mexico, Central and South America, and islands of the Caribbean.

The association's main purpose is to improve education in the South through accreditation, a nongovernmental and voluntary process of evaluation that seeks to improve educational quality and to assure the public that member institutions meet established standards. This activity is shared by three commissions of the association: the Commission on Colleges, the Commission on Secondary and Middle Schools, and the Commission on Elementary and Middle Schools. The association's role in African-American education in the South began in 1928, when the Association of Negro High School Education asked the Southern Association's help in developing a program of standardization for their schools. The College Commission received a similar request to do the same for African-American colleges. In 1929, the Southern Association's "Committee on Approval of Negro Schools," also known as the Highsmith Committee, began to inspect African-American institutions in the South.

A list of Class A and Class B African-American colleges appeared in the association's *Proceedings* in 1930. Class A schools were those meeting the full standards of the association for institutions of higher education, and Class B were those that did not then meet full standards, but whose general academic quality warranted the admission of their graduates to an institution requiring the bachelor's degree for entrance. Fisk University* was the only institution on the Class A list in the first year. In 1932, Atlanta University,* Morehouse College,* Spelman College,* and Hampton Institute* joined Fisk on the list of A-rated institutions. The committee approved twenty high schools in 1931, and thereafter a listing of both colleges and high schools appeared in the *Proceedings*. These A-rated schools and colleges together formed the Southern Association of Colleges and Schools for Negroes and worked with the Highsmith Committee for sixteen years.

As early as 1943, conversations between the Highsmith Committee and a committee of the association of A-rated schools discussed the desirability of the two associations working together to integrate the accreditation process. Recommendations were made in 1951 to dissolve the Highsmith Committee and to make the accreditation of African-American schools and colleges a regular function of the commission of the Southern Association of Colleges and Schools, and to dissolve the association of A-rated schools. In 1953, the first institutions accredited under this system became association members. As some colleges and schools needed more time to meet membership standards, the approved lists were held open until 1961 for colleges and until 1967 for secondary schools.

SELECTED BIBLIOGRAPHY

Donald C. Agnew, *Seventy-Five Years of Educational Leadership* (1970).

TERESA GREER

SOUTHERN EDUCATION FOUNDATION. Located in Atlanta, Georgia, the Southern Education Foundation (SEF) was created in 1937 when four philanthropic funds committed to improving education in the South were incorporated to form a single philanthropic entity. These funds were the Peabody Education Fund* (1867), created by George Peabody to assist in the education of "children of the common people" in "the more destitute portions" of the post–Civil War South; the John F. Slater Fund* (1907), the first philanthropy in the United States devoted to education for African-Americans; the Negro Rural School Fund* (1907), created by Philadelphia Quaker Anna T. Jeanes, which supported African-American master teachers who assisted rural southern schools; and the Virginia Randolph Fund (1937), created to honor the first of these "Jeanes teachers" with monies raised from Jeanes teachers across the South. For more than 125 years, the SEF and its predecessor philanthropies have worked to promote equity and quality in education in the South, primarily for African-Americans and disadvantaged citizens. The foundation's interests span all levels of education, from early childhood education to postgraduate and professional education.

As some of the most influential educational agencies of their day, SEF's predecessor organizations were able to attract to their boards individuals of great prestige, despite the fact that the goals of the funds did not reflect mainstream white opinion and sought to aid and uplift African-Americans in general and African-American education in particular. Among the most prominent board members were six U.S. presidents. They were Ulysses S. Grant, Rutherford B. Hayes, William McKinley, Grover Cleveland, Theodore Roosevelt, and William Taft.

The foundation has played an instrumental role in the establishment of public kindergartens in the South, in promoting minority participation in higher education, in supporting African-American teachers, and in setting a public policy agenda for educational reform in the South. SEF operates a number of programs that address several critical needs in education. Through the operation of its own programs, the foundation takes a direct and active role in promoting positive change in educational equity in the South. Currently, the foundation's largest programs are directed toward improving the quality and supply of minority teachers and toward school restructuring. In addition, the foundation also sponsors conferences, commissions research on educational issues, and administers philanthropic funds for other organizations concerned with education.

The foundation is recognized as a public charity as defined by the United States Internal Revenue Code and is a tax-exempt 501(c)3 organization. SEF operated as a private foundation from its founding until 1983, when the foundation applied to the IRS for an advance ruling for public charity status, which was awarded in 1988. The foundation is governed by a board of trustees, guided by advisory committees and task forces, and employs thirteen staff members and two consultants. The work of the Southern Education Foundation is funded by an endowment of approximately ten million dollars and through grants from corporations, foundations, and individuals. The foundation maintains an active role in fundraising and welcomes contributions of any size.

SELECTED BIBLIOGRAPHY

Southern Education Foundation, *Toward Equity and Excellence: A History of the Southern Education Foundation* (1987); Southern Education Foundation, *The Jeanes Story: A Chapter in the History of American Education, 1908–1968* (1979); Southern Education Foundation, *Jeanes Supervision in Georgia Schools: A History of the Program from 1908 to 1975* (1975).

DIANA W. DE BROHUN

SOUTHERN UNIVERSITY SYSTEM. The Southern University System is one of the largest predominantly black public universities in the nation, with campuses in Baton Rouge, New Orleans, and Shreveport, Louisiana, and a total campus area of 1,002 acres. Students come to Southern from all sixty-four parishes of Louisiana, from forty-six of the fifty states, and from at least forty foreign countries, pursuing degrees in the arts and humanities, the sciences, education, agriculture, business, home economics, nursing, public policy and administration, engineering, and law.

The Baton Rouge campus is the oldest and largest of the three institutions. Founded in 1880, it is a land-grant institution located on 884 acres, including an Agricultural Experiment Farm for research and teaching. Special emphasis is given on this campus to strengthening liberal arts training, test sophistication, computer literacy, and career preparation. The institution further emphasizes and supports the pursuit of knowledge through structured and formalized investigation. It maintains an environment that enhances research and creative activities by faculty and students through the recognition of scholarly accomplishments and the promotion of the university as a laboratory for exploration and experimentation of the highest order.

The New Orleans campus began operation in September 1959. In addition to the baccalaureate degree programs, associate degree programs are offered in computer science, stenography, social welfare, real estate, and substance abuse. Research and public service activities are designed to address the problems facing the urban community. Additionally, SUNO has one of the largest evening and weekend colleges among institutions its size in the state and is fully accredited by the Southern Association of Colleges and Schools. The graduate and undergraduate programs in the School of Social Work are fully accredited by the Council of Social Work Education.

The Shreveport–Bossier City Campus was founded in 1964 and today is a public two-year coeducational commuter community college. The academic base is formed by the divisions of business, humanities, natural science, social science, and freshman studies. Educational offerings include developmental courses, one-and two-year career-oriented programs in technical and semiprofessional fields, associate degrees, and transfer programs to enter a four-year college or university.

SELECTED BIBLIOGRAPHY

National Association for Equal Opportunity in Higher Education, *Profiles of the Nation's Historically and Predominantly Black Colleges and Universities* (1993).

SAMUEL L. MYERS

SOUTHWESTERN CHRISTIAN COLLEGE (SWCC). Southwestern Christian College in Terrell, Texas, is the only historically black college affiliated with the Churches of Christ in America. Its primary founder was the Reverend George Phillip Bowser, an African-American minister of that denomination. Early in the first decade of the twentieth century, Reverend Bowser launched his efforts to create a Church of Christ-sponsored institution of higher education for African-Americans. At the time, blacks were not admitted to that church's established colleges. Bowser first initiated a Bible school in his church, the Jackson Street Church of Christ in Nashville. This school was later moved to Silver Point, Tennessee, where it was named the Silver Point Christian School and housed in a single brick building. Financial difficulties led to the closing of the Silver Point school. Afterwards, Bowser moved around the country, opening Bible training schools in Louisville, Kentucky, Detroit, Michigan, and Fort Smith, Arkansas, as he went. However, like his earlier efforts, these schools were also underfinanced and short-lived.

Bowser's quest was taken up by younger African-American Church of Christ preachers whom he had once taught. These men began a movement to establish in the state of Texas the kind of school Bowser had envisioned. The first building to be used for this purpose was the Lake Como Church of Christ in Fort Worth, Texas, which became the new home of the Southern Bible Institute. In 1949, buildings of the defunct Texas Military College in Terrell were purchased, and the institute moved from Fort Worth to Terrell. The name of the school was changed to Southwestern Christian College in 1950.

SWCC's mission is threefold: to offer a well-rounded educational program that will motivate students to value academic excellence within the context of a commitment to moral and spiritual values; to assist disadvantaged students in making their transitions from high school to college; and to help students prepare for varied vocations in life as well as leadership roles in the Church of Christ. Its student body, while predominantly African-American, is culturally diverse, with students hailing from thirty-five states and several countries. As a result, the institution has developed a strong developmental studies program in English as a second language and for students who have deficiencies in reading and mathematics.

Fully accredited by the Southern Association of Colleges and Schools,* SWCC presently confers associates of arts and sciences degrees and bachelor's degrees in Bible and religious education. Its strengths lie in its rigorous academic program, internationally renowned chorus, and outstanding athletic programs in basketball and track and field.

JACK EVANS

SPELMAN COLLEGE. Spelman College in Atlanta, Georgia, is the nation's oldest undergraduate liberal arts college for African-American women. It is renowned for its academic excellence and the leadership and achievements of its students and alumnae. Since 1881, Spelman has grown to educate over 1,500 students from forty-six states, the District of Columbia, and thirteen foreign countries. Since 1988, Spelman has been included in *U.S. News & World Report*'s annual listing of the nation's best colleges and universities. Spelman recognizes its unique position in higher education and takes seriously its role as a preeminent resources for the education African-American women leaders. As part of the Atlanta University Center, Spelman benefits from access to and cooperation with five other schools, while offering special opportunities for the education of women.

SELECTED BIBLIOGRAPHY
National Association for Equal Opportunity in Higher Education, *Profiles of the Nation's Historically and Predominantly Black Colleges and Universities* (1993).

SAMUEL L. MYERS

SPINGARN, ARTHUR BARNETT (28 March 1878, New York, N.Y.–1 December 1971, New York, N.Y.). An attorney, National Association for the Advancement of Colored People* official, and bibliophile, Spingarn was educated at Columbia University, where he received the B.A. in 1897 and a law degree in 1900. Howard University* awarded him an honorary degree in 1941. Spingarn's career as an attorney spanned some seventy years and was devoted to addressing the problems African-Americans faced in the American judicial system. His legal career overlapped his service with the NAACP, an organization for which he was an early organizer. From 1911 until 1939, Spingarn was a leader of the NAACP's national legal committee and vice president. He was elected the third president of the organization in 1939 and served until 1966. In 1913 Spingarn, his brother Joel, who preceded him as NAACP president, and Joel's wife Amy inaugurated the Spingarn Medal to honor important contributions by distinguished African-Americans. He is credited with helping to secure the services of Charles Hamilton Houston* as the organization's first paid counsel.

During Spingarn's long tenure with the NAACP, many court battles were waged that were important to education, housing, and public accommodations and to addressing voting and other civil rights issues. The significant cases attacking segregation in education included *Missouri ex rel. Gaines v. Canada** (1938), *Sipuel v. University of Oklahoma** (1948), *Sweatt v. Painter** (1950), *McLaurin v. Oklahoma State Regents** (1950), and the watershed case *Brown v. Board of Education of Topeka, Kansas** (1954).

Spingarn was also widely known as a bibliophile and an authority on African-American literature and art. His extensive private library of African-American authors was acquired by Howard University in 1946 and is one of the cornerstones of the renowned Moorland–Spingarn Research Center.* The Spingarn Collection, the product of a thirty-five-year worldwide search, illustrates the rich legacy of black historiography and provides the foundation for much current into black history and culture. Spingarn also authored the *Crisis** magazine's annual review of books by black authors from 1936 to 1968. Spingarn died at his home in New York City. Memorial services were held at Frank Campbell's Funeral Chapel.

SELECTED BIBLIOGRAPHY

Arthur B. Spingarn Papers, Moorland-Spingarn Research Center, Howard University; *Current Biography* (June 1965); Beverly Gray, "White Warrior," *Negro Digest* (September 1962); Minnie Finch, *The NAACP: Its Fight for Justice* (1981).

THOMAS C. BATTLE

STEVENS SCHOOL. Thaddeus Stevens Elementary School was the first school in Washington, D.C., to be built using public funds primarily for the education of "colored" children. Located in the Georgetown section of Washington, D.C., the school, built in 1868, served the African-American community that historically had been located there. It is the oldest standing school built to provide free public education for African-Americans in the District of Columbia and is the oldest functioning public school in the system.

The District of Columbia abolished slavery in 1862, nine months before the Emancipation Proclamation was issued and three years before the Thirteenth Amendment prohibited slavery. That same year Congress passed an act stipulating that 10 percent of taxes collected from the District's African-American community be set aside to start a primary public school for African-American children. This tax would yield only $736 after two years. It became obvious that funds raised under the act of 1862 were not sufficient. The financial burden of educating the District's African-American community fell upon the local school system. A new act was passed in 1866, which set aside a portion of all tax revenues collected not only from the Georgetown community, but citywide. Five hundred thousand dollars was appropriated by Congress during this same year to supplement the cost of construction for African-American and white schools in Georgetown and the District. Stevens was built two years after this new act and six years after a federal act mandated that children in the District ages 6–14 receive at least three months of compulsory education.

William Syphax, a schoolboard trustee and a prominent African-American businessman, offered a resolution to school trustees that the new school be named the "Stevens School House" in memory of the late Thaddeus Stevens, a Republican Congressman from Pennsylvania. Although he died at the height of his popularity, he was known for his work for the common school movement and especially for his advocacy of the abolitionist cause.

There is strong evidence that Stevens was built on one of the three lots set aside by the board of trustees for "colored" schools. Erected at 21st and K Streets, in the Old West End, now part of the downtown business district, the building had a property value of $18,240 and was furnished for $2,900. The school originally consisted of twelve rooms and an assembly hall. In 1883, additions were made to the school to alleviate overcrowding, but in 1896 the central portion of the school had to be nearly torn down and rebuilt because of faulty workmanship. A new, taller facade was built that added extra classrooms and eliminated the bad conditions. This structure is still standing today.

The Stevens school is a monument to the Reconstruction Era in America. Its history and programs for youths continue to stand in the community. The school has been placed on the District of Columbia inventory of historic sites.

SELECTED BIBLIOGRAPHY
Board of Trustees of the District of Columbia Public Schools, *First Annual Report, 1874–1875*; Juanita Braddock, Elizabeth Shiro, and Patricia Coan, *Stevens on Stevens: Community Perspective* (1984); Henry Bullock, *A History of Negro Education in the South* (1967); Winfield S. Montgomery, *Historical Sketch of Education for the Colored in the District of Columbia 1807–1905* (1907); Carter G. Woodson, *The Education of the Negro Prior to 1861* (1915).

LYNN LONG

STEWART, DONALD M. (8 July 1938, Chicago, Illinois). An educator and administrator, Stewart is president of The College Board, a post he has held since January 1987. He earned his bachelor of arts degree at Grinnell College in 1959, with the highest honors in political science. He received a master of arts in political science as a Woodrow Wilson Fellow at Yale University in 1962. At Harvard University, he earned a master of public administration degree (1969) and a doctor of public administration degree (1975) at the Kennedy

School of Government. In addition, he studied international law, organization, and economics at the Graduate Institute of International Studies in Geneva, Switzerland, from 1960 to 1962 and completed the Advanced Management Program at the Harvard Graduate School of Business Administration in the summer of 1983.

Before coming to the College Board, Stewart had served for ten years as the sixth president of Spelman College,* the 113-year-old historically black women's college in Atlanta, Georgia. At the University of Pennsylvania from 1970 to 1976, Dr. Stewart served as executive assistant to the president, instructor in public policy analysis, associate dean of arts and sciences, and assistant professor in the Department of City and Regional Planning. During this period, he was also director or coordinator of programs in community leadership, continuing education, and higher education research at the College of General Studies and the Fels Center of Public Policy.

Stewart was a staff member of the Overseas Development Division of the Ford Foundation from 1962 to 1969, working on assignments in Lagos, Nigeria; Cairo, Egypt, and Tunis, Tunisia, as well as in the foundation's New York City office. He concluded his tenure at the foundation by serving as program officer in its Middle East–Africa Program.

Stewart is a trustee or director of the Martin Luther King, Jr., Center for Nonviolent Social Change; Grinnell College; Teachers College, Columbia University; and the Committee for Economic Development. He is a member of the Council on Foreign Relations and former chairman of the National Advisory Committee on Accreditation and Institutional Eligibility of the U.S. Department of Education. He also served as trustee and board chairman of the Educational Testing Service, and as director and vice chairman of the American Council on Education. He is a former Japan Society fellow and trustee and currently serves as a director of the New York Times Company, the Principal Group in Des Moines, Iowa, and the Campbell Soup Company. He is a member of the Board of Trustees of the Mayo Foundation and WNET-TV in New York City and a member of the Visiting Committee to the Graduate School of Education and the John F. Kennedy School of Government at Harvard University.

Stewart is married to the former Isabel Carter Johnson, an alumna of Wellesley College who is also an educator. They have two sons, Jay, a graduate of Harvard University, and Carter, a graduate of Stanford University. The Donald and Isabel Stewart Living and Learning Center on the campus of Spelman College is named in honor of Dr. Stewart and his wife.

CHARLES A. ASBURY

STILLMAN COLLEGE. Founded in 1876 by the Presbyterian Church in the United States in Tuscaloosa, Alabama, this private, four-year coeducational liberal-arts college represents an oasis of multiculturalism and the richness of the Christian experience and instills in its students a sense of values and moral responsibility. Fully accredited by the Southern Association of Colleges and

Schools* and the Alabama State Department of Education, Stillman awards the bachelor of arts and bachelor of science degrees in sixteen academic areas.
SELECTED BIBLIOGRAPHY
National Association for Equal Opportunity in Higher Education, *Profiles of the Nation's Historically and Predominantly Black Colleges and Universities* (1993).

SAMUEL L. MYERS

STORER COLLEGE. Storer College of Harper's Ferry, West Virginia, existed as an educational institution for African-Americans from 1867 to 1956. Plans for the college were initiated when John Storer, a philanthropic northern lawyer, pledged ten thousand dollars for the establishment of a school, which would eventually become a college, that would educate youth without regard to race or color. Most notably, this school was to be located in one of the southern states. Storer challenged "friends of the colored people in the Free Baptist denomination" to raise an amount equal to his donation prior to January 1, 1868. With influential support from General Oliver O. Howard of the Bureau of Refugees, Freedmen, and Abandoned Lands (the Freedmen's Bureau)* and others, this goal was met and exceeded well before the deadline.

Harper's Ferry was selected as the site for the new school when the federal government donated several acres of land and four large government mansions at the junction of the Potomac and Shenandoah Rivers. In late 1867, the state of West Virginia matched Storer's gift and incorporated the school, making it the first institution established in that state for African-American higher education. Ongoing financial support for the school came from the state and the Northern Baptist Association.

Until 1938, Storer provided high school training to African-American West Virginia youth who were not provided with such facilities in their local districts. In addition to its four-year high school course, it offered a two-year standard normal program for elementary school teachers, a regular two-year junior college course, and special work in agriculture and homemaking. For many years it was the state's only teacher-education institution for African-Americans.

In 1938, Storer became a degree-granting college. The college's first degrees were awarded in 1942 to a class of seven students. In 1946, the college was accredited by the West Virginia Board of Education for the purpose of granting A.B. degrees in elementary education and degrees in secondary education in the fields of science, social science, English, and home economics. This accreditation continued until the school's demise a decade later.

In 1955, after the *Brown v. Board of Education of Topeka, Kansas** decision declared racial segregation unconstitutional, the West Virginia State Board of Education suspended its funding of Storer College. Efforts to keep the school open failed, and Storer ceased operations in 1956. In 1960, legislation was enacted by Congress to incorporate the abandoned Storer College facilities and grounds, including the historic John Brown Fort, which was moved to a site on the college's thirty-acre campus in 1910, into the Harper's Ferry National Monument.

SELECTED BIBLIOGRAPHY

Vivian Verdell Gordon, "A History of Storer College, Harper's Ferry, West Virginia," *Journal of Negro Education* 30 (1961): 445–49.

FAUSTINE C. JONES-WILSON

SUDARKASA, NIARA (Gloria Marshall Clark) (14 August 1938, Fort Lauderdale, Florida). An anthropologist and college president, Sudarkasa was born in Fort Lauderdale, Florida. She was reared there and in New York City, where her mother owned a dry-cleaning establishment. Sudarkasa spent much of her childhood in Fort Lauderdale with her maternal grandparents, Alpheus and Tryphenia Evans, who were from the Bahamas. At age fourteen, she entered Fisk University* under a Ford Foundation Early Entrant Scholarship. After spending a semester as an exchange student at Oberlin College* in Ohio, she transferred there in her junior year and took courses in Caribbean and African studies. She soon found connections between the Bahamian themes of her childhood and Yoruba traditions and institutions. In 1957, after graduating from Oberlin in the top 10 percent of her class with a sociology major, Sudarkasa moved to New York. She received her master's in anthropology from Columbia University in 1959 and continued toward a doctorate. During her doctoral program, she studied the Yoruba language and culture at the University of London School of Oriental and African Studies and later in Nigeria. She received a Ph.D. in anthropology from Columbia in 1964. Arguing that women in traditional African societies have more honored roles than do women in Western societies, Sudarkasa conducted research in Nigeria, Ghana, and the Republic of Benin. She received fellowships and study grants from organizations such as the Social Science Research Council Fellowship (1973–74), a Senior Fulbright Research Scholarship to study in the Republic of Benin (1982–83), and Ford Foundation and National Endowment for the Humanities grants (1983–84). She has published numerous articles on African women (especially on Yoruba women traders), West African migration, and African and African-American families.

Sudarkasa spent the early years of her academic career at traditionally white institutions. She taught briefly at Columbia and then for twenty years at the University of Michigan, where she was known both for her scholarship and for her political activism in support of causes such as more black studies and the admission of more minority students. She directed the Center for Afro-American and African studies from 1981 to 1984, when she became associate vice president for academic affairs. She became president of Lincoln University* in Pennsylvania in 1986. Under her presidency, Lincoln University has developed extensive international programs, increased its applications and enrollment, and begun a capital campaign.

SELECTED BIBLIOGRAPHY
Christa Brelin and William C. Matney, eds., *Who's Who among Black Americans, 1992–
1993* (1992).

ELIZABETH L. IHLE

SUMNER, CHARLES (6 January 1811, Boston, Massachusetts–11 March 1874, Washington, D.C.). As a lawyer, lecturer, advocate of international peace, leader of educational and prison reform, organizer of the antislavery Whigs, founder of the Republican Party, antislavery leader, and pioneer of the Liberal Republican movement of 1872, Charles Sumner made an exceptional contribution to American history. Sumner's father, Charles Pinckney Sumner, was a lawyer and the sheriff of Suffolk County; his mother, Relief Jacob Sumner, worked as a seamstress. He grew up in Boston, and in August 1821 entered Boston Public Latin School. He graduated from Harvard University in 1830, and in 1834 he graduated from Harvard Law School. Sumner became known as a pedantic orator during his college career. After graduation he studied at home and later taught school.

Sumner was elected to the United States Senate from Massachusetts in 1851. In the Senate, he made repeated and spirited attacks against the South, arguing that slavery was a sin and that it was the duty of each state to abolish it. He consistently spoke out against the evils of slavery and favored freeing the slaves and giving them the right to vote. Sumner's vision of an emancipated America motivated his constitutional speeches opposing slavery. He believed the Constitution and the Union did not sanction a man being held as property. He wanted to educate and mobilize public opinion in the free states of the North so they would overwhelmingly join the moral fight against slavery.

Sumner led the Senate's opposition to President Abraham Lincoln's moderate plans for Reconstruction. Later, he also opposed President Andrew Johnson's postwar Reconstruction plans. Sumner contended that the defeated South was a conquered province outside the protection of the Constitution and that the Confederate states should provide constitutional guarantees of racial equality for African-Americans before being readmitted into the Union. He proposed that the freedmen be given homesteads from their former slavemasters' estates and that state legislatures should be required to maintain a system of public education open to all races. Sumner further contended that giving the freedmen the ballot and education would reverse past injustices. He argued that voting rights would give African-Americans manhood and that learning to read and write would enhance their dignity.

During the 1840s, Sumner worked with Massachusetts educator Horace Mann to improve the system of public education in that state. Mann's plan to achieve his primary educational objective of upgrading the curriculum and quality of instruction later became a model for the nation. Sumner worked with Mann to establish normal schools for teacher training and institutes of in-service teacher education in Massachusetts. He was also a zealous spokesman for prison reform and peace.

Sumner made his last speech before the Senate on 10 March 1874. He died of a heart attack in Washington, D.C., on the next day.

SELECTED BIBLIOGRAPHY

W. E. B. Du Bois, *Black Reconstruction in America, 1860–1880* (1973); David Donald, *Charles Sumner and the Coming of the Civil War* (1960); David Donald, *Charles Sumner and the Rights of Man* (1970); Edward L. Pierce, *Memoirs and Letters of Charles Sumner* (reprint 1969).

CONSTANCE A. BURNS

SUMNER SCHOOL. The Charles Sumner School, named in honor of the fiery abolitionist senator from Massachusetts, holds a significant place in the development of educational opportunities for African-Americans in the District of Columbia. This beautifully designed brick schoolhouse, located on M Street, Northwest, was built in 1871 to replace the dilapidated, two-story wooden building that had served as a school for the city's African-American children since 1866.

During the century that followed its dedication, the Sumner building housed its own elementary classes and a secondary school (Paul Laurence Dunbar High School*). The Dunbar school held its first commencement, the nation's first high school graduation for African-American students, at Sumner in 1877. Sumner also housed eight other primary and grammar schools along with the executive offices of the superintendent and board of trustees of the "colored" schools of the District of Columbia and Georgetown. Renamed the Myrtilla Miner Normal School in 1877, the former Sumner building served as the site of the city's first normal school, or teacher's college, for African-Americans. (The Miner school was later incorporated into the University of the District of Columbia*). Miner offered a broad spectrum of public and private educational and administrative activities, including adult education, night classes, and health clinics.

In 1986, the Miner School was placed on the District of Columbia Inventory of Historic Sites by the Joint Committee on Landmarks of the Nation's Capital. That same year, it was carefully renovated and renamed the Charles Sumner School Museum and Archives. In its collection may be found some of the early records of the D.C. Public Schools, pieces of Charles Sumner's correspondence, and other memorabilia. The building is frequently used as gallery space for local artists and by public and private groups for conferences and social events.

SELECTED BIBLIOGRAPHY

The District of Columbia Public Schools, *The Charles Sumner School* (commemorative booklet) (1986).

BARBARA DODSON WALKER

SWANN v. CHARLOTTE–MECKLENBURG BOARD OF EDUCATION, 402 U.S. 1 (1971). In this landmark decision, the U.S. Supreme Court upheld busing as a constitutional method of desegregating public schools within a school district. The Court also defined the obligations of local school authorities to implement desegregation efforts and reinforced the broad authority of the federal court to dictate the proper remedy for eliminating racially segregated public schools that create dual systems within school districts.

The city of Charlotte and surrounding Mecklenburg County, North Carolina, comprised a single, independent school district which had more than eighty-four thousand students in 107 schools during the 1968–69 school year. Approximately 29 percent of the twenty-four thousand students were African-American, most of whom (twenty-one thousand) attended schools within the city of Charlotte. Two thirds of those—about fourteen thousand students—attended twenty-one schools that were at least 99 percent populated by other African-American students. The district court ordered the school board to provide a plan to desegregate the faculty and student populations. The lower court became dissatisfied with the school board's plan and appointed its own expert to formulate a plan. The district court later received plans prepared by the U.S. Department of Health, Education, and Welfare and a "minority plan" submitted by four members of the nine-member school board.

Recognizing the many problems encountered by federal courts in effectuating *Brown v. Board of Education of Topeka, Kansas,** the Supreme Court reviewed the case in order to provide some guidance to lower courts in formulating acceptable desegregation plans. The Court made clear the broad powers of district courts in evaluating and formulating desegregation plans, stating that the lower court had broad power to fashion a remedy that would assure a unitary (desegregated) school system. The Court examined four means of assessing school desegregation remediation efforts: (a) the use of racial quotas, (b) the existence of single-race schools, (c) the presence of attendance zones, and (d) the use of transportation.

The Court rejected the claim that strict racial quotas must be utilized in assigning students to schools. The Court held that suitable desegregation efforts need not require strict adherence to racial quota requirements, stating that the constitutional command to desegregate schools does not mean that every community must always reflect the racial composition of the school system as a whole. Second, the Supreme Court warned that schools comprised of students of one race would raise the ire of the court. The Court stated that "schools all or predominantly of one race in a district of mixed population will require close scrutiny to determine that school assignments are not part of a state-enforced segregation." The Court emphasized that the district court and school authorities should make efforts to achieve the greatest possible degree of actual desegregation and should be concerned with the elimination of single-race schools. Third, the Court viewed as acceptable the pairing and grouping of noncontiguous school zones as a tool for breaking up a dual-school system. Finally, the Court held that busing students out of neighborhood schools is an appropriate tool for eliminating a dual segregated system, noting that "desegregation plans cannot be limited to the walk-in school."

The *Swann* decision clarified the requirements of *Brown* and, quite significantly, recognized mandatory busing as an appropriate method for achieving desegregated unitary school districts. Some critics argue that mandatory busing has contributed significantly to the social phenomenon called "white flight,"* the tendency of whites to move away from the inner city and into residential neighborhoods located in the outlying suburbs. Ironically, as a result of the white flight that followed court-ordered busing, separate and unequal school systems continue to exist, with predominantly African-American and Hispanic urban school districts generally having access to fewer funds and resources than predominantly white suburban districts.

SELECTED BIBLIOGRAPHY

Leon Jones, *From Brown to Boston: Desegregation in Education (1954–1974)*, vol. 1 and 2 (Bibliography) (1979); Gary Orfield, *Must We Bus? Segregated Schools and National Policy* (1978); Jeffrey A. Raffel, *The Politics of School Desegregation: The Metropolitan Remedy in Delaware* (1980); Judith F. Buncher, ed., *School Busing Controversy: 1970–1975* (Facts on File, 1975); Brian J. Sheehan, *Boston School Integration Dispute: Social Change and Legal Maneuvers* (1984).

LISA WILSON EDWARDS

SWEATT v. PAINTER, 339 U.S. 629 (1950). This case was brought by the National Association of Colored People* (NAACP) on behalf of Herman Sweatt. Sweatt petitioned that he was denied admission to the state-supported University of Texas Law School because of a state law that forbade admission of African-Americans to the school. Sweatt refused an offer made by the school to enroll in a separate law school established by the state for African-Americans and demanded admission to the regular University of Texas Law School.

A comparison of the two law schools revealed the following: The University of Texas Law School had sixteen full-time and three part-time professors, a student body of 850, a library of 65,000 volumes, a law review, moot court facilities, scholarship funds, an Order of the Coif affiliation, many distinguished alumni, and a rich, prestigious tradition. The separate Texas State Law School for Negroes had a faculty that included five full-time professors, twenty-three students, a library of 16,500 volumes, a practice court, a legal aid association, and one alumnus admitted to the Texas Bar. By maintaining separate and inferior facilities for African-American law students, the state effectively prevented any opportunity for interaction with the white lawyers, judges, and other officials who made up the overwhelming majority of the state's legal professionals.

The Supreme Court held that the legal education offered to Sweatt was not substantially equal to that which would be offered at the University of Texas Law School. Also, the Court proclaimed that the Equal Protection Clause of the Fourteenth Amendment required that Sweatt be admitted to the University of Texas Law School. This decision was a reversal of an earlier Texas trial court decision, which found that a newly established state law school for Negroes offered Sweatt advantages and opportunities for the study of law that were substantially equivalent to those the state offered white students at the University of Texas. The trial court denied Sweatt admission to the University of Texas Law School, and the Court of Civil Appeals affirmed, thereby leading to the Supreme Court reversal.

Sweatt v. Painter and a similar case, *McLaurin v. Oklahoma State Regents*,* examined the extent to which the Equal Protection Clause of the Fourteenth Amendment limits the power of a state to distinguish between students of different races in professional and graduate education in a state university.

SELECTED BIBLIOGRAPHY

Sweatt v. Painter, 339 U.S. 629 (1950); M. Yudof, D. Kirp, T. van Geel, and B. Levin, *Educational Policy and the Law: Cases and Materials* (1987).

                                                JOHNNY EDWARD BROWN AND WILLIAM C. AKINS

T

TALENTED TENTH. A term conceptualized and popularized by W. E. B. Du Bois,* it describes the 10 percent of African-Americans whom Du Bois judged to be exceptional in intellectual ability and character, who would be liberally educated to become race leaders. During the 1880s Booker T. Washington,* a Hampton Institute* graduate, was appointed principal of Tuskegee Institute.* In his 1895 Atlanta Exposition speech, Washington emphasized industrial education for blacks and accommodation to the existing racial status quo. White southerners and northern business men enthusiastically endorsed these concepts, and made Washington the most popular Southerner since Jefferson Davis. Among southern African-Americans, however, the speech caused sorrow and apprehension. Many believed that Washington was asking them to surrender their political power and educational opportunities for their youth.

Du Bois, a Harvard-educated Ph.D. from New England, was among Washington's most notable opponents. In 1903, Du Bois published *The Souls of Black Folk*, in which he asserted: ''The problem of the twentieth century is the problem of the color line.'' That statement was not only accurate prophecy but was also a summation of the conflict between Washington and Du Bois, who stated that Washington's Atlanta Compromise implied that southern whites could now continue oppressive social policies without intervention from northern whites and southern African-Americans. Du Bois gradually became the spokesman for those African-Americans who aspired to higher education and intellectual endeavors, as opposed to the developing peasant conservatism promoted by Washington and his supporters.

In 1903, Booker T. Washington published *The Negro Problem*, which included several essays by prominent African-Americans. Du Bois's entry, ''The Talented Tenth,'' emphasized the necessity of a liberal arts education in order to develop ''race men,'' an intellectual elite distinct from businessmen and artisans. Du Bois began the essay thus: ''The Negro race, like all races, is going to be saved by its exceptional men. The problem of education, then, among Negroes must first of all deal with the Talented Tenth; it is the problem of developing the Best of this race that they may guide the Mass away from the contamination and death of the Worst, in their own and other races.'' According to DuBois, the Talented Tenth rises and brings others with them; the worst that the unrisen could do would be to pull the risen down.

The most serious questions facing African-American leaders, however, were how to train the leaders of a struggling people, and how to increase the strength of the few who had achieved prominence. Du Bois believed that there could be only one answer: ''The best and most capable of their youth must be schooled in the colleges and universities of the land.'' He refused to argue subject matter or teaching methodology, but emphasized the crucial need to develop an educational system to improve the social and economic status of African-Americans. This need, along with the lack of trained African-American teachers, contributed to African-American educational institutions' concentration on normal school training, and strengthened support for Washington's educational philosophy.

Du Bois did not disparage the educational efforts of Washington and his followers. He did, however, recognize the contradiction represented by the level of educational attainment among the Tuskegee staff. He noted in his essay that ''Washington had as his helpers the son of a Negro Senator, trained in Greek and the humanities, and graduated at Harvard; the son of a Negro congressman and lawyer, trained in Latin and mathematics, and graduated at Oberlin . . . indeed some thirty of his chief teachers are college graduates, and instead of studying French grammars in the midst of weeds, or buying pianos for dirty cabins, they are at Mr. Washington's right hand helping him in a noble work. And yet one of the effects of Mr. Washington's propaganda has been to cast doubt upon the expediency of such training for Negroes, as these persons have had.''

Du Bois concluded his essay by stating that ''[t]he Talented Tenth of the Negro race must be made leaders of thought and missionaries of culture among their people.''

SELECTED BIBLIOGRAPHY

Frances L. Broderick, *W. E. B. Du Bois: Negro Leadership in Time of Crisis* (1959); Louis R. Harlan, *Booker T. Washington*, vols. 1 and 2 (1972, 1973); Winthrop Jordan, *White over Black* (1968); Julius Lester, ed., *The Thought and Writing of W. E. B. Du Bois* (1971); Elliot M. Rudwick, *W. E. B. Du Bois: A Study in Minority Group Leadership* (1961).

DAVID W. BISHOP

TALLADEGA COLLEGE. Founded in 1867, Talladega College is located in Talladega, Alabama. Although the curriculum is rooted in the liberal arts, it offers majors in most fields of interest to today's students. All of its programs, whether in the humanities, social science, the sciences, or mathematics, are excellent and distinctive. Further, the lecture recital program of the college, which brings nationally prominent scholars, politicians, and artists to the campus, adds a special dimension to Talladega's superior academic environment. Its relatively small size, location, highly credentialed faculty, select students, and rich legacy of achievements make Talladega College a training ground for scholars and leaders among men and women. Talladega College has been cited in statistical studies for its particularly high percentage of graduates who earn science doctorates, degrees in medicine, and doctorates in other difficult disciplines.

SELECTED BIBLIOGRAPHY

National Association for Equal Opportunity in Higher Education, *Profiles of the Nation's Historically and Predominantly Black Colleges and Universities* (1993).

SAMUEL L. MYERS

TEACHERS, AFRICAN-AMERICAN, CERTIFICATION AND LICEN-SURE. Teachers in all states are required to hold a license and to be certified to teach a particular subject or areas of the school curriculum. Licensure ensures that the providers of educational services meet minimal standards that will protect the public from harm. A certificate ensures a level of competence. Teachers are certified upon the recommendation of an institution that has an approved program to offer certification in that area. Such endorsements are provided by state departments of education or by the National Council for Accreditation of Teacher Education (NCATE), an affiliate of the American Association of Colleges for Teacher Education (AACTE). More than twelve hundred colleges and universities in the United States prepare K–12 teachers. In most states, there is an oversupply in almost all fields; yet the shortage of fully certified minority teachers continues to be a major problem for school districts in every region. The causes and cures for this problem are the source of intense debate in school reform literature.

Through interstate reciprocity agreements, states may agree to accept for licensure graduates from approved programs in other states. Most teachers enter the profession with a one-year renewable license. After three years, most teachers get a five-year renewable license. In instances where a teacher has not met certification standards and no certified teacher is available, an emergency certificate can be issued for one year while missing requirements are completed. Alternative routes to certification or emergency licenses may be used when regular requirements have not been met.

Competency or standardized tests are used by states to determine entry or continuation in the teaching profession or merit pay. They have been subjects of continuing debate about their impact on the dwindling numbers of minority teachers. The tests are usually on basic skills, specialty areas, or general professional knowledge. The National Teachers Examination* (NTE), the most widely used teacher competency test, was developed in the 1950s but was not widely required for licensure until the 1980s. Other competency tests are the Pre-Professional Skills Tests (PPST) and the CBEST test in California.

Before the 1960s, there existed little literature on the problems of teacher certification. Teachers, especially African-Americans, were poorly paid; and a normal school (2 year) diploma was still acceptable in much of the nation. Urban districts like Chicago, New York, and Philadelphia were the first to require four-year degrees; and many urban districts initiated local teacher exams to control entry into the ranks of the profession.

During most of the twentieth century, neither high school graduation nor postsecondary schooling was expected for most young people. Although segregation existed in most of the nation's schools and teacher corps, teaching was one of the few professions open to educated minorities and women. A succession of legislative actions in the 1950s and 1960s—the *Brown v. Board of Education of Topeka, Kansas** decision, the Civil Rights Act of 1964,* Executive Order 11246, and Title IX—drastically changed the educational landscape. Legally segregated school districts were dismantled, and women were legally entitled to enter most fields. As a result, there was increased migration from the rural South, women began to enter professions other than teaching, and one-race neighborhood schools were ruled unconstitutional.

Once the dual school systems were made illegal, southern districts began to embrace teacher competency tests as a means of determining which experienced teachers would be retained. Northern districts also embraced the competency tests, but primarily to control entry. In addition, many minority teachers were hired under emergency certification, with little opportunity for permanent slots unless they passed the competency tests. African-American teachers filed suit under Title VII of the 1964 Civil Rights Act to show that the tests had a disproportionate impact on minority teachers.

Standardized tests like the ACT and the SAT are used to "sort" students within schools and for admission to universities. During the civil rights era, African-American parents charged that in many schools, not only were the teachers white, thus providing few role models for minority youth, but advanced classes were also all-white, while remedial or special education classes were all or largely minority. During this era, testing for entry to a variety of occupations also became more prevalent. When minorities felt that other tests were used unfairly, these tests also were challenged. Under Title VII of the Civil Rights Act and *Griggs v. Duke Power Company,* teacher competency tests and other tests were placed under progressively more intense security.

The challenges to competency testing were most successful in showing that many experienced minority teachers and administrators who did not "pass" the tests nevertheless performed well in school and received satisfactory performance evaluations. The challenges also presented evidence that "pass" levels tended to be set where they most impacted minority test takers. The EEOC Guidelines required that the tests be "predictive of or significantly correlated with important elements of work behaviors which comprise or are relevant to the job or jobs for which the candidates are being developed" (Cohen, 1989). Meeting this guideline shaped most of the testing litigation.

In 1983, increasing criticism about the quality of instruction offered in the schools was captured most persuasively in a report by the U.S. Department of Education. The report asserted that America was "at risk" from "a rising tide of mediocrity'' in the nation's schools. Universities and school districts responded by making passing scores on teacher competency tests an additional requirement for initial certification or licensure. During the early 1960s and 1970s the Educational Testing Service (ETS) had clearly stated that the NTE should not be the sole criterion for teacher certification and should not be used as a performance predictor. ETS was especially concerned about the impact of the NTE on minority test-takers. In 1983, the state of Florida enforced for the first time a law that required that 80 percent of college students must pass subject-matter exams for teacher education programs to maintain their approved status. Thirty-eight programs in eighteen colleges lost approval. Most of the eighteen schools were African-American or had large minority enrollments.

As a second part of the reaction to *A Nation at Risk* and other reform reports that criticized the preparation of teachers, institutions began to also require the Pre–Professional Skills Test (PPST), a test of basic language and math skills, as an early screening device or for admission to teacher education programs. Minorities challenged the PPST effect as more important for the eventual certification of minority teachers than was the NTE. They argued that the PPST effectively screened out first-generation minorities who brought the nontraditional languages of their home communities to campus. Minorities also held that first-generation students were the traditional sources for teachers and that the PPST and other similar tests should not be used to prevent their certification as teachers.

By 1984, twenty-one states had tests or plans to test for admission to teacher education programs on college campuses. Among the larger states, Texas adopted the PPST as the only examination, and California adopted the CBEST, a similar test of reading, writing and math skills that was developed by the Educational Testing Service expressly for California. In 1983, only 26 percent of the African-American candidates passed the California tests, while two thirds of all applicants passed. That year in Texas only 16 percent of the African-American students passed the math skills test and 20 percent passed the writing test.

In the 1980s, some educators were increasingly convinced that competency testing could eliminate minority teachers and that future minority students could complete K–12 and never have a minority teacher. These educators responded by developing strategies to increase the success rates of minorities on teacher competency tests and by negotiating with state departments of education to provide alternatives to standardized tests to certify teachers, especially minority teachers. Increased success rates were achieved at Grambling State University* and Norfolk State University,* which became models for other institutions. During this decade, New Jersey and California became leading proponents of alternative routes to certification. These new routes allowed districts to structure programs that were tailored to success in the districts. They were used to eliminate large pools of emergency certificates and/or to address special needs, including a diverse teacher corps.

By the late 1980s, preemptory challenges of the PPST and the NTE were largely exhausted. Institutions began to seek other means to ensure that minority teachers could be certified. Research indicated that American schools, especially the largest urban districts, were becoming increasingly minority, that many more districts and the entire state of California would become "majority-minority," and that the number of certified minority teachers was decreasing. Urban school districts convinced many universities and state departments of education that teacher preparation programs should both increase the pool of minority teachers and ensure that all teachers were better equipped to teach the diverse cultures and languages in the schools.

The Ann Arbor case affirmed that black English was a legitimate form of discourse that could be used in schools. *Lau v. Nicholas* addressed the language rights of those children, some of whom were African-American, whose first language was Spanish. In the 1970s, Wisconsin, Minnesota, and Iowa established human relations codes for the certification of teachers. These codes required that multicultural education be infused in the curriculum and that preservice teachers have direct field experiences with learners from multicultural groups. The University of Wisconsin system, in its strategic plan for teacher preparation, required that each state institution submit an annual report that included efforts to increase the number of minority teachers (University of Wisconsin System, 1990).

On the national level, the National Council for the Accreditation of Teachers added a precondition for universities seeking national certification that addressed the preparation of a diverse corps as well as the need for infusion of multicultural content. The Middle States Association also added an infusion requirement that impacted the general education of teachers. Donna Gollnick and Arthur Wise, vice president and president of NCATE, and Howard Simmons, head of MSA, faced considerable criticism for these revisions. There were also a number of collaborative efforts to increase the certification rates of minorities. In one notable example, graduate schools of education at Columbia University, Harvard University, and Vanderbilt University collaborated with historically black colleges and universities in southern states to address the shortage of minority teachers.

By the 1990s, the rates of certification of minorities had improved. A 1988 survey of four-year institutions found that almost three fifths required a teacher competency test and, more important, that 71 percent of the minorities were passing these tests, compared to 90 percent for majority students.

SELECTED BIBLIOGRAPHY

Bernice Bass de Martinez, "Political and Reform Agendas Impact on the Supply of Black Teachers," *Journal of Teacher Education* 39, no. 1 (January-February 1988): 10–13; James E. Bruno and George Marcoulides, "Equality of Educational Opportunity at Racially Isolated Schools: Balancing the Need for Teacher Certification with Teacher Shortage," *Urban Review* 17, no. 3 (1985): 155–65; Charles W. Case, R. Jerrald Shive, Karen Spiegal, and Virginia M. Ingebretson, "Minority Teacher Education: Recruitment and

Retention Methods," *Journal of Teacher Education* 39, no. 4 (Summer 1988); "A Survey of Two Years of Action by 50 States and the District of Columbia to Reform the Education of Teachers," *Chronicle of Higher Education*, 10 April 1988, pp. 31, 33, 36; Judith H. Cohen, "Legal Challenges to Testing for Teacher Certification: History, Impact and Future Trends," *Journal of Law and Education* 18, no. 2 (Spring 1989): 229–65; Antoine M. Garibaldi, "Recruitment, Admission and Standards: Black Teachers and the Holmes and Carnegie Reports," *Metropolitan Education* 4 (1987): 17–23; Bernard R. Gifford, "Excellence and Equity in Teacher Competency Testing: A Policy Perspective," *Journal of Negro Education* 55, no. 3 (1986): 251–71; Patricia A. Graham, "Black Teachers: A Drastically Scarce Resource," *Phi Delta Kappan* 68 (1987): 598–605; Willis D. Hawley, "Toward a Comprehensive Strategy for Addressing the Teacher Shortage," *Phi Delta Kappan* 67 (1986): 712–18; Stafford Hood and Lawrence J. Parker, "Minority Bias Review Panels and Teacher Testing for Initial Certification: A Comparison of Two States' Efforts," *Journal of Negro Education* 58, no. 4 (1989): 511–19; Harvey Pressman and Alan Gartner, "The New Racism in Education," *Social Policy* (Summer 1986): 11–15; L. Jill Rambert, *The Impact of Historically Black Institutions on the Supply of Black Teachers*, Southern Regional Education Board (October 1989); G. Pritchy Smith, "The Critical Issue of Excellence and Equity in Competency Testing," *Journal of Teacher Education* 35, no. 2 (March–April 1984): 6–9; Herbert Teitelbaum and Richard J. Hiller, "Bilingual Education: The Legal Mandate," *Harvard Educational Review* 47 (1977): 138–70.

SHIRLEY F. STENNIS–WILLIAMS

TEACHERS, AFRICAN-AMERICAN, CHARACTERISTICS. Until the Civil Rights Movement expanded somewhat the employment possibilities for African-Americans, teaching and the ministry were two of the few occupations open to college-educated African-Americans. Unlike the ministry, however, teaching was open to men and women on an equal basis. In 1890, African-American women comprised slightly more than half of all African-American teachers in the United States. Twenty years later, more than two thirds of African-American teachers were females; and by 1960, 84 percent of all African-American elementary and secondary school teachers were women. Since the 1970s, the number of African-Americans entering the teaching profession has been gradually declining. In 1950, half of the African-American professionals in the United States were teachers. By 1977, however only 22 percent of the bachelor's degrees in education were awarded to African-Americans. By 1983, the number of degrees in education had declined even further, with only 9 percent of the bachelor's degrees in education being conferred on African-Americans. Between 1971 and 1986, the percentage of African-American teachers declined from 8.1 percent to 6.9 percent.

The reasons for this decline are complicated, but it can be attributed in part to increased teacher testing at both entry and exit stages of the teaching profession. In California in 1983, only 25 percent of African-Americans passed the examinations given to prospective teacher education candidates. In Florida, the pass rate for African-American teacher candidates in 1980 was 40 percent. In the same year in North Carolina, the failure rate of African-Americans was 87 percent. Comparable statistics on the low passing rates of African-American teacher candidates are available for other states, including Alabama, Texas, Pennsylvania, Georgia, Oklahoma, and Louisiana.

Another factor affecting the number of African-American teachers is the declining number of African-American students enrolling in and completing college. A third, less acknowledged factor influencing the numbers of African-American teachers was the desegregation of the nation's schools subsequent to the 1954 *Brown v. Board of Education of Topeka, Kansas** decision. One consequence of desegregation was that, between 1954 and 1970, approximately thirty-two thousand African-American teachers were displaced in the seventeen southern and border states affected by *Brown.*

Prior to the 1960s, many African-American teachers belonged to the American Teachers Association (ATA), especially those employed in states that maintained de jure segregated schools. Founded in 1904 as the National Association of Teachers in Colored Schools,* the American Teachers Association was comprised of state associations, many reorganized from previously existing organizations. The ATA held conferences for its members, focusing on improved teacher training and professional development. The organization also published the *Colored Teacher,* later renamed *The Bulletin,* a journal dedicated to issues concerning African-American teachers and students.

One of the primary accomplishments of the ATA was its involvement in litigation that resulted in equalization of pay for African-American teachers. The association provided moral, and in some cases, financial, support to members involved in the National Association for the Advancement of Colored People's* series of salary equalization lawsuits. In 1966, the ATA merged with the National Education Association.

The research on teacher characteristics and their relationship to teacher attitudes and behavior is substantial; however, due in part to differences in methodology and to small sample size, the results are inclusive. A 1988 review of thirty-six experimental and naturalistic research studies on teacher expectations concluded that, although teachers generally hold more negative attitudes about African-American pupils than about white pupils, in those few studies which compared African-American and white teachers' attitudes, African-American teachers held higher expectations for African-American pupils. Nevertheless, in one of the most widely cited qualitative studies of teachers' negative behavior toward African-American pupils (manifested in the placement of students in ability groups according to social class), the subject teacher was African-American. A few other studies of this type have also found that middle-class African-American teachers are biased against working-class pupils. Subsequent research, however, has found significant discrepancies in the extent to which social class, type of teacher training institution, and other factors shape the attitudes and behavior of African-American teachers toward African-American pupils of varying social classes.

Recently a small body of research has accrued that examines the pedagogy of excellent African-American teachers. This research, which takes the cultural integrity of the African-American community as its starting point, has found that such teachers frequently rely on the cultural and social underpinnings of the African-American community to strengthen their connections with students and their parents. Cultural solidarity and connectedness manifest in strong attachments to the African-American community, linking classroom content to students' own life experiences. These connected behaviors include the use of familiar community speech style and cultural patterns and a focus on the social development of the child, reflected in the teachers' willingness to assume personal responsibility for nurturing in students the prerequisite skills for success in school and society.

SELECTED BIBLIOGRAPHY

Samuel Etheridge, "Impact of the 1954 *Brown v. Topeka Board of Education* Decision on Black Educators," *Negro Educational Review* 30, nos. 3–4 (1979): 217–32; Michele Foster, "Constancy, Change, and Constraints on the Lives of Black Women Teachers: Some Things Change, Most Stay the Same," *NWSA Journal* 3, no. 2 (1992): 233–61; Michele Foster, "The Politics of Race: Through African-American Teachers' Eyes," *Journal of Education* 172, no. 3 (1990): 123–41; Michele Foster, "Education for Competence in Community and Culture: Exploring the Views of Exemplary African-American Teachers," *Urban Education* 27, no. 4 (1993): 370–94; Jacqueline Irvine, "Disappearing Black Educators," *Elementary School Journal* 88 (1988): 503–13; National Education Association, *Status of the American Public School Teacher 1985–1986* (1987); Thelma D. Perry, *History of the American Teachers Association* (1975).

MICHELE FOSTER

TEACHERS, AFRICAN-AMERICAN, RECRUITMENT, DESEGREGATION, AND SHORTAGES. The "separate-but-equal" doctrine established in 1896 by *Plessy v. Ferguson*,* while flawed, was not without its positive aspects. By affirming the legal concept of equal protection in education for African-Americans, *Plessy* provided a rationale for the establishment of a separate system of education, creating opportunities for those African-Americans who wished to pursue careers as teachers and administrators in "colored" schools. While school desegregation has been widely touted as a positive development in U.S. society, it has had some unanticipated long-term consequences. One of these is the negative impact it has had on the recruitment of and demand for African-American teachers.

As with *Plessy*, however, a major reason for the negative impact of the 1954 *Brown v. Board of Education of Topeka, Kansas** decision was the court system's reluctance to interfere in the decisions of white school administrators who resisted implementation of the law in a number of ways. After *Brown*, many school systems retained all of their white teachers, even those with only provisional certification, while dismissing many fully certified African-American teachers. An African-American teacher who retired or moved away was often replaced by a white teacher or not replaced at all. Culturally biased standardized tests were used to screen out disproportionate numbers of African-Americans, and African-American teachers were often placed in teaching positions outside their field so that they could be more easily fired on the basis of poor performance. The educational climate created by these resistance efforts has had a cumulative negative impact on the numbers of African-Americans in the field of education and on recruitment efforts to bring more African-Americans into the field.

The true impact of the *Brown* decision may never be accurately known because little or no effort has been made to determine how many African-American teachers lost their jobs in the two decades following *Brown*. However, estimates range from thirty-two thousand to thirty-eight thousand in the seventeen southern and border states affected by desegregation orders. This decline in African-American participation in the teaching force has continued in more recent years. In 1970, 12 percent of the teaching force was African-American, but by 1986, it had dropped to under 7 percent.

Among those African-Americans pursuing higher education, there is a trend toward selecting fields other than education. In the twelve years between 1966 and 1978, the percentage of African-American college students choosing education as a major dropped from 23 percent to 6.8 percent. While this may reflect the growth of other employment opportunities for persons of color, the long-term effects in the field of education have been detrimental.

The crisis in American education created by the declining numbers of teachers of color is compounded by the general lack of minority student recruitment and retention efforts at predominantly white institutions of higher education. As desegregation was implemented in higher education, these institutions drew increasingly larger numbers of African-American students, who in the past likely would have attended historically black colleges and universities (HBCUs). Given the traditional importance of HBCUs in the preparation and recruitment of African-American teachers, these trends gave added momentum to the rapid decline in the numbers of African-American teachers at all levels of education.

Unfortunately, the decline in the proportion of African-American teachers is occurring as the proportion of children of color in the nation's schools is increasing. One major rationale for efforts to increase the number of African-American and other teachers of color is the need for both nonwhite and white students to have such teachers serve as positive role models. The presence of nonwhite role models is vital to effective education, lest students receive implicit messages identifying authority figures as predominantly white.

SELECTED BIBLIOGRAPHY

Barbara Astone and Elsa Nunez-Wormack, *Pursuing Diversity: Recruiting Minority Students* (ASHE-ERIC Higher Education Report No. 7) (1990); Beverly P. Cole, ''The Black Educator: An Endangered Species,'' *Journal of Negro Education* 55, no. 3 (1986): 326–34; Samuel B. Ethridge, ''Impact of the 1954 *Brown v. Topeka Board of Education* Decision on Black Educators,'' *Negro Educational Review* 30, no. 4 (1979): 217–32; Sabrina Hope King, ''The Limited Presence of African-American Teachers,'' *Review of*

Education Research 63, no. 2 (1993): 115–49; Joseph Stewart, Jr., Kenneth J. Meier, Robert M. LaFollette, and Robert E. England, "In Quest of Role Models: Change in Black Teachers Representation in Urban School Districts, 1968–1986," *Journal of Negro Education* 58, no. 2 (1989): 140–52.

A. WILLIAM PLACE

TEENAGE PREGNANCY AND AFRICAN-AMERICAN EDUCATION.
Early, unplanned childbearing can seriously disrupt the educational careers of African-American adolescents. School can help to remedy the problems of adolescent childbearing through prevention and intervention programs. The public reaction to adolescent pregnancy and childbearing is often emotional, very negative, and clouded by demeaning stereotypes of African-American sexual behavior and family life. Current statistics, however, indicate that African-American adolescents are not significantly different from other American ethnic groups in their sexual behavior. Slightly more than half of both African-American (59%) and white (51%) adolescent females are sexually active.

In contrast, African-American adolescents have higher pregnancy and birth rates than their white counterparts. Although the majority of adolescents do not experience pregnancy or birth, the pregnancy rate for African-American adolescents (18.6%) is double that of white adolescents (9.3%). Similarly, the birth rate for African-American adolescents (9.5%) is approximately twice that of white adolescents (4.4%). Although rates of adolescent pregnancy and childbearing remain higher for African-Americans than for whites, the recent increases in these rates in the United States are the result of increases in white adolescents. In addition, U.S. adolescent pregnancy and childbearing rates are higher than in any other western industrialized nation; this is true even when African-Americans are excluded from the data and only whites are considered. Thus, adolescent childbearing is not a phenomenon limited to African-Americans; in fact, because the majority of the U.S. population is white, the majority of adolescent childbearers in the United States are white.

Pregnancy, childbearing, and childrearing during adolescence may interfere with the advanced education necessary for adult success in American society. African-American women who have their first child during adolescence have lower levels of educational attainment than do those who delay childbearing until after the adolescent years. While the educational attainment of adolescent childbearers has increased since the 1950s, this increase has been greater for African-Americans than for whites. Among African-American young adult women seventeen years of age or younger when their first child was born, only seventeen percent had graduated from high school in 1958, as compared to 61 percent in 1986. The corresponding rates for their white counterparts were 20 percent in 1958 and 54 percent in 1986. Among adolescent childbearers, African-Americans appear to have better educational outcomes than do other ethnic groups. Comparisons of adolescent childbearers in the National Longitudinal

Survey of Youth indicated that African-Americans achieve higher educational levels than do whites or Hispanics.

The conventional wisdom of the past was that a life of poverty is the inevitable outcome of adolescent childbearing. Continued education, however, is a key factor in the resilience of adolescent childbearers in their later lives. In a study of African-American women who took part in the National Survey of Family Growth, the number of years of education completed was a stronger predictor of women's income than was the experience of adolescent motherhood. Educational attainment has a stronger influence on adult women's economic well-being than does the age at which she has children. Further, a seventeen-year longitudinal study of African-American adolescent childbearers in Baltimore found a variety of outcomes in adulthood, illustrating that a successful adult life is possible for adolescent childbearers.

Many adolescent childbearers had difficulty in school before the pregnancy occurred. Adolescents may have lost interest in school or dropped out prior to the occurrence of a pregnancy. Thus, the educational problems of adolescent mothers may not be due solely to the pregnancy and its outcome. Educational difficulties of adolescent mothers may have their roots in earlier experiences. Similarly, the children born to adolescent parents may have educational difficulties, especially if they grow up in poverty. Educational outcomes of children of adolescent parents may not be substantially different, however, from those of children born to older mothers of the same socioeconomic and racial/ethnic background. Poverty creates difficulties for children, regardless of the mother's age.

The younger the adolescent, the more likely she is to experience negative outcomes from pregnancy. Older adolescents are more likely to become pregnant; only 0.5 percent of all adolescent childbearers are younger than fifteen years of age. Older adolescents may be close to high school completion or may have completed high school. African-American adolescent childbearers are likely to be unmarried. In the majority of cases, the father of a child born to an adolescent is an older, young adult male. Therefore, school-based programs for adolescent parents may miss many of the males involved in adolescent pregnancy.

The prevention of unplanned pregnancy in adolescence requires at least two different approaches, one focusing directly on the prevention of early sexual activity and pregnancy and one focusing indirectly on increasing adolescents' educational attainment and adult career options. Both types of programs can be delivered through the school or through a collaboration of schools, families, and communities.

First, programs focusing directly on pregnancy prevention are needed. The majority of African-American adolescents receive some form of sex education in their schools. These programs should begin early enough so that adolescents receive them before they become sexually active. Some sex education programs encourage adolescents to abstain from sexual activity. Clearly, abstinence is a strategy that will prevent pregnancy without fail. Some sex education programs, however, promote abstinence without providing adequate information about contraception. In spite of the promotion of abstinence as a goal, the majority of individuals will become sexually active during adolescence. Adolescents therefore need information about contraception. No evidence supports the idea that giving adolescents information about or access to contraception will increase sexual activity. Programs that provide information about reproduction should also include discussion of the personal relationship in which responsible sexual expression occurs.

Some high schools include clinics that provide, with parental permission, health services that include information on contraception. The provision of contraceptives in public schools is controversial, however, because of the possibility that adolescents may conclude that adults are encouraging sexual activity. This possibility must be weighed against the reduction of the risks of pregnancy and of sexually transmitted disease.

In addition to direct prevention programs, there is a need for programs that contribute indirectly to the prevention of unplanned pregnancy by enhancing school participation, academic achievement, and the school-to-work transition. Programs are needed to motivate adolescents to aim toward life goals that are incompatible with early pregnancy and childbearing. Adolescents need compelling reasons to delay pregnancy and childbearing. General educational improvement should be associated with reduced pregnancy rates. Adolescents who have high educational aspirations and who believe they can reach their educational and career goals are less likely to place themselves at risk for pregnancy than are adolescents whose future looks bleak.

Because prevention programs, at their best, are not 100 percent effective, intervention programs are needed for pregnant and parenting adolescents. Services are needed that enhance the education of the adolescents and the development and the education of their young children as well. Two important kinds of programs are those that provide prenatal care and those that provide child care for the children of adolescent parents.

With adequate prenatal care, many of the problems associated with adolescent childbearing would be lessened. When prenatal care and nutrition are adequate, medical risks are reduced to a normal level, except in pregnancies in adolescents younger than fifteen years old. Unfortunately, pregnant adolescents may not have access to appropriate care and may not begin prenatal care early in the pregnancy. Successful interventions with pregnant adolescents must include prenatal care.

African-American adolescents very rarely choose adoption as a pregnancy resolution. Consequently, adolescents who give birth are faced with the task of rearing a child; at the same time, they need to complete their schooling and prepare to enter the job market. Providing care for the child can be a problem for adolescents who are enrolled in school. Some schools have responded by providing on-site child care programs, which typically require a commitment from the adolescent parent to attend school, to participate in child development and other related classes, and to spend some time each day in the child care center. Other programs provide referrals for family day-care homes or child care centers outside the school.

Up-to-date statistics on adolescent sexual activity, pregnancy, and birth rates can be obtained directly from sources such as the Census Bureau, the Centers for Disease Control, and the National Center for Health Statistics. The National Center for Health Statistics regularly administers the National Survey of Family Growth, which samples adolescent as well as adult females. Organizations such as the Alan Guttmacher Institute, Center for Population Options, and the Children's Defense Fund* regularly compile reports of relevant data on adolescent pregnancy and childbearing.

SELECTED BIBLIOGRAPHY

Claire D. Brindis, Karen Pittman, Patricia Reyes, and Sharon Adams–Taylor, *Adolescent Pregnancy Prevention: A Guidebook for Communities,* Stanford Center for Research in Disease Prevention (1991); F. F. Furstenberg, J. Brooks–Gunn, and S. P. Morgan, *Adolescent Mothers in Later Life* (1987); Tom Luster and E. Dubow, "Predictors of the Quality of the Home Environment That Adolescent Mothers Provide for Their School-Age Children," *Journal of Youth and Adolescence* 19 (1990): 475–94; Diane Scott–Jones, "Adolescent Childbearing: Whose Problem? What Can We Do?" *Phi Delta Kappan* 75 (1993): 1–12; Diane Scott–Jones and Sherry L. Turner, "The Impact of Adolescent Childbearing on Educational Attainment and Income of Black Females," *Youth and Society* 22 (1990): 35–53; Dawn Upchurch and James McCarthy, "The Timing of a First Birth and High School Completion," *American Sociological Review* 55 (1990): 224–34; Charles Westoff, "Unintended Pregnancy in America and Abroad," *Family Planning Perspectives* 20 (1988): 254–61; Laurie S. Zabin and Sarah Hayward, *Adolescent Sexual Behavior and Childbearing* (1993).

                                                              DIANE SCOTT–JONES

TENNESSEE STATE UNIVERSITY. Tennessee State University in Nashville, founded in 1912, is an urban, land-grant institution of higher education devoted to teaching, research, and public service. It is accredited by the Commission on Colleges of the Southern Association of Colleges and Schools* and grants bachelor's degrees in forty-two academic areas, master's degrees in twenty-one areas, and doctoral degrees in public administration, administration and supervision, curriculum and instruction, and psychology. TSU is one of seven historically black institutions with a college of engineering, a school of nursing, a school of allied health professions, and a school of agriculture. In addition, students may select a major in the college of arts and sciences, the college of business, the college of education, or the graduate school. TSU boasts the largest School of Allied Health Professions in the state of Tennessee and one of the largest in the nation. Allied health has eight programs designed to prepare students for opportunities in health care administration and planning, medical technology, dental hygiene, speech pathology and audiology, medical records, respiratory therapy, physical therapy, and occupational therapy. Three of the programs are in collaboration with Meharry Medical College, only a few blocks from the TSU main campus.

SELECTED BIBLIOGRAPHY

National Association for Equal Opportunity in Higher Education, *Profiles of the Nation's Historically and Predominantly Black Colleges and Universities* (1993).

SAMUEL L. MYERS

TERRELL, MARY ELIZA CHURCH. (23 September 1863, Memphis, Tennessee–24 July 1954, Annapolis, Maryland). A teacher, school board president, social activist, and suffragist, Mary Church Terrell joined the crusade for racial equality and human dignity for African-Americans in the United States in the 1890s. Born Mary (Mollie) Church, she was the first of two children of Robert Reed Church and Louisa Ayers Church. Her father was a former slave who acquired his fortune through real estate and other business ventures and later became the South's wealthiest African-American. In 1884, Mary received a B.A. degree from Oberlin College* the only white college of that day that accepted African-American females. Although the faculty and students of Oberlin were active in the antislavery struggle, Church expressed little about racism or sexism while attending college. She joined in Oberlin's prestigious literary society and participated in its public debates; she also became an editor of the *Oberlin Review*.

In 1885, she became a member of the faculty at Wilberforce University* in Ohio, the first institution of higher learning for African-Americans. She moved to Washington, D.C., in the 1890s, and in 1891, she married Robert Terrell, a teacher, lawyer, and later a judge of the Municipal Court of the District of Columbia. After moving to the District of Columbia, Mary Church Terrell became the first African-American member of the school board in 1895 and the first president of the National Association of Colored Women in 1896. She was instrumental in gaining support for the provision of public services for African-American Washingtonians including child care, nursing schools, facilities for senior citizens, and programs for troubled youths. She was also active in the antilynching and women's suffrage movements and served as an advisor to government leaders on racial problems.

For more than sixty years this pioneer paved the way for better education and quality of life for the nation's African-American children. In 1953, at the age of ninety, Terrell led a committee that won a suit to end discrimination in Washington's hotels, restaurants, buses, and other public facilities.

SELECTED BIBLIOGRAPHY

Dorothy Sterling, *Lift Every Voice* (1965); Library of Congress, *Letters and Diaries*, Mary Church Terrell Papers; Paula Giddings, *In Search of Sisterhood* (1988); Leon Litwack and August Meier, eds., *Black Leaders of the Nineteenth Century* (1988).

CONSTANCE A. BURNS

TEXAS COLLEGE. Texas College grew out of the Phillips Academy, a Colored Methodist Episcopal (presently Christian Methodist Episcopal) Church–

supported elementary and secondary school for African-American children in Tyler, Texas (established 1894). In January 1895, the academy's offerings were expanded to remedy the limited educational opportunities available to African-Americans in eastern Texas during the latter part of the nineteenth century and the early decades of the twentieth century. The newly created institution, located on 101 acres, was divided into three academic units: elementary, secondary, and collegiate. Reverend O. T. Womack and Bishop Elias Cottrell served as the college's first administrators.

Texas College received its official charter in 1907. In 1909, the board voted to change the name of the college to Phillips University in honor of its chairman and the CME's then-presiding bishop, Henry Phillips. However, because of widespread objections from supporters, the name Texas College was restored in 1912. In 1932, the college was accredited by the Texas Department of Education. The next year, it added a normal school for the preparation of teachers. During the 1940s, a state and federally approved program in home economics was established. In 1948, the college received the highest rating given to any African-American college of that time by the Southern Association of Colleges and Schools. A graduate program in education, begun in 1951, was discontinued in 1959. During the 1990s, a community program for the in-service training of teachers was initiated.

Texas College is today a four-year baccalaureate degree-granting, coeducational, liberal arts college supported and controlled by a board of seventeen trustees elected by CME conferences throughout the United States. The school's open admissions policy makes it accessible to a board-based traditional and nontraditional student population. Though small, it continues to serve as an educational and cultural center for African-Americans in eastern Texas.

SELECTED BIBLIOGRAPHY

Daniel A. P. Murray Association, *The Murray Resource Directory to the Nation's Historically Black Colleges and Universities* (1993); Department of Interior, *Negro Education: A Study of the Private and Higher Schools for Colored People in the United States*, vol. 2 (1917); Cecil Eugene Evans, *The Story of Texas Schools* (1955); Dwight O. W. Holmes, *The Evolution of the Negro College* (1970); Charles Henry Phillips, *The History of the Colored Methodist Episcopal Church in America: Its Organization, Subsequent Development and Present Status* (1898).

                                                                                                    A. J. STOVALL

TEXAS SOUTHERN UNIVERSITY. Texas Southern University is located in the heart of Houston. Established as a state university in 1947, the institution's history actually began when Houston Colored Junior College opened in 1927. The junior college was transferred to the state of Texas following passage of a bill creating Texas State University for Negroes, and the institution's name was changed to Texas Southern University (TSU) in 1951. A fully accredited university, TSU offers students a wide range of undergraduate, graduate, and professional degree programs, including those leading to doctorates in several areas. The academic programs are organized into seven schools and colleges; a General University Academic Center and an honors program provide enhancement and instructional support. Faculty and students conduct research in a variety of disciplines, much of it through the university's Centers for Outreach and Research Program. The university also offers many services to facilitate student development and academic success, such as a variety of extracurricular activities, an annual series of cultural events, tutorial labs, internships, and mentoring programs.

SELECTED BIBLIOGRAPHY

National Association for Equal Opportunity in Higher Education, *Profiles of the Nation's Historically and Predominantly Black Colleges and Universities* (1993).

SAMUEL L. MYERS

TEXTBOOKS, AFRICAN-AMERICAN REPRESENTATION IN. African-Americans have been a neglected population in textbooks, starting with the first such works published in the early eighteenth century. The advent of space flight in the 1960s and the social turmoil of the era were both catalysts in the upheaval of the American educational system. Russia's launch of the Sputnik satellite, in particular, caused educators to examine the content of the curriculum and how American students were taught science, mathematics, and reading. The social and political concerns of the African-American community also demanded a closer look at what was being taught, especially to and about African-Americans. Over a period of years, attempts have been made to evaluate textbooks of all types to determine the incidence and treatment of African-Americans in these books.

Publications specifically written as instructional tools for children had their beginnings with *Orbis Pictus*, a history picture book written by John Amos Comenius in 1658. The hornbook, first used around 1550, was a textbook used to teach the alphabet, a list of vowels and syllables, the Lord's Prayer, and often short verses. During the mid-1800s, textbooks known as chapbooks or battledores replaced the hornbook. These books included both lessons and stories, and were said to be the forerunner of paperbacks and comic books. There is no evidence that Africans or African-Americans were included in any books published during this time.

Textbooks that include African-Americans to any great extent are usually history books published for use in social studies classes. African-Americans have been most represented in narratives related to the issues of slavery, the Civil War, and discrimination. Textbook authors often attempted to explain or rationalize racism, without presenting the full picture of how such discrimination against African-Americans evolved over time. History books written in the early twentieth century tended to ignore the significant contributions made by African-Americans in the development of the United States as a world power. African-

Americans seldom appeared in illustrations that were not related to slavery, the Civil War, reconstruction, or the Civil Rights Movement.

Researchers have analyzed history books written after 1930 to determine the incidence and treatment of African-Americans. Analysis of elementary-level American history textbooks used in Chicago, for example, revealed that there were four major events related to African-Americans that appeared in all the books analyzed. These events were the arrival of slaves at Jamestown in 1619, the invention of the cotton gin and the demand for more slaves, Lincoln's election and his concern about slavery, and the Emancipation Proclamation. Further references to African-Americans included the difference between field slave and house slave and Lincoln's speech on the continuance of a nation half slave and half free. Only four blacks were found mentioned by name: George Washington Carver, Matthew Henson, Ralph Bunche, and Haiti's Pierre Dominique Toussaint L'Ouverture. In a 1964 study of thirty-six history textbooks written for use in grades four through eight, African-Americans were included only in theme units related to legal segregation, discrimination, stereotypes, and racial harmony. By the late 1960s, some publishers began to include units addressing such topics as African-American achievement, violence and conflict, and peaceful resistance to deliberate acts of discrimination.

Studies of the depiction of blacks in high school–level textbooks have indicated that African-Americans were not portrayed at all in secondary U.S. history textbooks published prior to 1960. After 1960, text narratives related to African-Americans focused on slavery, reconstruction, and the Civil Rights Movement. Descriptions of African-Americans tended to be abstract and lacking in human dimension. The main focus was on events; no attempt was made to provide a historical perspective on social problems, African-American achievement, or positive interracial interactions. Textbooks published after 1981 have shown a sharp increase in text devoted to the African-American. However, the treatment of African-Americans generally still followed the traditional mode. African-American history was divided into two historical time periods, 1701–1864 (slavery) and 1866–1953 (reconstruction); less space was devoted to contemporary events such as the Civil Rights Movement.

However, social studies textbooks published since 1985 have improved significantly over previous textbooks in the inclusion of African-Americans in narrative text as well as in illustrations. This is not to say that African-Americans are being given equal or unbiased attention, but rather that the amount of text referring to them has increased dramatically. This is due in part to the outstanding achievements of many African-Americans in areas of endeavor that had been closed to them prior to the civil rights movement. Many history textbooks still rely on the depiction of a few prominent African-Americans to tell the entire story of the African-American experience. Although an improvement, this does not mean that adequate and accurate information has been provided about African-Americans and their history.

Mathematics and science textbooks, because they concentrate on teaching relatively abstract concepts, do not readily lend themselves to scrutiny for inclusion of African-Americans. However, elementary-level mathematics and science textbooks often use illustrations to support a concept; often these illustrations involve people. Mathematics and science textbooks and other materials published prior to the 1960s contained few if any illustrations that included African-Americans. Since the mid-1960s, based on the demand for more visibility in teaching materials, African-Americans began appearing in a limited way in mathematics and science textbooks for use by elementary school children.

Textbooks in the area of language arts are the first books children encounter when they enter school. The hornbooks, battledores, and chapbooks were the forerunners of the reading books used in schools today. Significant changes have been made in the structure of the reading development curriculum, and as a result the books themselves have also changed.

During the colonial period the Bible and other religious materials were used for instruction. This was followed in 1690 by *The New England Primer*, in 1783 by Noah Webster's *American Spelling Book* (also known as the *Blue-Backed Speller*), and in 1836 by *McGuffy's Readers*. *McGuffy's* became the most widely used reader, selling more than one million copies between 1836 and 1906. This six-volume set contained English language and grammar activities, poetry, and writings by prominent whites. African-Americans were totally excluded. *McGuffy's Readers* were superseded by books known as basal readers or "look-say" readers, developmental reading books that over time became the mainstay of language arts education. The most widely used series was the American Book Company's *Dick, Jane, and Sally*. This controlled-vocabulary series reinforced the concept of the middle-class nuclear family, typically a mother, father, and three children, supported by the father while the mother kept house. The family and everyone they came in contact with were white; no African-Americans existed in their world. This series defined the reading curriculum until the early 1960s, when the Writers' Committee of Detroit's Great Cities School Improvement Program wrote the *City Schools Reading Program*. This series for beginning readers depicted urban settings in which minorities were featured prominently. The writers felt that children needed beginning reading materials that presented real-life situations and characters that resembled their own families. Thus, this series presented African-American siblings Jimmy, Debbie, and David, and their friend Larry, who was white. As in the American Book series, theirs was an intact family consisting of three children, a mother, and a father.

After the inception of the *City Schools Reading Program*, many textbook publishers that previously had presented only the stereotypical white family hastened to add minorities to their series. This was done initially by using the same illustrations but darkening some of the character's faces and renaming them. Later, facial features and hair styles were changed to more closely approximate African-American features and hair texture. Although African-

American characters played very minor roles in the books, their inclusion was seen by publishers as adequately responding to the need to incorporate minorities, specifically African-Americans, in textbooks.

In the mid-1960s, the MacMillan Company published *The Bank Street Readers*, developed by the Bank Street College of Education in New York. These readers presented a variety of family situations, a cross-section of life in an urban center, and excursions into surrounding suburban areas. The stories and illustrations were multiethnic. As a result of the efforts of the *City Schools Reading Program* and the *Bank Street Readers* most basal reader publishers began to more fully incorporate African-Americans and other minorities in their books. However, depictions of the family remained the core of the stories until the whole focus of developmental readers changed.

During the 1980s, the teaching of developmental language arts skills changed; developmental reading evolved into a program that guided not only language arts skills but also concept development in all academic subjects. Accordingly, a drastic change was made in the content of developmental reading materials. Publishers no longer used a family format for their series, instead incorporating literature, social studies, mathematics, science, art, and music. The books, written by authors from various ethnic groups, contained folklore, history lessons, stories about inventors and their inventions, science lessons and experiments, and a variety of related concepts. Most publishers included African-American authors, folklore, and nonfiction material related to African-Americans.

There presently exist many different types of developmental reading programs and literature textbooks for secondary school students. Many school systems have instituted literature-based programs in which the developmental reading material comes from commercially published books; the teacher is then responsible for selecting those books that best meet students' needs. This gives teachers the opportunity to select books written for and about African-Americans as the major component of a reading program. The inclusion of such books on many secondary-level book lists, along with the opportunity for teacher selection, may mitigate somewhat the stereotypical presentations of African-Americans predominant in traditional American education.

Authors of textbooks for secondary schools and college classes historically have been white. Very few African-Americans were asked to write textbooks for major publishers, and it was extremely difficult for African-American authors to secure contracts to write general college textbooks. Thus, textbooks used in secondary schools and college classes were almost devoid of any treatment of African-Americans, with the exception of the cursory references contained in social studies materials. Literature books for English classes in secondary schools and college classes have in the past contained mostly works by and about whites. Occasionally a selection by a prominent African-American author such as Langston Hughes would appear in an American literature textbook, but the incidence was not widespread. However, with the introduction of African-American studies programs into the college and secondary school curriculum, there developed a need to publish books generic to such programs. This gave African-American authors entrance into major publishing companies, as publishers realized the extent of profits to be made from the proliferation of African-American studies programs in major universities throughout the world. Many African-American authors, after becoming well known for their books about their people, have branched out into other areas and have made it possible for other African-Americans to enter into the predominantly white world of educational publishing. However, there remain many inaccuracies, stereotypical depictions, and examples of underrepresentation of African-Americans in textbooks used in all types of educational institutions.

SELECTED BIBLIOGRAPHY

J. A. Banks, "A Content Analysis of the Black American in Textbooks," *Social Education* 33 (1969); J. Burack, "How Textbooks Obscure and Distort the History of Slavery," *Textbook Letter* 3, no. 5 (1992); J. Garcia and D. E. Tanner, "The Portrayal of Black Americans in U.S. History Textbooks," *Social Studies* (September-October 1985); M. Kane, *Minorities in Textbooks* (1970); P. E. Lovejoy, *Transformations in Slavery: A History of Slavery in Africa* (1983); R. C. Turner and J. A. Dewar, "Black History in Selected American History Textbooks," *Educational Leadership/Research Supplement* 6, no. 3 (1973).

DOLORES P. DICKERSON

THOMPSON, CHARLES H. (19 July 1895–21 January 1980). Charles H. Thompson, the first African-American to earn a Ph.D. in education (University of Chicago, 1925), began his teaching career at Howard University* in 1926. He spent the next forty years in continuous service to the university until his retirement in 1966.

Thompson's influence was felt throughout the Howard University community. He served as associate professor, professor, and chairman of the Department of Education, dean of the College of Liberal Arts, dean of the Graduate School, and founder and editor-in-chief of the *Journal of Negro Education.** As dean of the College of Liberal Arts, he instituted procedures that led to the selection of promising high school graduates through nationwide scholarship examinations. He inaugurated a freshman advisory system, improved the admissions process, studied and expanded the use of standardized tests, and helped in the development of faculty tenure policies and faculty improvement procedures. His annual reports to Howard's board of trustees are noteworthy for the particularly keen insights Thompson shared on the status and aspirations of African-Americans in higher education. In his later role of dean of the Graduate School, Thompson called for complete reexamination of the objectives, standards of admission and scholarship, and requirements for the master's degree. Under his guidance, programs leading to the degree of doctor of philosophy were begun. In 1966, Thompson completed the university's first comprehensive five-year self-study.

Not only did Thompson have wide and varied experiences as teacher, scholar, and administrator at Howard, but he served on a number of national educational boards and commissions and held memberships in many scholarly societies and professional organizations. He was a fellow of the American Association for the Advancement of Science and was listed in several national and international biographical dictionaries such as *Who's Who in America* and *International Who's Who*. He was also a member of the National Education Association, the American Association for Higher Education, the National Society for the Study of Education, and similar professional organizations in the field of education. He was a member of the National Board of the NAACP* for several years and, for an even longer period, a member of the NAACP Legal Defense and Education Fund, Inc. He served as a member of the U.S. National Commission for UNESCO (1946–49) and was a member of the American Council on Education Committee on Discrimination in Higher Education (1948–57). He also served as a member of a number of ad hoc government advisory committees and commissions over a period of more than twenty-five years.

Because of his special interest and competence in the field of ethnic minority education, he served as an expert educational witness in many of the segregation cases in the field of higher education. Particularly noteworthy were the *Sweatt** case in Texas in 1946 and the *Sipuel** and *McLaurin** cases in Oklahoma in 1947, three of the key cases in the outlawing of racial segregation. He was a consultant in developing the legal strategies that led to *Brown v. Board of Education** (1954).

In addition to editing the *Journal of Negro Education* for thirty-one years, Thompson was the author of over one hundred important scholarly articles and research papers, many of which were published in the *Journal*. He also served as an editorial consultant to *The Nation's Schools* (1943–50) and to the *World Book Encyclopedia* (1942–62).

After Thompson's death in 1980, an annual lecture-colloquium series was established in his name by the editorial/advisory board of the *Journal of Negro Education*. Thompson was married to Mae Stewart Thompson of Washington, D.C., whom he survived. Mrs. Thompson was a long-time physical education instructor in the District of Columbia Public Schools.

SELECTED BIBLIOGRAPHY

Program brochures, the Charles H. Thompson Lecture-Colloquium series (1980–present) (on file at the offices of the *Journal of Negro Education*, Washington, D.C.); Aaron B. Stills and Fay Flanagan, "Charles H. Thompson's Journal: To Protect and to Serve," *Journal of Teacher Education* 3, no. 1 (1990): 65–69; Charles H. Thompson, "Editorial Comment: Why a *Journal of Negro Education?*" *JNE* 1, no. 1 (1932): 1–4; Stephen J. Wright, "Editorial Comment: Charles H. Thompson—Founder and Seminal Editor-in-Chief of the *Journal of Negro Education*," *JNE* 48, no. 4 (1979): 447–48.

D. KAMILI ANDERSON

TOLLETT, KENNETH SCRUGGS (14 July 1931, Muskogee, Oklahoma). Distinguished Professor of Higher Education at Howard University* since 1971,

Tollett has contributed to the study of law and the legal profession. He received his A.B., J.D., and M.A. degrees from the University of Chicago and practiced law in Chicago from 1955 to 1958. At the age of twenty-eight, he became acting dean of the Texas Southern University School of Law and served as dean until June 1970. He was a visiting fellow at the Center for the Study of Democratic Institutions and a professor at the University of Colorado School of Law. He was chairman of the National Advisory Board and director of the Institute for the Study of Educational Policy (ISEP) at Howard, from March 1974 to March 1985.

Tollett has presented over a hundred major papers, including "Supreme Court Justice Thurgood Marshall: Mr. Civil Rights Advocate," given at the dedication ceremonies for North Carolina Central University School of Law in Durham (1980), and "Race Consciousness and Community: The Need for a Variety of Black Perspectives in the Civic or Public Deliberative Discourse," at the biennial meeting of the American Section of the International Association for the Philosophy of Law at the University of Utah (1990). He has published over a hundred articles, monographs, and letters in publications including the *Notre Dame Lawyer*, the *Black Law Journal*, the *Harvard Blackletter Journal*, and the *Wall Street Journal*.

Tollett has received many awards, such as the National Bar Association's C. Francis Stradford Award in 1968; the University of Chicago Alumni Association's Professional Achievement Award in 1972; and the National Association for Equal Opportunity in Higher Education's (NAFEO) Black College Act Award for "longstanding commitment to strengthening black colleges and universities" in 1987. His funded proposals and grants total nearly three million dollars.

ERICA E. TOLLETT

TOUGALOO COLLEGE. Tougaloo College in Tougaloo, Missippy, was founded in 1869 on the principle that it be "accessible to all." Tougaloo is today a four-year liberal arts, private coeducational and church-related institution. The school's history is firmly rooted in academic excellence and human freedom. Its students are trained for leadership and commitment. Tougaloo was cited in October of 1988 by *U.S. News and World Report* as one of the nation's best colleges. The September 1989 issue of *Money* magazine listed the school as one of the nation's best higher education buys. The tradition of promoting equality continued when in July 1991, the school hosted the 30th Commemorative Conference of the Freedom Riders. Its historic president's mansion was selected as one of eleven buildings on campuses of historically black colleges and universities to be restored by the Department of the Interior. Touglaloo offers a variety of courses and majors through the four divisions of the school: education, natural science, humanities, and social science. Over 50 percent of the school's graduates go on to graduate school.

SELECTED BIBLIOGRAPHY
National Association for Equal Opportunity in Higher Education, *Profiles of the Nation's Historically and Predominantly Black Colleges and Universities* (1993).
                                                                    SAMUEL L. MYERS

TRENT, WILLIAM JOHNSON, JR. (8 March 1910, Asheville, North Carolina–27 November 1993, Greensboro, North Carolina). Trent, Jr., received a B.A. in 1930 from Livingstone College* in Salisbury, North Carolina, where his father, Dr. William J. Trent, Sr.,* was president. In 1932, he received the M.B.A. degree from the Wharton School at the University of Pennsylvania. He did further graduate work in economics at the University of Chicago.

Trent taught economics while he served on the faculties of Livingstone (1932–34) and Bennett College,* Greensboro, North Carolina (1934–38), where he was also acting dean during his last year. He also coached basketball at both schools. From 1938 to 1944, he held government posts in Washington, D.C., during the administration of President Franklin D. Roosevelt, first as an advisor on African-American affairs to the Secretary of the Interior, Harold L. Ickes, and then as a race-relations officer in the Federal Works Agency.

In 1944, Frederick D. Patterson,* president of Tuskegee Institute (now Tuskegee University*) and founder of the United Negro College Fund (UNCF),* asked Trent to help him form this association of private black colleges. Trent promptly moved to New York, where he spent the next twenty years as the first executive director of the UNCF. In his years as executive director, Trent oversaw the raising of about seventy-eight million dollars to strengthen the best private black colleges. At that time, thirty-two colleges in eleven southern states were sharing the fund's income. By 1961, the fund was raising about two million dollars a year.

In 1961, Trent was named special ambassador by President John F. Kennedy to attend the ceremonies commemorating the independence of the nation of Upper Volta. From 1964 to 1975, Trent was assistant personnel director with an emphasis on affirmative action at Time, Inc. Concerned largely with race relations and minority issues, one of Trent's major projects was the recruitment of African-American employees for all positions in the company. In 1965 he served on the nineteenth selection board of the Department of State, and in 1967 he served on a foreign service inspection team in Japan.

While in New York, Trent was a member of St. Catherine's A.M.E. Zion Church and served on its trustee board. He also served as president of the board of St. Luke's Hospital in Manhattan. Trent served as a longtime board member and treasurer of the National Urban League and was on the boards of the Salvation Army, the College Placement Service, the Experiment in International Living, the New York Community Trust, and the Whitney M. Young, Jr., Foundation. When Trent returned to Greensboro in 1975, he worked in the development office of Bennett College. Trent was awarded honorary doctorates from Bennett College, Livingstone College, Morehouse College,* Atlanta University (now Clark Atlanta University*), Virginia Union University,* and Xavier College (now Xavier University*). In recognition of his commitment to education, the William J. Trent, Jr., UNCF Memorial Fund was established at Bennett College. Trent was also the posthumous recipient of the Frederick D. Patterson award from the UNCF.

He is interred in Evergreen Cemetery in Greensboro.

Trent is survived by his wife, the former Viola Scales, and their three daughters.

SELECTED BIBLIOGRAPHY

Christa Brelin and William C. Matney, Jr., *Who's Who among Black Americans* (1966); Lucille Arcola Chambers, *American's Tenth Man* (1957); Editors of Ebony, *The Negro Handbook* (1966); Rayford Logan and Michael R. Winston, *Dictionary of American Negro Biography* (1982); the most complete collections of materials on William J. Trent, Jr., are in the North Carolina Historical Room at the Greensboro Public Library; the Thomas F. Holgate Library at Bennett College, Greensboro, North Carolina; and in the W. C. Jackson library at the University of North Carolina at Greensboro.

ANDRE D. VANN

TRENT, WILLIAM JOHNSON, SR. (30 December 1873, Charlotte, North Carolina–12 June 1963, Salisbury, North Carolina). William Trent, Sr., was an educator, college president, and civic leader. He graduated from Livingstone College High School in 1894 and received his B.A. from Livingstone College* in 1898, where he also received an honorary M.A. degree in 1910. Trent embarked upon his first professional experience in higher education administration in 1899 when he became the president of Greenville Junior College in Tennessee. He later moved to Asheville, North Carolina, where he began his twenty-five-year career with the Young Men's Christian Association (YMCA). In Asheville he served as general secretary from 1900 to 1911, and in Atlanta, Georgia, as executive secretary from 1911 to 1925. While in Atlanta he continued his zeal and commitment to serve humanity by aiding in the establishment of the Atlanta Urban League and the Atlanta School of Social Work at Atlanta University in 1925. He is further remembered as being instrumental in organizing the first national NAACP* meeting in the South.

A nationally recognized figure within the African Methodist Episcopal Zion Church, Trent returned in 1925 to his alma mater, Livingstone College, where he became its fourth president and the first graduate to lead it. During his thirty-two-year reign, he accomplished several critical goals. He led a successful campaign to expand the campus, overseeing the erection of Price Memorial Building and several other buildings, and made the institution financially solvent. His most outstanding achievement was raising the academic standing of the college by gaining full accreditation, which led to its recognition as a true liberal arts college and theological seminary.

In 1951, in recognition of his deep commitment to children and his involvement in community affairs, the mayor of Salisbury, North Carolina, appointed

Trent to a six-year term on Salisbury City School Board of Education, where he became its first African-American member. He also served as a member of the Southern Inter-Racial Commission. In 1957, Trent retired due to poor health, but remained an active participant in the affairs of Livingstone College and the A.M.E. Zion Church.* He was considered by many to be, next to Bishop William Jacob Walls, the church's best oral historian. Trent was a member of the Omega Psi Phi and Sigmi Pi Phi fraternities, the Prince Hall Affiliated Masons, the Odd Fellows, and the Republican Party.

SELECTED BIBLIOGRAPHY

Richard Bardolph, *The Negro Vanguard* (1959); Lucille Arcola Chambers, *America's Tenth Man* (1957); William Jacob Walls, *The African Methodist Episcopal Zion Church: A Reality of the Black Church* (1974); Thomas Yenser, *Who's Who in Colored America* (1933).

ANDRE D. VANN

TUREAUD v. BOARD OF SUPERVISORS ETC., 116 F. Supp. 248 (1953); Reversed in 207 F.2d 807 (1953); Reinstated in 228 F.2d 895 (1953). Alexander Tureaud of New Orleans brought this suit to court in 1953 to obtain an injunction to prevent the State of Louisiana from refusing African-American students admission to Louisiana State University, then attended only by white students. The district court held, in line with the equal protection clause of the Fourteenth Amendment, "that the plaintiff and all others similarly qualified and situated are entitled to educational advantages and opportunities available within the state, at the same time, upon the same terms and substantially equal to those which the state provides and makes available to other residents and students of the state."

The state of Louisiana operated two separate university systems in 1953, one for whites and one for African-Americans. Louisiana State University had an admission policy barring nonwhites from its six-year combined program in the arts and sciences and law course. African-American students were expected to attend the separate Southern University and Southern University Law School, which were also maintained by the state of Louisiana.

This case was brought by Tureaud as part of a class-action suit, which, in effect, meant that any decision made in his case would apply to all Louisiana African-American citizens once a decision was made. Tureaud applied to Louisiana State University for admission to their combined six-year arts and sciences and law degree program and was summarily denied admission, on the basis that the school had a policy of not admitting African-Americans. The defendants in this case, the Board of Supervisors of Louisiana, stated that African-American students could obtain both an arts and sciences and a law degree at Southern University. As an alternative, African-American students could transfer to Louisiana State University after their first year of law studies if they were unhappy with Southern University.

Tureaud contended that the program offered at Southern University was not "substantially equal" to the education one would receive at Louisiana State

University. In its analysis, the Court pointed to criteria outlined in *Sweatt v. Painter** (339 U.S. 629), a Supreme Court case, and decided that the level of education to be received at Southern University did not equal the level offered at Louisiana State. An African-American student who was not satisfied with the Department of Law at Southern University but who wished to obtain a combined degree was required to go to Southern University for two years in an arts and science program, transfer to Louisiana State for a year of law, and *then* be awarded his degree from Southern. A white student, pursuing the same course of education, would be allowed to begin and end his studies at Louisiana State without transferring from one school to the other.

Applying the criteria outlined by the Supreme Court in *Sweatt*,* the district court concluded that Louisiana's "denial of admission, solely on the basis of his race, denies those rights guaranteed to plaintiff by the Fourteenth Amendment, and that such denial would inflict irreparable injury upon the plaintiff." The district court granted the temporary injunction suspending Louisiana State University's policy of banning African-Americans from the combined program solely on the basis of race.

This decision was an important step for African-Americans towards delegitimizing state-operated "separate but equal" institutions of higher learning, which were segregated along racial lines.

SELECTED BIBLIOGRAPHY

Constitution of Louisiana, Article XII, Section 1, 1921; Loren Miller, *The Petitioners: The Story of the Supreme Court of the United States and the Negro* (1966); *Sweatt v. Painter*, 339 U.S. 629, 70 S.Ct. 848, 94 L.Ed. 1114; *U.S. Constitution, Equal Protection Clause, Amendment V*, as applied to the states through the Fourteenth Amendment.

BEVERLY BAKER–KELLY AND RACHEL GABRIEL

TUSKEGEE UNIVERSITY. Tuskegee University, located in central Alabama and founded in 1881 by Booker T. Washington,* is one of the most famous universities in the United States Current programs, including both undergraduate and graduate instruction, which are organized around seven colleges and schools: College of Arts and Sciences; School of Agriculture and Home Economics; School of Business; School of Education; School of Engineering and Architecture, with options in aerospace science engineering, chemical engineering, electrical engineering, and mechanical engineering; also architecture and construction, School of Nursing and Allied Health; and School of Veterinary Medicine. Army and Air Force ROTC programs are also available. Substantial outreach service programs, along with a sizeable research component, combine to make Tuskegee a comprehensive institution. The university is fully accredited by the Southern Association of Colleges and Schools*; the following programs are accredited by national professional agencies: architecture, chemistry, dietetics, engineering, extension service, nursing, occupational therapy, social work, and veterinary medicine.

SELECTED BIBLIOGRAPHY
National Association for Equal Opportunity in Higher Education, *Profiles of the Nation's Historically and Predominantly Black Colleges and Universities* (1993).

SAMUEL L. MYERS

U

UNDERACHIEVEMENT. The various reform reports of the 1980s reminded America and its educators that many students, including those identified as gifted and talented, were failing to achieve to their academic potential. Underachievement includes dropping out of school, having poor grades and low grade-point averages, and failing to pass school proficiency tests. Most definitions of underachievement assume that only students who score highly on a standardized intelligence, ability, or achievement test but perform more poorly than expected in school (e.g., they get low grades) are underachievers. However, these definitions generally ignore the fact that many capable African-American learners do not necessarily perform well on standardized instruments. They also reveal a lack of agreement as to whether one should assess underachievement by comparing (a) IQ test scores with grades, (b) IQ test scores with ability test scores, (c) achievement test scores with grades, (d) achievement test scores with ability test scores, (e) ability test scores with grades, or (f) any combination of the above. Thus, whether a student should be identified as gifted or an underachiever is a relative consideration, not a definitive one.

The difficulty of defining underachievement among African-American students is complicated by the reality that identified characteristics of underachievement are usually established on white middle-class students and, thus, do not necessarily fit characteristics common among African-American students, particularly those from economically disadvantaged backgrounds. For example, gifted students from economically disadvantaged backgrounds learn quickly through experience and generalize it to other areas of their lives in order to make this learning meaningful and relevant. They also learn better in informal settings and cooperative groups.

African-American students also confront social, cultural, and psychological barriers that contribute to or exacerbate underachievement. Moreover, those identified as gifted are in psychological jeopardy, primarily because they often feel and are perceived as being different from their already marginalized peers. Negative peer pressure has been shown to sabotage the achievement of many capable African-American students, particularly those who fear being accused of "acting white." These gifted African-American students find themselves in a double or even triple quandary, which can ultimately hinder their achievement.

Vague and indefensible definitions of giftedness and underachievement compound identification problems and thus increase the already high probability that African-Americans will be underrepresented in gifted programs or over-represented in special education classes for the learning disabled, behavioral disordered, and emotionally mentally retarded. The use of appointed score ranges on an IQ or achievement test as the only or primary criterion for gift-edness and underachievement can significantly hinder African-American children's chances for inclusion in gifted programs. At the same time, it can guarantee their being placed in special education programs and otherwise not receiving needed and appropriate services. More attention to learning styles, authentic assessment, multicultural assessment, and multicultural education, for example, must be incorporated into the schools and educational practices to help African-American students reach their potential in school and life, rather than remaining at risk for underachievement and school failure.

SELECTED BIBLIOGRAPHY

B. Bricklin and P. M. Bricklin, *Bright Child—Poor Grades* (1965); B. Fine, *Undera-chievers: How They Can Be Helped*, 1st ed. (1967); M. J. Fine and R. Pitts, "Intervention with Underachieving Gifted Children: Rationale and Strategies," *Gifted Child Quarterly* 24 (1980): 51–55; D. Y. Ford, "The American Achievement Ideology as Perceived by Urban African-American Students: Explorations by Gender and Academic Program," *Urban Education* 27, no. 2 (1992): 196–221; D. Y. Ford and J. J. Harris III, "Black Students: At Promise, Not 'at Risk' for Giftedness," *Journal of Human Behavior and Learning* 7, no. 2 (1990): 21–30; S. Fordham, "Racelessness as a Factor in Black Stu-dents' School Success: Pragmatic Strategy or Pyrrhic Victory?" *Harvard Educational Review* 58, no. 1 (1988): 54–84; S. Fordham and J. U. Ogbu, "Black Students' School Success: Coping with the "Burden of 'Acting White,' " *Urban Review* 18, no. 3 (1986): 176–207; A. G. Hilliard III, "Standardization and Cultural Bias as Impediments to the Scientific Study and Validation of 'Intelligence,' " *Journal of Research and Development in Education* 12, no. 2 (1979): 47–58; G. T. Kowitz and C. M. Armstrong, "Under-Achievement: Concept or Artifact?" *School and Society* 89 (1961): 347–49; R. R. Lind-strom and S. San Vant, "Special Issues in Working with Gifted Minority Adolescents," *Journal of Counseling and Development* 64 (1986): 583–86; R. A. Mickelson, "The Attitude-Achievement Paradox among Black Adolescents," *Sociology of Education* 63 (1986): 44–61; D. A. Saurenman and W. B. Michael, "Differential Placement of High-Achieving and Low-Achieving Gifted Pupils in Grades Four, Five, and Six on Measures of Field Dependence–Field Independence, Creativity, and Self-Concept," *Gifted Child Quarterly* 24 (1980): 81–86; R. L. Thorndike, *The Concepts of Over- and Under-Achievement* (1963).

DONNA Y. FORD

UNDERCLASS. Prior to the 1960s, the social atmosphere of the inner cities was one of a sense of community and positive neighborhood identification. There were explicit norms and sanctions against aberrant behavior. During the

1960s, along with other factors, the reduction of various types of blue-collar jobs resulted in deteriorating social conditions in the inner cities. Most working and middle-class individuals moved out of the inner cities after obtaining mainstream occupations, leaving the lower class behind. The latter, usually referred to as the underclass, is frequently characterized by low aspirations, poor education, family instability, illegitimacy, unemployment, crime, drug addiction, alcoholism, frequent illness, and early death. The deterioration within this underclass is observed in several aspects of this group's family life, social structure, and attributes of individuals. Some documented problems include the ever-increasing numbers of female-headed families and few positive role models, as well as a lack of self-reliance and self-respect associated with welfare dependency, prolonged poverty, and social disorder.

The underclass may be defined as a group of racially and socially isolated low-income families and individuals who, in an attempt to survive, create lifestyles that are adaptations of traditional values. These modified values tend to reduce the group's ability to utilize positive coping strategies as defined by the larger society and to utilize optimally the available resources. Between the 1960s and 1990s, the status of the underclass, a group that is largely made up of African-Americans and other nonwhites, has been the subject of considerable political and ideological debate. An understanding of the underclass and its creation may be viewed from several perspectives.

Those defined as politically liberal tend to relate the plight of the underclass to broader societal problems such as social class, racial isolation, subordination, and discrimination. Conservatives tend to emphasize the differences in group values and the failure of the underclass to compete for available resources as an explanation of the underclass group's experiences. In referring to the existence of the underclass, conservatives describe the group as a people locked into a culture of poverty and welfare. While conservatives have remained steadfast in their position, liberals have changed the direction of their focus and energy over the years. They struggle with the stigma and demoralization resulting from the manner in which low-income African Americans were depicted in several reports, particularly Senator Moynihan's report of 1965. Liberals strongly opposed Moynihan's and other reports, arguing that they presented negative images that fuel racist arguments and imply blaming the victims. Subsequently, liberals began to embrace selective evidence that emphasized the ability of lower socioeconomic groups to adapt, survive, and flourish against all odds. While liberals were emphasizing the more acceptable characteristics of the underclass, the social and economic gaps between urban low-income African Americans and middle-class and upper-class Americans continued to widen. This resulted in both economic and social isolation of the underclass as well as disillusionment and economic deprivation. Supporting the arguments proffered by liberals and conservatives are the determinists and behaviorists, respectively. Similar to the liberals, determinists assert that society is primarily responsible for the status of the underclass because society determines the individual's behavior. Behaviorists, like conservatives, emphasize individual factors such as cultural history and personal attitudes.

The growth of the underclass has been attributed to several factors. For example, this group's numbers increased tremendously because of economic developments that were the direct result of a resurgence of racism, and shifts in the job market from a manufacturing based economy to a technological and service economy. In addition, the legacy of more than two hundred years of slavery, lynching, poll taxes, and Jim Crow laws resulted in the creation of this deprived group. Therefore, the tendency of conservatives and behaviorists to stress individual characteristics, attitudes, and behavior seems to represent a myopic view that considers only the manifestations of a complex situation without consideration of its root causes. Evidence to support the premise that the problem of the underclass is primarily a structural, societal one is seen in the fact that even when legislative barriers are removed, a system of economic and social inequality persists for an indefinite period of time.

Further, statistical data point to the fact that African Americans and other minority group members comprise a great proportion of the underclass. According to the recent comparative economic and social measures, only 9 percent of white Americans are classified as poor, compared with just over 30 percent of African-American and 28 percent of Hispanics. The unemployment rate for minority groups is about twice that of whites, and this rate worsens as blue-collar work evaporates or is exported. White-collar jobs make up 59 percent of all U.S. employment; blue-collar jobs make up 22 percent, and service occupations 19 percent. The public schools fail to produce graduates with skills that match available jobs, and dropout rates among the underclass are high. It is estimated that 45 percent of Hispanics and 35 percent of African-Americans drop out of high school. There is a strong correlation between schooling and income. Most dropouts earn approximately two thirds the median annual income of a high school graduate and less than half that of a college graduate.

The existence of the underclass can be explained by both historical and contemporary racism and individual factors such as family structure, family history (especially welfare dependency), and personal attitudes and behavior. The cycle of poverty seems to be a self-perpetuating phenomenon as the culture of poverty is both an adaptation to conditions imposed by the larger society and the perpetuation of low socioeconomic status from generation to generation. The deleterious effects of underclass status may be observed in the following categories of members: those who are angry and openly reject society's dominant values; those who make a living through illegal means; those who are passive and depend on welfare and government support; those who are resigned to their status while using unhealthy coping strategies such as reliance on drugs; and those who depend on marginal and often unreliable means of economic support.

SELECTED BIBLIOGRAPHY
K. Auletta, *The Underclass* (1982); W. J. Wilson, *The Truly Disadvantaged: The Inner City, the Underclass, and Public Policy* (1990).

SYLVIA WALKER AND ADA VINCENT

UNITED NEGRO COLLEGE FUND (THE COLLEGE FUND/UNCF). The College Fund/UNCF is the oldest and most successful higher education support organization in the United States. Founded in 1944 by Tuskegee Institute (now University)* president Frederick D. Patterson* as a fundraising organ for twenty-seven private historically black colleges and universities, it has grown into a comprehensive organization whose mission is to raise funds, provide program services, and offer technical assistance to its members, their students, and faculty. The College Fund/UNCF today offers more than 350 programs for the institutions within its network, which include forty-one of the nation's 103 historically black colleges and universities. These programs range from scholarships to curriculum development, college preparation, and faculty development.

Membership in The College Fund/UNCF is limited to historically black, private, accredited, four-year colleges, universities, and professional schools. Member colleges are located in ten southern states, Ohio, and Texas. More than 54,000 students attend College Fund/UNCF member institutions annually.

The importance of the organization's mission is echoed in its longtime slogan, ''A Mind Is a Terrible Thing to Waste,'' which emphasizes the importance of scholarship assistance for African-American students seeking higher education. The College Fund/UNCF estimates that approximately 90 percent of these students require financial aid in order to attend or complete college. Forty percent are the first in their families to attend college. Roughly 50 percent are from families with gross annual incomes of less than $30,000.

Since its founding, The College Fund/UNCF has raised more than $1 billion for its member institutions. In 1995, it was ranked among the top quarter of national charities surveyed by *The Chronicle of Philanthropy* and ranked number one among nonprofit educational groups according to the same survey. In October 1995, The College Fund/UNCF concluded its most ambitious capital drive, ''CAMPAIGN 2000: An Investment in America's Future,'' which raised $280 million, exceeding its $250 million goal by 12 percent. Also in 1995, the organization achieved an all-time low cost ratio of 15.85 percent.

One of The College Fund/UNCF's most prominent activities in recent years has been its annual marathon television scholarship fundraising event. Hosted by renowned singer-entertainer Lou Rawls, the ''Lou Rawls Parade of Stars'' has told the organization's story to millions of television viewers and showcased top-flight entertainment since 1980. In January 1995, the show raised $12.2 million in cash and pledges, bringing the fifteen-year total to more than $132 million raised to assist deserving college students.

More than 250,000 men and women have graduated from The College Fund/ UNCF institutions since 1944, including such prominent alumni as civil rights leader Dr. Martin Luther King, Jr.; former U.S. Ambassador to the United Nations and former Atlanta mayor Andrew Young; Marian Wright Edelman, president of the Children's Defense Fund*; Olympic track star Edwin Moses; Carl Ware, senior vice president of Coca-Cola Company; Dr. Ruth Simmons, president of Smith College; and Hazel O'Leary, U.S. Secretary of Energy.

The College Fund/UNCF is presently headed by former Pennsylvania Congressman William H. Gray, III, who assumed the office of president and chief executive officer in 1991. He replaced Dr. Christopher Edley, who led the organization for almost twenty years prior, beginning in 1973.

TERHEA WASHINGTON

UNITED STATES v. COOK COUNTY SCHOOL DISTRICT, 286 F. Supp. 786 (N.D. ILL), 404 F.2d 1125 (7th C. 1968). This was the first of several cases holding that, to remedy the effects of past racial discrimination, school officials must give affirmative consideration to racial factors in allocating faculty and staff members, assigning students, and deciding other pertinent matters of educational policy, including location and construction of schools, transportation of pupils, and the educational structure of the district. The court reasoned that the detrimental effect of racial segregation in schools is the same whether the segregation is coerced or coincidental.

This particular action began when the U.S. Attorney General brought suit against the Chicago school system for alleged racial discrimination in 1968. At that time, the Chicago school system was one of the most segregated in the country. The school district argued that segregation was not caused by law but was due to the residential housing patterns of Chicago in which the races chose to separate themselves, i.e., the resulting school segregation had de facto rather than de jure origins. The U.S. District Court found that the segregation present in the Chicago school system was a violation of the 1964 Civil Rights Act* and the Fourteenth Amendment of the Constitution. The court reasoned that the school district had violated the Fourteenth Amendment by instituting affirmative policies that segregated the races by the drawing of attendance zones, transportation of students, and selection of school sites. In addition, the court found that the school district had perpetuated segregation in its hiring practices for teachers and in the busing of white children living in African-American attendance zones to white public schools. Also, the court found that the 1964 Civil Rights Act applied to Chicago school districts even if state and local law had never condoned segregation, as the school district's affirmative acts of discrimination had altered the school system from a constitutional de facto system to an unconstitutional de jure system. Finally, the court granted the government's motion for preliminary injunction against the school district from engaging in discriminatory practices and ordered that the school district act affirmatively to remedy the past situation by developing a desegregation plan.

The Cook County case was significant for both its political and legal aspects. Its legal significance was that a school district's practices could be found to be unconstitutional under the Fourteenth Amendment even though there had never been a law establishing segregation. Its political significance was that it was the first of many cases in the late 1960s and early 1970s dealing with desegregation in the North and West. These cases caused great conflict and further fractured the fragile political coalition of white liberals, working-class urban ethnics, and African-Americans that had helped achieve the civil rights victories of the 1960s.

SELECTED BIBLIOGRAPHY

Civil Rights Act of 1964, 401 et seq., 42 U.S.C.A. 2000, et seq.; Comment, "Public School Desegregation and the Contours of Unconstitutionality: The Denver School Board Case," *Colorado Law Review* 45 (1974): 456; Laurence H. Tribe, *American Constitutional Law* (1978); Note, "Demise of the Neighborhood Plan," *Cornell Law Review* 55 (1970); Peck and Cohen, "The Social Context of DeFacto School Segregation," in O. Schroeder and D. Smith, eds., *De Facto Segregation and Civil Rights* (1965), 186 n. 49; R. M. Rader, "Demise of the Neighborhood School Plan," *Cornell Law Review* 55 (1970): 594–610; U.S. Commission on Civil Rights, *Racial Isolation in the Public Schools* (1957).

BEVERLY BAKER–KELLY AND J. GABRIEL EDMOND

UNITED STATES v. JEFFERSON COUNTY BOARD OF EDUCATION, 372 F.2d 836 (1966). In *United States v. Jefferson County Board of Education*, the U.S. Court of Appeals for the Fifth Circuit addressed the unfulfilled legacy of the *Brown* decision. *Jefferson County* was actually the consolidation of seven district court cases. Each of these cases involved school districts in the southern states that were charged with not implementing an adequate desegregation plan. The issues addressed by the Court involved the nature of the duty of school districts to desegregate public schools; the effect that the passage of the Civil Rights Act of 1964* and the promulgation of desegregation standards by the Department of Health, Education, and Welfare (HEW) had on school integration standards; and, fundamentally, the scope and depth of school desegregation required to meet Constitutional standards.

In the years following the *Brown* decision its mandate was met with widespread intransigence in the South. Various means of inhibiting the progress of integration were utilized. As *Brown* had stated that African-American children were "personally" entitled to a desegregated education, the ruling was often interpreted narrowly to mean that African-American children were able to apply to white schools on an individual basis and that the fact that they were able thereby to gain limited entry constituted desegregation. Some southern school boards utilized a dual zoning system, wherein separate schools were built in both primarily African-American and primarily white neighborhoods, the former staffed with African-American teachers and the latter with white teachers. Some states neutralized the effect of court-ordered desegregation by issuing grants to children attending private schools, by facilitating the flight of white students from the public school systems, or by passing so-called freedom-of-choice statutes, whereby schools were "integrated" by giving students the option to transfer between schools.

In *Jefferson County* the Court denounced this institutionalized unwillingness to effect school desegregation, holding that "the law imposes . . . an absolute duty to integrate. . . . [R]acial mixing of students is a high priority educational goal." In regard to the effect of the Civil Rights Act of 1964 and the HEW Guidelines, the Court determined that "[t]he national policy is plain: formerly . . . segregated public school systems . . . must shift to unitary, nonracial systems." The HEW Guidelines were determined to be "minimum standards," by which the "transition . . . to a unitary integrated system may be carried out effectively, promptly, and in an orderly manner."

This case is noteworthy in its finding that true desegregation requires integration. This case was repetitioned twice to the Court (in 1967 and 1969). Both times the Court reaffirmed its initial judgment. This decision has been heralded by the NAACP Legal Defense Fund and other civil rights organizations as the most significant case since *Brown* because the court in effect made integration compulsory in order to help achieve a racially nondiscriminatory school system.

SELECTED BIBLIOGRAPHY

Wendy R. Brown, "The Convergence of Neutrality and Choice: the Limits of the State's Affirmative Duty to Provide Equal Educational Opportunities," *Tennessee Law Review* 60 (Fall 1992): 63–133; Kevin Brown, "Has the Supreme Court Allowed the Cure for De Jure Segregation to Replicate the Disease?" *Cornell Law Review* 78 (November 1992): 1–83; Frank T. Read, "The Bloodless Revolution: The Role of the Fifth Circuit in the Integration of the Deep South," *Mercer Law Review* 32 (Summer 1981): 1149–66.

BEVERLY BAKER–KELLY AND RICHARD MOLLOT

UNITED STATES v. MONTGOMERY COUNTY BOARD OF EDUCATION, 395 U.S. 225 (1969). Lawyers for a group of African-American parents in Montgomery County, Alabama, filed this case on 11 May 1964. The purpose of the litigation was to enjoin the Montgomery County Board of Education from continuing to operate a dual public school system in which black children were segregated from white children on school buses and in schools, white teachers were teaching white students, and black teachers were teaching black students. On 31 July 1964, District Court Judge Johnson concluded that the board was indeed operating racially segregated schools in violation of the U.S. Constitution. He ordered integration of some grades by September 1964. In response to that order, a few African-American students were admitted.

However, annual court proceedings and county board of education reports revealed to the court that the Board of Education was not expeditiously and fully desegregating Montgomery County schools, nor had it fulfilled its fourteen-year-old obligation under *Brown I* and *Brown II* to integrate its school system. Thus, in March 1968, Judge Johnson found that conditions were substantially the same as in 1964. He warned the board that further undue delay in desegregation would not be tolerated. Since the board had failed to comply with its own desegregation plan, Judge Johnson amended the plan by enumerating specific guidelines for desegregation. The board accepted most of the guidelines except an order to integrate the faculty to match the ratio of white to African-American faculty members that existed throughout the school system.

The court of appeals modified the trial court's order by stating that although faculty desegregation was necessary, the board would only be required to substantially or approximately meet the trial court's ratio requirement. The Supreme Court disagreed and its justices opined that, for fifteen years, the board had ignored its ruling in *Brown*. It ruled that faculty and staff desegregation was an important part of achieving a desegregated school system. It decided that Judge Johnson's order should stand without modification because that order created the best course, through his specific and expeditious commands, for bringing about a completely unitary school system.

The significance of *U.S. v. Montgomery County Board of Education* is twofold. First, it is the seminal case that holds that desegregation by racially balancing students is not enough and that faculty desegregation is an important aspect of eliminating dual school systems. Second, Judge Johnson's plan for desegregation represents the first effort by a court to specify exacting requirements for desegregation. After the Supreme Court issued its ruling, courts of appeals throughout the country ordered faculty integration.

SELECTED BIBLIOGRAPHY

Carr v. Montgomery County Board of Education, 232 F. Supp. 705 (M.D. Ala. 1964) (board enjoined from operating segregated schools); *Carr v. Montgomery County Board of Education*, 235 F. Supp. 306 (M.D. Ala. 1966) (court-ordered implementation of desegregation plan by fall of 1967 including desegregated faculty assignments); *Carr v. Montgomery County Board of Education*, 289 F. Supp. 647 (M.D. Ala. 1968) (Judge Johnson's desegregation plan); *Montgomery County Board of Education v. Carr*, 400 F. 2d 1 (5th Cir. 1968) (judge's lament that ratio should not have been modified); *Carr v. Montgomery County Board of Education*, 377 F. Supp. 1123 (M.D. Ala. 1974) (students permitted to attend elementary schools in their neighborhood); *Carr v. Montgomery County Board of Education*, 511 F.2d 1374 (5th Cir. 1975) (adopted the neighborhood school plan); P. Altbach and K. Lomotey, *The Racial Crisis in American Higher Education* (1991); C. Willie, *School Desegregation Plans That Work* (1984); F. T. Read, "Judicial Evolution of the Law of School Integration since *Brown v. Board of Education*," *Law & Contemporary Problems* 39 no. 1 (1975): 7–49; P. Gewirtz, "Remedies and Resistance," *Yale Law Journal* 92 (1983): 585, 597; J. H. Wilkinson, "The Supreme Court and Southern School Desegregation, 1955–1970: A History and Analysis," *Virginia Law Review* 64, no. 4 (1978): 485, 550.

CYNTHIA R. MABRY

UNITED STATES v. WALLACE, 218 F. Supp. 290 (N.D. Ala. 1963). On 5 June 1963, Judge Syebourn Lynne of the United States District Court for the Northern District of Alabama issued an injunction directing that Vivian J. Malone, David M. McGlathery, and other persons of color be permitted to enroll at the University of Alabama. The injunction was issued two weeks after the court ruled that its earlier decision, *Lucy et al. v. Alabama*,* remained the controlling law and that the dean of admissions at the University of Alabama could not prevent the enrollment of any person on the basis of color or race. By issuing its injunction permitting Malone and others to enroll, the federal court exercised its authority and power over the state governor, George C. Wallace, and prevented him from interfering with and obstructing the law.

SELECTED BIBLIOGRAPHY

Jack Bass, *Unlikely Heroes* (1981); Jack Bass, *Taming the Storm* (1993); *United States v. Wallace*, 218 F. Supp. 290 (N.D. Ala. 1963); *Lucy v. Alabama*, 134 F. Supp. 235 (N.D. Ala. 1955).

PATRICIA O. ROTH

UNITED STATES v. YONKERS BOARD OF EDUCATION, 837 F.2d 1181 (2d Cir. 1987). This case is one of a series of related suits in the fight to end segregation in the city of Yonkers, New York. In the relevant portion of this lengthy opinion, most of which concentrated on issues surrounding discrimination in public housing, the Second Circuit Court of Appeals upheld the use of district-wide magnet schools to remedy intentional racial segregation by the city and its board of education.

In the part of its opinion relevant to education, the Second Circuit first addressed challenges to the system-wide desegregation order advanced by the board, focusing on two points in support of its holding. First, it determined that by disproportionately assigning minority faculty to schools with high concentrations of minority students, by discriminating in the placement of minorities in special education, and by refusing to invoke its contractual right to stem the exodus of more experienced white teachers to schools outside of minority neighborhoods, the board contributed to district-wide segregation. Second, it opined that even where a segregative practice such as the disproportionate placement of African-American students in what became identified as minority schools was limited to one building, it often had secondary effects elsewhere; for example, difficulties arose when students were reassigned in anticipation of the opening of a new school. Consequently, the Second Circuit ruled that by cooperating in the city's effort to maintain segregated neighborhoods, which contributed to school segregation, the district was properly ordered to implement a system-wide remedy.

United States v. Yonkers Board of Education predates, but is consistent with, the Supreme Court's later ruling in *Missouri v. Jenkins*, to the extent that both upheld the remedial use of magnet schools in the fight against school segregation. Yet, however reasonable the judicial opinions in *Yonkers* may be, they have been unable to resolve the dispute. In fact, at the start of the 1993–94 school year, district court judge Leonard Sand, who has presided over the trial litigation since its inception, found that vestiges of segregation remained. Thus, based on disparities in test scores and dropout rates, he ordered the district to overhaul its curriculum and to address the way in which it prepares its teachers to interact with diverse students. *Yonkers* remains a significant decision, which illustrates how vigilant federal courts will continue to retain jurisdiction over school desegregation cases until such time as this invidious form of discrimination is eradicated.

SELECTED BIBLIOGRAPHY

"Yonkers Must Step Up Effort, Federal Judge Says," *School Law News*, 10 September 1993, p. 3.

CHARLES J. RUSSO AND J. JOHN HARRIS III

UNIVERSITY OF ARKANSAS AT PINE BLUFF. The University of Arkansas at Pine Bluff (UAPB) is the second oldest state-supported institution of higher education in Arkansas and one of only two with a land-grant mission. Beginning in 1873 as Branch Normal College, it continued from 1927 until 1972 as Arkansas Agricultural, Mechanical, and Normal College, at which time it joined four other campuses to comprise the University of Arkansas system. The university has distinguished itself as an institution that provides a quality education for all of Arkansas citizens. Degree programs in more than forty areas are offered in the School of Education; the School of Arts and Sciences; and the School of Business and Management. A fifth school of computer science, technology and pre-engineering has been approved. Degree programs in more than forty areas are offered through these schools. Three nondegree divisions complete this academic structure: University College, which coordinates a special freshman studies program; Continuing Education, which arranges evening and weekend courses; and Military Science, which prepares students who desire a career in the U.S. Army. The campus covers a 220-acre tract in Pine Bluff.

SELECTED BIBLIOGRAPHY

National Association for Equal Opportunity in Higher Education, *Profiles of the Nation's Historically and Predominantly Black Colleges and Universities* (1993).

SAMUEL L. MYERS

UNIVERSITY OF MARYLAND v. MURRAY, 169 Md. 478 (1936); *Pearson et al. v. Murray*, 182 A. 590 (1936). On 15 January 1936, the Maryland Court of Appeals ruled that the Board of Regents of the University of Maryland had to admit Donald Gaines Murray, an African-American citizen of Maryland, as a law student in the University of Maryland Law School (UMLS). Murray, a 1934 Amherst graduate and a resident of Baltimore, applied to (UMLS) even though it was the state-supported law school designated for white students only. Although he qualified for admission, the university's Board of Regents denied him admission solely on the basis of his race. Thurgood Marshall* recommended Murray's case to Charles H. Houston* of the National Association for the Advancement of Colored People* (NAACP). Houston accepted the case as the NAACP's test case to challenge state actions that provided inequality in the graduate and professional training of African-American college graduates.

Murray's legal counsel (Houston, Marshall, and William I. Gosnell) successfully argued that the Board of Regents' exclusion of Murray from UMLS denied him equal protection as guaranteed by the Fourteenth Amendment of the U.S. Constitution. The Board of Regents acknowledged that the law school was for white students only and that Maryland had not established a separate law school for African-American students. The Board of Regents' main dispute was that Maryland afforded black college graduates "equal" treatment by providing them with scholarships to attend graduate and professional schools outside the state rather than at the University of Maryland. Thus, the leading issue in the *Murray* case was whether the Board of Regents could maintain the separation of races and exclude African-American students from the only state-supported law school by furnishing them scholarships for studying outside the state at law schools open to blacks.

Although the court acknowledged that Maryland could choose its own system for providing equality in the legal training of its African-American and white citizens, the court ruled that Maryland's out-of-state scholarship program did not adequately provide black students with a legal education "substantially equal" to the legal education afforded white students at UMLS. The court concluded that Maryland's out-of-state scholarship program was inadequate for several reasons. First, the out-of-state scholarships only covered tuition, and Murray would be at an economic disadvantage having to pay travel and incidental expenses to commute or move to the nearest out-of-state law school accepting black students (i.e., Howard University* Law School). (If admitted to UMLS in Baltimore where Murray resided, Murray would not have to incur the additional expenses.) Second, there was no guarantee that Murray would receive a scholarship, because it was questionable whether sufficient funds had been appropriated to ensure scholarships to every African-American applicant. Third, the out-of-state option would not provide Murray with the advantages of studying Maryland laws and observing Maryland's judiciary, legal practitioners, and courts, where he intended to practice.

The court noted in its decision that there was no statutory authority to establish a separate law school for African-Americans, hence, it could not fashion a legal remedy to provide for such a school. Because of the inadequacy of Maryland's out-of-state scholarship program to provide equal treatment and because a separate law school for African-Americans had not been established within the state, the Court concluded that equality meant the Board of Regents must admit Murray to the only state-supported law school available, the University of Maryland Law School.

The *Murray* court stated in its decision that it would not review the constitutionality of "whether with aid in any amount it is sufficient to send the negroes outside the state for like education" (169 Md. at 487). However, the *Murray* case provided the legal and social precedent by which other out-of-state scholarship programs would be judicially scrutinized. As the NAACP's first successful judicial attack on inequality in professional and graduate training for African-American college graduates, the *Murray* case was the legal cornerstone for the landmark U.S. Supreme Court decision, *Missouri ex rel. Gaines v. Canada*,* 305 U.S. 337 (1938).

SELECTED BIBLIOGRAPHY

Genna Rae McNeil, *Groundwork: Charles Hamilton Houston and the Struggle for Civil Rights* (1983); Jean L. Preer, *Lawyers v. Educators: Black Colleges and Desegregation in Public Higher Education* (1982); Charles Hamilton Houston, *Crisis* 43 (March 1936): 79; *Afro-American Newspaper*, 14 September 1935, p. 4; 25 January 1936, p. 6.

ANDREA D. WILLIAMS

UNIVERSITY OF THE DISTRICT OF COLUMBIA. The University of the District of Columbia (UDC), the nation's only exclusively urban land-grant institution of higher education, opened in 1977. However, the roots of the university date back to 1851, when Myrtilla Miner opened a school to prepare "colored girls to teach." The system of public higher education in Washington moved through several phases and mergers until, in 1976, the board of trustees of UDC was seated and began implementing the consolidation of three public higher education institutions—D.C. Teachers College, Federal City College, and Washington Technical Institute—into a single University of the District of Columbia. UDC is a commuter institution. Its academic programs are arrayed under a five-college structure—business and public management, education and human ecology, liberal and fine arts, life sciences and physical science, and engineering and technology. In addition, it maintains a division of continuing education and a university college. The university maintains a deep respect for traditional values of higher education, while also providing education for the growing numbers of largely urban-based, nontraditional students who must be prepared for excellence in this technological age.

SELECTED BIBLIOGRAPHY

National Association for Equal Opportunity in Higher Education, *Profiles of the Nation's Historically and Predominantly Black Colleges and Universities* (1993).

SAMUEL L. MYERS

UPWARD BOUND. The Upward Bound program came into existence as a result of the Higher Education Act of 1965, Public Law 89-329. Its continued existence was authorized by the Higher Education Amendment of 1992, Public Law 102-325. This program is administered by the Department of Education under the Office of the Assistant Secretary for Postsecondary Education. The purpose of this program is to instill high school students with the skills and motivation required for the successful completion of post–high school education. Its primary objective is to improve the academic performance and motivational levels of the participants so that upon completion of the program these students may graduate from secondary schools and successfully compete in postsecondary educational programs. Upward Bound strives to compensate for academic deficiencies and cultural differences to enhance scholastic success. A variety of services are offered, including class instruction in writing, reading, and mathematics. Additionally, assistance is offered in the areas of personal counseling, tutorial services, high school class selection, and university alternatives.

Children from low-income families, potential first-generation college students, and veterans in need of academic support are the eligible participant target groups served by this program. Potential first-generation college students from low-income families make up two thirds of attendees. Enrollees must be between thirteen and nineteen years of age and have completed the eighth grade but not have entered the twelfth grade. As a result of this program, many African-Americans and other minorities who otherwise may not have had the chance have successfully completed high school and college.

The Upward Bound program consists of three components. The first phase of the program is held during summers for high school students. The second operates during the summer preceding the last year of high school and continues throughout the academic year and concludes prior to high school graduation. The third, called "the Bridge," is conducted during the summer immediately following high school graduation and prior to college entrance. During each phase of the program, students are challenged to reach their potential.

The project has more than five hundred sites nationwide. The federal government provides funding to higher education institutions, consortiums of higher education institutions, agencies, and organizations to administer Upward Bound. In rare instances, secondary schools may qualify for participation in Upward Bound.

CYNTHIA ROSS

V

VIRGINIA STATE UNIVERSITY. Virginia State University, located in Et-trick, near Petersburg, was founded on 6 March 1882, when the legislature passed a bill to charter the Virginia Normal and Collegiate Institute, exclusively for the education of ''persons of color.'' Thus, Virginia State University became America's first fully state-supported four-year institution of higher learning for African-Americans. In 1902, the legislature revised the charter act to curtail the college program and to change the name to Virginia Normal and Industrial Institute. In 1920, the land-grant program for African-Americans was moved from Hampton Institute* to Virginia Normal and Industrial Institute. In 1923, the college program was restored, and in 1930 the name was changed to Virginia State College for Negroes. The institution was renamed Virginia State College in 1946, and finally the legislature passed a law in 1979 to provide the present name, Virginia State University. Today, the university is a coeducational comprehensive institution. It boasts historic and emerging centers of excellence in the sciences, business, fine arts, engineering technology, aquaculture and small farm research, telecommunications, and the Honors College.

SELECTED BIBLIOGRAPHY

National Association for Equal Opportunity in Higher Education, *Profiles of the Nation's Historically and Predominantly Black Colleges and Universities* (1993).

SAMUEL L. MYERS

VIRGINIA UNION UNIVERSITY. Virginia Union University, located in Richmond, was founded in 1865 to provide high-quality educational opportunities for the newly emancipated. Today, the small liberal arts university offers students of every race and economic group the chance to develop their minds and spirits as they pursue programs of study that lead to either a B.A. or a B.S. degree in the natural and social sciences, mathematics, education, psychology, business, and the humanities. Its School of Theology offers master's and doctoral degrees. Virginia Union University has consistently produced well-qualified graduates, many of whom hold positions of leadership throughout the

United States and other countries. It is accredited by the Southern Association of Colleges and Schools* and is a member of the United Negro College Fund.* The university is a member of the National Collegiate Athletic Association Division II and the Central Intercollegiate Athletic Association, participating in intercollegiate competition in six men's and five women's sports.

SELECTED BIBLIOGRAPHY

National Association for Equal Opportunity in Higher Education, *Profiles of the Nation's Historically and Predominantly Black Colleges and Universities* (1993).

SAMUEL L. MYERS

VOCATIONAL–TECHNICAL EDUCATION, AFRICAN-AMERICANS AND. Vocational–technical education proponents and critics agree that occupational and technical education programs have the potential to provide a vehicle through which employment needs of non–college-bound African-American youth and adults can be more adequately met. Although African-Americans have experienced a long and varied history in vocational–technical education programs, both proponents and critics note that vocational education has not been totally responsive to the needs of African-Americans. Inadequate employability skills, the high unemployment rate, and underemployment among African-American youth and young adults indicate that vocational–technical programs have been less than successful in addressing the needs of the African-American community. Consequently, African-Americans have not enrolled in vocational–technical training programs in large numbers. Various theories and explanations have been advanced to explain the limited participation of African-Americans in vocational–technical training programs, and several strategies to improve this level of participation have been proposed.

African-American participation in vocational–technical education began during the period of slavery. Apprenticeship programs were made available to slaves in 1619 when they arrived as indentured servants in colonial America. These apprenticeship systems were used to teach slaves the vocational skills they needed to make and keep plantations self-supporting. Instruction was provided in such areas as carpentry and weaving. Slaves were also involved in such skilled positions as stonemasons, blacksmiths, artisans, inventors, and potters and in such unskilled labor positions as cooks, maids, butlers, and gardeners. Following the Civil War, numerous private industrial colleges, including Lincoln University,* Fisk University,* Hampton Institute,* and Tuskegee Institute* were established with resources donated by northern whites and philanthropists. Agriculture, domestic science, and industrial education were included in the curricula of these schools. In 1881 Tuskegee Institute began the successful extension efforts that flourished under the leadership of Booker T. Washington* and George Washington Carver.

During this same period, abolitionist-statesman Frederick Douglass advocated expanding African-American participation in vocational and industrial training. Private liberal arts colleges began to offer manual-training courses for African-

Americans during the 1880s. From 1865 to 1900, numerous African-American colleges and training schools (forerunners of high schools) were founded. In 1890, the Morrill Act* provided funding for seventeen African-American land-grant colleges. These institutions became primarily responsible for preparing teachers and leaders, including vocational educators, to staff African-American high schools.

Manual training for African-Americans was offered in public secondary schools from 1910 to the 1930s. This development has been partially attributed to Booker T. Washington's philosophy regarding the importance of manual arts to the economic sufficiency of the African-American community. Even though the Niagara Movement* founded by W. E. B. Du Bois* in 1905 opposed Washington's position on philosophical and political bases, the movement also called for manual and vocational education for African-Americans. Although the impact of the Washington–Du Bois debates on shaping African-American participation in vocational education is unclear, many historians acknowledge that these debates did indeed influence African-American attitudes toward vocational education.

Federal funding for trade and industrial education in historically black institutions of higher education was made available in the 1930s. More recent vocational education legislation, specifically the Carl D. Perkins Vocational and Applied Technology Education Act of 1990, directed more federal funds to school districts and colleges in low-income communities. An intended outcome of this act and of other vocational education legislation passed after 1963 has been the increased involvement of persons of color in vocational-technical education.

Despite this rich tradition, African-American students, teachers, administrators, and policymakers are currently underrepresented in vocational–technical education programs at all educational levels. Substantial gains were made in minority student enrollment in vocational–technical education programs in the late 1970s. For example, in 1977 the percentage of African-Americans in such programs was 14.6 compared to 12 percent representation of African-Americans in the total U.S. population. However, recent statistics document declining African-American enrollment in secondary vocational–technical programs. Sponsored by the National Center for Education Statistics, a comparative study of high school sophomores in the United States from 1980 to 1990 showed that the percentage of African-American sophomores enrolled in vocational–technical education programs dropped from 34.1 percent to 6.2 percent over the ten-year period, while the percentage of African-American sophomores enrolled in general education programs increased from 39.0 percent to 42.9 percent. On a more positive note, the percentage of African-American sophomores enrolled in college preparatory or academic programs also increased, from 26.9 percent to 40.9 percent. For all sophomores over the ten-year period, the percentage of enrollment changed from 46.0 percent to 50.8 percent for general education programs, from 33.1 percent to 41.3 percent for college preparatory or academic programs, and from 21.0 percent to 7.9 percent for vocational–technical education. These trends are similar to the enrollment trends for African-American sophomores; however, African-American enrollment in vocational–technical education has decreased at a much sharper rate than the overall sophomore enrollment in these programs.

African-American teachers are also underrepresented in the nation's elementary, secondary, and higher education classrooms. Although total enrollment in teacher preparation programs has increased in recent years, the teaching profession is not attracting minority teachers to its ranks. The American Association of Colleges for Teacher Education has estimated that, by the year 2000, approximately one third of the school population will be minority students and less than 5 percent of all American teachers will be persons of color. Similar scenarios are expected for secondary and postsecondary vocational–technical classrooms. In 1989–90, only 7.4 percent of beginning vocational teachers in the United States were African-American, while 88.9 percent were white, 2.0 percent Hispanic, and 1.7 percent other. An added problem is the disproportionate distribution of African-American faculty in relation to the African-American population. For example, William Young examined minority vocational–technical teacher representation in rural and urban areas in Illinois, Kansas, and Mississippi and concluded that, although minority teachers were well represented in urban vocational–technical programs, minority teachers were vastly underrepresented in all three states, specifically in rural areas.

Vocational–technical educators also point to the lack of African-American representation among the field's decision-makers. Few African-Americans serve as administrators and counselors or as members of vocational–technical advisory councils. Until 1977 there was no organized national organization charged with representing African-American concerns in the field. However, in 1977 the National Association for the Advancement of Black Americans in Vocational Education (NAABAVE) was founded with the overriding mission of providing national leadership in promoting greater participation of African-Americans in all aspects of vocational–technical training.

Why are vocational–technical education services not used by African-Americans? Authors have advanced many hypotheses to describe their restricted involvement. Social, economic, and demographic developments have been singled out as contributing factors to this limited participation. For example, vocational–technical educator and researcher Ferman Moody has observed in 1980 that cultural deprivation, immediate gratification, fatherless families, broken homes, and welfare dependency are characteristics that impede African-Americans' advancement in vocational–technical education programs. Moody also noted that to fully understand African-American perceptions of vocational–technical education, a better knowledge about blacks' vocational history is necessary, as is understanding about the extent to which slavery, racism, segregation, denial, rejection, and exploitation have affected African-Americans' success in contemporary vocational–technical education programs.

Additionally, the negative image associated with vocational–technical education programs has led many parents, not just African-American parents, to advise students against enrolling in these programs. The consensus of a survey conducted by Charles Nichols in 1980 was that the adverse image of vocational–technical education was the pervading reason that it was not meeting the needs of African-Americans. Nichols concluded that African-Americans view the field as appropriate for someone else's children or as "dead-end" education for people who cannot achieve in other arenas. It is difficult for students whose parents hold such negative attitudes to regard it as a route to skilled employment.

To help counteract the negative perceptions students receive from parents, African-American teachers are needed in schools to provide role models and counsel students regarding vocational–technical training opportunities. However, as noted earlier, African-American teachers and administrators are underrepresented in these programs, as they are in all education programs at all levels. Certainly this scarcity of African-American vocational–technical educators contributes to the decreasing minority student enrollments at both secondary and postsecondary levels. The need to recruit more minority teachers in all areas is acute. Clearly, unless more persons of color are recruited into vocational–technical teaching, students will have fewer role models to convince them that they, too, can succeed in these fields.

To reverse the declining participation of African-Americans in vocational–technical education, several approaches must be considered: (a) Improve the image of vocational–technical education among the African-American population. As noted earlier, vocational–technical education is viewed by many African-Americans as a second-class education that leads nowhere or, at best, to low-paying jobs with little future. Additionally, the image that vocational education programs are designed for disadvantaged, low-achieving individuals abounds. Educators must demonstrate that vocational–technical education reaches out to those who are highly motivated as well. These negative viewpoints of vocational–technical education must be considered. (b) Improve the programmatic nature of vocational courses by offering realistic, quality programs that are tied directly to labor-market needs. Programs must be reviewed and revised continuously to keep pace with the changing labor market. Individuals must be convinced that the sophisticated technologies of the 1990s are available to them through today's vocational–technical programs. (c) Employ capable, caring, and knowledgeable school leaders. Involve more African-Americans in such leadership roles as teachers, counselors, and administrators. (d) Involve interested and supportive employers from business and industry, policymakers, former students, parents, and community groups and organizations in the program to serve as role models for young students and to serve on advisory councils. Secure African-Americans for representation among these constituency groups. (e) Ensure that schools in predominantly African-American areas have facilities, equipment, and instructional and management staff comparable to schools located outside these areas. (f) Direct more emphasis on placement initiatives that will result in jobs for African-American graduates. (g) Attract African-Americans to vocational–technical teacher education positions in higher education and to teaching positions at secondary and postsecondary levels. It is imperative that persons of color provide effective role models for students in secondary and higher education classrooms.

The success of African-Americans in vocational–technical education programs is at a critical juncture. Clearly, vocational–technical education has not responded appropriately to the needs of the African-American community. We must not only recognize this crisis; we must work diligently and be committed to doing something about it.

SELECTED BIBLIOGRAPHY

"Data File," *Vocational Education Journal* 66 (September 1991): 41–44; James Jennings, "Minorities and Voc Ed: The Challenges," *Vocational Education Journal* 66 (April 1991): 20–21, 45; Reynaldo L. Martinez, Jr., "A Crisis in the Profession: Minority Role Models in Critically Short Supply," *Vocational Education Journal* 66 (April 1991): 24–25, 46; Ferman Moody, "The History of Blacks in Vocational Education," *Voc Ed* 55 (January 1980): 30–34; National Center for Education Statistics, *America's High School Sophomores: A Ten Year Comparison 1980–1990* (June 1993); Charles F. Nichols, Sr., "How Well Are We Serving Black America?" *Voc Ed* 55 (January 1980): 22–24; "Sex and Racial/Ethnic Characteristics of Full-Time Vocational Education Instructional Staff," *National Center for Education Statistics Bulletin* (November 1982); William C. Young, "Too Few Black Americans in Vocational Education," *Vocational Education Journal* 64 (April 1989): 12–14.

ROSETTA F. SANDIDGE

VONTRESS, CLEMMONT E. (22 April 1929, Kentucky). Clemmont E. Vontress received the B.A. degree from Kentucky State University* (1952, French and English); the M.A. (1956, counseling) and Ph.D. (counseling) from Indiana University. He has also done additional graduate work (1952–53, French and Spanish) at the State University of Iowa.

A university professor for more than twenty-six years, Vontress is currently professor of counseling at George Washington University, where he teaches or has taught graduate courses such as counseling theory and techniques, organization and administration of counseling services, cross-cultural counseling, career counseling, and group counseling. Previously, he was a professor of counseling at Howard University* (1965–69), director of counseling, Crispus Attucks High School, Indianapolis, Indiana (1958–65), English teacher, George Washington High School, Indianapolis, Indiana (1956–57), and instructor of English and typing, U.S. Army Education Center, Hammelberg, Germany (1954–55). He has also been a visiting professor at Atlanta University (now Clark Atlanta University)* (1965), Virginia Polytechnic Institute and State University (1978; 1987), Kuwait University (1983), and Johns Hopkins University (1983).

Vontress is a member of several professional organizations, including the District of Columbia Counseling Association; the American Counseling Association; the Association for Multicultural Counseling and Development; the Association for Religion and Value Issues in Counseling; and the American Psychological Association. He has also been a member of the editorial boards of the *Personnel and Guidance Journal* (1969–72) (currently, the *Journal of Counseling and Development*) and the *Journal of Negro Education** (1966–73). In 1971, Vontress received the National Capital Personnel and Guidance Association's Counselor Educator of the Year award; in 1974, he received the same organization's Award for Outstanding Publications; and in 1991, he was installed as Honorary Life Member and Distinguished Scholar of Chi Sigma Iota, the international counseling and professional honor society.

Vontress has written more than seventy books, chapters, book reviews, and articles in professional journals. Included among these works are *Counseling Negroes* (1971); "Racial Differences: Impediments to Rapport," *Journal of Counseling Psychology* (1971); "Barriers in Cross-Cultural Counseling," *Counseling and Values* (1974); "An Existential Approach to Cross-Cultural Counseling," *Counseling and Values* (1974); "An Existential Approach to Cross-Cultural Counseling," *Journal of Multicultural Counseling and Development* (1988); and "Traditional Healing in Africa: Implications for Cross-Cultural Counseling," *Journal of Counseling and Development* (1991).

FREDERICK D. HARPER

VOORHEES COLLEGE. Voorhees College, founded in 1897 by Elizabeth Evelyn Wright, is a coeducational liberal arts college located in Denmark, South Carolina. Affiliated with the Episcopal Church, Voorhees was the first predominantly black institution in South Carolina to achieve full accreditation by the Southern Association of Colleges and Schools.* Historic facilities and a tree-shaded, park-like setting, situated on 350 acres, give Voorhees one of the most attractive campuses in the country. Four academic divisions at Voorhees offer a wide choice of courses and preparation for an almost unlimited number of careers. The divisions are business, humanities, natural sciences, mathematics and computer science, and social sciences.

SELECTED BIBLIOGRAPHY

National Association for Equal Opportunity in Higher Education, *Profiles of the Nation's Historically and Predominantly Black Colleges and Universities* (1993).

SAMUEL L. MYERS

VOTING RIGHTS ACT OF 1965, EDUCATION IMPLICATIONS OF THE. The Voting Rights Act of 1965 is generally considered to be one of the most successful pieces of civil rights legislation ever enacted in the United States. Yet controversy and debate over the meaning, the fairness, and the enforcement of the act and its subsequent amendments animate its history. While African-American voter registration and participation in the electoral process has increased substantially, school board membership remains disproportionately white. The impact of the act on public education may be viewed at two levels.

First, the act may be viewed in the broad context of its contribution to increasing minority participation in the democratic process. Second, its educational impact may be viewed as having opened the door for increased minority group membership on local school boards and assisting in the inclusion of minorities in the local educational decision-making process.

For 250 years after their arrival in the United States as slaves, most African-Americans in the United States were not allowed to vote. Prior to the Civil War, free African-American men were disfranchised in all but six northern states, and African-American women could not vote anywhere in America. After the Civil War, between 1865 and 1869, African-Americans remained mostly disfranchised in the North, and suffrage was severely restricted in the South. In 1869 Congress proposed the Fifteenth Amendment to the United States Constitution, which guaranteed African-Americans the right to vote. The triumph of the passage of the Fifteenth Amendment was short-lived for African-Americans in the South, however, as whites quickly revolted against the enfranchisement of African-Americans. This resistance took the form of the rise of the Ku Klux Klan and the enactment of legislation that mandated new voting requirements, such as literacy tests and poll taxes, effectively disenfranchising most African-Americans. Beginning in the early 1900s groups such as the National Association for the Advancement of Colored People* (NAACP) struggled against African-American disfranchisement. But disfranchisement and discrimination against African-Americans continued for decades, and not until World War II did large-scale changes in racial attitudes begin to take place.

Congress passed three pieces of civil rights legislation, in 1957, 1960, and 1964, that variously supported and protected African-American voting rights. But these acts were marked by the absence of effective federal involvement in the enforcement of African-Americans' right to vote. The battle to gain equal suffrage was also waged outside Congess. During the 1960s, organizations such as the Southern Regional Council, the Congress of Racial Equality, the Student Nonviolent Coordinating Committee (SNCC), and the Southern Christian Leadership Conference fought white resistance to increased African-American voter registration throughout the South. These groups' efforts met with violence and resistance by white citizens and police. Media coverage of these events focused the nation's attention on the Civil Rights Movement, creating a climate of outrage that assisted President Lyndon Johnson in garnering political support for a new voting rights act, designed to allow the Justice Department to take direct action to protect the right of African-Americans to vote. In August of 1965, Congress passed the Voting Rights Act of 1965, and a proud President Johnson (who was a southerner) signed the bill on 6 August 1965.

The Voting Rights Act of 1965 was enacted by President Johnson in order to eliminate racial discrimination in the American electoral process by removing obstacles to African-American registration and voting. The core of the act was found in sections 4 and 5, which designated certain areas (covered states) of the country where voting discrimination had been widespread and flagrant, suspended literacy tests and other similar tests in those areas, and prohibited any changes in voting procedures in those areas without clearance from the Attorney General or approval from the United States District Court for the District of Columbia. The act was upheld by the Supreme Court in the 1966 *South Carolina v. Katzenbach* case. The high court found the act's suspension of literacy tests and its preclearance provisions to be constitutional.

The impact of the act on African-American registration and voting was enormous. In the South, African-American voter registration increased from 29 percent of the voting-age population in 1964 to 52 percent in 1967. By comparison, white registration increased from 73 percent to 79 percent during the same period. In all of the targeted southern states, African-American voter turnout in the 1965 and 1968 presidential elections increased, in some instances by as much as 20 percent. Though the act resulted in increased African-American participation in the electoral process, it did not resolve the issue of dilution of the African-American vote. Vote dilution, the practice or effort of diminishing the impact of minorities' voting strength, took many forms after the passage of the act. Since 1965, the reshaping of political and school districts to maintain white voting power and the use of at-large school board elections both have been challenged as electoral devices that dilute minority groups' equal participation in the political process. In at-large elections, school board members are elected on a city-or county-wide basis, effectively preventing a minority group from electing a preferred candidate. In ward elections (single-member districts), school board members are elected from geographically based single districts; where a majority of the voters are minorities, they are likely to be successful in electing a minority preferred candidate.

Twenty-seven years after the enactment of the Voting Rights Act, school board members were still disproportionately white, as were school board presidents. In 1992, 94 percent of all school board members were white, as were 97 percent of all school board presidents. Numerous claims of voting discrimination under the Voting Rights Act have been brought, challenging at-large school board elections, including legal challenges in Florida, California, Arkansas, Alabama, Virginia, Texas, South Carolina, Pennsylvania, Delaware, and Massachusetts. Since the act was passed in 1965, minority plaintiffs have challenged vote dilution practices under section 2 of the act. The proof required to establish a claim of vote dilution has changed several times during this period. In 1980, in *Mobile v. Bolden,* the Supreme Court held that, in order to establish a vote dilution violation under section 2 of the act (or under the Fourteenth or Fifteenth Amendments), plaintiffs were required to prove that officials maintained or adopted the challenged electoral device, such as an an at-large election system, with the intent to discriminate against minority voters. This test placed a high evidentiary burden on plaintiffs, as they had to probe the racial motives of lawmakers, public officials, and entire communities in order to prove discriminatory intent. In 1982, in response to the Supreme Court's decision in *Bolden,* Congress amended section 2 of the act, replacing the discriminatory intent standard with a "results test." The amended act allowed plaintiffs to prevail by showing that, under the totality of the circumstances, the challenged electoral procedure had the result of denying a minority group equal opportunity to participate in the political process and to elect representatives of their choice.

In 1986, the Supreme Court considered the amended section of the act in the case of *Thornburg v. Gingles*. In this extremely important voting rights case, the Supreme Court held that three objective factors must be present to make a claim of vote dilution caused by an at-large (multimember-district) election procedure: (a) the minority group must be sufficiently large and compact to constitute a majority in a single-member district; (b) the minority group must be politically cohesive; and (c) the white majority must normally vote as a block, in a way sufficient to defeat the minority group's choice of candidates. The *Gingles* test has been applied by lower courts in vote dilution cases involving school board election schemes in order to establish a violation of the act. Courts have indicated a clear preference for single-member district (ward) voting over multimember at-large school board elections. Courts have viewed single-member districts as electoral devices that maximize minority voting strength. Consequently, numerous discriminatory school board election systems have been struck down and eliminated by the federal judiciary. Courts have stopped short of creating a minority group right to proportional representation.

In most of the cases brought under the act challenging at-large school board elections, African-Americans maintaining the lawsuit have been seriously underrepresented. Although African-American citizens have achieved some school board electoral success, nationwide, the inability to elect African-American candidates in numbers that reflect the percentage of African-American population indicates continuing racial bias in voting, despite gains achieved under the act. In summary, the act has been viewed largely as a success in increasing minority participation in the electoral process, but it has fallen short in securing African-American a genuine voice on their local school boards.

SELECTED BIBLIOGRAPHY

Lorn S. Foster, ed., *The Voting Rights Act* (1985); Bernard Grofman and Chandler Davidson, eds., *Controversies in Minority Voting* (1992); Bernard Grofman, Lisa Handley, and Richard Niemi, *Minority Representation and the Quest for Voting Equality* (1992); Lani Guinier, "The Triumph of Tokenism: The Voting Rights Act and the Theory of Black Electoral Success," *Michigan Law Review* 90 (1991): 1077; *Harvell v. Ladd*, 958 F.2d 226 (8th Cir. 1992); James Scott McClain. "The Voting Rights Act and Local School Boards: An Argument for Deference to Educational Policy in Remedies for Vote Dilution," *Texas Law Review* 67 (1988): 139; *Mobile v. Bolden*, 446 U.S. 55 (1980); *South Carolina v. Katzenbach*, 383 U.S. 301 (1966); *Thornburg v. Gingles*, 478 U.S. 30 (1986).

JOSEPH R. MCKINNEY

WARREN COURT. Many people were surprised when President Dwight D. Eisenhower appointed Earl Warren as chief justice of the Supreme Court in 1953. Warren, a California governor, was known more as a moderately conservative politician than as a legal scholar. Few analysts could have predicted that he would emerge as a strong defender of civil rights and the architect of decisions that would reshape American society. As chief justice for fifteen years, Warren led a judicial revolution that reshaped many social and political relationships in America. Rather than focusing on legal theories, Warren was more interested in the basic fairness of decisions. In addition to Earl Warren, in 1953–54 the other justices on the Court were Felix Frankfurter, Hugo L. Black, Stanley F. Reed, William O. Douglas, Tom C. Clark, Robert H. Jackson, Harold H. Burton, and Sherman Minton.

As helmsman of the Court, Warren convinced the other justices to issue a unanimous judgment for change in the *Brown v. Board of Education of Topeka, Kansas** case in 1954. Rejecting the ''separate but equal'' doctrine that had prevailed since the *Plessy v. Ferguson** decision in 1896, he stated that ''separate educational facilities are inherently unequal.'' Unanimity, which Warren believed essential in such explosive situations, subsequently became the hallmark of all Supreme Court decisions on racial equality. Warren believed that the Supreme Court should rule on the basis of modern interpretations of the Constitution rather than on the basis of past rulings only. To those who firmly believed in the doctrine of *stare decisis*—the principle that precedent governs—this was a radical approach. Yet, many of the Warren Court decisions established ideas that are taken for granted today, such as the unlawfulness of racial segregation. Although Warren probably is best remembered for his role in *Brown*, he did not consider it the most important case decided by the Court under his leadership. According to several sources, Warren considered the case of *Baker v. Carr* (1962) to be the most significant decision of the Court during his tenure.

Before the 1960s, the Court had long refused to get involved in voting rights but, with *Baker*, it plunged in and decided that unequal election districts were discriminatory and violated the Fourteenth Amendment. This case, and the arm-load of reapportionment cases that followed, not only gave us the phrase "one man, one vote," it also shifted the country's center of gravity from the hinter-lands to the cities. The Warren Court also was responsible for sweeping changes in the area of criminal procedure. In *Miranda v. State of Arizona* (1966), Warren ruled that the police, before questioning a criminal suspect, must inform him of his right to remain silent and to have counsel present and that confession ob-tained in defiance of these requirements is inadmissable in court.

One of the Warren Court's most vocal critics was Richard M. Nixon, who throughout the 1968 presidential campaign ran against Warren and his Court as much as against his Democratic rival, Senator Hubert Humphrey. Nixon won the election in November 1968, and it was clear that his recommendations for appointments to the Supreme Court would be conservative. In an attempt to ensure that he would be replaced by a liberal, Warren submitted his resignation to President Lyndon B. Johnson, but the Senate rejected Johnson's nominee. The Court, just before Warren's resignation, was composed of justices John Marshall Harlan, Hugo L. Black, William O. Douglas, William J. Brennan, Jr., Abe Fortas, Potter Stewart, Byron R. White, and Thurgood Marshall.*

Consequently, with Warren's resignation on his desk, President Nixon was given the opportunity to name the next chief justice. He appointed Warren E. Burger, who took his seat on the Court in 1969. The turning away from the Warren Court, however, was orchestrated and controlled not by Burger but by Potter Stewart (appointed by President Eisenhower in 1958) and Byron White (appointed by President John F. Kennedy in 1962), both of whom had served on the Warren Court; Lewis F. Powell, Jr. (appointed by President Nixon in 1971), and considered the most moderate of the four Nixon appointees (the other two were Harry A. Blackmun, appointed in 1970, and William H. Rehnquist, appointed in 1971); and by John Paul Stevens (appointed by Gerald R. Ford in 1975). The center gained control. Yet, in the twenty-five years since Warren's resignation in 1969, his legacy has shown remarkable resilience. For many, much of the credit for the architecture of the Court's post-Warren jurisprudence goes to William J. Brennan, Jr. (appointed by President Eisenhower in 1956), who is said to have been the "strategist" of the liberal Warren Court era.

SELECTED BIBLIOGRAPHY

Bob Woodward and Scott Armstrong, *The Brethren* (1979); Richard Kluger, *Simple Justice* (1976).

JOYCE WALKER–JONES

WASHINGTON, BOOKER TALIAFERRO. (5 April 1856, Hale's Ford, Vir-ginia–14 November 1915, Tuskegee, Alabama). Booker T. Washington was the founder and president of Tuskegee Institute (now Tuskegee University*), which he led for thirty-four years. Washington was the leading spokesman for African-American education during the period 1895-1915. He was an advisor to three U.S. presidents and served on the boards of two distinguished black institutions of higher education and several civic organizations. Thousands of high schools across the nation are named in his memory, as are many institutions in Africa.

Washington was born into slavery on a small plantation in rural Franklin County, Virginia. His mother's name was Jane; his father was unknown to him and was reputed to be a white man. Booker had an older brother, John, and a younger sister, Amanda. Booker lived in slavery for nine years, until the family moved to Malden, West Virginia, in 1865. His elementary education in Malden was periodic and on a low level; however, in 1872 he was admitted to Hampton Normal and Industrial Institute (now Hampton University)* on probation. Washington developed a close and personal relationship with the principal and founder of Hampton, General Samuel C. Armstrong.* Washington earned his undergraduate degree from Hampton in 1875. After graduation he returned to Malden in 1878 to accept a teaching position that lasted three years. Washington left Malden to enroll in a school for African-American Baptist preachers, Wayland Seminary in Washington, D.C. After eight months, he returned to Hampton to teach in July 1879. His duties involved supervising the Indian dormitory and setting up Hampton's first night school at a salary of twenty-five dollars per month.

In 1880, General Armstrong received a request from Macon County, Alabama, to send a white man to Tuskegee to set up a normal school for African-American residents. Lewis Adams, a black tinsmith, and George Campbell, a white businessman, had secured a state charter and two-thousand dollars per year to establish the Normal School for Colored Teachers in Tuskegee. Armstrong responded with a strong recommendation for his best teacher and former student, Booker T. Washington. When Washington arrived in Tuskegee in June 1881, there were no plans, buildings, or materials awaiting his inspection. He was met by Lewis Adams, who would become his first friend and advisor. Through Adams, cooperation was secured for the use of a dilapidated building next to the local African Methodist Episcopal church. The Normal School for Colored Teachers was officially opened on 4 July 1881, with thirty students. During the first month, Washington contracted to purchase an abandoned plantation of one hundred acres for five hundred dollars.

Washington's most outstanding achievements can be summarized under three major categories. First is his influence on the philosophy and practice of education for African-Americans, achieved largely through public-speaking tours across the country and the broad distribution of his written works. Second are the organizational efforts of groups and campaigns that Washington promoted at the regional and national levels including key assistance provided to other black institutions. Third is the capacity-building and expansion of Tuskegee from a basic-literacy and family-living focus (normal) to a certificated skills-training emphasis (industrial).

Washington's public-speaking career was launched in 1884 by his address to the National Education Association in Madison, Wisconsin. In 1885, he began publishing the *Southern Letter* as a monthly organ to enlist support from a targeted audience. Washington was a prolific writer. He wrote editorials and articles for major newspapers. He published fourteen major books. His most popular book, *Up from Slavery* (1901), was translated into five languages and became an international classic. The best-known and most controversial of his early speeches was the 1895 Atlanta Exposition Address.* Designed to improve race relations, the speech was applauded by southern whites, northern white philanthropists, and black supporters. However, a small group of African-American intellectuals were extremely critical of his speech for what they claimed to be its "accommodating" tendencies and the implication that blacks were willing to accept second-class citizenship. Despite these criticisms, Washington continued to receive widespread support for his educational ideas and deeds from a growing African-American middle class and a large constituency of southern and northern whites.

Washington's impressive organizational efforts, outside of developing the Tuskegee school, include setting up the National Negro Business League in 1900 in Boston. He was elected president of that organization and held the position for life. In 1904 Washington started the Rural School Improvement Program with initial financial assistance from the Jeanes Fund* and later the Rosenwald Fund.* In 1910, he began a series of rural improvement speaking tours throughout the South to encourage self-help approaches to farming and family living. A common theme in these speeches was an emphasis on land ownership.

Washington was unselfish in his assistance in helping other black colleges. Notably, his service as a advisor and trustee to Fisk University* (1909–15) and Howard University* (1907–15) had an impact on their development. In 1915, he helped to restore Howard's annual federal appropriation after a southern congressman deleted it from the appropriations bill. He also served on the board of the National Urban League* (1910–1915).

Some of the most important programs started at Tuskegee during the years of expansion under Washington's leadership include the Bible Training School (1881) and the Night School (1883). A farmer's conference was organized in 1890. Tuskegee's hospital and nurse training school were established in 1892, with the latter being the first to be started in the state, white or black. An Agricultural Experiment Station was established at Tuskegee in 1896. A group of graduates and teachers were sent to Africa to introduce cotton cultivation in 1900. The year 1906 witnessed the expansion of extension services with the initiation of the Jesup Agricultural Wagon (a movable school) and the inauguration of the Farmer's Demonstration Project (1907). The Baldwin Farms Project, designed to sell forty-acre plots to Tuskegee graduates for a farming network, was established in 1914. Negro Health Week was kicked off at Tuskegee in 1915, the year of Washington's death, reportedly from hardening of the arteries, high blood pressure, and kidney disease. At the time of it's founder's passing Tuskegee Institute had an endowment of two million dollars, 3,000 acres of land, 1,537 regular students and 197 faculty members, and offered 38 different trades and an annual budget of three hundred thousand dollars.

Washington received two honorary degrees: an M.A. from Harvard University, 1896; and a Ph.D. from Dartmouth College, 1901. He married three women: Fannie N. Smith (1882), Olivia A. Davidson (1886), and Margaret J. Murray (1892). Three children were born, one daughter with Fannie (Portia, 1883) and two sons with Olivia (Booker Jr., 1887, and Ernest, 1889). Washington was buried in the Tuskegee Institute Cemetery.

SELECTED BIBLIOGRAPHY

Virginia L. Denton, *Booker T. Washington and the Adult Education Movement* (1993); Shirley Graham, *Booker T. Washington, Educator of Hand, Head and Heart* (1955); Louis R. Harlan, *Booker T. Washington: The Making of a Black Leader, 1856–1901* (1972); Louis R. Harlan, *Booker T. Washington: The Wizard of Tuskegee* (1983); Tuskegee Archives, the Booker T. Washington Collection.

EDWIN HAMILTON

WASHINGTON, MARGARET MURRAY. (1861 or 1865, Macon, Georgia). Margaret James Murray was born in Macon, Georgia. Her mother was a washerwoman, and her father an Irish immigrant who died when Margaret was a child. She graduated from Fisk University's preparatory and college courses after eleven years of part-time study and work. In 1889 she accepted a teaching position at Tuskegee Normal and Industrial Institute.* The following year she became "lady principal" at Tuskegee. In 1891 she married Tuskegee's principal Booker T. Washington,* who, widowed from his second wife in 1887, had three small children.

Margaret Murray Washington continued to teach after her marriage and also took on other responsibilities, both on and off campus. She was largely responsible for Dorothy Hall, an industrial department for women at Tuskegee. In 1895 she organized the Tuskegee Woman's Club, which held weekly mothers' meetings, providing child care and offering classes and lectures to adult women. The club took special interest in the poor workers on a nearby plantation. The club opened a school for the children, ran boys' and girls' clubs, and began a newspaper-reading club for men.

Tuskegee held an annual African-American conference, which excluded women. In 1910, Mrs. Washington and other women met separately to design a Town Night School to reach adults unable to attend Tuskegee. The school taught reading, cooking, sewing, carpentry, bricklaying, and other skills. For two years, Tuskegee embraced the effort as an extension program, but when the institution stopped supporting the Night School, the Tuskegee Women's Club took it over, offering as many as 103 night classes.

Mrs. Washington was present at one of the first national efforts to unite African-American women's club in 1895, when a group of one hundred women created the National Federation of Afro-American Women. Mrs. Washington was elected president of the federation, which united thirty-six clubs in twelve states. A similar effort resulted in the concurrent formation of the National League of Colored Women. The following year, 1896, the Federation and the

League joined to become the National Association of Colored Women (NACW), electing Mary Church Terrell* as its first president. Mrs. Washington was president of NACW from 1912 to 1916 and also served for many years as editor of NACW's newsletter, *National Notes.*

In the 1920s, Margaret Washington was involved in the Council for Interracial Cooperation (CIC), a foundation-funded effort to unite African-Americans and whites. At a meeting held in Memphis in 1920 to discuss the formation of a women's division of the CIC, she was one of three African-American club-women invited to speak. Her remarks included a reference to African-American women's indebtedness to white Southern women. However, her comments were refuted by another African-American woman, Charlotte Hawkins Brown,* who said that Mrs. Washington represented "the most conservative type of Negro woman." Later in the conference, Washington again adopted a conciliatory stance. Prior to the meeting, Lugenia Burns Hope and other African-American clubwomen wrote a position paper stating their agenda for the CIC women's group. A white woman edited this position paper before reading it to the assembly, without consulting the African-American women. The edited version was considerably watered down. It took out the reference to voting rights, eliminated a statement that black women should have all the rights and privileges of white women, and added an ambiguous section on lynching. Some African-American women at the meeting, including Hope, were angry and refused to accept the edited version. Mrs. Washington, however, called for cooperation. In the end, nothing from the conference was printed.

In the 1920s, Margaret Washington was instrumental in the creation of the International Council of Women of the Darker Races. This group, recognizing the importance of education, aimed to disseminate knowledge of the history and achievements of peoples of color around the world. It worked on curriculum integration by organizing teachers, recommending reading lists, and lobbying school boards.

SELECTED BIBLIOGRAPHY

Hallie Q. Brown, *Homespun Heroines and Other Women of Distinction* (1926, 1988); Paula Giddings, *When and Where I Enter* (1984); Eleanor Hinton Hoytt, "International Council of Women of the Darker Races," in D. C. Hine, E. B. Brown, and R. Terborg-Penn, eds., *Black Women in America* (1993); Kathleen Thompson, "Margaret Murray Washington," in D. C. Hine, E. B. Brown, and R. Terborg-Penn, eds., *Black Women in America* (1993).

MARGARET A. NASH

WATSON, BERNARD CHARLES (4 March 1928, Gary, Indiana). An educator, foundation executive, and civic leader, Bernard Watson received his undergraduate degree from Indiana University, an M.Ed. from the University of Illinois, and a Ph.D. from the University of Chicago. He also studied at the Advanced Administrative Institute of Harvard University. Watson served as president and chief executive officer of the William Penn Foundation for twelve years prior to his retirement in December 1993. Under his leadership, the foundation's assets increased in value from $133 million to $587 million, and its annual grantmaking budget from $9 million to $35.7 million. A significant proportion of these grant funds was awarded for programs to improve educational opportunities for African-American youth. Among the recipients were the School District of Philadelphia, many colleges and universities (including several historically black institutions), and other organizations such as PRIME (Philadelphia Regional Introduction for Minorities to Engineering). Some of the programs funded included summer enrichment programs on college campuses, designed to interest eighth, ninth, and tenth graders in mathematics and science, as well as retention programs for minority students majoring in math, science, and engineering. Several of these grants also addressed one of Watson's chief concerns: the disproportionately low number of African-Americans holding Ph.D.s and teaching at the college level. Upon retirement, Watson became chairman of the board of the Healthcare Management Alternatives (HMA) Foundation. He was also appointed the Presidential Scholar of Temple University and is currently at work on a number of projects relating to issues of public policy, particularly those affecting minorities and the poor.

Prior to his work in philanthropy, Watson had a distinguished career as an educator. He served as a teacher and administrator in the public schools of Gary, Indiana, and later became the deputy superintendent of schools in Philadelphia, the nation's fourth largest city. He then moved to Temple University, also in Philadelphia, where he was the organizing chairman and professor of a new department of urban education in the Graduate School of Education. From 1976 to 1982, he was Academic Vice President of the University. In 1967, Watson was appointed by President Lyndon Johnson to the National Council on Education Professions Development, and in 1980, President Jimmy Carter appointed him to the National Council on Educational Research. He currently serves on a third presidential commission, the National Advisory Council for Historically Black Colleges and Universities, having been appointed by President Bill Clinton in 1984. Watson has served on numerous boards and commissions, both local and national, many of them concerned with improving educational opportunity. For many years he has been the senior vice chairman of the board of the National Urban League,* and he was a member of the William T. Grant Foundation Commission on Work, Family, and Citizenship, which studied and made recommendations on the problems of non–college-bound youth.

Watson is married to the former Lois Lathan, also an educator, and is the father of two children, Barbra and Bernard, Jr.

DOROTHY I. BLANCHARD AND FASAHA M. TRAYLOR

WATSON, JOHN BROWN (ca. 1872, Smith County, Texas–6 December 1942, Pine Bluff, Arkansas). Educator, YMCA worker, insurance executive, bank receiver, and college president, Watson, after profiting from the meager educational advantages offered near the farm where he was brought up, studied at Bishop College in Marshall, Texas. He became a teacher in his native county in 1898. After studying at Colgate from 1900 to 1901, he entered Brown University, where he graduated in 1904. For five years thereafter he taught at Morehouse College* in Atlanta, Georgia. While at Morehouse, Watson taught three people who later became distinguished college presidents, including Mordecai W. Johnson,* who served for many years as president of Howard University* in Washington, D.C.

Watson left the classroom in 1909 and for the next eight years served as a YMCA worker. Finding that this work did not offer a great future, he entered the insurance business in Atlanta, Georgia, in 1921, working as the receiver of the Atlanta State Savings Bank until 1923. At the conclusion of this service, he returned to education as president of Leland College, Baker, Louisiana, where he functioned so successfully that in 1928 he was called on to head the state-funded Arkansas Agricultural, Mechanical, and Normal College for Negroes at Pine Bluff (now the University of Arkansas at Pine Bluff*).

At the time of his appointment to the AM&N presidency, the college was run down; indeed, it had never been adequately equipped. Watson spent the remainder of his life in the development of the college's educational facilities. When he arrived, he found a student body of only thirty-six students and a handful of teachers; but during the fourteen years that he labored at the post, he built a new physical plant of several modern brick buildings and teacher cottages. He also increased the enrollment to approximately seven hundred students, served by some forty full-time faculty, representing the best staff available from the nation's historically black colleges. During his tenure at AM&N, Watson was instrumental in bringing a new sense of respectability to the campus. Prior to his coming, many citizens chose to send their children out of state or to other in-state colleges rather than enroll them at AM&N. Within the first years of his tenure, Watson succeeded in reinstating the school's four-year bachelor's program, moving the college to its present location, and reorganizing the faculty in standard academic departments and divisions. Through his exceptional work, Watson established his reputation as a strong leader, a strict disciplinarian, and a man of strong educational convictions.

SELECTED BIBLIOGRAPHY

Gordon D. Morgan, *Lawrence A. Davis: Arkansas Educator* (1985); J. W. Leslie, *Pine Bluff Commercial Newspaper* (9 and 16 July 1972); Frederick Chambers, *Historical Study of Arkansas Agricultural Mechanical and Normal College, 1873–1943*, Ph.D. diss., Ball State University (1970); Martin E. Mantell, *Lay Well the Foundation: A Short History of UAPB* (1977); Marion Etoile Watson, The Watson Century Collection, Brown University, Providence, Rhode Island.

                                                                          HENRY W. PENNYMON, SR.

WEST VIRGINIA STATE COLLEGE. West Virginia State College (WVSC) in Institute, West Virginia, is located in the state's center of government, industry, business, and population. It serves the greatest number of students in the

Kanawha Valley and is a resource center for this metropolitan area. The college provides a broad spectrum of undergraduate degree programs for a diverse population of residential and commuting students. Especially noteworthy is the comprehensive schedule of classes offered to an exceptionally large population of evening students. It responds to additional educational and career needs with nontraditional courses and programs and cooperative education internships. Founded in 1891, the college attained national prominence as an institution of higher education for African-Americans, and it continues to serve as a center of black culture.

Voluntary integration in 1954 created a distinctive living laboratory of human relations at WVSC and attracted a racially and culturally diverse student body, faculty, and staff. The college cherishes its reputation for safeguarding academic freedom, for being innovative in its scholarship programs, and for removing barriers to education and leadership for women, minorities, and the handicapped. A distinguished accreditation record testifies to its concern for quality in its academic and cocurricular programs. With its general education core, WVSC seeks to develop among its students a high level of competence in English and mathematics, an increased appreciation of the liberal arts, and an expanded awareness of a respect for the contributions of women and minorities to our society. The college's curriculum also places emphasis on contemporary technology and its roots in modern science.

SELECTED BIBLIOGRAPHY

National Association for Equal Opportunity in Higher Education, *Profiles of the Nation's Historically and Predominantly Black Colleges and Universities* (1993).

SAMUEL L. MYERS

WHARTON, CLIFTON R., JR. (13 September 1926, Boston, Massachusetts). The son of a college Latin and French professor and a forty-year veteran of the U.S. Foreign Service, Clifton R. Wharton, Jr., attended the Boston Latin School, graduating in 1943, and from there went to Harvard University, where he earned a B.A. in history, graduating cum laude in 1947. After earning his M.A. in International Affairs from the Johns Hopkins University in 1948, he obtained a position at the American International Association for Economic and Social Development. He worked there until 1953, when he left to enroll in a doctoral program in economics at the University of Chicago, where he earned another M.A. and the Ph.D. in 1956 and 1958, respectively.

In 1957, Wharton joined the Agricultural Development Council, working with its agricultural economics efforts in Malaysia, Vietnam, Thailand, Laos, and Cambodia. He was appointed director of the council's American Universities Research Programs in 1964, acting director of the council in 1966, and vice president in 1967. After leaving the council, Wharton served as a trustee of the Rockefeller Foundation from 1970 to 1987. He was chairman of the foundation's board from 1982 to 1987.

Wharton began his career in higher education as visiting professor at the University of Malaysia and later at Stanford University. In 1970, he was named the president of Michigan State University (MSU) in East Lansing, thereby becoming the first African-American to head a predominantly white university in the United States. After eight years at MSU, Wharton assumed the chancellorship of the State University of New York (SUNY) system, with its sixty-four campuses, nearly four hundred thousand students, and annual budget of over $2.5 billion. In this position, he focused on decreasing SUNY's bureaucratic structure and strengthening the caliber of its graduate programs. He held the SUNY chancellorship from 1978 until 1987, when he accepted the position of chairman and chief executive officer of Teachers Insurance and Annuity Association–College Retirement Equities Fund (TIAA–CREF) and became the first African-American to head a Fortune 100 company.

Founded in 1918 by industrial magnate Andrew Carnegie, TIAA–CREF is a nonprofit, private pension fund providing retirement, life insurance, and disability plans for college and private school educators. During his six-year tenure as CEO, Wharton reorganized the fund's corporate structure and spearheaded programs aimed at increasing responsiveness and offering more flexible financial options to customers. The company's assets doubled during his period of leadership. Wharton stepped down as head of TIAA–CREF in 1993, leaving an annual salary of approximately $1 million, to accept the nomination by President Bill Clinton to be U.S. Deputy Secretary of State.

Although Wharton's appointment was enthusiastically endorsed in many circles, it was vilified by others, who claimed he was "an underqualified diversity hire." Attacks on his qualifications disregarded his three decades of experience in international affairs in Latin America and Southeast Asia with the United Nations, National Academy of Science, and State Department, with appointments under four previous presidents. Others, noting Wharton's academic background, claimed that he would be a figurehead with little responsibility. Amid mounting controversy, Wharton served ten months at the State Department, where his duties encompassed foreign aid and departmental management. He steered the review, realignment, and refocusing of the Agency for International Development, chairing the task force that sought to reevaluate the role of U.S. foreign assistance in the post–Cold War era. He emphasized the elimination of hunger, poverty, and illness; enhancement of educational opportunities; and expansion of the economic position of women in countries receiving both rapid-response and long-term assistance. The combination of partisan attacks on his competency, journalistic reports of administrative displeasure, a rumored personality conflict with Secretary of State Warren Christopher, and nonsupport from the White House led Wharton to tender his resignation in November 1993.

Wharton is author, coauthor, or editor of over fifty articles in professional journals, as well as four books on topics ranging from education to agricultural economics. He has served on the boards of directors of several major corporations and organizations including Time, Inc., the Corporation for Public Broadcasting, the Federal Reserve Bank of New York, the Ford Motor Company, and the New York Stock Exchange and is an active member of the National Urban League, the National Association for the Advancement of Colored People,* and his local country club.

Wharton is married to the former Delores Duncan of New York City and Danbury, Connecticut. She is the founder, chair, and CEO of the Fund for Corporate Initiatives, Inc., a nonprofit organization dedicated to advancing the role of women and minorities in corporate America, and serves as a trustee or board member of the Massachusetts Institute of Technology, the Fashion Institute of Technology, the Kellogg Company, and Gannett Co., Inc. The couple have two sons, Clifton III and Bruce.

SELECTED BIBLIOGRAPHY

Caroline V. Clarke, "What's Next for Wharton?" *Black Enterprise* 24, no. 11 (June 1994): 30; B. Denise Hawkins, "Clifton Wharton, Jr., Takes His Education, Business, and Economics Background to World Arena," *Black Issues in Higher Education* 9, no. 23 (14 January 1993): 6; Teachers Insurance Annuity Association–College Retirement Equities Fund Press Package (January 1994); "The $70 Billion Man: Clifton Wharton Used a Velvet Touch to Transform TIAA–CREF into a Dynamic Financial Powerhouse," *Black Enterprise* 19, no. 11 (1 June 1989): 100.

NATAKI H. GOODALL

WHITE FLIGHT. This term describes the voluntary withdrawal of white people, particularly those who are middle class, from housing, schools, and school districts that are desegregating. The result is that racially segregated schools become desegregated for a brief period, then resegregated because of the departure of white pupils. White parents who flee from desegregated schools say they do so because they fear that the quality of education offered their children will decline; their children may experience physical violence or emotional problems; their children's values and those of other races are too dissimilar related to academic achievement, and/or social/sexual behavior and their children will suffer as a result. These parents may also fear that their property values will decline in desegregating areas. White flight occurs most frequently in districts with an African-American enrollment of more than one third and when busing plans call for white students to attend formerly black schools.

School-district officials planning for student reassignment and bus transportation take into account the possibility that whites will withdraw their children and therefore make desegregation impossible. However, some officials have used this possibility as an excuse to avoid careful, realistic policies for school desegregation, thereby forcing the courts to make judgments about school district planning. The result has been the institution of court-ordered desegregation plans in such cities as Boston, Denver, Memphis, Dallas, Houston, and San Francisco; in general, court-ordered desegregation plans have been controversial. Parents are still free to move as they see fit; the result is a growing number of one-race schools or schools populated primarily by students of color irrespective of race or ethnicity.

Large urban schools and school districts increasingly are populated by students of color, and by the children of the working class or the poor. Increasing numbers of the African-American middle class have moved to the suburbs since the passage of the Fair Housing Act of 1968*; their children therefore attend suburban schools. Others of this group who remain in cities have chosen to educate their children in parochial or private schools, not the public schools, because of fear of crime, other maladaptive behaviors, or drugs.

Voluntary school desegregation plans, including magnet schools and freedom-of-choice options, sometimes bring white and African-American middle-class students back into urban public schools.

SELECTED BIBLIOGRAPHY

Christine H. Rossell and Willis D. Hawley, "Understanding White Flight and Doing Something about It," in Willis D. Hawley, ed., *Effective School Desegregation: Equity, Quality, and Feasibility* (1981); Daniel U. Levine and Robert J. Havighurst, *Society and Education*, 7th ed. (1989).

FAUSTINE C. JONES–WILSON

WILBERFORCE UNIVERSITY. Founded in 1856, Wilberforce University is the oldest private African-American liberal arts college in the nation. It was named in honor of the great eighteenth century abolitionist, William Wilberforce. WU is affiliated with the African Methodist Episcopal (AME) Church and was early guided by its leaders, including A.M.E Bishop Daniel A. Payne,* its founder and second president. Located in southwest Ohio, WU provides academic excellence for people of all religious faiths, creeds, and colors, especially African-American men and women. Its mission is to develop the total person while preparing him or her for today's complex job market and society at large through a liberal arts education and a cooperative education program. WU is one of three higher education institutions in the nation to have a comprehensive cooperative education program for all students.

In 1988, WU initiated a program that sends WU students to an Israeli kibbutz for the summer. On the kibbutz, students work in a self-contained community in factories that produce and repair water meters. The program now encompasses several other projects: WU students studying at Hebrew University in Jerusalem and WU students teaching Israeli youth English. Because of its success, plans are being made to invite students from other historically black institutions to participate in the innovative program.

SELECTED BIBLIOGRAPHY

National Association for Equal Opportunity in Higher Education, *Profiles of the Nation's Historically and Predominantly Black Colleges and Universities* (1993).

SAMUEL L. MYERS

WILLIAMS, LORRAINE ANDERSON (6 August 1923, Washington, D.C.). History professor, social science program chairman, editor, department chairman, university vice president, and civic leader Lorraine Williams received her

B.A. (1944) and M.A. (1945) from Howard University.* In 1955, she was awarded the Ph.D. from American University. Her area of specialization is the intellectual history of the Civil War and Reconstruction eras.

Williams joined the faculty at Howard University in 1946 as an instructor in the Social Science Program of the College of Liberal Arts, teaching intellectually gifted students. In 1962, she chaired the program, a post she held until 1969. Appointed chairman of the Department of History at Howard University in March 1970, Williams embarked upon a program of unprecedented expansion of the department. New courses were added, research flourished, and a greatly increased number of both graduates and undergraduates completed the program in history.

Williams was awarded funds from the Howard University-sponsored Research Program in 1970 to create new and revised courses, including urban history, African history, and comparative history. In August of that year, the Graduate School of Arts and Sciences awarded her a grant to undertake curriculum research in Africa. As a result, she traveled to Senegal, Ghana, Nigeria, and Kenya. From this experience, Williams strengthened the curriculum in African history at Howard and laid the foundation for future cooperation between Howard and African universities.

Williams was appointed vice president for academic affairs at Howard University on 1 October 1974. In this capacity she was responsible for undergraduate, graduate, and graduate professional programs as well as the research institutes, the Howard University Press,* and the academic support services. In 1974 she spearheaded the establishment of a major research institute, the Institute for the Study of Educational Policy. In 1976, under her leadership, Howard's Graduate School of Arts and Sciences was inaugurated as an autonomous unit with its own faculty and budget; and in 1978 the University Library System acquired its one millionth volume. In May 1983 after nearly forty years of service, Williams retired from Howard University.

Williams is a member of the board of directors of the American Council on Human Rights, the NAACP,* the American Association of University Women, the National Urban League,* and the National Council of Negro Women, where she as served as national historian (1959–60) and national vice president (1961–62). She served two terms as national president of the Sigma Gamma Rho Sorority (1959–62; 1967–71), and led that organization to greater involvement in community training programs, support of education, and civil rights. In 1978, President Jimmy Carter appointed her a member of the U.S. Circuit Judge nominating panel for the District of Columbia.

Williams is the author of numerous scholarly works. She has been published in the *Journal of Social Science Teachers*, the *Journal of Negro History*, and the *Journal of Negro Education*.* In 1966, she coauthored *A Teaching Aid for College Courses in Social Sciences*, published by the New York Times Company. From 1967 to 1969, she served on the Board of Educational Advisors to

The *New York Times* and from 1974 to 1976 she served as editor of the *Journal of Negro History*.
SELECTED BIBLIOGRAPHY
Lorraine Anderson Williams, *Howard University: The Academic Affairs Division Annual Report to the President of Howard University* (1980); Michael R. Winston, *Howard University: The Department of History, 1913–1973* (1973).

OLIVE A. TAYLOR

WILLIAMS, LUCELIA ELECTA (29 February 1824, Deerfield, Massachusetts–22 December 1895, Deerfield). Educator, administrator, and school founder, Lucelia E. Williams was the daughter of a farmer. No record survives of her education. She was a common-school teacher in Massachusetts, but does not appear to have attended a normal school, a not-unusual circumstance in that era. In 1864, at forty years of age, Williams joined a remarkable group of northerners, African-American and white, who journeyed into the South, in the midst of war, to open schools and teach the freed slaves. She taught in Beaufort, South Carolina, in that year. She went on to teach in Richmond and Petersburg, Virginia, and in Washington, D.C.; in 1867, she was assigned by the American Missionary Association* (AMA) to Hampton, Virginia. Her sister, Philomela A. Williams, joined her in Hampton.

The Williams sisters were initially teaching in one of the elementary-level schools in Hampton; but before the year's end Samuel Chapman Armstrong,* later to gain fame through his notions of industrial education developed at Hampton Normal and Agricultural Institute (now University),* had tapped Lucelia Williams to organize the normal school in his proposed institute. She took hold of the effort with energy, soliciting books for a library, developing a curriculum, ordering furniture for the school and arranging for its delivery, and looking after other details in Armstrong's frequent absences. She opened the normal school in April 1868, with twenty-three students; a year later her department of the institute had grown to sixty-four.

Williams appears to have fallen out with Armstrong over questions of the proper education for African-Americans because she advocated a rigorous academic education, a position at odds with Armstrong's vision of an education appropriate for people of color. Lucelia and Philomela taught Latin and algebra to one student in their spare time, leading Armstrong to threaten his expulsion and apparently prompting the ouster of the sisters.

Despite Williams' prominent role in the founding of Hampton Institute, its official histories make no mention of her. However, on the strength of her work at Hampton, in the autumn of 1869 the AMA assigned Williams to Jacksonville, Florida, to organize and open a teacher-training school for the freedmen, to be named after Lincoln's secretary of war, Edwin M. Stanton. She was the first woman the AMA entrusted with such a task. Opened in November, Stanton Normal School soon had seven teachers and three hundred students, the first secondary school for African-American students in Florida. Williams served as principal of Stanton Normal School for seven years before retiring to Massachusetts with her sister. Stanton Normal School went on to distinguish itself in the education of Florida's African-Americans. James Weldon Johnson served as principal of the school in later years, after having received his own education there.

Williams died of natural causes and is interred at South Deerfield, Massachusetts.

SELECTED BIBLIOGRAPHY

Ronald E. Butchart, "Williams, Lucelia E.," in John A. Garrity, ed., *American National Biography* (1994); Ronald E. Butchart, "Recruits to the 'Army of Civilization': Gender, Race, Class, and the Freedmen's Teachers, 1862–1875," *Journal of Education* 172, no. 3 (1990): 76–87.

RONALD E. BUTCHART

WILSON, REGINALD (27 February 1927, Detroit, Michigan). A nationally renowned scholar and leader on race and equity issues in higher education, Wilson received his Ph.D. in educational psychology (1971), his M.A. in clinical psychology (1958), and his B.S. in special education (1950), all from Wayne State University. He was honored as a Distinguished Alumnus of Wayne State University in 1980 and is a recipient of the Anthony Wayne Award and the Distinguished Service Medal of the City of Detroit.

Wilson is the founding director of the Office of Minority Concerns (OMC) at the American Council on Education (ACE). He was named Senior Scholar of the ACE in October 1988, after serving as the director of the OMC for seven years. As Senior Scholar, he provides training and guidance to the faculty, staff, administration, and governing boards of hundreds of college and universities in an attempt to expand educational and employment opportunities for people of color. He has also served as a policy analyst and strategist to state higher education commissions, to the U.S. Department of Education, and to the Congress, working on such issues as desegregation, student financial aid, and minority scholarships.

Prior to coming to ACE Wilson was the president of Wayne County Community College in Detroit. Other higher education career positions include director of the Center for Black Studies, University of Detroit; associate dean of testing, Oakland Community College; director of research, test development and evaluation, and associate professor of psychology, Oakland Community College; and associate director of Upward Bound,* Oakland University. Prior to his entry into higher education, Dr. Wilson was the chief psychologist of the Special Education–Vocational Rehabilitation Project and psychologist for the Detroit Public Schools. He is licensed as a psychologist in Michigan and Washington, D.C., and has done volunteer work with homeless shelters in the District of Columbia.

Dr. Wilson is the author of *Civil Liberties in the United States* (1988) and coauthor (with Jonas Chenault and Charles A. Green) of *Human Behavior in* *the Urban Community* (1967). He has also contributed articles to such scholarly publications as the *Journal of Negro Education*,* the *Journal of Black Studies*, and the *Harvard Education Review*.

DEBORAH J. CARTER

WINSTON, MICHAEL RUSSELL (26 May 1941, New York, New York). An historian, educator, university administrator, and foundation director, Michael Winston was educated at Howard University* (B.A. magna cum laude, 1962) and the University of California, Berkeley (M.A., 1964, and Ph.D., 1974), where he was a Woodrow Wilson Fellow and a John Hay Whitney Fellow. In the summer of 1962, he studied English history at the University of Edinburgh, Scotland, as a Moten Fellow.

Winston's major academic interests have been modern European history, the comparative analysis of modernizing elites in nonwestern societies, race and culture contacts since the eighteenth century, and the history of higher education in the United States. His academic appointments and activities have included instructor, the Department of History, Howard University (1964–66 and 1970–71); research assistant, the Centennial History of Howard University project (1965); teaching assistant, the Department of History, the University of California, Berkeley (1966–68); and assistant dean and lecturer in history (1968–69), assistant professor of history (1971–73), director of research, Department of History (1972–73), and associate professor of history, College of Liberal Arts, Howard University (1974–90). He has also served as executive assistant and associate director at the Institute for Services to Education (1965–66).

From 1973 to 1983 Winston directed Howard's newly reorganized Moorland–Spingarn Research Center,* where his vision had a profound impact upon its growth and development as the largest repository of research collections documenting the history and culture of people of African descent in the Americas, Africa, and Europe. Appointed a fellow of the Woodrow Wilson International Center for Scholars in 1979, he undertook research on the history of African-American colleges and universities in the United States. In 1983 Winston was appointed vice president for academic affairs at Howard University and served until 1990. He is currently president of the Alfred Harcourt Foundation.

Winston has been a consultant to many research organizations, foundations, universities and government agencies, including the American Academy of Arts and Sciences, the Joint Center for Political Studies, the Ford Foundation, the National Science Foundation, the National Institute of Education, the Smithsonian Institution, Xavier University,* Yale University, the British Universities Summer School Program, the National Endowment for the Humanities, the NAACP Legal Defense Fund, Inc., The Library of Congress, and the Council on Foreign Relations. He has been a member of the board of directors of Harcourt Brace Jovanovich, Inc., the world's largest publisher of scientific, medical, and educational books and scholarly journals. From 1980 to 1984 he served on the Council of the Program on American Society and Politics of the Woodrow Wilson International Center for Scholars.

Winston's writings include *The Negro in the United States*, vol. 2 (with Rayford W. Logan, 1970); *The Howard University Department of History, 1913–1973* (1973); *The Dictionary of American Negro Biography* (coedited with Rayford W. Logan, 1983); and *Historical Judgments Reconsidered* (coedited with Genna Rae McNeil, 1988).

SELECTED BIBLIOGRAPHY

Michael R. Winston Papers, Moorland–Spingarn Research Center, Howard University; *Who's Who Among Black Americans* (various editions).

THOMAS C. BATTLE

WOMEN'S STUDIES, AFRICAN-AMERICAN. African-American women have engaged in self-conscious explorations of their social, cultural, and historical situation since at least the nineteenth century. In poetry, fiction, essays, speeches, and political discourse and less formally in spoken word and song, African American women have described and analyzed the meanings of being simultaneously black and female in the United States.

Not until the early 1970s, however, did African-American women writers, scholars, and activists begin to define black women's studies as a specific and complex field of intellectual inquiry. Toni Cade Bambara's anthology, *The Black Woman*, published in 1970, was the first contemporary collection to bring together writing that directly addressed the experience of being both black and female and the impact of racism and sexism upon the lives of black women. In the early 1970s young African-American women scholars, inspired by the struggles for black and women's liberation and by the newly emerging field of women's studies, began to research, teach, and write about black women. During this period the lives of African-American women were generally overlooked in the contexts of African-American studies* and women's studies, and there was a huge amount of new and exciting research to be undertaken.

Literary works by African-American women writers were a rich source of already existing primary material, and much of the earliest research in African-American women's studies focused upon literature. In 1972 and 1973, writers Alice Walker and Barbara Smith taught courses on black women writers at Boston area colleges. In 1972, the *College Language Association Journal* published Ora Williams's "A Bibliography of Works Written by American Black Women," and it was published the following year in book form. In 1975 Mary Helen Washington published *Black-Eyed Susans: Classic Stories by and about Black Women*, the first collection of short fiction by black women.

Soon black women in other disciplines, most notably history, began to research and publish work about African-American women. Sharon Harley, Darlene Clark Hine, Eleanor Smith, and Rosalyn Terborg Penn were among the first to write about black women's history and were also organizers of the Association of Black Women Historians, founded in 1979. As the 1970s proceeded, the numbers of college courses, research papers at scholarly conferences, and publications on African-American women continued to increase.

In 1982, Gloria T. Hull, Patricia Bell Scott, and Barbara Smith published the collection *All the Women Are White, All the Blacks Are Men, But Some of Us Are Brave: Black Women's Studies*. It was the first work to name African-American women's studies as a specific academic pursuit; and its essays, bibliographies, and course syllabuses served as a catalyst for what became in the 1980s a recognized field. The virtual renaissance of African-American women's literature that also occurred in the 1980s helped to increase popular consciousness of black women's history, culture, and issues in nonacademic settings. This burgeoning of writing and work in other artistic genres and the growth of an explicitly black feminist movement were significant components in providing a context in which African-American women's studies could grow. Black lesbian feminists were often at the forefront of articulating political issues that affected all black women and in initiating groundbreaking work in the field of African-American women's studies.

The growth of African-American women's studies also saw the rise of various controversies about its priorities and practice. There were varying points of view about the role of feminism in African-American women's studies. Some black women who were committed to teaching and writing about black women were not comfortable with the term feminist and adopted the term *womanist* or Africana women's studies. Other practitioners strongly identified as African-American feminists and saw feminism as an important stance from which to carry out their work. Questions were raised about who could work most effectively in this area; and, although most African-American women did not want to restrict participation by white women and black men, there were still tensions about African-American women's studies being appropriated by outsiders whose commitment was to career advancement as much as to the subject matter itself. Homophobia and heterosexism sometimes caused divisions, despite black lesbians' significant contributions to the field. Black men in male-dominated African-American studies departments sometimes blocked black women's efforts to introduce subject matter about African-American women. White women in women's studies were often both racist and elitist and completely excluded the experiences of women of color and working-class white women.

Although these and other questions about the direction of African-American women's studies continue to be raised, it has become an exceedingly vibrant and significant field. In the 1980s, major academic and community conferences on African-American women began to be held all over the country. In 1981, Kitchen Table: Women of Color Press, the only U.S. publisher for women of color, was founded by Audre Lorde and Barbara Smith and published major anthologies that are widely used in college courses, including those focusing on African-American women. *SAGE: A Scholarly Journal on Black Women* was founded in 1984 by Beverly Guy–Sheftall and Patricia Bell–Scott and is based at Spelman College.* It continues to be the only publication of its kind devoted exclusively to the experience of black women.

Although there are currently no African-American women's studies departments and programs, the field has flourished in its nearly two decades of existence. African-American women scholars have forged links with scholars of African origin who are also researching and writing about black women in the African diaspora. The institutionalization of multiculturalism and of greater diversity in university curricula (and the debates that have accompanied these changes) are in part the result of the successful establishment of African-American women's studies and other courses about heretofore marginalized groups. In January 1994 a landmark conference, ''Black Women in the Academy: Defending Our Name,'' was organized by Evelynn Hammonds and Robin Kilson at MIT and was attended by over two thousand women scholars, primarily African-Americans. The conference's large attendance, challenging dialogue, and widespread media coverage are just one indication of how successfully African-American women's studies has grown from the initial efforts of a handful of visionary African-American women.

SELECTED BIBLIOGRAPHY

Gloria T. Hull et al., eds., *All the Women Are White, All the Blacks Are Men, But Some of Us Are Brave: Black Women's Studies* (1982); Darlene Clark Hine, ed., *Black Women in America: An Historical Encyclopedia* (1993); Patricia Hill Collins, *Black Feminist Thought* (1990); *SAGE: A Scholarly Journal on Black Women*, vols. 1 (1984–94).

BARBARA SMITH

WOODSON, CARTER GODWIN (19 December 1875, New Canton, Virginia–3 April 1950, Washington, D.C.). Carter Godwin Woodson was born to John Henry Woodson and Eliza Riddle Woodson, former slaves who, although illiterate, imbued in Carter and his eight brothers and sisters a profound respect for learning and the importance of the work ethic. The poverty experienced by the Woodson family allowed little time for Carter Woodson and his siblings to attend school. Carter attended a one-room country school very sporadically, because he had to work long hours on the farm to help his parents provide the basic necessities for the family. Through the assistance of his uncles, Morton Riddle and James Buchanan Riddle, Carter Woodson was able to learn the basics of geography, spelling, arithmetic, and United States history. In 1892, Woodson left New Canton, Virginia, and migrated to Huntington, West Virginia, where he joined his brother, Robert Henry Woodson, and worked with him in the coal mines. While working in the mines and through involvement in self-study, Woodson was able to complete Huntington High School in a year and half.

Woodson's love of learning, acquired from his parents and uncles, enabled him to achieve superior academic success. He earned a bachelor of literature degree at Berea College* in Kentucky, in 1903; earned his B.A. (1907) and M.A. (1908) degrees in history at the University of Chicago; and, after a period of concentrated research and teaching, earned his Ph.D. degree in history at Harvard University. His doctoral dissertation was entitled *The Disruption of Virginia*. Woodson, following W. E. B. Du Bois, had the distinction of being the second African-American to earn a Ph.D. in history from Harvard University. He later studied at the Sorbonne and the University of Paris.

Woodson made inimitable and lasting contributions in the fields of education and history. He served as supervisor of education in the Phillipines in 1903; as a principal of the District of Columbia's Armstrong High School in 1918–19; as Howard University's* Dean of Liberal Arts in 1919–20; and as dean of education at West Virginia Collegiate Institute (now West Virginia University) in 1920–23. Woodson's most enduring contributions were as a prolific writer of African-American history, a relentless advocate of truth, and an unyielding supporter of African-American pride and solidarity. He founded the Association for the Study of Negro Life and History, now called the Association for the Study of Afro-American Life and History,* in Chicago on 9 October 1915, along with Dr. George C. Hall, J. E. Stamps, W. B. Hartgrave, and A. L. Jackson. The Association for the Study of Afro-American Life and History, the *Journal of Negro History*, the *Negro History Bulletin*, and the Associated Publishers, all founded by Woodson, served as catalysts in bringing national and worldwide attention to the problems and contributions of African-Americans. He also started what was then called Negro History Week in February 1926. This one-week observance, changed to Black History Month in 1976, is now observed in elementary and secondary schools, institutions of higher education, and churches throughout the nation and many parts of the world.

Woodson's trenchant grasp of African-American life and history enabled him to write twenty-one books and over four hundred monographs, speeches, and book reviews pertaining to African-American life and history. Some of his notable works include *The Negro in Our History, The Story of the Negro Retold*, and *The Negro Church*. His scholarly work served to inspire and encourage prominent scholars such as L. D. Reddick, John W. Davis, Charles H. Wesley, Rayford W. Logan, and John Hope Franklin. Woodson's academic achievements and selfless work for African-American uplift led to the NAACP* awarding him its coveted Spingarn Medal in 1926.

Woodson never married, but he was viewed by many of his scholarly admirers as "married" to his beloved Association for the Study of Afro-American Life and History. He worked untiringly to make certain that African-American people would not "become a negligible factor in the thought of the world and stand in a danger of being exterminated." Considered by many as a "scholar's scholar" and universally regarded as the "Father of Black History," Woodson made a towering contribution to the serious, systematic study of African-American life and history. Alone in his residence at 1538 Ninth Street, NW, Washington, D.C., Woodson died of a heart attack on 3 April 1950. His funeral was held at Washington's historic Shiloh Baptist Church, and he was buried in Lincoln Memorial Cemetery in Suitland, Maryland.

SELECTED BIBLIOGRAPHY

Ralph W. Bullock, *In Spite of Handicaps* (1927); W. E. B. Du Bois, "A Portrait of Carter G. Woodson," *Mainstream* 3 (June 1950): 19–25; John Hope Franklin, "The Place of Carter G. Woodson in American Historiography," *The Negro History Bulletin* (May 1950); Rayford W. Logan, "Carter G. Woodson: *Phylon* Profile," *Phylon* 6 (1945): 315–21; Hubert E. Potter, *A Review of the Life and Times of Carter G. Woodson* (1956); L. D. Reddick, "Carter G. Woodson (1875–1950): An Appreciation," *Phylon* 11 (1950): 177–79; Anthony Scally, *Walking Proud* (1985); Charles Wesley and Carter G. Woodson, *The Story of the Negro Retold* (1959); Carter G. Woodson, *The Negro in Our History* (1928).

SAMUEL L. BANKS

WORK, MONROE NATHAN (15 August 1866, Iredell County, North Carolina–2 May 1945, Tuskegee, Alabama). A bibliographer, sociologist, minister, teacher, and writer, Work was one of eleven children of slave parents, Alexander and Eliza (Hobbs) Work. In 1876, young Work's family moved to Kansas, where his father obtained a 160-acre farm near Ashton, a town ten miles west of Arkansas City. In his early teens, Work had to interrupt his studies to take care of his invalid father and ill mother. After his mother died in 1889 and his father went to live with another sibling, young Work resumed his studies. At the age of twenty-six, he graduated from high school. In 1892, unable to obtain a teaching position, Work became interested in the church. He was subsequently ordained and given a pastorate in the African Methodist Church at Wellington, Kansas, where he worked for only a few months. In September 1893, Work staked a claim to one half of a 160-acre block of free land given to interested parties in southern Kansas. Two years later, Work sold his real estate acquisition to further his education.

In late 1895, Work entered the Chicago Theological Seminary to study for the ministry. In three years, he had redirected his interest. Consequently, Work pursued an educational career at the University of Chicago, graduating in 1902 and 1903 with B.A. (philosophy) and M.A. (sociology) degrees, respectively. From 1903 to 1907, he taught English, history, and pedagogy at Georgia State Industrial College in Savannah. He then began to conduct research, writing articles on African and African-American life. His interest in research and the collection of meaningful data enhanced his awareness of the need for a comprehensive bibliography of African and African-American authors. Creating such a listing years later proved to be a worthwhile endeavor.

In 1908, Work joined the faculty at Tuskegee Institute,* in Alabama. Booker T. Washington,* the most influential African-American in the United States at that time, employed him as director of the Department of Records and Research. Work's task, to gather data relative to the African-American and establish a bureau of information on graduates and former students, afforded Work the opportunity to influence African-American life and race relations. One of his major contributions stems from the establishment of this information bureau. At

Tuskegee, Work built up a priceless collection of information on African-Americans. In 1912, he edited and published *The Negro Year Book*,* an invaluable handbook of facts regarding the development and condition of African-Americans, which included an extensive bibliography. Carnegie Corporation* responded to increased reader interest in the handbook by issuing additional grants to Work.

In 1928, Work's *A Bibliography of the Negro in Africa and America* was published. It was a comprehensive handbook that listed valuable books, pamphlets, and articles on blacks in Africa and America. Such a listing enabled Work to publish countless articles in various journals on topics from folklore to labor. Work was also involved in programs for the improvement of African-American life in Savannah and wrote the first *Health Week Bulletin*. He also published statistics and other data on lynching.

On 27 December 1904, Monroe Work married Florence E. Hendrickson of Savannah. They had no children. In 1945 he died of natural causes in Tuskegee.

SELECTED BIBLIOGRAPHY

Monroe Work, "Preface," *Bibliography of the Negro in Africa and America* (1928); Anson Stokes, "Introduction," *Bibliography of the Negro in Africa and America* (1928); Jessie Guzman, "Monroe Work and His Contributions," *Journal of Negro History* (October 1949); Dorothy Porter's "Monroe Work," Monroe N. Work Papers, Manuscript Collection, Tuskegee Institute.

JOYCE BLACKWELL–JOHNSON

WRIGHT, JAMES SKELLY (14 January 1911, New Orleans, Louisiana–6 August 1988, Bethesda, Maryland). A federal judge and civil rights activist, Wright received his Ph.B. degree in 1931 and J.D. degree (1934) from Loyola University, New Orleans. A federal judge in New Orleans from 1949 to 1962 and thereafter in Washington, D.C., Wright was a social reformer unapologetic about his role as an activist judge. He was responsible almost single-handedly, through his decision in *Bush v. Orleans Parish School Board*, 138 F. Supp. 337 (E.D. LA. 1956), for the desegregation of the New Orleans school system in the wake of *Brown v. Board of Education of Topeka, Kansas*.* Long before *Brown*, however, Wright had already desegregated Louisiana's higher education facilities. Within a year of his appointment to the federal bench, he issued a landmark ruling directing the enrollment of African-Americans at Louisiana State University Law School in Baton Rouge. In 1954, the year of the *Brown* decision, the law school graduated its first African-American students, one of whom was Ernest Morial, the first African-American elected to the Louisiana legislature and later the first African-American mayor of New Orleans. Wright also ordered LSU to accept African-Americans into its graduate schools, medical school, and undergraduate colleges—all decisions that predated *Brown*. In 1957, he ordered desegregation of the New Orleans bus and streetcar systems.

Desegregation of the New Orleans public schools took ten years, from 1952 to 1962, and was sometimes referred to as the Second Battle of New Orleans.

Over its course, the *Orleans Parish School Board* case required forty-one separate judicial decisions, an average of one decision every three months. It culminated finally in Wright issuing a May 1960 order setting a specific date for the beginning of desegregation of the New Orleans grade schools, the first such final order issued in the South. Wright's plan was one sentence long: beginning in September 1960, first-grade students could attend the formerly all-white or all–African-American schools nearest their homes. Wright's decision resulted in the passage of twenty acts by four special sessions of the Louisiana legislature, all seeking to block his order. Each law was subsequently stricken by the three-judge federal court on which Wright sat. As a result, Wright became the focal point of one of the most intensive campaigns of harassment and abuse ever suffered by a federal judge. His life was frequently threatened, burning crosses and coffins were placed on his lawn, and he was shunned by many white citizens. United States marshals eventually were required to live with him and his family twenty-four hours a day. Ultimately, after Wright entered injunctions against the governor, the state legislature (and each individual member), the New Orleans superintendent of schools and the state attorney general, compliance followed.

Southern senators blocked the Kennedy administration's plans to elevate Wright to the United States Court of Appeals for the Fifth Circuit in New Orleans. As a result, he was appointed to the United States Court of Appeals in the District of Columbia in 1962. On the D.C. circuit, he demonstrated the same commitment to eliminating the effects of racial discrimination as he had in New Orleans. In *Hobson v Hansen*,* he invalidated the District of Columbia's track system for its public schools as unfairly discriminating against underprivileged minority students by separating them on the basis of their courses of study and thereby thwarting their prospects for securing higher education. In the course of his ruling, he amassed 118 pages of empirical and sociological data to support his conclusions that the tracking system condemned lower-income African-American youth to a hopelessly compromised second-class education.

Wright's concern for equality of opportunity and evenhandedness in the application of the law to rich and poor manifested itself in other areas as well. He ruled in favor of the rights of slum tenants to withhold rent for leaky and rat-infested dwellings and to report landlords' housing code violations without risk of eviction. He also provided remedies for beleaguered consumers threatened with repossession of goods for their failure to meet payments under "unconscionable" installment contracts. In another case, Wright travelled to the bedside of a critically ill patient to determine whether she should be required to receive a blood transfusion over the religious objections of her relatives. He ordered the transfusion, and the patient recovered.

Wright served as Chief Judge of the U.S. Court of Appeals for the D.C. Circuit from 1978 to 1981, was the recipient of numerous awards and honorary degrees, and authored many scholarly articles on legal and nonlegal subjects.

SELECTED BIBLIOGRAPHY
Arthur Selwyn Miller, *A "Capacity for Outrage": The Judicial Odyssey of J. Skelly Wright* (1984); Arthur Selwyn Miller, ed., *On Courts and Democracy: Non-Judicial Writings of J. Skelly Wright* (1984); Jack Bass, *Unlikely Heroes* (1981); J. W. Peltason, *Fifty-Eight Lonely Men* (1971); F. Read and L. McGough, *Let Them Be Judged: The Judicial Integration of the Deep South* (1978); "Memorial Tributes," *George Washington Law Review* 57 (1989): 1029–62; "Symposium, Judge J. Skelly Wright," *Hastings Constitutional Law Quarterly* 7 (1980): 857–999.

EDWARD M. CHIKOFSKY

WRIGHT, RICHARD ROBERT (16 May 1855, Dalton, Georgia–2 July 1947, Philadelphia, Pennsylvania). An educator, high school principal, and association founder, Wright received a B.A. degree from Atlanta University (now Clark Atlanta University*) in 1876 and was awarded an honorary M.A. from his alma mater in 1879. He also studied at Cambridge University (1895), Harvard University (1896), the University of Chicago (1900), and the Wharton School of Finance at the University of Pennsylvania.

Between 1872 and 1876, Wright taught at various county schools in rural Georgia, but following his graduation from Atlanta University he took charge of an American Missionary school in Cuthbert, Georgia (1876–80). In 1876, he founded and was the first president of the Colored Teachers Association, which established Howard Normal School and elected Wright as principal (1876–80). In addition to holding these two positions, Wright was the founder and first president of the South-West Georgia Teacher's Association (1877–95), was the first principal of Ware High School in Augusta, the only publicly supported high school for African-Americans in Georgia (1880–91) and the first president of Savannah State, the first state college for African-Americans in Georgia.

R. R. Wright was one of the leading organizers and founding members of the American Association of Colored Youth (1889) and the National Association of Teachers in Colored Schools* (1904), serving as the second president of the latter organization from 1908 to 1910. He organized and was elected president of the National Association of Principals and Presidents of A and M Colleges for Colored Youth (1902) and was reelected when the association became the Association of A and M Colleges and Schools of Higher and Secondary Education (1905). Wright was a founder of the Atlanta University Alumni Association and member of the school's board of trustees, which elected him vice chairman (1869–1907). He conceived and initiated the movement that culminated in the organization of the American Negro Academy* in 1897 and was founder and first president of the Colored Farmer's Congress (1898), the Georgia State Industrial Fair Association (1900), and the Georgia Agricultural and Industrial Association (1905).

In conjunction with his educational work and organizational activities, Wright established several newspapers in Georgia, the *Journal of Progress* (Cuthbert, 1878–81), the *People's Defense* (Augusta, 1883–85), and the *Weekly Seminar*

(Savannah, 1885–95). In 1883 he cofounded and served as president of the Georgia Colored Press Association and was instrumental in its reorganization into the Georgia Press Association (1892), as well as in the creation of the Negro Newspaper Syndicate.

Wright moved to Philadelphia in 1921, where he opened the Citizen and Southern Bank, entered the University of Pennsylvania, and organized and led the National Negro Bankers Association (1924). He also served as president of the Philadelphia Business League, was a member of the Philadelphia Chamber of Commerce, and in 1941 organized the National Freedom Day Association.

SELECTED BIBLIOGRAPHY

"Slave to Banker: Major Wright, 91, Most Amazing Negro Living in American Today," *Ebony* (November 1945); 43–47; J. W. Gibson and W. H. Crogman, *Progress of a Race* (1902); William N. Hartshorn, ed., *An Era of Progress and Promise, 1863–1910* (1910); Elizabeth Ross Haynes, *The Black Boy from Atlanta* (1952); June O. Patton, "Major Richard Robert Wright, Sr., and Black Education in Georgia, 1855–1920," Ph.D. diss., University of Chicago, 1980.

JUNE O. PATTON

WRIGHT, STEPHEN J., JR. (8 September 1910, Dillon, South Carolina–16 April 1996, Baltimore, Maryland), an educator, administrator, and college president, Wright earned a bachelor's degree at Hampton Institute* in 1934, a master's degree at Howard University* in 1939, and a Ph.D. at New York University in 1943. Wright began his professional career as a teacher in the Kennard High School in Centreville, Maryland, in 1934 and became principal of the Douglass High School in Upper Marlboro, Maryland, in 1936. He began the higher education phase of his professional career at North Carolina Central University* in 1939 as director of student teaching, becoming chair of the Department of Education in 1943. In 1944, he accepted an appointment as professor of education and director of the Division of Education at Hampton Institute and served from 1945 to 1953 as professor of education and dean of faculty at Hampton. From 1953 to 1957 he was president of Bluefield State College* (West Virginia); from 1957 to 1966, president of Fisk University*; from 1966 to 1969, president of the United Negro College Fund*; and from 1970 to 1976, vice president of the College Entrance Examination Board, retiring in 1976.

Wright's public and professional service over the years included membership and leadership positions on a number of boards, including Meharry Medical College* (1962–67), Hampton University (1963–68), Shaw University* (1965–67), West Virginia State College* (1970–76), Paterson (N.J.) State College (1960–74), the University of Richmond (1975–82), the American Council on Education (1962–66), the Education Testing Service (1964–68), the National Council on the Humanities (1968–74), the Arms Control and Disarmament Advisory Committee (1968–69), President Lyndon Johnson's National Library Commission (1966–68), the New Jersey State Board of Higher Education (1975–76), the Virginia State Council (board) for Higher Education (1982–90), president of the Association of Colleges and Secondary Schools (for Blacks) (1956–57), and chairman of the National Education Association's Educational Policies Commission (1964–67). Wright also served as an expert witness in lawsuits involving equal educational opportunity, including *Brown v. Board of Education of Topeka, Kansas.* His professional writings were published in the *Journal of Negro Education*,* the *Saturday Review*, the *Harvard Educational Review, Educational Record* and the *Journal of Higher Education*, among others.

Wright's professional honors and awards included election to Phi Delta Kappa; distinguished alumni awards from Hampton, Howard, and New York universities; the Frontiers International's Professional Educator of the Year Award; the National Association for Equal Opportunity in Higher Education's Leadership in Higher Education Award; the Brotherhood Citation of the National Council of Christians and Jews; and the F. D. Patterson* Award for Distinguished Service for the United Negro College Fund.* He received honorary degrees from fifteen colleges and universities.

He was married to the former Rosalind Person, and resided in Hampton, Virginia.

CHARLES A. ASBURY

WYGANT v. JACKSON BOARD OF EDUCATION, 476 U.S. 267 (1986). This case is the only Supreme Court ruling on de facto segregation and faculty assignment schemes. In *Wygant* the Court struck down a local school board's attempt to maintain a racially integrated faculty in the face of layoffs by extending preferential retention protection to minority teachers. A provision in the 1972 collective bargaining agreement between the Board of Education in Jackson, Michigan, and its teachers granted preferential protection against reductions in force to less-senior minority faculty members. It did so as a means of easing racial tensions in the community that had spilled over into the schools. Under the terms of the contract the parties voluntarily agreed that, if layoffs became necessary, those with the most seniority would be retained, except that at no time could there be a greater percentage of minority teachers laid off than the current proportion of minority faculty employed in the district.

When layoffs became necessary in 1974, the board failed to follow the agreement. Subsequently, in a suit by minority teachers, a state court ordered the district to comply with the terms of the contract. After another round of furloughs in 1982, both the Federal District Court for Eastern Michigan and the Sixth Circuit Court of Appeals upheld the contract in the face of challenges by laid-off senior teachers. The courts ruled that the racial preferences did not violate the Equal Protection Clause of the Fourteenth Amendment since they were intended to remedy societal discrimination by providing role models for minority students. The Supreme Court granted *certiorari* "to resolve the important issue of the constitutionality of race-based layoffs by public employers."

As a plurality decision, *Wygant* is ultimately less than satisfying. The only Supreme Court case on the bounds of voluntary affirmative action plans and de facto segregation, it fails to provide clear direction. While the plurality in *Wygant* clearly favored hiring plans rather than layoffs as a means of remedying the effects of discriminatory practices, none of the three opinions in the five-member majority opined that a race-conscious affirmative action plan is a per se violation of equal protection. Yet, the Court was unable to articulate standards under which a governmental program designed to provide assistance to minorities is permissible. Thus, faced with the resegregation of public schools and the prospect that litigation similar to *Wygant* may be forthcoming, educators must await further guidance from the Supreme Court as they seek to remedy inequitable and discriminatory hiring practices.

SELECTED BIBLIOGRAPHY

Wygant v. Jackson Board of Education, 476 U.S. 267.

CHARLES J. RUSSO

X

XAVIER UNIVERSITY. Xavier University of Louisiana, located in the heart of New Orleans, is the only predominantly black U.S. institution of higher learning operated under the auspices of the Catholic Church.* The university is administered under a combined lay/religious board of trustees, faculty, and administration. Today its student population is nearly 50 percent non-Catholic and 10 percent white. The university offers training in more than three dozen academic and professional fields and is comprised of a college of arts and sciences, a college of pharmacy and a graduate school. The educational program at Xavier is liberal arts-oriented, with all students required to take a core of prescribed courses in theology and philosophy, humanities, communications, history, behavioral sciences, mathematics, and natural sciences, in addition to more intensive work in their respective majors. Its College of Pharmacy, one of only two pharmacy schools in Louisiana, annually educates 15 percent of all African-American pharmacy students in the United States. Xavier's premedical students are also highly regarded, enjoying an acceptance rate of better than 80 percent at medical and dental schools throughout the country.

SELECTED BIBLIOGRAPHY

National Association for Equal Opportunity in Higher Education, *Profiles of the Nation's Historically and Predominantly Black Colleges and Universities* (1993).

SAMUEL L. MYERS

Y

YALE CHILD STUDY CENTER. The Yale Child Study Center is a part of the academic department of Yale University and the School of Medicine and is also affiliated with the Department of Child Psychiatry at the Yale New Haven Hospital. Located in New Haven, Connecticut, the Center was created in 1911 by one of America's earliest and most influential leaders in child development, Dr. Arnold Gesell. It was established to generate new knowledge and inform educational and social policy through the scholarly and scientific study of children and families. Its faculty is comprised of an array of researchers, practitioners, and scholars who coordinate and direct numerous intervention programs addressing the academic, psychosocial, and psychoemotional needs of New Haven's inner-city student population.

One highly touted activity of the Yale Child Study Center is the Comer School Development Program (commonly known as the Comer Process*). Directed by and named for African-American psychologist Dr. James Comer,* this program brings parents, staff, students, and community members together to improve school climate, enhance student self-concept, and increase achievement at targeted inner-city schools. The program has received much national acclaim for its positive impact on the achievement and psychosocial adjustment of African-American children. The Bush Center for Child Development and Social Policy Research is a component of the Child Study Center that engages in educational reform initiatives, including Head Start* and other early intervention programs, parental leave, and school safety.

Another successful program of the Yale Center is the Healthy Tomorrows–Katharine Brennan Health Connection, which provides child- and family-centered mental health consultation for students at New Haven's predominantly African-American Katharine Brennan Elementary School. Additionally, the Center operates several school-based outpatient clinics that provide unique, easily accessible, mental health services to inner-city children and families in New Haven. Twelve such satellite clinics, serving a thirty percent African-American clientele, were initiated in 1992. Yet another center effort, Project Leap, offers an alternative to the streets for youth from four of the city's inner-city schools. Students from six area colleges serve as Project Leap teacher-counselors charged with raising the academic performance of participating youth. Further, the center sponsors support programs for children who are at risk of out-of-home placement and their parents. Individuals suffering from multiple stresses such as AIDS and drug abuse–related problems are also supported through education, training, and clinical intervention.

Since its inception, the Yale Child Study Center has been committed to improving the quality of life of inner-city children and families. With its unique interdisciplinary approach to research and intervention, it is today one of the world's leading institutions for training professionals for service in impoverished urban communities.

SELECTED BIBLIOGRAPHY

James Comer, *School Power: Implications of an Intervention Project* (1980); James Comer, "Reflections on Child Development and Education," in Derek L. Burleson, ed., *Reflections and Personal Essays by 33 Distinguished Educators* (1991); Sharon Kagan, *United We Stand: Collaboration for Child Care and Early Education Services* (1991).

VALERIE MAHOLMES

SELECTED BIBLIOGRAPHY

Abraham, Henry J. *Freedom and the Court* (1967).

Abramowitz, Elizabeth. *Equal Educational Opportunity for Blacks in U.S. Higher Education: An Assessment* (1975).

———. *The Status of Black Women in Higher Education* (1977).

———. *More Promise Than Progress: A Continuing Assessment of Equal Opportunity in Higher Education* (1979).

Adams, Frank, and Myles Horton. *Unearthing the Seeds of Fire: The Idea for Highlander* (1975).

Akoto, A. *Nationbuilding: Theory and Practice in Afrikan Centered Education* (1992).

Allen, Walter Recharde, and Reynolds Farley. *The Color Line and the Quality of Life* (1987).

Allport, Gordon. *The Nature of Prejudice* (1985).

Altbach, Philip G., and Gail P. Kelly, eds. *Education and Colonialism* (1978).

Altbach, Philip G., and K. Lomotey. *The Racial Crisis in American Higher Education* (1991).

American Association of Colleges for Teacher Education. *Minority Teacher Recruitment and Retention: A Call for Action* (1987).

American Association of Medical Colleges. *Minority Students in Medical Education* (December 1991).

———. *Participation of Women and Minorities on U.S. Medical School Faculties 1980–1990.* Faculty Roster System (1991).

Anderson, James D. *The Education of Blacks in the South, 1860–1935* (1988).

Ani, M. *Yurugu: An African-Centered Critique of European Cultural Thought and Behavior* (1994).

Aptheker, Herbert. *A Documentary History of the Negro People in the United States* (1964).

Arnez, Nancy L. *Cultural Linguistic Approach to Education* (1972).

———. *Partners in Urban Education: Teaching the Inner City Child* (1973).

Asante, Molefi K. *Afrocentricity* (1980).

———. *The Afrocentric Idea* (1987).

———. *Kemet, Afrocentricity and Knowledge* (1990).

Astin, Alexander. *Minorities in American Higher Education* (1982).

Astone, Barbara, and Elsa Nunez-Wormack. *Pursuing Diversity: Recruiting College Minority Students* (ASHE-ERIC Higher Education Report No. 7) (1990).

Austin, Frank E. *The History of Segregation* (1956).

Baird, R. M. *Bigotry, Prejudice and Hatred: Definitions, Causes, and Solutions* (1992).

Baker, Houston. *Black Studies, Rap and the Academy* (1993).

Ballard, Allen B. *The Education of Black Folk: The Afro-American Struggle for Knowledge in White American* (1973).

Banks, James A. *Multicultural Education: Theory and Practice.* 2d ed. (1988).

———. *Introduction to Multicultural Education* (1994).

Bardolph, Richard. *The Negro Vanguard* (1959).

———, ed. *The Civil Rights Record: Black Americans and the Law, 1849–1970* (1970).

Barnett, Marguerite R. and James A. Hefner. *Public Policy for the Black Community* (1976).

Bass, John, and Jack Nelson. *The Orangeburg Massacre* (1984).

Bates, P., and T. Wilson. *Effective Schools* (1989).

Beaumont, Andre G., ed. *Handbook for Recruiting at the Traditional Black Colleges* (1975).

Bell, Derrick A., Jr. *Race, Racism and American Law* (1973).

Bempechat, J. *Fostering High Achievement in African-American Children: Home, School, and Public Policy Influences* (1992).

Bender, Lois W. *Fostering Minority Access and Achievement in Higher Education* (1987).

Benedict, Ruth. *Race: Science and Politics* (1959).

Bennett, Lerone, Jr. *Before the Mayflower: A History of the Negro in America, 1619–1962* (1962).

Bentley, George R. *A History of the Freedmen's Bureau* (1955).

Berke, Joel S. *Answers to Inequity* (1974).

Berry, G. L., and C. Mitchell-Kernan, eds. *Television and the Socialization of the Minority Child* (1982).

Berry, Mary Frances. *Twentieth Century Black Women in Education* (1982).

Billingsley, Andrew. *Black Families in White America* (1968).

Binkin, Martin, and Mark J. Eitelberg. *Blacks and the Military* (1982).

Blackwell, James E. *Mainstreaming Outsiders: The Production of Black Professionals* (1981).

———. *Networking and Mentoring: A Study of Cross-Generational Experiences of Blacks in Graduate and Professional Schools* (1983).

———. *The Black Community: Diversity and Unity.* 2d ed. (1985).

Blaustein, Albert, and Robert L. Zangrando, eds. *Civil Rights and African-Americans: A Documentary History* (1968, 1991).

Bond, Horace Mann. *The Education of the Negro in the American Social Order* (1934).

Bowser, Benjamin P. *Black Male Adolescents: Parenting and Education in Community Context* (1991).

Broderick, Francis L. *W. E. B. Du Bois: Negro Leader in Time of Crisis* (1959).

Brookover, W. B., and L. W. Lezotte. *Changes in School Characteristics Coincident with Changes in Student Achievement* (1977).

Brown, Hugh Victor. *A History of the Education of Negroes in North Carolina* (1961).

Brown, Letitia Woods. *Free Negroes in the District of Columbia, 1790–1846* (1972).

Bullock, Henry Allen. *A History of Negro Education in the South from 1619 to the Present* (1967).

Buncher, Judith F., ed. *School Busing Controversy: 1970–1975*. Facts on File (1975).

Butchart, Ronald E. *Northern Whites, Southern Blacks, and Reconstruction: Freedmen's Education, 1862–1875* (1980).

Carson, Clayborne. *In Struggle: SNCC and Black Awakening of the 1960's* (1981).

————, ed. *The Student Voice 1960–1965* (1990).

Carter, Deborah J., and Reginald Wilson. *Ninth Annual Status Report 1990 on Minorities in Higher Education* (1991).

————. *Minorities in Higher Education: Tenth Annual Status Report* (1991).

————. *Minorities in Higher Education: Twelfth Annual Status Report* (1993).

Chase, Alan. *The Legacy of Malthus: The Social Costs of the New Scientific Racism* (1977).

Children's Defense Fund. *Children out of School in America* (1974).

————. *School Suspensions: Are They Helping Children?* (1975).

Chipman, S. F., and V. G. Thomas. *The Participation of Women and Minorities in Mathematical, Scientific and Technical Fields* (1984).

Chubb, John, and Terry Moe. *Politics, Markets and American's Schools*. Brookings Institute (1990).

Clark, Septima. *Ready from Within: Septima Clark and the Civil Rights Movement* (1986).

Clewell, B. C., and B. Anderson. *Women of Color in Mathematics, Science and Engineering: A Review of the Literature* (1991).

Cole, Johnetta B. *Conversations: Straight Talk with America's Sister President* (1993).

Coleman, James S., *Equality and Achievement in Education* (1990).

Coleman, James S., E. Campbell, C. Hobson, J. McPartland, A. Mood, F. Weinfield, and R. York. *Equality of Educational Opportunity* (1966).

College Entrance Examination Board. *Equality and Excellence: The Educational Status of Black Americans* (1985).

Commission on Minority Participation in Education and American Life. *One-Third of a Nation* (1988).

Cornelius, Janet Duitsman. *"When I Can Read My Title Clear": Literacy, Slavery, and Religion in the Antebellum South* (1991).

Council of Independent Black Institutions. *Positive African Images for Children: The CIBI Social Studies Curriculum* (1990).

Cross, George Lynn. *Blacks in White Colleges: Oklahoma's Landmark Cases* (1975).

Cross, William E., Jr. *Shades of Black Diversity in African-American Identity* (1991).

Cruse, Harold. *The Crisis of the Negro Intellectual* (1967).

Davis, Allison. *Social Class Influences upon Learning* (1948).

————. *Leadership, Love, and Aggression: How the Twig Is Bent* (1983).

Davis, Allison, and John Dollard. *Children of Bondage: The Personality Development of Negro Youth in the Urban South* (1940).

Davis, Cyprian, OSB. *The History of Black Catholics in the United States* (1990).

Davis, John P. ed. *The American Negro Reference Book* (1966).

Davis, Marianna W. *Contributions of Black Women to America* (1981).

Denton, Virginia L. *Booker T. Washington and the Adult Education Movement* (1993).

Department of Interior. *Negro Education: A Study of the Private and Higher Schools for Colored People in the United States*, vol. 2 (1917).

DeVore, Donald E., and Joseph Logsdon. *Crescent City Schools: Public Education in New Orleans, 1841–1991* (1991).

Diamond, Paul R. *Beyond Busing: Inside the Challenge to Urban Segregation* (1985).

Drago, Edmund L. *Initiative, Paternalism and Race Relations: Charleston's Avery Normal Institute* (1990).

Drake, St. Clair, and Peter Omari. *Teaching Black: An Evaluation of Methods and Resources* (1971).

Du Bois, W. E. B. *The Souls of Black Folk: Essays and Sketches* (1903).

Edelman, C. *The Economic Status of Black America: The State of Black America* (1989).

Edelman, Marian Wright. *The Measure of Our Success* (1992).

Edmonds, Helen G. *Black Faces in High Places: Negroes in Government* (1971).

Embree, Edwin, and Julia Waxman. *The Story of the Julius Rosenwald Fund: Investment in People* (1949).

Emerson, Thomas I., David Haber, and Norman Dorsen. *Political and Civil Rights in the United States: A Collection of Legal and Related Materials* (1967).

Engs, Robert Francis. *Freedom's First Generation: Black Hampton, Virginia, 1861–1890* (1979).

Evans, Cecil Eugene. *The Story of Texas Schools* (1955).

Finch, Minnie. *The NAACP: Its Fight for Justice* (1981).

Fiol-Matta, Liza, and Mariam K. Chamberlain. *Women of Color and the Multicultural Curriculum: Transforming the College Classroom (with a Segment on Puerto Rican Studies)* (1994).

Fischer, Roger A. *The Segregation Struggle in Louisiana, 1862–1877* (1974).

Fleming, John E. *The Lengthening Shadow of Slavery: A Historical Justification for Affirmative Action for Blacks in Higher Education* (1976).

Fleming, John E., Gerald R. Gill, and David H. Swinton. *The Case for Affirmative Action for Blacks in Higher Education* (1978).

Franklin, Vincent P. *The Education of Black Philadelphia: The Social and Educational History of a Minority Community, 1900–1950* (1979).

Futrell, Mary Hatwood. *Educational Choice* (1991).

Gabel, Leona C. *From Slavery to the Sorbonne and Beyond: The Life and Writings of Anna J. Cooper* (1982).

Gay, Geneva, and Willie L. Baber, eds. *Expressively Black: The Cultural Basis of Ethnic Identity* (1987).

Geiss, Immanuel. *The Pan-African Movement* (1974).

Georgia Association of Jeanes Curriculum Directors. *Jeanes Supervision in the Georgia Schools: A Guiding Light in Education* (1975).

Gibbs, J. T. *Young, Black, and Male in America: An Endangered Species* (1988).

Gibson, J. W., and W. H. Crogman. *Progress of a Race* (1902).

Glen, John M. *Highlander: No Ordinary School* (1988).

Goggin, Jacqueline. *Carter G. Woodson: A Life in Black History* (1993).

Goldberg, David Theo, ed. *Anatomy of Racism* (1990).

Goldman, Roger, with David Gallen. *Thurgood Marshall: Justice for All* (1992).

Gossett, Thomas F. *Race: The History of an Idea in America* (1963).

Graham, Shirley. *Booker T. Washington, Educator of Hand, Head and Heart* (1955).

Gutman, Herbert. *The Black Family in Slavery and Freedom, 1750–1925* (1976).

Haas, Lawrence J. *The Washington Almanac* (1992).

Hacker, A. *Two Nations: Black and White. Separate. Hostile. Unequal* (1992).

Hale, Janice E. *Black Children: Their Roots, Culture and Learning Styles* (1986).
————. *Unbank the Fire: Visions for the Education of African American Children* (1994).
Hamilton, Edwin. *Adult Education for Community Development* (1992).
Harlan, Louis R. *Booker T. Washington: The Making of a Black Leader, 1856–1901* (1972).
————. *Booker T. Washington: The Wizard of Tuskegee, 1901–1915* (1983).
Harris, J. J., and M. A. Kendall. *Facilitating Equity through the School Superintendency: Leadership, Equity, and School Effectiveness* (1990).
Harris, T. H. *The Story of Public Education in Louisiana* (1924).
Hawley, Willis D., ed. *Effective School Desegregation: Equity, Quality, and Feasibility* (1981).
Heath, S. B. *Ways with Words: Language, Life and Work in Communities and Classrooms* (1983).
Herskovits, Melville J. *The Myth of the Negro Past* (1958).
Hill, R. A., and B. Blair. *Marcus Garvey: Life and Lessons* (1987).
Hilliard, Asa G., III, ed. *Testing African American Students* (1991).
Hilliard, Asa, III, and Barbara Sizemore, eds. *On Saving the African American Child* (1984).
Hine, Darlene Clark, Elsa Barkley Brown, and Rosalyn Terborg-Penn, eds. *Black Women in America: An Historical Encyclopedia* (1993).
Hogan, Rev. Peter. *Josephite History, The Josephite Harvest* (1992–93).
Hollins, Etta R., Joyce E. King, and Warren C. Hayman, eds. *Teaching Diverse Populations: Formulating a Knowledge Base* (1994).
Holmes, Dwight O. W. *The Evolution of the Negro College* (1970).
Holmes, F. *Prejudice and Discrimination* (1970).
Horst, Samuel L. *Education for Manhood: The Education of Blacks in Virginia during the Civil War* (1987).
Horton, Aimee I. *The Highlander Folk School: A History of Its Major Programs, 1932–1961* (1989).
Huggins, Nathan I. *Afro-American Studies: A Report to the Ford Foundation* (1985), passim.
Harris, Robert, et al. *Three Essays: Black Studies in the United States* (1990).
Hughes, Larry W., William M. Gordan, and Larry W. Hillman. *Desegregating America's Schools* (1980).
Hull, Gloria T., et al., eds. *All the Women Are White, All the Blacks Are Men, But Some of Us Are Brave: Black Women's Studies* (1982).
Human Affairs Commission. *South Carolina's Blacks and Native Americans* (1976).
Hundley, Mary Gibson. *The Dunbar Story (1870–1955)* (1965).
Institute of the Black World, eds. *Education and Black Struggle: Notes from the Colonized World* (1974).
Irvine, Jacqueline J. *Black Students and School Failure* (1990).
Jacoway, Elizabeth. *Yankee Missionaries in the South: The Penn School Experiment* (1980).
James, C. L. R. *A History of Negro Revolt* (1983).
Jaynes, Gerald David, and Robin M. Williams, Jr., eds. *A Common Destiny: Blacks and American Society* (1989).

Jencks, C., et al. *Inequality: A Reassessment of the Effect of Family and Schooling in America* (1972).

Johnson, Charles S. *Patterns in Negro Segregation* (1943).

Johnson, James P., Janet L. Sims, and Gail A. Kostinko. *Mordecai Wyatt Johnson: A Bibliography of His Years at Howard 1926–1960*. Moorland-Spingarn Research Center (1976).

Johnson, S. T. *The Measurement Mystique* (1979).

Joint Center for Political and Economic Studies Press. *The Inclusive University* (1993).

Jones, J. *Prejudice and Racism* (1972).

Jones, Lance. *The Jeanes Teacher in the United States 1908–1933* (1933).

Justiz, Manuel J., Reginald Wilson, and Lars G. Bjork, eds. *Minorities in Higher Education* (1994).

Kambon, K. K. K. *The African Personality in America: An African-Centered Framework* (1992).

Kamin, Leon J. *The Science and Politics of IQ* (1974).

Kane, M. *Minorities in Textbooks* (1970).

Kardiner, Abram, and Lionel Oversey. *The Mark of Oppression: Explorations in the Personality of the American Negro* (1951).

Karenga, Maulana. *Introduction to Black Studies* (1993).

Katz, Michael B. *The Undeserving Poor: From the War on Poverty to the War on Welfare* (1989).

Kellogg, Charles Flint. *NAACP: A History of the National Association for the Advancement of Colored People* (1967).

———. *NAACP*. vol. 1, *1909–1920* (1976).

King, Kenneth. *Pan-Africanism and Education: A Study of Race Philanthrophy and Education in the Southern States of America and East Africa* (1971).

Kirp, David. *Just Schools: The Idea of Racial Equality in American Education* (1982).

Kluger, Richard. *Simple Justice: The History of Brown v. Board of Education and Black America's Struggle for Equality* (1976).

Kunjufu, J. *Critical Issues in Educating African-American Youth: A Talk with Jawanza* (1989).

Leavell, Ullin W. *Philanthropy in Negro Education* (1950, reprint 1970).

Lewis, David Levering. *W. E. B. Du Bois: Biography of a Race, 1868–1919* (1993).

Lincoln, C. Eric, and L. H. Mamiya. *The Black Church in the African-American Experience* (1990).

Litwack, Leon, and August Meier, eds. *Black Leaders of the Nineteenth Century* (1988).

Logan, Rayford W., and Michael R. Winston, eds. *Dictionary of American Negro Biography* (1982).

Lovejoy, P. E. *Transformations in Slavery: A History of Slavery in Africa* (1983).

Low, W. A., and Virgil A. Clift. *Encyclopedia of Black America* (1981).

Lowery, Charles D., and John F. Marszalek. *Encyclopedia of African American Civil Rights from Emancipation to the Present* (1992).

Marcus, Laurence R., and Benjamin D. Stickney. *Race and Education: The Unending Controversy* (1981).

Margo, Robert A. *Race and Schooling in the South, 1880–1950* (1990).

Mather, Lincoln Frank, ed. *Who's Who of the Colored Race: A General Biographical Dictionary of Men and Women of African Descent* (1915).

Matney, William C., ed. *Who's Who among Black Americans* (1988).

Mayberry, Bennie B., ed. *Development of Research at Historically Black Land-Grant Institutions* (1977).

Mayberry, B. D. *The Role of Tuskegee University in the Origin, Growth and Development of the Negro Cooperative Extension System 1881–1990* (1989).

McAdam, Doug. *Freedom Summer* (1988).

McAdoo, H., ed. *Black Families* (1988).

McNeil, Genna Rae. *Groundwork: Charles Hamilton Houston and the Struggle for Civil Rights* (1983).

McPherson, James M. *The Abolitionist Legacy: From Reconstruction to the NAACP* (1973).

Meier, August. *Negro Thought in America, 1880–1915: Racial Ideologies in the Age of Booker T. Washington* (1963).

Meier, August, and Elliott Rudwick. *Black History and the Historical Profession, 1915–1980* (1986).

Meier, Kenneth, J. Stewart, and R. England. *Race, Class and Education: Second-Generation Discrimination* (1989).

Metropolitan Life Survey of the American Teacher. *Violence in America's Public Schools* (1993).

Miller, Loren. *The Petitioners: The Story of the Supreme Court of the United States and the Negro* (1966).

Montgomery, Winfield S. *Historical Sketch of Education for the Colored in the District of Columbia 1807–1905* (1907).

Moorland Foundation. *The Arthur B. Spingarn Collection of Negro Authors* (1947).

Morgan, David R. *Desegregating Public Schools: A Handbook for Local Officials* (1982).

Morris, Frank L., Sr. *The New Slavery: The Denial of Doctoral Opportunities for African-American Students in American Universities in a de facto Low-Wage American Economy* (1992).

Morris, Robert C. *Reading,'Riting, and Reconstruction: The Education of Freedmen in the South, 1861–1870* (1981).

National Association of State Universities and Land-Grant Colleges. *Leadership and Learning: An Interpretive History of Historically Black Land-Grant Colleges and Universities* (n.d., circa 1993).

National Center for Children in Poverty School of Public Health. *Five Million Children: A Statistical Profile of Our Poorest Young Citizens* (1991).

National Commission for Excellence in Education. *A Nation at Risk: The Imperative for Educational Reform* (1983).

National Council for Black Studies. *Black Studies Core Curriculum* (1981).

National Science Foundation. *Women and Minorities in Science and Engineering* (1990).

Neby, Indus A. *The Development of Segregationist Thought* (1968).

Neiman, Donald G. *To Set the Law in Motion: The Freedmen's Bureau and the Legal Rights of Blacks, 1865–1868* (1979).

Nelson, Dana D. *The World in Black and White: Reading Race in American Literature, 1638–1867* (1992).

Neufeldt, Harvey G., and Leo McGee, eds. *Education of the African American Adult: An Historical Overview* (1990).

Newbold, N. C., ed. *Five North Carolina Negro Educators* (1939).

Neyland, Ledell W. *Historically Black Land-Grant Institutions and the Development of Agriculture and Home Economics 1890–1990* (1990).

Oakes, J. *Keeping Track of How Schools Structure Inequality* (1985).

————. *Lost Talent: The Underparticipation of Women, Minorities, and Disabled Persons in Science* (1990).

————. *Multiplying Inequalities: The Effect of Race, Social Class, and Tracking on Opportunities to Learn Science and Mathematics* (1990).

Ogbu, John U. *The Next Generation: An Ethnography of Education in an Urban Neighborhood* (1974).

————. *Minority Education and Caste: The American System in Cross-Cultural Perspective* (1978).

Omi, Michael, and Howard Winant. *Racial Formation in the The United States: From the 1960s to the 1980s* (1986).

O'Neill, Timothy. *Bakke and the Politics of Equality* (1978).

Orfield, Gary. *Must We Bus?: Segregated Schools and National Policy* (1978).

————. *Public School Desegregation in the United States, 1968–1980* (1983).

Orfield, Gary, and Carole Ashkinaze. *The Closing Door* (1991).

Passow, A. Harry. *Toward Creating a Model Urban School System: A Study of the Washington, D.C., Public Schools* (1967).

Pearson, W., Jr. *Black Scientists, White Society, and Colorless Science: A Study of Universalism in American Science* (1985).

Pelham, J. *Factors Affecting Retention in Science-Based Curriculums at HBCUs* (1991).

Peltason, Jack. *Fifty-eight Lonely Men: Southern Federal Judges and School Desegregation* (1971).

Piliawsky, Monte. *Exit 13: Oppression and Racism in Academia* (1982).

Ploski, Harry A., and James Williams. *The Negro Almanac: A Reference Work on the African-American* (1989).

Potter, Hubert E. *A Review of the Life and Times of Carter G. Woodson* (1956).

Preer, Jean L. *Lawyers v. Educators: Black Colleges and Desegregation in Public Higher Education* (1982).

Pride, R., and J. Woodard. *The Burden of Busing: The Politics of Desegregation in Nashville, Tennessee* (1985).

Prothrow-Stith, D., and M. Weissman. *Deadly Consequences: How Violence Is Destroying Our Teenage Population and a Plan to Begin Solving the Problem* (1991).

Pruitt, Ann S., ed. *In Pursuit of Equality in Higher Education* (1987).

Rambert, L. Jill. *The Impact of Historically Black Institutions on the Supply of Black Teachers* (October 1989).

Ramirez, M., III, and A. Castaneda. *Cultural Democracy, Bicognitive Development and Education* (1974).

Richardson, Joe M. *Christian Reconstruction: The American Missionary Association and Southern Blacks, 1861–1890* (1986).

Rowan, Carl T. *Dream Makers, Dream Breakers: The World of Justice Thurgood Marshall* (1993).

Rowe, Cyprian L. *Crisis in African Studies: The Birth of the African Heritage Studies Association* (1970).

Salomone, Rosemary. *Equal Education under Law* (1986).

Schroeder, Oliver, Jr., and David T. Smith. *De Facto Segregation and Civil Rights* (1965).

Schuman, Howard, Charlotte Steeh, and Lawrence Bobo. *Racial Attitudes in America: Trends and Interpretations* (1985).

Scott, Hugh J. *The Black School Superintendent: Messiah or Scapegoat?* (1980).

Sedlacek, William E., and Glenwood C. Brooks, Jr. *Racism in American Education: A Model for Change* (1976).

Sherer, Robert G. *Subordination or Liberation?: The Development and Conflicting Theories of Black Education in Nineteenth Century Alabama* (1977).

Sindler, Allen. *Bakke, DeFunis, and Minority Admissions: The Quest for Equal Opportunity* (1978).

Smedley, Katherine. *Martha Schofield and the Re-education of the South, 1839–1916* (1987).

Smith, Bob. *They Closed Their Schools: Prince Edward County, Virginia, 1951–1954* (1965).

Smith, G. Pritchy. *Recruiting Minority Teachers* (1992).

———. *Report to the Education Seminar: NAACP* (1992).

Smith, Jessie Carney. *Black Academic Libraries and Research Collections: An Historical Survey* (1977).

Southern Education Foundation. *The Jeanes Story: A Chapter in the History of American Education, 1908–1968* (1979).

———. *Toward Equity and Excellence: A History of the Southern Education Foundation* (1987).

Spencer, Samuel R., Jr. *Booker T. Washington and the Negro's Place in American Life* (1955).

State of New York, Office of Education Performance Review. *School Factors Influencing Reading Achievement: A Case Study of Two Inner City Schools* (March 1974).

Stone, Donald P. *Fallen Prince: William James Edwards, Black Education and the Quest for Afro-American Nationality* (1990).

Takaki, Ron. *A Different Mirror: The Making of Multicultural America* (1993).

Task Force on Black Cultural and Academic Excellence. *Saving the African American Child* (1984).

Thomas, Gail E., ed., *Black Students in Higher Education* (1981).

Thompson, Daniel C. *The Negro Leadership Class* (1963).

———. *Private Black Colleges at the Crossroads* (1973).

Tushnet, Mark V. *The NAACP's Legal Strategy against Segregated Education, 1925–1950* (1987).

United States Commission on Civil Rights. *Equal Protection of the Laws in Public Higher Education* (1957).

———. *Racial Isolation in the Public Schools* (1957).

———. *Racial Isolation in the Public Schools*, vol. 1 (1967).

———. *Your Child and Busing* (1972).

———. *Reviewing a Decade of School Desegregation 1966–1975: Report of a National Survey of School Superintendents* (1977).

———. *Toward an Understanding of Bakke* (1979).

Urban, Wayne J. *Black Scholar: Horace Mann Bond, 1904–1972* (1992).

Washington, V., and U. J. Oyemade. *Project Head Start: Past, Present and Future Trends in the Context of Family Needs* (1987).

Weber, G. *Inner City Children Can Be Taught to Read: Four Successful Schools* (1971).

Weinberg, Meyer. *Minority Students: A Research Appraisal* (1977).

Weinstein, Allen. *The Segregation Era, 1863–1954* (1970).

Whalen, Charles, and Barbara Whalen. *The Longest Debate: A Legislative History of the 1964 Civil Rights Act* (1985).

Wilkerson, Doxey A. *Special Problems of Negro Education* (1939).

Wilkinson, J. Harvie, III. *From Brown to Bakke: The Supreme Court and School Integration, 1954–1978* (1979).

Williams, George W. *History of the Negro Race in America, 1619–1880* (1968).

Williams, Juan. *Eyes on the Prize* (1988).

Williams, Leslie, and Doris Pronin Fromberg, eds. "African Influences in Ancient Contributions to Child Care and Early Education (Prior to A.D. 1750)," in *Encyclopedia of Early Childhood Education* (1992).

Williams, Robin M., Jr., and Gerald D. Jaynes. *A Common Destiny: Blacks in American Society* (1989).

Willie, Charles V. *The Sociology of Urban Education* (1978).

———. *School Desegregation Plans That Work 7* (1984).

Willie, Charles V., and Susan L. Greenblatt. *Community Politics and Educational Change: Ten School Systems under Court Order* (1981).

Willie, Charles V., Antoine M. Garibaldi, and Wornie L. Reed, eds. *The Education of African-Americans*, vol. 2 (1990).

Wilson, Reginald, ed. *Race and Equality in Higher Education* (1982).

Wilson, Reginald, and Deborah J. Carter. *Eighth Annual Status Report on Minorities in Higher Education* (1989).

Wilson, Reginald, and Sarah E. Melendez. *Minorities in Higher Education: Third Annual Status Report* (1984).

Wilson, W. J. *The Truly Disadvantaged: The Inner City, the Underclass, and Public Policy* (1990).

Woodson, Carter G. *The Education of the Negro Prior to 1861* (1919).

———. *Mis-Education of the Negro* (1933, reprint 1977).

Work, Monroe N., ed. *Negro Year Book: An Annual Encyclopedia of the Negro 1937–38* (1937).

Yenser, Thomas, ed. *Who's Who in Colored America 1933 to 1937: A Biographical Dictionary of Notable Living Persons of African Descent in America* (1937).

Zigler, E., and S. Muenchow. *Head Start: The Inside Story of America's Most Successful Educational Experiment* (1992).

Zimet, M. *Decentralization and School Effectiveness: A Case Study of the 1969 Decentralization Law in New York City* (1973).

INDEX

ABOUT THE EDITORS AND CONTRIBUTORS

CHARLES B. ADAMS is a graduate of the University of Pennsylvania and is currently a student at Howard University School of Law, Washington, D.C.

RUSSELL L. ADAMS is chairman of the Afro-American Studies Department, Howard University, Washington, D.C.

WILLIAM C. AKINS is the Assistant Superintendent of the Austin Independent School District in Austin, Texas.

DOROTHY L. ALEXANDER is a professor in the College of Education at Grambling State University, Louisiana.

WALTER R. ALLEN is a professor of sociology at the University of California, Los Angeles.

DENISE A. ALSTON is a senior policy analyst in the Professional Standards and Practice Division of the National Education Association in Washington, D.C.

D. KAMILI ANDERSON is the associate editor of the *Journal of Negro Education*. Her publication credits include the "Literature" chapter in *Black Arts Annual: 1987–1988* (*1989*) and numerous book reviews, news and feature articles in *Black Issues in Higher Education*, *Belles Lettres*, *New Directions for Women*, *Conditions*, the *Journal of Negro Education*, *Sage* and *Small Press*.

ANSELM J. FINCH ARCHER is a senior writer and researcher with Mississippi Writers Associates Limited in Lexington, Mississippi.

CHALMERS ARCHER, JR., is a professor of education at Northern Virginia Community College in Manassas, Virginia.

NANCY L. ARNEZ is a professor emerita, School of Education, Howard University, Washington, D.C.

CHARLES A. ASBURY is a professor emerita of education at Howard University. His articles have appeared in journals such as the *Negro Educational Review*, the *Journal of Research and Development in Education*, the *Journal of Negro Education*, and the *Review of Educational Research*.

BEVERLY BAKER-KELLY is a scholar-in-residence at the George Washington University School of Law.

DENISE ANITA BALTIMORE is a Juris Doctor candidate at the District of Columbia School of Law.

The late SAMUEL L. BANKS was the director of the Baltimore, Maryland, City Public Schools Department of Compensatory and Funded Programs.

ROSELLA HUGHES BARDLEY is a former teacher and guidance counselor; she retired as principal of Eliot Junior High School, Washington, D.C.

GERRI BATES is a professor in the Department of English at Howard University, Washington, D.C.

THOMAS C. BATTLE is director of the Moorland-Spingarn Research Center at Howard University, Washington, D.C.

BRUCE BEEZER is the associate dean for academic affairs and professor in the College of Education and Psychology at North Carolina State University.

DERRICK A. BELL, JR., is a visiting professor at New York University in the School of Law and a former professor of law at Harvard University.

BRENDA BERNADINE BELL-BROWN is an associate professor of education at Merrimack College in North Andover, Massachusetts.

PATRICIA BELL-SCOTT, professor of family development, women's studies, and psychology at the University of Georgia, is cofounding editor of *SAGE: A Scholarly Journal on Black Women*.

BARBARA L. BERNIER is a member of the District of Columbia and Pennsylvania bar associations and an associate professor at the Roger Williams University School of Law.

ESME BHAN is a museum specialist, National African-American Museum, the Smithsonian Institution, and a former research assistant in the Moorland-Spingarn Research Center, Howard University, Washington, D.C.

DAVID W. BISHOP retired as professor emeritus from the Department of History, North Carolina Central University, Durham.

JOYCE BLACKWELL-JOHNSON is an instructor in the Department of History at North Carolina Central University, Durham.

DOROTHY I. BLANCHARD is the assistant to the Presidential Scholar of Temple University, Philadelphia, Pennsylvania.

DEVARA KOLOM BODOG is a law student at Howard University, Washington, D.C.

JOHNNY EDWARD BROWN is the deputy superintendent for educational programs for the Cleveland, Ohio, public schools.

WALTER M. BROWN retired as dean of the School of Education at North Carolina Central University, Durham.

CONSTANCE A. BURNS joined the U.S. Army Center of Military History in Washington, D.C., as the curator of education in 1991.

RONALD E. BUTCHART is professor and program director of education programs at the University of Washington–Tacoma Campus, Tacoma.

LORETTA M. BUTLER is a researcher for the Office of Black Catholics, Archdiocese of Washington, D.C.

DEBORAH J. CARTER is the associate director of the American Council on Education, Washington, D.C., and a doctoral candidate at the University of Maryland, College Park.

KRINER CASH is superintendent of Martha's Vineyard Public Schools and is the former associate dean of the School of Education, Howard University, Washington, D.C.

MICHAELE F. CHAPPELL is assistant professor of mathematics education, Department of Secondary Education, University of South Florida, Tampa.

ERICA JOCELYN CHEW is a former television news producer and now works full-time as a writer.

EDWARD M. CHIKOFSKY is an adjunct professor of law, Washington College of Law, the American University, and Fordham University School of Law.

ELIZABETH CLARK-LEWIS is director of the Public History Program and associate professor of history, Howard University, Washington, D.C.

VERNON F. CLARKE is an independent filmmaker based in Atlanta.

TERENCE COLES is a graduate of Norfolk State University and is currently a student at Howard University School of Law.

ARNOLD COOPER is dean of the College of Education and Human Services at Clarion University in Pennsylvania.

WILLIAM R. CRUMPTON is a master's degree candidate at North Carolina Central University, concentrating in African-American history.

FRANCENA D. CUMMINGS is director of the Southeastern Regional Vision for Education Consortium for Mathematics and Science Education, Tallahassee, Florida.

WALTER G. DANIEL is professor emeritus and editor emeritus, School of Education, Howard University, Washington, D.C.

ERMA GLASCO DAVIS is a retired educational administrator, Detroit, Michigan, public school system, and former adjunct professor, Marygrove College, Detroit.

HILDA ANDREA DAVIS is a retired professor of English and dean of women who taught at Palmer Memorial Institute, Shaw University, Talladega College, the University of Delaware, and Wilmington College.

JOHN DAYTON is an assistant professor in the Department of Educational Leadership at the University of Georgia.

DIANA W. DE BROHUN is communications officer at the Southern Education Foundation in Atlanta, Georgia.

JANET DEGGES is an intern in the Office of Communications at Oberlin College, Oberlin, Ohio.

TOMIKA DEPRIEST is a researcher and writer for local and national publications, video production companies, and other commercial entities.

DOLORES P. DICKERSON is associate dean of the School of Education, Howard University, Washington, D.C.

EDNA C. DIGGS is curator at the National Afro-American Museum and Cultural Center, Wilberforce, Ohio.

JOSEPH T. DURHAM is a professor of education at Morgan State University, Baltimore, Maryland.

HENRY DUVALL is the director of communications for the Council of the Great City Schools, Washington, D.C.

TIMOTHY K. EATMAN is a doctoral candidate at the University of Illinois–Urbana in the College of Education, Department of Educational Policy Studies.

J. GABRIEL EDMOND is a graduate of the University of Miami and is currently a student at Howard University School of Law.

LISA WILSON EDWARDS is an appellate attorney in the Civil Rights Division of the U.S. Department of Justice in Washington, D.C.

MIRIAM R. EISENSTEIN is a lawyer for the Department of Justice, Washington, D.C.

JACK EVANS is president of Southwestern Christian College, Terrell, Texas.

BARBARA FLEMING is director of the Office of Planning, Research, and Retention at Central State University in Wilberforce, Ohio.

JOHN E. FLEMING is director of the National Afro-American Museum and Cultural Center in Wilberforce, Ohio.

DONNA Y. FORD is an assistant professor at the University of Virginia in the Curry School of Education, Charlottesville, Virginia.

ED FORD is the director of public relations at Berea College in Berea, Kentucky.

TYRONE FORMAN is a Patricia Roberts Harris Doctoral Fellow in the Graduate Program in Human Development and Social Policy, Northwestern University, Evanston, Illinois.

MICHELE FOSTER is an associate professor of African-American and African Studies and Education at the University of California-Davis.

H. JEROME FREIBERG is a professor of education at the University of Houston, Houston, Texas.

FRANCINE FULTON is a doctoral candidate in the Special Education Program, Temple University, Philadelphia, Pennsylvania.

MICHAEL FULTZ is an associate professor of education at the University of Wisconsin, Madison, where he specializes in the history of African-American education. His writing has appeared in such publications as the *Teachers College Record*, the *Harvard Educational Review*, and the *Journal of Negro Education*.

RACHEL GABRIEL is a graduate of the American University and is currently a student at Howard University School of Law.

BETTYE J. GARDNER is a professor of history at Coppin State College, Baltimore, Maryland.

ANTOINE M. GARIBALDI is vice president for academic affairs and professor of education at Xavier University, New Orleans, Louisiana.

DERRICK GILBERT is a doctoral student in the Department of Sociology at the University of California-Los Angeles.

NICHOLAS GLASS is a doctoral student in the Department of Educational Policy Studies at the University of Wisconsin–Madison.

LINA R. GODFREY is a professor in the Department of Home Economics at the University of Arkansas-Pine Bluff.

NATAKI H. GOODALL is a master's degree candidate in the Department of History at North Carolina Central University.

TERESA GREER is editor of association publications for the Southern Association of Colleges and Schools in Decatur, Georgia.

LUETHEL TATE GREEN is a consultant to school health services in Washington, D.C.

JUDITH BERRY GRIFFIN is the president of A Better Chance, Inc., and is a former appointee to the Department of Education during the Carter administration.

MARGARET E. HALE-SMITH is assistant director of lifelong education in the Office of the Vice President for University Outreach at Michigan State University, East Lansing.

MARY ELLEN HAMER is director of the Office of Communications, South Bend Community School Corporation, South Bend, Indiana.

EDWIN HAMILTON is a graduate professor, School of Education, Howard University, Washington, D.C.

FREDERICK D. HARPER is a professor in the School of Education, Howard University, Washington, D.C.

EDGAR W. HARRIS is director of public relations and alumni affairs at Mary Holmes College in West Point, Mississippi.

J. JEROME HARRIS served as the superintendent of the Atlanta public schools from 1988 to 1990.

J. JOHN HARRIS III is a professor and the dean of the College of Education, University of Kentucky at Lexington.

JANETTE HOSTON HARRIS is a professor of history at the University of the District of Columbia and former president of the Association for Study of Afro-American Life and History.

JOSEPH E. HARRIS is Distinguished Professor, Department of History, Howard University, Washington, D.C.

PATRICIA HALL HARRIS is an administrative assistant, School of Education, Howard University, Washington, D.C.

BERTHA N. HARRISON retired as an assistant professor from the Department of Home Economics, University of Arkansas–Pine Bluff.

NORRIS M. HAYNES is an associate professor of the Child Study Center and director of the Research and School Development Program at Yale University, New Haven, Connecticut.

JOHN M. HEFFRON is an associate professor in the Department of Educational Foundations at the University of Hawaii-Manoa.

RONALD D. HENDERSON is director of the Research Division at the National Education Association and is the former director of Desegregation Studies at the National Institute of Education.

EARL F. HILLIARD, JR., is a student in the JD/MBA program at Howard University in Washington, D.C.

MICHAEL R. HILLIS is a research assistant for the Center for Multicultural Education at the University of Washington.

DARLENE CLARK HINE is the John A. Hannah Professor of American History at Michigan State University in East Lansing.

JULIUS W. HOBSON, JR., is assistant director, Division of Congressional Affairs, American Medical Association, in Washington, D.C.

DAVID JULIAN HODGES is a professor in the Division of Programs in Education, Hunter College in New York.

HAROLD W. HORTON, SR., is the associate director of the William Monroe Trotter Institute at the University of Massachusetts–Boston.

WILLIE T. HOWARD, JR., is professor and dean emeritus, School of Education, Howard University, Washington, D.C.

MICHELLE R. HOWARD-VITAL is vice chancellor of the Division of Public Service and Extended Education at the University of North Carolina at Wilmington.

HARRIET HUNTER-BOYKIN is an associate professor in the School of Education and Human Development at George Washington University, Washington, D.C.

ELIZABETH L. IHLE is a professor of secondary education, library science and educational leadership at James Madison University in Harrisonburg, Virginia.

VIVIAN W. IKPA is an associate professor of educational administration and policy studies at Temple University, Philadelphia, Pennsylvania.

SYLVIA M. JACOBS is a professor and chair of the Department of History and Social Science at North Carolina Central University. Her previous books include *The African Nexus: Black American Perspectives on the European Par-*

titioning of Africa, 1889–1920 (1981), and *Black Americans and the Missionary Movement in Africa* (1982), both published by Greenwood Press.

FRANCES JAMES-BROWN is a professor of mental health, retardation, and chemical dependency at Columbus State Community College, Columbus, Ohio.

RENEE JEFFERSON is a project director at the National Urban League in New York, N.Y.

SHARON D. JOHNSON is head of acquisitions/periodicals at Woodward Library in Austin Peay State University, Clarksville, Tennessee.

BEVERLY W. JONES is a professor of history and director of the Institute for the Study of Minority Issues at North Carolina Central University, Durham.

DENEESE L. JONES is an assistant professor in the College of Education, Curriculum, and Instruction at the University of Kentucky in Lexington.

EVONNE PARKER JONES is an associate professor of English at Northern Virginia Community College, Annandale.

TRACEY T. JONES is a research assistant for the Center for Disability and Socioeconomic Policy Studies and the *Journal of Negro Education*, Howard University, Washington, D.C.

WAYSON R. JONES, a musician and writer, is the publications assistant at the *Journal of Negro Education*, Howard University, Washington, D.C.

FAUSTINE C. JONES-WILSON is a professor emerita of education at Howard University and editor emerita of the *Journal of Negro Education*. Her books include *The Changing Mood in America: Eroding Commitment?* (1977) and *A Traditional Model of Excellence: Dunbar High School of Little Rock, Arkansas* (1981). She is also the author of numerous articles, book chapters, editorials, and book reviews.

DONALD FRANKLIN JOYCE is the dean of library and media services at Austin Peay State University, Clarksville, Tennessee.

JOYCE ELAINE KING is associate vice chancellor for academic affairs and diversity programs, University of New Orleans, Los Angeles.

LARRY LEFLORE is an associate professor at the University of Southern Mississippi, Hattiesburg.

WILBERT LEMELLE is president of the Phelps-Stokes Fund, New York, and is a former president of Mercy College, New York.

VALINDA W. LITTLEFIELD is a Ph.D. candidate in the Department of History, University of Illinois–Urbana.

LISA R. LOCKHART is the coordinator of the Literacy Brigade at the Septima Clark Center for Urban Literacy, Columbus, Ohio.

KOFI LOMOTEY is the chairman of the Department of Administrative and Foundational Services at Louisiana State University in Baton Rouge.

LYNN LONG is assistant principal at Martin Luther King, Jr., Elementary School, Washington, D.C.

CYNTHIA R. MABRY, formerly assistant general counsel for the Washington Metropolitan Area Transit Authority, is currently research instructor in law at New York University.

VALERIE MAHOLMES is currently the assistant director of research with the Comer School Development Program in New Haven, Connecticut.

FRANK L. MATTHEWS is the publisher of *Black Issues in Higher Education* and a former assistant senior vice president and law professor at George Mason University, Fairfax, Virginia.

LANCE MCCREADY is a Ph.D. candidate in Educational Studies at Emory University, Atlanta, Georgia.

S. GARRETT MCDOWELL earned his Ph.D. in political science from the University of California at Berkeley.

JOSEPH R. MCKINNEY is an associate professor, Department of Educational Leadership, Ball State University, Muncie, Indiana.

GENNA RAE MCNEIL is a professor of history at the University of North Carolina at Chapel Hill.

CARROLL L. MILLER is a professor and dean of the Graduate School emeritus, Howard University, Washington, D.C.

RICHARD MOLLOT is a student at Howard University School of Law, Washington, D.C.

EVELYN K. MOORE is the executive director of the National Black Child Development Institute in Washington, D.C.

SHARON E. MOORE is assistant professor in the Department of Sociology/ Social Work at Seton Hill College, Greenburg, Pennsylvania.

HARRY MORGAN is a professor at West Georgia College, Carrollton.

LORENZO MORRIS is an associate professor of political science, Howard University, Washington, D.C.

ZAKIYYAH MUHAMMAD is the founder of the Universal Institute of Islamic Education, a former director of education for Clara Muhammad Schools, and currently a research associate with Dr. C. Eric Lincoln on his upcoming study, "Islam in the African-American Experience."

MABEL LAKE MURRAY is the NAACP National Teachers Examination Coordinator in Baltimore, Maryland.

SAMUEL L. MYERS is president of the National Association for Equal Opportunity in Higher Education (NAFEO) and was formerly president of Bowie State College.

DEBORAH H. NAJEE-ULLAH is an associate professor of development studies and assistant director of Atlanta Math Project, Georgia State University.

MARGARET A. NASH is a graduate student in educational policy studies at the University of Wisconsin.

CYNTHIA NEVERDON-MORTON is professor of history at Coppin State College, Baltimore, Maryland.

JAMES E. NEWBY is an associate professor of education, Department of Educational Administration and Policy, at Howard University, Washington, D.C.

FLORENCE MARGARET NEWELL is assistant professor in the College of Education at the University of Cincinnati in Cincinnati, Ohio.

JULIE BURNETT NICHOLS is a graduate student in the Department of Educational Policy Studies at the University of Illinois at Urbana.

DIANNA NIXON is a graduate of Columbia University and is currently a student at Howard University School of Law, Washington, D.C.

PEDRO A. NOGUERA is an assistant professor in the School of Education at the University of California at Berkeley and is the former president of the Berkeley School Board.

MARGO OKAZAWA-REY is a professor in the School of Social Work at San Francisco State University. She has worked with school and community organizations in the development of strategies that promote multicultural awareness and empowerment for communities of color. She is the author of several articles and book chapters, and is a coeditor of the forthcoming book, *Roots of Racism/ Stories of Resistance*: *Critical Perspectives on Multicultural Education*.

CHARLOTTE L. ORANGE, a professor at Virginia State University in Petersburg, Virginia, received her doctorate in special education from the University of Michigan.

LAURA H. G. O'SULLIVAN is a law student in the School of Law at Howard University in Washington, D.C.

EURADELL L. PATTERSON is a teacher employed by Oakland Unified School District, Oakland, California.

JUNE O. PATTON is a professor of history and public policy at Governor State University in University Park, Illinois.

LIZ PEAVY is the director of the Septima Clark Center for Urban Literacy in Columbus, Ohio.

JUDY PELHAM is a psychologist at the Philadelphia Child Guidance Center and has been a consultant to public schools and a teacher at the graduate school level.

HENRY W. PENNYMON, SR., is a retired educator who taught at Tuskegee Institute, Alabama, and in the Joliet, Illinois, public schools.

NICOLE PETERS is a law student at Howard University Law School, Washington, D.C.

CHRISTINE P. PHILLIPS is an assistant professor of career counseling in the School of Business, Howard University, Washington, D.C.

TENITA SHERRELL PHILYAW received her bachelor of arts degree from North Carolina State University in 1992 and is currently a graduate student at North Carolina Central University.

A. WILLIAM PLACE is an assistant professor of educational administration at the University of Dayton, Ohio.

THERESA RECTOR retired from Howard University, Washington, D.C., after twenty-seven years as associate editor and business manager of the *Journal of Negro Education.*

JACQUELINE K. REED is in the Office of Research and Evaluation for Prince George's County Public Schools.

HAROLD O. ROBINSON is pastor of the Spottswood A.M.E. Church and book editor of the A.M.E.–Zion Quarterly Review.

CYNTHIA ROSS, a student at Howard University School of Law, is the former international news editor of the *Barrister,* the official newspaper of Howard University School of Law, Washington, D.C.

PATRICIA O. ROTH is a faculty member at the American University in Washington, D.C.

STEVE ROYSTER is an attorney with the Department of Justice, Civil Rights Division, in Washington, D.C.

CHARLES J. RUSSO is a professor and chair of the Department of Educational Administration, School of Education, University of Dayton.

ROSETTA F. SANDIDGE is an assistant professor in the Department of Curriculum and Instruction and Special Programs Coordinator in the College of Education at the University of Kentucky.

HUGH J. SCOTT has served as dean of programs in education at Hunter College of CUNY since 1975; he is a former superintendent of schools in Washington, D.C. (1970–73).

DIANE SCOTT-JONES is an associate professor of psychology at Temple University, Philadelphia, Pennsylvania.

PORTIA SHIELDS is an associate professor of education and dean of the School of Education, Howard University, Washington, D.C.

MWALIMU J. SHUJAA is an associate professor in the Department of Educational Organization, Administration, and Policy at the State University of New York at Buffalo.

JANET SIMS-WOOD is the assistant chief librarian of the Reference/Reader Service Department in the Moorland-Spingarn Research Center at Howard University in Washington, D.C.

DIANA T. SLAUGHTER-DEFOE is a professor of education and social policy in the School of Education and Social Policy and a professor of African American studies at Northwestern University in Evanston, Illinois.

BARBARA SMITH is a scholar-in-residence at the Schomburg Center for Research in Black Culture where she is researching her book on African-American lesbian and gay history.

CAROL J. HOBSON SMITH has retired from the U.S. Department of Education, Washington, D.C.

ELAINE MOORE SMITH is an assistant professor of history at Alabama State University in Montgomery.

ROLAND B. SMITH JR., is the executive assistant to the president and an associate professor of sociology at the University of Notre Dame, Notre Dame, Indiana.

PETER A. SOLA is a professor in the School of Education, Howard University, Washington, D.C.

MYSCHELLE W. SPEARS is an assistant professor in the Department of Curriculum and Instruction in the School of Education, Howard University, Washington, D.C.

LISA STARK is an attorney with the Department of Justice in Washington, D.C.

ALICE STEELE-ROBINSON is the director of elementary curriculum and Title I for the Cabarrus County Schools, Concord, North Carolina.

JAMES W. STENNETT is a graduate student at Mississippi State University, Mississippi State.

SHIRLEY F. STENNIS-WILLIAMS is the dean of the School of Education at Edinboro University of Pennsylvania.

DONALD P. STONE, an independent scholar, is owner and operator of Snow Hill Press, Snowhill, Alabama, and is currently working on a biography of Booker T. Washington.

A. J. STOVALL is an associate professor of political science and director of the Wilbur N. Daniel African American Culture and Research Center at Austin Peay State University in Clarksville, Tennessee.

CAROLYN STROMAN is the associate dean of the School of Communications and associate professor in the Department of Human Communications Studies in the School of Communications, Howard University, Washington, D.C.

OLIVE A. TAYLOR is an assistant professor of history and director of the undergraduate program, Department of History, Howard University, Washington, D.C.

JULIUS E. THOMPSON is an assistant professor of Black American Studies and History at Southern Illinois University at Carbondale.

MARY F. TOLIVER is a Ph.D. candidate in research methodology, Department of Counseling and Educational Psychology, Loyola University, Chicago, Illinois.

ERICA E. TOLLETT is the senior public policy analyst for the National Black Child Development Institute, Washington, D.C.

KENNETH S. TOLLETT is the Distinguished Professor of Higher Education and former director of the Institute for the Study of Educational Policy at Howard University, Washington, D.C.

FASAHA M. TRAYLOR is a senior program officer at the William Penn Foundation, Philadelphia, Pennsylvania.

CAROLYN HOLLOMAN TROUPE, a retired school administrator and college instructor, served for many years in the public schools of Washington, D.C., and at Towson State University, Baltimore, Maryland.

KIMBERLEY A. TURNER is the director of programs, Howard University Research and Training Center for Access to Rehabilitation and Economic Opportunity, Center for Disability and Socioeconomic Policy Studies, School of Education, Howard University.

ANDRE D. VANN is an adjunct instructor of history in the Department of History and Social Science at North Carolina Central University, Durham.

ADA VINCENT is the director of substance abuse outpatient programs with the Center for Mental Health, Inc., Washington, D.C.

JACQUELINE E. WADE is the executive director of the National Council for Black Studies, Inc., Columbus, Ohio.

CHARLES W. WADELINGTON is the minority interpretations specialist for the North Carolina Division of Archives and History/Historic Sites Section for the Department of Cultural Resources in Raleigh.

BARBARA DODSON WALKER is the national president of the Afro-American Historical and Genealogical Society, Inc., Washington, D.C.

SYLVIA WALKER is the director of the Center for Disability and Socioeconomic Policy Studies and professor of education, Howard University, Washington, D.C.

JOYCE WALKER-JONES is a senior attorney at the U.S. Equal Employment Opportunity Commission in Washington, D.C.

PETER WALLENSTEIN is an associate professor of history at Virginia Polytechnic Institute and State University, Blacksburg.

TERHEA WASHINGTON is the assistant director of communications marketing at The College Fund/UNCF.

WILLIAM H. WATKINS is an associate professor of education at the University of Illinois, Chicago.

BERNARD C. WATSON retired as president and CEO of the William Penn Foundation and is a former vice president of Temple University, Philadelphia, Pennsylvania.

EARLE H. WEST is a professor emeritus and former associate dean of the School of Education, Howard University, Washington, D.C.

ANDREA D. WILLIAMS is an attorney for the U.S. Department of Transportation and a 1992 graduate of Howard University School of Law, Washington, D.C.

LAWRENCE H. WILLIAMS is an associate professor of Africana studies and history at Luther College, Decorah, Iowa.

LEE E. WILLIAMS II is a professor of history and director of the Office of Multicultural Affairs at the University of Alabama, Huntsville.

REGINALD WILSON is a senior scholar at the American Council on Education in Washington, D.C.

MICHAEL R. WINSTON is the president of the Jovanovich Foundation, Silver Spring, Maryland, and is the former director of the Moorland–Spingarn Research Center at Howard University, Washington, D.C.

ROBERT WITHERSPOON is a former training specialist and education and human resources consultant for the Education Net and served as the organization's executive director from 1978 to 1992.

ISBN 0-313-28931-X

90000>

EAN

9 780313 289316

HARDCOVER BAR CODE